W9-ANT-642

# MEMOIR AND LETTERS

OF

# CHARLES SUMNER.

*Charles Sumner*

From a Photograph by Allen, 1873.

# MEMOIR AND LETTERS

OF

# CHARLES SUMNER.

BY

EDWARD L. PIERCE.

VOL. IV.

1860—1874.



BOSTON:
ROBERTS BROTHERS.
1893.

Reprinted by Mnemosyne Publishing Co., Inc. Miami, Florida

**First Mnemosyne reprinting 1969**

**Reprinted from a copy in the**
**Fisk University Library Negro Collection.**



Library of Congress Catalog Card Number:
71-83949

Printed in the United States of America

# CONTENTS OF VOL. IV.

## CHAPTER XLIX.

1863–1864.



## CHAPTER L.

1864–1865.



## CHAPTER LI.

1865–1866.



## CHAPTER LII.

1866–1867.

## CHAPTER LVII.

1871–1872.



## CHAPTER LVIII.

1872–1873.



## CHAPTER LIX.

December 1, 1873 — March 11, 1874.



## APPENDIX.

# MEMOIR AND LETTERS

OF

# CHARLES SUMNER.

## CHAPTER XLIV

SECESSION. — SCHEMES OF COMPROMISE. — CIVIL WAR. — CHAIRMAN OF FOREIGN RELATIONS COMMITTEE. — DR. LIEBER. — NOVEMBER, 1860–APRIL, 1861.

THE secession movement had been definitely planned before the election of Mr. Lincoln, and its leaders were as well satisfied with this result as were his own supporters. They had even connived at it by a division of the Southern vote, so as to make a pretence for revolution. Immediately after the election was made known, they proceeded actively to consummate their purpose in open and secret measures. On December 15 appeared the address of Jefferson Davis, Benjamin, Slidell, Wigfall, and other leaders of secession in Congress, invoking the Southern people to organize a Southern confederacy; avowing that "the primary object of each slaveholding State ought to be its speedy and absolute separation from a union with the hostile States." South Carolina took the lead, and seceded five days later, followed the next month by Mississippi, Florida, Alabama, Georgia, and Louisiana. Texas completed her secession February 1. The disunion sentiment was advancing in Arkansas, North Carolina, Virginia, and Tennessee, — States which, however, postponed the final act till after President Lincoln's call for troops. There were threatening signs also in Missouri, Kentucky, and Maryland. Delaware alone among slave States seemed securely held to the Union.

The disunion sentiment was not confined to the slaveholding States. The identification of the Democratic party with the slaveholding interest for a long period had poisoned the minds of many of the Democratic leaders at the North. Treasonable sentiments were uttered by Franklin Pierce, Caleb Cushing,

Fernando Wood, Horatio Seymour, and Chancellor Walworth;[1] and Daniel E. Sickles, in his speech in the House, Dec. 10, 1860, set up the city of New York as a barrier against the march of national troops for the maintenance of the Union. Journals of great influence, notably the New York "Herald" and Albany "Argus," stimulated the conspiracy with harangues which justified the seceders and denied to the government the right to reduce them to submission by force.[2]

As soon as the secession began, a panic prevailed at the commercial centres of the North; the money market was severely strained; the banks were on the brink of suspension; Southern trade, then a very important factor in the general business of the country, stopped altogether; and many a merchant who had enjoyed a solid prosperity stood appalled at the prospect of bankruptcy.[3] The fright extended beyond the supporters of Bell, Breckinridge, and Douglas, even to some of Lincoln's supporters, who if possible would in view of the Southern uprising have recalled their votes. Public meetings were held in the great cities, in which, in the name of the Union, not only a surrender to the demands of slavery was insisted upon, but even the right of free speech was assailed.[4] Because of his antislavery position, George William Curtis was not allowed to deliver a lyceum lecture in Philadelphia, and the use of the hall which had been engaged was refused at the instance of the mayor. An antislavery meeting in Boston was broken up by a mob composed of roughs and business men, who for the moment were allies; and the mayor, who was in sympathy with these assailants of free speech, pleaded his inability to protect the meeting. A prominent journal of the city justified the outrage, and notified the two senators from Massachusetts that they

[1] Greeley's "American Conflict," vol. i. pp. 388-393, 512. Cushing made, November 26, an inflammatory speech at Newburyport, which affirmed the right of secession, and denied the right of the government to coerce the seceders. (Boston "Post," November 27, 28, 29.) His letter, November 19, justifying the complaints of the seceders is printed in the Boston "Advertiser," November 21. Henry Wilson replied to him at length in a trenchant letter, which reviewed his earlier and better record. New York "Tribune," December 26.

[2] Greeley's "American Conflict," vol. i. pp. 395, 396. James Gordon Bennett's later change of front is described in Thurlow Weed's Memoir, vol. i. pp. 616-618.

[3] George Livermore wrote Sumner, December 12: "It is an awful time for merchants, — worse than in 1857; and if there is not some speedy relief, more than half the best concerns in the country will be ruined." Nevertheless, while counselling moderation in speech, he expressed himself strongly against any backing down.

[4] Greeley's American Conflict, vol. i. pp. 363-367.

would not hereafter have a hearing in the city.[1] Bankers and brokers muttered warnings to the new Administration that it would be left without funds if it refused to compromise with secession.[2]

The master spirits in Buchanan's Cabinet when Congress met were secessionists, — Cobb, Secretary of the Treasury, who left it bankrupt December 10; Floyd, Secretary of War, who after ordering the transfer of ordnance from Pittsburg to Ship Island and Galveston, and obstructing the reinforcement of the national forts at the South, resigned on the 29th; and Thompson, Secretary of the Interior, equally disloyal with Floyd, who lingered till January 8. Black, the Attorney-General, gave an elaborate opinion, November 20, strung with sophistries, denying the right of the government to maintain itself by armed force in the insurgent States. The President refused, against the appeal of the loyal members of his Cabinet, to reinforce the forts in the harbor of Charleston. From such a Cabinet, in which he could no longer remain with honor, even Cass, Secretary of State, after a career of subserviency to the South, withdrew, December 14, to be succeeded by Black. The notion of State supremacy, which recognized an allegiance to the State on the part of its citizens higher than any due from them to the nation, had so corrupted the minds of officers of the army and navy from the South that a painful uncertainty prevailed as to the loyalty of Southern men holding high commands in either service. Many, to their honor be it said, never wavered in fidelity; but when in the spring of 1861 Robert E. Lee, bound as he was by triple ties of education at the national expense, oaths of allegiance, and kinship to Washington, drew his sword against his country, the suspicion of Southern officers was found to be well justified.

President Buchanan, in his message to Congress, laid the original blame for existing troubles altogether on the loyal people of the free States, attributing them to the moral and political agitation against slavery; and although disavowing the right of secession as a theory, he denied the right of the government "to coerce a State into submission which is at-

1 Boston "Courier," December 4: "Nor do we believe that our people will listen hereafter to the fierce tirades of Phillips and his crew, to the empty platitudes of Sumner, or the insolent bravado of Wilson."

2 Sumner's speech in the Senate, Feb. 12, 1861. Works, vol. v. p. 473.

tempting to withdraw." His remedies — as if enough had not been done in that direction — were an express recognition, in the Constitution, of slavery in the slave States, the admission of the Calhoun doctrine of the constitutional sanction of slavery in the Territories, and a reaffirmation of the right to recover fugitive slaves. So far did he go as to proclaim that in case the free States did not repeal their personal liberty laws, "the injured States, after having first used all peaceable and constitutional means to obtain redress, would be justified in revolutionary resistance to the government of the Union." Such language at such a time was a direct encouragement of rebellion. Fortunately for his fame, he ended the year better than he began the session. On the voluntary retirement of three traitors from his Cabinet he called to the vacant places three loyal men, — Edwin M. Stanton, Joseph Holt, and John A. Dix; and from that time they, in conjunction with Black, — now improved in his conception of public duty and constitutional law, — largely directed the President's action. Though from the beginning of the new year to his last day in office he left undone, to the infinite injury of his country, what he ought to have done, he was no longer a plaything in the hands of secessionists.

The rapid advance of secession in the South, and the treasonable exhibitions in the North, produced a sense of bewilderment and helplessness among loyal people. It was a period distinguished by hesitation, unsteadiness of action, confusion of ideas, and changes of position; a season of perplexity, "men's hearts failing them for fear," — all natural enough when patriotic men were confronted by unexampled terrors. The threats of secession, which had hitherto seemed mere bravado, were now found to have a real and hostile meaning. The movement had swept over the cotton States, and appeared likely to carry all the slave States by force of sympathy. It was impossible to measure the extent to which the masses of the Democratic party in the North were in accord with their pro-slavery leaders, or to know of a certainty how much there was in Franklin Pierce's prediction, in his letter to Jefferson Davis a year before, that the fighting when it came would not be south of Mason and Dixon's line only, but would be also between two classes of citizens at the North.[1] Above all, it was not in human vision

[1] Other Northern Democratic leaders made similar predictions. Von Holst, vol. vii. p. 284.

to foresee what latent heroism and endurance were to become manifest in the free States in the event of a long, bloody, and costly civil war. The conditions of this extraordinary period thus briefly noted show how much at that time Republican statesmen had to withstand, and may help this generation to accord due honor to those who stood firm, and to deal charitably with those who wavered and temporized.

The anxious question pressing on loyal people during the winter of 1860–1861 was how to secure a peaceful and orderly inauguration of Mr. Lincoln, and how during the critical interval to hold the border slave States, as well as Tennessee and North Carolina, from joining the Confederacy. Sumner wrote, January 9, to F. W. Bird, who had advised an appeal by the Republican members of Congress to the people, stating the dangers of the government: —

"In the logic of events violence must have reached the capital before February 1, had not the President and General Scott taken steps to counteract it. Ten days ago everything tended to that catastrophe; for two days I thought it inevitable; I am not sure now that it can be avoided. But a movement of troops from the North would be a hostile step which would surely precipitate events. Our situation, locked within the slave States, exposes us to attack before protection can come from the North. This cannot be changed. Of course, I shall not shrink from any responsibility; but the time has not come for the appeal which you desire. Events will travel with fearful rapidity. Very soon all slavedom will be in a blaze, — Virginia as much as any other State, embittered by the teachings of Wise and Mason.

"General Scott says: 'Since the 2d of January, — yes, sir, since the 2d of January,' the President has done well. Jeff. Davis says that but two men in Washington are frightened, — the President and Scott. I enjoyed Andrew's message. At last Massachusetts is herself!"

Horace Greeley, appalled with the prospect of civil war with an uncertain issue, hastened to bid the insurgent States to "go in peace," while at the same time rejecting any compromise. He treated secession as a revolutionary right, and discountenanced coercive measures for keeping the seceding States in the Union.[1] Wendell Phillips, in a passionate harangue, affirmed

[1] New York "Tribune," Nov. 9, 26, 30, Dec. 17, 1860; Feb. 23, 1861. Greeley says in his History that "several other Republican journals, including some of the most influential, held similar language, and maintained a position not unlike that of the 'Tribune.'" Later, in the New York "Tribune," Aug. 23, 1865, Greeley explained his position in 1860–1861. The Boston "Advertiser" (Nov. 12, Dec. 12, 1860; Jan. 24, 1861), a conservative journal, published leaders of the same tenor as the "Tribune's" articles. Among Sumner's correspondents who favored non-resistance to secession were Dr. Samuel G. Howe, John G. Whittier, Rev. James Freeman Clarke, and Rev. John Pierpont. Mr. Clarke published

the right of the slave States, "upon the principles of 1776," to decide the question of a separate government for themselves.[1] Thurlow Weed, on the other hand, contemporaneously with Greeley's prompt declaration, proposed to reach a peaceful issue in another way, — by acceding to the substance of the claims of the seceders. He proposed in his newspaper, as a compromise, a new fugitive-slave law, the surrender of the prohibition of slavery in the Territories, the admission of States whether free or slave, as they might come, and the protection of slavery by the government in territory lying south of 36° 30′, — a solution in the main like that which was urged later by Mr. Crittenden.[2] General Scott, head of the army, communicated, Oct. 29, 1860, his views in a formal paper to President Buchanan, and to Floyd, Secretary of War. While advising the immediate garrisoning of Southern forts, — a wise counsel, which the dilatory and irresolute President did not heed, — he proposed to yield to secession except in the case of "interior States," whose withdrawal would produce "a gap" in the Union. He even assumed to advise, as a better alternative than force, a division of the country into four confederacies, the boundaries of which he proceeded to define. A few months later, March 3, 1861, he recommended to Mr. Lincoln, by letter to Mr. Seward, the adoption of the Crittenden propositions, naming peaceable separation as one of the alternatives.[3] At the Pine Street meeting in New York, where W. B. Astor, A. A. Low, D. S. Dickinson, Edwards Pierrepont, Wilson G. Hunt, and S. J. Tilden took part, an address to the South, drawn by John A. Dix, and resolutions were

an anonymous pamphlet at the time (a letter addressed to Sumner) on "Secession, Concession, or Self-Possession," in which he said: "We cannot coerce a State to remain in the Union against its will; we must not attempt to do this." Whittier's poem (Jan. 16, 1861), "A Word for the Hour," is in the same vein. He wrote Sumner, March 13, 1861: "The conflicting rumors from Washington trouble me. I am for peace, not by conceding our principles, but by simply telling the slave States 'go,' — border ones and all. I believe in the irrepressible conflict."

[1] April 9, 1861, at New Bedford; Schouler's "History of Massachusetts in the Civil War," vol. i. pp. 44–47. Phillips said, "I maintain on the principles of '76 that Abraham Lincoln has no right to a soldier in Fort Sumter." To apply to him his favorite expression, he "remembered to forget" the inclusion of this address in his volume of speeches.

[2] Albany "Evening Journal," November 30, December 1 and 15; Greeley's "American Conflict," vol. i. p. 360; Weed's "Life," vol. ii. pp. 303, 313. George E. Baker wrote to Sumner, December 3, from Albany, that "no influential man agreed with Mr. Weed's view, and that it had no support in the rural districts." The Boston "Journal," Jan. 9, 17, 1861, was not opposed to the restoration of the Missouri Compromise line and the non-prohibition of slavery south of 36° 30′. Greeley afterwards questioned the wisdom of the overtures made by himself and Weed. "American Conflict," vol. i. p. 361.

[3] New York Tribune, Oct. 24, 1862; Scott's Autobiography, p. 626.

adopted, in which the right of slaveholders — not to be interfered with by federal or local legislation — to carry their slaves into the Territories and hold them there was affirmed, and the Southern States were treated as an injured party which had been denied its rights under the Constitution.[1]

Propositions of compromise were offered in Congress as soon as it met in December, and committees on the subject were appointed, — one of thirteen in the Senate and another of thirty-three in the House, Thomas Corwin of Ohio being chairman of the latter. The most noted of the schemes, which was presented December 18, came from Crittenden of Kentucky, — a most respectable and patriotic statesman, who, however, under the limitations of his training and associations could not comprehend the moral and political antagonism to the extension and perpetuity of slavery which animated the free States. He proposed by a constitutional amendment to prohibit slavery in territory north of 36° 30′, but to establish or recognize it as existing in territory south of that line, both as to territory hereafter[2] acquired as well as to that now held, imposing on the territorial government the duty to protect it; to disable Congress from abolishing slavery in the District of Columbia so long as it existed in Maryland and Virginia, or in any places within its jurisdiction situated in slave States, or from prohibiting members of Congress or federal officers from bringing their slaves into the District and holding them therein as such; to prohibit any future amendment to the Constitution which should authorize Congress to interfere with slavery in the States; to disfranchise free negroes in all the States (a provision added by Douglas and accepted by Crittenden); and to authorize masters to take slaves from one slave State to another, or to a slave Territory, — all these safeguards of slavery to become unalterable provisions of the Constitution. Besides these constitutional changes, his scheme affirmed anew the constitutional validity of the Fugitive Slave Act, imposed on Congress the duty to indemnify the owners of escaped slaves, and called for the repeal of the personal liberty laws of the States. Its only recognition of the spirit of humanity was an expression in favor of the execution

[1] Memoirs of John A. Dix, vol. i. pp. 346-360. Dix and Tilden were Free Soilers in 1848. Dix approved the Crittenden Compromise. Coleman's "Life of J. J. Crittenden," vol. ii. p. 237.

[2] Mr. Crittenden said, February 12, that he did not intend to insist on the term "hereafter" if it stood in the way of a settlement.

of the laws against the African slave-trade.[1] This plan of compromise as a whole went further than any Republican in the Senate would go, and was lost by a single vote, — its passage being defeated by the withdrawal of senators from the seceding States, or their refusal to vote. It was supported by Douglas, and by the Democratic and Southern Whig senators, including Mason, Hunter, and Wigfall, who had not yet left the Senate. It was this scheme which received the approval of the city council of Boston and twenty-three thousand petitioners from Massachusetts.

Mr. Seward came to Washington at the opening of the session, looking to compromise as the solution of the troubles, and on himself as the great peacemaker, almost divinely appointed; but on his arrival he found his Republican associates sturdy and non-compliant, and he seemed to think them as much at fault as the seceders. His temper of mind may be caught from three extracts from his letters. Dec. 3, 1860: "The Republican party to-day is as uncompromising as the secessionists in South Carolina. A month hence each may come to think that moderation is wiser." Jan. 13, 1861: "Two-thirds of the Republican senators are as reckless in action as the South." January 21: "Mad men North and mad men South are working together to produce a dissolution of the Union by civil war. The present Administration and the incoming one unite in devolving on me the responsibility of averting those disasters. My own party trusts me, but not without reservation. All the other parties, North and South, cast themselves upon me."[2] This singular estimate of his own position will shortly reappear in this narrative.

Mr. Seward took an opportunity to address the Senate January 12, just after the holidays. It was already known that he was to be Secretary of State in the new Administration, and it was assumed that he would speak with authority as to its purposes, though in this respect public expectation was at fault. Mr. Lincoln was tolerant and catholic in selecting and trusting men, but he put his conscience and judgment in no man's keeping. The main part of Seward's speech was an appeal for the

[1] Works, vol. v. pp. 437-439; Wilson's "History of the Rise and Fall of the Slave Power," vol. iii. pp. 71-82. The Crittenden Compromise was incidentally a topic of debate in the Senate, Feb. 9, 1864, when Sumner, Wilson, and other senators took occasion to reaffirm what they had said against it in 1861.

[2] Seward's "Life," vol. ii. pp. 496-497: Weed's "Life," vol. ii. p. 308.

Union, often eloquent and pathetic, and only briefly and near the end did he propose remedies. These were the organization of the Territories and their admission as States without conditions as to slavery, which was a surrender of the position held by the Republican party from its birth; an unalterable amendment of the Constitution prohibiting Congress from interfering with slavery in the States; and a convention — one, two, or three years later — to revise the Constitution. Incidentally he advised the revision of the Fugitive Slave Act and of the personal liberty laws of the free States. The speech had the characteristics of Seward's style; it was grave and impressive, and marked throughout by a certain vagueness and subtlety. It was difficult for either side to find out from his language exactly what was in his mind, and how far he proposed to go.[1] He read the speech before its delivery to Sumner, who pleaded with him in vain to reconsider his purpose.[2]

Sumner wrote to Dr. Howe, January 17: —

"I trust that Massachusetts continues unseduced by any proposition of compromise or concession, in whatever form or name. My best energies have been devoted to keep our men *firm*, FIRM, FIRM. My solicitude is so great that it has touched my health, but I cannot help it. Seward read me his speech four days before its delivery. When he came to his propositions, I protested with my whole soul, for the sake of our cause, our country, and his own good name, and I supplicated him to say no such thing. I do not speak, for such a speech as I should make would be seized by the conservative press, and be made the apology for the conduct of the slave States. To a member of the House who inquired what 'concession' I was willing to make, I said, 'There is one: I will consent to be silent yet a little longer.'"

The course of Charles Francis Adams, then serving his first term in Congress, was incomprehensible, and his explanations then made did not explain it. For nearly twenty years he had been a leader in the political movement against slavery,[3] always in the advance; and while like Sumner and Wilson keeping within constitutional lines, he was as radical as they in promoting measures to protect fugitive slaves, being the author of

1 The New York "Tribune," February 4, took issue with Seward, and found a parallel to his course in Webster's "Seventh of March" speech. The New York "Independent," February 7, contains S. H. Gay's criticism of the speech; but the editor a week later took a more favorable view of it. Seward spoke again briefly January 31. Mrs. Seward did not approve her husband's "concessions." Seward's "Life," vol. ii. p. 496.

2 Letter to John A. Andrew, Jan. 17, 1861. Works, vol. v. p. 455.

3 Wilson's "Rise and Fall of the Slave Power," vol. i. pp. 481, 485, 491, 585, 622, 642, 645, 649; vol. ii. pp. 119, 147, 344, 347, 348.

the first Act of the kind in his State,—in insisting on the prohibition of slavery in all the Territories, irrespective of conditions of climate and population, and its abolition in all national territory, notably in contests with Webster and Winthrop,—in denouncing the Compromise measures of 1850, and especially the Fugitive Slave Act, the immediate and complete repeal of which he had advocated. He stoutly insisted in 1854 that the Nebraska bill should be opposed, not so much as a breach of compact, but rather as the rejection of the Free Soil principle that slavery should be excluded from the Territories by national prohibition.[1] He took part in the Free Soil national conventions of 1848 and 1852, and the Republican convention of 1856; and when elected to Congress in 1858, he was understood to hold the most advanced constitutional positions against slavery. He held such positions during the first session of his term; and when he was leaving Boston for Washington in December, 1860, he signified to his friends that he should still maintain them against the expected pressure for compromise. The key to his new departure is most likely to be found in his personal and political intimacy, begun at Washington, with Mr. Seward; and their speeches in the session of 1860-1861 bear intrinsic evidence of a common understanding as to a course of action which was more in harmony with the character of Seward than with that of Adams.

Adams, as member of the Corwin committee of Thirty-three, moved two propositions, December 28 and 29,[2]—one a constitutional amendment excluding any amendment of the Constitution concerning slavery unless proposed by a slave State and adopted by all the States; and the other the admission of New Mexico as a State without restricting her action as to slavery.[3] The constitutional amendment proposed a new safeguard for slavery, and put the slaveholding interest in a superior position in the government. It was a late day in the history of

[1] Letter to Sumner, March 17, 1854.

[2] Mr. Adams, in his letter to G. H. Monroe, April 17, 1861, states that the propositions, prepared by others, were handed to him by Corwin, who thought they would have more effect coming from him than from any other member of the committee. It is likely that they were drawn by Seward, who had moved the amendment to the Constitution in the Senate committee of Thirteen.

[3] Mrs. Seward, who had decided views of her own, wrote to Sumner from Auburn: "I am grieved and surprised by Mr. Adams's proposition to give New Mexico to slavery. Three hundred thousand square miles of God's earth is a high price for the questionable advantage of a union with the slave States."

civilization to travel in that direction. An historian calls this proposition, as moved by Seward in the Senate and by Corwin in the House, "an act of moral self-abasement on the part of the North."[1] The other proposition admitted New Mexico, altogether unripe for membership in the Union,[2] although she had already in 1859 legalized slavery and adopted a barbarous slave code.[3] Within two weeks Mr. Adams, however, voted in committee against his two propositions when they came up again for final action, justifying his change of position on the ground that they had not been accepted as satisfactory by the recusant States; but they were carried in the committee against his negative vote.[4] Within three weeks from this action, he made a speech in the House, January 31, in which he returned to the support of the propositions he had offered and later rejected.[5] In this speech he maintained the inability of Congress to prohibit slavery in the Territories in the face of the Dred Scott decision, although he had denied its validity in a public address at Philadelphia, in which he had assailed the Buchanan Administration for its efforts to palm off as law extra-judicial opinions of a slaveholding bench of judges.[6] Mr. Adams, in letters to his constituents, treated as "an unrepealed and unrescinded contract"[7] a clause of the Compromise of 1850 which provided for the admission of New Mexico with or without slavery, as its

[1] Von Holst, vol. vii. p. 431.

[2] New Mexico is not thought thirty and more years later to be fit for admission. Arizona, then included in her limits, is also still a Territory.

[3] Von Holst, vol. vii. pp. 199, 227. The Boston "Courier," holding an extreme Southern position, approved, February 2, Mr. Adams's propositions, saying: "It is certain that these propositions include the principle of everything for which the South has contended."

[4] Journal of the Committee of Thirty-three. New York Tribune, Dec. 30 and 31. 1860: New York Herald, December 31; New York Evening Post, Jan. 15, 1861.

[5] Everett, Winthrop, and A. A. Lawrence, members of the Boston Union Committee, sat near Adams as he was speaking; and when he closed, Everett gave him congratulations and approval. Another hearer was Cassius M. Clay, who approved Adams's propositions in an address in Washington, January 26; New York "Tribune," January 28. Adams in this speech indicated his disposition to abandon the personal liberty laws of the States. Everett approved the Crittenden Compromise in a letter to the author of it; but Winthrop's reply was guarded. Coleman's "Life" of J. J. Crittenden, pp. 238, 239.

[6] Adams, in a letter to F. W. Bird, Feb. 16, 1861, though regarding Judge Taney's opinion as a *dictum*, thought it sure to be adopted by the court. Lincoln's Administration, however, rejected it altogether, and treated negroes as citizens. Opinion of Edward Bates, Attorney-General; McPherson's "History of the Rebellion," p. 378; Sumner's Works, vol. v. pp. 497, 498.

[7] Letter to E. L. Pierce, Jan. 1, 1861. Mr. Adams's action was reviewed by E. L. Pierce in the Boston "Atlas and Bee," Jan. 9, 1861; and the same journal published a leader, February 19, concerning it.

constitution prescribed at the time of admission. But the opponents of that Compromise at the time, and the Republican party later, always treated that provision, as well as a similar one in the Nebraska bill, as purely legislative declarations, subject to repeal and to be repealed whenever the pro-slavery power should be overthrown. On this view they acted when they prohibited slavery in all the Territories by the statute which President Lincoln approved June 19, 1862. Mr. Adams supported his propositions and others of the committee of Thirty-three by votes in the House, — some of his colleagues from Massachusetts joining with him, but the greater number separating from him.[1] He used no persuasions with them, and seemed indifferent as to their action.

In the committee of Thirty-three, two members alone — Washburn of Wisconsin and Tappan of New Hampshire — stood firmly against all compromise. Five however — Washburn, Tappan, Morrill, Kellogg, and Robinson — were against the admission of New Mexico as a slave State. Of the different reports, Wilson says in his History: "With the exception of the report signed by Washburn of Wisconsin and Tappan of New Hampshire, which alone had the true ring of freedom and fealty to human rights, each of the eight reports was apologetic and deprecatory in tone, — conceding much, sacrificing Northern self-respect, and ignoring as if they did not exist all claims of justice and humanity."[2] None of the House measures were considered in the Senate except the constitutional amendment, somewhat changed from the form proposed by Mr. Adams, which passed both houses by bare majorities, and was acted on only in two States.

In the midst of the general panic and demoralization there were senators and representatives who stood firmly for maintaining the historic positions of the Republican party. They included two-thirds of the Republican senators, but a smaller proportion of the Republican members of the House, where there

[1] McPherson's "History of the Rebellion," pp. 57-62; Congressional Globe, pp. 1262-1264, 1284, 1285, 1327, 1328, 1330. In the House, John Sherman, Schuyler Colfax, and William Windom voted for the proposed constitutional amendment. John Sherman agreed with Adams as to the admission of New Mexico without the prohibition of slavery. R. H. Dana, Jr., in speeches at Manchester, N. H. (February 19), and Cambridge, Mass. (February 11), took substantially Adams's view. Boston "Advertiser," February 20; Adams's "Biography" of Dana, vol. ii. pp. 252, 253. Governor Andrew is also understood to have communicated to Mr. Adams his approval of the latter's course at this time; but the anti-slavery men of Massachusetts were as a body against compromise.

[2] Vol. iii. p. 31.

was much shifting of position.[1] Of this type in the Senate were Sumner, Wilson, Trumbull, Wade, and Preston King; and in the House, Thaddeus Stevens, John Hickman, G. A. Grow, Roscoe Conkling, and Owen Lovejoy; and among Massachusetts members, Alley, Buffinton, Burlingame, Eliot, and Gooch. At such a period the steady courage of Sumner was of inestimable service in saving the country from the disaster of compromise and surrender.

The intimacy between Sumner and Adams, which began in 1845, and had been very close during the political conflicts of fifteen years, now came to an end. There was a scene in which Adams resented Sumner's protest against his support of compromise, the details of which are not known. It was Mrs. Adams's desire that the public should not take note of the altered relations of the two friends, and at her request Sumner assisted in a reception at her house; but their intercourse then ended. The parting was a grief to Sumner, who always clung to old friends. His private letters at the time, which speak freely of individuals, make no mention of Mr. Adams, and he was equally reserved in conversation. Adams was in a few weeks on his way to England, there to render a diplomatic service to his country second to no other in our history, or second only to that of Franklin. Nothing, except one or two formal notes, passed during his absence between him and Sumner, although during the same period the latter's correspondence with the friends of the United States in England was voluminous. After Mr. Adams's return in 1868, they met if at all only casually, neither calling on the other. Mutual respect, however, continued, and each refrained from all public criticism of the other.[2] If Adams had been the candidate in 1872 against General Grant, he would have been supported by Sumner with entire cordiality. In 1874 Adams paid a tribute to Sumner's memory at a meeting of the Massachusetts Historical Society,—a service which Sumner, if he had been the survivor, would have as sincerely rendered to the memory of Adams.[3]

[1] New York Times, January 23; February 5.

[2] Both were members of the Saturday Club in the years 1870–1873, and probably met at its monthly dinners; but it is not remembered that they conversed together at these reunions. Both were with the club April 27, 1861, and Oct. 27, 1873. Longfellow's "Life," vol. ii. p. 365; Adams's "Biography" of Dana, vol. ii. p. 360. Adams's letter, March 13, 1874, to a Faneuil Hall meeting, contains an appreciative estimate of Sumner.

[3] Mr. Adams, after his return from Europe, did not resume his former political relations, and he was at one time the Democratic candidate for governor. His confidential intercourse with his old Free Soil associates ended in 1861, except that he took the chair at

The peace conference of delegates from the free States and the border slave States, including Tennessee and North Carolina, called at the instance of the Legislature of Virginia, was in session at Washington from February 4 to February 27. Ex-President John Tyler, who well represented its spirit, was its president, and Salmon P. Chase led the non-compromisers on the floor. The majority voted propositions of compromise in the line of the Crittenden scheme; but Congress gave no heed to them. A considerable number of the members of the Massachusetts Legislature voted against the State's taking part in the conference, and Sumner agreed with them, being the only member of the Massachusetts delegation in Congress who declined to recommend the appointment of delegates. It was feared that the conference would distract the loyal sentiment of the country, and embarrass Mr. Lincoln's Administration. On the other hand, it was thought ungracious to keep aloof from a conference in which the border States were to join; and there was also some apprehension that in the absence of regular delegates the State might be misrepresented by volunteers.[1] Sumner was in a measure reconciled to the overruling of his judgment by the sturdy character of the delegates whom Governor Andrew appointed.[2]

Sumner was resolute against all these attempts at compromise. He believed it to be the right and duty of the elected Administration to take possession of the government and to administer it upon the principles which it had professed before the election, without receding in any degree and without compromise in substance or form. A parley with treason, a submission by lawful authority to conditions imposed by armed insurgents, involved a dissolution of all government. The Union, blessed as it was, would not as the price of its existence justify a wider area for slavery or new muniments for its perpetuity. Sumner deplored the distraction which the compromising spirit produced; and when he saw the friends and allies of a lifetime failing in the supreme moment, he put his trust, under Providence, not in the fidelity of leaders, but rather in the madness of the slaveholders. He took no optimistic view of the situ-

a Free Soil Reunion at Downer Landing, Aug. 9, 1877. The publication of his diary at some future period is likely to throw light on his action in the winter of 1860-1861.

1 Everett, Winthrop, and other members of the "Union" committee from Boston, then in Washington, were mentioned in the newspapers as likely to be invited to take seats in the absence of duly appointed delegates.

2 Works, vol. v. p. 461.

ation, but at the outset faced the worst. In the early part of 1861 he looked upon a slaveholders' rebellion as the probable outcome of Republican success in the national election. As soon as South Carolina began (in November) her formal proceedings for secession, he believed the cotton States would all follow her.[1] Before January ended he was convinced that all the slave States would join the Confederacy, except Maryland and Delaware, which would be held by the government as the route to Washington, and perhaps also Missouri. He saw that civil war was inevitable, and did not deceive himself, or attempt to deceive others, with the notion that it was to be a short one, — one of sixty or ninety days; but he believed that it was to be one which would task the full energies of the loyal people, with possible reverses at the beginning, with alternations of victory and defeat, with prolonged suspense, but with certain and absolute triumph at the end, crowned and glorified by the abolition of slavery.[2] His faith did not spring from natural buoyancy of spirits; it was not assumed in order to encourage his countrymen or keep foreign powers from intermeddling; it was to no considerable extent based on a comparison of the government's resources with those of the insurgents, — but it came from, and was maintained by, an inborn conviction that in a world governed by moral law such a cause as theirs could not succeed, and such a cause as the nation's could not fail.[3]

A great pressure was brought to bear upon Mr. Lincoln, before he left his home at Springfield, to make some declaration in favor of a compromise, especially with a view to hold the border States; but he resolutely refused, regarding any concession in the face of menace as a destruction of the government. He made known his opposition to any division of the Territories by the Missouri Compromise line, or the adoption of

[1] Many leaders of Northern opinion regarded with a light heart the initial movements for secession. Von Holst, vol. vii. pp. 233-239.

[2] Works, vol. v. pp. 449-467, where Sumner's letters to Governor Andrew and others at this time are given. His letter to Rev. E. E. Hale, dated Dec. 30, 1860, was read by the latter at Faneuil Hall, March 14, 1874. The ' North American Review" (1879), vol. cxxix. pp. 125, 375, 484, gives anonymous reminiscences from "The Diary of a Public Man," some of which describe interviews with Sumner at the time. They are manifestly false in certain points, and as a whole, like all anonymous testimony, entitled to no credit. They are the subject of criticism in G. T. Curtis's "Life of Buchanan," vol. ii. pp. 391, 395.

[3] Greeley's despairing state of mind at times is revealed in his letter to Lincoln, July 29, 1861. Nicolay and Hay's "Life of Lincoln," vol. iv. p. 365.

the dogma of popular sovereignty.[1] In his speeches during his journey from his home to the national capital there was no suggestion of compromise or of a surrender of any Republican position. When he reached Washington, all hope of the passage of compromise measures vanished. Among his titles to national gratitude, none is greater than his fidelity in this eventful moment of our history.

Sumner wrote to John Jay, Jan. 22, 1861: —

"I am much more afraid for our cause than for our capital Events march; and I do not see how the secession of thirteen or fourteen States can be arrested. But pray keep the North firm, — this is my daily prayer."

To F. W. Ballard, January 26: —

"This is a trying ordeal. History will protect the men who now stand firm. No compromise will now hold. Mr. Lincoln is perfectly firm. He says that the Republican party shall not with his assent become 'a mere sucked egg, all shell and no meat, — the principle all sucked out.' Pray keep our friends at Albany *firm, firm, firm,* — not 'a pepper corn.'"

To F W. Bird, January 28: —

"I read every word, although your letter was one of thirty brought me at the same time. I see the future clearly, — all bright for freedom, if the North will only keep its tranquillity and firmness. If Massachusetts begins a retreat, I know not where it will stop; there is nothing of freedom in the North which will not be endangered. God guard her from any backward step! I have written to Pierce[2] an off-hand letter, giving my sentiments on the madness which would now repeal the safeguards of freedom. I trust that if there is anybody at the State House who cares for my opinion, and who inclines to this madness, he will at least hesitate well, and not act hastily. Freedom is about to have her greatest peril, to be followed by results of unspeakable importance. Men will press compromise, but, I am happy to believe, in vain. *The question is to be settled now.*

"Virginia will secede, carrying with her all the rest, except perhaps Maryland, which will be retained by the national capital. There are some who think this cannot be done, but that the revolution which carries Maryland will seize the capital. Perhaps February will be an eventful month. I have not spoken, because I could say nothing which would not be perverted by the compromisers as an attempt to widen the breach. Meanwhile I insist upon an inflexible 'No' to every proposition. 'No,' 'No,' 'No,' let the North cry out to every compromise and to every retreat."

1 New York "Tribune," Jan. 30, 1861. Nicolay and Hay's "Life of Lincoln," vol. iii. pp. 258, 259, 279-288, 327 *note.* This general statement concerning Mr. Lincoln's position must be qualified by a reference to the closing sentence of his letter to Seward, Feb. 1, 1861: "Nor do I care much about New Mexico if further extension were hedged against." Nor was he at any time concerned about the oppressive and unconstitutional legislation of 1850 for the rendition of fugitive slaves.

2 Henry L. Pierce, then a member of the Legislature.

To Whittier, February 5: —

"I deplored Seward's speeches.[1] The first he read to me, and I supplicated him not to make it. The true-hearted here have been filled with grief and mortification. People are anxious to save our forts, to save our national capital; but I am more anxious far to *save our principles*, which leaders now propose to abandon, as Mr. Buchanan proposed to abandon Fort Sumter. The public pride arrested the latter; I hope the public conscience may arrest the former. My old saying is revived in my mind. *Backbone*, — this especially is needed here. If we are saved, it will be by events, and not by men. The inordinate demand of the slave States will make it next to impossible to appease them; even compromise cannot go so far. If they asked less we should be lost. Pray keep Massachusetts firm and strong. She must not touch a word of her personal liberty laws. The slightest act of surrender by her would be a signal for the abasement of the free States."

To John Jay, February 5: —

"I am filled with grief and oppressed with mortification when I see what is going on [the surrender of principles]. But my faith is yet strong that God will guide us safely to the end, and uphold our cause even when men desert it."

To F. W. Ballard, February 9: —

"I fear nothing now but compromise. 'The thing I am afraid of is fear,' says old Montaigne; and he was very wise."

To John Jay, March 27: —

"Everything tends, as I have foreseen, to a break-up of the Union. But Seward is infatuated; he says in sixty days all will be well."

Sumner kept aloof from the debate on the crisis, yielding with some reluctance to the counsels of friends, who thought that if he gave his views his motives would be misconceived, and he would be accused of a purpose to increase the excitement.[2] But he was not altogether silent. A few days after the session began he read to the Senate, with brief comments, an original private letter of Andrew Jackson, written in May, 1833, to Rev. Andrew J. Crawford, in which, referring to the attempt of South Carolina at nullification (then recently arrested), he said that "the tariff was only the pretext, and disunion and a Southern confederacy the real object," and added that "the next pretext will be the negro or slavery

[1] January 12 and 31.

[2] Notes of an undelivered speech prepared in February show his tone of mind at the time. Works, vol. v. pp. 481–483.

question."[1] The letter was thus first made known to the country when its prediction was being fulfilled.

The panic at this time was nowhere greater than in Boston, where popular demonstrations in favor of compromise were made. Seward's speech and Adams's propositions had turned the public mind in that direction, and the masses of men do not at such a time discriminate between different schemes. The supporters of Bell, Douglas, and Breckinridge, being in a majority, took the lead in urging the Crittenden plan, and they carried along with them some unreflecting Republicans. Among the callers of a "Union" meeting in its support were William Appleton, Albert Fearing, James M. Beebe, and Josiah G. Abbott. The meeting was held February 5, in Faneuil Hall, with Mayor Wightman in the chair; and among the speakers were J. Thomas Stevenson, B. R. Curtis, and H. F. Durant.[2] A committee, of which Everett, Winthrop, and A. A. Lawrence were members, went to Washington to promote the adoption of the Crittenden propositions. Everett and Lawrence called on Sumner, and the former with much emotion urged him to enlist in some scheme of compromise; but they found that he could not be moved.[3] The city council by formal vote approved the Crittenden scheme. A petition in its support, with more than twenty thousand names procured in the cities and towns of the State, was, after being wrapped in the American flag, presented, February 12, by Mr. Crittenden in the Senate. Sumner, though keeping aloof from debates, was unwilling that the State should be put in a false position, and after Crittenden had presented the petition, took occasion at once to explain the character and effect of the propositions approved by it, — "going," as he said, "beyond the Breckinridge platform, already solemnly condemned by the American people in the election of Abraham Lincoln;" and he gave as the best apology for the petitioners their ignorance of the character of the propositions.[4] Two things only, he maintained,

1 Works, vol. v. pp. 433-436. Mr. Crawford, then living at the South, was harassed by his neighbors on account of the publication of this letter, and shortly after destroyed the original. It came to Sumner's hand through W. L. Burt, of Boston, a kinsman of Lucius Wilcox, of Canandaigua, N. Y., a son-in-law of Mr. Crawford.

2 Seward and Adams were applauded at the meeting. Durant denounced Sumner, and referred to the break between him and Adams. At a "workingmen's" meeting, so called, held February 19, in the same place, in support of the compromise, Seward's and Adams's names were applauded, and Sumner's received with groans and hisses.

3 Works, vol. v. pp. 444, 463. New York Times, January 25.

4 The Boston "Courier," February 4, said that it was a libel on Massachusetts for Sumner to say that her people did not approve the Crittenden Compromise.

were all-sufficient for the present crisis: "First, that the Constitution of the United States as administered by George Washington shall be preserved intact and blameless in its text, with no tinkering for the sake of slavery; and secondly, that the verdict of the people last November, by which Abraham Lincoln was elected President of the United States, shall be enforced without price or condition."[1] To the suggestion coming from some quarters that the bankers and merchants of New York and Boston would not lend money to the government unless a compromise was made, he replied that after the recent example of France, the people would promptly meet the emergency by a popular loan; and he added with emphasis, "There is but one thing now for the North to do, — it is to stand firm." A colloquy with Crittenden ensued, in which the latter upbraided Sumner for not proposing amendments to his (Mr. C.'s) plan, or offering one of his own, accusing him of "sitting sullen and silent here for one month or more with his breast full of resentment." Sumner replied that he had voted for Senator Clark's substitute, which expressed precisely his convictions.[2] The city council of Boston passed a vote, February 7, declaring the senator's statement with regard to the petitioners "undignified, unbecoming a senator and a citizen of Boston, and untrue." He was however sustained by several of the leading journals of the city in his comments on the petition, and he received many letters, several from the signers themselves, verifying what he had said.[3] E. L. Pierce wrote, February 14: —

"Your speech in the Senate was just the thing. It was uncompromising, and therefore was right. It was brief; and no speech at this time should be long. It dealt with the present; and this is no time for historical speeches. It was temperate, as we should be; it was firm, as the occasion requires."

R. W. Emerson wrote, February 27: —

"Peace and prosperity adhere to your truth and firmness, as they ought. I am always consoled in the bad times by your fidelity. . . . May the Highest Wisdom and Strength keep and guide you!"

Sumner called on President Buchanan with reference to the offer of aid to the government formally made by the State of

1 Works, vol. v. pp. 468–480. In a debate in the Senate, Feb. 9, 1864, Sumner reiterated his views of the Crittenden Compromise.

2 "That the provisions of the Constitution are ample for the preservation of the Union and the protection of all the material interests of the country; that it needs to be obeyed rather than amended," etc.

3 Works, vol. v. pp. 477–480.

Massachusetts; and inquiring what else the State could do for the good of the country, the President replied, "Adopt the Crittenden propositions." The senator's answer was, that such were the unalterable convictions of the people of the State that they would never adopt propositions which protected slavery in the Territories, and disfranchised large numbers of her citizens. The interview then ended without further discussion.[1]

Sumner interposed an objection to the House resolution which by an irrepealable and unamendable amendment to the Constitution excluded Congress forever from interfering with slavery in the States, so as to prevent its being hurried through; and the next day he had a correction made in the journal which had failed to record his objection. It passed at the end of the session by the exact two-thirds vote required. Among the negative votes were those of Sumner, Wilson, Foot, Trumbull, Wade, Preston King, and Z. Chandler. Seward and Fessenden did not vote. In presenting, February 18, petitions opposed to compromise, Sumner added comments of his own in approval. He expressed his dissent, February 25, from one which prayed for national interference with slavery in the States.

During the winter there was a determined effort in Massachusetts to repeal the personal liberty law of the State. An appeal to that effect, signed by Chief-Justice Shaw, recently retired from office, B. R. Curtis, Joel Parker, George Ticknor, and a large number of persons of high standing, was published in the papers and presented to the Legislature. It was supported by leading Boston journals. George Ashmun, who had presided at the national Republican convention, in an open letter to Mr. Winthrop urged the repeal. Governor Banks, yielding to the pressure, in a farewell message recommended the repeal; while his successor, Governor Andrew, took the opposite position, though willing to assent to the revision of any doubtful provision. Sumner was most earnest in his protests against a repeal, insisting that any questions concerning the statute should be left to the courts, and that a repeal under menace would be a humiliation. His letters, which were freely shown among members of the Legislature, were thought to have saved the statute.[2]

[1] Works, vol. v. pp. 448-449.

[2] The statute was amended in one particular, where by a certain construction it might involve a conflict between national and State officers, — this amendment being desired by Governor Andrew. Rhode Island repealed her personal liberty statute; but Vermont stood firm.

To A. G. Browne, who wished him to come to Boston to assist in preventing the repeal of the personal liberty law, he wrote, January 24, declining on account of duties at Washington : —

"But, believe me, I would do much, and suffer too if need be, to save our beloved Commonwealth from the shame of a backward step. There is not a personal liberty law or habeas corpus statute on her books which will not be mentioned among her glories when these events come to be written."

He wrote, January 29, a long and earnest letter to Henry L. Pierce, then a member of the Massachusetts House of Representatives, and afterwards serving with him in Congress : —

"I was glad when you were chosen to the Legislature; but I did not know then that I should have the special occasion for gratitude which fills me when I think that you are there to meet with steadfast opposition all those timid counsels which seek to overthrow our Massachusetts safeguards of personal liberty; for I did not then imagine that the Republican party, fresh from its greatest triumph, would be willing to sacrifice these safeguards. . . . If the influence of the surrender were confined to Massachusetts I would try to bear it, — cover my face with my hands, concealing my shame. But I see clearly that it would be the signal of a surrender of still other things throughout the free States. If Massachusetts yields anything now to the outcry of the traitors, other States will yield everything. My conviction of this is so strong that I sincerely feel that you, who are now defending our Massachusetts laws, are defending the most vital principles of human liberty in every State of the Union. . . . This I know: Massachusetts can gain nothing by the proposed system of surrender; but if it is entered upon she will lose her high place as the steadfast, fearless, and uncompromising friend of human rights, and she must lose something of her self-respect. I write at my desk while we are discussing the railroad to the Pacific. The bill has just passed the Senate; this is good news. But every triumph of civilization increases my pride in Massachusetts, which has done so much for it on this continent. God grant that she may not take a backward step, and set her face towards barbarism!"

To E. L. Pierce, who had maintained before the legislative committee the conformity of the personal liberty laws with the national Constitution, he wrote, February 7 : —

"I honor and thank you much for your speech, which is able, well-sustained, and eloquent. If the scales have been doubtful, this powerful effort ought to determine the question. But I trust that at last our Massachusetts honor is safe. Do give me some assurance that it is so. At this moment not a letter of our personal liberty law must be touched. If anything is really commanded, — and I insist that it is not, — pray save us from this humiliation, at least till after the 4th of March. Of course, it will be easy for the committee to keep back their report. People here fear compromise. I am anxious; but in my judgment nothing can pass which will really satisfy the seceders. I think we shall be saved. When the cause has been won, you cannot be forgotten among those who have nobly served it; but won or lost, there is a satisfaction in serving such a cause. God bless you!"

Sumner's correspondents — and they were very numerous at this time — were, with few exceptions, opposed to any compromise, and many of them were explicit in their disapproval of the propositions of Seward and Adams. But the writers, whether for or against concession, were all groping in darkness and uncertainty, — some thinking a separation likely, with more or less friction or collision, and then a possible reunion, but none foreseeing civil war and great armies facing each other from the Potomac to the Red River. Parke Godwin expressed the prevailing thought in a letter, Dec. 4, 1860: —

"As to our public affairs, I am greatly in the dark. Principles I see clearly; but I do not see what is likely to be the practical upshot of the crisis. The best way, doubtless, is to adhere to the right, and let the all-wise Disposer bring out the issues in his time."

None wrote at the time more thoughtfully than John Jay, who kept urging the necessity of precautions for securing Mr. Lincoln's inauguration in accordance with regular and customary forms, for keeping open the way to the capital, and for holding the forts and navy-yards. He wrote, December 31: —

"Is it Charles Francis Adams of Massachusetts who consents that New Mexico shall be cursed with slavery, and recommends to the Republican party to deny their principles, and do this great wickedness in order to appease a State in armed rebellion, and mollify others that are insulting and outraging to the last extent Northern citizens within their borders? Let the slave-power extort from our fears one sacrifice of the principles on which we fought and won this last great battle, and their triumph and our humiliation will be complete."

No one was firmer in this crisis than S. P. Chase, already elected again to the Senate, and just completing his second term as governor of Ohio. His phrase, "Inauguration first, adjustment afterwards," became a watchword of uncompromising Republicans; and in that spirit he acted in the Peace Conference, where he dissented from the majority of the Ohio delegation. He wrote to Sumner, Jan. 23, 1861, deploring Seward's speech,[1] and ending, "My faith is fixed; no compromise now,

[1] He had by letter (Jan. 11, 1861) endeavored to dissuade Seward from making a compromise speech. Schuckers's "Life of S. P. Chase," p. 202.

and no proposition of adjustment until the executive department of the government is ours." And three days later he wrote again: —

"The surrender will not save the Union; firmness, decision, moderation, will, — if anything will. If my voice could be heard in the Senate I would protest with all my power against the surrender of New Mexico to slavery, — than which it is difficult for me to conceive of anything more repugnant to our professions before the people, as well as against an amendment of the national Constitution touching slavery in the States."[1]

The various schemes of compromise, agitated in the winter of 1860–1861, had no sensible effect in appeasing the Southern temper, and probably never varied the course of a single Southern man; and they dropped from the controversy when armed conflict opened at Fort Sumter. The Union was to be maintained not by fencing with propositions, but by the patriotism and endurance of the free States.

Sumner during this anxious period conferred often with General Scott and the loyal members of Buchanan's Cabinet — Stanton, Holt, and Dix — in reference to the safety of the capital and measures necessary to secure a regular and peaceable inauguration of President Lincoln.[2] He was, in frequent letters to Governor Andrew, most urgent that Massachusetts should offer pecuniary aid to the government in its strait, — a measure which was carried.[3]

Later in the session the Morrill tariff bill was passed. Sumner made an effort without success to put engravings, paintings, and statuary on the free list, as well as books which had been printed thirty years. He advocated a lower duty on books than the fifteen per cent proposed by the bill, and expressed his preference for admitting all books free. He was opposed by Hale of New Hampshire, Baker of Oregon, and Clingman of North Carolina, but assisted by Douglas.[4] He continued while in the Senate, whenever the question came up, to contend for free books and free works of art and free instruments for use in scientific education, and was finally successful in freeing

1 Other correspondents who condemned all compromise were B. R. Wood and G. E. Baker of Albany; David Dudley Field and Joshua Leavitt of New York; F. W. Bird, G. S. Boutwell, W. Claflin, J. T. Buckingham, Dr. Samuel Cabot, and E. L. Pierce of Massachusetts.

2 Works, vol. v. pp. 454, 457–459.

3 Works, vol. v. pp. 455, 458, 465, 466.

4 February 18, 19, 20. Congressional Globe, pp. 987, 1030, 1047–1051.

books thirty years old from duty.[1] He sought to free ornamental trees and shrubs, saying of the trees that "we should encourage them all, till Birnam wood do come to Dunsinane."[2] He was always, as he said, for a free list in the tariff as large as possible.[3] He joined with his colleague Wilson in voting for lower duties on imported wool,[4] — both acting in harmony with their position in the passage of the tariff act of 1857. At the extra session in July, 1861, he opposed raising the duties imposed in the Morrill Act by ten per cent, taking the ground that the increase, while not likely to add to the revenue, would naturally repel from us the sympathies of the laboring classes of Europe.[5] Fessenden, however, thought that foreign opinion should not be taken into account. Sumner also proposed to relieve from the higher duty goods in the course of transportation at the time of the passage of the Act.[6] At a later session, that of 1867, he voted and spoke for lower duties on coal, so that he was accused by another senator of having made a "free trade" speech.[7] He regarded the high duties on imported goods levied during the war as temporary and provisional.[8] He showed, as will be seen in the review of the next session, the same liberality in the treatment of the internal tax system. Some later expressions indicate his temper of mind on the general question of a protective tariff. He wrote to Lieber, Jan. 17, 1863: —

"I don't understand your anxieties about protection. I see no pressure on this question from New England or elsewhere. Besides, the duties rendered necessary for revenue will constitute an all-sufficient protection. What more will be thought of? If you see any danger ahead on this account, pray indicate it precisely, that I may do what I can to meet it. You know that I am

1 July 8, 1862; Works, vol. vii. pp. 166-168, June 2 and 6, 1864; Works, vol. viii. pp. 471-474, June 17, 1864; Works, vol. ix. pp. 28, 29, Feb. 27, 1865; Works, vol. ix. pp. 336-339, Jan. 24, 1867; Works, vol. xi. pp. 83-90, Jan. 30, 31, 1867; Congressional Globe, p. 862, 913, June 30, 1870; Works, vol. xiii. pp. 471-473, March 27, 1872; Works, vol. xv. pp. 61-64; also for free books in foreign languages, Jan. 31, 1867; Globe, p. 914; May 28, Globe, pp. 3957, 3958.

2 May 27, 1872. Congressional Globe, pp. 3899, 3900.

3 March 26, 1872. Congressional Globe, p. 1977.

4 Feb. 19, 1861; Congressional Globe, pp. 1026, 1027. He voted, July 12, 1866, in association with his colleague, Mr. Wilson, for the postponement of a tariff for the increase of duties, — a measure chiefly promoted by the wool-growing interest, and meeting with little favor from New England manufacturers.

5 July 29, 1861. Works, vol. v. pp. 502-508.

6 July 26, 29. Congressional Globe, pp. 278, 318.

7 Jan. 29 and 30, 1867; Works, vol. xi. pp. 91-97; Congressional Globe, p. 855.

8 June 16, 1864. Works, vol. ix. pp. 26, 27.

no partisan of protection, and that on that whole question I am absolutely independent."

And again a week later: —

"I do not understand your anxiety about protection in New England. Wilson and myself are not its partisans, and I am ready to move in any policy which is liberal and just, — especially to the West."[1]

Sumner was with the other senators present at Mr. Lincoln's inauguration, March 4. The Senate, meeting the same day to act on the appointments of the new Administration, remained in session till late in the month. Sumner was at the time mentioned for the English mission, and Governor Andrew and other persons of influence desired his appointment; but he put aside the suggestion peremptorily, preferring his place in the Senate to any other. The Senate listened to the disunion speeches of Clingman, Wigfall, Mason, and Breckinridge, and to speeches hardly less mischievous from Douglas and Bayard. Douglas was bitter in the extreme towards Wilson, Fessenden, and Hale; and Wilson in a brief reply justly called his speech "mischievous," "wicked," and "unpatriotic." This was the last of his career, as he died a few weeks after the session closed. The Republicans generally kept silent in the debate. They were now in a majority by the withdrawal of senators from the seceded States, and entitled to the chairmanship of the committees and a majority of members of each committee. It fell to Bright of Indiana, who nine years before had explained the exclusion of Chase, Hale, and Sumner by saying that they were "outside of any healthy political organization," to move the new list on which the two parties had agreed. Sumner was made chairman of the committee on foreign relations, taking the place of Mason, who had held the post since 1851. His associates were Collamer, Doolittle, Harris, Douglas, Polk, and Breckinridge. He was also placed on the committees on private land claims and patents. His colleague, Wilson, became chairman of the committee on military affairs. Sumner, exercising the customary right of a chairman, designated as clerk of his committee Mr. Ben Perley Poore, not at the time a per-

[1] He recurred to the subject briefly in a letter to John Bright, May 21, 1866, *post*, p. 289. W. D. Kelley, in his eulogy in the House, April 27, 1874, took exception to Sumner's "theories of trade and finance, — free trade and the limitation of the medium of exchange to a volume of paper money so restricted that it might ever be interchangeable with gold." Mr. Kelley had probably no evidence of Sumner's views except his public action.

sonal or political friend, and only an acquaintance for a short time, but supposed by long residence abroad to be specially competent for the duties, — requiring, however, Mr. Poore to ascertain whether his appointment would be satisfactory to Douglas and Breckinridge, the Democratic members of the committee.[1] He excluded liquors from the committee room, and caused the side-board to be removed in which they had been kept. From the beginning he was prompt in calling the committee to order, taking the chair punctually at the moment; saw to it that matters for its consideration had been well matured, and held it strictly to the business in hand. By his efficiency he kept its docket clear, so that the regular sessions were sometimes omitted. He was deferential towards his associates, as well when he differed from them as when he agreed with them, and whether his personal relations were friendly with them or not. On all questions foreign or domestic he carried a level head in the midst of enthusiasm or frenzy, well assured of the future, and confident that time and reflection would restore sobriety of judgment. Political opponents as well as friends have borne willing testimony to his conduct in the committee.[2]

The first matter on which the committee was called to act was the San Juan question, — the disputed boundary between Vancouver's Island, a British possession, and the United States, on which Sumner made a report proposing arbitration. The dispute, however, remained open until the treaty of Washington in 1871.[3]

Sumner's new position was altogether congenial to his tastes. There were no subjects with which he was so competent to deal as with those belonging to his committee. Knowledge of international law acquired in early studies, personal intercourse with public men abroad, and constant interest in European affairs, kept up in correspondence and in intercourse with foreign ministers at Washington, combined to give him rare equipment for the post.[4] The appointment was received with general favor.[5]

[1] Boston Journal, March 21, 1871.

[2] See testimonies of senators in "North American Review," July and August, 1878, pp. 69-75.

[3] Works, vol. v. pp. 484-491.

[4] *Ante*, Memoir, vol. i. p. 150. Gideon Welles, in a review of political history in 1875, wrote: "Mr. Sumner was a scholar, and better read on the subject of our foreign relations, international law, our treaties and traditions, than any other man in Congress. He better filled the position of chairman of the committee on foreign relations than any of his associates could have done." North American Review, July, 1887, p. 78.

[5] Works, vol. v. pp. 484, 485.

He, as well as other Republican senators, now assumed responsibility for public affairs, and their capacity for legislation was to be tested. Hitherto their work had been chiefly one of criticism, obstruction, and protest; it was henceforth to be initiative and practical.

Naturally, Sumner was specially concerned for our representation abroad. He wrote to F. W. Bird, March 10: —

"There is chaos in our foreign system. But it is of incalculable importance that our cause should be represented at every European government with all the character, skill, and persuasion which we can command. But I fear that this exigency is not comprehended."

While not making it a rigid rule, Sumner thought it desirable that a minister should be able to speak the language of the country to which he was accredited. He was impatient with two notions which are apt to prevail at Washington, — that appointments to diplomatic posts are fit rewards for party service, and that they should also be distributed equally among the States and sections.[1] He valued most highly the accomplishments of George P. Marsh, who was appointed to the Italian mission, on account of his familiarity with languages and his rank among *savans*. He pleaded in vain with Mr. Lincoln for Theodore S. Fay's retention at Berne,[2] and also failed in securing for Motley the mission to the Hague. He approved the appointment of Carl Schurz to Madrid, and also procured that of secretary of legation at the same court for Mr. H. J. Perry, without the latter's request or knowledge, — deeming Mr. Perry's previous experience in the same office, and his attainments in the Spanish language, to be of special advantage to our country. He was very desirous that John Jay should receive an important mission, in view of his personal fitness, his unselfish patriotism, and his devotion to the antislavery cause; but unfortunately his name and that of Motley were both presented for the Austrian mission after Motley had failed to secure the mission to the Hague, and Burlingame had been transferred from Vienna to Pekin. Sumner was embarrassed by the rivalry of the two friends ("brothers" to him, to use his own expression); but while meaning to keep the balance between the two, he never-

[1] He wrote to an applicant for a foreign post, July 4, 1861: "Nobody who wishes to succeed should hail from Massachusetts or New York. Their claims are said to be exhausted."

[2] *Ante*, vol. ii. p. 120, *note*.

theless said enough to give the impression to the President and Secretary of State that he favored Motley. Jay, who should have had the appointment, bore the disappointment in a manly way.[1] It was Sumner's weakness that he put too high a value on literary distinction even in diplomatic service, where, combined with practical qualities, it undoubtedly adds to a minister's power.

Sumner as chairman of the committee on foreign relations and Seward as Secretary of State were for the next eight years to remain in agreeable personal relations, and to co-operate in public business and friendly offices;[2] but they were rarely to be in sympathetic relation on questions concerning slavery and reconstruction. There were also to be differences of opinion on matters of foreign policy. Seward, adept as he was in domestic politics, was at times erratic, visionary, and impulsive; and his judgment was disturbed by romantic ideas both of his own relation to events and of the methods by which the Civil War might be averted or speedily ended. His earliest State papers embarrassed the government, and had to be partially withdrawn or explained. His assurances that slavery was not concerned in the conflict will be hereafter referred to; but his theory of the relation of the nation to the States, in which he came very near to Buchanan's, was no less objectionable. He wrote Mr. Adams, our minister at London, April 10, two days before the bombardment of Fort Sumter, that "the federal government could not reduce the seceding States to obedience by conquest," and that "only an imperial and despotic government could subjugate thoroughly disaffected and insurrectional members of the State," — an unfortunate declaration, which misled European powers as to our system of government.[3]

Seward's character was complex; it is difficult to understand it, and it is possible to misjudge him. At the outset as secre-

[1] Mr. Jay was appointed to Vienna eight years later.

[2] It is hardly worth while perhaps to take note of a statement that the President and secretary were in the habit of playing upon the senator, enticing him to the support of their measures by making him think they were his own rather than theirs. No instance is given, and no authority for such a statement; and its only basis, if it has any, is Washington gossip, which is not history. The relations of both Lincoln and Seward to Sumner, and all they are known to have said of him, show that in case of difference of opinion neither of them pretended to any art of overcoming his adverse view other than by convincing his judgment.

[3] F. W. Newman's Miscellanies, vol. iii. p. 196; London "Morning Star," May 11, 1869.

tary he opposed the relief of Fort Sumter, and continued to oppose it against the positive opinions of his associates,—Chase, Blair, and Welles. On April 1 he submitted to the President, without the latter's invitation, what is justly called "an extraordinary state paper, unlike anything to be found in the political history of the United States." After saying that "we are at the end of a month's administration, and yet without a policy, either domestic or foreign," he urged as the ruling idea of a policy at home that "we must change the question before the public from one upon slavery, or about slavery, for a question upon union or disunion;" and that the occupation of Fort Sumter, which was regarded as a slavery or party question, should be terminated "as a safe means for changing the issue." Next, as a foreign policy, he "would demand explanations from Spain and France, categorically, at once" (for what he did not say); and "if satisfactory explanations are not received" from them, he "would convene Congress and declare war against them." He "would also seek explanations from Great Britain and Russia [for what he did not say], and send agents into Canada, Mexico, and Central America to rouse a vigorous continental spirit of independence on this continent against European intervention." The letter then proceeded to a still more extraordinary recommendation:—

"For this purpose it must be somebody's business to pursue and direct it [this policy] incessantly. Either the President must do it himself, and be all the while active in it, or devolve it on some member of his Cabinet. Once adopted, debates on it must end, and all agree and abide. *It is not in my especial province; but I neither seek to evade nor assume responsibility.*"

Eccentricity, almost unsoundness of mind, might fairly be suspected in one who could make such astounding propositions,—wars with two foreign nations, to be added to a civil war; hostile demonstrations at the same time against two other powers; a practical abdication by the President of his functions, and an assumption by his secretary of something like a dictator's office, or of a consul's extraordinary power conferred in time of danger, to take measures for the protection of the State!

The President answered promptly, saying as little as he could, treating his secretary with the utmost delicacy, objecting to the charge of lack of policy, and replying to the suggestion of concentration of power with the single comment: "I remark that if this must be done, I must do it."[1] It is not strange that the President afterwards sought other advice than his secretary's when critical foreign questions were pressing for solution. Notwithstanding the incident, which must have left on his mind permanent distrust of the secretary's discretion, he decided wisely as well as generously that one with Seward's large and varied powers could, if kept under proper control and oversight, be made very useful to the country; and Seward continued to hold his place securely. The secret of the correspondence was well kept, not being revealed during the lifetime of the parties to it.

Mr. Lincoln intervened at times to amend by interlineations and erasures the official papers of the Secretary of State, often crude and extravagant, — notably one of the earliest, that of May 21, 1861, to Adams, portions of which, written it is said under irritation, were "phrased with an exasperating bluntness, and certain directions were lacking in diplomatic prudence."[2] Sumner was in Washington when this despatch was under consideration, and it is likely that the President advised with him concerning its modification.

There was unfortunately in the critical period of 1861-1862 a conviction prevailing in England that Seward was personally hostile to that country, and bent on war with it. It may be accounted for by the tone of some of his official papers, as that of his letter, Oct. 14, 1861, to Lord Lyons; his proneness to suggest war or a rupture of friendly relations as an event likely to follow conduct of which we complained; his circular to the Northern governors concerning fortifications on the lakes, which gave apprehensions of a contemplated invasion of Canada; and perhaps also his style of conversation with diplomats and other foreigners, often mere badinage, which was interpreted to have a hostile meaning not intended by him. But this distrust, whatever its cause, existed in fact; and there was danger that it might precipitate serious difficulty with foreign powers at a time when our burdens could not be increased without national disaster and ruin.[3] Weed, in his semi-official visit to England and France,

[1] Nicolay and Hay's "Life of Lincoln," vol. iii. pp. 444-449. Seward's biographer does not explain or comment upon his remarkable suggestions of foreign wars, and his readiness to take the responsibility for their direction. Seward's "Life," vol. ii. p. 535.

[2] Nicolay and Hay's "Life of Lincoln," vol. iv. pp. 269-277.

[3] N. W. Senior's letter to Sumner, Dec. 10, 1861; Reid's "Life" of W. E. Forster, vol. i. p. 344; Walpole's "Life" of Lord John Russell, vol. ii. p. 342. According to Earl Russell, "Lord Lyons reported that, incredible as it might appear, the American Secretary

discovered this prevailing impression concerning Seward, and did his best in private conversation and a letter to the London "Times" to remove it.[1] The Duchess of Sutherland evidently wrote with the same thought her letter to Seward, Dec. 8, 1861.[2] Cobden, however, took him less seriously, thinking him "a kind of American Thiers or Palmerston or Russell, talking to Bunkum."[3] The Duke of Argyll, a member of the British cabinet, the only member altogether sympathetic with our cause, wrote to Sumner as early as June 4, 1861: —

"I write a few lines very earnestly to entreat that you will use your influence and official authority to induce your government, and especially Mr. Seward, to act in a more liberal and a less reckless spirit than he is supposed here to indicate towards foreign governments, and especially towards ourselves. I find much uneasiness prevailing here lest things should be done which would arouse a hostile spirit in this country. So far as I know, this uneasiness is founded rather on things said than on things yet actually done. But Mr. Seward knows Europe less well than you do; and the very natural state of violent excitement of your people just now leads many of us to fear that he may be disposed to do high-handed and offensive things which would necessarily lead to bad blood, and perhaps finally to rupture. I rejoice that at such a critical time you are at the head of the body which on foreign relations is able to control the government, because I know how anxious you will be to be just and considerate in your dealings.[4] I only wish you had been in Seward's place. There is a great fear here that he has got it into his head that the English people can't and won't take offence at anything the American government may do to their ships or their people. Now, this is a great mistake. I believe there is no desire stronger here than that of maintaining friendly relations with America. But there are points on which our people are very sensitive; and if they saw themselves touched on these points in honor or interest, the irritation would be extreme, and could not be controlled. I write this to you as a private and a very valued friend, for your own private use and guidance. I am sure we shall do all we can here to keep the peace, and I feel sure that you will do the same. But I have not equal confidence in the government of the United States."

Shortly after Sumner's return from a visit to Washington in May, 1861, he mentioned in conversation the distrust of Seward prevailing abroad as well as in some quarters at home; and he

of State really hoped to overawe England and France by threatening language." Bright wrote to Sumner, Nov. 29, 1861: "There is a feeling among our ministers that Mr. Seward is not so friendly in his transactions with them as they could wish. I hope this is not so."

[1] Seward's "Life," vol. iii. pp. 29, 30, 37; Weed's "Life," vol. ii. pp. 355–361.

[2] Seward's "Life," vol. iii. p. 32.

[3] Morley's "Life" of Cobden, vol. ii. p. 386.

[4] Cobden expressed the same confidence in Sumner in his letter to Lieut.-Colonel Fitzmayer, Dec. 3, 1861. "Life," pp. 386, 387.

wrote privately to Lieber to the same effect. But it is not true, as has been stated, that he sought to undermine the secretary in correspondence with English friends and in conversation with foreign diplomats. On the other hand, he did his best in that correspondence to make it appear that Seward, whatever expressions he might have used, was not in fact hostile to England, and that the President also was friendly and pacific towards that country as well as France.[1]

The change of Administration brought a horde of competitors for the offices. The civil service doubtless needed renovation, and many office-holders, even at the North, were so infected with Southern sympathies that their retention was undesirable. The civil service reform had not then been thought of, so that there was no check to the pressure for office. The Massachusetts delegation, meeting in Boston, assigned the important appointments for the State ; and Sumner, still at Washington, took the list to the President, saying that while it did not in all respects represent his views he approved its immediate adoption, deeming it most important that in the existing exigency of public affairs all controversy as to the offices should be ended at once. The appointments thus recommended were forthwith made.

The Postmaster-General, Mr. Blair, adopted the rule of allowing the senators each to name the postmaster for his place of residence. The Boston post-office was sought by three persons, who were backed by an array of names on their petitions and by political influence,—all three active in politics, and two of them editors of city journals. Sumner, turning from these applicants, selected John G. Palfrey, who had retired from political activity and was without any considerable political support, — making the selection on the ground that Dr. Palfrey, while as qualified for the post as the other candidates, had for a long period rendered eminent service to the cause of freedom, notably in his writings as also in his example as the liberator of inherited slaves.[2] Sumner's action in this appointment illustrates his exceptional way of disregarding considerations personal to himself. Palfrey was not one who could ever serve him in return, while the defeated applicants might, if disposed, prove at some time formidable adversaries. It may be safely said that Sumner never assisted

[1] *Post*, p. 60.

[2] Dr. Palfrey by letter, Jan. 9, 1866, acknowledged himself indebted solely to Sumner for the appointment. The doctor died in 1881 at the age of eighty-five.

in an appointment with the slightest thought of its bearing on his own political fortunes.

While catholic in his estimates of men, and desirous to introduce those of different types into the public service, he was readily enlisted in behalf of those who had served the anti-slavery cause; and among the appointments he promoted were those of John Pierpont, clerk in the treasury department; Professor C. D. Cleveland, consul at Cardiff; H. R. Helper, consul at Buenos Ayres; Seth Webb, consul at Port-au-Prince, William S. Thayer, consul in Egypt; and Anson Burlingame, minister to China. His influence secured a place on the Sanitary Commission for Dr. Samuel G. Howe; but though exerted from the beginning, it failed to make him minister to Greece,—a country with which Dr. Howe was identified in his youth.

Sumner, as was his habit, lingered at Washington after the close of the session; and he was still there April 13 (the day Fort Sumter was surrendered), and even later, on the 15th, when the President issued his proclamation calling for seventy-five thousand troops. He left the capital on the 18th, and stopped in Baltimore, taking a room at Barnum's Hotel. His presence in the city becoming known, a riotous crowd gathered in search of him; and the proprietor insisted that he should leave at once, as his longer stay would be perilous to his property as well as to the guest. The latter, however, claiming his rights as a traveller, was conducted to a secluded chamber, no one but the proprietor and one of his assistants knowing where he was. He left at an early hour the next morning for Philadelphia, meeting on the way the Sixth Regiment of Massachusetts volunteers. "It was," he said, "the first regiment of volunteers he had seen; and he was struck by the gayety of soldier life, which overflowed as the train passed." At Baltimore the regiment encountered a secession mob like the one which had hunted the senator, and while fighting its way through the city lost four men killed and thirty-six wounded.[1] The intelligence of this encounter, April 19, reached Philadelphia before Sumner arrived there. On the night of that day the regiment was quartered at Washington in the Senate chamber.[2] On the 21st Sumner visited in New York the armory of the New York Seventh, which had left

[1] Order was restored May 13, when General Butler took military possession of the city.

[2] Sumner gave a vivid and detailed account of his experiences in Baltimore in a note to his Works, vol. v. pp. 492-494.

the preceding afternoon. It was occupied by the Third Battalion of Massachusetts Rifles, commanded by Major Charles Devens (afterwards distinguished in military and judicial life), at whose request he addressed the troops. His speech was inspiring, — a summons to a soldier's duty and a pathetic tribute to those who had just fallen in Baltimore, closing with the watchword, "Massachusetts, the Constitution, and Freedom."[1] At last a war had come which the author of "The True Grandeur of Nations" thought honorable and worthy of every patriot's blessing.

The correspondence between Sumner and Dr. Lieber — the latter now a professor in Columbia College, New York — was resumed in January, 1861, after a suspension of nearly eight years. It was opened again by a note from Lieber, which at his request Sumner destroyed as soon as he had read it. From that time they were in frequent correspondence, letters between them passing several times a week during the war and reconstruction periods. Sumner often sought Lieber's stores of knowledge on history and public law; and he was happy to do good offices for the doctor in securing appointments in the army for two of his sons. They were as friendly and confidential as in the early days, and both rejoiced in their restored relations.[2] The suspension of their correspondence in 1853 would not be referred to in this Memoir but for an explanation given in a letter of Dr. Lieber printed in his "Life and Letters," pp. 296, 297. The doctor living in Columbia, S. C., twenty-two years (from 1835 to 1857), came to take a milder view of slavery than he carried there from the North, and dissented altogether from Sumner's radical treatment of the subject. Moreover, his exile, as he thought it was, was not favorable to geniality of temper. His early friendship for Sumner was indeed genuine; but it was one thing to enjoy the society of an aspiring youth and make use of him, and quite another to see him rise to a distinction far beyond his own. He objected to the style and substance of Sumner's addresses on war and slavery, and wrote to him on his election to the Senate that he did not rejoice in the event. Sumner bore this patiently, and there was no break, though the old re-

[1] Works, vol. v. pp. 494-496.

[2] A letter from Lieber in 1862 began with "My old and restored friend."

lation was weakened. He was grieved to see his friend become the apologist of slavery, as he thought him to have become, and plainly said so in letters to him; also, according to the doctor's account, sending by mail antislavery newspapers with marked passages. This was not agreeable to Dr. Lieber, who closed the correspondence. Sumner, to his credit, kept silent as to the breach, and his version of it does not exist. He always took to heart a broken friendship, and maintained a strict reserve concerning it. Lieber's second letter to Sumner, after the correspondence was renewed, requests the senator's intervention in favor of his son, a soldier in the Union army.[1] It somewhat corroborates Sumner's view of Lieber's conformity to Southern opinions that one of his sons entered the Confederate army. How Sumner was always trying to serve Lieber will be seen from a letter to him written from Boston, July 17, 1849: —

"I do not understand you; you are an enigma. Have I offended you in any way? Since your return from Europe I have heard of your writing to Longfellow, often to Howe, sometimes to Hillard, but never a line to me; and now comes a stray sheet, without date, without signature, without beginning, without end, without one word of friendship or one symptom of regard. I have sent you such poor publications as I had to offer, valuable only as containing cherished opinions and feelings; but you do not let me know even that they have come to hand. But let that pass. I have longed to write to you of late to speak of some matters interesting to you, but I did not feel encouraged to do so. I wished to tell you what Sparks said about the professorship of history. Shortly after he had been chosen to the presidency he came to see me, and spoke freely of his duties. I then inquired about his professorship, and asked him on his resignation to consider your claim for the post. He thanked me, but said that the place would not probably be filled for a long time, or if it were filled it would be at half-price with a salary of a thousand dollars only, — in short, he said the college could not make it an object for you; and so ends this scene.

"At a meeting of the trustees of the Blind Asylum, met to consider Howe's application for leave of absence and the appointment of a substitute, I suggested to the trustees that they must begin to look about for a successor, and mentioned you. I said that if you would consent to take the place, and dedicate to it your great powers, you would make the school a pharos for the blind everywhere. The trustees who were present seemed to receive the suggestion with great interest. If you would make up your mind that the place would be acceptable to you in 1851, I think that you could have it."

[1] Lieber's "Life and Letters," p. 318.

## CHAPTER XLV.

### AN ANTISLAVERY POLICY. — THE "TRENT" CASE. — THEORIES OF RECONSTRUCTION. — CONFISCATION. — THE SESSION OF 1861-1862.

SUMNER was in Washington ten days in the latter half of May, 1861, when he conferred with the President and General Scott, and was in his seat when the extra session opened, July 4, going to Washington a fortnight before it began. Forty-four senators were present, including those from Maryland, Missouri, Kentucky, and Tennessee. Among the Southern senators were Breckinridge, who was soon to join the rebellion, and Andrew Johnson,[1] who stood almost alone among them as a Southern man of positive loyalty. The seceded States were not represented. Among Northern senators were Wilson of Massachusetts, Morrill and Fessenden of Maine, Hale of New Hampshire, Foot and Collamer of Vermont, Preston King of New York, Wilmot of Pennsylvania, Trumbull of Illinois, Wade and Sherman of Ohio, and Chandler of Michigan. The presence most missed was that of Douglas, who died June 3.[2] The committee on foreign relations consisted of Sumner (chairman), Collamer, Doolittle of Wisconsin, Wilmot, Browning of Illinois, Polk of Missouri, and Breckinridge. Sumner's frequent motions for executive sessions showed that the committee was busy with its appropriate work. There was a general disposition to limit the action of Congress during this session to measures directly related to the prosecution of the war, with which Sumner expressed his concurrence in presenting an antislavery memorial. Schemes of confiscation were started; and Sumner introduced two bills for the punishment of conspiracy against the United States and the confiscation of the property of persons engaged in it, — which, however, made no reference to slavery.

1 Sumner, July 24, in asking to have Johnson's resolution as to the objects of the war lie over, took occasion to express great respect for him.

2 The session of July 9 was set apart for eulogies on Douglas, in which Trumbull and Collamer took part. Sumner, though inclined to pay tributes to deceased associates, remained silent.

The session closed August 6. Sumner on his way to Massachusetts made visits to Mr. Jay at Bedford and Mr. Fish at Garrison's. When he reached Boston his first duty — a deeply sad one — was to visit the home of Longfellow, from which had been removed by tragic death the poet's wife, a noble and accomplished woman, his own constant and loyal friend for twenty years. He wrote, July 11: —

"DEAREST LONGFELLOW, — God bless and comfort you! I am overwhelmed with grief, and long to be with you. Nothing but duties here, which cannot be postponed, prevents me from going on at once!"

And again, July 21: —

"DEAREST LONGFELLOW, — Daily, hourly, constantly I think of you, and my thoughts end with myself; for I cannot forget my own great and irreparable loss. In all visions of life I have always included her, for it never occurred to me that I should be the survivor, and I counted upon her friendship to the last. How strong must be your grief, I know and feel in my heart. But your happiness has been great, and the memories which remain are precious. I long to talk with you, and to enter into all this experience so trying, and help you to bear it, if I can. I must go with you to Mount Auburn. I hear of the children with great interest; they will be to you a comfort and consolation. I wish Charley would write me about you, and tell me how you are doing. I have been unhappy away. I wish I had seen her once more; but duties here stood sentinel in the way. Mr. William Appleton and myself have been together a good deal to talk of this bereavement. He is well. God bless you!"

To R. Schleiden, May 5: —

"This generous uprising of the North is a new element of force, which foretells the subjugation of the rebels. I do not doubt the result. I never believed that the North would be practically divided when the conflict came; but I did not expect the ferocious unity and high-strung determination which are now witnessed. . . . I feel proud of the activity and vigor displayed by my State."

Again, June 2: —

"I do not doubt that England will settle down into just relations to our government if she is not prevented by sinister influences. There has been precipitation on her part, caused naturally by our short-coming here, and also by the London 'Times.' The two especial things on which the South relied were (1) division at the North and (2) recognition by the great powers. The failure with regard to the last will be as great as with regard to the first. What then will the South do? It must yield at last. The end is certain; and also the extinction of slavery."

To Lieber, June 23: —

"I have no dread of Congress. The session will be very brief, — a week or ten days; both houses in secret session; everything prepared in advance: (1) An army bill; (2) Navy bill; (3) Loan bill and war taxes on the free list, with perhaps an income tax; (4) Bill for treason, and to arrest supplies for traitors; and (5) Bill of embargo and non-intercourse for the whole Southern coast in lieu of the blockade, which is a great mistake. Such at least is my programme which I have submitted to the President and his Cabinet; and I hope it will be carried out without a single speech, or one word of buncombe, so that our short session may be a mighty act. Our foreign relations especially concern me. The statement in the message will be 'all's well.'"

Prince Napoleon, who had come in his yacht to the United States, visited Washington in the last days of the extra session. His sympathies were with the cause of the Union and of the abolition of slavery; and he was greatly attracted to Sumner, both on account of common sentiments and the senator's interest in the public life and literature of France.[1] Sumner was one of the guests at a banquet given to the prince in Boston in September, and late in the same day, as he was setting sail, bade him good-by on board his yacht.

The government abstained scrupulously during the early months of the Civil War from acts and declarations which implied an antislavery purpose, and even expressly disavowed such a purpose. This policy was thought necessary, not only to hold the border slave States, where what was called loyalty was largely lukewarm and uncertain, but also to retain in the free States the support of the masses hitherto opposed to the Republican party. There was a division, too, among the Republicans, — many of whom in the Middle States and the more southern of the Western States, sufficient in number to reduce the party by their defection to a minority, had no sympathy with antislavery opinions, and desired the war to be strictly one for the Union without interference with slavery. The army also, private soldiers as well as officers, was at the time far from being inspired by antislavery sentiments; and it was the common talk of the camp that the war was for the Union only, and that slavery would remain untouched.

During this period, officers of the army in formal orders declared it to be their duty and purpose to suppress and crush out servile insurrections. Some were reported to have offered to

1 Col. Ferri Pisani's "Lettres sur les États-Unis d'Amérique," pp. 121, 122.

return fugitive slaves to their masters.[1] The war department required McDowell to forbid the harboring of fugitive slaves in camps, or their accompanying the troops on a march; this was at the President's instance, though the fact of his interposition was at his request kept from the public.[2] Negroes were forbidden to leave Washington except on proof of freedom. The Attorney-General, in a letter of instructions, recognized the duty of marshals to return fugitive slaves. The Secretary of the Interior at a public meeting denied the right of the government to interfere with slavery in South Carolina. The Secretary of War abstained from approving General Butler's doctrine that the slaves of rebels should be treated as "contraband of war," and cautioned him against interfering with the slaves of peaceable citizens, or preventing the voluntary return of fugitive slaves. The President himself revoked General Fremont's order emancipating the slaves of rebels within his command in Missouri, and later revoked a similar order of General Hunter issued in South Carolina. These revocations greatly disturbed the antislavery men; but emancipation was clearly a matter of general policy which he had a right to retain in his own hands.

A similar spirit pervaded our diplomatic correspondence. Just before the attack on Fort Sumter (April 10), Seward instructed Adams "not to consent to draw into debate before the British government any opposing moral principles which may be supposed to lie at the foundation of the controversy between those (the Confederate) States and the federal Union;" and a week after the surrender (April 22) he instructed Dayton that "the Territories will remain in all respects the same whether the revolution shall succeed or shall fail; the condition of slavery in the several States will remain just the same whether it shall succeed or shall fail." These disavowals of any moral issue in the contest made our cause appear one of empire only, and tended to repel foreign sympathy and remove the greatest im-

[1] Halleck's order excluding fugitive slaves from the lines of his army came later, — Nov. 20, 1861. The reason given in the order for the exclusion was that they carried information to the enemy; whereas, instead of doing so, they brought information to our government. The President expressed to the writer, Feb. 15, 1862, much impatience at the hesitation of the Senate to confirm Halleck's nomination as major-general on account of this order. As to the military orders and other official action concerning fugitive slaves at this time, see McPherson's "History of the Rebellion," pp. 234–260.

[2] Nicolay and Hay's "Life of Lincoln," vol. iv. pp. 390, 391.

pediment to foreign intervention.[1] In less than a year the mistake was confessed when Seward in a letter to Adams, Feb. 17, 1862, took note of the prejudice which the cause of the Union had suffered in Great Britain and France "from the assumption that the government which maintained it is favorable, or at least not unfavorable, to the perpetuation of slavery;" and he proceeded to set forth the results hostile to slavery which the war had brought to pass.[2]

Among radical antislavery men there was from the beginning of the Civil War a conviction that it would if prolonged prove the destruction of slavery in the rebel States; and they would not have been satisfied with any settlement which did not insure its extinction. Most of them, however, were content for a while to await the progress of events, and united with the mass of citizens on the simple issue of preserving the Union without pressing on the Administration measures hostile to slavery, — protesting, however, in the mean time against any disclaimers of an antislavery policy or purpose by the government. They were nevertheless uneasy at the manifestation of any disposition to protect it, or to save it from the natural results of war. Their restiveness was shown in Congress in Lovejoy's resolution "that it is no part of the duty of the soldiers of the United States to capture and return fugitive slaves," which passed the House, July 9, by a vote of ninety-three yeas to fifty-five nays;[3] but this was almost their only demonstration during the first three months after the assault on Fort Sumter.

The defeat of the Union forces at Bull Run, July 21, marks an important change in popular feeling. While it mortified the national pride and dissipated the hope of a speedy close of the war, it led the people to reflect more seriously than before on

[1] Lord Shaftesbury in a speech at a public meeting (reported in the London "Times," July 25, 1861) attributed to the absence of an antislavery policy the want of sympathy for our cause in England, and said: "There was no honest feeling on the subject of slavery in America except among the Abolitionists, headed by that great and good man, Charles Sumner." The Duchess of Argyll wrote Sumner, Dec. 1, 1861, that while foreigners who had been close observers of American politics might be expected to see that the Civil War might become one of liberation, "Americans had no right to expect the world at large to believe that it is what many of its leaders are asserting that it is not." In January, 1862, Weed found that our cause lacked moral support in France as well as in England from the want of an avowed antislavery policy. Seward's "Life," vol. iii. p. 57.

[2] In his despatch, May 28, 1862, he stated the reasons for his change of instructions on slavery, and testified to the negro's help to the Union cause; but later, July 5, he condemned those who urged a proclamation of emancipation. *Post*, p. 110.

[3] Lovejoy, answering Sumner's note of congratulation, wrote, July 11: "Our conservative people were timid and vexed, but they had to vote right at last."

the character of the struggle and the necessity of putting the national cause on the highest ground, and of bringing to the rescue of the country all possible moral and physical forces. This change of sentiment appeared in the debates and action of Congress on the proposition to declare free the slaves of rebels employed by them for military purposes, which passed the Senate, July 22, the day after the disaster, and became a law on the last day of the session.[1] It was the first of a series of laws against slavery, and was aptly characterized by Breckinridge, its leading opponent, as the beginning of "a loosing of all bonds." Sumner, referring a few months later to the fact that it passed the Senate the day after the defeat, said: "In the providence of God there are no accidents; and this seeming reverse helped to the greatest victory which can be won."[2]

Sumner believed from the first that the Civil War would end slavery, and ought to end it; and as already seen, he foresaw that civil war was inevitable. In his view a policy of emancipation was an essential part of our case as it was to stand before the world, absolutely necessary to enlist foreign sympathy and prevent European intervention. With that policy left out he believed that success in the field was not possible, and that the war would be "a vain masquerade of battles." He was not impressed with the objections to the avowal of an antislavery policy which weighed on the minds of many patriotic men. He was content, however, to wait for a favorable moment, though utterly opposed in the mean time to any acts or declarations which gave or promised protection to slavery. Two days before the bombardment of Fort Sumter, when President Lincoln mentioned to him in confidence the decision to provision and hold the fort, he hinted his own conception of what was to come in the pregnant reply, "Then the war-power will be in motion, and with it great consequences." In May, when driving one evening with the President alone in the latter's carriage, he brought up the subject of slavery, telling the President that he was right then in his course, but that he must be ready to strike when the moment came. The time he thought had come when the first considerable conflict of the two forces took place at Bull Run; and he then desired the President at

[1] Sumner called, May 26, 1862, for the instructions to commanding generals in pursuance of this provision. Works, vol. vii. p. 82.

[2] Address, Nov. 27, 1861. Works, vol. vi. p. 113.

once to take the step openly and irrevocably. What occurred then he stated subsequently as follows: —

"On the day of the disaster he was with the President twice, but made no suggestion then. On the second day thereafter, when the tidings from all quarters showed that the country was aroused to intense action, he visited the President expressly to urge emancipation. The President received him kindly, and when Mr. Sumner said that he had come to make an important recommendation with regard to the conduct of the war, replied promptly that he was occupied with that very question, and had something new upon it. Mr. Sumner, thinking that he was anticipated, said, 'You are going against slavery?' 'Oh, no, not that,' he replied impatiently. 'I am sorry,' said Mr. Sumner; when the President, with increasing impatience, reminded him of the evening drive in his carriage, and then retorted, 'Did you not then approve my course?' 'Certainly,' said Mr. Sumner, 'at that time; but I said also that you must be ready to strike at slavery, and now the moment has come. Of this I have no doubt.' And he proceeded to urge his reasons, but could not satisfy the President. The interview, which was late in the evening, did not terminate till midnight." [1]

Sumner was impatient during the rest of the summer and early autumn with "the policy of forbearance" towards slavery, which, as he thought, gave moral strength to the rebellion; and he determined to arrest it by an appeal to the country. He chafed under the undue influence of Kentucky and other border slave States over the Administration; and he was sorely grieved at the President's revocation of Fremont's proclamation. He wrote Dr. Lieber, September 17, six days after the issue of the order revoking it: —

"The London 'Times' is right. We cannot conquer the rebels as the war is now conducted. There will be a vain masquerade of battles, a flux of blood and treasure, and nothing done! Never has there been a moment of history when so much was all compressed into a single line and brought directly under a single mind. Our President is now dictator, imperator, — which you will; but how vain to have the power of a god and not to use it godlike! I am sad, for I know that we are to spend energy and resource of all kinds, and accomplish nothing until there is a change of policy."

To Dr. W. H. Russell, of the London "Times," he wrote, September 16: —

"Let me add that I have been astonished at the minuteness of criticism directed against your account of the panic [at Bull Run], which I regarded very much as a battle-piece by Wouverman with his perpetual white horse.

1 Works, vol. vi. p. 31. The editor of the New York "Evening Post" of March 12, 1874, recalled President Lincoln's statement to him that in drives to the Soldiers' Home Sumner was accustomed to press the issue of a proclamation of emancipation.

If I can judge from what I hear, people are much less sensitive with regard to your errors of fact than with regard to the tone in which you wrote. They feel that this is not friendly; that it is *de haut en bas;* that you write down upon us, — and this you can imagine is not pleasant. It becomes more conspicuous from its contrast with the real cordiality of one or two recent French writers, who have struck chords which I wish had been struck by an Englishman. I hear from different quarters that the war will soon be ended. I do not see it so;[1] and if slavery is left to itself, I think you are right in the horoscope you cast. But help us to a breath of generous, strengthening sympathy from Old England, which will cheer the good cause and teach everybody that there can be no terms of any kind with a swarm of traitors trying to build a State on human slavery."

Sumner accepted the invitation to address the annual State convention of the Republican party at Worcester in October, given to him by William Claflin, chairman of the State committee, and afterwards governor of the State. Mr. Dawes (since senator) presided. Governor Andrew received his second nomination, which was made by acclamation. The great hall was filled with delegates and spectators, — an audience which was divided in opinion, a part in favor of, and a part opposed to, a radical antislavery policy, but all thoughtful, patriotic, and devoted to the government.

The speech was not long, but it was emphatic in every sentence, and showed from beginning to end intense earnestness.[2] Exhibiting slavery as the sole cause and main strength of a rebellion hitherto maintaining itself on land and sea, Sumner insisted that it should be struck down with every power within the grasp of the government. These were some of his passages: "Slavery is our Catiline, being to this war everything, — inspiration, motive-power, end and aim, be-all and end-all. . . . It is often said that war will make an end of slavery. This is probable; but it is surer still that the overthrow of slavery will make an end of the war. . . . It is not necessary even, borrowing a familiar phrase, to carry the war into Africa; it will be enough if we carry Africa into the war in any form, any quantity, any way. . . . A simple declaration that all men within the lines of the United States troops are freemen will be in strict conformity with the Constitution and also with precedent. The Constitution knows no man as slave. . . . There

[1] Sumner from the beginning put no faith in the prediction of a "three months' war." Memoir of W. H. Channing by O. B. Frothingham, p. 309.

[2] Works, vol. vi. pp. 1–29.

is a higher agency that may be invoked, which is at the same time under the Constitution and above the Constitution, — I mean martial law in its plenitude, and declared by solemn proclamation."

Though not definitely proposing the arming of the slaves, he called attention to that resource by describing parallel cases in Greek and Roman history in which the assistance of slaves had been effective, and gave instances in which American generals in earlier wars had treated fugitive slaves as freemen. He denied "any sanction under the Constitution for turning a national camp into a slave-pen, or for turning military officers into slave-hunters." He invoked, with citations from his speeches in Congress, the authority of John Quincy Adams in favor of the power to emancipate slaves by martial law. He was willing to compensate loyal owners, saying, "Never should any question of money be allowed to interfere with human freedom. Better an empty treasury than a single slave. A bridge of gold would be cheap if demanded by the retreating fiend." He did not assume to say that the hour had come for using the mighty weapon, leaving the decision to those with whom the responsibility rested; but he reminded his hearers "that there are times when *not to act* carries with it greater responsibility than to *act*."

The speech was strongly applauded, the applause often compelling the speaker to pause, sometimes in the middle of a sentence; and there were no unfriendly responses. Those who had been for ten or twenty years or more contending against slavery responded most warmly to this first demonstration against a too slow and hesitating policy; but a large number of delegates were unsympathetic with the main propositions, and there were others who, though respecting the speaker and agreeing with the ends he sought, felt that the time had not come for that open and direct assault on slavery which he advocated. The resolutions were silent on the subject; and the Rev. James Freeman Clarke's effort to add to them declarations corresponding with the speech, though not reaching a vote, disclosed a strong opposition. It is uncertain what their fate would have been on a division. Among the delegates there were, it is quite likely, some who, though concurring generally with their senator, thought it sufficient for him to take the advanced position without any action of the convention, — in number large enough to have prevented a majority vote in their favor.[1]

Sumner's citations from Greek and Roman history underwent criticism in newspaper articles, the tone of which disclosed that the writers were less interested in historical verity than in weakening his position as a public man.[2] Indeed, the unwelcome reception which the speech met with in conservative quarters revealed the purpose to replace him in the following year with a senator of less positive convictions on the slavery question.

The speech was printed in the New York "Tribune" and other journals, and appeared in large pamphlet editions, and through various modes of publication reached the country. In other States and in Europe[3] it encountered the same differences of opinion as in Massachusetts. It was the subject of wide discussion in the press. The distinctly antislavery journals of the Free Soil type approved it, while not only the Democratic press but the Republican press of conservative Whig traditions were clamorous against its doctrines. The political journals of Boston joined in denouncing it, and their attacks exceeded the limits of good taste, — one of them reprobating his "insane counsels," and another deeming him "a fit inmate of an insane asylum." They pronounced his proposed interference with "the social system of the South" as fatal to loans of money and enlistments of men, leading to the unutterable horrors of servile insurrection, and alienating the loyal elements in the border slave States. They went so far as to take positions adverse to emancipation, from which they were obliged to recede in less than a twelvemonth. One said, "Proclaim the policy of emancipation, and all hope of a reconstruction of the Union will be crushed out." The Republican journals of

[1] Sumner's old Free Soil associates were not quite unanimous in supporting his view. Mr. Jay in a letter advised awaiting the progress of events and the development of opinion among war Democrats; R. H. Dana, Jr., signified his dissent (Adams's "Biography" of Dana, vol. ii. pp. 259, 260; Boston "Advertiser," October 26); and even Governor Andrew regarded both Sumner's and Dr. Clarke's action as untimely. The Boston "Advertiser," October 4, called Sumner's "an unfortunate speech."

[2] Boston "Advertiser," October 3 and 10. Charles C. Hazewell came to Sumner's defence in his "Review of the Week" in the Boston "Traveller," October 19. In a note to the speech (Works, vol. vi. pp. 30–64) Sumner printed a large number of extracts from newspapers and letters addressed to him, showing the conflict of opinion at the time. The letters which warmly approved the speech were generally from Free Soilers and others who had been long identified with the antislavery movements.

[3] It was printed in the London "News" at the instance of Martin F. Tupper.

Massachusetts, outside of Boston, however, generally approved the speech.[1] Indeed, except in rare instances, the senator did not in his whole career receive the cordial support of the press of his own city, usually controlled by the conservative and commercial classes.

Sumner was among statesmen the first to demand the policy of emancipation. His address has a historic place as the first formal declaration in any high quarter in favor of that policy. It stimulated thought in that direction, organized antislavery sentiment in the North, and crystallized public opinion. Its effects were soon seen in military orders and in speeches from public men, which pointed to a thorough policy against slavery.[2]

An editor who was then and had long been Sumner's critic, William Schouler, author of the "History of Massachusetts in the Civil War," wrote, Feb. 18, 1869, of this speech: —

> "I am struck with wonder at the clear comprehension which you had of the magnitude of the war at the beginning, and of the true and only means by which it could be conducted to a proper termination. Your speech reads to-day like a sacred prophecy. For it you were assailed; but it was true nevertheless, and the country came at length to your defence by adopting your statesmanship."

Shortly after the convention (in less than three weeks), Sumner delivered an address, or lecture, in Boston, entitled "The Rebellion, its Origin and Mainspring,"[3] which during the same and the next month he repeated in several cities of Massachusetts, and also in Providence, Albany, and Philadelphia. Such was the impression which it made on the public that he was urged to deliver it a second time both in Boston and Philadelphia; and he consented to repeat it in the former city, but not in the latter. Its final delivery was at Cooper Institute in New York, November 27. The hall was crowded with an audience the best which that great city could supply. The scene was the more brilliant from the presence of ladies in larger numbers than had ever been seen on such an occasion in New

[1] The Springfield "Republican," however, took the same view as the Boston journals.

[2] Secretary Cameron's instructions, Oct. 14, 1861, to Brigadier-General T. W. Sherman, and the latter's proclamation at Port Royal; Colonel John Cochrane's address to his regiment, Nov. 13, 1861, with Mr. Cameron's approving remarks; Wendell Phillips's lecture on "The War for the Union," in December, 1861; G. S. Boutwell's Address, Dec. 16, 1861, in "Speeches and Papers relating to the Rebellion," p. 123. Cameron's annual report in December, 1861, as prepared contained an argument for emancipation and the arming of slaves, but the President required him to modify it.

[3] Works, vol. vi. pp. 65–118.

York. The platform was thronged by men already or since eminent in public life, or in various departments of professional, business, or literary activity. The chairman, William Curtis Noyes, of high rank at the bar, on taking the chair, gave a sketch of the career of James Otis, the patriot leader of the Revolution, in fame and suffering for the cause of liberty the counterpart and forerunner of the orator of the evening, whom he introduced as "the advocate and friend of all, of whatever rank or condition or color; the scholar, the philanthropist, the martyr, the statesman." Nothing could exceed the enthusiasm which greeted the senator as he stepped forward.

The address was of the same purport as the speech at Worcester, though more extended and elaborate. It identified slavery and disunion in our past history as well as in the present struggle, and with a view to prevent further compromise pronounced against the concessions to slavery proposed at various periods, and notably after Mr. Lincoln's election. The stress of his argument was upon the institution of slavery as the sole cause of all the trouble, and the sole support of the rebellion. He said: —

"All must see, and nobody will deny, that slavery is the ruling idea of this rebellion. It is slavery that marshals these hosts and breathes into their embattled ranks its own barbarous fire. It is slavery that stamps its character alike upon officers and men. It is slavery that inspires all, from general to trumpeter. It is slavery that speaks in the word of command, and sounds in the morning drum-beat. It is slavery that digs trenches and builds hostile forts. It is slavery that pitches its wicked tents and stations its sentries over against the national capital. It is slavery that sharpens the bayonet and runs the bullet; that points the cannon and scatters the shell, — blazing, bursting unto death. Wherever this rebellion shows itself, whatever form it takes, whatever thing it does, whatever it meditates, it is moved by slavery; nay, the rebellion is slavery itself, — incarnate, living, acting, raging, robbing, murdering, according to the essential law of its being."

He insisted that with the advance of our armies emancipation was a military necessity; and with greatest emphasis he asserted the absolute need of moral forces as our allies in the struggle. He said: —

"It remains for us to encounter the rebellion calmly and surely by a force superior to its own. To this end something more is needed than men or money. Our battalions must be reinforced by ideas, and must strike directly at the origin and mainspring. . . . Reason and sentiment both concur in this policy, which is according to the most common principles of human conduct.

In no way can we do so much at so little cost. To the enemy such a blow will be a terror; to good men it will be an encouragement; and to foreign nations watching this contest it will be an earnest of something beyond a mere carnival of battle."

The audience approved the address by a resolution adopted by acclamation.[1] Sumner signified his purpose at the time to renew the discussion in the Senate, a pledge which he fulfilled. "From this time forward," as he wrote some years later, "he never missed an opportunity of urging emancipation, whether in addresses before the people and in the Senate, or in direct personal appeal to the President. In the last he was constant, rarely seeing the President without in some way presenting the all-absorbing question."[2]

This address encountered the same line of criticism which followed the one delivered at Worcester; but the public mind had become more familiar with the topic, and an antislavery policy was now finding more general favor.

Among Sumner's letters at this period was one to John Bright, October 15:[3]—

"Your letter was so interesting and satisfactory that I could not forbear sending it to Mr. Seward, who has returned it to me with a letter which I enclose. Perhaps I cannot share fully the sanguine tone with which he writes. From the beginning he has seen our affairs in this way. I have not. The South will fight like desperadoes, and I see no chance of closing the war without striking at slavery. I know all the difficulties in the way; but the difficulties from inaction are greater. I do not suggest a scheme of outright emancipation, but something that may wear and weaken slavery and make its extinction inevitable. To this at least everything now points; and it would be hastened by any disaster. Meanwhile the good people of England owe to us their good wishes. We are fighting the battle of civilization, and their public men and newspapers should recognize and declare the true character of the conflict. It is not necessary that emancipation should be openly on our flag. It is enough that we are fighting against men seeking to found a new government with slavery as its corner-stone, claiming outlying territories for slavery, and sure also if successful to open the slave-trade. And yet this wicked rebellion has found backing in England. The effect of public declarations in England has been most irritating here. I have kept my temper, and with the President and Mr. Seward have stated the case always in the interest of that good-will between our two countries which it is my desire to cultivate.

1 Sumner was entertained after the address at Curet's restaurant, 764 Broadway, where his views were approved in brief remarks by distinguished guests, — fully by Mr. Noyes, and with some reserve by Mr. Evarts.

2 Works, vol. vi. p. 64.

3 Mr. Bright wrote to Sumner September 6, — the beginning of their correspondence on the Civil War.

Several times I have been obliged to oppose the Secretary of State, who has been disposed to a course of much harshness. Even if England has no sympathy for our government, her best interests are bound up with our success. In this way soonest cotton can be had. Our forces are already vast, and they are becoming powerful in discipline. Our fleet also is considerable. It will be difficult for our people to forget the last five months of coldness and cold-shoulderism which we have received from England; but it is not too late to soften the aversion which has been produced. At this moment people are very hopeful. There is a consciousness of strength. Business, too, has revived. It would be cheaper for England to support her three millions of operatives for an indefinite time than to plunge into war for the sake of these rebels."

To R. Schleiden, November 3: —

"You will observe that I propose no crusade for abolition, or, according to your language, no change of programme, making it a war of abolition instead of a war for the preservation of the Union. I accept the latter formula, but insist that the Union can be preserved only by striking at slavery. In short, abolition is not to be the object of the war, but simply one of its agencies. Mr. Cameron's instructions are practically a proclamation of freedom to the slaves where the expedition lands; and not only this, an invitation to take part 'in squads and companies.' And this is beyond the Act of Congress and only by virtue of martial law. Indeed, he goes beyond Fremont."

To John Jay, November 10: —

"Since Fremont's proclamation, it has seemed to me the issue has been fairly presented and the opportunity given to speak out. And I do not think that you or I ought to miss the opportunity. The cause needs all possible influence from talent, character, position, statement, everything. It is to be presented strictly as a measure of military necessity, and the argument is to be thus supported rather than on grounds of philanthropy. At the same time I do not hesitate in declaring also that thus you will do an act of justice. So shall you subdue the rebel masters while you elevate the slave."

There was danger during the first year of the war and even till January, 1863, when the President's pledge for the nation was finally given, that with a cessation of hostilities slavery would remain untouched. While Sumner, as he avowed, would not have had war declared or carried on for the direct purpose of freeing the slaves, he was determined that universal abolition as well as a restored Union should be the benign compensation for the destruction of life and treasure. He saw the great opportunity for his country and humanity, and he seized it. Meantime he did all he could to push public opinion forward and shut off all chance of retreat, by urging to that end antislavery statutes, executive and military orders, and a proclamation of freedom to the slaves, and, above all, by creating, through argument and appeal, an unconquerable will among the people that slavery and rebellion should share a common fate. At a period of distraction and hesitation, — with Seward resisting, great masses of men hostile or unconcerned on the subject, the border slave States demanding the maintenance of the old order of things, — it was of infinite advantage that one statesman of foremost rank held resolutely and perseveringly to this great purpose. It was Sumner's prophet-like voice and determination which prepared the way for Lincoln's proclamations, and made them the events they became.

The military situation at this time was not hopeful. The Union forces had met in October, 1861, with a terrible disaster at Ball's Bluff in Maryland. They had encountered reverses in Missouri and Mississippi. They had lost ground even in Kentucky, and the rebel camp was at Bowling Green. McClellan was mustering and drilling a large army in Virginia which was as yet only defending Washington and preparing for an advance in the spring. The navy had won positions at Hatteras and the important point of Hilton Head; but it remained to be seen to what extent they were to serve in breaking the military power of the rebellion. Grant's effective work in the West was yet in reserve. No substantial victory had removed the depression which set in after the defeat at Bull Run; and the rebels, as well as their partisans in Europe, were full of high hope. The current of hostile British opinion was growing stronger against us during these continued reverses.

Just at this time the "Trent," a British mail and passenger steamer, — when in the Bahama Channel, bound from Havana to Nassau, two neutral ports, — and having among its passengers Mason and Slidell, Confederate envoys accredited to England and France respectively, who were proceeding on their missions with despatches and two secretaries, was boarded, November 8, by Captain Wilkes of the United States naval ship the "San Jacinto," who, acting without instructions, took the four persons from the steamer, and leaving her to go on her way, brought them to the United States, where, by the order of our government, they were confined in Fort Warren in the harbor of Boston. The Secretary of the Navy, Mr. Welles, promptly justified the capture, and only regretted that the vessel was not taken as well. According to him, Mr. Seward, though refraining from any public expression, was "elated and jubilant over the capture," and did not conceal his approval of Wilkes's act.[1] The House of Representatives, meeting within a month, as its first act, after verifying the titles of members to their seats, passed unanimously, and without even a reference, a joint resolution approving Captain Wilkes's "brave, adroit, and patriotic conduct;" and though there was not wanting a distrust in some quarters of the expediency or legality of Captain Wilkes's act, public opinion, as expressed by the press and even by publicists, very generally applauded it. Among those who in Massachusetts gave it sanction were Edward Everett, Theophilus Parsons, Caleb Cushing, C. G. Loring, George Sumner, Joel Parker, B. F. Thomas, G. T. Bigelow, R. H. Dana, Jr.,[2] and the editors of that conservative journal, the Boston "Advertiser."

It was, indeed, a perilous moment, perhaps the most perilous, in our Civil War. Public opinion in Great Britain had been running strongly against us, and a large party in that country was watching for a pretext to push intervention in favor of the rebellion. "Three fourths of the House of Commons," as Cobden wrote, "will be glad to find an excuse for voting for the dismemberment of the great republic."[3] He wrote to Bright, December 6: "I doubt whether another year's blockade will be borne by the world. What say you? If you agree, you should let Sumner know." The Cabinet, while maintaining the forms of neutrality, was largely influenced against us by the pressure of great interests. This hostile sentiment now saw its opportunity, and showed itself in the bitter and vindictive appeals of the press. The Confederates had enlisted Louis Napoleon in their behalf, and they were now jubilant with the prospect of a British alliance and of the breaking of the blockade.

The British government, by Earl Russell, then head of the foreign office, at once (November 30) demanded the surrender of the four persons, with a suitable apology; and as subsequently ascertained, it directed the same day, by private instructions, Lord Lyons, its minister at Washington, after seven days' delay in complying with the demand, to break up his legation and leave Washington, and to communicate at once

1 "Lincoln and Seward," by Gideon Welles, p. 185. "The Cabinet generally coincided in expressing gratification and approval." Nicolay and Hay's "Life of Lincoln," vol. v. p. 26.

2 Adams's "Biography" of Dana, vol. ii. p. 259.

3 Morley's "Life of Cobden," vol. ii. pp. 388–390.

with the British navy in American waters, and with the governors of all British possessions in America. It hastened to despatch troops to Canada and to put the navy in readiness. Refusing discussion and negotiation, it peremptorily laid down its ultimatum, and took initial steps for war.[1] It encouraged the war spirit among the people by withholding Seward's letter to Adams of pacific purport, which was written immediately after the transaction and promptly communicated to Earl Russell.[2] The government and people of the United States, already taxed to their utmost in a civil war, were on the brink of a foreign war with the greatest naval power in the world. The prospect was dark indeed; and intense anxiety and depression prevailed among our people when the determination of the British government became known by the demand being communicated December 19.

Sumner was in Boston when the tidings of the seizure of Mason and Slidell arrived. When others were exulting he said at once, without hesitation, "We shall have to give them up;" and while dining with friends he repeated this opinion.[3] As soon as he reached Washington he sought the President and Secretary of State, and was relieved to find that as yet they had taken no position, and were awaiting a communication from the British government. He found the President anxious, notwithstanding the current of opinion in the country in favor of the capture, in which his Cabinet, except Mr. Blair, joined. The President then as always was receptive to what Sumner had to say on foreign affairs, — often giving greater heed to his views than to Mr. Seward's.[4] While the matter was pending the senator was almost daily with the President, and often with the secretary, constantly urging that every honorable effort should be made, not only to settle the present difficulty, but to remove

1 Adams's letter to Seward, Nov. 29, 1861, shows that the former was expecting shortly instructions to close his mission.

2 Seward's "Life," vol. iii. p. 21.

3 G. H. Monroe in Hartford "Courant," Nov. 22, 1873.

4 Mr. Welles, in his "Lincoln and Seward" (p. 185), says: "The President had doubts, misgivings, and regrets, which were increased after an interview with Senator Sumner, with whom he often — sometimes to the disgust and annoyance of Mr. Seward — advised on controverted or disputed international questions, and especially when there were differences between himself and the Secretary of State." Such was his confidence in Sumner's judgment that he sometimes struck out passages from the secretary's despatches to which the senator objected. ("Reminiscences of Abraham Lincoln, collected by A. T. Rice," Paper by John B. Alley, p. 579.) Sumner assured Cobden of Seward's pacific disposition, but Cobden was distrustful. Morley's "Life of Cobden," vol. ii. pp. 386, 391.

altogether British distrust, which he felt to be a great obstacle to our military operations. On Christmas day — the day before final action on the demand — he read to the President and Cabinet while in session the letters he had just received from Bright and Cobden concerning the capture.[1]

Sumner was anxious to prevent the negotiation being embarrassed by premature discussion in Congress. He sought to have the joint resolution from the House commending Captain Wilkes referred to his own committee rather than to the committee on naval affairs, of which Hale of New Hampshire was chairman, but yielded to its reference to the latter committee rather than raise a debate at an unseasonable time. Hale, when the subject was under consideration in the Cabinet, and on the day of final action, but before it was known, took occasion in the Senate to denounce in advance any proposition to surrender Mason and Slidell as a national humiliation. His ill-timed outburst was alarming in the critical condition of things. Sumner replied briefly, stating his confidence in a peaceful and honorable adjustment, and the subject being in safe hands advised an adjournment of the discussion till the question should be presented in some practical form, or at least on evidence.[2]

The same day that these remarks were made in the Senate, December 26, Mr. Seward notified Lord Lyons that Mason and Slidell would be delivered up. The decision was right, but the grounds he took had no support in principle. He treated the rebel diplomatic agents and the despatches they carried as contraband of war, and therefore liable to seizure on a neutral vessel, and found Captain Wilkes's act only illegal on account of his inadvertency in not bringing her into port as a prize. He also made the extraordinary declaration that "if the safety of the Union required the detention of the captured persons, it would be the right and duty of this government to detain them," — adding that the persons themselves had become unimportant on account of the effectual check and waning proportions of the rebellion.[3]

The ground taken by Mr. Seward was untenable; and the omitted act, which he asserted would have made the capture

[1] Nicolay and Hay's "Life of Lincoln," vol. v. p. 35.
[2] Works, vol. vi. pp. 161, 162.
[3] It is not credible that Mr. Seward seriously took this view of the military situation.

legal, would if performed have only aggravated the illegality.[1] The assertion also of the right to hold the men in case of a national exigency was a notice that our government might repeat the act at any time in its discretion. Mr. Fish, then in private life, wrote Sumner, December 29:—

"The state department's letter to Lord Lyons scarcely justified the declaration attributed to you in your gentle rebuke to Hale that the matter was in able hands. In style it is verbose and egotistical; in argument, flimsy; and in its conception and general scope it is an abandonment of the high position we have occupied as a nation upon a great principle. We are humbled and disgraced, not by the act of the surrender of four of our own citizens, but by the manner in which it has been done, and the absence of a sound principle upon which to rest and justify it. . . . We might and should have turned the affair vastly to our credit and advantage; it has been made the means of our humiliation." [2]

The British government received the surrender with the explanation as a sufficient reparation; but Earl Russell, with a view to exclude the inference that Mr. Seward's positions were acquiesced in, replied, Jan. 23, 1862, denying that the Confederate envoys, as diplomatic agents, or their despatches, were contraband of war; and referring to Mr. Seward's assertion as to what would have been done if the safety of the Union required it, he said that Great Britain would not have submitted to the detention "however flourishing might have been the insurrection in the South, and however important the persons captured might have been." The principle on which the transaction should have been placed has been clearly stated by Dr. Woolsey: "That there is no process known to international law by which a nation may extract from a neutral ship on the high sea a hostile ambassador, a traitor, or any criminal whatsoever; nor can any neutral ship be brought in for adjudication on account of having such passenger on board." [3]

The immediate difficulty was disposed of, and the public anxiety was relieved; but it was very desirable that some one who

1 The Duke of Argyll, writing Sumner, Jan. 10, 1862, said that if Mr. Seward's position were adopted, the two nations would be at the point of war every week; and he stated that the English case rested on the broad principle maintained in the French despatch, "that a packet running *bona fide* from one neutral port to another neutral port cannot contain contraband of war, and that despatches or communications of any kind from one belligerent to a neutral power are not contraband, and are not liable to seizure or detention as such."

2 Gideon Welles wrote of Mr. Seward later: "He was always ready, always superficial, not a profound thinker, nor with any pretensions to the scholarly culture and the attainments of Sumner." North American Review, July, 1887, p. 78.

3 International Law, § 199.

could speak with authority should put our action on sound principles of international law. No public man at the time was so adapted to this duty by his position and training as Sumner. In moving, January 6, a reference of the President's message and the correspondence on the "Trent" case, he indicated his purpose to address the Senate, briefly remarking that Great Britain in her reclamation had rejected her own in favor of American precedents. On his motion, the reference was made the special order for the 9th at one o'clock, when he took the floor. The public were deeply interested in the subject. There had been changes of feeling corresponding to the successive phases of the transaction, — first, enthusiasm when Captain Wilkes's act was reported; then concern and alarm at the prospect of a foreign war; then acquiescence in the surrender with a sense of humiliation. The novelty of the subject added to the attractions of the speaker in drawing to the Senate a large and distinguished audience. The galleries were filled; Chase and Cameron of the Cabinet, and the foreign ministers (except Lord Lyons, whom etiquette kept away), were on the floor. The senators, who in ordinary debates were much engaged in writing, apparently negligent of what was said, turned towards Sumner's seat and listened while he spoke for nearly two hours.[1] He did not once name Mason and Slidell, but spoke of them as "the two old men, citizens of the United States, and for many years senators, — arrogant, audacious, persistent, perfidious, — one author of the Fugitive Slave bill, and the other chief author of the filibustering system which has disgraced our national name and disturbed our national peace." His main position was that neither Mason and Slidell, not being persons in military service, nor their despatches, were contraband of war, or liable to seizure on a neutral vessel according to declared American principles and practice.[2] He, however, reviewed at length our contention with Great Britain concerning the impressment of American seamen, which was enforced by that power in the wars with France at the close of the last and early in the pres-

[1] Mrs. Mary Clemmer Ames gave an account of the scene in the Springfield "Republican."

[2] Despatches being carried with the knowledge of the owner or master to the enemy may be contraband under some circumstances. (Woolsey's "International Law," § 199; Mountague Bernard's "Notes on some Questions suggested by the case of the 'Trent.'") Dr. Woolsey, in a published letter of Jan. 11, 1862, approved Sumner's speech as free from the errors of Seward's despatch.

ent century, with the result that the British pretension justified Captain Wilkes, while our constant assertion of neutral rights was against him; and he welcomed England to her new stand upon American principles, which it was our duty to abide by even at the cost of national disappointment and the surrender of two conspicuous leaders of the rebellion. It was, however, hardly worth while to give so much prominence, even as an *argumentum ad hominem*, to an old pretension which, though not formally disclaimed, had been long practically abandoned; but Sumner as well as Seward was constrained by anxiety to put the argument in a way that would reconcile the people to the surrender, showing that we were maintaining our old position while Great Britain was reversing hers. The speech closed with suggestions for the amelioration of maritime law, the abolition of privateering, the immunity of private property at sea as on land, and the abolition of contraband of war and of the right of search.[1]

The speech met with great popular favor, and called out approving responses from publicists and jurists. It was especially grateful to conservative people of the commercial and professional classes, who had always been repelled by what they thought to be Sumner's too exclusive devotion to moral questions, and who had been disturbed by his recent demonstrations in favor of the policy of emancipation. Some of them expressed surprise to find that one who had hitherto appeared to be only an abolition agitator was indeed a statesman of large and sound views; and they were reassured in their confidence in the government by the close connection of one so clear-headed and well-balanced with our foreign affairs.[2]

The senator received testimonies of approval from a long list of correspondents, — among whom were John Bigelow, N. P. Tallmadge, Francis B. Cutting, Parke Godwin, R. H. Dana, Jr., Henry L. Dawes, Julius Rockwell, George T. Bigelow, Emory Washburn, John H. Clifford, James Russell Lowell, Charles E. Norton, Prof. Henry M. Torrey, John M. Read, and Wayne

1 He added to the speech in later editions a passage in favor of the abolition of commercial blockades, — one of Cobden's favorite ideas. Works, vol. vi. pp. 216, 217; Letters of Cobden to Sumner (MSS.), Dec. 6 and 12, 1861; Jan. 23, 1862.

2 The Boston "Advertiser," which had justified the capture and opposed a surrender, printed only a brief summary of the speech, while printing entire that of B. F. Thomas in the House which sustained Captain Wilkes. The New York "Tribune" printed Sumner's speech in full.

MacVeagh. From this large collection of tributes only two can be given.

Theodore D. Woolsey wrote: —

"Having just read with pleasure your speech on the 'Trent' case, as given in the 'Tribune' of yesterday, I feel moved to express to you my satisfaction that you have given the affair such a shape, and have tacitly exposed some of Mr. Seward's errors."

Hamilton Fish wrote: —

"*Exactly* right. You have done justice to the question, to the country, its history, its policy, and its late action. On such ground as you have placed the subject we stand proudly before the world. Your speech stands out in grand contrast to the official letter. It should be circulated largely in England among the class who will read it. The British press will not publish it in full unless you can bring, through some of your friends, an influence to bear. Cannot you do so?"

Sumner wrote to Mr. Bright, December 23: —

"I wish that I could see the future in our relations with England. Does England mean war? The impression here is that she does; and two foreign ministers have given to-day the opinion that she does. If this be so, then must I despair. It is said that if the 'Trent' question is adjusted, even on English terms, another pretext will soon be found. Can this be so? All this is to me inexpressibly painful; for I am almost a Quaker in principle. Besides, my sympathies have always been thoroughly English, — so much so as to expose me to frequent criticism. Thus on every account I protest against such a contest; but I fear that it is coming. I cannot write this without emotion. You have done all that you can, I do not doubt, and so has Cobden. On my part I have tried. Your letter, and also Cobden's, I showed at once to the President, who is much moved and astonished by the English intelligence. He is essentially honest and pacific in disposition, with a natural slowness. Yesterday he said to me, 'There will be no war unless England is bent upon having one.' Lord Lyons has left his instructions, which are not yet answered; but it is not known what will follow in the event of the answer not being categorical. Will Lord Lyons then withdraw and the war begin, — perhaps Copenhagen be enacted anew? I fear, while there has been no want of courtesy, there has been want of candor and fairness on the part of the English government. If this act were anything but an accident, there might be an apology for the frenzy which seems to prevail. The President himself will apply his own mind carefully to every word of the answer, so that it will be essentially his; and he hopes for peace. But if the English government chooses to take advantage of our present misfortunes and to attack us in our weakness, it will be for the future historian to judge the act. Of course, such conduct will leave behind an ineradicable, undying sting. I speak simply of the fact which must for a long time be in the way of harmony between our two countries. Do you remember the visit of the Prince of Wales? Think of the reciprocal sympathy then abounding to be changed, I fear, into hate.

I cannot bear the thought. What I can do to prevent this will be done sincerely and earnestly. We are inexpressibly grateful for your good, noble words. There is no suggestion of compromise; it is impossible."

To Lieber, December 24:[1] —

"The articles in the [New York] 'Herald,' proposing to give up the emissaries, but to remember the incident and call England to account hereafter, will be in the way of peace. If England sees that war is inevitable sooner or later, she will accept it now. The only chance of peace is that the settlement shall be complete and without mental reservations which shall hereafter be forged into thunderbolts. Of course, I say this daily to the President, who is essentially pacific. Such a Congress as you suggest is impracticable. The Congress of Paris went as far as possible at that time. We must wait until the exigency is greater or civilization more advanced. Of course, I should like to propose such a Congress, but not unless it can be presented in a practical form. Think of it, and tell me (1) what propositions you would submit, and (2) how would you enlist the other nations.

"War with England involves — (1) Instant acknowledgment of rebel States by England, followed by France; (2) Breaking of the present blockade, with capture of our fleet, — Dupont and all; (3) The blockade of our coast from Chesapeake to Eastport; (4) The sponging of our ships from the ocean: (5) The establishment of the independence of rebel States; (6) Opening of these States by free trade to English manufacturers, which would be introduced by contraband into our States, making the whole North American continent a manufacturing dependency of England. All this I have put to the President.

"I have proposed to the President arbitration. But in her present mood England will not arbitrate; and it has been suggested also that no nation can submit to arbitration a question with regard to its own subjects. But let us make a precedent. Seward is tranquil and confident; but, *me judice*, no man can penetrate the future. Passion is too strong, and we are too little informed of the real purposes of England.

"Your suggestion with regard to improvement in maritime law is so much in harmony with my own constant aspirations that I am unwilling to dismiss it. Pray, put it in practical form, or at least develop it more at length. I see impediments at this moment to a movement in Congress on this subject. But my anxious desire is to associate with our decision about Mason and Slidell some triumph of our traditional policy with regard to maritime rights. Of course, this must come from the Administration, and I have to-day urged it."

To Mr. Bright, December 30: —

"I know not which to be most grateful for, your speech or your letters. All of the letters, including that of December 14, I have sent to the President, who told me to-day that he had just read your speech. You already know

[1] Lieber's answer, dated December 27, will be found in his "Life and Letters," pp. 323–325.

the settlement of the 'Trent' case. But will the British cabinet and the exacting British people, fired by bad newspapers, be satisfied? I fear not. Then there goes with the settlement Mr. Seward's unhappy declaration to Mr. Adams that he has never believed a recognition of the rebel States could take place 'without producing a war between the United States and the recognizing powers.' Of course, such a suggestion is not sanctioned by international law, and I have to-day protested to the President against it. It is, however, only an opinion of one man. And yet I should be inexpressibly pained if the British government took this step. Let them leave us to ourselves. The contest must go on; there is no thought of compromise or arrangement. And with its progress the slavery question becomes more prominent. Against war, as I am, never could I urge a war for emancipation; but with war forced upon us I accept emancipation as one of the agencies by which it may be brought to a close; and I see clearly that the war will then have a character which it now wants. If there are difficulties in this step, there are greater difficulties without it.

"But I wander from our case. I spoke with the President several times on arbitration, and proposed Prussia, or, better still, three learned publicists of the Continent to sit in judgment. But it was necessary that the case should be decided at once. Its pendency caused a paralysis upon all our naval and military movements against the rebellion, which gave us a foretaste of the certain effect of a British war. . . . Let me say, I am shocked by the readiness with which the people and government of Great Britain have commenced war; for what are all these armaments and troops in motion but the beginning of war on an opinion given by the Crown lawyers, — in other words, on a point of law which it needed lawyers to detect? There is bad blood in England; and I fear that the case of the 'Trent' was only the present opportunity for it, and that another will soon be found. Of course in this mighty war, with so many points of contact and of question between the two countries, there is constant danger of collision. It may occur any day unless both governments put confidence in each other, and sincerely cultivate peace. This is our desire, believe me; I know intimately the views of the President and of his Cabinet. If there have been incidents or expressions which may be taken in a different sense, be assured they do not represent the policy of the Administration. I am in earnest in this statement, and make it with the amplest knowledge.

"Have you read Count Gasparin's article on the question? Oh that such a voice could come from the British government! If this accursed slave-driving rebellion prevails, and slavery becomes incarnate in a new government, it will be England and France who will have done the deed 'without a name.' God bless you!"

To Mr. Cobden, December 31: —

"I cannot thank you enough for your constant and most instructive letters down to 12th December. Not a word has been lost. I have read them all to the President; and the most important I read to the President and his whole Cabinet assembled Christmas day to consider the 'Trent' case; at the same time I read John Bright's letters. All were full of gratitude to two such good friends who, true to the best interests of their own country, so truly watched for us also. Will the settlement of the 'Trent' case be accepted in England as definitive? I fear not. The war fever is too intense; and I fear there is a foregone determination in the public mind to have war with the United States. Can this be so? This must be stopped. We are in earnest for peace. I can speak for the President and his Cabinet. If there have been incidents or expressions giving a different impression, they must be forgotten.[1] Last evening at a dinner by the Secretary of War, where were Seward, Chase, and two or three senators, while we were seated at table the President entered and took a seat at the table. I have never seen or known such an incident before, for our Presidents have some of the reserve of sovereigns. The conversation was much of it on the 'Trent' case. Speaking of the course of England, Seward said he had no memory for injuries, and that in surrendering Mason and Slidell he did it in good faith, — laying up nothing for future account or recollection. I mention this conversation and the surrounding circumstances that you may know the inner sentiments of our Cabinet, and especially of the man who is most suspected by Englishmen. Seward may be careless or hasty; he is not vindictive. The President is naturally and instinctively for peace, besides being slow to conclusions. He covets kindly relations with all the world, especially with England. I say this confidentially, for I have seen him almost daily and most intimately ever since the 'Trent' question has been under discussion. Pardon me for pressing this upon you; it is necessary that your government should be cured of its distrust. Unless this is done, you will continue your preparations, and we shall be kept with your great British sword hanging over us. Meanwhile our efforts against the rebellion will be pressed. For a moment we have been checked by the question with you. So long as that continued unsettled, all our expeditions were held back; now they will start. It is believed that we shall occupy New Orleans by the 1st of February, and also other important places. There must be soon a decisive battle in Kentucky, where the government has an army of one hundred thousand men under an able general. If England and France had not led the rebels to expect foreign sympathy and support, our work would be easily accomplished. Meanwhile the slavery question will be associated more and more with the war.

"The President now meditates an early message to Congress, proposing to buy the slaves in the still loyal States of Missouri, Kentucky, Maryland, and Delaware, and then to proclaim emancipation with our advancing armies.[2] These States, which are still contested by the rebels, would then be fixed to the Union, and we should deal exclusively with the cotton States. You see the magnitude of the questions which now occupy us. It is hard that with complications such as history has scarcely ever recorded, our position should be embarrassed by foreign nations. There are six hundred and sixty thousand men in arms under the pay of the national government, and not a single conscript. But you conceive the terrible responsibilities of this enormous force.

[1] This, as well as a like sentence in the letter to Mr. Bright just preceding, doubtless refers to certain expressions of Mr. Seward in correspondence and conversation, which had been interpreted in England in a hostile sense.

[2] The message was sent in March 6, 1862.

To sustain it will task the finances of our country. Already our banks have suspended specie payments under the anticipated return from England of American securities. It is deplorable that so much of bad influence should come to us from England.

"We must strive to extract as much as possible for maritime rights out of the unfortunate 'Trent' affair. I shall do what I can. The attention which the subject has received will prepare the way for reform. I note well your suggestions about our blockade.

"You know I am for peace *quand même*, and especially with England. I believe that all the circumstances and considerations in extenuation of the British outbreak have been stated by me to the President as strongly as they could have been stated by Lord Palmerston. I know them intimately and completely, and I desire that the President should know them. They explain but do not justify British conduct. You, of course, will bear with me in saying this. On reaching Washington for the opening of Congress, I learned from the President and from Mr. Seward that neither had committed himself on the 'Trent' affair, and that it was absolutely an unauthorized act. Seward told me that he was reserving himself in order to see what view England would take. It would have been better to act on the case at once, and to make the surrender in conformity with our best precedents; but next to that was the course pursued. Nothing was said in the message nor in conversation. Lord Lyons was not seen from the day of the first news until he called with his letter from Lord Russell. The question was not touched in the Cabinet. It was also kept out of the Senate, that there might be no constraint upon the absolute freedom that was desired in meeting it. I may add that I had cultivated with regard to myself the same caution. The letter of my brother George, which the 'Times' announced as inspired by me, was written in my absence from Boston, and I first saw it in a newspaper which I read in the train. These circumstances will let you see how little there was of study or effort against England. Meanwhile the British fever has gone on, and I doubt not our answer will find your navy and army panting to be unleashed against us, and disappointed at the result. Telling the President a few days ago that it was now important to drive out from the British government their distrust of his Administration, and to plant confidence instead, he said at once, with perfect simplicity: 'I never see Lord Lyons. If it were proper I should like to talk with him, that he might hear from my lips how much I desire peace. If we could talk together he would believe me.' . . . There is another question pending at this moment in my committee, — the President and Cabinet declining to act, — what we shall do on the Mexican side. That fleet of England, France, and Spain in the Gulf of Mexico means no good to us."

To Mr. Bright, Jan. 9, 1862: —

"Yours of 21st December made me grateful again. We all look with curiosity to the reception of our recent act in England. I think the fire-eaters will have all their fire taken from them. What will they do next? I am not without my fears that we have obtained a truce only. Among us there has been loose talk with occasional menace, but the result has been accepted with singular tranquillity. As for our Cabinet, I assure you confidently, knowing what I say, that there is no idea of war or rupture with England, and that nothing is now hoarded for future animosity when it may be more convenient; and my sincere desire is that your Cabinet may be in the same mind, and sincerely and actively. If so, then permanent peace is assured. The general feeling is that England took advantage of our weakness. I say 'general,'—perhaps that is too strong; but this I often hear; and I confess that it does not seem like the conduct of a magnanimous people to make a *casus belli* at once on a point of law, when we are embarrassed by domestic difficulties. But on the point of law I have not doubted you were right, and according to American principles too. Perhaps you will see a speech of mine on this topic. I hope that I have not spoken too freely of my mother country. My earnest desire was to do something for peace; but I was obliged to arouse the patriotism and self-respect of my own countrymen by associating the surrender with American principles. I think that we shall soon have news from some of our expeditions."

The debate on the seizure of the "Trent" was not continued in the Senate; and Sumner's speech was left to stand as the statement of the American case.[1] His position as the authority on foreign affairs was from this time firmly fixed in the Senate, until his controversy with President Grant nine years later. One of the senators — Mr. Morrill of Vermont — said with emphasis, when Sumner was no longer a member of the committee, that his administration of its business during the period he remained chairman was "masterly."[2] Another associate, Dixon of Connecticut, who had no sympathy with his advanced antislavery position, expressing his fear lest the country should become embroiled in difficulties with France by certain proceedings in New Orleans, wrote, Nov. 15, 1862, beseeching Sumner to exert his influence for peace, adding: "Your views on foreign

[1] Elaborate notes in Sumner's Works (vol. vi. pp. 162-168, 219-242) review the disputes and print extracts from newspapers and correspondence. English opinion was discontented with Sumner's treatment of the English precedents. (London "Times," Jan. 25, 1862.) Its contributor, W. V. Harcourt, writing under the pseudonym of "Historicus," weakened his argument by personalities, which he modified in a volume published later. Henry Reeve, in a letter to Sumner, January 28, attributed to him a misconception of the English precedents, and claimed that the English position was what Sumner denied it to be in a passage of his speech found in Works, vol. vi. p. 175. A correspondent of the New York "Tribune," Jan. 13, 1862, mentions that the foreign ministers at Washington commended Sumner for his tact, and regarded the speech as "forming a chapter in the law of nations." Mr. Dana thought the speech "the best thing for Sumner's popularity and reputation he had done," though not wholly approving his argument. Adams's "Biography" of Dana, vol. ii. pp. 261-263.

[2] In a conversation with the writer. Mr. Conness said in the Senate, Feb. 6, 1868: "Without any disrespect to the other members of the committee, I had really begun to believe that the honorable senator [Sumner] was the committee." Sumner answered from his seat, "Oh, no; not at all."

affairs are so just and wise that I thank God you are in the influential position you hold in relation to them."

In January Sumner moved in the Senate, without the customary reference, the confirmation of Mr. Cameron, then Secretary of War, as minister to Russia, and of E. M. Stanton as his successor in the Cabinet; but the Senate referred the nominations. He supported the former's confirmation in debate against certain charges affecting his official integrity. Mr. Cameron was confirmed, with considerable opposition, however, from Republican senators. Sumner, who had been in close relations with Stanton during the winter of 1860–1861, when he was a member of Buchanan's Cabinet, cordially welcomed him to his new post.

This was the first session in which Sumner was able to make his opposition to slavery effective in legislation and national policy, and what follows will show how he used his opportunity. When he reached Washington, before the session opened in December, 1861, he was gratified to find that a positive policy against slavery had gained ground with the Administration. Chase, hitherto the only decided antislavery man in the Cabinet, was always his cordial ally. Cameron, the retiring Secretary of War, and Stanton, who was soon to succeed him, had come to the same conviction. The President was, however, still cautious. Sumner regretted to find that his message, read to him before it was sent to Congress, was silent on the great theme;[1] and he was grieved to hear from the President's own lips that he had stricken from Cameron's report its recommendation of the arming of slaves.[2] He saw, however, that the President meant to move against slavery, though slowly, and with special consideration of the border slave States. He called often on Mr. Lincoln to press the question, in one or more interviews during each week, and conferred with Chase as to his state of mind. The President then and always took kindly to Sumner's pressure, and never misconceived his earnest and positive manner, — telling the senator early in the session that he was ahead of himself only a month or six weeks.[3] They were not so near together as that, and hard work was yet to be done; but the ground had been broken, and from that time

[1] One paragraph, however, hinted at compensated emancipation and colonization.
[2] Works, vol. vi. p. 391.
[3] Works, vol. vi. p. 152.

the progress was steady. The chief difference at the time was that Sumner and men of his type did not see the advantages which then impressed the President of dealing tenderly with the lukewarm and even doubtful loyalty of the slaveholding opponents of the Administration in the border slave States.

Later, in December, the President communicated to Sumner his plan for inducing the border slave States to accept a project of voluntary emancipation, — one of gradual abolition, assisted by a national contribution. Sumner did not himself believe in any gradual scheme, or in the practicability of compensation on a large scale, or in the President's project for colonization; but he looked upon this forward movement as an earnest of better things to come. On the morning of the day, March 6, when the President was to send in his message, the senator received a request from him to come to him as soon as convenient after breakfast. At the interview the President read the draft of the message. Sumner gave his own opinion against gradualism, and also designated a certain passage which was subject to a mischievous construction. The President, as Sumner was proceeding to put it in a different shape, volunteered to strike it out; and as Sumner continued to study the paper, at length interrupted in a pleasant way, saying: "Enough; you must go, or the boys [the private secretaries] won't have time to copy it."[1] This, the President's own favorite measure, was approved by a joint resolution of Congress; but it did not take effect as a law. It, however, testified to the country his genuine interest in the subject. On July 4 Sumner urged the President to commemorate the day by declaring emancipation and calling the slaves to our aid; but there were to be some weeks' delay. He lingered at Washington after the season closed in order to have a freer opportunity to impress the President's mind.[2]

The two men, President and senator, were unlike in temperament, unlike in theoretic positions; and the one had a weightier responsibility than the other. The President kept his eye intent on saving the Union, and would have saved it, if it had been the shorter way, without freeing any slave.[3] Sumner was as intent as the President on the same end; but in his belief there

[1] Works, vol. vi. pp. 391, 392.

[2] Sumner desired the President to call for colored troops, even before the Act of July 17, 1862, which expressly authorized them. Speech in the Senate, Feb. 10, 1864; Works, vol. viii. p. 90.

[3] Letter to Greeley, Aug. 22, 1862.

was from the first no way to it except through emancipation; and although opposed to beginning a war for emancipation, he would not after the Confederacy had taken up arms have welcomed any settlement which did not absolutely insure the freedom of every slave. The question may be safely left to this and other generations, in a country without a master or a slave, governed by one law of liberty and citizenship, whether he was right or not in his aspiration and purpose. It was easy for him to co-operate with the President and to bide his time; for he saw, as all saw, that the roots of Mr. Lincoln's character were sound, and that his coming up to the great duty could be only a question of time. While waiting anxiously for the President to move forward, he bore unstinted testimony to his sincerity of purpose and to the sureness of his finally acting aright.[1]

The consummation, however, which Sumner so greatly desired was now near at hand. On July 13 the President revealed to Seward and Welles on a drive that he had about come to the conclusion that the emancipation of the slaves by proclamation was "a military necessity absolutely essential for the salvation of the nation." On the 22d he submitted to the Cabinet his draft of a proclamation declaring free, Jan. 1, 1863, slaves held in States persisting in the rebellion; but he yielded then to Seward's point that it would be wise to postpone it till after some military success.[2] Chase wrote to Sumner, August 12: "The President's mind undergoes, I think, a progressive change in the line of a more vigorous policy and more decisive enfranchisement." The President carried out his purpose September 22, five days after the battle of Antietam, — submitting his preliminary proclamation to his Cabinet, deciding the question then wholly himself, and asking advice only as to phrases and details. Sumner received the announcement with profound satisfaction, being quite content with the grounds on which the proclamation was based, and making no complaint of its limitations of territory to States and parts of States still contumacious, which were sure to give way before political and military necessities.

[1] Letter of Sumner to ———, June 5, 1862. Works, vol. vii. pp. 116-118.

[2] Seward's correspondence and other evidence show that he was opposed to the step on other grounds than that of timeliness, and that he was out of sympathy with those who, to quote his own words, had "long and importunately clamored for" a proclamation of emancipation. *Ante*, pp. 39, 40; *post*, p. 110; Seward's "Life," vol. iii. pp 118, 135; Welles's "Lincoln and Seward," p. 210; Nicolay and Hay's "Life of Lincoln," vol. vi. p. 128; Owen Lovejoy's letter to W. L. Garrison, Feb. 22, 1864, "Liberator," April 1, 1864.

The general judgment now is that the President's advance in an antislavery policy came as early and was as rapid as the state of public sentiment admitted; but this view does not impeach the wisdom of antislavery men who, by earlier agitation in favor of that policy, prepared the way for his decisive step in September, 1862. If they had left the field to the border State men and Northern conservatives, he would have had no public opinion to support him. They were also clearly right in their position that during the waiting period there should be no declarations or action adverse to an antislavery policy by the President or Congress, or by generals in the field, or in correspondence with foreign powers.[1]

This proclamation, followed by the later one of January 1, 1863, yields in importance to no event in American or even in modern history. It had not, indeed, the sanction of States as a constitutional provision, or of Congress as a statute, or of a high tribunal as a rule of law. It could not perhaps have been pleaded in any court as securing the liberty of a single slave. But in its significance and effect it stands before any edict, secular or ecclesiastical, since Constantine proclaimed Christianity as the religion of the Roman world. It was the voice of a great nation, uttered in solemn form at the supreme moment of its history, pledging itself to the cause of universal freedom.

The President had much at heart at this time a plan for colonizing emancipated slaves in tropical countries, — calling the attention of Congress to it, directing diplomatic correspondence, and engaging in an attempt to settle a ship-load of the colored people, collected in Washington and its vicinity, on Île de Vache in the West Indies. The expedition came to grief, and the President from that time saw the impracticability of his plan.[2] Sumner discreetly avoided any direct issue with him as to this idea, well assured that he himself would come to see that it was a delusion.

The third day of the session Sumner called attention to General Halleck's exclusion of fugitive slaves from his camp and lines, and severely condemned it. The same day he took occasion, in supporting Wilson's resolution for the release of fugitive

[1] Mr. Schurz's "Essay" on Lincoln, pp. 77, 93, implies a criticism of the pressure which was made on the President by "the radical antislavery men." This class includes Mr. Schurz himself, as his letter from Madrid to Sumner, Nov. 14, 1861, shows, in which he urged the adoption of a policy of emancipation.

[2] New York Tribune, Aug. 25, 1862; September 13 and 14.

slaves from the Washington jail, to denounce the slave code of the District of Columbia, with the view of preparing the public mind for abolishing slavery in the District. "This was the first open word against slavery in the District since the breaking out of the rebellion."[1] The next week he took part in the tributes to two senators recently deceased, — Bingham of Michigan and Baker of Oregon, the latter of whom, while serving as an officer, had fallen at Ball's Bluff. President Lincoln came to the Senate to listen to the eulogies on Colonel Baker. Sumner drew the characters of the two senators, and particularly emphasized their relations to the slavery question.[2] The fate of Baker he ascribed directly to slavery; and in the line of his recent appeals to the public, he called for the striking down of "slavery, — the barbarous enemy of our country; the irreconcilable foe of our Union; the violator of our Constitution; the disturber of our peace; the vampire of our national life, sucking its best blood; the assassin of our children, and the murderer of our dead senator." Mr. Jay recognized the intent of the eulogies, saying of them, "They are not only eloquent tributes to the dead, but powerful appeals to the living." Later in the session, May 15, 1862, Sumner paid a tribute to Goldsmith F. Bailey, a deceased member of the House from Massachusetts, whose election he had materially aided at the time the former member, Eli Thayer, had adopted Douglas's notion of settling the slavery question in the Territories by the vote of the inhabitants.[3]

Very early in the session he moved a resolution for legislation forbidding the army to be employed in the surrender of fugitive slaves, — a subject in which his colleague, chairman of the committee on military affairs, took a special interest.[4] A few months later during the same session the measure passed as an article of war. Sumner wrote to F. W. Bird, March 12, of this article: "It is a triumph; it is the best act of the session; had it existed originally, it would have been next door to military emancipation." He moved his resolution in consequence of representations from Governor Andrew and other correspondents that certain officers, some of them from Massachusetts, had been returning fugitive slaves; and mentioned at the time Brigadier-General Charles P. Stone, who took notice of the reference in an insulting letter. General Stone was not long

[1] Works, vol. vi. pp. 119, 120, 121–123.
[2] Works, vol. vi. pp. 124–139.
[3] Vol. vi. pp. 504–509.
[4] December 18. Works, vol. vi. pp. 145–149.

after taken into custody, and his arrest and prolonged confinement were attributed to Sumner, who took occasion later to disclaim in the Senate any connection with the circumstance.[1] Later in the session he recurred at length to the unfriendly conduct of certain army officers towards fugitive slaves.[2]

Sumner had the privilege of connecting his name with the suppression of the slave-trade. Seward conferred with him on the subject, and negotiated a treaty with Great Britain for a mutual and restricted right of search and for mixed courts. Sumner was present at the state department when Seward and Lord Lyons signed it. He pressed its consideration in his committee and in the Senate. In a speech, April 24, he reviewed the legislation and negotiations concerning the subject, as well as the objections to the pending treaty.[3] The ratification passed without dissent; and Sumner hastened to the state department to inform the secretary of the vote. Seward leaped from his lounge, where he had been sleeping, and exclaimed: "Good God! the Democrats have disappeared! This is the greatest act of the Administration." Lord Lyons came in the evening to Sumner's lodgings "overflowing with gratitude and joy."[4] Later in the session Sumner secured legislation giving effect to the treaty.[5] The honest co-operation of the two great nations sealed the fate of the slave-trade. A few years later the mixed courts, instituted for its suppression, being without business, were discontinued. On the day the treaty was ratified,[6] Sumner carried in the Senate (after a pressure of some weeks, "against open opposition and cold shoulderism") the acknowledgment of the independence of Hayti and Liberia, prevented a long time by the pro-slavery interest, which feared the recognition of States made up of negroes or founded by insurgent slaves. He moved

[1] April 21, 1862. Works, vol. vi. pp. 148, 149. Mr. Blaine, while exonerating Sumner fully from responsibility for General Stone's confinement, and condemning the latter's letter as "ill tempered and abusive," treats at length the injustice done him by a long confinement without cause made known to him or ever found to exist. ("Twenty Years in Congress," vol. i. pp. 381-395.) Mr. Blaine says: "Aside from Mr. Sumner's public denial on the floor of the Senate, — which of itself closed the issue, — he was never known to be guilty of an act of revenge; that passion belongs to meaner natures."

[2] May 1, 1862. Works, vol. vi. pp. 489-498.

[3] Works, vol. vi. pp. 474-486.

[4] The Duchess of Argyll by letter, May 18, congratulated Sumner on the result.

[5] At the next session he introduced, March 3, 1863, a joint resolution further to give effect to the treaty, which was carried. He recurred briefly to the treaty in debate, March 9, 1868.

[6] He wrote to Dr. Lieber: "Rarely has the Senate done so much in a single day."

promptly the reference of so much of the President's message as concerned the subject to his committee, and had the papers produced from the files of the Senate. After opposition in the committee, which he was finally able to overcome, he reported, February 4, a bill authorizing the diplomatic representation of our government to those republics, and spoke at length in its favor, — describing the two countries, their history and productions, and maintained their title to recognition.[1] The bill passed by a large majority. Its chief opponent was Garrett Davis of Kentucky, Sumner's antagonist in such debates, who expressed his disgust at the constant recurrence of the slavery question, and who could imagine no sight so dreadful as that of "a full-blooded negro" in Washington society. Sumner's promotion of the measure received formal recognition both in Hayti and Liberia; and the former republic, as late as 1871, manifested its gratitude for his continued interest in its welfare by the presentation of a medal, and by an order for his portrait to be placed in its capitol.[2] In 1866 he reported a bill for establishing diplomatic relations with Dominica, the other part of the island, the object of which was effected by an appropriation in the consular and diplomatic bill.[3]

It was a very busy session for his committee, in which foreign relations, treaties, nominations for diplomatic posts, intervention in Mexico, and the abolition of the slave-trade were dealt with, involving almost daily executive sessions, and an amount of labor equal to that done in open Senate.[4]

Sumner spoke, March 31, in favor of his colleague's bill for the abolition of slavery in the District of Columbia.[5] The bill made compensation to the loyal owners of slaves not exceeding three hundred dollars for each slave, and, what was of doubtful propriety, contained a provision, moved by Mr. Doolittle, according to the wish of the President, for the transportation to Hayti or Liberia of such as desired to emigrate to those countries. The

[1] Works, vol. vi. pp. 445–473. Sumner was instructed on Haytian affairs by Benjamin C. Clark, a Boston merchant, consul of Hayti at that port, who died in 1863. The senator received many letters from him during this session. The senator's hearty satisfaction with the passage of this measure is mentioned in Dr. William Hague's "Life Notes of Fifty Years," p. 165.

[2] Works, vol. xiv. pp. 306–309; vol. xv. pp. 270–272.

[3] Works, vol. x. p. 270.

[4] He was a member also of the committee on land claims and of the committee on patents.

[5] Works, vol. vi. pp. 389–438.

speech reviewed the origin of slavery in the District, and dwelt on the irrational basis of the institution generally, — denying to it constitutional existence in all places within the exclusive jurisdiction of Congress. As in his view there could be no property in man, he preferred to consider the grant of money as a *ransom* [1] for the slave rather than as compensation to the master. The speech had one defect, which marred its unity, — a diversion from the main topic into a review of white slavery in the Barbary States, covering ground which he traversed some years before in a lecture.[2]

Frederick Douglass wrote to Sumner: —

> "If slavery is really dead in the District of Columbia, and merely waiting for the ceremony of 'Dust to dust' by the President, to you more than to any other American statesman belongs the honor of this great triumph of justice, liberty, and sound policy. . . . I take nothing from the good and brave men who have co-operated with you. There is or ought to be a head to every body; and whether you will or not, the slaveholder and the slave look to you as the best embodiment of the antislavery idea now in the councils of the nation."

The bill, which was opposed chiefly by Garrett Davis and other border State men, passed both Houses by a considerable majority. The President was understood to have doubts as to some of its provisions, and to hesitate in approving it.[3] During the suspense Sumner said to him: "Do you know who at this moment is the largest slave-*holder* in this country? It is Abraham Lincoln; for he holds all the three thousand slaves of the District, which is more than any other person in the country holds," and expressed surprise that the President could postpone the approval a single night.[4] Mr. Lincoln signed the bill, but stated in a message objections relative to the rights of certain owners under disability, which were met by a supplementary bill.

The bill which formed the new State of West Virginia out of the old State of Virginia, instead of an absolute prohibition of slavery, provided only that children born after a certain time should become free, and, as modified, fixed certain ages when slaves should become free. Sumner undertook to substitute an

1 O. A. Brownson thought this term happily chosen.

2 Works, vol. i. pp. 383-485.

3 The cause of the delay may have been only to give the slave-owners in the District, who were very much opposed to it, an opportunity to be heard. New York "Evening Post," April 16, 1862.

4 Works, vol. vi. p. 393.

absolute prohibition. Though there were supposed to be only ten thousand slaves within the limits of the proposed State, he declared himself unalterably opposed to any more slave States, and insisted that however small the number, all history showed that "it takes but little slavery to make a slave State with all the virus of slavery."[1] Failing to change the terms of the bill, he voted against the admission. A number of Republican senators, including Trumbull and Wilson, voted with him. Curiously enough, he often encountered in his antislavery efforts the sharpest criticism or the most strenuous resistance from senators who had the reputation of holding advanced antislavery positions, — and in this instance from Hale and Wade.

Sumner proposed an amendment to the internal tax bill, taxing slaveholders for their slaves, which encountered from several Republican senators constitutional objections, chiefly as levying a capitation tax.[2] Hale condemned it as recognizing property in man, — an inference which Sumner avoided by treating it as levied on a *claim*, and as recognizing a fact rather than a right. Sherman, who led in opposition to the amendment, took Sumner to task for not being sufficiently considerate and restrained in his description of slaveholders as a class. Sumner's proposition prevailed after a debate, but was lost on a later vote.[3] Consideration for the border slave States rather than constitutional scruples determined the final action of the Senate.

Congress was not yet ready for the repeal of the Fugitive Slave Act; but meantime Sumner watched every opportunity to restrict its operation and prepare the way for its repeal. He was strenuous in preventing any recognition of it in new legislation;[4] and in calling attention to the attempts of masters to recover slaves in Washington, he introduced a resolution to prevent their seizure in the District of Columbia, to which the clause in the Constitution as to the escape of persons held to service did not apply.[5]

1 June 26, July 1 and 14, 1862. Works, vol. vii. pp. 122-127.

2 May 28 and June 6, 1862. Works, vol. vii. pp. 93-109.

3 Among the senators voting with him were Anthony, Fessenden, Foot, Grimes, King, Trumbull, Wade, and Wilmot. Among those voting against the amendment were Hale and Wilson.

4 Feb. 25, 1862. Works, vol. vi. pp. 378-380.

5 May 23, 1862. Works, vol. vii. pp. 78-81.

At this session he entered in the Senate on that contest for civil equality, irrespective of color, which he began in an argument before the Supreme Court of Massachusetts in 1849, and which he was to continue to the last day of his life. On this question he showed to the end the perseverance of the youth who carried to completion the plan of a pedestrian journey when his companions one after another left him to continue it alone.[1] When appropriate bills were pending, he moved and advocated amendments to remove the disability of colored persons as witnesses in the courts of the United States, including proceedings for confiscation,[2] and as carriers of mails.[3] In these efforts he encountered unexpected resistance from Republican senators and representatives, sometimes on the ground that his motions were likely to defeat a beneficial measure, — for instance, from Hale and Clark of New Hampshire and Foster of Connecticut as to the removal of the former disability, and from Colfax in the House as to the removal of the latter. He secured the enfranchisement of colored people as witnesses in the District of Columbia by an amendment to the supplementary bill abolishing slavery in the District; and he had only to wait for their full competency being established in all national courts. He called attention by resolution to the exclusion of colored persons from the benefit of the patent laws; but no action was found necessary, as the government under the changed views on the slavery question rejected the doctrine of the Dred Scott decision.[4]

Theories of reconstruction were broached as early as the first year of the war. Among the people, and even among Republican leaders, there was a belief that after the war, likely to be brief, the States in revolt would resume their place in the government with no substantial change in their polity, and that the legal condition of slaves could be reached only through State action. Sumner from the first took a radical view of the change effected by the rebellion. He considered that these States, with their State machinery usurped, and with no legal officers, — all of whom had repudiated the authority of the United States, — had ceased to exist, and, to use his phrase, had committed

[1] *Ante*, vol. i. p. 69.

[2] April 3. Works, vol. vi. pp. 442-444; May 12 and June 28, vol. vi. pp. 502, 503; July 3, 7, and 15, vol. vii. pp. 152-161.

[3] March 18, 1862. Works, vol. vi. pp. 385-388.

[4] Dec. 16, 1861. Works, vol. vi. p. 144.

"State suicide."[1] Two consequences followed, — first, that their statutes had become lifeless parchments; secondly, that Congress became invested with the same plenitude of power over them as over Territories never yet organized into States. His conclusion was that the slaves had become free by the extinction of all State laws, including those which supported slavery; and that Congress ought to assume for the present complete jurisdiction over the vacated territory, like any territory belonging to the United States, as an inseparable part thereof, and to hold it as such till it saw fit in its discretion to restore such territory to statehood. The phrase "State suicide" found little favor; it startled conservative minds; and it went counter to the idea of historical continuity, which is always a national aspiration, — the idea, as Chief-Justice Chase at a later day called it, of "an indestructible Union of indestructible States." But while Sumner's formula was not accepted, Congress in fact afterwards worked upon his idea in the extra-constitutional proceedings for reconstruction which followed.[2] The theory which found most favor was that the States controlled by the rebellion were out of practical relations to the government, to be restored only when Congress admitted them to representation.

The subject of reconstruction first appeared in the Senate in Sumner's resolutions of Feb. 11, 1862,[3] which declared that the seceded States had abdicated all rights under the Constitution, and become *felo de se*, or lapsed; and therefore slavery, as a peculiar local institution, without any origin in the Constitution or in natural right, but dependent solely on local laws, had ceased to exist; and Congress should assume jurisdiction over the vacated territory, and proceed to establish therein republican forms of government.[4] These propositions occasioned much

[1] "Call it suicide, if you will, or suspended animation, or abeyance, — they have practically ceased to exist." Speech, May 19, 1862. Works, vol. vii. p. 14.

[2] Democratic senators were accustomed to rally Republicans on their later conversion to Sumner's doctrines as to the power of Congress over the rebel States which they had at first repudiated. Hendricks did this in a passage with Sherman and Fessenden, Jan. 30, 1868. (Congressional Globe, p. 860.) Doolittle upbraided (Feb. 24, 1868) Republican senators for deserting him in resisting Sumner's ideas, which he said "had not only educated but had Sumnerized the Senate." Works, vol. vi. p. 311.

[3] See his speech, July 11, 1867. Works, vol. xi. p. 397.

[4] Works, vol. vi. pp. 301–318. Harlan of Iowa and Harris of New York introduced at this session radical bills for reconstruction. The latter's bill met Sumner's views; but he took exceptions to some amendments of the judiciary committee which recognized "the laws and institutions" of the seceded States. Congressional Globe, Feb. 17, 1862, p. 843; July 7, Globe, p. 3139; Works, vol. vii. p. 162.

excitement in the Senate, and Republican leaders — Sherman, Fessenden, Dixon, and Doolittle — were prompt to disavow emphatically any responsibility of the Republican party for them. Sherman went so far as to say that they acknowledged the right of secession, and he could draw no distinction between them and the doctrines of Jefferson Davis. Willey and Carlile of Virginia, representing border State allegiance, imputed disloyalty to Sumner, and also likened him to Jefferson Davis. He encountered similar criticism outside of the Senate, as well from some supporters of the Administration as from its opponents.[1] Peace was as yet so far in the distance that the question had not become a practical one; but Sumner always thought it wise to break ground early, and prepare the public mind for an approaching issue.[2] The step he took at this time stimulated conservative antagonism to him in his own State, which took shape in the autumn.

He wrote to Lieber, March 29: —

"I was penetrated with joy when I found that it was only the left arm that your brave boy had lost. Only! But this is a great loss; and yet last evening at a restaurant there was a young man, of most gentlemanlike appearance, who had lost his left arm, and I watched him with constant interest, so that I could hardly eat my dinner. He was gay and easy, and made his single arm do the work of two. His hand when he entered was gloved; but he contrived to unglove it, and then, with a friend of his own age, enjoyed his champagne and dinner, beginning with oysters. I do not know who he was.

"Assuming that our military success is complete, and that the rebel armies are scattered, what next? Unless I am mistaken, the most difficult thing of all, — namely, the reorganization. How shall it be done, — by what process? What power shall set a-going the old governments? Will the people

1 The New York "Evening Post," March 13, 1862, wrote an elaborate leader against it. Joel Parker, professor at Cambridge, treated the offer of the resolutions as an act of treason, and more mischievous than open adhesion to slavery. ("North American Review," April, 1862, p. 463.) Sumner's undelivered speech on his resolutions became an article in the "Atlantic Monthly," October, 1863 (Works, vol. vii. pp. 493–546), to which Montgomery Blair, Attorney-General, replied in a speech at Rockville, Md., October 3. The resolutions, however, were supported in the New York "Tribune," Feb. 25 and March 15, 1862, by O. A. Brownson, the Catholic writer, and by a public meeting in Cooper Institute, March 6, 1862, where James A. Hamilton took the chair. (Works, vol. vi. pp. 376, 381–384.) Sumner's article was approved in letters from Judge John Appleton of Maine, Isaac N. Arnold of Illinois, and Thaddeus Stevens. Mr. Blair, in letters to Sumner, September 24 and November 28, while maintaining at length his public criticisms, avowed his personal friendliness. Mr. Lincoln's comments on the opposite views of Sumner and Blair are given in his "Life," by Nicolay and Hay, vol. ix. p. 336.

2 Two years later (Feb. 8, 1864) he called by resolutions for irreversible guaranties and a constitutional prohibition of slavery in loyal as well as disloyal States. Works, vol. viii. pp. 75–79.

co-operate enough to constitute self-government? I have positive opinions here. If successful in war, we shall have then before us the alternative: (1) Separation; or (2) subjugation of these States with emancipation. I do not see any escape. Diplomatists here and abroad think it will be separation. I think the latter, under my resolutions or something like."

The confiscation bill consumed a large part of the time of Congress during the session. It was a new field of legislation; and there was great perplexity in determining the source and extent of the power of Congress. It was a period when the most intelligent and foresighted were groping their way as well on points of expediency as of legality. Congress on the last day of the session (July 17) passed a comprehensive act confiscating the real and personal estate of rebels and emancipating their slaves. The same act, and another act concerning the militia which passed the same day, authorized the President to employ persons of African descent for the suppression of the rebellion in such manner as he might judge best, in any military or naval service.

Sumner had no hesitation as to the power of Congress, which, as he argued, combined in the event of rebellion and war both rights of sovereignty and rights of war, — the former governed by the Constitution, but the latter, being outside of the Constitution and not subject to its provisions, limited only by the principles of international law which define the rights of belligerents. The two sources being combined, he saw ample power in Congress to declare and establish the freedom of the slaves within the limits of the rebel States. As those States had in his view ceased to exist, Congress had succeeded to the power to govern the territory and to exercise therein all the functions and incidents of sovereignty; and also holding all the rights of a belligerent, it could emancipate and protect in their freedom the slaves of enemies, in the exercise of an unquestionable right of war.[1] He took part in the discussion at different times, making two elaborate speeches, and on the day before the session closed spoke in favor of a resolution to explain and construe the confiscation bill so as to meet certain doubts of the President, which, though the senator did not share them, were supposed to stand in the way of its approval.[2] How much he thought of the policy of freedom embodied in the measure a

[1] Mr. Collamer took issue with him in the debate.

[2] May 19, 1862 (Works, vol. vii. pp. 1–77); June 27 (pp. 128–147); July 16 (pp. 182–186).

few expressions will show. In his first speech in the debate he said: —

"God in his beneficence offers to nations, as to individuals, opportunity, *opportunity*, OPPORTUNITY. Never before in history has he offered such as is ours here. Do not fail to seize it. The blow with which we smite an accursed rebellion will at the same time enrich and bless; nor is there any prosperity or happiness it will not scatter abundantly throughout the land." [1]

On the last day but one of the session he said [2]: —

"I have never, from the beginning, disguised my conviction that the most important part of the bill concerns emancipation. To save this great part, to secure this transcendent ally, to establish this assurance of victory, and to obtain for my country this lofty crown of prosperity and glory, I willingly abandon all the rest. The navigator is called sometimes to save his ship by casting part of the cargo into the sea. But whatever the difference between the President and Congress, there are two points on which there is no difference: blacks are to be employed, and slaves are to be freed. In this legislative proclamation the President and Congress will unite; together they will deliver it to the country and to the world. It is an occasion of just congratulation that the long debates of the session have at last ripened into a measure which I do not hesitate to declare more important than any victory achieved by our arms. Thank God! the new levies will be under an inspiration which cannot fail. It is the idea of freedom, which, in spite of all discomfiture, past or present, must give new force to the embattled armies of the republic, making their conflicts her own. Sir, from this day forward the war will be waged with new hopes and new promises. A new power is enlisted, incalculable in influence, strengthening our armies, weakening the enemy, awakening the sympathies of mankind, and securing the favor of a benevolent God. The infamous Order No. 3,[3] which has been such a scandal to the republic, is rescinded. The slave everywhere can hope. Beginning to do justice, we shall at last deserve success."

Sumner's only interest in confiscation was thereby to accomplish emancipation, and break up large estates so as to obtain secure homes for the colored people. As a punishment, he had no faith in it from the beginning. He said, June 27, 1862: —

"But I confess frankly that I look with more hope and confidence to liberation than to confiscation. To give freedom is nobler than to take property. . . . There is in confiscation, unless when directed against the criminal authors of the rebellion, a harshness inconsistent with that mercy which it is always a sacred duty to cultivate. . . . But liberation is not harsh; and it is certain, if properly conducted, to carry with it the smiles of a benignant Providence." [4]

On different occasions he treated measures of confiscation and political disability as temporary expedients, belonging to

[1] May 19. Works, vol. vii. p. 76.
[2] July 16. Works, vol. vii. pp. 185, 186
[3] Halleck's, Nov. 20, 1861.
[4] Works, vol. vii. p. 146.

a period of transition, and to be discontinued when the exigency had passed.[1] He discountenanced a notion quite popular at the time, that rebels at the close of the war were to be tried for treason and hung. "People talk," said he, "flippantly of the gallows as the certain doom of the rebels. This is a mistake. For weal or woe, the gallows is out of the question. It is not possible as a punishment for this rebellion."[2]

In the midst of all the passions of war Sumner maintained his serenity of mind. Looking forward to a time when soldiers now in hostile ranks would serve under the same colors, he offered a resolution, May 8, 1862, as pertinent to an inquiry of General McClellan, declaring it inexpedient that the names of victories obtained over our fellow-citizens should be placed on the regimental colors of the United States.[3] His colleague Wilson, as if to make a point, offered five days later a resolution of opposite tenor; but General Scott, the highest military authority then living, recorded his contemporaneous judgment in favor of Sumner's proposition, pronouncing it "noble, and from the right quarter."[4] Three years later he took ground against placing in the Capitol "any picture of a victory in battle with our own fellow-citizens."[5] This, too, encountered the opposition of his colleague as well as that of Howe of Wisconsin, but his action was approved by General Robert Anderson; and again, as before, military authority was with him, and not with his civilian critics. In harmony with his action on these points was his treatment of the question of retaliation, to be referred to hereafter. Caleb Cushing shortly before his death remarked concerning Sumner, that though "the protagonist" in Congress against slavery, he was the only Republican statesman who adhered to broad and liberal views, and pointed as an instance to the distinction between him and his colleagues in his view of the proper use of battle-flags.[6]

[1] Remarks, July 13, 1867 (Works, vol. xi. p. 408); June 18, 1868 (Congressional Globe, p. 3247).

[2] Speech, May 19. Works, vol. vii. p. 70.

[3] Works, vol. vi. p. 499. Sumner's renewal of the proposition, Dec. 2, 1872 (Works, vol. xv. p. 255), and the censure passed upon him by the Legislature of Massachusetts and subsequently recanted, will be related hereafter.

[4] Scott's "Autobiography," pp. 188–190. The House had, Feb. 22, 1862, refused to have captured rebel flags presented in its hall on the occasion of Washington's Farewell Address being read.

[5] Feb. 27, 1865. Works, vol. ix. pp. 333–335.

[6] In an interview with E. L. Pierce, Dec. 4, 1878.

Sumner was from the first strenuous in his contention that all attempts at reconstruction should be initiated and controlled by Congress; and he questioned the appointment of military governors for seceded States, made by the Secretary of War at the President's instance (those of Edward Stanly for North Carolina and Andrew Johnson for Tennessee), in the spring of 1862.[1] The former took a position against schools for colored children as forbidden by "the laws of the State;" and Vincent Colyer, who had opened such schools near Newbern, went to Washington and invoked the senator's aid.[2] Sumner sought the President at once, tracing him to the war department. As he made his complaint he discovered an impatience in Mr. Lincoln which he had not encountered before, the latter exclaiming, "Do you take me for a school-committee man?" "Not at all," replied Sumner; "I take you for President of the United States; and I come with a case of wrong, in attending to which your predecessor George Washington, if alive, might add to his renown." The President took this in good part, and changing his tone, proceeded to consider the case. Sumner afterwards called the attention of the Senate to Stanly's proceedings, in remarks and resolutions which denied the authority of the Executive to appoint military governors.[3]

Sumner spoke at length on the proposition to make treasury notes legal tender, — admitting the constitutional power, but fearful of the abuses incident to its exercise, and doubtful whether an exigency justifying a resort to it existed in the present case. He yielded in conclusion to the opinion of Mr. Chase, the Secretary of the Treasury, that the exigency was im-

[1] Works, vol. vii. p. 112.

[2] Colyer too hastily left his post; and if he had persevered in his enterprise, it is not likely that he would have been interfered with (New York "Tribune," June 18; Boston "Advertiser," June 27). He died at Contentment Island, Conn., in July, 1888. Sumner recurred to the subject of military governors in his article for the Atlantic Monthly, October, 1863 (Works, vol. vii. pp. 494-501). Stanly wrote to Sumner, March 18, 1864, taking exception to the latter's reference to himself in the article, and denying that he closed the schools. Sumner replied at length, Jan. 29, 1865. The senator did not agree with the governor's construction of his own acts, but they stated their opposite views in language of mutual respect.

[3] June 2 and 6, 1862 (Works, vol. vii. pp. 112-115, 119, 120). Sumner's protest stopped the practice of appointing military governors; and on account of it Mr. Stanton withdrew the offer of a similar appointment for South Carolina to E. L. Pierce made through Mr. Chase, who desired this appointment to be made as an offset to that of Stanly, and hoped by means of it to secure in the reorganized State a recognition of the negroes as citizens and voters.

perative, but insisted that a remedy so full of danger must be regarded as a temporary expedient.[1]

He took part in the debate on the expulsion of Polk[2] of Missouri and Bright[3] of Indiana, both senators being accused of participating in or giving countenance to the rebellion; and also in the debate on the admission of Stark of Oregon, to whom disloyal conduct was imputed.[4] He spoke in favor of the title of Lane of Kansas to his seat, maintaining that he had not lost it by accepting what was alleged to be an incompatible office.[5]

The Internal Tax bill was full of novel points, and required the most laborious and minute attention. Sumner intervened with motions, suggestions, and remarks oftener than any senator not on the committee which reported it, and as often as any member of it except Fessenden the chairman, — giving attention to nice points of phraseology as well as to the rates of taxes. He spoke against a tax on cotton, — it being an agricultural product, and the tax being likely to embarrass the manufacture of cotton goods,[6] — and succeeded in reducing it, and at one time in striking it out altogether. His constituents — mill-owners in Fall River, Lowell, and Lawrence — were greatly interested in this measure. He succeeded, with Dixon's co-operation, in carrying a lower rate of duty on fire and marine insurance[7] (that on life insurance being exempted without controversy), contending that the duty was a tax upon a tax, a tax upon a premium, and a tax on something which was in itself almost a charity. He received

[1] Feb. 13, 1862. Works, vol. vi. pp. 319–345. The speech was thought to have removed the doubts as to the passage of the bill. (New York Tribune, February 14.) He treated the currency question more fully July 11, 1868. Works, vol. xii. pp. 443–480.

[2] December 18. Works, vol. vi. pp. 150, 151. He had paired with Polk, March 4, 1861.

[3] Jan. 21 and Feb. 4, 1862. Works, vol. vi. pp. 252–289. Bright's offence was the giving of a letter of introduction to Jefferson Davis, March 1, 1861, similar in purport to a letter of Caleb Cushing, which some years later insured his rejection as chief-justice. Sumner disavowed personal feeling, which Bright attributed to him. He treated particularly in his speech the kind of evidence competent in such a case. He led the debate, Feb. 13, 1868, in co-operation with Conness, Edmunds, Howard, and Sherman, against the admission of Philip F. Thomas, senator-elect from Maryland, specifically on the ground that he had permitted a minor son to leave home to enlist in the Confederate army, and had provided him with money as he left; but Thomas's resistance, as a member of Buchanan's Cabinet, to the relief of Fort Sumter, and his resignation when it was decided to send provisions to the garrison, was the underlying motive with senators for excluding him. He was refused a seat, although his right was maintained by the votes of Anthony, Fessenden, and Frelinghuysen. Works, vol. xii. pp. 257–269.

[4] Feb. 18, 26, June 5, 1862. Works, vol. vi. pp. 346–364.

[5] Jan. 13, 1862. Works, vol. vi. pp. 242–251.

[6] May 27 and June 4. Works, vol. vii. pp. 84–92.

[7] May 24, 26, and June 4, Congressional Globe, pp. 2334–2337, 2346, 2552, 2556.

for his efforts in this direction the thanks of the insurance companies of Boston. He spoke briefly for taxing receipts for passengers, but not for freight;[1] for a higher duty on whiskey and tobacco;[2] a lower duty on salt;[3] and the exemption of paper from tax as a tax on books.[4] In later sessions he sought reductions in the internal taxes, and particularly the repeal of the income tax,[5] and in that of 1871-1872 proposed the entire abolition of the system, which in his view had then come to be a political machine.[6]

This session was the most remarkable of all the sessions of the Congress of the United States.[7] The duties of Congress at this time were extraordinary in novelty and variety. It reorganized and supported a great army for the suppression of the greatest of rebellions, and a navy for the protection of our commerce and the blockade of our entire coast. It confronted at the beginning a foreign war threatened by Great Britain. It exhibited wise statesmanship no less than capacity for war. It

1 May 24, Congressional Globe, p. 2333.

2 May 22, Congressional Globe, pp. 2283, 2315; May 27, Globe, p. 2367.

3 June 5, Congressional Globe, p. 2579.

4 May 23, June 5, Congressional Globe, pp. 2317, 2579.

5 March 17, 1868, Congressional Globe, p. 1918; April 7, 1870. Works, vol. xiii. pp. 370-374. June 22 and July 1, 5, 1870, Globe, pp. 4709, 5095, 5100, 5236.

6 Dec. 11, 1871, March 21, 26, and June 4, 1872, Congressional Globe, pp. 45, 1856, 1857, 1977, 4216.

7 To various miscellaneous matters not mentioned elsewhere, Sumner gave attention during the session, — speaking in favor of a bill restoring without salvage property to loyal owners which had been captured by the rebels and afterwards recaptured, and giving his opinion against the policy of prize-money in any case (June 30, 1862, Works, vol. vii. pp. 148, 149); in favor of creating the rank of admiral without increased pay (July 2, 1862, vol. vii. pp. 150, 151); in favor of treating a majority of the senators elected and holding seats as a constitutional quorum without counting the vacant seats of senators from the seceded States (July 12, 1862, vol. vii. pp. 169-175; see vol. ix. pp. 489-492); in favor of the substitution of linen paper for parchment in the enrolment of bills, with a sketch of the use of parchment from early times, and a statement of the superior conveniences of paper now generally adopted in the States (May 16, Works, vol. vi. pp. 510-521; he recurred to this subject April 17, 1867, Congressional Globe, p. 849; Jan. 27, 1871, Globe, p. 775; and Feb. 20, 1874, Globe, pp. 1664-1667); against the extension in hearings before committees of the common law rule exempting a witness from testifying if the answer would criminate himself (Jan. 22, 1862, Works, vol. vi. pp 290-292); against a five minutes' limit to speeches in secret sessions of the Senate (Jan. 27 and 29, 1862, Works, vol. vi. pp. 293, 294); in favor of having the country represented at the International Exhibition in London, Jan. 31, 1862, Works, vol. vi. pp. 295-292); against regulating Congressional mileage in the army bill (Feb. 6, Works, vol. vi. pp. 299, 300); in favor of an inquiry as to the treatment of Union officers and soldiers killed at Manassas (April 1, 1862, Works, vol. vi. pp. 439-441); and making a report in favor of assisting by a loan Mexico in her resistance to foreign intervention, then threatened by England, France, and Spain (Feb. 19, 1862, Works, vol. vi. pp. 365-375). Other subjects to which he gave attention were claims of consuls for indemnity, the transportation of foreign mails, the proper number of staff officers, and the discharge of State prisoners.

prohibited slavery forever in all national territory, thus ending a great controversy; made freemen of the slaves in the District of Columbia; established by law a policy of emancipation from which no retreat was possible; gave hope to the colored race in the recognition of Hayti and Liberia; struck the final blow at the African slave-trade. It created a system of internal revenue unknown to the country for more than a generation; secured to actual settlers free homesteads on the public domain; added a department of agriculture to the national system; authorized a railway to the Pacific Ocean, thus to clasp the continent with iron bands; affixed penalties to crimes against the nation, but freely offered pardon and amnesty. In the midst of extraordinary responsibilities, it did not neglect the duties of routine legislation. Whoever shall hereafter study its record will pass lightly over the personal bickerings which come up here and there in the debates, while he contemplates the grand result so creditable to its authors and so fruitful of benefit to mankind.

Sumner was always interested in beneficent internal improvements, especially in those which were immediately connected with the advance of civilization. As early as 1853 he gave a God-speed to a railway from the Atlantic to the Pacific, by sending a "Fourth-of-July" toast to the mayor of Boston, in which he treated it as "marking an epoch of human progress second only to that of the Declaration of Independence."[1] This enterprise was then regarded — at a period when as yet the Kansas-Nebraska question had not made the intervening territory familiar to the public mind — as visionary, or only practicable at some distant day. Ten years later, and six years before its consummation, he wrote to persons who were promoting it:[2] —

"I have always voted for the Pacific Railroad; and now that it is authorized by Congress, I follow it with hope and confidence. It is a great work; but science has already shown it to be practicable. Let the road be built, and its influence will be incalculable. People will wonder that the world lived so long without it. Conjoining the two oceans, it will be an agency of matchless power, not only commercial, but political. It will be a new girder to the Union, a new help to business, a new charm to life. Perhaps the imagination is most impressed by the thought of travel and merchandise winding their way from Atlantic to Pacific in one unbroken line; but I incline to believe that the commercial advantages will be more apparent in the opportunities the railroad will create and quicken everywhere on the way. New homes and

[1] Works, vol. iii. p. 228. [2] Ibid., vol. vii. pp. 318, 319.

new towns will spring up, making new demand for labor and supplies. Civilization will be projected into the forest and over the plain, while the desert is made to yield its increase. There is no productiveness to compare with that from the upturned sod which receives the iron rail. In its crop are schoolhouses and churches, cities and States."

Sumner took a genuine interest in E. L. Pierce's administration of the Sea Islands of South Carolina. He wrote to him, Feb. 28, 1862: —

"We have to-day ordered the printing of your report, which forthwith becomes a 'document,' and among the best. I am proud of it. There is great ignorance in the chamber in regard to the pending cotton bill, and I fear there will be delay in considering it. But I shall try to press it. You are aware that it was prepared by Mr. Olmsted,[1] an admirable man."

Again, March 2: —

"The Secretary of the Treasury told me yesterday that he had given you full power with regard to the slaves at Port Royal. This is an eminent trust."

And again, June 7: —

"I am very busy; not a minute for anything but work. This tax bill has absorbed me lately, and everything else also. But I have had time to hear of your success, for it comes to me constantly from so many tongues. You have done an excellent work, and laid a foundation for fame. Chase speaks of your doings always with great interest and confidence. He authorized me to use his name in proposing you to the Secretary of War for governor of that region."

Sumner wrote to Mr. Bright from Boston, August 5: —

"I wish I could sit by the seashore and talk with you again. It is hard to write of events and of persons with that fulness and frankness which you require. The letters which I enclose from Mr. Atkinson,[2] a most intelligent and excellent person, will let you see the chance of cotton from the South. Do not count upon it. Make your calculations as if it were beyond reach. His plan of opening Texas reads well on paper; but thus far we have lost by dividing our forces. We must concentrate and crush. The armies of the South must be met and annihilated. If we start an expedition to Texas there will be another division. Climate, too, will be for the present against us. The correspondence between General Butler and Mr. Johnson will show you that government puts no restraint upon the sale of cotton; it is the perverseness of the rebels that does it all.

"Congress has adjourned. After a few days in Washington to see the President and Cabinet, I have come home, glad of a little rest, but to find new cares here. Our session has been very busy. You, who follow our fortunes so kindly, doubtless know what has been done for freedom, for reform

[1] Frederick L. Olmsted. [2] Edward Atkinson, of Boston.

generally, and also in the way of organizing our forces and providing means. There have been differences of opinion on questions of policy, especially on slavery. This was to be expected. But the bill of confiscation and liberation, which was at last passed under the pressure from our reverses at Richmond, is a practical act of emancipation. It was only in this respect that I valued it. The Western men were earnest for reaching the property of the rebels. To this I was indifferent, except so far as it was necessary to break up the stronghold of slavery. I wish that the Cabinet was more harmonious, and that the President had less *vis inertiæ*. He is hard to move. He is honest but inexperienced. Thus far he has been influenced by the border States. I urged him on the 4th of July to put forth an edict of emancipation, telling him he could make the day more sacred and historic than ever. He replied: 'I would do it if I were not afraid that half the officers would fling down their arms and three more States would rise.' He is plainly mistaken about the officers, and I think also with regard to the States. In the Cabinet, Chase, who enjoys and deserves public confidence more than any other member, also the Secretary of War and Secretary of the Navy, are for this policy. The last call for three hundred thousand men is received by the people with enthusiasm, because it seems to them a purpose to push the war vigorously. There is no thought in the Cabinet or the President of abandoning the contest. Of this be sure. It will be pushed to the full extent of all the resources of the republic, including, of course, the slaves. Strange it seems to me that I, who so sincerely accept the principles of peace, should be mixed up in this terrible war. But I see no way in which England can get cotton speedily except through our success. England ought to help us with her benedictions, for she is interested next to ourselves. But her adverse sympathies help put off the good day. All here are grateful to you for your strong and noble words. God bless you! I say with all my heart."

To the Duchess of Argyll, August 11: —

"At last I am at home, after eight months of uninterrupted labor at Washington. The late Congress was one of the most important legislative bodies of which there is any record. Few have acted on so many important measures, relating to army, navy, tariff, taxation; and then the great questions of a railroad to the Pacific; a free homestead on the public lands to all actual settlers; emancipation in the District of Columbia; prohibition of slavery in all the outlying Territories; the liberation of slaves coming within our lines, and the tender of compensation to loyal slaveholders for the freedom of their slaves; the acknowledgment of the independence of Hayti and Liberia, and the slave-trade treaty. Here is enough for an epoch.

"In this unhappy war our government has recently met with reverses; but nothing has occurred to modify in the least the purposes of the President or of any member of the Cabinet, except, if possible, to render them more determined to employ all the agencies needed to subdue the rebellion. I stayed in Washington some days after Congress, in order to confer intimately with the Administration. I saw them all, and was much with the President, so that I feel acquainted with their purposes *au fond*. That they will persevere, I pray you not to doubt.

"The President's great difficulty now is as to arming the blacks. He invites them as laborers, but he still holds back from the last step to which everything irresistibly tends. He says, 'Wait; time is essential.' That is, after an interval of time we shall be able to do what he thinks we cannot do now. Of course, he assumes that in the last resort every agency must be employed; and the country expects this. I am against emancipation by war, and I have always been against any interference with slavery in the States; but I have clearly seen from the beginning that only in this way can our war be ended.

" . . . I owe the duke a letter also. Thanks for your frankness. Write me unreservedly. I know your sincerity and goodness so well that I cannot misunderstand you."[1]

[1] The Duchess in her letter of July 12 had written her conviction that the attempt to overcome the rebellion had become hopeless, and her earnest desire to have it given up.

# CHAPTER XLVI.

## QUALITIES AND HABITS AS A SENATOR. — 1862.

SUMNER was from the beginning of his career in the Senate an interesting, and he had now become the most conspicuous, figure at the Capitol. His seat was first inquired for by visitors.[1] Person, fame, suffering, accomplishments, character, the confidence of men, all united to put him in the front and to keep him there. His associates in the Senate, when his presence no longer imposed reserve, testified to the power of his personality.[2] On the day when they summed up his relations to the body in which he had long served, they recalled "his manly beauty and manly strength,"[3] "his imposing presence on the outer circle of the Senate,"[4] and "the grand intonations of his far-sounding voice."[5] One said: "He was a man of such mark in his mere exterior as to arrest at once the attention of a stranger and make him a chief among ten thousand."[6] Another said: "You will remember his commanding presence, his stalwart frame (six feet and four inches in height), the vigor and grace of his motions, the charm of his manners, the polish of his rhetoric, the abundance of his learning, the fervor and impressiveness of his oratory. He was every inch a senator, and upheld with zeal and fidelity the dignity, privileges, and authority of the Senate."[7]

[1] Pall Mall Gazette, Dec. 26, 1866. The correspondent remarked upon the public interest in Sumner, — greater than in any other senator, — as also upon his qualities of intellect and character, saying that his motto might well be "Frangi non flecti."

[2] Eulogies in Congress, April 27, 1874. Congressional Globe, pp. 3399-3406, 3409-3419.

[3] G. F. Hoar. [4] J. S. Morrill. [5] O. D. Conger. [6] D. D. Pratt.

[7] E. R. Hoar. Edward Dicey, who visited the United States at this period, described the senator as "that great, sturdy, English-looking figure, with the broad, massive forehead, over which the rich mass of nut-brown hair, streaked here and there with a line of gray, hangs loosely; with the deep blue eyes, and the strangely winning smile, — half bright, half full of sadness. He is a man whom you would notice amongst other men, and whom not knowing you would turn round and look at as he passed by you. Sitting in his place in the Senate, leaning backwards in his chair, with his head stooping slightly over that great broad chest, and his hands resting upon his crossed legs, he looks in dress and attitude and air the very model of an English country gentleman. A child would ask him the time in the streets, and a woman would come to him unbidden for protection." ("Federal States," vol. i. pp. 236-237.) Mrs. Janet Chase Hoyt, daughter of Chief-Justice Chase, incorporates the above description into one of her own, adding further details of Sumner's manner in the society of friends. New York "Tribune," April 5, 1891.

Edward Everett, in a eulogy, likened the fidelity of John Quincy Adams to his seat in the House of Representatives, to that of a marble column of the Capitol to its pedestal;[1] and the same tribute is Sumner's due. No private errand and no listlessness kept him from his public duty; and he attended with severe punctuality the sessions of his committee and of the Senate. When the Internal Tax bill, which had consumed many days of discussion, was pending (nearly six months after the session began), he remarked that he had not been absent from his seat three minutes since it was taken up, or half an hour since the session began.[2] Near the end of the session he spoke forcibly against a final adjournment until the public business was completed, pointing out that Congress was by several weeks short of the limit which it was accustomed to reach when members were paid by the day instead of by the year.[3] In declining an invitation to attend a public meeting in the city of New York, he said, "A senator cannot leave his place more than a soldier." [4]

It has often occurred in the Senate, — and it occurred many times during this session, in which the duties of patriotism were most exacting, — that it was obliged to adjourn for want of a quorum, or for want of the attendance of a sufficient number to make its action decisive. Sumner's vacant chair, while he was in health, was never an obstruction to public business. Again and again, at this and at other sessions, as the official record shows, he protested against an early adjournment in the afternoon, and urged that the Senate go on with its calendar.[5] His

1 Senator Casserly referred, March 31, 1871, to Sumner as the senator "whom I do not see in his seat, which is very unusual, by the way."

2 May 30, 1862. Works, vol. vii. pp. 110, 111.

3 July 12 (Works, vol. vii. pp. 176–179). He had made similar remarks May 22 (Congressional Globe, p. 2225). The New York "Evening Post," June 7, 1862, had an article of the same tenor.

4 July 14, 1862. Works, vol. vii. pp. 180, 181.

5 Henderson of Missouri (May 16, 1868, Congressional Globe, p. 2494) referred to Sumner's constant votes against adjournments until after five or six, P. M., and against final adjournments even in July or August, saying, "If the senator had his way, he would remain here forever and ever." Edmunds said in relation to his opposition, April 17, 1869 (Globe, p. 726), "I never knew the day to come when my friend from Massachusetts really thought the Senate ought to adjourn;" and three days later (Globe, pp. 733, 734) he referred to Sumner's chronic difficulty about adjournments. Similar pressure from Sumner, with similar resistance from other senators who recalled his uniform position on the suspension of business, will be found in the record of later sessions (June 25, 1864, Globe, p. 3263; July 2, 1864, Works, vol. ix. pp. 55–63; July 26, 1866, Globe, pp. 4166, 4167; Dec. 14, 1868, Globe, p. 68; Dec. 15, 1869; May 5, 6, and 20, 1870, Globe, pp. 137, 3239, 3274, 3277, 3653; Feb. 15, 1871, Globe, p. 1262). Thurman's tribute, April 27, 1874 (Globe, p. 3400), referred to Sumner's high estimate of the effect of full discussion.

persistence in opposing a limitation of the session, even under the oppressive heat of the summer, brought him sometimes into collision with senators who, though not laggards, took a less exacting view of official duty, or who thought, sometimes quite rightly, that enough had already been done, and what remained would ripen for better action during the vacation.[1] Sumner's superlative fidelity may be thought finical, but it attests the seriousness with which he regarded all public duties.

Sumner's presence in the Senate was always one of dignity, such as became the office and place. He never descended to frivolity; he did not, as is the habit of restless members, keep passing from seat to seat, indulging in small talk with one or another, but remained mostly in his own;[2] he listened with respect to what his associates said in debate;[3] his manners were uniformly decorous, as opponents in the worst of times admitted; and the stranger in the gallery looking down on the scene recognized in him the impersonation and ideal of a leader in what has been regarded, in view of its constitution and functions, as a parliamentary body second to none in the world.

John Bigelow, already referred to, a writer and public man distinguished for critical observation of men and affairs, wrote in his journal on shipboard, in February, 1861, his estimate of Sumner, given in reply to a fellow-passenger who had made some criticisms on the senator: —

"First, he was the most accomplished man in public life in America; second, the ablest orator in Congress; third, of unblemished private character; fourth, of unblemished public character, which no breath of calumny had ever reached, and whom no one had ever dared approach with a dishonorable proposition; fifth, a man whose zeal and talents had been expended, not upon selfish schemes, but upon measures and policies looking to the improvement of the condition of society, — such ends as, whatever differences of opinion may prevail as to the adaptation of his means to secure them, must possess the sympathy and respect of all good citizens; sixth, he is

[1] July 2, 1864 (Works, vol. ix. pp. 55–63; Globe, p. 3502). June 25, 1864 (Globe, p. 3263). March 31 and April 7 and 8, 1869 (Globe, pp. 384, 607, 609).

[2] Douglas's swagger up and down the aisles is still remembered. Wilson was never so unhappy as when obliged to stay in his seat. Sumner's uniform observance of rules and courtesies in the Senate was referred to in tributes in Congress, April 27, 1874, by Pratt of Indiana in the Senate (Congressional Globe, p. 3403), and by E. R. Hoar in the House (Globe, p. 3410). He was accustomed to make protests against scandalous conduct in the Senate, — as Abbott's threat of a duel with a senator, and the drunkenness of Senator Saulsbury and Vice-President Johnson.

[3] Thurman said of him in his tribute, April 27, 1874 (Congressional Globe, p. 3400), "He spoke often and elaborately himself; and he was the best, and perhaps the most courteous, listener among us to the speeches of others."

very amiable; and seventh, a man whose decorum of character and whose talents have done and are doing more than those of any other man in the Senate to arrest the gradual decline of that body in the estimation of the country, in itself a service which those who feel the important rôle the Senate ought to play in our constitutional system know how to appreciate."

Mr. Bigelow added in 1886 the following memorandum to complete what he had said twenty-five years before: —

"Though a man of strong feeling, Mr. Sumner was distinguished for the marvellous control which he always exerted over his passions. In this respect he had an advantage over most of the conspicuous public men of his time. He never seemed to entertain — at least I never saw him exhibit — any resentment. When the names of his political assailants were mentioned in his presence, he took his revenge with a smile.

"No statesman of his time so completely and effectively expressed the anti-slavery sentiment of the free States.

"He was fond of applause, — rather too fond of it; but he sought only such applause as he thought he deserved. His ends were always of the best. His name is not associated, so far as I can recollect, with any public effort which did not have for its end the welfare of his country, by means entirely consistent with the highest standards of dignity and honor.

"It would have been well, I think, if Sumner had held some important executive or administrative office, — that of governor of Massachusetts, or a member of the Cabinet at Washington, for example, — that he might have familiarized himself with the difficulties which every servant of fifty millions of masters, be he ever so pure and wise, must always encounter in trying to have his own way."

Sumner had a comprehensive intelligence, which always sought to throw on the question in hand all the light of history and philosophy. Among American statesmen, those whom he most resembled in this respect are Jefferson, Edward Livingston, and John Quincy Adams. He never valued his own opinion so highly that he was not ready to sit at the feet of the masters of science. He was always prone to test public questions, not by apparent and transient exigencies, but by principles permanent and fundamental. It was for this reason that during the Civil War and reconstruction period he consulted so often Dr. Lieber, a publicist, living apart from political management, whose knowledge and counsels other public men would not have thought worth seeking.

Sumner believed it to be the statesman's part to lead the people, and not merely to follow them. He recognized, indeed, that measures and policies, in order to prevail, must have the support of public opinion; but he did not in advance study the drifts and currents of that opinion. He trusted the instincts of the people, and believed that what was right and true and wise would after statement, appeal, and agitation be approved by them. As these pages will show, he often advanced while others hesitated, and secured positions which afterwards they thought it safe to occupy. In the midst of popular frenzy he held firmly to his convictions, waiting serenely for the "sober second thought."

Sumner's sense of moral rectitude was supreme in the direction of his public conduct; and next to that sense was his allegiance to fixed principles of law and policy in opposition to temporary considerations of expediency and opinion. On details and minor points he was ready to yield; but he did not believe in piecemeal legislation, and he always held fast to the substance of a good measure, believing it was wiser to force small men and weak men to do their duty than to let them have their way. He was incapable of any indirection or political trick. In no public act was he ever governed by the slightest reference to his own personal interest or fortunes. Equity, patriotism, and human rights were his inspirations, and the expression of his face was that of conscientiousness and sincerity. This is the testimony not merely of old and intimate friends, or of men tempered like himself, but of critical observers not bound to him by personal relations. It was often given in his lifetime, and more freely when death had set the seal on his career. Not denying to many of their contemporaries a certain measure of these noble qualities, their fullest development must be found in our time in two kindred characters,—John Bright and Charles Sumner.[1] What Bright did for Eng-

[1] See estimates in W. H. Channing's "Life," by O. B. Frothingham, p. 367; "Pall Mall Gazette," Dec. 26, 1866; Harper's Weekly, March 24, 1866; New York "Herald," Dec. 28, 1871, containing an article, in the characteristic style of that journal, from a correspondent who mingles praise and dispraise. J. W. Forney wrote of Sumner ("Anecdotes of Public Men," vol. ii. p. 262): "We are all human; the best, like the worst, are controlled more or less by personal motives. But Sumner, I insist, was the supreme exception to this rule. I never knew any man less moved by selfish instincts. True, he had a lofty self-consciousness, or self-assertion; he liked to speak of his achievements, and he had the precision and the positiveness of a close reader and thinker. But he was not a self-seeker. He never intrigued for place; he never catered to public opinion. Nobody ever believed his course was governed other than by love of country. He was one of the boldest and most generous supporters of every progressive measure; and yet nobody ever charged that he or any of his friends had any connection with the legislation he advocated." Senator Pratt said, April 27, 1874: "No lobbyist ever approached him with doubtful propositions. No one could count upon his vote unless the measure was one which commanded his approbation from his sense of its justice and fitness." See "National Republican," Feb. 18, 1872.

land Sumner did for the United States,—each insisting always on the supremacy of the moral sentiments in government and the intercourse of nations, and each leaving a character stamped ineffaceably on the civilization of the English-speaking race.

It was thought that Sumner's ideal side was too greatly developed to admit of the working of the executive faculties in legislation. There is an indisposition to admit various capacities in the same person. *Est mos hominum ut nolint eundem pluribus rebus excellere;* and Sumner's confessed addiction to great principles stands in the way of the recognition of his ability to deal with the routine of ordinary work. It is easy, however, to push this criticism too far. He had not, indeed, like many public men, been bred in childhood to the drudgery of farm or workshop, and he missed something by this exemption. He did not remain long enough at the bar, nor was he devoted enough to his profession while he remained in it, to acquire that various knowledge of all pursuits which comes naturally to a lawyer in full practice. By the bent of his nature, also, he was inclined to moral and political speculations rather than to executive detail. Other qualities and habits, however, served him in overcoming these limitations. He learned prudence, economy, and fidelity in his father's house; he could not bear the thought of being in debt; he was from the start a hard worker; he was never hasty in judgment, but weighed well all questions of action and conduct, so that friends who sought his advice in trouble found him a wise counsellor; he was thoughtful in the little things as well as the great things of life; he was methodical in habit as in the working of his faculties; he kept an open mind for all knowledge, whether coming from books, letters, or conversation; he was thorough in preparation, and exhausted the subject in hand; and, above all, he was supremely conscientious in doing in the best way, to its full completion, every private or public service which he undertook. If he had not that liking for details, that interest in statistics, tables, and calculations, or in legal niceties, which is marked in some public men,—notably the senators from Vermont for a generation,—he largely made up for the defect by scrupulous fidelity in investigation, and close attention to each piece of business from its beginning to its end. If he were to oppose or seek to modify a tax in a revenue bill, he was always present at the critical moment, and never losing heart with one failure, renewed his motion at every later stage. If he had engaged to promote an appointment, he was not content with an assent to his request by the head of the department, but he followed the papers in their course from bureau to bureau till he saw the commission drawn and signed. A constituent, who visited Washington to look after his interest in a pending bill, could, after he had shown the justice of his case and obtained the senator's promise of attention to it, go home with entire confidence that the promise would be kept with no further reminder, even though the matter might not in the course of business be reached for months. He carried earnestness and will into all he did, and succeeded where others of less heart and force failed. A manager of the sanitary commission[1] relates how, arrested by red tape at the war department, he sought in his despair the senator, who overcame all obstacles in an hour, and saw delivered to the manager the needed pass for the relief steamer up the Potomac. It came about from his fidelity and the general confidence in his efficiency that the people of his State confided to him their interests in pending legislation, or in business with the departments, rather than to others who had passed their lives in professional, industrial, or commercial pursuits.[2] One great secret of his power, as was remarked by a shrewd critic of public men, was his intense personality, "his great and overmastering qualities," which brought him at times into collision with other senators, but which nevertheless made him "one of the powers and estates of the country."[3]

The period of Sumner's chairmanship of the committee on

[1] W. A. Hovey, of Boston.

[2] The Congressional Globe's Index for the session (1860–1862) will show how much more Sumner attended to the details of the internal tax bill than his colleague, who had been a manufacturer, but was lacking in method. George B. Upton, a leading Boston merchant for a long period, familiar with public men, a friend of Webster, and long regarding Sumner as a mere enthusiast, thus gave his testimony in a letter, Jan. 28, 1869: "I neglected to say a single word in relation to your re-election to the Senate. Whatever differences of opinion have heretofore existed, or may now exist, I desire to put this simple testimony in writing, that of all the gentlemen who have formerly represented Massachusetts, or who now have that honor, either in the Senate or House of Representatives, it has not been my good fortune to know one who has been as prompt and kindly attentive to the applications of his constituents as yourself."

[3] Warrington's (W. S. Robinson) Pen Portraits, pp. 517–520. This writer said: "It would be difficult to name a man, — and this is the universal testimony of those who have been to Washington on business, and have asked Mr. Sumner's aid, — it would be difficult, if not impossible, to find a man so industrious, methodical, thorough, energetic, and successful in attending to pure matters of business. This is the simple fact, and no exaggeration whatever. His great practical talent excels that of almost every man we have ever sent to Congress."

foreign relations was fruitful in business appropriate to the sphere of that committee. It was his duty to scrutinize, report, and explain treaties on a large variety of topics, which when ratified became laws of the land. They concerned naturalization, citizenship, extradition, postal relations, commerce, and navigation, the suppression of the slave-trade, claims of American citizens against foreign governments or of foreigners against our own, and cessions of territory. The disposition of such questions required a practical talent, in which he was not found wanting. While a member of the committee on the District of Columbia, he reported and carried through bills relating to the various interests of the District. Several statutes removing the disability of colored citizens were his handiwork. The consolidation of the statutes of the United States was his first thought, and was finally effected by his constant pressure.

Some critics, remembering that Sumner stood at some time in the way of their pretensions, or solicitous that their unrenowned services should not be overlooked, have suggested as a limitation to his sphere that he did not draw many statutes.[1] This mechanical work falls largely to the solicitors of the departments, or to promoters of bills;[2] and Sumner did as much of it as most men holding his relation to general affairs, — as much, for instance, as Webster or Seward. Wilson probably did not, while chairman of the committee on military affairs during the Civil War, draw one of the bills reported by him, — all being supplied by the Secretary of War, whose proper business it is to adjust the details of the military system.

The mass of senators and representatives at that time were accustomed to leave Washington immediately after the adjournment.[3] Sumner never left when the session ended, but habitually remained at the capital several weeks to bring up correspondence in arrears, post documents, and explore public questions which awaited action. He was not, it is true, encumbered with the family or business ties which called some of his associates to their homes; but he was in this prolonged assiduity altogether an exception among those who were as free as himself.

1 General Butler's Book, p. 314; G. S. Boutwell in the Boston "Globe," Sept. 28, 1890.

2 The bankrupt bill, which has long engaged the attention of Congress, was drawn by an eminent judge, — John Lowell, of Boston.

3 The custom has been somewhat modified by the greater number of members who have become renters or proprietors of houses.

Sumner's style was deliberate. He sometimes introduced topics or reflections which he thought relevant, though they bore only remotely on his argument. He drew occasionally on former speeches for materials. To the last of his life, as in his youth, what he wrote or spoke was marred by quotations from prose and poetry, sometimes extended beyond the limits of good taste. But he never rambled, never continued speaking because he did not know where to end, never spoke longer than he intended when he rose, never uttered a sentence which did not express a thought clear and important to his own mind. Any habitual reader of the debates of Congress will readily note what vices of parliamentary speaking he escaped.

While senator he had always a large correspondence, and never larger than now, — letters not only from his wide circle of personal friends, American and foreign, but from thousands whom he never saw.[1] A few he answered, but the greater number were recognized only by a copy of some speech, with an autograph frank and a memorandum of "thanks" on the envelope. He delighted, as few delight, in such burdensome recognitions from correspondents, known and unknown. He was unhappy if snow or freshet kept back the postman's morning packet; and all who invaded his breakfast hour — the time when his intimate friends most sought him — recall the zest with which he opened and read letter after letter (now and then handing one to the visitor) from his miscellaneous correspondents, — Cobden, Bright, and the Duchess of Argyll; a dozen or twenty faithful friends who wrote of affairs in Massachusetts; old Abolitionists in all parts of the country, well known or obscure, — indeed, from thousands of all conditions who had thoughts and anxieties which they wished some one in Washington to share.

He was the only public man in Washington who had a European correspondence of any public value. Bright and Cobden, almost our only two friends of eminence in England, reported to him drifts of opinion important to be known by our government, and gave sincere counsels as to what it was best for us to do. The Duchess of Argyll, reflecting the views of the duke, then in the Cabinet, did the same. These letters as soon as received

[1] The letters received which he preserved, beginning with those received in his youth, were filed in letter-books, one hundred and eighty-two in number, each containing two or three hundred letters. They are an important source of this biography.

were read to the President and his advisers, and were most useful in guiding their action. To these three correspondents he wrote often and most earnestly, — maintaining, spite of slowness and shortcomings, the moral grandeur of our cause, and protesting against the unfriendly, or, at least, unsympathetic action of the British government. To other Englishmen he wrote at intervals with appeals of like tenor; and he also conducted a correspondence with the Count of Paris after his return from this country to France. Sumner's intimate communication with foreigners, at a time when foreign opinion and action were so important to us, is not among the least of his services to his country during our civil contest.[1] He was likewise in communication with a large proportion of the legations and consulates of the United States, from which came statements of their needs and the aspect of our Civil War as it was regarded at their posts, and advice as to modes of enlisting foreign opinion in our favor.[2] No one outside of the state department had at command equal sources of information of this kind.

He was the one senator to whom advanced antislavery men looked for the expression and promotion of their views; and every mail at this time, and indeed during his entire service in Congress, brought him a large number of letters from this class, in which they stated, often at great length, their hopes and fears, and their interest in the various measures concerning slavery.[3]

Sumner's rooms while he was in the Senate were more sought than those of any member of either house. Among the visitors were writers for public journals, friends from Massachusetts, politicians from all parts of the country, survivors of the old antislavery guard, and distinguished foreigners. They often came late in the evening and stayed long; and his only way of dismissing them was, when he was on familiar terms with his caller, to turn to the unfinished work on his desk. "For a busy man," wrote Forney, "he was the most accessible I ever knew."

[1] He kept an eye from the beginning of the Civil War on foreign opinion, and pleaded that the secret service fund should be used to instruct foreign journals.

[2] Among correspondents of this class at this time were John Bigelow, Henry Adams, J. E. Harvey, W. S. Thayer, Seth Webb, Jr., J. S. Pike, B. Taylor, J. R. Giddings, T. Corwin, Carl Schurz, H. J. Perry, C. D. Cleveland, and B. R. Wood.

[3] Wendell Phillips delivered a lecture in Washington in March, 1862, probably his first visit to the capital. He had an interview with Mr. Lincoln, and was introduced by Sumner on the floor of the Senate, where he was greeted by Mr. Hamlin, the Vice-President, who left the chair to take his hand.

How he could accomplish all his tasks, and yet give so much time to miscellaneous visitors, was something of a mystery. It was, however, his midnight vigils which brought up the arrears. The newspaper men were generally very friendly to him. He held tightly the secrets of the Senate notwithstanding he had no respect for the system of closed doors; but as far as consistent with a senator's oath, he talked freely and instructively to all who came to him. After he had a house of his own, which was not till 1867, he explained to Dr. Howe a *contre-temps* by which a well-known scholar whom he had wished to see had been refused admission, and added: —

"I am impatient and nervous, weary, fatigued, and unhappy, beginning the day weary and ending it weary. From the time I take my seat at the breakfast table interruptions begin; and such is the succession of visitors that during this vacation I have been detained daily at the table where I breakfasted till three o'clock P. M., without an opportunity of putting pen to paper or leaving the room. At dinner I try to be alone, unless with guests, and the domestic says to callers at this time that I am engaged. . . . I doubt if any one is as much beset by help-seeking visitors as myself, nor is anybody equally accessible. The President and members of the Cabinet receive at their offices during an hour or two. I begin with the morning and end at midnight, intermitting an hour for dinner. What my manner is to them, all this considered, I leave to the judgment of those who see me most. To some I am impatient, at times very impatient, as they insist upon absorbing my time; but I doubt if anybody in Washington hears so many with greater patience or kindness. My duties now are onerous, and I need one hundred hours daily instead of twenty-four.

"I had not heard of H.'s death. Such is my feeling about life that he seems to have obtained rest. I have a sense of relief for the persons thus preferred. He is taken beyond our trials, where ingratitude and falsehood will cease. Good-by! Again a Happy New Year!"

There was at this time an enormous pressure for places in the home and foreign service of our government, and also for appointments and promotions in the army. These aspirants, as well as citizens who had business with the departments, often eminent in position and of disinterested patriotism, were unable to obtain access to them except through senators and representatives. Sumner, as the files of letters received by him show, bore his full share of this burden. He and his colleague were the medium of communication between Governor Andrew and the government.[1]

[1] The files of the governor's office at the State House contain many letters from Sumner on public business.

Literary men as well as antislavery men, irrespective of the States they lived in, felt they had a special claim on Sumner. Motley was urgent with him for a mission, first at the Hague and then at Vienna. Fay hoped, though vainly, to be saved by him from the competition of place-seekers. Bayard Taylor, wishing to succeed Cameron at St. Petersburg, wrote from that capital, Aug. 18, 1862: "Take my importunity in good part; there are so few senators who are scholars!"

It was a time when relatives were always at Washington on their way to look for wounded or sick soldiers, or to recover their bodies from fields and hospitals. Sumner, however much it might invade his time, was always glad to serve them by procuring passes or otherwise. When any of his friends met with bereavements, his habit was to send a letter of solace. The files of his correspondence contain many replies from those whose griefs he sought to assuage. The brother of Rev. Arthur B. Fuller, killed at Fredericksburg, whose widow's petition for a pension he promoted, wrote to him: "As often as my brother's widow receives her pension for herself and little ones, she will think of the senator from Massachusetts."

Sumner's admirers often named their children for him. His replies to them, when they announced this kind of recognition, were of uniform tenor, and one written in 1865 may be given as a specimen: —

> "Don't make a mistake. Never name a child after a living man. This is the counsel I give always and most sincerely. Who knows that I may not fail? I, too, may grow faint, or may turn aside to false gods. I hope not; but this is one of the mysteries of the future. Therefore name your boy some good Christian name. It may be Charles if you will, for that is general; but do not compel him to bear all his days a label which he may dislike. I once met a strong antislavery youth who bore the name Martin Van Buren. He was born while New York sat in the Presidential chair, and his father named him after the chief of the land. But the youth did not find the sentiments of the late M. V. B. such as he wished to be associated with. Somebody in the play says in anger to his son: 'I'll unget you!' Don't do this. Simply unname him."

Samuel Hooper entered, in December, 1861, the House as a member from a Boston district, and continued a member during the rest of the senator's life. He was a wealthy merchant, and his associations and sympathies hitherto had been those of the capitalists, who as a class had not looked with favor on Sumner. Daily intercourse, as was often the case, changed Mr. Hooper's view of the senator, and he came to be his cordial and confidential friend, so remaining to the end. He dispensed a liberal hospitality; and in his house at Washington, as well as at Boston and on the seashore, Sumner was always welcome to lodge or dine.[1] Later in these pages it will become necessary to refer to a near connection between the two friends.

Two or three incidents in family and friendship may be noted here, — the death in March, 1862, of another of the "Five of Clubs" (Felton, of whose funeral Mr. Thies sent an account); the disability of George Sumner, stricken with paralysis, and after medical treatment in Northampton coming back to the old home in Hancock Street; a cordial letter from Agassiz in the autumn urging attendance at the dinners of the Saturday Club at Parker's.

[1] The intimacy which he had enjoyed with the family of Mr. Adams, already Minister to England, was now transferred to Mr. Hooper's, at whose house he dined at least once or twice a week from 1861 to 1874.

## CHAPTER XLVII.

### THIRD ELECTION TO THE SENATE.

WHEN the session of Congress ended, July 17, 1862, the military situation was no more hopeful than at the beginning. Grant had indeed won a substantial victory at Fort Donelson; New Orleans had been taken; and Farragut with his squadron held command of the Lower Mississippi. The reduction of Vicksburg was essential to the opening of the river; but that point could not yet be attained. The hope of the nation had centred for months on McClellan's army, which, after a final reverse before Richmond, retired to Harrison's Landing, where it remained when the session closed.[1]

Sumner's term was to expire March 4, 1863, and the choice of his successor was to be made by the legislature elected in November, 1862. His other re-elections were not contested; but this time a spirited movement to defeat him was under way early in the year, and broke out openly in the summer. The Democratic party, though supporting the prosecution of the war under the patriotic impulse of the masses, was generally hostile to the Republican leaders, who were attempting, as it alleged, to make the war "an abolition war." But standing alone, it was in Massachusetts too reduced in numbers to carry an election. From another quarter, — from the remains of the Bell-Everett party, and from some Republicans who were such from circumstances and not from antislavery conviction, — came the most virulent opposition to Sumner's re-election. These "odds and ends" started what they called a People's Party, aimed against both Sumner and Governor Andrew; but as the task of defeating both was found to be too heavy, they finally directed the main assault on Sumner.[2] They nominated for governor

1 Antislavery senators were charged with interfering with McClellan's plans, and Wilson in an open letter denied the charge for himself and his colleague.

2 The articles in the New York "Herald" in July, 1862, are an expression of a general feeling among people of lukewarm loyalty against not only Sumner but other public men of antislavery position.

Charles Devens, an officer in service, a Republican by political connection, but of limited political activity, and the Democrats adopted him and the other candidates named by the People's Party.[1] The movement had the important aid of the Springfield "Republican," whose proprietor was absent for a vacation in Europe, and who lived to regret the part his journal took in the canvass.[2] Ultra-conservatism made its last struggle; and conspicuous among its leaders was Professor Joel Parker of Cambridge, whose judicial temper was upset by Sumner's "State-suicide" doctrine, and who combined with his ability as a jurist antipathy to those who found more power in the Constitution to deal with slavery than he could find.[3] As soon as the opposition began to show itself there was a rally on the other side. Sumner could always rely upon a reserved force among the people, a force consisting of those with whom the moral sentiments were uppermost, — Liberty Party men of 1844, Conscience Whigs of 1845 to 1847, Free Soilers of 1848 and 1852, — classes abounding in men of intellectual vigor. They comprised the clergy in large numbers, teachers of advanced schools, and most of the editors of the country press. If idealists, they were not idealists only, and they were a match for practised party men in using effectively the weapons of political warfare. As a body they were governed by no selfish considerations, and they went into a contest with a determined spirit, which meant not only the support of their own candidate, but war upon his assailants. They were to be feared beyond their numbers in any conflict in which they took part, and politicians looking to preferment thought it prudent not to put themselves in their way.

This body of Sumner's supporters, it should be remembered, was made up of men to whom he had never done a favor by help to office or otherwise, and who expected no such favor in the future; but during his career, at the slightest warning of

1 The People's Party, at a mass convention in Springfield, October 24, presented as candidate for senator C. F. Adams; but at his instance his name was withdrawn by his son. (Boston "Advertiser," October 28.) The hostile movement outside of the party was thought to have helped Sumner within it. Boston "Advertiser," October 14, November 5.

2 "Life and Times of Samuel Bowles," vol. i. pp. 357–359. Dr. Holland, who was antipathetic to Sumner, was at this time the managing editor. The "Republican," in 1862, opposed an emancipation policy.

3 A coadjutor and townsman of Judge Parker, John C. Dodge, who was an eminent lawyer, confessed, after reading the first two volumes of this Memoir, in a letter to the author, that he had misjudged Sumner for many years, and now saw his character in a better light.

any attempt to assail or weaken his position, they came at once to his rescue. The mainspring of their loyalty is easily found; and it is creditable alike to him and to them. They had been inspired, many of them in youth, by his noble sentiments, his courageous statements of moral truth, his unconquerable will in the warfare with slavery; and when aroused, they made a formidable power, such as no other statesman has been able to command. Jackson, Clay, and Webster drew to themselves hosts of friends by their personal and intellectual qualities; but Sumner stands almost alone as a public man whose great support was the moral enthusiasm of the people.

The Republican State convention met at Worcester, September 9, and Sumner's supporters were ready for the first encounter. They decided to make the issue openly upon him in the convention. This direct appeal to the people in the nomination of a senator was contrary to custom in Massachusetts; but it had a distinguished precedent in another State,—in Illinois, where Lincoln in 1858 was nominated as the Republican candidate against Douglas. Sumner thought it unseemly to mix personally in the contest within the party, and declined an invitation to attend the convention in a letter read by Mr. Claflin to the delegates, which invoked an earnest support of the government, but did not omit to add an appeal for the policy of freedom, which he deemed essential to success.[1] The chair was occupied by Alexander H. Bullock, afterwards governor,—a most accomplished person, and though heretofore holding very conservative views, now one of Sumner's firmest friends. His opening address laid stress on the necessity of an antislavery policy, and its growing favor with the people, saying: "We have been forced beyond the conditions which define the functions of a State in health, and are groping amid the issues of life and death." The leader among the delegates opposed to Sumner's nomination was R. H. Dana, Jr., who during the period of 1860–1865 was having one of his periodic attacks of high conservatism. He was strongly opposed to any declaration of emancipation as the policy of the government, even upon the ground, or as he called it under cover, of military necessity, and also to measures of confiscation whose chief intent was the

[1] Works, vol. vii. pp. 187–190. T. D. Eliot, a Massachusetts member of Congress, at a public meeting on the evening preceding the convention, answered at length the charge that Sumner was not a practical legislator, citing his services in various matters.

freedom of the slaves.[1] Sumner's relations with him and his family had been intimate for many years; and he was at the time United States district attorney, — an appointment which the senator had taken pleasure in promoting.[2] These relations hampered Mr. Dana, and he withheld from the convention the real grounds of his opposition, confining himself to the narrow point of expediency, — that the nominating resolution would not do the senator any good.

When the customary motion for a committee on resolutions was made, Dana, fearing the composition of such a committee, moved as a substitute a brief resolution supporting the government in the prosecution of the war. J. Q. A. Griffin[3] promptly moved an amendment, which approved the conduct of the two senators from Massachusetts, and nominated Sumner for re-election as "a statesman, a scholar, a patriot, and a man of whom any republic in any age might be proud." He maintained his substitute in a trenchant speech, in which he handled roughly Dana and others co-operating with him. Mr. Griffin never took part in any controversy outside of his own State, and he died before the full fruition of his powers;[4] but in a rich combination of logic, humor, and sarcasm, no lawyer or politician of Massachusetts at that time equalled him. He had a quick-witted sense of the currents of a popular assembly, and a strong and impressive voice, which he used effectively in saying: "Remember, it is our duty not only to sustain the arms of the generals in the field, but likewise to sustain the President in his seat, the Cabinet in its councils, the governor in his chair, and *above all the fearless legislator in his duty.*" Other delegates, among them George F. Hoar, followed in the same line; and the resolutions were referred to a committee, of which Griffin was chairman and Dana a member. In committee Dana opposed without success the contested resolution, and another which called for the extermination of slavery as the principal

[1] Letters of Mr. Dana to Sumner in manuscript, June 4 and Sept. 13, 1862; Adams's "Biography" of Dana, vol. ii. pp. 259, 263.

[2] Adams's "Biography" of Dana, vol. ii. pp. 257. Dana expressed surprise that Sumner was for some time less cordial than before; but he could hardly have expected a different result from his leadership in a movement of such a personal character against the senator. (Ibid., p. 265.) Indeed, Dana, if the positions had been reversed, would have been less tolerant than Sumner. The coldness, however, was but temporary. Sumner afterwards had no sincerer friend and admirer than Dana. Ibid., vol. ii. pp. 339, 340, 361, 363.

[3] F. W. Bird, William Claflin, and other supporters of Sumner had selected Griffin in a conference as their leader in the convention.

[4] He died in 1866 at the age of forty.

support of the rebellion. When the report was made to the convention, a motion to strike out the resolution nominating Sumner received but few votes, and the series was unanimously adopted. The attempt to discredit Sumner as a Republican was a signal failure. From this day the movement against him, so far as it was kept up, was outside of the party.

The points made against Sumner in the discussions of the newspapers and opposition speakers were, in the first place, that he had sought to make the war an antislavery war, and in that way to prevent a union of all loyal citizens in support of its prosecution; and secondly, that he was not "a practical man," and was so absorbingly devoted to his views on the slavery question that he could not attend to the business interests of his constituents. Said one speaker: —

> "We want men in the halls of Congress, in the House of Representatives, and above all and beyond all in the Senate chamber, who will attend to those interests, and not be continually, as they have been, sir, attending to mere wild speculations and recondite theories. Do not the people cry out, 'For God's sake, give us somebody who believes there is something to be attended to in the wants of a million and a quarter of white men, women, and children!'"

This was said by J. G. Abbott, a Free Soiler of 1848, now full of rancor against his former sentiments and his old associates.[1]

There was an attempt in the beginning of the canvass to detach support from Sumner on the pretence that he was an obstruction to the Administration, which had adopted a policy the opposite of his, — that of letting slavery alone, and prosecuting the war on the sole issue of the Union; but this argument was effectually silenced by the President's Proclamation of Emancipation, September 22, which followed by a few days the Republican convention.[2] A report, studiously circulated, that the senator was in personal as well as political antagonism to the President was completely met by a letter from Sumner, which was widely published.[3]

1 W. S. Robinson ("Warrington"), in his "Pen Portraits," pp. 521, 522, says: "I should like to have him [the reader] look back and read the speeches of Joel Parker and Leverett Saltonstall, who tried by that movement to make the war a war for the 'flag' only, and not for freedom and regeneration. Charles Sumner was the great central figure of that contest, and from that time forward to the end of reconstruction he was the great civic hero of the crisis."

2 It had already been submitted to the Cabinet before the convention met, but the fact was not known to the public.

3 Works, vol. vii. pp. 116–118; New York "Tribune," June 16. This letter was brought before the public by the senator's friend, Mr. Alley.

Sumner as well as his friends saw the importance of his going to the people himself; and he accepted invitations to address meetings in several principal places, twelve at least, in the State, — among them one at Faneuil Hall, Boston,[1] at noon day, where he could face an assembly of large commercial interests, and one at Springfield, where Mr. Bowles's newspaper had with all its influence made hardly any impression on Republican voters. In both cities, as well as in the other places where he spoke, he was received with the same old-time cordiality and enthusiasm. One of less courage, perhaps one with more tact, would under the circumstances have shaped his address so as to ward off the familiar criticism that he was too much absorbed in the slavery question to do wisely and effectively the general work of a statesman. Bnt it was not in his nature to avoid a personal issue by indirection of any kind. With that absolute fearlessness which was a part of himself, he took the recent proclamation for his text, and showed at length how the measure was essential as a military necessity, replying at the same time to the various objections urged against it. Looking forward beyond the end of the Civil War, he maintained that there could be no perfect union, no assured peace, no assimilation of the people North and South, without converting slaves into freemen. Among his sententious passages are these: —

"Without the aid of the slaves the war cannot be ended successfully. Their alliance is therefore a necessity. . . . The force of the rebellion may be broken even without appeal to the slaves. But I am sure that with the slaves our victory will be more prompt, while without them it can never be effectual completely to crush out the rebellion. It is not enough to beat armies. Rebel communities, envenomed against the Union, must be restored, and a widespread region quieted. This can be done only by removal of the disturbing cause and the consequent assimilation of the people, so that no man shall call another master. . . . A united people cannot be conquered. Defeated on the battle-field, they will remain sullen and revengeful, ready for another rebellion. This is the lesson of history. . . . The Unionists of the South are black. Let these be rallied, and the rebellion will be exposed not only to a fire in front, but also to a fire in the rear. . . . Heavy battalions are something, but they are not everything. Even if prevailing on the battle-field, which is not always the case, the victory they compel is not final; it is impotent to secure that tranquillity essential to national life. Mind is above matter, right is more than force; and it is vain to attempt conquest merely by matter or by force. If this can be done in small affairs, it cannot in large;

[1] Works, vol. vii. pp. 196–246. He spoke again briefly, October 31, in Faneuil Hall, with Richard Busteed.

for these yield only to moral influences. . . . Let the war end on the battle-field alone, and it will be only in appearance that it will end, not in reality. Time will be gained for new efforts, and slavery will coil itself to spring again. The rebellion may seem to be vanquished, and yet it will triumph. The Union may seem to conquer, and yet it will succumb. The republic may seem to be saved, and yet it will be lost, — handed over a prey to that injustice which, so long as it exists, must challenge the judgments of a righteous God." [1]

In the beginning he spoke, but only briefly, of the criticisms to which he had been recently subjected, — recalling Burke's address to the electors at Bristol as appropriate to similar accusations against himself, to the effect that he had overdone in "pushing the principles of general justice and benevolence too far;" and he challenged scrutiny of his record at all points in disproof of the imputation that he had neglected the business interests of his constituents. Affirming his fidelity to those interests, as well as to the great cause he had served, he stated that during a service of more than eleven years he had never for once visited home while Congress was in session, or been absent for a single day, unless when suffering from the disability which followed the assault in 1856; and during the recent session he had not been out of his seat a single hour.

Among his critics who had imputed to him a neglect of the material interests of his State was Linus Child,[2] to be recalled as an opponent of the "Conscience Whigs" of 1846, who had in behalf of the cotton manufacturers visited Washington during the recent session especially to prevent a tax on the production of cotton. Having found in Sumner his most effective support, he wrote him on his return a grateful letter, acknowledging the great obligations of his clients to the two Massachusetts senators for their efficient service in protecting a great New England interest; and he reported to the manufacturers his peculiar indebtedness to Sumner. Shortly after, Mr. Child sought Sumner's influence for an internal revenue appointment, and failing to receive it turned against him, first speaking against him in the Republican convention, and then, changing his party, he took the chair at the People's Party convention. The senator in speeches read his letter as a direct contradiction to his charge of neglect of the business interests of his constituents.

1 The speech delighted Dr. Thomas Guthrie of Edinburgh, who made it a topic of public prayer in a church service. Letter of the Duchess of Argyll to Sumner, Dec. 3, 1862.

2 *Ante*, vol. iii. p. 126.

Sumner found eloquent and able support in different directions in the newspapers of his State; in Wendell Phillips, who called him "the Stonewall Jackson of the Senate, . . . patient of labor, boundless in resources, terribly in earnest;" in John G. Whittier, who dwelt upon the many sides of his character and his various attainments, his stainless life, with no use of his high position for his own personal emolument; in Horace Greeley, who in leaders in the "Tribune" set forth the importance to the whole country of his re-election, laying stress on his character for integrity and sincerity, respected alike by enemies and by friends, and who later in an article in the "Independent" reviewed his career at length.[1] When the lines had been distinctly drawn, the result was no longer doubtful. Governor Andrew's plurality exceeded twenty-seven thousand. The Legislature in January following re-elected Sumner by a vote of two hundred and twenty-seven to forty-seven for all others,—nearly five to one, most of the minority voting for J. G. Abbott. On the evening of the election the senator was waited upon by delegations, whom he addressed briefly; and a similar greeting, which he declined, was offered him at Washington. The public journals of the country, and numerous congratulatory letters from distant places, recognized the result as an important event.[2]

Other States were not as steadfast as Massachusetts in 1862. The Administration was outvoted in New York and New Jersey,—States which had chosen Republican electors, and now elected governors[3] hostile to it; and it encountered defeat in Pennsylvania, Ohio, Indiana, and Illinois. Several causes contributed to this disaster,—chiefly the want of success in the field, the incidents of increased taxation, derangement in the currency, and the imminency of a draft. The disaster on the Rappahannock was at hand. Greeley gives the opinion in his History that during the year following July 4, 1862, a majority of the people, outside of the soldiers in the field, would have voted for peace, and a still larger majority against emancipation.[4] This is a conjecture; but it indicates the depression

1 Works, vol. vii. pp. 237, 238, 243, 244.

2 New York "Tribune," Nov. 8, 1862; Jan. 16, 1863. The last notice reviewed his career, and contrasted the circumstances of his first entrance into the Senate in 1851 and his present position.

3 Horatio Seymour and Joel Parker.

4 Vol. ii. p. 254.

which McClellan's and other failures brought on the public mind. Conservative Republicans assigned as a cause of the reaction the radical policy which Congress had adopted on the slavery question at its late session, and it is altogether probable that it repelled a considerable number of voters.

Sumner wrote to Mr. Bright, October 28: —

"I wish I were at Llandudno, where for a day I could talk on our affairs and enjoy a little repose. The President is in earnest. He has no thought of any backward step; of this be assured. Since I last wrote you I have been in Washington, when I saw him daily, and became acquainted precisely with his position at that time. There is nobody in the Cabinet who is for 'backing-down;' it is not talked of or thought of. The President was brought slowly to the proclamation; it was written six weeks before it was put forth, and delayed, waiting for a victory, and the battle of Antietam was so regarded. I protested against the delay, and wished it to be put forth — the sooner the better — without any reference to our military condition. In the Cabinet it was at first opposed strenuously by Seward, who from the beginning has failed to see this war in its true character, and whose contrivances and anticipations have been those merely of a politician who did not see the elemental forces engaged. But he countersigned the proclamation, which was written by the President himself, as you may infer from the style. The old Democracy (more than half of which is now in armed rebellion) are rallying against the proclamation. At this moment our chief if not our only danger is from the division which they may create at the North. The recent elections have shown losses for the Administration; but I do not think it possible that we can be without a determined working majority in the House, who will not hearken to any proposition except the absolute submission of the rebels. The hesitation of the Administration to adopt the policy of emancipation led Democrats to feel that the President was against it, and they have generally rallied. I think a more determined policy months ago would have prevented them from showing their hands. The President himself has played the part of the farmer in the fable, who warmed the frozen snake at his fire. But from this time forward our whole policy will be more vigorous; and I should not be astonished to see the whole rebellion crumble like your Sepoy rebellion, which for awhile seemed as menacing to your Indian empire as ours has been to our republic. I believe I have avoided in my letters any very confident prediction. I have never seen our affairs with Mr. Seward's eyes; but I have from the beginning seen that our only chance against the rebellion was by striking slavery; and it seemed to me that these mighty armaments on both sides, and their terrible shock, were intended to insure its destruction. It is time for it to come to an end. I am grateful to you that you have kept your faith in us, and I pray you to persevere. I write to you sincerely, as I feel; and I beg you to believe that I would not excite any confidence which I do not believe well founded. Of course, we have before us the whole reconstruction of Southern society. I have seen it so from the beginning; but I have hope that our people will rise to the grandeur of the occasion. The colonization delusion is from Montgomery Blair, postmaster-general, who has made a convert of the President; but thus far I have thought it best to allow it to have a free course, and thus to avoid a difference with the President. Our generals are inefficient, but our troops are excellent. I have loved England, and now deplore her miserable and utterly false position towards my country. God bless you!"

To the Duchess of Argyll, November 12: —

"You will hear of the elections. In Massachusetts the vote has been all that I could desire. In New York it has been bad, — worse for us than the bloodiest defeat; for it will unquestionably encourage the rebellion and those who sympathize with it at home and abroad. But it is easy to explain the change without supposing any vital change of sentiment. More than three-fourths of the soldiers in the army, most of them voters, are for the Administration. Had they been at home, the result would have been largely different. Then the people were deceived by the cry from the opposition that there must be more vigor in the war. But it now remains for the Administration to put all possible energy into the war, and to break its back before spring. I see the way to this more clearly now than ever. (1) The true policy has been declared; (2) the general who has been our military incubus, McClellan, is at last removed; (3) the country insists upon vigorous, determined action.

"I know not what disappointments may be in store, and I think you will bear witness that while I have not doubted the final result, I have never been sanguine with regard to the immediate present. But I am now more hopeful than at any former moment. . . . Of course, it must take long to trample out all this rebellion in its embers as well as its flames; but I shall not be suprised to see it subdued soon.

"Various expeditions are on foot which promise us all the seaports, while our large army moves into the enemy's country. Meanwhile we are startled by the news of rebel ships built and equipped in the Mersey and the Clyde on an unprecedented scale.[1] I hope that these will not be allowed to aggravate our foreign relations. I am at a loss to understand why good people in England should gravitate so strongly to sympathy with a miserable slave-government, which if it should be established would be a most offensive slave-trading oligarchy, which a true Englishman, such as I have known and admired, would scorn. You hear something of the feeling here on this point. Men who have always stood by England as son by father are now embittered. I hear their complaints in silence, or answer only by a soft word; but I have my sorrows when I observe the manifestation of opinion in England. A great mistake has been made; pray do not let it go further! How will it look in history, that in the great strife where slavery was in issue England was on the wrong side? Pardon my frankness. Next to my own country right, I long to see England right, honestly, sincerely. But I wish I could talk of these things; there is much that I cannot write. God bless you! Remember me most kindly to your mother the duchess. Pray let us keep the peace in all things as completely as possible."

[1] Sumner's first reference to these ships.

In a letter to Mr. Bright, of the same date, similar in substance to the one written to the duchess, he said: —

"Opinion with you seems to be growing worse and worse, — more utterly prejudiced and senseless. The English heart seems given to the brutal slave-masters. Our trials have been great; but I confidently point to our efforts, which amidst all failures show transcendent resources. It is to our credit that we had so long and carefully been absorbed in the arts of peace that we wanted generals to command. How was it with England in the Crimea?"

To the Duchess of Argyll, November 17: —

"I hope that the English position will be so firmly fixed that it cannot be swayed to the support of slavery, and that the old English sentiment will be quickened to that honorable life which is such a pride to all who truly love England. I do not desire England to step from her neutrality; but I believe that her generous historian hereafter will regret bitterly, if this terrible war to prevent the establishment of a vulgar slave empire and the re-opening of the slave-trade shall be closed without her sympathies being recorded in harmony with her best and most glorious past. Of course, in putting down this rebellion we are putting down a government whose life is slavery; and now, thank God, we shall put it down by freedom!

"All that I hear now is more cheering. Mr. Chase, who has for a long time taken gloomy views, writes me full of confidence and hope; and there is a general feeling that the war is to be pushed with irresistible vigor. Do not suppose me unconscious of the enormous difficulties which under the most favorable circumstances we must encounter. The whole social system of the South must be reorganized. No wisdom and no courage can be too great for this enterprise. I do not consent yet to renounce the good-will of England. Surely the friend of Garibaldi, the critic of Neapolitan tyranny, and the patron of Italian unity may find an occasion for these sentiments on this side of the Atlantic. With me nothing is clearer than this: as no man stands in the way of another, so no nation stands in the way of another. Therefore I share no jealousy of any other power. Let all thrive and prosper. England will be greater if our Union is preserved than if it is destroyed. But it will not be destroyed.

"The late elections will doubtless encourage the rebellion; but they have also encouraged the Administration. The President accepts their lesson, and is determined to press forward. . . . But these delays and disasters were needed in order to compel emancipation. How many dreary conversations I have had with the President on this theme, beginning sixteen months ago! But McClellan's failure did more for the good cause than any argument or persuasion. God bless you!"

Sumner attended in the autumn of 1862 the annual dinner of the Hampshire County Agricultural Society at Northampton, where he was called up by Erastus Hopkins, an accomplished orator and steadfast friend of the senator. Their acquaintance went back to the time when they were fellow-pupils at the Boston Latin School. Sumner recalled, as he began, his pedestrian excursion, as a Harvard student, to the Connecticut valley, whose beauties he then saw for the first time.[1] He paid a tribute to the farming industry, and enforced the duties of patriotism, paramount among which he put the support of the war and the policy recently announced by the President.[2] He was not in the habit, like most public men, of attending such meetings; and the only other similar occasion when he was present was at Dedham, where however he did not speak.

[1] Memoir, vol. i. pp. 61, 62.
[2] October 14. Works, vol. vii. pp. 248–254.

## CHAPTER XLVIII.

SEWARD. — EMANCIPATION. — PEACE WITH FRANCE. — LETTERS OF MARQUE AND REPRISAL. — FOREIGN MEDIATION. — ACTION ON CERTAIN MILITARY APPOINTMENTS. — PERSONAL RELATIONS WITH FOREIGNERS AT WASHINGTON. — LETTERS TO BRIGHT, COBDEN, AND THE DUCHESS OF ARGYLL. — ENGLISH OPINION ON THE CIVIL WAR. — EARL RUSSELL AND GLADSTONE. — FOREIGN RELATIONS. — 1862-1863.

THE third session of the Thirty-seventh Congress began Dec. 1, 1862, and ended March 3, 1863. Early in the session there was a movement for the displacement of Mr. Seward as Secretary of State. It came from a wide-spread feeling in the country, as well as in Congress, that he was wanting in earnest convictions as to the character of the great struggle; that he was an obstruction to a decided policy, and a paralyzing influence in the Administration. As was then believed, and has since been found to be true, he had opposed in the Cabinet the issue of the proclamation of emancipation. Sumner had been on the whole friendly to him, — more so than most of the senators. He was, indeed, sorely grieved at the secretary's exclusion, in his diplomatic correspondence, of "opposing moral principles"[1] from the Civil War at its beginning, and at his further assurance that slavery was to remain untouched by the conflict;[2] but Seward had added a grave cause of offence. In a despatch to Mr. Adams, July 5, 1862, which had recently come to Sumner's attention, he treated armed rebels ("the extreme advocates of African slavery") and loyal antislavery men ("its most vehement opponents") as "acting in concert together to precipitate a servile war, — . . . the former by making the most desperate attempts to overthrow the federal Union; the latter by demanding an edict of universal emancipation as a lawful and necessary if not, as they say, the only legitimate way of saving the Union."[3]

[1] *Ante*, p. 39.
[2] *Ante*, p. 39.
[3] Curiously enough, when Mr. Seward sent his despatch, July 5, 1862, the President was already brooding on a proclamation of emancipation, which he mentioned to two of his secretaries eight days later, and formally presented to his Cabinet, July 22.

The general dissatisfaction of the Republican senators with Mr. Seward took formal shape in a caucus which was convened shortly after the session began. They took unanimous action (Mr. King of New York alone not voting), which it was supposed would effect his withdrawal from the Cabinet. Without naming him, it was agreed to call upon the President to make such changes in his Cabinet as would secure unity of purpose and action, and include in it only the cordial and unwavering supporters of a vigorous and successful prosecution of the war. The committee of the caucus, consisting of Collamer, Trumbull, Howard, Harris, Grimes, Pomeroy, Fessenden,[1] Sumner, and Wade, waited on the President, December 18. Collamer presented the formal paper which had been agreed upon, and the senators individually stated their objections to Mr. Seward's continuance in the Cabinet. When Mr. Lincoln's attention was called, probably by Sumner, to the despatch of July 5, he expressed surprise, and disclaimed any knowledge of it, — a disclaimer which he subsequently repeated to Sumner.[2]

The President stood firmly by the secretary, and the effort to displace him proved futile. It received a check in an unexpected quarter, — from one of the secretary's associates. Mr. Seward on hearing of it sent to the President his resignation before the senators had their interview with him; and Mr. Chase, who singularly enough saw fit to construe the terms of the request as including himself, took occasion also to resign. The President by a joint letter to both secretaries requested them to resume their places. Seward promptly assented without consulting Chase, and the latter then followed with a withdrawal of his resignation.[3]

[1] Fessenden's unfavorable opinion of Seward at an early date is given in his letter, Feb. 2, 1858, to J. S. Pike. "First Blows of the Civil War," p. 379.

[2] New York "Tribune," March 2, 1863. There was a controversy between the New York "Tribune" and New York "Times" as to Seward's practice in submitting despatches to the President before they were sent. (New York "Tribune," February 25, 26, and 28.) The articles in the "Tribune," signed "Truth and Courage," were written by James W. White, a member of the New York bar.

[3] The details of this movement against Seward are found in the newspapers, — New York "Tribune," Dec. 22 and 23, 1862, Jan. 10, 1863; New York "Evening Post," Dec. 20, 22, 1862; Boston "Journal," Jan. 14, 1863; in Schuckers's "Life of S. P. Chase," pp. 473–475; Welles's "Lincoln and Seward," pp. 81–85; and Nicolay and Hay's "Life of Lincoln," vol. vi. pp. 263–272. The last account referred to needs confirmation as to some details, particularly in the statement which includes "Grimes, Sumner, and Trumbull as attacking the Cabinet *generally*." This is not true of Sumner, who is known to have been earnest in his support of Chase and Stanton, and is not known to have had special objection to other members except Seward. He had agreeable relations with Blair, who desired

The defeat of McClellan's army before Richmond in June, 1862, marks an important stage in the controversy concerning emancipation and the arming of negroes, whether free or slave. This appears in the debates in the Senate, July 9 and 10, particularly in the speeches of Sherman, Fessenden, Collamer, and Rice of Minnesota,[1] — none of whom had been disposed hitherto to move in that direction. Congress passed two acts which expressly authorized the employment of persons of African descent in the military or naval service. The President called, July 4, for three hundred thousand volunteers, and ordered a month later a conscription. Before the year ended voluntary enlistments, except under the offer of high bounties, had practically ceased, and the quotas could be filled only by drafts. Good citizens, whatever theoretic opinions they might have held on the slavery question, saw the necessity of resorting to every means for maintaining the army. Those who feared that in a draft the lot might fall on themselves were no longer unwilling that colored volunteers should take the places which they themselves might be forced to take as conscripts. The Secretary of War by an order, August 25, authorized Brigadier-General Saxton, commanding at Beaufort, S. C., to enlist slaves, and in January, 1863, gave a similar authority to Governor Sprague of Rhode Island and Governor Andrew of Massachusetts. With the beginning of the new year the enlistment of colored soldiers became the fixed policy of the government. To the same period belong Mr. Lincoln's proclamations of emancipation of Sept. 22, 1862, and Jan. 1, 1863. This was the act and the policy which Sumner had continued to urge on the President ever since July, 1861, and had from time to time in speeches, resolutions, and bills pressed on the country and on Congress. It was the doom of the institution whose struggle for supremacy brought him into public activity. Hereafter his contest was to be with the inequalities and caste distinctions which it left behind.

him to be appointed to the Cabinet after Blair himself had been compelled to leave it. (Nicolay and Hay, vol. ix. p. 349.) His cordial understanding with Welles appears in the latter's book on "Lincoln and Seward." From Bates he obtained a decisive opinion as to the pay of colored troops. Sumner's only reference to the attempted displacement of Seward, discovered in his correspondence, is a single sentence of a letter to Dr. Lieber, Jan. 23, 1863: "The pressure for the expulsion of Seward increases by letters and fresh arrivals."

1 A committee of senators, headed by Trumbull, waited on the President to urge more vigorous measures, — among them the arming of negroes. New York "Tribune," July 21, 1862.

He wrote to E. L. Pierce, Dec. 3, 1862: —

"If there be anything in the message which you do not like, treat it as surplusage.[1] The operative part is the last paragraph, where the President announces and vindicates emancipation. The country will be saved!"

To his colored friend, J. B. Smith, on Christmas day: —

"I am happy to assure you that the President will stand firm. He is now in favor of employing colored troops to occupy the posts on the Mississippi River, South Carolina, and the Southern places."

To Dr. Howe, December 28: —

"You will be glad to know that the President is firm. He says that he would not stop the proclamation if he could, and he could not if he would. Let New Year's day be a day of jubilee!"[2]

The year 1862 closed disastrously to our arms; and the first half of the next year was discouraging to the patriot heart. Vicksburg in the West still resisted siege and assault. In December, 1862, our army was defeated at Fredericksburg under Burnside, and in May, 1863, at Chancellorsville under Hooker. Rebel war-vessels, built and equipped in England, with more in process of construction, were destroying our commerce; and our slow progress in the suppression of the rebellion was stimulating unfriendly opinion in England and France to press intervention. It was a period of despondency among soldiers and among the people. Many of Sumner's correspondents describe the deep and prevailing gloom in the community. He, however, never lost heart, even in the darkest hours. He expected reverses, assured of ultimate success. The basis of his trust in our final triumph was, as already stated, largely *moral*, — "in the providence of God," to which he often referred. He would not believe it possible that a conspiracy founded on slavery as a corner-stone could ever prevail; and his confidence was assured when our government at last, by declaring emancipation and arming the slaves, had placed itself before mankind openly and irrevocably on the side of freedom.

McClellan was relieved from command in November, 1862, and from that time took no part in the war. Late in January

[1] An allusion to the President's plans for colonizing the colored people and for compensated emancipation.

[2] Sumner received from Mr. Lincoln the pen with which the proclamation was signed, and delivered it to George Livermore, of Cambridge, who had expressed a desire to preserve it. "Reminiscences of Abraham Lincoln, collected by A. T. Rice," p. 230.

following he accepted an invitation to visit Boston, where he was entertained with elaborate receptions (one at Mr. Everett's), and presented with a pitcher and a sword. Governor Andrew and other members of the State government were ignored in the festivities. It was almost the last effort of the expiring conservatism of Boston to rally on the old lines. The plot was already in progress to put McClellan forward as the opposing candidate to Lincoln in the election of 1864.

Sumner wrote to the Duchess of Argyll, Jan. 4, 1863: —

"I send you a 'monthly' containing three cantos of Longfellow's translation of Dante. I always thought the 'Paradiso' dull and difficult, although at times beautiful with thought and poetry. This translation shows the original as it is in metre, language, and thought. 'The Planting of the Apple Tree'[1] seems to me an exquisite poem by a true poet who loves England, and therefore grieves now.

"We are now occupied with the great question what to do for the new-made freedmen, that their emancipation may be a blessing to them and to our country. It is a vast problem, on which we need sympathy and good-will. A happy New Year to you! Some wish for war in Europe, because France and England will then see their duty towards us. I long that these countries may see their duties; but I am against war everywhere, and with my whole heart."

To Lieber, January 17: —

"These are dark hours. There are senators full of despair, — not I. The President tells me that he now fears 'the fire in the rear' — meaning the Democracy, especially at the Northwest — more than our military chances. But I fear that our army is everywhere in a bad way. I see no central inspiration or command; no concentration, no combination which promises a Jena."

Again, January 23: —

"There can be no armistice, although Greeley has favored mediation, to which an armistice must be an incident. The war will go on. The storm prevented a great battle last Tuesday. I found Stanton last evening cheerful, — confident that we should soon have Vicksburg. The army at Fredericksburg is now 180,000 men, — 68,000 horses and mules, for which there is daily forage, including 16,000 cavalry and 6,000 wagons. Where in history was such a force, thus appointed, gathered together? Stanton says it ought to be able to go on its belly to Richmond. . . . Is it not wretched in McDougall to bring forward those resolutions about France and Mexico? He has entreated me to let them be taken up and discussed. I shall stop the discussion if I can, and so told him."

[1] By William C. Bryant.

To John Jay, May 18: —

"The mist has not yet cleared away from our recent battlefield,[1] and there are events and men still obscured by it. I hope for the best. If the Seventh regiment would welcome the African regiment[2] it would be an epoch as good as a victory, and the sure herald of many victories. If that regiment could do this service it would contribute more to the war than when it hurried to Washington. Of this there can be no doubt. History would so record the act.

"I return the letter of the prince,[3] which I read carefully to the President, who liked it much, and said of it that it was the letter of a most sensible man. It confirms me in my opinion that the question will yet be presented in Europe whether such a new nation as these slave-mongers are now building can ever be recognized."

Sumner introduced, February 9, a bill for the enlistment of slaves and others of African descent.[4] No report was made upon it; but a year later the proposition became a part of an enrolment act.[5] Later in the year he appealed to colored men to enlist.[6]

President Lincoln's recommendation of national aid to emancipation in slave States led to a bill granting aid to the State of Missouri, which in its final shape, as it came from the judiciary committee, allowed the alternative of gradual or immediate emancipation. Sumner made a strenuous effort to rid the bill of the principle of gradualism.[7] He insisted that a war measure, which the bill was claimed to be, must be instant and not prospective in its operation, and that a *gradual* war measure was an absurdity in terms. Unless the work was done at once, he saw ahead the certainty of controversy and the possibility of reaction. He said: —

"Gradualism is delay, and delay is the betrayal of victory. If you would be triumphant, strike quickly; let your blows be felt at once, without notice or premonition, and especially without time for resistance or debate. Time deserts all who do not appreciate its value. Strike promptly, and time

1 At Chancellorsville.

2 The Fifty-fourth Massachusetts, under Colonel Shaw, was about to pass through New York on its way to the South.

3 The Count of Paris, who had written to Mr. Jay concerning the purposes of the French government towards the United States.

4 The bill was commended in a leader in the New York "Tribune," Feb. 12, 1863.

5 Nearly a year earlier, May 26, 1862, Sumner offered a resolution looking in the same direction (Works, vol. vii. p. 83); and in his speech at Faneuil Hall, Oct. 6, 1862, he urged the arming of slaves. Works, vol. vii. p. 214.

6 Works, vol. vii. pp. 325, 326.

7 Feb. 7 and 12, 1863. Works, vol. vii. pp. 266–277.

becomes your invaluable ally; strike slowly, gradually, prospectively, and time goes over to the enemy."

Only eleven senators on one vote and ten on another voted against the alternative of gradual emancipation. Among them were Fessenden, Grimes, Harlan of Iowa, Lane of Indiana, Pomeroy, and Wade. Wilson voted with Sumner at one stage and against him at another. Sumner, though failing to have the obnoxious provision stricken out, voted for the bill on its final passage, trusting that it would be satisfactorily amended in the House. It did not, however, come to a final vote in that body. Congress had little heart in the President's favorite idea of compensating slave-owners,[1] and the measure was not again agitated.[2]

Mr. Stanton appointed a commission to investigate the condition of the negroes coming within our lines, and to propose methods for protecting and assisting them. Sumner hoped much from it. Its results were, however, inconsiderable; events rather than theories were to settle the problem. Sumner wrote to F. W. Bird, March 19: —

"At last the Freedman's Commission is organized, — Dale Owen, Howe, McKaye. . . . I have seen the commissioners, and like them much. They are excellent and admirable, and enter upon the work generously and nobly. They have invited Howe to meet them in New York at once, in order to plan

[1] Mr. Lincoln adhered to the last to his plan of compensated emancipation, and revived it at a Cabinet meeting, Feb. 5, 1865, in which it found no favorable response. Nicolay and Hay, vol. x. pp. 133-137.

[2] Miscellaneous matters to which Sumner gave attention at this session were as follows: Facilities for soldiers obtaining tobacco, which he opposed, Feb. 25, 1863, — a service which called out a grateful letter from the anti-tobacco enthusiast, Rev. George Trask; the exemption from conscription of clergymen, which he advocated, Feb. 16, 1863 (Works, vol. vii. pp. 303-306), — making a similar effort at the next session, Jan. 14 and 18, 1864 (Congressional Globe, pp. 204-255); other points in the conscription bill, Feb. 16, 1863 (Globe, pp. 985, 986, 988); the bill creating the national bank system, Feb. 9, 1863; the reported sale of colored freedmen by the rebels, Dec. 3, 1862; sale of land in the Sea Islands of South Carolina forfeited for taxes, with reference to the interests of freedmen, Jan. 9 and 26, 1863 (Globe, pp. 245, 507, 508); the bill to punish correspondence by American citizens resident abroad with the Confederate government or its agents, Jan. 7 and Feb. 13, 1863 (Globe, pp. 214, 925); carrying into effect the convention with Peru for the settlement of claims, Feb. 24 and 26, and March 3, 1863 (Globe, pp. 1235, 1301, 1489, 1512); derangement of mails between New York and Washington, Jan. 7, 1863 (Globe, p. 215); indemnity to the owners of a French brig for injury in a collision with a United States war vessel, Dec. 10, 1862 (Globe, p. 52); the mission to Bolivia, Jan. 28, 1863 (Globe, p. 568); the taking of depositions to be used abroad, Feb. 27, 1863 (Globe, p. 1335); the union of the Mississippi River and the Red River of the North by canal navigation, Jan. 28, 1863 (Globe, p. 562); "justice to a widow on Sunday morning," Feb. 28, 1863 (Globe, p. 1391); an hospital and ambulance corps, Dec. 3, 1862 (Works, vol. vii. p. 255; Boston "Journal," June 30, 1863, replying to Dr. H. I. Bowditch).

their work. They propose to visit South Carolina and Louisiana, and perhaps also the West Indies. I doubt not that their report will be a contribution to civilization."

One of Sumner's greatest public services — and it was an inestimable service — was his constant effort during the Civil War to hold back the Senate from any action likely to imperil peaceful relations with England and France. The Confederates saw in a war between the United States and either of those powers their opportunity, — indeed their best, if not their only, prospect of success. The French emperor had seized the occasion of our extremity to attempt the conquest of Mexico, and the time he had chosen made his scheme all the more offensive to the American people. His operations in that country were contrary to the traditional idea of our people, which has always been set against the extension of European dominion on this continent. Nevertheless, the burden of a foreign war at this time would have been fatal to the Union cause; and existing conditions imposed on our government, in its relations with foreign powers, the duty of discreet forbearance, so far as was consistent with honor. Sumner had always the cause of Mexico at heart, and was even disposed to go further than most of his associates in the Senate in befriending her by financial assistance;[1] but he strenuously opposed during the Civil War all attempts to embroil our government in a conflict with France.[2] He was able to hold within safe bounds the Senate, where his personal influence acted directly; and he could also arrest there the inconsiderate measures of the House, — a body in which on foreign questions the judgment yields readily to the demand for spirited action.

McDougall of California offered resolutions in the Senate in January, 1863, condemning French intervention in Mexico, and requiring the withdrawal of French troops from that country. Sumner opposed them as untimely, and calculated to give aid and comfort to the rebellion.[3] He thought there was madness

[1] Report in the Senate, Feb. 19, 1862, Works, vol. vi. pp. 365–375; Address at the Cooper Institute, Sept. 10, 1863, Works, vol. vii. p. 368.

[2] After the withdrawal of the French troops, Sumner opposed ill-considered action calculated to disturb our relations with France (Jan. 15 and 16, 1867, Congressional Globe, pp. 459, 487); but he proposed that our government should offer its good offices to Mexico by way of mediation between the contending parties in that country. April 20, 1867, Works, vol. xi. pp. 354, 355.

[3] Feb. 3, 1863, Works, vol. vii. pp. 257–261.

in a proposition which openly challenged war with France when all the national energies were needed for the suppression of the rebellion. When that was accomplished, "the whole continent would fall naturally, peacefully, and tranquilly under the irresistible influence of American institutions." He said: —

"I forbear from details at present; I wish to avoid them unless rendered necessary. I content myself with saying that the resolutions either mean something or they mean nothing. If they mean nothing, surely the Senate will not enter on their discussion. If they mean anything, if they are not mere words, they mean war, — and this no common war, but war with a great and adventurous nation, powerful in fleets and armies, and still constant in professions of amity and good-will. Sir, have we not war enough already on our hands without needlessly and wantonly provoking another? For myself, I give all that I have of intellectual action and will and heart to the suppression of the rebellion; and never by my consent shall the Senate enter upon a discussion the first effect of which will be aid and comfort to the rebellion itself."

Sumner's motion to lay the resolutions on the table prevailed by a vote of thirty-four yeas to ten nays.

McDougall, irrepressible on this subject, and not restrained by a patriotic sense of responsibility, introduced a year later (Jan. 11, 1864) his "belligerent proposition," — now more decisive in its terms than before, as it affirmed the duty of the government to declare war against France if the French troops were not withdrawn by March 15 of the same year. It was referred to the committee on foreign relations, where it remained without report under Sumner's "judicious chairmanship."[1] McDougall was restive under the oblivion to which his measure was consigned, and made several attempts to revive it by a vote to discharge the committee; but in this he was defeated, May 27, by a decisive vote. Sumner committed to a similar burial Wade's resolution of inquiry on Mexican affairs; and McDougall confessed his own inability "to resist the tide of power" in the Senate held by the chairman of the committee on foreign relations.[2]

As has been well said, "the committee on foreign affairs of the House of Representatives had a chairman of a very different temper from Mr. Sumner, — Henry Winter Davis, who was equally distinguished for his eloquence and his ardor, his tenacity of opinion and his impatience of contradiction." He

1 Nicolay and Hay's "Life of Lincoln," vol. vii. p. 407.

2 June 28. Congressional Globe, p. 3339.

carried, April 4, 1864, as soon as reported, and without debate except brief remarks in its support from himself and Samuel S. Cox (a public man whose besetting frailty was that of habitual trifling with serious things), a resolution which, after referring to French intervention in Mexico, declared against "any monarchical government erected on the ruins of any republican government in America, under the auspices of any European power." The resolution passed unanimously,—one hundred and nine in the affirmative; and the members were so anxious to go on record in its favor that all absent members were on Morrill's motion allowed the next day by formal vote to be counted upon it. The resolution when received in the Senate was referred to Sumner's committee, which as before made no report; but though sanctioned only by the House, it proved mischievous. The French minister in Washington at once requested an explanation from Mr. Seward, and the secretary in his reply, while stating that the resolution truly interpreted the unanimous sentiment of the people of the United States, explained in substance that the direction of the foreign policy of the government belonged to the executive department, which did not contemplate any change of policy in regard to the war between France and Mexico. This assurance quieted the French government, whose foreign minister, M. Drouyn de l'Huys, had asked Mr. Dayton, at their first meeting after intelligence of the resolution had reached Paris (Mr. Seward's explanation not yet being known), "Do you bring us peace or war?"

When the correspondence of the state department became public, Davis reported in the House from his committee, June 27, a resolution affirming that Congress has a constitutional right to an authoritative voice in matters of foreign policy, and that its declarations, "while pending and undetermined, are not a fit topic of diplomatic explanation with any foreign power."[1] The resolution went over to the next session, when the members having become more thoughtful, it was laid on the table, Dec. 15, 1864, by six majority. Davis at once resigned his place on the committee, after saying that Seward had "slapped the House of Representatives in the face in his correspondence with the French government, and the House of Representatives

[1] Davis's report in full is copied in McPherson's "History of the Rebellion," pp. 350–354.

says it will not even assert its dignity;" but the House refused to excuse him. Four days later, however, the resolution passed; but a sense of responsibility being now active among a portion of the members, the part which reflected on "the diplomatic explanation" encountered opposition, and passed by only ten majority. This resolution also, on reaching the Senate, went to Sumner's committee, where it was safely kept for the rest of the session, and was not heard of again. If in that critical period any one of several senators or representatives who might be named, then leaders in those bodies, had held his place, it is fearful to contemplate the embarrassments and perils which might have come to pass in our foreign relations.

Mr. Seward quite early in the Civil War became a partisan of privateering as an auxiliary force in naval operations. At his instance, Mr. Grimes, of the committee on naval affairs, though himself at the time opposed to the measure, introduced, July 12, 1862, in the Senate a bill for granting letters of marque and reprisal. At the next session he reported from the committee a bill for the purpose, and having changed his opinion in the mean time, supported it, Feb. 17, 1863, by a speech. Mr. Chase, at first unfriendly to it, now accepted it as a method of reducing the war expenses. Enterprising merchants in New York, some of whom were lacking in character and responsibility, pressed the scheme openly or covertly. Grimes saw in it a mode of enlisting private enterprise in aid of the government, calling privateers "the militia of the seas;" and he was supported in debate by McDougall and Collamer. Sumner thought the measure of evil import from the beginning. As soon as the bill came to light he sought Lieber's views, saying, "I wish to do what is best for the country and civilization."[1] In the debate he contested the measure earnestly and pertinaciously.[2] He opposed this resort to "licensed rovers seeking prey," as an expedient once prevailing in maritime wars, but now discountenanced by the highest authorities and rejected by civilization; as demoralizing to the parties engaged in it, who were stimulated by booty; as a two-edged sword, likely to be turned against us hereafter; as uncalled for by any exigency, the rebels having no commerce to reward privateers. But the objection which, in view of plots for intervention, concerned him most at the time was the danger

[1] Lieber's opinion was rather in favor of the measure.

[2] Feb. 14 and 17, 1863. Works, vol. vii. pp. 278-300.

that the privateers in the exercise of their powers, particularly that of search, were likely to embroil us with foreign nations, and give them an excuse or pretence for interfering in our conflict. His efforts to defeat the bill as well as to limit its scope by amendment were without avail, and on the final vote only eight senators joined him. The bill passed the House without debate or division, and remained a law till it expired by its own limitation three years later.[1]

As soon as the bill had been approved Seward sought to put it into effect, and prepared forms and regulations for the purpose. Sumner thought it so fraught with mischief that he continued his resistance by a direct appeal to the President and members of his Cabinet, by an open letter to the Board of Trade of the city of New York,[2] and by prompting leaders in the "Tribune" and "Evening Post" of that city, as also in the "National Intelligencer." He remained in Washington for some weeks after the session closed, largely for the purpose of arresting proceedings under the act. In his appeals to the President, repeated at short intervals, he was fortified by letters from John Bright and the American banker in London, Joshua Bates.[3] Mr. Lincoln was impressed with his representations, and invited him to state his views at a meeting of the Cabinet, but on Sumner's doubting the expediency of this step, requested him to see the members individually. The senator found Welles, Blair, and Bates receptive to his views; but Chase remained firmly against him. He had an unpleasant interview with Seward, who did not conceal his satisfaction that he had achieved a personal triumph over the senator.[4] The secretary had chafed under Sumner's superior influence with the President, and had once remarked, when the senator's opinion had been quoted by the President against him, that "there were too many secretaries of state in Washington." Mr. Welles, to whom the sub-

[1] Grimes did not take kindly to Sumner's resistance to his bill; and their strenuous contention against each other's views at this time throws light on Grimes's later criticisms on Sumner.

[2] March 17, 1863. Works, vol. vii. pp. 313-315.

[3] In a letter to R. Schleiden, March 16, Sumner wrote: "I took to the President last evening Woolsey's 'Manual of International Law,' and called his attention to two pages on privateering, in order that he might see how it is regarded by one of our moralists and instructors. He read the condemnation aloud until his eyesight failed; then I finished the passage." Adams in a letter to Seward, March 27, 1863, "deprecated any present resort to so doubtful a remedy."

[4] Mutual explanations followed, and their personal relations were not disturbed, as is shown by a letter of Seward to Sumner, May 12, 1863.

ject was referred in the Cabinet, entered heartily into Sumner's view, and expressed himself in an elaborate letter to Mr. Seward, March 31, 1863. As Mr. Seward did not submit this letter to the President, the latter called for it, and sending for the senator, they read together the letter and discussed the subject of privateering and reprisals. Sumner's protests were at last effective. According to Mr. Welles, this interview of the senator with the President, and his own conference with him concerning the application of a Prussian adventurer (the only one filed under the Act), "terminated the privateer policy, and closed the subject of letters of marque and reprisal during the rebellion." [1]

Mediation and intervention in our Civil War, sometimes with the suggestion of force in the background, had been considered by foreign powers. The French emperor, whose mind was set upon interfering in the contest, by a despatch, dated Jan. 9, 1863, to the French minister at Washington, formally offered to mediate between the United States and the Confederates.[2] These offers, though firmly rejected by the President and Secretary of State, were an encouragement to the rebellion; and it was thought that the time had come for our government, with a view to end such plots, to take the position by an authoritative declaration that under no circumstances would any foreign power be admitted to a part in the contest. Sumner, therefore, prepared elaborate resolutions for adoption by Congress. He carried them through his committee after some days of chaos and discord, with very slight amendment.[3] Only five votes were given against them in the Senate, and those five from senators who had little or no sympathy with the government in its struggle. The resolutions, while approving foreign mediation on international questions, pronounced it unreasonable and inadmissible in domestic troubles, and declared that any proposition from a foreign power for the purpose of arresting the efforts of the national govern-

[1] Welles's "Lincoln and Seward," pp. 145-164; New York "Tribune," February 27, March 11, 17, 27, and April 3, 1863; New York "Evening Post." February 21. Referring to another question, — the disposition of public mails found on private vessels violating the blockade, — which was under consideration in 1862-1863, Mr. Welles mentions (p. 90) the "great confidence" President Lincoln had in Sumner's "superior intelligence and information on questions of international law," and his habit of consulting the senator on "conflicting and troublesome subjects with foreign powers."

[2] He had by a despatch, Oct. 30, 1862, sought the co-operation of England and Russia for the same purpose. Earl Russell's reply, November 13, was that the effort was premature.

[3] Reported February 28, passed March 3. Works, vol. vii. pp. 307-312.

ment to suppress the rebellion was in effect an encouragement to it, was calculated to prolong and embitter the conflict, and would if repeated be regarded as an unfriendly act. They attributed to the hope of foreign support the continued vitality of the rebellion, and expressed the regret that its chiefs had not been assured by foreign powers that a new government, "with slavery as its acknowledged corner-stone, and with no other declared object of separate existence, is so far shocking to civilization and the moral sense of mankind that it must not expect welcome or recognition in the commonwealth of nations."[1] And finally, the United States, "awaiting with well-assured trust the final suppression of the rebellion, . . . hereby announce as their unalterable purpose that the war will be vigorously prosecuted, according to the humane principles of Christian nations, until the rebellion is overcome; and they reverently invoke upon their cause the blessing of Almighty God."

Sumner declined to debate the resolutions when objected to by Powell, Saulsbury, and Carlile, but contented himself with saying that though agreed upon by the committee without any suggestion from the Administration, they met the entire and cordial approval of Mr. Seward. They passed the House by a large majority, and were sent, as was required by the last resolution, to our ministers abroad to be communicated to foreign governments.[2]

One incident concerning the resolutions — the assent of Garrett Davis of Kentucky to them in committee, notwithstanding the prominence they gave to the pro-slavery inspiration of the rebellion — is worthy of note. From the beginning of the Civil War Mr. Davis had been the most indefatigable opponent of antislavery measures; and he and Sumner had been on that account often opposed to each other in debate. Their relations were, however, very friendly in the Senate, as well as co-operative in the committee.[3] Davis's sincerity of conviction was apparent

[1] This doctrine was embodied in a resolution drawn by Mr. Lincoln, to be transmitted by Sumner to John Bright. Sumner's "Eulogy on Lincoln," Works, vol. ix. pp. 403, 404.

[2] Mr. Greeley had advocated in the New York "Tribune" the submission of the questions involved in the contest to a neutral power, — Switzerland, for instance, and in letters to Sumner, March 16 and Sept. 24, 1863, expressed his grief that the latter had rejected in the present instance the remedy of arbitration as a substitute for war which he had on other occasions supported. Sumner commented briefly on the subject of mediation, Jan. 16, 1863, in connection with W. C. Jewett's petition. Congressional Globe, p. 348.

[3] On Feb. 28, 1863, some pleasantry passed between them in the Senate on Mr. Davis's mentioning that Sumner and himself had been named together as "Abolitionists." Congressional Globe, pp. 1376, 1377.

in his manner and conduct; and although he could look at the great events passing only from his Kentucky standpoint, he was a true patriot, and thoroughly loyal to his country. He remained in the Senate till his death, late in 1872. Among his eulogists none paid to his memory a warmer tribute than his associate from Massachusetts, so often his antagonist, who was soon to follow him.[1] On that occasion Sumner said: —

"Time is teacher and reconciler; nor is it easy for any candid nature to preserve a constant austerity of judgment towards persons. As evening approaches, the meridian heats lose their intensity. While abiding firmly in the truth as we saw it, there may be charity and consideration for those who did not see it as we saw it. . . . Here let me be frank. Nothing could make any speech for slavery tolerable to me; but when I think how much opinions are determined by the influences about us, so that a change of birth and education might have made the Abolitionist a partisan of slavery, and the partisan of slavery an Abolitionist, I feel that while always unrelenting toward the wrong we cannot be insensible to individual merits. In this spirit I offer a sincere tribute to a departed senator, who, amid the perturbations of the times, trod his way with independent step, and won even from opponents the palm of character."

Lieber, who was not always appreciative of his friend's style in state papers and speeches, wrote now with enthusiasm: —

"This moment — 5 o'clock P. M. the 5th of March — I received, my dear Sumner, your resolutions concerning interference. They are not resolutions concerning interference; they are a proclamation of the people through their assembled representatives, — a proclamation worthy of their dignity and the grandeur of their cause. I know something of historical documents; this is one of the calmest, most collected, most faultless, as if America herself had said it, her left [hand] on her sword, her right stretched forward to the multitude of nations. I cannot write on them as they deserve, because their perusal has thrown me into a mood which makes me desirous to pace up and down through my three rooms rather than write; but I could not help writing these grateful words at once. There is a trumpet blast in the resolutions, and yet a blast as that of a herald followed by the person of America."

Sumner wrote to Mr. Jay, March 2: —

"My resolutions were discussed in committee three days, two hours each day. The first day, all was confusion; and Mr. Garrett Davis said he would not sanction anything which had slavery in it. I despaired; but at last, after some modifications, chiefly with regard to slavery as the origin and mainspring of the rebellion, the resolutions were unanimously adopted. I was surprised at the result; it seemed as if the millennium was at hand. Seward came to me to-day and expressed the desire that I should press them to a vote, which I hope to do to-night. The President, I understand, is pleased with

[1] Dec. 18, 1872. Works, vol. xv. pp. 261-265.

them. My hope was to do something to lift the tone of our foreign relations. I beg you to believe me grateful for the kind and good help which you gave me.

"It looked as if Clay[1] would be rejected. He pressed his case, and interested the President, till at last on Saturday Seward came to me with a most urgent message from the President to let him pass. Other members of the committee were spoken to also. So I was authorized to report him; but I have not yet done it."

A special session of the Senate, lasting ten days, was held as soon as the Congress expired. Sumner now entered on his third term.

One of the treaties ratified at this session was with Belgium for the capitalization of the Scheldt dues. The king communicated through the Belgian minister at Washington his thanks to Sumner for his efforts in securing its ratification.

Sumner's public action concerning individuals was never affected by former personal controversies, and he kept his balance well where under the influence of his antislavery sentiments he might be expected to lose it. His character in this respect is illustrated by a case which occurred at this time. Col. T. G. Stevenson, of Boston, when serving in South Carolina early in 1863, expressed a passionate opinion against the policy of arming negroes, and his own unwillingness to serve with them; and upon the outburst becoming known he was put under arrest, Feb. 10, 1863, by General Hunter, who deemed the expressions disloyal.[2] At the time of the arrest his nomination as brigadier-general was pending in the Senate. He was the son of J. Thomas Stevenson, a conservative of the most rigid type, who will be remembered as a leader of the "Cotton Whigs" in 1845-1847, and a participant in the prison-discipline dispute of the same period, — always bitterly opposed to Sumner;[3] and his kinsfolk, as well as himself, had joined in the social exclusion practised against Sumner at that time. One evening as the senator was returning from dinner to his apartment, he saw by the dim light of the street lamp some one standing at his door whom he recognized as Colonel Stevenson's father, with whom he had not passed a word for many years. Stevenson requested an interview, and Sumner invited him to his room. The father pleaded an hour or more

[1] Cassius M. Clay, nominated for the Russian mission.

[2] Boston Journal, Feb. 28, March 17, 1863; Boston Commonwealth, March 27, 1863; New York Tribune, March 17; D. W. Bartlett in New York Independent, June 11.

[3] *Ante*, vol. iii. pp. 91, 92, 124.

for his son, presenting testimonials for him, and withdrawing in his behalf the expressions alleged against him. Sumner sat a silent listener, answering only that the father ought to take pride in a son so dutiful as he had described, and that the case would be considered, but withholding any intimation as to his own action. The same evening General Burnside called and earnestly testified to the young man's loyalty, ability, and courage, his regret for the thoughtless words he had spoken, and his entire willingness to serve with negro troops. That night Sumner reflected on the case, and the next morning communicated to Mr. Hooper, the member from Boston, his purpose to support the nomination; and as he did nothing by halves, he moved the confirmation, and persuaded by personal appeals other senators who had been opposed to it to withdraw their opposition. It was the last day of the special session, when a single objection would have prevented action. It was understood and publicly stated at the time that Sumner's active intervention alone secured the confirmation. Two letters of thanks came from the family, — one from the father, who was still in Washington, and one from an aunt of the general, Hannah E. Stevenson, well known as the constant friend of Theodore Parker. The young man was at the time serving with colored troops in South Carolina, where he enjoyed the confidence of Colonel Shaw and other officers of colored regiments. When at home on leave in the summer, he called on the senator, thanked him for his good offices, and bore emphatic testimony in behalf of colored soldiers.

Some of the radical antislavery men openly condemned Sumner's support of Stevenson's confirmation. Wendell Phillips, hitherto among Abolitionists exceptionally kindly towards him, denounced him in speeches,[1] and went so far as to break off personal relations with him, even, as is stated, passing him on the street without recognition. Sumner felt hurt at Phillips's harshness, saying to a friend: "Wendell Phillips *knows* me; he knows me, and he ought not to speak of me as he does." Phillips's first overture was in a letter to Sumner in March, 1865, in which he warmly commended the latter's resistance to the admission of Louisiana with a constitution which disfranchised colored people. Henceforward nothing marred their friendship.

1 At New York, May 11, 1863. "Speeches and Lectures," pp. 559–562; also in a note as well as in the speech.

Sumner's action on another military appointment the year before also deserves mention,—that of Brigadier-General Isaac I. Stevens, a leader of the Breckinridge Democrats in 1860, now serving at Beaufort, S. C., whose confirmation had been suspended on account of a distrust of his loyalty, as well as on account of certain personal objections. The senator received a letter from E. L. Pierce, then in charge of freedmen on the Sea Islands, bearing witness to the general's cordial and effective co-operation in that work, as well as to his ability and devotion as an officer. As soon as the letter came to hand, Sumner called up the case, read the letter in the Senate, and moved the confirmation, which was carried. The senator's casting aside of personal or partisan prejudice in these two instances was justified by the event. Both officers fell on the field,—Stevens at Chantilly in Virginia, Sept. 1, 1862, and Stevenson at Spottsylvania, May 10, 1864.

Antislavery people were in 1863 anxious to have General Fremont called from retirement and put in command of a large body of colored troops. Sumner introduced to the President a body of gentlemen who visited Washington for the purpose, and he did what he could to further the plan. The President in a letter to Sumner showed his desire to advance the wishes of the deputation. Fortunately for the country these well-meant efforts came to no result. The final judgment upon Fremont is a distrust of his capacity for important civil or military duties.

Sumner remained in Washington till July,—nearly three months after the Senate had adjourned, and long after all the members of Congress, excepting those serving on the committee on the conduct of the war, had left for their homes. His time was well spent in watching closely public affairs, exerting influence against the issuing of letters of marque and reprisal, advising with the President concerning foreign despatches as they arrived; and his salutary influence on our foreign relations while he lingered at the capital, particularly in keeping the peace with England and France,[1] was recognized in public journals and letters from constituents. At the same time he was gathering materials for an address on foreign affairs to be delivered in the autumn, and maintaining our cause in full letters to Cobden, Bright, and the Duchess of Argyll.[2] He kept up close

[1] New York Tribune, July 9.

[2] Those were intended to set right the duke, then in the Cabinet.

relations with the foreign ministers resident at Washington,—Lord Lyons, Mercier, Schleiden, and Baron Gerolt the dean of the corps, the last named always his cordial friend; and he was a favorite guest at their family as well as their state dinners. Lord Lyons, though not at all earnest for our cause, was not unfriendly to it, and our country was on the whole fortunate in having him at this critical period as the representative of Great Britain in Washington. When his intercourse with public men more or less in sympathy with the rebellion was questioned, Sumner put the better construction upon it, as will be seen in his letter to Lieber.[1]

Partly for amusement, and partly for practice in French, Sumner allowed his time to be taken by conversations with Gustave Paul Cluseret, a Frenchman always in search of revolutions, made a brigadier-general in our Civil War at a period when commissions were lavishly and inconsiderately given, and later a minister under the French Commune. Like all such adventurers, he was full of complaints against everybody, which he poured on the senator in frequent calls and in letters of enormous length.

Another foreigner often seen at Sumner's lodgings during the first year or two of the Civil War, whose visits were about this time discontinued, was Adam Gurowski,[2] a Polish count, learned, but of unbridled speech, almost a madman when in passion,—"the terrible count," as Longfellow called him. He appeared in Cambridge in 1850, where his learning and liberal sentiments commanded the friendly interest of Longfellow, Felton, and Parsons. The last named procured for him the opportunity, when his English was still very broken, to deliver in the Harvard Law School some lectures on the civil law, which few attended and none understood.[3] Afterwards he lived mostly in New York and Washington. Sumner once climbed to an attic in New York to find him, when he lay ill and alone. In 1861–1862, at Sumner's instance, Seward gave the count a place in his department as translator, rather from sympathy with his misfortunes than from any service he rendered. He haunted Sumner's study at all hours, coming often in the evening and hanging on till past midnight, breaking in on important business and interrupting all work. Sumner's patience with bores

[1] *Post*, p. 138. [2] 1805–1866.
[3] The writer, then a law student, was one of the count's few hearers.

was proverbial; but it had a limit, and the count passed it. One day, worn out with his constant intrusion, and smarting probably under some offensive expressions, the senator bade him leave,[1] — the only time he was ever known to have shown the door to an unwelcome visitor. Gurowski in his published diary[2] vented his spleen both on Sumner and on Seward, the two best friends he had in Washington, though in each case there was a grain of truth in his satire.[3] Poverty and exile had taken all sweetness from the count's nature, if ever there was any there. In his last illness at Washington, Mrs. Charles Eames,[4] well remembered for her gracious and friendly spirit, took pity on his solitude and forlornness, and gave him a chamber to die in; and among those gathered under her roof to witness the last offices, some of whom had felt his shafts, she was the only mourner.

Sumner wrote to Mr. Cobden, March 16, 1863: —

"I am anxious, very anxious, on account of the ships building in England to cruise against our commerce. Cannot something be done to stop them? Our people are becoming more and more excited, and there are many who insist upon war. A very important person said to me yesterday: 'We are now at war with England, but the hostilities are all on her side.' I know the difficulties of your laws, and how subtle and pertinacious is the temptation of money-making; but it would seem as if there should be a way to prevent the unparalleled outrage of a whole fleet built expressly to be employed against us. Of course in this statement I assume what is reported and is credited by those who ought to be well informed. A committee from New York waited on the President yesterday and undertook to enumerate ships now building in English yards professedly for the Emperor of China, but really for our rebels. The case is aggravated by the fact that their armaments are supplied also by England; and their crews also, for it is not supposed that there will be a rebel sailor on board.[5]

"To-day the Cabinet consider whether to issue letters of marque under the new statute. I have seen the President twice upon this question, which I regard as grave, for it is intended as a counter-movement to what is done in England. Even if no mischief ensue, I am sure it will be a bad precedent, which I deplore with my whole soul. I found myself powerless against it in the Senate, for there was a 'war fever,' and you know how irresistible and diabolical that becomes. But the President is prudent and pacific, and has listened most attentively to my objections. The original idea is Seward's,

1 Perley's (B. P. Poore's) Reminiscences, vol. ii. pp. 137-141.

2 Diary, from 1861 to 1865.

3 He criticised Sumner's speeches for their minutiæ of research and superfluous erudition. Diary, vol. ii. pp. 56, 69, and 219.

4 *Ante*, vol. iii. p. 264.

5 Mr. Cobden, immediately on receiving this letter, called on Lord Russell to urge greater circumspection on the government, and particularly the watching of ships which were said to be building for the Chinese; and his cautions were well received.

who drew the first bill. I said to Grimes, the senator who urged the measure, 'How can you push so zealously a measure of Seward, whom you dislike?' To which he replied: 'The substitute I shall move is drawn by General Butler.' I read to the President your last letter. He enjoys the change in English sentiment, but was astonished that your public meetings were not called under this device: 'No fellowship with a new government founded on the perpetuity of slavery.'"

To Mr. Bright, March 30: —

"Still detained at Washington. I send you merely a glance at our present situation. We are anxious but hopeful with regard to both the great expeditions. At Charleston all must be ready. The preparations are vast beyond the knowledge of the public, with ironclads and a numerous fleet and untried contrivances. Where so much is at stake and the enemy has had such opportunity, perhaps we should not be too sanguine. Our naval authorities express themselves to me as confident; but I see that they are now more than ever impressed by the magnitude of the undertaking, — take it all in all, the greatest naval enterprise in history. On the Mississippi effort of all kinds is lavished on both sides. Here, too, our military men are confident. The delays are disheartening, but our people are tranquil. The Democracy is falling into line with the government, and insisting upon the most strenuous support of the war. Our finances are now promising. Mr. Chase was with me yesterday, and so contented with their condition that he thinks of a fortnight's vacation with his daughter. He told the President a few days ago that he attributes our financial success first and foremost to the Proclamation, and only secondly to the financial measures adopted. Had the anti-slavery policy been adopted earlier, our position would have been much better. For the delay Mr. Seward is in great measure responsible. The President is naturally slow, and therefore disposed to harmonize with the hold-back policy.

"I have just read Lord Russell's letter on the Proclamation, cold and unsympathizing, and determined not to see the difficulties of our terrible struggle. His argument that it makes slavery legal and illegal at the same time is futile. In the excepted places it leaves slavery as it was, doing nothing with it. I regretted the exception, but it is not obnoxious to the criticisms of Lord Russell. What a sad page of history Englishmen are making! But my chief anxiety now is on account of the ships said to be building for the rebels in England. If half of what is reported be true, then is the future dark; I do not like to penetrate it. If those ships get to sea our commerce is annihilated; but this would be the most trivial of the terrible consequences. Mr. Canning said once in the House of Commons:[1] 'If a war must come, let it come in the shape of satisfaction to be demanded for injuries, etc. But, in God's name, let it not come in the paltry, pettifogging way of fitting out ships in our harbors to cruise for gain! At all events, let the country disdain to be sneaked into a war. If I wished for a guide in a system of neutrality, I should take that laid down by America,' etc. Pray avert this result."

[1] April 16, 1823.

Again, April 7: —

"I have passed an anxious and unhappy week; for all the signs are of war, more surely than in the time of the 'Trent.' I have read Lord Russell's letters. They are bad and mischievous, and seem intended to provoke. I must believe that the number of ships building is exaggerated; but if there be any, and if they are allowed to sail and to depredate upon our commerce, so far as any now remains, you must see at once the exasperation which will ensue. The question has been considered by our Cabinet. There is no difference of opinion, not the least; and it is now thought by many that the British ministry means war, since everybody is supposed to mean the natural consequences of his conduct. . . . All look forward to action of the most decisive character should those ships come out. England will then have thrown herself into the arms of slavery, and our war will assume new proportions, involving perhaps all Europe. There will be no hesitation here. Our purpose, now more fixed than ever, is to prevent the establishment of a disgusting slave-empire on our borders, and we shall continue our efforts against all the allies it may enlist, and make our appeal to the civilized world. We have bad news from Vicksburg, and the President reports bad news from Charleston; but we are not disheartened. These are the vicissitudes of war. Our people are now more than ever united and determined. The rebels are enfeebled and famished. There is no person in the Administration who doubts the result. Our only present anxiety comes from England. If England were really 'neutral,' our confidence would be complete. But this is no contest for 'neutrality,' and here is the mistake made at the beginning. It belonged to England, as a leader of civilization, to declare at once that a disgusting slave-empire, ready for the slave-trade itself, could not expect fellowship. But the *moral element* has been ignored; and Lord Russell writes irritating letters against those who are in deadly struggle with slavery. I hear but one sentiment, whether from the President, his Cabinet, or members of the Senate (as far as any are here now). I try to tranquillize the sentiment; but I clearly see that as events now tend, all who talk peace will be powerless. The 'Trent' affair was not in this age a *casus belli;* I never so regarded it, and was always convinced that it must be adjusted. But I cannot see our present difficulties in this light. If English vessels are permitted to destroy our commerce so that it will cease to exist, there is an event which in itself must have great consequences, among which will be the inevitable *contre-coup*. That of England will disappear next, and this world of ours will be turned topsy-turvy. Whatever may be the vicissitudes, I am sure that freedom must prevail. And this is my consolation as I cast this gloomy horoscope."

To the Duchess of Argyll, April 7:[1] —

"Just as I was about to write to you, I am gladdened by your letter of 19th March, which in its tone is so inconsistent with that war which we are now expecting from England. But first let me express the pleasure I had in

[1] He had written the duchess a full letter, March 24, on the progress of the war, and the Confederate cruisers which were being fitted out in England.

Tennyson's ode.[1] I have read it aloud again and again, and always with fresh delight. It is exquisite, and the best thing of the kind that I can recall in all literature. In perfect contrast, I put Lord Russell's recent despatches, which I have read with grief unspeakable. . . . On their character, and the inevitable tendency of our relations with England, there is but one opinion in the Cabinet. Not a single member hesitates in conclusion; nor does the President. When I read those papers I was amazed and saddened. The danger from the 'Trent' never to my mind was so menacing. There are various propositions for immediate action, all of which I have opposed with my whole soul, willing still to hope for peace, although I feel keenly the force of the remark that 'war has already begun, with hostilities all on one side.' Our commerce is next to the largest which the world has ever seen; and this is about to be driven from the ocean by ships in which every plank and rope, and every arm, from the knife to the cannon and the crew, are British, and nothing but the pirate officers rebels. This in itself is an important fact, and must have corresponding consequences. If I write thus freely to you, it is because I wish you to see the occasion of my anxiety.

"I have been much with the President, and know intimately his desires and purposes. He is most pacific in nature, and is slow; but he has no doubt as to the action which duty and public opinion will require. Of course it is assumed that England will acknowledge the slave-empire, and that the co-operation which now exists will become open alliance. It will be for us, seeking the exclusion of such a monster-empire from the family of nations, to meet the combined hostilities of slavery. I cannot bear the thought that England should be on that side: that Louis Napoleon should be there is natural. Already I see the signs that the contest, if it be not arrested, will be marked by an intensity and exasperation which will find limits only in the strictest requirements of international law. I write to you plainly, but I cannot disclose the extent of my sorrow as I see the inevitable drift of events. The dreams of my life will be disappointed. I have longed for peace everywhere, but especially with England. I have labored always for it, and now in daily counsels I still labor for it; nor am I unheard. But the course of events in England and the tone of Lord Russell's despatches will render me powerless.

"Meanwhile the present war goes on, with the vicissitudes incident to war, such as England felt in the Peninsular and then again in the Crimean; but there is now an intenser unity among our people, and a determination to go forward without wavering. Our purpose is fixed. Notwithstanding all temporary checks, the slave-empire, just ready to commence slave-trading, shall not be allowed to exist on our borders; and we shall insist against all the allies slavery may find, and make our appeal to the world. I know the opinion of every member of the Cabinet intimately. There is not one who for a moment thinks of abandoning the contest, or who doubts the result.

"The mistake of European powers has been that they ignored the moral element in this terrible war, — as if there could be neutrality where one side sought to defy civilization, and claimed welcome on an odious principle for the first time declared as the corner-stone of a government. And our reverses

[1] A Welcome to Alexandra.

have been misconstrued. They have been the chastisement and expiation imposed by Providence for our crime towards a long-suffering race. Had we succeeded early, we should not have suffered according to our deserts. We must lose other battles, and bury more children; but the result will be attained. The rebels are now famishing, and my information leads to the belief that with the overthrow of one of their large armies the bubble will burst. Only this morning I have had with me a Union man from Arkansas, who assures me that in a few weeks that State, which has always been mad for slavery, will be ready to choose members of Congress, — ready, as he expressed it, 'to wipe out slavery.' Nothing troubles us now but England. All the rest we have measured and are prepared for. Remember, my dear friend, I am no idolater of the Union; I have never put our cause on this ground. But I hate slavery; and never through any action or non-action of mine shall a new slave-empire be allowed to come into being to insult God and man." [1]

Again, April 13: —

"Yours of the 26th, my dear duchess, has come this morning, and I make haste to report the feeling of to-day in season for the bag, which will leave in an hour. I have just come from the President. He had expected a repulse at Charleston. Some weeks ago he revealed to me his want of confidence in the expedition, although the navy department were always most confident. To-day the President is more hopeful. The 'Keokuk,' which was sunk, was the feeblest of all. The other vessels stood the storm of shot, — new and of extraordinary force, made in England. The captain, who is here, tells me that never in war was there such a pelting by shots of such force. That the ships, always excepting the 'Keokuk,' stood this pelting is the present ground of hope. If they could have passed the impediments in the water and extricated themselves from the focus of the batteries, it is thought they would have put a different face upon the transaction. The present purpose is to deal with the impediments, so as to give the ships an opportunity. I tell you what I hear. It may be that further knowledge and counsel may change the plans. I cannot disguise my own conviction, entertained for a long time, that Charleston is to be taken on the field of battle, [2] — that is, by breaking the chief army of slavery; and this we are now permitted to believe will be done. Our army near Washington, under Hooker, will move in a day or two. All concur in representing it in admirable condition, hardy, well disciplined, well fed, and ready for action, — one hundred and fifty thousand men with more than sixty thousand animals, horses and mules. Its general

[1] The duke replied, April 24, 1863, at length to this letter. He found nothing in Lord Russell's despatch which was objectionable, and commended as favorable to us his recent reply in the House of Lords, March 23, to Lord Stratheden (Campbell). He treated the escape of the "Alabama" as "an accident," and giving no cause of quarrel. He claimed that a neutral could sell unarmed ships to a belligerent, and that such was the case of the "Alabama." He regarded with astonishment Sumner's undying confidence in our success, though he should rejoice to see it justified by the event. The duchess replied also on the 29th in much the same vein, though now, as always, with the greatest personal sympathy with and interest in her correspondent.

[2] The prediction proved true. Charleston fell in February, 1865, with the advance of Sherman's army.

is confident, and he is very dashing. If he accomplishes what is expected, the whole card-castle of slavery may tumble. But whatever may be the result here or elsewhere, our purpose is fixed. The slave-mongers shall not build their government at our side; nor will we consent to their coming into the family of nations. I am almost a Quaker, not by extraction, but by sentiment; but I believe that if ever it was justifiable to take the sword, it is to prevent the establishment of such a piracy.

"Let me say frankly and most kindly where I think England has erred. It is twice. First, she declared neutrality between the two parties, — fatal mistake, from which Lord Russell's speech[1] is the beginning of extrication. There can be no just neutrality between the two parties. You will not accept this view; but I ask you to think of it. Such a government, founded on such a pretension, seeking admission into the fellowship of Christian States, should have been told at the beginning that there was no place for it. To this England will yet come, unless the 'Alabama' carries her completely into the embrace of the slave-mongers, so that her cause and theirs will be one. The next mistake of England is that having declared neutrality, she has not been true to it. I do not allude now to the ships, though to us that case is flagrant; but I allude to the declarations of at least two of her ministers,[2] made long ago, that separation was inevitable. The direct tendency of their declarations was twofold: first, to encourage the slave-mongers, and to give hope and confidence to slavery wherever it was; and, secondly, by an infirmity of human nature, to bind these ministers, who had thus made themselves prophets, to desire the verification of their prophecy. And all this was more noteworthy when it was considered that the same ministers, while thus assuming the triumph of the slave-mongers, had not one word of regret for this terrible defeat of civilization itself. 'La neutralité n'existe plus dès qu'elle n'est pas parfaite.' I doubt if old Count Bernstorff, who made this remark, would have called such a neutrality 'perfect;' and not being 'perfect,' according to him it is nothing.[3]

"And now pardon me, — I write freely, that you may see how one who does not view England unkindly is constrained to judge recent events. Lord Russell's speech[4] is in the right direction; but why was it not uttered a year ago? Those words would have gone far then to cut off hope from the slave-mongers, and so doing, would have hastened the doom of slavery, and saved bloodshed incalculable. It is hard, very hard, to know that without English assistance slavery could never have stood forth in its present armor. You will think me unreasonable, and that I only see one side. I am charged here with seeing always the English side; but from the beginning there has been but one side to this terrible conflict. I will not borrow divine words, and say all who are not for us are against us; but I do say that from the beginning — and now since the President's Proclamation more than ever — we were entitled

1 March 23, in which Earl Russell contended, in reply to Lord Stratheden (Campbell), that an offer of mediation would be premature, and a recognition of the Confederates unfriendly to the United States; and he also maintained that there was no case for the intervention of foreign powers.

2 Gladstone and Russell.

3 Quoted by Sumner in an Address, Sept. 10, 1863. Works, vol. vii. p. 348.

4 March 23, in the House of Lords.

to the good wishes of all who really hated slavery. Strange idea, that slavery would be doomed by allowing it triumph, predominance, and power, with welcome and honor and hospitality in the family of nations![1] No, my dear friend, there is but one way: civilization requires, on our allegiance, that this great wrong shall not be with our sanction. Reading Lord Russell's speech, I feel tranquil for the time. Surely he cannot mean to carry England into war with us, as his other acts had made me fear. But the last debate and Lord Palmerston's speech[2] make me sad again. Mr. Seward says that the first speech, with the conversation of the next day reported by Mr. Adams, was a rainbow;[3] but now again we have darkness and storm. But I believe on this question England at last must come right; in this faith I live. God bless you!"

Again, April 17: —

"I write now by this intermediate packet merely in my anxiety. Perhaps I shall not be able to write much longer, — certainly not, unless there is a change on the other side of the water in certain public tendencies; and yet, as I reflect upon the case, I settle in the conviction that war between us is impossible, because English statesmen will reflect upon the direful consequences, — inconceivable desolation, shaking institutions at home, all for the sake of slavery and to support slave-mongers. . . . I have set my face against any act by which the English government could have the least ground of offence against us. For this policy I have pleaded strenuously. I did this for the sake of peace and for the sake of England; but I did it also because it is my desire, if the war comes which England now menaces, that the United States shall be absolutely without reproach, and that the terrible responsibility shall all be on the side of the supporters of slavery.

"Most firmly believing in the providence of God, I look forward to the overthrow of the slave-mongers, no matter what allies they may secure. It cannot be that he will desert his cause, and allow crime to organize itself ostentatiously in the very civilization of the nineteenth century. We have more to suffer; we have deserved it for our hardness of heart. Perhaps England also has more to suffer. But I am sure that in the end the slave-mongers must be suppressed. My present most earnest hope is that they may not enlist others in the destruction which awaits them."

Again, April 21:[4] —

"I fear that I have written you too warmly; but you will accept my letters as the record of the hour. Two objects I have had at heart: first, the

[1] A reference to Gladstone's theory.

[2] March 27.

[3] Mr. Adams, March 26, 1863, transmitted to Mr. Seward a copy of Lord Russell's speech of March 23, mentioning its better spirit, and the next day reported a long interview with him. On the 28th he transmitted a report of the debate of the 27th, which included speeches of W. E. Forster, Bright, the Solicitor-General (R. Palmer), Layard, and Lord Palmerston. The debate related to the sailing of the "Oreto" ("Florida") and the "Alabama," and to the capture of the "Adela" and the "Peterhoff" by the United States.

[4] Sumner wrote the same day a letter of a similar tenor to Cobden.

extinction of slavery; and secondly, peace, especially with England; and both seemed about to be defeated through the English government. We are all more tranquil now, — not from any positive assurance of peace from England, but more from the conviction that the English government will not open that interminable chapter of war which many even think now already opened on their side. The French minister,[1] who was with me for two hours yesterday, thinks that the ships will not be allowed to leave, and that there will be no trouble; and this is Lord Lyons's opinion. Baron Gerolt, the Prussian, and *doyen* of the diplomatic body here, who understands our affairs better than any of his associates, writes to his government, so he tells me, that England ought not to provoke a war with this government; that it would be a terrible conflict; and he adds that he does not doubt, if we are not interfered with by England, that the Federal power will be re-established. He had a conversation yesterday with Lord Lyons, which was quite satisfactory.

"It has seemed to us an obvious duty of the English government to take the responsibility of enforcing its own statute of neutrality, which is little more than the requirement of international law, and that it was enough for us to direct attention to the reported fact. Some of our Cabinet were so strongly of this opinion that they were unwilling that our minister or agents should take any further steps, and insisted that after what had passed the English government should be left to do as they pleased, and we should simply wait the result, it being generally understood that the sailing of the ships would be a declaration of war. I insisted most earnestly that while I did not differ from others as to the obvious duty of the English government, yet, as it had become a question of peace or war, I would not stand upon any form; that I would employ agents, attorneys, and counsel; institute law proceedings, — in short, do all that we thought the British government ought to do, so far as we might be able to do, whether in courts or out of courts. The President at last adopted this view, and Mr. Evarts,[2] who is a very eminent lawyer, without a superior in the country, has been despatched to do all that he can, in consultation if possible with your law officers or with others, to arrest the guilty vessels. He is a friend of Mr. Seward, who had hoped that he would take his place in the Senate; but he has never been in public life, and is purely a professional man. I think that his visit will do good; and I am so much interested in it that I shall give him a letter to the duke, and also to Mr. Gladstone, whom I admire, notwithstanding his deflection from the line where I should like to see him.

"I may err, — it may be that I shall be disappointed; but I feel sure that slavery cannot prevail. Blood and treasure will be lavished, and tears will flow in torrents; but justice will be established at last, before this war can end. In this conviction I am firm. I do not speak of sixty or ninety days, nor do I see any immediate prospect of this peace; but I am none the less certain that it must come.

"The duke's article on Lord Dalhousie[3] makes me hungry for the next.[4] I have read it with intense interest, and have enjoyed the way in which it is

[1] M. Mercier.

[2] William M. Evarts.

[3] "India under Lord Dalhousie." Edinburgh Review, January, 1863, pp. 1–42.

[4] "India under Canning." Edinburgh Review, April, 1863, pp. 444–497.

done, and the sentiment which enters into it, as well as the subject. It has revived in my mind the tragedy of 1857, when British empire in India was thought by many to be more doubtful than ours in the slave States. I recall a pleasant interview with Lady Havelock at Harrow, who told me that she had put aside among unopened parcels a present from the United States for her husband, reserving it for her children; and she dwelt with emotion on the flags at half-mast in New York when the news of his death was received. But I doubt if history will attach to British supremacy in India an importance and sacredness comparable with the cause of antislavery, now imperilled from England. You will read the Adjutant-General's speech [1] to the soldiers. Our policy is fixed; there can be no retreat. Let us have the God-speed of all who hate slavery!"

To Mr. Cobden, April 26:—

"I see but one course for England. Let her act upon her antislavery history, and let the slave-mongers know that they can expect nothing from her. Say it frankly and openly, the sooner the better. Their only hope is England. Such a declaration, besides its perfect consistency with the traditional policy of England, would be glorious for her; and it would do more than anything else to bring back that temper of peace which ought to prevail between our two countries."

To the Duchess of Argyll, April 26:—

"The duke's speech [2] was like himself, and has been much admired. You will, perhaps, note the account of it in a private letter printed here in Washington. But I long to have him take the ground, where at last England must come, that she can have nothing to do with a pretended government founded in a violation of human rights. That done, the war will soon be ended, and slavery too, and the old feeling here towards England may be won back.

"Our government is now not only hopeful but confident. We do not doubt the result. For the first time, our position is fixed. The Secretary of War told me yesterday that our rolls showed eight hundred thousand men under arms,—all of them paid to February 28, better clothed and better fed than any soldiers ever before. He knows well that we may be doomed to other reverses; but he is sure that the war can end in only one way, and he now thinks very soon. But besides our army, we have a credit which is adequate to all our needs; and we have powder and saltpetre sufficient for three years, even if our ports should be closed, and five hundred thousand unused muskets in our arsenals, and the best armorers of the world producing them at the rate of fifty thousand a month. Then, better still, our policy is clear. After much seeming uncertainty, you have its antislavery character openly announced,—(1) by the Proclamation; (2) by the resolution of Congress adopted with unequalled unanimity; [3] (3) by the speech of the Adjutant-

[1] Address of Lorenzo Thomas, Adjutant-General, to Union soldiers at Lake Providence, La., April 8, 1863, where he was organizing colored troops.

[2] At Edinburgh, April 1.

[3] Concerning intervention, Feb. 28, 1863. *Ante*, pp. 122, 123.

General of the national army calling negroes to the service; (4) by communications with foreign governments. There we stand. It will be for foreign governments to interfere on the side of slavery if they think best. . . . Meanwhile we await the change in England. Let it be soon, — soon for the sake of civilization; soon for the sake of peace. I am so much of an Englishman that I say freely, soon for the sake of England herself. The letter against letters of marque[1] which I enclose was to the New York Chamber of Commerce. My policy has at last prevailed. There will be no letters, at least for the present. Mr. Seward has been obliged to yield."

To Lieber, May 3:[2] —

"Of course I always listen to you, especially on any topic within the domain of history or public law, with the disposition to assent at once. You conquer as soon as you come upon the ground. And Mr. Binney has an authority peculiar to himself also. You know that I have always regarded him as the first lawyer our country has produced. Others may have had as much law; but none have had as much of everything which makes the consummate lawyer. And yet I must say frankly that I think you are both mistaken in your judgment of Lord Lyons. If you had expressed regret that the British minister had not openly and magnanimously declared his sympathy with our cause, I should agree with you. I regret it much. But you speak of him as 'tampering with our enemies,' and 'holding covert intercourse with disloyal men;' and this very serious charge is founded on his receiving New York Democrats, perhaps John Van Buren and Horatio Seymour, immediately after their triumph at the polls last autumn, while he listened to their complaints and theories.[3] If these men at that time talked of peace and of mediation, they did nothing more than they had done at public meetings and in newspapers, with the acquiescence if not sympathy of many calling themselves Republicans. This is melancholy, but it is the fact. Our government has never proceeded against them, nor has anybody suggested such proceedings. But any well-founded criticism of Lord Lyons must assume that these Democrats were guilty of something beyond political obliquity.

"I take it that no publicist will now question that a foreign minister may cultivate relations with a constitutional opposition in countries where constitutions exist; that he may listen to its opinions and its plans, and through its leaders inform himself. This at least has been the habit in France, England, and the United States. From the time I took my seat in the Senate, when I was almost alone, and in the Administration journals often denounced as a traitor, I had such relations with the foreign ministers here, especially of England and France. I think that they were more intimate with me than with any supporters of the Administration, and I assure you I never failed to talk my treason to them. But I never supposed that they in this way made themselves obnoxious to censure. Had I been a revolutionist, an 'enemy,'

1 Works, vol. vii. p. 313.

2 Reply to Lieber's letter, April 19, 1863, printed in Lieber's "Life and Letters," pp. 331-333.

3 A less favorable view of Lord Lyons's conferences in New York is taken in Nicolay and Hay's "Life of Lincoln," vol. vi. pp. 84-88.

or 'disloyal,' they could not have listened to me; but so long as my conversation was on topics which entered into the differences of party, they were free to listen, as I was free to talk. Last autumn the opponents of the Administration reached the verge of disloyalty. Just at that moment when a popular election had seemed to sanction their ideas, Lord Lyons arrived, and he listened to them, and reported what they said. . . .[1]

"It is not fair to say in reply that the course of the Democrats was fatal to the republic. You and I think so, and history will record it; but I doubt not that many sincerely thought our course fatal. It is enough that the difference between us, owing to our public calamities, had become a party difference. Thank God! this day has passed. But there is another piece of statesmanship, difficult as any we have had, — to keep from war with England. For success here we must avoid dropping any new ingredients into the cauldron. And this is why I trouble you with my dissent.

"Suppose the Duc de Noailles, the French ambassador in London, before France acknowledged our Independence, had received the visits of the Marquis of Rockingham, Lord Chatham, Mr. Burke, Mr. Fox, and Mr. Wilkes. I can well imagine the anger of George III., who knew little of law or constitution; but I doubt if Lord North would have complained. Of course, in entertaining such relations, the minister exposes himself to the dislike of the government in power; and it will be for him a question of tact and policy to determine how far he can go without impairing the influence which he ought to preserve. But no constitutional government will deny him this intercourse. . . .

"I have always thought McClellan incapable as a general, and without any sentiment for liberty. This is his mystery. Both were needed. There is no doubt here about Hooker. He told Judge Bates, at the time of the visit with the President, that he 'did not mean to drive the enemy, but to bag him.' It is thought he is now doing it."[2]

To Mr. Cobden, May 19: —

"There seems to be a better feeling on both sides. We begin to feel that you do not mean war with us. But why does Lord Russell write such letters? . . . It is not enough to keep the peace now. We must see that there are no occasions of difference left outstanding, no sarcasms which will be remembered only to be hurled back. But your foreign minister makes me sad with regard to the future. I know too much of public opinion and of individual opinion not to see danger ahead. To Lord Lyons I say: 'Avoid making questions if possible; and if they must be made, put them in such a form as to leave behind the least possible record or souvenir.' There have been conflicting opinions about our Potomac army. The latest report from those who have visited it is most encouraging. The army is strong and confident. I think there will be a movement soon, but the rough and wooded character of Virginia makes difficulties unknown in Europe. Military men doubt if there

[1] The omitted paragraph contains a citation from Wicquefort and a statement of the reply of Joseph Bonaparte, when ambassador at Rome, to revolutionists in that city.

[2] The letter was written on the day of Hooker's defeat at Chancellorsville. He did not prove equal to so high a command.

can be a decisive battle where there is no field on which the troops can be marshalled. Happy country where there is no battle-field! But I cease to watch very closely single events in this war; it is the result which I keep in view, and this is sure. I expect further disaster, and now deliberately make up my mind to it. But this can only postpone without changing the final day. Perhaps it is needful in order to carry out the transition which is now in progress."

To Lieber, May 20: —

"I perused your code[1] when you first sent it to me. . . . It is an epoch, and marks the civilization of the country and age. Perhaps it may be called high-water mark, for it is of inconceivable importance to have these principles settled in the hard text of an articulated document, which is next to a statute. I congratulate you upon this work, which will give you fame. More than this, it will be useful."

To the Duchess of Argyll, June 2: —

"The country is tranquil, while war seems to be putting forth new efforts on all sides. The North was never more prosperous; there is nothing in its streets or its fields to show the contest in which we are engaged. Wages are high, business is active, and every form of industry is well rewarded. The havoc of death reminds society of distant battles, and also the lame and maimed in the streets tell the same story; but in all these cases personal sorrow or loss is tempered by the thought that it has been for our country in a noble cause, — nobler than any before in history. So that the North thus far has not felt the war. Of course, it will go on; for, as I constantly write, there can be but one end to it. Any other would cover us all, and England too, with humiliation. God grant that England may not see too tardily where all the logic of her history, all the suggestions of her truest interest, and all the requirements of civilization lead! Historicus[2] writes now with clearness, carefulness, and truth. I wish I could say the same of some of his earlier essays, which had neither.[3] There was one at least which contained a flagrant misstatement, from which a little care would have saved him. But he is a fine spirit, who was then, like many others, under a temporary hallucination.

"Vicksburg is to be besieged. Our military men are confident. For myself, I look to the end, which I know is sure."

Again, June 8: —

"Our only source of anxiety is in Europe. It is announced this morning, under the telegraphic head, that France and England are considering again a proffer of mediation in our affairs. Of course, every such proffer, if possible, and every report of such an idea must tell for the slave-mongers. We are tranquil with regard to our war. Nobody connected with the government doubts the result if we are left to ourselves; nor, indeed, is it supposed that European

[1] Instructions for the Government of the Armies of the United States in the Field.
[2] W. V. Harcourt.
[3] Works, vol. vi. pp. 226-228.

interference can do more than make the contest more bloody and bitter. It can have but one end, sooner or later. But these reports from Europe make us feel that you are determined to make us suffer more, to spend more money, and to sacrifice more lives. If your foreign office were truly inspired, it would send the slave-mongers packing; that would be the greatest act of Lord Russell's career. Let him do this, and his name will be linked forever with the final extinction of slavery and the pacification of a continent. Our treasury is now in good condition. Mr. Chase told me yesterday that he had paid everything, and had five millions surplus, with money coming in daily. If it be said gold is at a premium, so it was in England in 1812."

To John Curwen, London, July 6 : —

"I accept with pleasure the position with which you honor me in your association for the help of freedmen.[1] I am glad to see the name of Buxton in the place which it ought never for a moment to have abandoned. I have liked Mr. Charles Buxton much. He seemed true, earnest, and intelligent when I had the good fortune to talk with him. But I have not been able to comprehend him of late, — except that so many others have backslided too; ay, and the fast-anchored isle itself has slipped from its moorings. It is sad to reflect on the relations of England to this terrible war. When its history comes to be written, there will be pages which all true Englishmen would wish to blot out with their tears. Strange that Mr. Charles Buxton[2] did not see that he yielded to the very argument which the slave-mongers brought against his noble father. Let him have faith in the cause; and, above all, do not let him for a moment sanction the idea of a slave-breeding, slave-trading government to flaunt in the face of civilization. And, pray, save England that I have loved from the unutterable degradation of any further coquetry with this intolerable, Heaven-defying iniquity!"

The month of July, 1863, marks a turning point in the Civil War. The American people on their national anniversary were gladdened with the tidings of the capitulation of Vicksburg and of Lee's retreat from Gettysburg. Great battles were yet to be fought, and reverses as well as victories were in store; but the tide had at last turned. Government and people were inspired with confidence; the most intelligent of the Confederates, though still hoping for the best, saw that the chances were against them; foreign cabinets and statesmen were from that time cautious in the exhibition of unfriendliness. Our cause was now identified with the noblest aspirations of mankind. It had become the cause not only of union, but of liberty also; and not the cause of one nation only, but of civilization.

[1] Sumner had been asked the use of his name as an officer of a society in England in aid of the freedmen.

[2] Charles Buxton was a vacillating politician. John Bright once said of him: "I should not like to go out tiger-hunting with Buxton; he might leave me to the tiger."

Sumner wrote to E. L. Pierce, Beaufort, S. C., July 1: —

"Horace Greeley, sometimes called General Greeley, is the author of General Gillmore's appointment.[1] . . . There will be no change there until he has had his trial. Hooker was relieved at his own request; but he was led to make the request by a disagreement with Halleck. Meade was the choice of the generals, and also of Hooker himself, and so seems to begin with the confidence of the military men. I am inclined to think him a solid soldier, who understands his business, perhaps of the Wellington type, and wearing spectacles. Chase was sorry that Hooker felt obliged to take the step he did. There has been talk of danger from the rebels, who are pretty near I keep at my desk. Butler is here, anxious, and not finding things to his satisfaction."

He wrote, July 29, to the same correspondent, who had written from Beaufort, S. C., concerning the assault on Fort Wagner by the Fifty-fourth Massachusetts (colored), led by Col. Robert G. Shaw: —

"I have just received your beautiful and touching letter on the Fifty-fourth Massachusetts Tell all of that regiment that you see that I honor them much: *Sic iter aa — Libertatem!* I cannot be consoled for the loss of Shaw. But where better could a young commander die than on the parapet of an enemy's fort which he had stormed? That death will be sacred in history and in art.

"The God of battles seems latterly to smile upon us. I am content that he should not smile too much. I fear our victories more than our defeats. There must be more delay and more suffering, — yet another 'plague' before all will agree to 'let my people go;' and the war cannot, must not, end till then."[2]

To Mr. Bright, July 21: —

"I have read the debate of the 30th of June.[3] Your last words touched the whole question to the quick. The guilt of this attempt is appalling; but next to the slave-mongers is England, with a grinning neutrality. My friend Mr. Gladstone dealt with the whole question as if there were no God. Englishmen may doubt. I tell you, there can be but one end to this war. I care not for any temporary success of the slave-mongers, they must fail; but English sympathy is a mighty encouragement. You will note our success in the Southwest; everything there is against the rebellion. There is pretty good reason to believe that Charleston will soon be ours. Lee's army has lost

[1] To the Department of the South.

[2] Sumner was interested in the project of an equestrian statue of Colonel Shaw, and contributed a paper to the Boston "Advertiser," Oct. 2, 1865 (Works, vol. ix. pp. 493-497), in favor of the statue, proposing as its site the terrace in front of the State House in Boston. He took part in a public meeting for the purpose, and was appointed a member of the committee to carry out the plan. It was suspended for many years, but was revived in 1891.

[3] On Roebuck's motion for the recognition of the Southern Confederacy. Bright's Speeches, vol. i. p. 267.

thirty thousand men, and I am inclined to think now must be much demoralized. We are too victorious; I fear more from our victories than our defeats. If the rebellion should suddenly collapse, Democrats, copperheads, and Seward would insist upon amnesty and the Union, and 'no question asked about slavery.' God save us from any such calamity! If Lee's army had been smashed, that question would have been upon us. Before this comes, I wish two hundred thousand negroes with muskets in their hands, and then I shall not fear compromise. Time is essential; so great a revolution cannot come to a close at once. By next steamer we send you Mr. Whiting[1] — an admirable lawyer, in the full confidence of the President, and my personal friend, agreeing with me positively in policy and object — to take the place of Mr. Evarts, to advise our minister to confer with your Crown lawyers and government, and to state our case. Nobody in England from here has known so much of the intimate opinions of our government or of its policy. He has been the legal adviser of our war department. I send you a pamphlet[2] by him. I hope that he may have good opportunities. Pray, announce his visit to Cobden and Forster. He is amiable, social, and true as steel on slavery, determined that the war shall end only with slavery. I long to write you about our Cabinet in reply to yours of the 27th of June. I wish we could sit together on the seashore."

Again, August 4: —

"I do not write to you of victories or reverses; for all these you will read in the newspapers. Whether victory or reverse, I know well that there can be but one end to the war: the rebellion will be put down. There are two things which make me anxious. First, I fear that devil of compromise. I do not think the danger is great; but any such danger is terrible. The longer our triumph is postponed, the more impossible this becomes. Our present policy is, therefore, (1) Two hundred thousand negroes under arms; (2) The admission of a Gulf State with an altered constitution abolishing slavery (Florida is ready to take this step; it may be in six or eight weeks;[3] this will be a controlling precedent); and (3) To insist that there can be no talk of admission into the Union except on the basis of the actual condition at the moment, with slavery abolished by the Proclamation. We fear the Secretary of State may intrigue the other way.

"The second cause of anxiety is in our relations with England. Your government recklessly and heartlessly seems bent on war. You know how the Democracy, which it now courts, will turn and rend it, while the Irish

[1] William Whiting, of Boston. He was distinguished at the bar as counsel in patent causes. He died in 1873 at the age of sixty, before taking a seat in Congress, to which he had been elected.

[2] The War Powers of the President, etc.

[3] Mr. Chase desired E. L. Pierce in May, 1863, to take a position in the service of his department at the South, in order to assist in organizing Florida as a free State. It was proposed to occupy the State with colored troops, — the Fifty-fourth Massachusetts to be the first to be sent there. The troops were, however, needed elsewhere, and the project was suspended. Mr. Pierce, however, went to the South, as Mr. Chase requested, to await events, and was on Morris Island at the time of the assault on Fort Wagner, July 18, 1863.

have at last their long-sought opportunity. A leading merchant said to me this morning that he would give fifty thousand dollars for a war between England and Russia, that he might turn English doctrines against England. The feeling is very bitter. When we are disengaged, who can arrest it? A just policy of kindness and good-will might do something to win back the true relations; but it ought to be adopted at once. The draft will be enforced. These rioters[1] are the present allies of the London 'Times.'"

To Mr. Cobden, September 4: —

"Your letter of the 7th of August is my last news from England. You seem tranquil. Gold is beginning to rise here, and a few days ago the agent of the Barings came to consult me about our foreign relations, saying that he was so anxious that he hesitated to give credits; but his anxiety was put on the uncertainty about the ironclads. We hear nothing authentic with regard to them. Evarts was here a few days ago, anxious, but with the impression that they would not be allowed to sail. But I think the public generally is more excited about Louis Napoleon, who has put himself in a direction which must eventually bring him in collision with us. Meanwhile, the war goes on; not as fast as the public expected, but fully as fast as I expected. In the military council which ordered the present attack on Charleston last June, the chairman, General Halleck, doubted the result, but thought there was no harm in trying; the others were confident. I do not think success will come early or easy. It is not proposed to move against Mobile until cool weather. The movement of Rosecrans is very important; his army is excellent, and he is a good officer. A movement in Texas is preparing. I accept the idea of delay, and even of reverse; but the end is sure, and I have so regarded it ever since the President's Proclamation. But I am inclined to think that 'time' is an essential element of a conflict which has become a social revolution.

"I do not differ from you when you say that you never would have counselled a war for emancipation. Nor I; indeed, I have done nothing but accept the conditions imposed by the other side. Of course, I would not surrender to slavery. There was a moment when, perhaps, it was possible to let the States go; but I doubt. Since then the thing has been morally impossible; the war must be fought out. This is sad enough to me! It costs me a pang to give up early visions, and see my country filled with armies, while the military spirit prevails everywhere. Everywhere soldiers come forward for offices of all kinds, from the Presidency to the post of constable; and this will be the case from this time during my life.

"You will read the President's letter.[2] It is like him, unique and characteristic; but he states the case very well. It has given assurance that there is no chance of compromise. Of course not; every day makes the end of slavery more certain."

[1] In New York in July, 1863, on the occasion of the draft. The negroes were the marked victims of outrage.

[2] Aug. 26, 1863, to the Illinois Union convention.

To R. Schleiden, September 6: —

"Your note was most instructive. You were right, — there will be no war on account of poor Poland. What means the policy of the emperor on this continent? I fear trouble ahead. The President's recent letter was all that I had ever promised. It is his best production. If there had been any doubt about the way in which the war will close, that letter must have removed it.

"I wish I had been at Washington to pay my respects to Mrs. Ward, the new bride. To all the baron's family [Gerolt's], and above all to himself, I owe homage. He is the friend of my country, and a wise counsellor; and he has always been with me most kind and indulgent. I am sorry that he too should be tried by the unsettled condition of his own country. What means the Austrian emperor's playing the liberal? But it is a good idea to ask to see Germany *ein ganze* — undivided. I hope this too may come. I miss my weekly talk and instruction."

To Mr. Bright, September 22: —

"The news from Rosecrans is not all that we desire; but I have great confidence in his military ability and in his 'holdfast character,' — and yet I confess that to my military eye, so far as I may judge such things, his position does not look right. But what then? His defeat would only postpone, not change, the result. At Charleston General Gillmore has done all that for the present he can do; he now waits for the navy. This is stopped, not by batteries and fire, but by ropes under the water, which are contrived to foul the screws of the monitors, by which they would be rendered unmanageable, so as to drift ashore. I am astonished that means have not been devised for the removal of this network; but thus far they have not succeeded. I think, however, the necessary contrivance will not be long wanting. With that, I understand there will be nothing serious to prevent the ironclads from going to Charleston. You will observe that the elections, as they have occurred, are for the Administration. Chase writes me from Washington that 'things are looking better and better' there. Our only anxiety is for England and France. Nobody can measure the complications which either of these powers may cause. The feeling towards England among those who have been most Anglican is of intense disappointment and sorrow. The Irish and Democrats are naturally against England; but the merchants and the educated — those who depend upon English books and enjoy the thought of English life — are now thoroughly aroused. I doubt if any ministry since Lord North's has made such a mistake as Lord Russell's. It might have buckled this great and growing power in perpetual amity; but it has pushed it aside, with insult. I long for England thoroughly to reconsider her course towards us. She must take a new start, or all who love peace here will be powerless. Meanwhile the prosperity of the North is great. Travel is immense; every conveyance, whether the largest steamer or the largest train, is crowded to repletion. Incomes are large; A. T. Stewart of New York says that his income has been at least four millions of dollars, and he has paid as income tax two hundred thousand dollars. This is the largest that I know of."

To R. Schleiden, September 25: —

"Yesterday Mr. Hooper's only son died; he had failed fast from a consumption. My poor brother still lingers; it seems as if each day must be his last. I read to him your amusing letter, which I thought he enjoyed much. For more than twenty days he has taken no food.

"I am sorry that the German sky does not look brighter to you; but I can well imagine your solicitudes. I fear that Rosecrans has met with a disaster;[1] but you know I have said that I expected defeat, with perhaps the loss of an army. Perhaps this is necessary to bring about the perfect consummation which under Providence is as certain as time. My letters from England yesterday are in better tone than ever. The rams will be stopped, and Lord Russell will be 'civil.' There is softening towards us; but what will Louis Napoleon do?"

To Mr. Bright, October 6: —

"If Lord Russell wants cotton let him withdraw all support, material and moral, from the rebellion; and let him begin by withdrawing his prophecies against us. Nothing is clearer than this: that the policy of the British government has prolonged the contest, and thus put off the day when the mills and operatives of Lancashire can count upon a supply of cotton. It is this government which has been their greatest enemy. Every blockade-runner, and all talk of mediation or recognition, is a coquetry, which gives encouragement to the rebellion. I am always sure, if my feet are planted on a moral principle, that I cannot be permanently defeated, — such is not the providence of God; and I am sure that those whose feet are not planted on a moral principle cannot stand permanently. But, pray, where are the feet of England? They should have been planted at the outset on the principle that slavery is wrong, and that therefore, in harmony with her great history, she would have nothing to do with it. There should have been no paltering with it, no encouragement to this wickedness. At this moment I am more solicitous about France and England than about our military affairs. In the latter there is a temporary check, and you know I said long ago that I was prepared for further disaster; but this can only delay, and not change, the result. Foreign intervention will introduce a new, vast, and incalculable element; it would probably provoke a universal war. You will observe the hobnobbing at New York with the Russian admiral. Why is that fleet gathered there? My theory is that when it left the Baltic, war with France was regarded as quite possible, and it was determined not to be sealed up at Cronstadt; if at New York, they could take the French expedition at Vera Cruz. The emperor of Russia has done well in emancipating the serfs, and I doubt not himself and his empire are both elevated by the act and better prepared for good things. But I am not a Russian; I believe yet in Western civilization. But England and France must retrace their steps."

It will be seen that in his foreign correspondence Sumner did his best to arouse the moral sentiment of England in our

[1] Near Chattanooga.

behalf, and to warn against the calamities for which, in case of intervention or other unfriendly action, Great Britain would be held responsible. With his early prepossessions for English life, he was sorely grieved at the course of the English government, the current of English opinion, and the unsympathetic and even hostile declarations of public men. If his warnings had been heeded in high quarters, that country would have been saved from a sad piece of history ending with the award at Geneva.

The letters of Bright and Cobden frankly stated our difficulties as they appeared to the English people, and suggested points where we should be on our guard. As soon as received, Sumner read or sent them to the President. Bright from time to time applied to him for information as to our plans and policy, which would enable him to make more positive statements in our behalf, and to assure the English people that our government would persevere in its policy of freedom.

Alone among eminent Englishmen, Bright was from first to last in our Civil War the unhesitating, unwavering, and fearless champion of our cause, full of faith and courage at all times.[1] Cobden wrote to Sumner, Feb. 12, 1862: "I hardly know anybody, except our courageous friend Bright (who rather likes to battle with the long odds against him), that thinks you can put down the rebellion."[2] Cobden at first had leanings towards the South, influenced by his free-trade sentiments and his repugnance to war, but he soon came right under the inspiration of Bright.[3] He had been impressed during his visits to this country with the material resources of the free States, and did not share the common English opinion that the suppression of the rebellion was improbable; but he had no faith, when that result should be reached, in the pacification of the revolted States. He was not in sympathy with some of our military methods, particularly the blockade, which he thought an unnecessary interruption of the pursuits of peace, and sure, if the contest were prolonged, to bring on foreign intervention.[4] Thus hampered

1 See his speeches, Dec. 4, 1861, and Dec. 18, 1862. "Speeches by Rt. Hon. John Bright," edited by T. Rogers, vol. i. pp. 194, 195, 224, 225.

2 See Cobden's letter to Paulton, January, 1862, in Morley's "Life of Cobden," vol. ii. p. 390.

3 Morley's "Life of Cobden," vol. ii. pp. 372, 373.

4 Letter of Cobden to Sumner, in manuscript, July 11, 1862. Morley's "Life of Cobden," vol. ii. p. 401. The Duke of Argyll wrote Sumner, July 12, to the same effect.

by economical opinions and want of faith, he was less aggressive in our behalf than he might otherwise have been.

The Duchess of Argyll wrote often to Sumner, and the duke occasionally. Both were personally sympathetic, and wished well to our country and the antislavery cause; but they had little faith, for the first two years of the war, in our success, and they believed that the South, if overcome by armies, would be unsubdued in spirit, — "a very large Ireland." They explained, without justifying, currents of English opinion adverse to us; and the duke firmly resisted Sumner's contention that the British proclamation of neutrality and the demand for the surrender of Mason and Slidell were unfriendly acts. He rejected also Sumner's contention that the pro-slavery basis of the Confederacy should have affected the question of belligerency. The duchess lamented Sumner's unfriendliness to England, — a sentiment which he earnestly disavowed in his replies. She as well as the duke thought him unjust in his reflections on Earl Russell, who, as they claimed, was after all friendly to our country, notwithstanding casual expressions which seemed the contrary, and who had in their view maintained faithfully the neutrality of England. The duchess's letters were always tender and sympathetic, glowing often with religious fervor. Of all Sumner's friends, not one at any period of his career had a deeper interest in his welfare. She wrote, May 8, 1862: "My hope and prayer is that you may come out of the fiery trial stronger, freer, happier than before. I hope we may meet in this life again." Again, May 30, 1863: "Your confidence in the overthrow of slavery is a blessed one to have, and God grant that your eyes may see the day! but his are the means, his the instruments. When you lay suffering and helpless, the cause made perhaps more progress than it may make by war; but it is impossible not to see that the cause *is* making way. God help and bless you!" Again, July 21, 1864: "I do hope for your victory, and for the spirit of mercy, of kindness, to the many who have fought for this bad cause so well." Again, August 5, 1865: "Your trees here are flourishing.[1] I remember with thankfulness how unlikely it then seemed when you planted them that your health would bear the strain of public life; and since then how much wear and tear it has borne! and 'as thy day, so shall thy strength be,' has been proved. God bless you!"

[1] *Ante*, vol. iii. p. 552.

Robert Ingham expressed, July 2, 1862, regret that the London "Times" misrepresented English opinion of our conflict, particularly that of the middle classes. He wrote, Feb. 19, 1864: —

"As to the general feeling of the country, I incline to my early impression. Amongst those who were never favorable to your institutions the cause of the Confederates was popular; and this feeling has been somewhat widened and strengthened by sympathy with the weaker power and with the dauntlessness of their resistance. But then the Parliamentary friends of the government and the industrious middle and working classes are largely in your favor; and with them too the sentiment is becoming stronger as your government (guided, I must say, my friend, by your authority and consistent example) has made it more apparent than at first that justice to the negro is now involved in your success. It is, however, always irksome for me to write as if I were a cold bystander on these subjects, knowing how your 'life is hidden' in this cause, — how commanding and responsible your position, and how poignantly your loving heart must have suffered at the inevitable calamities which must have befallen many friends."

Again, Oct. 25, 1865: —

"No one has a title to witness with purer joy the successful close of your great contest; for from the first you proclaimed the cause of the abolition of slavery — the cause of your noble exertions throughout your life — as your object in the war, and the sole reward to be looked to."

William E. Forster wrote, Nov. 22, 1861, heartily in our favor, approving Sumner's recent speech at Worcester, and expressing the hope that our government would soon hoist the standard of emancipation. Harriet Martineau complained, Nov. 18, 1862, that American opinion treated England unfairly as compared with France, as the former country had resisted the latter's pressure for breaking the blockade and for intervention. Martin F. Tupper, though of positive antislavery convictions, wrote, Nov. 9, 1862, that it would be better to let the South go than to attempt a forced union. Earl de Grey (later Marquis of Ripon), who succeeded G. C. Lewis as Secretary of War, answered, June 14, 1863, Sumner's note of congratulation, and while withholding an expression of opinion on our contest, joined heartily in Sumner's hope for a continuance of unbroken peace between the two nations.

Several English friends with whom Sumner came into intimate relations during his first visit to Europe were now far apart from him. The Wharncliffes were open partisans of the

South.[1] Brougham spoke of Sumner angrily, and denouncing the attempt to suppress the rebellion, said that our people were "stark mad." The Grotes regarded our cause with disfavor; so also did Senior, who wrote only to upbraid us for our shortcomings, saying, "But as soon as you get rid of them [Southern politicians heretofore charged with being responsible for our brusque treatment of other nations], your language becomes more insulting, your threats become more precise, your tariff becomes more hostile, and at last your conduct becomes more outrageous." Henry Reeve was equally intemperate, ranking the Confederates with Washington and Franklin, and promising their recognition if they were not conquered in three months, — an act to be concurred in by all the great powers of Europe, to which, as he wrote, we should have to submit or go to war with all mankind. Joseph Parkes held from the beginning that acquiescence in secession was better and wiser than civil war; and he justified the attempt of the seceding States to obtain independence. He was silent from January, 1861, to October, 1863, and then replied to a recent note from Sumner introducing William Whiting, of Boston. He had heretofore disapproved Sumner's style of dealing with slavery and its supporters, and he was now full of cynicism in his views of our great conflict.[2] He had no patience with Sumner's treatment of the course of the English people and government, in his speech in New York, September 10, and could scarcely believe that it came from "the Charles Sumner of ancient days, who talked peace and good-will as the Christian feeling and true policy of our two nations of common origin, race, language, interest, and religion." Mrs. Parkes, however, as became one of American birth, added a postscript, saying that herself and her daughter were "stanch Northerners."

It was a surprise and grief to Sumner to see English opinion run so strongly against us. As he had expected more from this source than others, his sense of disappointment was greater than theirs; and the England of his youth was never the same England to him again. Saddest of all was the cold shoulder of

1 The Marchioness of Drogheda, daughter of Sumner's old friend John Stuart Wortley, was an exception, and was outspoken and constant for the cause of the Union. She and her husband came to Boston in 1865, where Sumner met them.

2 A later letter of May 12, 1864, though cordial in assurances of friendship, was of the same tenor.

scholars and philanthropists.[1] Men like Earl Russell and the Buxtons gave as an excuse for their want of sympathy at the beginning that we disavowed an antislavery policy, and later when that policy was announced they reprobated it as inviting servile insurrection. Gladstone and the Bishop of Oxford (son of Wilberforce the philanthropist) affected to believe that the extinction of slavery was more likely to follow the success than the defeat of the insurgents. Others, whose better instincts inclined them to our side, laid great stress on every incident of the conflict which did not agree with their notions of propriety, — such as the sinking of obstructions in Charleston harbor, the inclusion of chloroform and medicines among articles contraband of war, or General Butler's order inflicting deserved punishment on women in New Orleans who insulted Union soldiers on the streets. A sentimentalism, strange in a people whose career has been one of invasion and empire, all at once overcame them, and they expected in our case all the amenities of peace to be maintained amid the passions and agonies of civil war.

The sympathy with the Southern Confederacy which pervaded the English people (outside of the working classes and a part of the middle class) was a mystery to our people at the time, and even now is not easily understood.[2] Several influences set the current against us, and they may be classified as follows: —

1. The privileged classes, nobility and landed gentry, feared the power and example of our republic;[3] to them it was a "standing menace." They had also a sentiment of fellowship

[1] Among those in our favor were Goldwin Smith, Thomas Hughes, Mill, Huxley, Fawcett, R. M. Milnes, and F. W. Newman. R. M. Milnes wrote to C. J. MacCarty, Jan. 20, 1862: "I am in a minority of two or three, the House of Commons and society being all Southern;" and to George von Bunsen, Feb. 6, 1862: "Parliament meets to-day, with no great prospect of change of any kind. The feeling about America is intensely Southern, and I with my Northern sympathies remain in greater isolation than ever." Lord Houghton's "Life," vol. ii. pp. 76, 77.

[2] The writer has asked many intelligent Englishmen to explain English feeling towards us at this time, and they have seemed uniformly puzzled by the inquiry.

[3] Bright, in his address at Rochdale, Dec. 18, 1862, mentions that in private, when a candid opinion was given, it was said that "the republic is too great and powerful; and that it is better for us — not by 'us' meaning you, but the governing classes and the governing policy of England — that it should be broken up." Lord Cranworth, who in a moderate way shared the opinions of his class, wrote to Sumner, March 13, 1865: "I will not attempt to conceal from you that we think Europe, and more especially England, will be safer from the horrors of war if you are to continue two great nations than if you are all to be reunited as one great fighting nation."

with the slaveholding class. Their sympathies acted on others in social relation with them.

2. Manufacturers hoped by our dismemberment to obtain free trade with the South. The trade connections of Liverpool and Manchester, and other commercial centres ramifying through the kingdom, made English capital almost a unit against our cause.

3. The Morrill tariff act of 1861 was a fresh grievance. Lord Russell, in his first interview with Mr. Adams, May 18, 1861, touched upon "the high protective tariff recently enacted;" and Mr. Adams assured him that "it was intended rather for revenue than for protection, and that if it failed in bringing revenue it would not be maintained for the sake of monopoly and restriction."[1]

4. The contest on the part of the South was assumed to be one of State rights, and therefore justified by the example of the colonies in our Revolution.

5. The declarations of our government at the beginning of the war of its purpose not to interfere with slavery, announced by Congress, by the President, and by Mr. Seward in his despatches, promoted the idea that the contest was purely one for the unity of the government, and repelled the active support of liberal minds. While some, like John Bright, saw the inevitable tendency of events to emancipation, others did not see it. With some this was a genuine reason, and with others a pretence.

6. Certain national sentiments were misapplied, namely, sympathy for the "under dog," or "weaker party."[2] Some "peace men," overlooking that the first step was taken by the insurgents, charged most perversely on the government the sole responsibility for the bloodshed.[3]

7. Our government, under pro-slavery administrations, had been wanting in due respect for other nations, as in the invasion of Mexico and the Ostend Manifesto.

8. The participation of large numbers of our people in the English-Irish controversy, often with an official or semi-official sanction.

[1] Lord Russell to Lord Lyons, May 21, 1861.

[2] Lord Cranworth, in his letter to Sumner, March 13, 1865, gives this sentiment — "a morbid sympathy, perhaps" — as an explanation of English sympathy with the rebellion.

[3] John Bright used to tell the story of a "peace man" of his acquaintance who was beside himself in rage at our government for the bloodshed, all of which he charged against it.

9. The belief was honest with some, and "father to the thought" with others, that the Southern people would surely maintain their independence. Our form of government was thought the least adapted of any to such a strain, and the resources of the free States were not comprehended. The belief in our failure was from the first widespread, and at times almost universal.[1]

10. The London "Times," which then swayed English opinion far more than at a later period, was a potent influence against the American cause.[2]

English public opinion was notably affected by the proclamations of emancipation of September, 1862, and January, 1863. The change was at first most marked among the masses, — among those who were swayed by democratic instincts, — but it soon appeared in the altered tone of the leading journals and of public men. Great meetings were held to express sympathy with our cause; and the moral and religious sentiment of the country, particularly among Non-Conformists, set strongly in our favor.[3] Sumner's correspondents recognized the change for the better. Bright wrote to him, as early as Dec. 6, 1862: "The antislavery sentiment here has been more called forth of late, especially since the proclamation was issued; and I am confident that every day the supporters of the South among us find themselves in greater difficulty owing to the course taken by your government in reference to the negro question." Cobden described in his letter to Sumner, Feb. 13, 1863, the scene in Exeter Hall January 29, where the multitude applauded the new policy of freedom; and he wrote that the recognition of the

[1] Lord Derby said in the House of Lords, Feb. 6, 1863: "I declare my firm conviction that there is no possibility of establishing the Union between the North and the South." Cobden wrote to Bright, Sept. 8, 1863: "Some shallow and indiscreet members of our aristocracy exclaimed at the outbreak of the Civil War, 'The republican bubble has burst;' but the experience of the last two years shows that, whether in peace or war, the republic, instead of a bubble, is the greatest and most solid fact in history. It is to be hoped that gradually our educated mob of the clubs will become, however unwillingly, acquainted with the warlike resources of America." The probable division of the United States was an inherited English idea. Coleridge gave expression to it in his "Table Talk," p. 201 (Jan. 4, 1833).

[2] An American living in London during the war collected in scrap-books all the leaders, correspondence, telegrams, and items concerning the United States which appeared in the "Times." Mr. Bright, who saw them once, used to say that "there were more lies between those covers than between any others ever known."

[3] A paper signed by thirteen thousand five hundred people of Birmingham, expressing sympathy with the United States, was presented to Mr. Adams, Feb. 27, 1863, by a committee which was introduced by Mr. Bright. New York "Tribune," March 17, 1863.

South by England on the basis of negro slavery had become an impossibility.[1] The victories of Vicksburg and Gettysburg in July confirmed this direction of public opinion.

Two English statesmen, members of the Cabinet, — Earl Russell (Foreign Secretary) and Gladstone (Chancellor of the Exchequer), — both of whom Sumner had met in a friendly way, sorely disappointed him in their attitude on our contest. The former took occasion to say at an early day that our government and the insurgents "were contending, as so many of the States in the Old World have contended, the one side for empire, and the other for independence."[2] His despatches were, in Sumner's view, "hard, curt, captious, cynical." The fitness of these terms appears in Russell's criticisms of the Proclamation of Emancipation, Jan. 17, 1863, which four years later he publicly withdrew.[3] His neglect to detain the "Alabama" for some days after he had received Sir Robert Collier's opinion, while waiting for that of the Crown lawyers, brought the countries to the brink of war, and cost England heavily in the subsequent award of damages. This delay he admitted late in life to have been an error.[4] While his feelings do not appear to have inclined him decidedly to one side or the other, he treated the contest with an air of indifference, though without any definite purpose of hostility to either party; and on a review of his whole course he appears to have endeavored to maintain a fair neutrality.[5] Certainly he was effective in resisting a strong party which was always pressing for intervention. Few, if any, of his class and rank would have been likely to have done better for us in his position than he did;[6] but more was expected from him than from them on account of the liberal opinions of which he had been at other times the supporter.

Gladstone, unlike Russell, had no direct official relation to our contest, and he came as a volunteer before the public when

1 Joshua Bates, in his letter to Sumner, May 13, testified to this change of public opinion. Adams recognized it in his letters to Seward, May 7 and June 5, without, however, mentioning the cause.

2 At Newcastle, Oct. 14, 1861.

3 At the Garrison breakfast, St. James's Hall, London, June 24, 1867.

4 "Recollections and Suggestions" (Boston, 1875), pp. 235, 334.

5 His speeches in the Lords, April 29, 1864, and March 23, 1865, justify this better view of him.

6 Mr. Bright said to E. L. Pierce that Earl Russell was our friend, though badly surrounded. In letters to Sumner, April 24 and May 2, 1863, he describes Russell as meaning well, but weak and changeable.

he sought to produce a popular impression against us. There is evidence that very early in the struggle he had been free in personal intercourse in expressing his sympathy with the Southern insurrection;[1] but he first gave his views to the public early in 1862, — at first in a guarded, and later in a more positive, manner; venturing further than any member of the Cabinet, and, according to Mr. Adams, "transcending the line of policy" which it had agreed upon.[2] There is no way so effective in carrying opinion against a cause as to make it appear hopeless, and Mr. Gladstone chose that way. At Leith, January 11, he said: "All thinking men had come to the conclusion that the party apparently the strongest had committed themselves to an enterprise which would probably prove to be beyond their strength." At Manchester, April 24, before the Chamber of Commerce, he argued from historical analogies that the North could not succeed in its gigantic enterprise, and that it was impossible to conquer a people set upon independence; refused to see in the struggle any question of freedom or slavery; or if such an issue were to be admitted, he rebuked the idea that free institutions were to be propagated at the point of the sword, or the horrors of war bent to philanthropic ends; reaffirmed Russell's declaration that the contest was on one side for empire and on the other for independence; and set aside the claim of Americans to sympathy on the politic ground that Englishmen could not be expected to risk the permanent hostility of six or ten millions of the Southern people who might hereafter become a great nation.[3] His treatment of the American question was throughout captious and cynical. The London "Times" responded heartily to his espousal of the cause of the Confederates, saying: "The view taken by Mr. Gladstone of American affairs is so entirely in accordance with that which we have long advocated, that we do not scruple to adopt that portion of his speech as our own."[4] But as if enough had not been said, he returned to the theme again at Newcastle, October 7, when he

[1] Letters of a London correspondent of the New York "Evening Post," Sept. 20 and Oct. 27, 1862. Adams wrote to Seward, Oct. 10, 1862: "From the first there has been little doubt on which side his [Gladstone's] sympathy was. But the present is the first occasion upon which he has ventured to touch upon the slave portion of the controversy. His idea that the force of the slave tenure will be diminished by the withdrawal of that portion of the governing power which had heretofore been applied to sustain it in the free States is as ingenuous as it is sophistical."

[2] Adams to Seward, Oct. 17, 1862.

[3] London Times, April 25.

[4] London Times, April 28.

said: "There is no doubt that Jefferson Davis and other leaders of the South have made an army; they are making, it appears, a navy;[1] and they have made what is more than either, a nation." This triumphant tone showed where his heart was. He affected to believe, and sought to make others believe, in face of the antislavery measures of Congress and Mr. Lincoln's Proclamation of Emancipation, that the slaves would be better off, and their final liberation nearer, by a division of the country into two sections. He declared in Parliament, June 30, 1863, his belief that "the restoration of the American Union by force is unattainable," and again denounced (after Lincoln's Proclamation) "the emancipation of the negro race as an object that can be legitimately pursued by means of coercion and bloodshed." Sumner well said of Gladstone's prophecies: "British statesmen, forgetting for the moment moral distinctions, forgetting God who will not be forgotten, gravely announce that our cause must fail. . . . Opinions are allies more potent than subsidies. . . . Nothing is more clear than that whoever assumes to play prophet becomes pledged in character and pretension to sustain his prophecy."[2]

Mr. Gladstone, while, as Mr. Adams wrote, "expressing his individual opinions and giving loose to his personal sympathy with the chief of the rebels,"[3] produced the impression that the British government was about to intervene between our government and the insurgents.[4] He must have foreseen the natural effect of his declarations, and indeed by making them appears to have intended to prepare the way for recognition and intervention. Merchants in Manchester, assuming that the event was near at hand, began to start enterprises on the strength of his prediction and supposed authority. They applied to him for a more definite statement, and he answered that he had only said pointedly at Newcastle what he had said nine months before at Leith, that the effort of the "Northern States" was a "hopeless" one; and he suggested that there was an interval between opinions and the steps which give them effect.[5] Shortly after, in an

[1] Supposed to be a reference to the rebel rams then in construction in England, or already escaped. Adams to Seward, October 10.

[2] Address in New York, Sept. 10, 1863. Works, vol. vii. pp. 351, 352.

[3] Adams to Seward, Oct. 17, 1862.

[4] Adams to Seward, Oct. 10 and 17, 1862.

[5] Letters in his behalf by C. L. Ryan, October 16 and 18. London "Times," October 20 and 24.

open corespondence with Prof. F. W. Newman, he called the struggle of our government to maintain itself "a hopeless and destructive enterprise." [1]

Mr. Adams, disturbed by the tendency to intervention which Mr. Gladstone's speech at Newcastle had encouraged, and apprehensive that it foreshadowed imminent action of the Cabinet, made it the subject of a conference with Earl Russell.[2] The character and effect of the speech were such that our minister, as he wrote, began to consider "the condition of his travelling equipage," and regarded the close of his mission as likely to be at hand. Earl Russell intimated to Mr. Adams for himself, and on behalf of Lord Palmerston and other members of the Cabinet, regret that the speech had been made.[3] Sir George Cornewall Lewis, another member, undertook to neutralize its effect in a public address of his own;[4] and the official organ, the "Globe," drew a distinction between Mr. Gladstone and the ministry in regard to the sentiments he had expressed.[5] These disavowals in high quarters made public men more cautious; and, as Mr. Adams states, there came to be a general opinion that Mr. Gladstone had been "very indiscreet."

Mr. Bright wrote to Sumner, October 10, 1862: —

"I write to you from a feeling of anxiety. You will see what is being said here by public men who speak on your question, and most of all, and *worst of all*, by your old acquaintance and friend Mr. Gladstone. He has made a vile speech at Newcastle, full of insulting pity for the North, and of praise and support for the South. He is unstable as water in some things. He is for union and freedom in Italy, and for disunion and bondage in America. A handful of Italians in prison in Naples, without formal trial, shocked his soul so much that he wrote a pamphlet, and has made many speeches upon it; but he has no word of sympathy or of hope for the four millions of the bondsmen of the South! I have known for months past that he talked of a European remonstrance, or mediation, or recognition, or some mischief of that kind; but I

1 Dec. 1, 1862. Professor Newman's letter, November 28, calls Gladstone "the admirer of perjured men." Gladstone's rejoinder of December 4 was published in the London "Star." (New York "Tribune," December 12 and 20.) Mr. Gladstone's pro-slavery sympathies and partiality for the Southern rebellion were treated in "Letters on the American Rebellion," by Samuel A. Goddard, of Birmingham, contributed to English journals at the time, and since published in a volume, pp. 181–193, 252–259, 281–285.

2 Adams to Seward, October 24.

3 Seward to Adams, October 24.

4 October 14, before the Herefordshire Agricultural Society. He died April 13, 1863; and, as Seward wrote to Adams, May 4, on account of his firm, just, and dignified course in regard to our national affairs, his death was mourned as profoundly in this country as in England.

5 The Duchess of Argyll wrote to Sumner, December 6, that Gladstone's Newcastle speech "grieved" the duke and herself.

did not expect that he would step out openly as the defender and eulogist of Jeff. Davis and his fellow-conspirators against God and man. He *has* spoken, as you will see by the time you receive this; and what he has said will encourage the friends of the South here to increased exertions to promote something hostile to your government and people. Palmerston and Russell, I fear, will not need much pressure to induce them to do anything they dare do on behalf of the permanent disruption of your Union."

Union victories put an end to Mr. Gladstone's hostile prophecies. Mr. Bright wrote to Sumner, Sept. 11, 1863: —

"It would be curious to have a speech from Gladstone now. Perhaps *he* is beginning to doubt whether Jeff. Davis has made a nation. There is much cleverness mixed with little wisdom, or much folly, in some men, and our chancellor seems to be one of them. I think I shall make a selection from the writings of the 'Times' and the speeches of our public men, and publish them, that their ignorance and folly may not be forgotten."

In contrast with Gladstone's evil prophecies and undisguised sympathy with the Confederates was the steady support which John Bright, Richard Cobden, and William E. Forster gave to the American cause, although they had no sources of information not open to their distinguished contemporary. Bright at the very hour when the English temper was most excited by the seizure of Mason and Slidell, not then surrendered, appealed to his country in a speech at Rochdale, Dec. 4, 1861: —

"Now, whether the Union will be restored or not, or the South achieve an unhonored independence or not, I know not, and I predict not. But this I think I know: that in a few years, a very few years, the twenty millions of freemen in the North will be thirty millions, or even fifty millions, — a population equal to or exceeding that of this kingdom. When that time comes, I pray that it may not be said amongst them that in the darkest hour of their country's trials England, the land of their fathers, looked on with icy coldness, and saw unmoved the perils and calamities of their children. As for me, I have this to say: I am but one in this audience, and but one in the citizenship of this country; but if all other tongues are silent, mine shall speak for that policy which gives hope to the bondsmen of the South, and which tends to generous thoughts and generous words and generous deeds between the two great nations who speak the English language, and from their origin are alike entitled to the English name."

Again at Birmingham, Dec. 18, 1862, Bright, after referring to Gladstone's opposite prediction and belief, gave his own better hope: —

"I cannot believe, for my part, that such a fate will befall that fair land, stricken though it now is with the ravages of war. I cannot believe that civilization, in its journey with the sun, will sink into endless night in order to gratify the ambition of the leaders of this revolt, who seek to

'Wade through slaughter to a throne,
And shut the gates of mercy on mankind.'

I have another and a far brighter vision before my gaze. It may be but a vision; but I will cherish it. I see one vast confederation stretching from the frozen North in unbroken line to the glowing South, and from the wild billows of the Atlantic westward to the calmer waters of the Pacific main; and I see one people and one language and one law and one faith, and over all that wide continent the home of freedom and a refuge for the oppressed of every race and of every clime."

In his letters to Sumner during the war, Mr. Gladstone guarded himself against any expressions in favor of our government. He wrote of "the power and energy displayed in the wonderful but dreadful contest." He refrained, Jan. 3, 1862, from "entering on the gigantic question of the convulsion now agitating the American continent." As to the black race he wrote later, that "whichever way the war ends, it will leave the prospects of that race at least materially better than it found them," with no intimation that their fate would be better in the hands of a government which had proclaimed emancipation than in those of one founded on slavery as a corner-stone. Even after the capture of Vicksburg and Lee's retreat from Gettysburg, in letters of Nov. 5, 1863, and Feb. 1, 1864, he treated the re-establishment of the Union as "a contingency wholly unattainable," saying at the last-named date, "Ever since the development of an earnest purpose in the South, my opinion has remained absolutely the same."

Some years after the contest had ended, and when no man's word in our behalf was needed, Mr. Gladstone offered error of insight "into the nature and working of the American Union" as his excuse, with that facility of speech in reconciling adverse positions and explaining changed opinions for which he has since been remarkable.[1] After all, no different course was to be expected from this statesman. His parliamentary career began with apologies for African slavery,[2] and his family interest in a West India plantation made him easily the admirer of Jefferson Davis.

[1] To C. Edwards Lester, Oct. 8, 1867. New York "Evening Post," Dec. 28, 1868.

[2] May 17 and June 2, 1833. Address to electors of Newark, Oct. 9, 1832. Smith's "Life of W. E. Gladstone," chap. iii.

Sumner delivered, September 10, an address in New York on "Our Foreign Relations," in compliance with an invitation which had been given to him in February. While it was intended to assist our own people in understanding points in controversy, of which they had only an inadequate idea, its chief purpose was to affect foreign opinion by a clear and forcible statement, and thus arrest movements looking towards intervention, now the chief, indeed the only, hope of the rebels. He desired to exhibit to the English people, misled by their journals and public men, in the strongest light possible, the proslavery origin and character of the Confederacy, and to create against it a moral sentiment which cabinets would be obliged to respect. The occasion was exigent. The "Florida" and the "Alabama" were on the sea, — both having issued from English ports. Iron-clads building for the Confederates at Birkenhead were nearly completed. Earl Russell refused, September 1, to stop them, and Mr. Adams replied the day after receiving the refusal, "This is war!" The French emperor was pressing the English government to join him in intervention; and while the Cabinet held back from that step, its resistance could not be counted upon in the event of some new grievance, some new pressure of interests, or some disaster to our arms. As yet there had been no comprehensive review of our foreign relations, and the official correspondence published in fragments here and in England gave the public an inadequate idea of the points in controversy. Sumner wrote afterwards: —

> "Anxious to arrest the fatal tendency, he was not without hope that he might obtain a hearing in England, especially from the Cabinet, to most of whom he was personally known; but if unsuccessful in the last frank effort for peace, then he trusted that his speech would be a vindication of his country on the issue forced by England, and an appeal to the moral sentiments of the civilized world. On this account he dwelt especially on slavery, and the impossibility in a civilized age of recognizing a *new* power openly proclaiming this barbarism as its corner-stone." [1]

Of all American statesmen then active in public life Sumner was thought to be the most English in his tastes; [2] and among them he was almost the only one who had any considerable English acquaintance. For many English friends he felt an affection equal to that which he felt for any of his own countrymen. He was, as was often remarked in both countries,

[1] Works, vol. vii. p. 474.

[2] Edward Everett was in retirement.

the last of our public men from whom an indictment against England was to be expected; but Sumner never counted personal ties or social embarrassments when what seemed to him a high public duty called upon him to act.

The hall of Cooper Institute was filled with three thousand people on the appointed evening, and an equal number who sought the entrance doors were unable to obtain admission. The most eminent citizens of New York were on the platform. David Dudley Field, in introducing the orator, spoke of him as one "whose name is an introduction and a passport in any free community between the Atlantic and the Pacific seas," and then presented him amidst long-continued cheers of welcome. Sumner kept his audience till nearly eleven o'clock, his Address exceeding in length any which he had ever made.[1] He reviewed the queen's proclamation of neutrality, — "a precipitate, unfriendly, and immoral concession;" the menace of war on the occasion of the seizure of the "Trent;" the various unfounded complaints made against our government in official despatches; Russell's and Gladstone's prophecies of our failure and defeat, significant of their hopes and wishes; the fitting out of Confederate cruisers issuing one after the other from British ports, thus making England "the naval base" of the Confederacy; and the official tone of the British foreign office in discussing our cause, — "hard, curt, captious, cynical." He treated the hostile policy of the French emperor as shown in his attempts at mediation and his crusade at such a time against Mexico. He then reviewed at length intervention in foreign and civil wars as illustrated in history, — sometimes entered upon in the interest of liberty and sometimes in the interest of oppression, sometimes limited to good offices and sometimes carried to the extent of force, — stating in this connection the conditions under which revolted States may be recognized as independent nations, and denying that the rebel States had reached any stage which justified such recognition. He argued with great earnestness that whatever fellowship might ordinarily be accorded to new powers, and whatever intercourse with existing governments which sustained slavery might be toler-

[1] Works, vol. vii. pp. 327–392. A considerable part of the Address as printed must have been omitted in delivery. The reading of the Address as found in Sumner's Works would have occupied over four hours. The Address as there printed contains only a few passages not found in the first edition, which was issued by the Young Men's Republican Union.

ated, a Christian civilization required that a new power built by the confession of its creators on slavery as a corner-stone should be excluded peremptorily and indignantly from the family of Christian nations.[1] He pleaded that England by her traditional devotion to the protection of the African race, and France by her professed championship of "ideas," were pledged to maintain such exclusion. The latter part of the Address was an argument against the title to belligerent rights on the ocean of a rebel power which was unable to complete its captures by a legal adjudication essential to their validity, and which, without access to prize courts, uniformly burned captured ships.[2] Such cruisers, "all built, rigged, armed, and manned in Great Britain," availing themselves of British ports as "their naval base of operations and supplies, . . . never touching a port of the pretended government," were only "mere gypsies of the sea, disturbers of the common highway, outlaws and enemies of the human race." Here, however, he left open the question what should be "the fate of these ocean incendiaries." He closed with a picture of what the republic was to be, freed from slavery and triumphant over rebellion. "Born in this latter day, and child of its own struggles, without ancestral claim, but heir of all the ages, it will stand forth to assert the dignity of man; and wherever any member of the human family can be succored, there its voice will reach."

The Address, as was usual with Sumner's efforts of this kind, was marked by amplitude of historical review and intense moral earnestness. Epithets were heaped on the new slave empire to make it odious in the sight of mankind, and to repel all sympathy and fellowship with it. Notwithstanding its length, three New York journals and two in Boston found a place for the Address entire in their columns the day after its delivery.[3] A large edition was at once issued by the association before which Sumner spoke. The Address drew forth approval from the journals of the country, nearly always unqualified. Mr. Greeley

1 The Duke of Argyll, in a letter to Sumner, September 30, refused to admit in international intercourse a distinction between a new slave country and an old one.

2 Earl Russell and other English critics did not touch this point. The Duke of Argyll, however, in his letter of September 30, admitted that there was force in the contention. The Confederates alleged, in justification of their habitual destruction of captured vessels, the stringent blockade of their ports; but the validity of this excuse has not been passed upon judicially or settled by diplomacy. Dana's Wheaton, p. 487, *note*.

3 Allibone, author of the "Dictionary of Authors," in a letter to Sumner mentioned that it had taken twenty and a half columns in the New York "Tribune."

made it the subject of a contribution to the "Independent" of New York. It called out grateful and enthusiastic expressions in numerous letters from citizens and public men, including Seward, Chase, Corwin, Cameron, and Senators Anthony and Howe;[1] from Giddings, who, writing from Montreal, put his hope in Sumner more than in any public man; and Palfrey the historian, who counted the speech an epoch, not only in the pending contest, but in the history of the law of nations.[2]

Sumner's Address encountered criticism in England on these grounds: (1) It did not take into account the differences of opinion among the English people, and ignored the sympathy with our cause on the part of large masses of them, and particularly of the workingmen, who had suffered from the blockade, and on the part of certain English leaders, — Bright, Cobden, and Forster in Parliament, and Spurgeon, Newman Hall, and Baptist Noel in the pulpit. But Sumner was dealing with the nation as a unit, represented by its official heads. He was not writing an historical review after the contest had ended, in which a moral judgment on a people ought to take note of differences of opinion among them; but he was seeking in the midst of the contest to bring a foreign government to a sense of its obligations. (2) It condemned sharply the government of Great Britain, and let off easily that of France, although the former country had resisted the latter's pressure for interference in the contest. But our difficulties came from Great Britain, where the Confederate cruisers were fitted out; more was expected from the English people because of unity of race and language and better knowledge; and besides, in France the emperor's will, and not public opinion, governed. (3) It undertook to test international duty by moral principles rather than by accepted political rules, and erred in assuming that the nations were bound to discriminate against the Confederacy on account of the immorality of its pro-slavery origin and basis. This criti-

[1] Senator Howe of Wisconsin wrote of it: "Such conciseness of statement, such fulness of research, such wealth of illustration, such iron logic, heated but unmalleable, I really do not think are to be found in any other oration, ancient or modern. . . . No single man has ever so grandly struggled against the barbaric tendencies of a frightfully debauched generation. I cannot certainly foresee the future; you may be worsted in this encounter, but I know the world will be better for it." The author of the letter did not then foresee that ten years later he was to take the lead in removing the senator thus praised from the chairmanship of the committee on foreign relations.

[2] Numerous extracts from opinions of the address are given in Works, vol. vii. pp. 474–492.

cism, so far as it was just, would apply equally well to Sumner's treatment of all law, international or municipal, statute or customary, which did not conform to his moral ideas.

The Address received wide attention in England.[1] It met, naturally enough, with intemperate criticism from the London "Times" and other journals which were supporting the Confederacy. The tone of newspapers which were in sympathy with our country was deprecatory. Such were the "Daily News," the "Scotsman," and the "Guardian" and "Examiner" of Manchester. Admitting the truth of much which he said, and bearing witness to his character and high aims, these friendly journals insisted that, from his position at home and his peculiar knowledge of the English people, he should have calmed rather than inflamed public feeling in his own country; that he did not take into account the exigencies of the British government and its essential neutrality, which had called out passionate complaints from the Confederates and led to the withdrawal of their emissary, Mason, from London;[2] that he laid undue stress on the *time* of the issue of the queen's proclamation of belligerency, which must at any rate have shortly come, and which had the sanction of our own treatment of the rebels as belligerents. As soon as the Address came to hand, Earl Russell commented upon it at a public dinner.[3] Sumner at one time contemplated a reply, but came to the conclusion that his lordship's comments were not of sufficient gravity to justify one.

The Address grieved sorely some of Sumner's dearest friends in England. The Argylls wrote with undiminished personal regard, but both sorrowing that he had treated England unfairly. The duchess wrote, September 22: "Alas that it has come to this, that you should have felt it right to charge England as you have done in a public assembly! Was the fire not hot enough already?" And in this and later letters she maintained her protest with justifications and apologies. The duke also in his letter of September 30 deprecated the Address for its probable

1 An edition of one thousand copies, printed in this country, was sent by the Union League Club to Mr. Dudley, United States consul at Liverpool, for distribution among members of Parliament. A French translation of the Address abridged appeared in Paris, and was commended in the "Siècle" by Henri Martin.

2 Mason took leave in a farewell, which was printed contemporaneously with these reviews.

3 At Blairgowrie, September 26.

effect in both countries, and defended Earl Russell. He wrote in an excellent spirit, rejoicing in our recent successes, saying: "Pray continue to write as freely as ever, and as you see I am now doing. I take all you say, never forgetting from whom it comes, and always trying to see matters as they may justly seem to you." Cobden questioned, in a friendly and temperate way, the wisdom of the Address,—particularly in its effect in making England appear in a worse light than France,[1] and in its omission to bring prominently forward the alliance in sentiment between the American people and the English masses, led by the intellect and moral and religious worth of the kingdom. A few English friends, and only a few, were not disturbed by the speech,—as T. B. Potter, who thought it "glorious," and Prof. F. W. Newman, who associated it as "an historical memorial side by side with the proclamation of freedom," promotive of peace, and by a timely warning stimulating the British Cabinet to stop the sailing of the Confederate armed steamers from English ports.

Notwithstanding the irritation which the Address produced in England, as well among the friends of our cause as among its enemies, its permanent effect was to open the eyes of the British people to our case, and to put the government in fear of future difficulty if unfriendly demonstrations were continued, and Confederate war-ships built in England were allowed to leave her ports. Already, before his Address, but without Sumner's knowledge at the time, the Cabinet had shown itself affected by the military results at Vicksburg and Gettysburg.[2] On September 8, two days before Sumner spoke, Earl Russell, who had refused a week before to interfere, announced to Mr. Adams that instructions had been issued to prevent the departure of the two Confederate rams from Liverpool.[3] This was the turning-point in the course of the Cabinet. Adams wrote to Seward, October 16, that "the government has within the past week adopted mea-

[1] W. E. Forster made the same criticism in a letter, October 13, 1863. Forster's "Life," by T. Wemyss Reed, vol. i. pp. 360, 561.

[2] Bright wrote to Sumner, September 11: "You will hear by this mail that the iron-clad steam rams are detained by the government; I believe there is no doubt of this. I suppose the changed position of your affairs has helped our foreign office to the decision they have come to. Lord Russell has just made a short speech at Dundee, and he has said nothing foolish, which shows that there is an opening of the eyes among our statesmen as to the prospects of your war."

[3] If Sumner had known of this change of action, the tone of some parts of his Address might have been different. Cobden wrote to him: "You were, I suspect, speaking under the impression that the iron-clad rams would be allowed to leave."

sures of a much more positive character than heretofore to stop the steam rams."

Sumner wrote to Lieber, September 15: —

"I was sorry not to see you [in New York]. But especially should I have been glad could I have had the advantage of your counsels on the many topics of fact, law, and history which I undertook to treat. I spoke on two accounts: First, because it seemed to me that the country needed light; that the people were groping from ignorance of what England had done, and also from ignorance of law and history applicable to our own case. And, secondly, I spoke in the hope of reaching France and England, — people and cabinets. To the latter I am personally known as a lover of peace, so that my austerity will mean more than the New York 'Herald.' The speech is stereotyping, and the plates will be all cast to-day, to be published in New York. Several of the points, I think, are new. I ask your particular attention to that about ocean belligerency, where, I think, I am impregnable. But if I am right, what a blunder-crime do I throw upon England! Seward writes me that he has read my speech 'without once stopping,' and that I have 'performed a very important public service.' . . . I had intended to speak without notes; but I found my brain, exhausted perhaps by labor, did not grapple with the text, so I read for the first time before such an audience. I was recalled to Boston to be near my poor dying brother. Greene is here to be with him."

Again, October 24: —

"It has not gone in England much differently from what I expected. I knew too well (1) the prejudices of country and (2) the prejudices of party to suppose that I could speak as plainly as I did without giving pain and perhaps exciting anger. All supporters of the government must be against me at present, while the fit is on them. Of the independent Liberals I was doubtful. Some I supposed would be with me, and some against me. Professor Newman, personally a stranger, writes me, full of thanks, and predicts that the speech must do great good; so also writes an eminent business man of Manchester. But you tell me that G. Smith is the other way. I am sorry; for I admire and honor him much, and should be proud of his sympathy. But I feel that the whole question, in all its bearings, was one which I was more competent to decide than my critics. I know England and America well, and I know the tendencies of my own country. On my conscience, after a constant and minute private correspondence on all the topics of my speech, I felt that the time had come when the case should be plainly stated to England by a friend who meant peace and not war. My speech was a warning, with a pleading for peace; but misconception and misrepresentation have planted in many persons a false idea of it."

Cobden wrote, October 8, expressing admiration for the masterly ability of the speech, but adding, however, on the score of policy, — "I was, I confess, rather beset with the feeling of *cui bono* after reading your powerful indictments against England and France together; it should have been your policy to have kept them asunder." To this letter Sumner replied, November 6, as follows:—

"I have your letter on my speech. Not for controversy, but for statement, I reply to your *cui bono:* (1) As regards my own country. People here had a right to expect from me a statement of the case. There was a feverish and indignant feeling against Great Britain, without much knowledge. The facts which I set forth, none of which can be questioned, are now accepted as an exhibition of what your government has done. The effect has been excellent; for the people now understand the points in discussion. Instead of exciting them, I think that speech allayed existing excitement, followed as it was by a change in England. (2) As regards England. It was important that your government and people should know how those in our country most friendly felt with regard to their conduct. For months we have done all that could be done, and Lord Russell down to the 9th of September[1] (I spoke the 10th of September) gave no hint that we should not have war; indeed, the inference from his course was that we should have war,—for the departure of those rams would have been tantamount to a declaration of war by Great Britain against the United States. For weeks before I spoke, bankers and leading business men had revealed to me their anxieties, and the agent of a great English house[2] had told me he could not venture to open credits. It was time that something was said openly and plainly. I knew too well the prejudices of country and of party not to see that such an exposition would draw down upon me abuse and misrepresentation. But it seemed clearly my duty, and I am glad I did it. I know England well, and I know my own country; being somewhat behind the scenes, too, I felt that I could judge what was needed, not to soothe for the moment, not to gratify personal feelings, but to secure the great object of my heart,—solid peace between our two countries. I have often told you that the tendency here will be to war just as soon as our rebellion is suppressed. My hope is that England will so far reconsider her course and fraternize with us that war will be impossible; but there can be no hope of this unless the truth is put before her plainly. It is painful to me on such a grave occasion to lose the sympathy of English friends, especially of those who have stood by us so well; but all that has occurred, and especially the smart of Lord Russell, shows the good that has been done. People who resent my accusations, and deny even their truth, will think twice before they give occasion for their repetition. Lord Russell will change his war policy,—I call it such, for it tended inevitably to war. But I have said too much on a personal matter. Let me add, in reply to your suggestion, that the frankness which the occasion required did not allow me to make the distinction which you suggested between England and France; both were offenders, and it was necessary to tell them so.

"Meanwhile our elections are for emancipation and the Union. Our armies are moving slowly,—too slowly; but no reverse can change the inevitable result, which is just as sure as the multiplication table,—how soon, I know not. Whiting has returned to cheer us with good news from England

[1] Speech at Dundee.
[2] The Barings.

that no more 'Alabamas' will be allowed to make England a naval base. He enjoyed his day with you. But Lord John and the attorney-general[1] insist upon defending the concession of belligerency on the ocean to rebel slave-mongers without a prize court. That folly shows that there is more work to be done. We are all agreed against that. Here is the first great offence; Evarts puts this as No. 1. To take back this bloody folly will be bad for your Cabinet; but sooner or later, in some way or other, it must be done."

To R. Schleiden, September 14: —

"Truly, Germany united would be a great power, with a great history; with an early romance and Heldenbuch, with Minnesingers and Reinecke Fuchs, with Luther and Albert Dürer, and then with Goethe and Schiller. I should like to see it a plural unit. Such a people — so numerous, so educated, so strong if united — must make a powerful and irresistible nation. If I were a German I should strive for this unity; therefore I enter into your solicitudes. But where does it all tend? Will unity be accomplished? And, still further, will it be a true, liberal, and just unity, not the compression of superior force?"

Again, November 2: —

"I enjoyed last evening the inauguration of our new organ[2] from Germany, not inferior in size, and it is said superior in tone, to any in the world. As I looked at its vast proportions, observed its massive columns of sound, and then again its smaller pipes, and then listened to the swelling, pealing melody which filled the immense hall, I said to myself, That organ is the image of Germany as it ought to be, with all its massive columns in place, and its smaller pipes also; while now our Deutschland is like these same columns and pipes all out of place, each trying to play for itself, and making perpetual discord. There are some who wish to see our American organ in the same unhappy German condition; but they will not be indulged. The organ will be reconstructed and cleaned; and until Germany learns the beauty of unity, it will be the first of the world.

"I hear how my friends in England are pained; I expected it all. But no more pert letters will be written by Lord Russell. Lord Palmerston is much more occupied in watching Louis Napoleon than watching the United States, — so a friend writes, who dined with him at Walmer Castle. Lord Brougham deplores my 'delusion.'"

Among Sumner's correspondents in this country who wrote to him concerning questions with England were the well-known lawyers and publicists, Theophilus Parsons, Charles G. Loring, and George Bemis, — all of whom were in general accord with his views, and took part in the public discussion. Of these, Mr. Bemis, who replied to "Historicus" (Sir William V. Har-

1 Sir Roundell Palmer at Richmond, Yorkshire, Oct. 15, 1863.

2 Placed in the Music Hall, Boston, but several years later removed.

court), was the most active and the best read. Sumner put confidence in his judgment and learning, and from this time often consulted him on questions with Great Britain.

One product of Sumner's vacation was a magazine article on Franklin's life in Paris as ambassador of our country, which began with tracing the pedigree of the famous line concerning him, "Eripuit coelo fulmen sceptrumque tyrannis," and gave sketches of Franklin's friends and contemporaries in France, with observations on the remarkable impression he made on the French people. It closed with a contrast between him and John Slidell, the Confederate emissary to the French emperor.[1]

Sumner became at this time a member of the Union Club, Park Street, then recently organized, and often took his dinners there for the rest of his life when he was in Boston. The year before, he was formally admitted to the Saturday Club,[2] whose membership included Emerson, Longfellow, Agassiz, Lowell, Benjamin Peirce, Motley, Whipple, Judge Hoar, Felton, Dr. Holmes, R. H. Dana, J. M. Forbes, and others.[3] He had been its guest before at times, but he now when in Boston dined regularly with it at Parker's on its club day, the last Saturday of the month. On other Saturdays he dined at times at Parker's, with a political club of which his friend F. W. Bird was the leader; but his frequent dining with this club belongs to a period three or four years later.

George Sumner, who had been smitten with paralysis two years before, died, October 6, at the Massachusetts General Hospital. Charles was with him daily after his return from Washington, except at the time of his address in New York, being then called home by the tidings of George's rapid decline. Longfellow and Dr. Howe were frequent visitors to their friend's room at the hospital, and George W. Greene came occasionally from his Rhode Island home. To Mrs. Waterston, Charles wrote, October 3: "I should have been to see you, and

1 Atlantic Monthly, November, 1863; Works, vol. viii. pp. 1–38. Slidell did not return to the United States; he died in London in 1871.

2 He dined with the Saturday Club April 27, 1861. Agassiz, referring to Longfellow's absence from the club since his wife's death, wrote to Sumner, Dec. 20, 1863: "Longfellow promised to come back to the club next Saturday. I wish you were with us; we shall drink your health. Answer in thought when you go to your dinner that day, the 26th of December."

3 This club is commemorated in Adams's "Biography" of Dana, vol. ii. pp. 162–170, 360.

also to Quincy, except that every evening I have been with my poor brother, who now is visibly passing away, so that I was obliged to forego all the gratification of society. During the last week my brother has failed constantly; he can no longer converse, but simply says a few words. It seems as if the thread of life cannot spin for many days, even if it can for hours." Charles was at the bedside at the final moment, and wrote the next day to Mr. Waterston: "My poor brother was at last released from his trials yesterday afternoon, and we shall bury him from my mother's house to-morrow at two o'clock precisely. You and Mrs. Waterston were always kind to him and to me. The funeral will be private; but I should be sorry if friends like you should not be informed of the time. If I could reach Mr. Josiah Quincy, I should let him know also." Of the five brothers, Charles alone remained; but his mother and his sister Julia were still living.

Sumner was pressed to address political meetings during the autumn in New England and the West. A letter of great urgency, signed by Senators Preston King and Harris, Thurlow Weed, Governor Morgan, and Hiram Barney, besought him to give several addresses in the State of New York; he was asked to preside at the Republican State convention in Massachusetts. These requests were declined, and engagements to deliver a lecture were given up on account of the critical condition of his brother's health.

## CHAPTER XLIX.

LETTERS TO EUROPE. — TEST OATH IN THE SENATE. — FINAL REPEAL OF THE FUGITIVE-SLAVE ACT.—ABOLITION OF THE COASTWISE SLAVE-TRADE. — FREEDMEN'S BUREAU. — EQUAL RIGHTS OF THE COLORED PEOPLE AS WITNESSES AND PASSENGERS. — EQUAL PAY OF COLORED TROOPS. — FIRST STRUGGLE FOR SUFFRAGE OF THE COLORED PEOPLE. — THIRTEENTH AMENDMENT OF THE CONSTITUTION. — FRENCH SPOLIATION CLAIMS. — TAXATION OF NATIONAL BANKS. — DIFFERENCES WITH FESSENDEN. — CIVIL SERVICE REFORM. — LINCOLN'S RE-ELECTION. — PARTING WITH FRIENDS. — 1863-1864.

THE following extracts are given from letters written by Sumner early in the session which began in December, 1863: —

To Mr. Bright, December 15: —

"I have just received the Manchester 'Examiner,' containing the speeches at Rochdale,[1] which I have read gratefully and admiringly. Cobden's positive testimony must tell for us; and let me add that I like him the better the nearer he gets to the position that recognition is a moral impossibility. If this were authoritatively declared, the case would soon be closed. It is because the gate is still left open that the public is vexed by constantly receiving reports that in the event of Federal reverses there will be recognition. No Federal reverse can be an apology for such a crime. . . . Our friends are confident; there are no doubters. Besides, the battle of 'ideas' has been fought in the last Congress; it only remains that we should carry forward the 'ideas' that have been adopted. . . . The most determined Abolitionists now are in the slave States; and naturally, for with them it is a death grapple! But how great and glorious will be this country when it is fully redeemed, and stands before the world without a slave, — an example of emancipation!"

To George Bemis, December 18: —

"I have received a visit of three hours from the French Minister,[2] in which he told me plumply that he thought now as at the beginning that the war must end in separation, and that France was ready at any time to offer her 'good offices' to bring about peace. When he said this I snapped my fingers. But does not this explain the precise policy of the emperor?"

[1] By Cobden and Bright.

[2] M. Mercier.

To Lieber, December 28: —

"Your German sky lowers with war. Can it be avoided? My letters assure me that Germany at last is a unit, and that it will stand by Schleswig-Holstein. Schleiden, who is very intelligent, is openly for war. He says that the connection of the provinces with Denmark must be cut. This is war. Motley writes from Vienna that in his opinion war is inevitable. Mercier leaves Washington to-day. *Inter nos*, he will tell the emperor that the Mexican expedition is a mistake, and that he ought to withdraw it; but that the national cause here is hopeless, and that the war will end in separation! This I have from his own lips."

To W. E. Gladstone, Jan. 1, 1864: —

"I begin the year with my acknowledgments of the kindness of your letter, and with my best wishes. A happy New Year to you and to your family! A happy New Year also to all England; for my heart is always with England. Winter has come, and our soldiers are preparing their huts for winter quarters. But I learn that General Grant will not go into winter quarters; he means to trouble the rebellion without giving it time to rest.[1] This is more practicable in the milder climate where he is than in Virginia, which is on the isothermal line of Crimea. But our politics seem to have something of the tranquillity of our neighboring army. Never since I have been in public life has there been so little excitement in Congress. The way seems at last open. Nobody doubts the result. The assurance of the future gives calmness.

"Some who come direct from General Grant declare that the war can be ended on the 4th July next. For myself, I have never seen when this war would be ended; for I was unable to estimate the courage and force the resistance might derive from foreign nations. But it has been clear to me always that there was but one way in which it could end; and I have felt sure that could foreign nations see it in its true light there could be no difference on the question. The rebellion is simply slavery in arms, making pretensions utterly without precedent in history, — revolting, indecent, impious. If the rebellion could in any way be distinguished from this crime, then it might have a chance of success. But I do not believe, I cannot believe, that in this nineteenth century a just Providence will allow such a crime to flourish, or will continue to it the favor of foreign powers. No reverse of arms, no failure or national misfortune, can shake this firm conviction. There have been gloomy days, and it has been hard to see friends cut off, so many victims to slavery supplied, and [the rebellion] encouraged from Europe; but my confidence has not been disturbed. It has often seemed to me that if we had failed, there must have been at the last moment a shudder in England at the awful responsibility of taking by the hand a bloody power, the co-mate of Dahomey; and that the English heart would have said, 'No! in the name of Heaven, no!' Meanwhile our own efforts have relieved England from any such final responsibility. But my heart yearns to see the country

[1] Sumner wrote to Lieber, Dec. 28, 1863: "Grant will continue active; he has a military genius."

that I love pronounce the word which will hasten the end of our domestic war, and make any foreign war impossible, — all of which is in her power. Rarely in history has any nation been so situated as to do so much for another nation and for civilization, to say nothing of the infinite profit to herself. I hope I do not write to you too frankly. I should not write so if I had less confidence in your sincerity and goodness.

"I have been pained to learn that the Duchess of Sutherland, whose kindness to me enabled me to see you whom I already honored much, is still ailing. I hope that her generous nature may be spared yet longer to soften and quicken our social life. I am sure that she will rejoice when slavery, now in arms, is cast down, never to rise again. I think she would be glad to help at this overthrow. The date of your letter (Hawarden) reminds me of a pleasant day which I can never forget."

To W. W. Story, Rome, January 1: —

"A happy New Year to you and yours! I think of you constantly, and always with affection, and vow letters. But my life is so crowded that I have found myself dropping correspondence that did not come under the head, if not of business, at least of public interest. The 'Psyche'[1] is superb, and I enjoy it much. You know the bronzes were lost on the coast of Spain. . . . Of course I watch your ascending glory. Nobody followed with intenser interest your English success, and now I am preparing for something grander; for George R. Russell tells me that your 'Saul' is the finest statue he ever saw. The time will come when all you have done will be recognized. . . . I am vexed that the Quincy statue[2] is not on its way to a pedestal. It ought to be set up while the hero yet continues among us. . . . Shortly before leaving home I walked through the grounds of the old house[3] in Cambridge where I enjoyed so much. It was marked 'To let.' The past all came back, and I was filled with a pleasing melancholy. Longfellow was with me, and we talked of your father and of you. . . . You have now another minister at Rome,[4] — a pleasing gentleman, with whom I think you will mingle more cordially than with any other on the list. I counselled against any minister in Rome;[5] but if one was to be appointed I declared you to be able to do us the most good. But Massachusetts has already more than her quota according to the proportions in which offices are distributed. . . . This will be a free country. Be its sculptor. Give us — give mankind — a work which will typify or commemorate a redeemed nation. . . . After a painful illness, my only surviving brother, George, has gone, leaving me more than ever alone. My mother is infirm, and my sister is in California. God bless you, dear William! Give my love to Emmeline and Edith, of whom I hear brilliant things."

1 A copy of the antique, for which Sumner had given Story a commission.

2 The committee in Boston, who gave Story the commission, did not raise the necessary funds; but the statue was in 1878 placed in Sanders Theatre at Cambridge, through a bequest of George Bemis.

3 Judge Story's.

4 General Rufus King, of Wisconsin, 1814-1876.

5 For the sake of Italian unity, Sumner wished to have diplomatic relations with the Vatican discontinued, and on that view, at a later date, had the appropriation for the mission omitted.

To Samuel Wilberforce, Bishop of Oxford, February 5: —

"I cannot receive any message of friendship from England, especially from one who was always so kind to me, and, more than all, who bears such relations to the cause which is so dear to me, without confessing how much it touches me. Embracing with my whole heart the hope for peace between our two homes, and happy in every word which helps the removal of slavery, or which shows that this end is sincerely sought, I was glad to hear through an admirable friend[1] that you still thought kindly of me, and had not allowed the perplexities of an unparalleled contest to weaken your interest in the cause of the slave. I have always hoped most earnestly that our English friends would at last see this terrible battle in its true light, and that the generous, noble sympathies which in times past have been bestowed on efforts against African slavery would be given to those who slowly, reluctantly, and sorrowfully have taken the sword in self-defence against this iniquity. From all that we hear, it seems as if the cloud which hung over England is passing away. God be praised!

"I know not when this war will end; but I have long seen that it can end only in one way. It cannot be in the order of Providence that African slavery, rebel and belligerent, drenched with slaughter and smeared with blood, shall be welcomed and embraced by any civilized power, least of all by one which has grown great and glorious under the teachings of your name. In this trust I follow the fortunes of the rebel war waged against the national government with all the bad passions of slavery, — sad enough that we have been summoned to such a trial, very sad at times that our burden has been so much increased by misunderstanding abroad, but always taking counsel of my hopes, of the lessons of justice, and of the ways of Providence to man. There is a day sure to come which must make you happy and triumphant; it is when African slavery is extinguished. Then at last shall we be of one mind."

To Rev. John Douglass, Pittsburg, January 22:[2] —

"Duties will keep me here, so that I cannot be with you to listen to the arguments and counsels by which you will inaugurate your new movement. Let me say frankly that I know not if it be practicable to accomplish all the change in the Constitution which you propose; but I am sure that the discussion cannot be otherwise than advantageous. It can never be out of season to explain and enforce mortal dependence on Almighty God, or to declare the liberty and equal rights of all men, — in other words, to assert the Fatherhood of God and the brotherhood of man. Here are the two great commandments which no Christian can forget. In one is the duty and grace of piety, and in the other the duty and grace of humanity."

[1] The Duchess of Argyll.

[2] This letter was written in reply to a request for the senator's opinion as to the propriety of an amendment of the Constitution recognizing the Supreme Being, afterwards called for by a meeting held at Allegheny, Penn., Jan. 27, 1864. (New York "Tribune," Feb. 1, 1864.) Sumner's answer disturbed some of his Hebrew friends, who expressed their dissent in letters to him. John Sherman approved, Feb. 8, 1869, in the Senate such recognition.

To Frank Ballard, Dec. 29, 1864: —

"I am astonished at what you say of my favoring any proposition to disfranchise anybody. It is all an invention or misapprehension. I have said that I should not object to a recognition of God by formal words in the Constitution, — thus, for instance, saying, 'We, the people of the United States, acknowledging God as the ruler of nations,' etc. This is all; I take it no Hebrew would differ with me on this point. The President had a clause in this sense prepared for his last message; but it was abandoned lest it might embarrass the other constitutional amendment. But you can quiet your Hebrew associates with regard to me."

Loyalty in the Civil War was tested by what was known as "the iron-clad oath," prescribed by Act of Congress, July 2, 1862, under which all persons in the civil and military service were required to take an oath which affirmed past loyalty, as well as pledged future allegiance to the government. At the special session in March, 1863, and at the regular session, which began in December of the same year, Sumner contended that this statute applied to senators.[1] He and other Republican senators took the oath voluntarily; but as the Democratic senators maintained that the Act did not apply to members of Congress, and declined to take it, Sumner moved and carried a rule of the Senate requiring senators to take this oath; he also introduced and carried a bill requiring it of attorneys appearing in the courts of the United States. As usual in such debates Sumner was reminded — this time by Hendricks and Garrett Davis[2] — that he had been disloyal in his course upon the rendition of fugitive slaves; and he met the familiar thrust by distinguishing between "refusing to play the part of a slave-hunter" and "joining in rebellion against his country."

This session was signalized by the absolute repeal of the Fugitive Slave Act, which more than any other event had brought Sumner into public life, and which he had made ineffectual efforts to have repealed ever since he entered the Senate. He moved, Jan. 13, 1864, a special committee on slavery and freedmen, and became its chairman. His Republican associates were Howard of Michigan, Pomeroy of Kansas, Gratz Brown of Missouri, and Conness of California. He introduced a bill to repeal all fugitive-slave acts, which was referred to the committee; and its first report was a bill for the repeal, accompanied by an

[1] March 5, 1863; Jan. 25, 1864. Works, vol. viii. pp. 53–72.

[2] Davis said, Jan. 13, 1864, that Sumner, when he took his oath, had "treason in his heart and upon his lips." The same reminder came from Davis in the debate of Feb. 19, 1868, on the right of Philip F. Thomas to a seat in the Senate.

elaborate argument against the constitutionality, of the fugitive-slave legislation of Congress.[1] The bill encountered not only Democratic opposition, led by Buckalew, Hendricks, and Reverdy Johnson, but also resistance from a number of Republican senators, led by Sherman and Foster, who sought to save the statute of 1793. Sherman's amendment, excluding this early statute from repeal, — legislation which in his view was constitutional and preserving the rights of the Southern States, — prevailed, April 19, by a vote of twenty-four to seventeen, several Republicans voting affirmatively.[2] Sumner still wished the bill carried, notwithstanding its exclusion of the Act of 1793 from repeal; but Brown and Conness of his committee refused to support it after the amendment had passed, and it was laid aside. Two months later, however, a bill as broad as the one reported by Sumner's committee passed the House and reached the Senate. Sumner reported this bill promptly from his committee, and resolutely pressed its consideration against dilatory motions and appeals for the substitution of other business. Saulsbury wanted "one day without the nigger." Reverdy Johnson pleaded the absence of Davis, who desired to speak. A contest of physical endurance was at hand. The end was reached June 23, when, after Davis's speech, the Senate, reversing its former action, refused to save the Act of 1793, — some Republicans who had opposed its repeal changing their votes, and others not voting. The repeal of both Acts was then consummated by a vote of twenty-seven to twelve. The nays were mostly Democrats; but among Republicans, Collamer, Doolittle, Foster, and Sherman withheld their votes. President Lincoln signed the bill on the 28th.[3]

Sumner wrote to Mrs. Child: —

"The repeal of all fugitive-slave acts is of immense importance for us abroad;[4] but its practical importance at home is not great, except that every blow at slavery is practically important, so that it is difficult to measure it."

[1] Feb. 29, 1864: Works, vol. viii. pp. 118-175. Sumner took the radical ground in the report that the clause in the Constitution relating to persons "held to service or labor" did not apply to fugitive slaves. (*Ante*, p. 392.) Lieber questioned in a letter this peculiar interpretation, and Sumner replied to him at length, March 14 and 17, 1864, maintaining that on the principle of the "Somerset" case slavery was so odious and contrary to natural right that it could not be legalized or recognized by inference or indirect language.

[2] Sumner's deep regret at this result is expressed in his letter, April 23, 1864, printed in W. L. Garrison's "Life," vol. iv. p. 118.

[3] Full notes to Sumner's Works (vol. viii. pp. 403-406, 415-418) state the final proceedings in detail.

[4] Earl Russell stated in the House of Lords, April 29, 1864, that the retention of this Act had repelled sympathy for the federal cause.

Sumner's first motion to repeal the Fugitive Slave Act was made Aug. 26, 1852, when it received only three votes besides his own. His second motion for the repeal was made July 31, 1854, when ten senators voted for it; and his third was made Feb. 23, 1855, when nine senators voted for it.[1] After a struggle of twelve years his courage and pertinacity prevailed. He said in debate, April 19, 1864: —

> "Often, in other times, I have discussed these questions in the Senate and before the people; but the time for discussion is passed. And permit me to confess my gladness in this day. I was chosen to the Senate for the first time immediately after the passage of the infamous Act of 1850. If at that election I received from the people of Massachusetts any special charge, it was to use my best endeavors to secure the repeal of this atrocity. I began the work in the first session that I was here. God grant that I may end it to-day!"

Sumner succeeded at this session in carrying what he had proposed in 1862, — the abolition of the coastwise slave-trade, now left, as he said, "the last support of slavery on the statute-book." He had reported a bill for the purpose, but as it could not be reached in due course, he availed himself, as in other instances, of the appropriation bill, moving his bill as an amendment to it, and fortifying himself against the objection of irrelevancy with precedents, — among them his own amendment for the repeal of the Fugitive Slave Act in 1852, which Mr. Hunter, then in charge of the bill, did not object to as untimely.[2] Hendricks, as a thrust at Republican senators, expressed surprise that any one should oppose the senator's proposition on the ground of materiality, or want of connection with the pending bill, as he had succeeded in similar cases before, and would do so eventually in this; and so it proved. His amendment, lost at one stage, prevailed when he renewed the effort at another, and became law. Collamer was his hearty coadjutor in the debate, replying to Reverdy Johnson. Sherman and Trumbull, wishing "to keep legislative matter off the appropriation bill," voted against the amendment.

The advance of our armies had brought within our lines great numbers of negroes, formerly slaves; and individuals and associations interested in their welfare pressed on Congress the importance of a special department in the government charged with the duty of aiding and protecting them during the transi-

[1] *Ante*, vol. iii. pp. 303, 304, 393, 412.
[2] June 24 and 25. Works, vol. ix. pp. 30-38.

tion period. The House passed, March 1, 1864, a bill, reported by Eliot of Massachusetts, which established a freedmen's bureau under the war department. Sumner's committee, to which it was referred in the Senate, reported his substitute, which placed it under the treasury department, already charged with the abandoned lands in the insurrectionary districts, which were at the time, or likely to be hereafter, largely occupied by the freedmen.[1] The Democrats in both Houses were as a body opposed to any bureau, and there was more or less distrust of the measure among Republicans.[2] Sumner pressed it with his characteristic pertinacity, and it was carried, June 28, by a vote of twenty-one to nine, with a number of Republican absentees. Among those not voting was Grimes, whose argument implied distrust of the scheme in any shape. He had confined himself in debate to objections, mostly captious, to some provisions, and to strained interpretations of others, contending also that the powers of supervision, instead of protecting the negroes, would promote their continued subjection. He and Sumner had many spirited encounters, and Grimes's temper and manner at times reminded spectators that he had not forgotten the heats of a former debate, when Sumner resisted his bill for the issue of letters of marque and reprisal. The burden of defending the bill, both as to its substance and details, fell mostly on Sumner; and observers noted his alertness on the floor, and his capacity for a running debate, which had developed with him as with other Republican senators under the responsibilities of government.

The House did not proceed with the bill at this session; but at the next, in February, 1865, a committee of conference, of which Sumner was a member, reported a bill creating an independent "department of freedmen and abandoned lands." This passed the House, but Sumner was unable to carry it in the Senate, where Hale of New Hampshire and Lane of Indiana now joined Grimes in opposition. On the last day of the session another committee of conference agreed on a bill which placed

1 Eliot thought, and so expressed himself in letters to Sumner, that the House bill having passed by a narrow majority should not have been hazarded by amendments in the Senate, and the New York "Tribune," April 12, 1864, as well as Sumner's correspondents, — John Jay, Charles E. Norton, John M. Forbes, and E. L. Pierce, — took the same view; but Sumner's reply was that his committee was adverse to the House bill, he being one of the only two members who had sustained it in committee.

2 Horace Greeley wrote Sumner, Feb. 7, 1865, in opposition to the measure.

the bureau in the war department, limited its term to one year after the war, and reduced its scope. In this form it passed without debate or division, and was one of the last acts approved by Mr. Lincoln. General O. O. Howard was appointed commissioner. The bureau became a distinctive part of Republican policy, and a year later it was found necessary to enlarge its powers, and strike out the limitation of its term, by a bill which passed Congress over President Johnson's veto. The bureau was maintained till Jan. 1, 1869, and did good service as "a bridge from slavery to freedom." [1]

Sumner kept up continuously the contest for civil equality which he began in the session of 1861-1862. The street railway companies of the District of Columbia provided special cars for colored people, and excluded them from all others; and the exclusion was rigidly enforced under circumstances involving inconvenience, discomfort, and humiliation to those people. Sumner attacked the discrimination as a whole and in detail, taking advantage of applications for charters, and even of general acts, to which his propositions were hardly relevant. He had little active support among his associates; but few of them cared to record themselves when brought to the issue in favor of race prejudice and a relic of slavery. Among the statesmen of the time he was the one who pressed the cause of the colored people, their absolute equality of right, in season, and as many thought out of season, deaf to considerations of expediency, heedless of antipathy, undismayed by obstruction or defeat, unwearied and aggressive to the last. His efforts at the first regular session after the war began have been mentioned.[2] At the next — calling attention to an exclusion under distressing circumstances which had recently occurred — he procured an amendment to a charter for a street railway between Washington and Alexandria, forbidding discrimination on account of color in the carriage of passengers. The amendment passed by only one majority, several of the Republican senators — Anthony, Howe, and Lane among them — voting against it.[3] It was concurred in by the House, and became part of the Act of March 3, 1863. At the session now under review, he carried the same amendment to two charters, succeeding after spirited contests by a small majority in each case, — defeated at one stage and pre-

[1] Works, vol. viii. pp. 475-524; Wilson's "History of the Rise and Fall of the Slave Power." vol. iii. pp. 455-504.

[2] *Ante*, p. 72.

[3] Feb. 27, 1863. Congressional Globe, p. 1328.

vailing at a later one.[1] The opposition of Saulsbury, Powell, and Willey abounded in ribaldry. Republican senators — Trumbull, Sherman, Doolittle, and Grimes, as well as Reverdy Johnson — contended that an express prohibition was superfluous, as the exclusion was already forbidden by the common law; but this contention overlooked the opposite practice and judicial view prevailing in the slave and also in some of the free States. Sherman objected on the ground of the embarrassment to which the proprietors of the railway would be subjected. Sumner reminded Trumbull that the argument of supererogation had not bound him at other times, as he had advocated the Wilmot Proviso, although it only affirmed what was already law under a true view of the Constitution. To Grimes, now prone to oppose what Sumner urged, who asked what advantage would accrue from the amendment to the colored people, who would still be compelled to go to law to enforce it, Sumner answered: "The company will not dare to continue this outrage in the face and eyes of a positive provision of statute; that is the answer."

These prohibitions in special statutes did not, however, cover the ground, and the question kept recurring. At the next session, Jan. 17, 1865, Sumner moved his amendment to an Act incorporating another company, and Democratic senators alone voted against it. Foster and Sherman now joined him, and Grimes and Trumbull did not vote. A few days later he carried a general provision, forbidding exclusions on account of color on the railways of the District of Columbia, in the shape of an amendment to a bill amending the charter of an existing company, overcoming the objection made by Dixon, Conness, and Hale that his proposition was irrelevant, — and, as was often the case, failing at one stage of the bill, and at another, as the reward of his pertinacity, carrying his amendment. This Act took effect March 3;[2] but as one of the companies maintained

[1] Feb. 10, 25, March 16, 17, June 21, 1864; Works, vol. viii. pp. 103-117. The amendment was rejected, June 21, by fourteen to sixteen, — Foster, Grimes, Sherman, and Trumbull voting nay; but moved again by Sumner on the same day, it passed by a vote of seventeen to sixteen.

[2] Sumner treated the exclusion of colored persons from the ordinary railway carriages as a corporate malfeasance, even at common law, and before the statute of March 3 took effect sought, Feb. 20, 1865, the repeal of the charter of a company which enforced the exclusion. (Congressional Globe, pp. 915, 916.) He called attention in the Senate, Feb. 10 and 17, 1868 (Globe, pp. 1071, 1204), to a similar denial of right. He sought in the session of 1869-1870 the repeal of the charter of a medical society in Washington because of its exclusion of colored physicians as members. Dec. 9, 1860, Works, vol. xiii. pp. 186-188; March 4, 1870, Globe, pp. 1677, 1678.

the exclusion in defiance of the statute, the senator notified its managers of his purpose to move the forfeiture of its charter, and further, made a formal complaint against them to the law-officer of the District. This ended the contest, and from that time all the cars on street railways in the District were as free to one race as to the other.

Sumner had in 1862 secured the competency of colored persons as witnesses in the District of Columbia, but failed then to prevent their exclusion in other national tribunals, which, according to the practice, followed in the States the local laws, then excluding in the former slave States the testimony of such persons. He now introduced, Feb. 8, 1864, a bill to prohibit the discrimination in all the courts of the United States, and later reported it from the committee on slavery and freedmen, with an elaborate argument in its favor, which reviewed the statutes and decisions of the slave States, noted the history of the exclusion of witnesses in other countries, and set forth the injustice and irrational character of a disability imposed on the ground of color.[1] A few days before making the report he had advocated the inclusion of the prohibitory provision in a bill authorizing colored persons to carry the mails.[2] Failing to get his bill before the Senate, he moved it as an amendment to an appropriation bill, making a brief speech in its favor, and pressing it against the appeal of senators, who feared that any new impediment to the bill so late in the session would peril it.[3] Again his pertinacity prevailed, notwithstanding the reasonable objection that his amendment was not germane. He regarded this law, securing equality in the courts, as the most important of all in establishing the manhood and citizenship of the colored people. In the following August he wrote to Mrs. Child: "Among all the measures concerning slavery which have prevailed at the late session, I regard as first in practical value the overthrow of the rule excluding colored testimony. For this result I have labored two years."

The rate of pay for colored troops, particularly those enlisted for Massachusetts regiments, became a subject of controversy which involved a question of construction, — whether they were to be paid thirteen dollars a month, like other soldiers, or only

1 February 29, Works, vol. viii. pp. 176–216.

2 February 26, 29, Congressional Globe, pp. 837, 838, 868.

3 June 25, Works, vol. ix. pp. 39–46.

ten, under the Act of July 17, 1862, which provided the smaller sum for persons of African descent employed under it. The Secretary of War, confirming an opinion of Mr. Whiting, the solicitor of that department, placed them under this Act; but Governor Andrew strenuously contended that they came under the general acts which determined the pay of enlisted men, and should be paid equally with other soldiers. He, as well as Sumner, urged the secretary to rectify his action, but without avail; and Stanton became very impatient under their persistency. The question was then carried into Congress, on a joint resolution reported by Wilson. The Senate was favorable to equality of pay; but Fessenden and some other senators were indisposed to a retrospective provision.[1] Finally the controversy, after lasting for some months, was settled by a reference to the attorney-general, Mr. Bates, who decided in favor of the claim of the colored troops to equality of pay. Many letters on the subject passed between Governor Andrew and Sumner, and the former thanked the senator for his "constant advocacy" of a just measure. Neither Stanton nor Whiting intended injustice to the colored troops; but the different statutes raised a doubt which they gave in favor of the government, while fuller discussion led the attorney-general to an opposite conclusion.

At this session began the controversy in Congress concerning the suffrage of colored persons. The occasion was a bill providing a government for the Territory of Montana. The Senate struck out the discrimination of color; but the House, where the Republican majority was not large, insisted upon retaining it. After two committees of conference, the Senate yielded by a vote of twenty-six to thirteen. Some Republicans were influenced by the consideration that the issue was not a practical one, as there were no negroes in the Territory, and others probably were hampered by the existence of a similar discrimination in their own States. Sumner was very earnest in the discussion, and on two different days contended against the exclusion of colored men from suffrage.[2] To the objection that the question was not a practical one, he replied: "But it is said that there are no persons in the new Territory to whom the principle is now applicable. This can make no difference. It is something to declare a principle; and I cannot hesitate to say that at this moment the

[1] Feb. 10, 29, and June 11, 1864. Works, vol. viii. pp. 84–102.
[2] March 31 and May 19, 1864. Works, vol. viii. pp. 236–243.

principle is much more important than the bill. The bill may be postponed, but the principle must not be postponed." One incident of the debate was an encounter, sharp but friendly, between Sumner and Reverdy Johnson as to the merits of the Dred Scott decision, — "an atrocious judgment," as Sumner called it, — in which Johnson bore witness to his personal regard for Sumner, and the courtesy he had received from him.[1]

Sumner struggled hard at the same session, in the consideration of two bills amending the city charter, to include the colored people among the electors of the city of Washington; but the Senate was deaf to his entreaties, even rejecting the inclusion of colored soldiers.[2] Those like Morrill of Maine, Grimes, and Wade, who thought the proposition untimely, and those who were opposed to it altogether, made the majority. His own colleague was among those whom he could not persuade. Sumner, in protesting against the exclusion of the colored people from the suffrage, said: "At this moment of revolution, when our country needs the blessing of Almighty God and the strong arms of all her children, this is not the time for us solemnly to enact injustice. In duty to our country and in duty to God, I plead against any such thing. We must be against slavery in its original shape, and in all its brood of prejudice and error." Four years later, in the Senate, Mr. Doolittle, distinguishing Sumner from his colleague Wilson, who had at the beginning taken an opposite view, said of Sumner that he had "always been in favor of pushing negro suffrage; he was the originator of that notion; he is the master of that new school of reconstruction." [3]

Public opinion in the free States was now calling for a universal prohibition of slavery. Sumner presented the petition of the Women's National League, with one hundred thousand signatures, praying for an Act of Congress emancipating all persons of African descent in the United States, and he commended it in brief remarks.[4] A constitutional prohibition, however, could

[1] Sumner recalled in this debate his early association with Marshall. *Ante*, vol. i. pp. 124, 125.

[2] May 12, 26, 27, 28, 1864. Works, vol. viii. pp. 458-469.

[3] June 6, 1868, Congressional Globe, p. 2898. Sherman in the debate, Feb. 10, 1870 (Globe, p. 1181), put Sumner as the very first in the Senate to advocate and maintain the necessity of giving to the colored people of the Southern States the right to vote.

[4] Feb. 9, 1864. Works, vol. viii. pp. 80-83.

be the only sure method which would secure the end. On his way to Washington in December, when the session was about to begin, Sumner sketched to Henry C. Wright, a fellow-passenger between Fall River and New York, the form of a petition for an amendment of the Constitution declaring that "slavery shall be forever prohibited within the limits of the United States." Two days later, Mr. Wright procured its adoption at a meeting of the American Antislavery Society in Philadelphia, and this is supposed to have been the first public movement for the thirteenth amendment.[1]

Early in the session resolutions for such an amendment were proposed by Ashley of Ohio and Wilson of Iowa in the House, and by Henderson of Missouri in the Senate. Sumner himself offered two forms. He moved a reference of the subject to his own committee on slavery and freedmen, but yielded to Trumbull's suggestion that it belonged more properly to the committee on the judiciary, expressing as his chief desire that prompt action should be taken. Trumbull, adopting the formula of the Ordinance of 1787, reported as the proposed amendment that "neither slavery nor involuntary servitude, except as a punishment for crime, whereof the party shall have been duly convicted, shall exist within the United States, or any place subject to their jurisdiction." Sumner preferred a scientific to a traditional form, and thought the one reported to imply a sanction of slavery as a punishment of crime, — a penalty deemed humane at the time of the Ordinance, but now discarded.[2] His own substitute provided that "all persons are equal before the law, so that no person can hold another as a slave;" and later he suggested as another form, "Slavery shall not exist anywhere within the United States." Trumbull could not see why Sumner "should be so pertinacious about particular words," and Howard objected to the latter's formula as more French than American. Sumner, on appeal from Trumbull, withdrew his proposition, though afterwards regretting that he had not insisted on the striking out of the words which, as he thought, implied a sanction of slavery as a punishment of crime. He

[1] Works, vol. viii. p. 351. H. C. Wright's letter to Sumner in manuscript, May 17, 1866.

[2] The proposed sale of negro convicts in Maryland was an occasion of his subsequently recurring to his criticism of the form of the amendment. (In the Senate, Jan. 3 and Feb. 20, 1867, Works, vol. xi. pp. 54-58.) He also initiated, Jan. 3, 1867 (Works, vol. xi. pp. 52, 53), a prohibition of peonage in New Mexico.

addressed the Senate in favor of the amendment,[1] and the same day it passed by a two-thirds vote. Among those who supported it ably in debate was Reverdy Johnson. The success of the amendment in that body was assured; and Sumner's speech took a wide range, — touching upon various topics concerning slavery, its illegality under the Constitution as it was, the impropriety of compensating slave-owners, judicial perversions of the Constitution, and historical affirmations of equality before the law. While supporting the amendment *ex majore cautela*, he believed that slavery no longer existed *de jure*, and that the judiciary or Congress was competent to affirm the fact. He was troubled by the uncertainty of the fate of the amendment, and was not disposed to waive the right to a summary treatment of the question. He said, "Nothing against slavery can be unconstitutional," — a phrase which showed his disposition to treat morally rather than judicially legal and constitutional questions.[2] He said in debate, Jan. 5, 1865, on another bill: "I cannot close without declaring again my opinion that Congress at this moment is complete master of the whole subject of slavery everywhere in the United States, even without any constitutional amendment."[3] The amendment failing in the House at this session was carried in the next, in January, 1865; but it was not till December 18 of that year that it received the assent of a sufficient number of States, and was proclaimed a part of the Constitution.[4]

The passage of antislavery measures which Sumner pushed was attributed to his "acknowledged leadership" in the Senate, and they would have failed "under the direction of any senator less tenacious in his convictions of public duty, or less capable of enforcing them by argument." He compelled associates who were at heart opposed to them and sought to evade them to come to their support in the end, forcing them to go on record until they yielded. Under such pressure they changed their votes or withdrew to the lobby, fearing that their positions at home would be endangered with antislavery constituents who put

[1] April 8, 1864. Works, vol. viii. pp. 347–401.

[2] Sumner moved, July 1, 1864, the adoption of the Proclamation of Emancipation as a statute, proposing it as an amendment to the reconstruction bill; but it was lost. (Works, vol. ix. pp. 47–50.) He had already reported his proposed amendment as a bill.

[3] Works, vol. ix. p. 197.

[4] Sumner maintained in resolutions, Feb. 4, 1865, that only the States *de facto*, excluding those controlled by the rebellion, should be counted as a part of the whole number. Works, vol. ix. pp. 233–235.

their faith in this early and indomitable leader of their cause. Observers by no means in sympathy with the measures themselves recognized Sumner's power over reluctant associates as "a new illustration of the supremacy fairly achieved by those who wish strongly where they wish at all."[1] It is best, however, to note in this connection that senators whose votes had been thus forced naturally chafed under this kind of discipline, and some of them bore from that time a grudge which they were to wreak when the opportunity came.

Sumner's associates in the Senate, even those of antislavery convictions, were at times weary with his constant urging of antislavery measures; and his persistency in that direction encountered some criticism in journals of his own party. Some thought that there was a loss of moral power in dividing the attention between different measures instead of putting the whole force into a constitutional provision. Others, however, believed, and this was his own view, that the agitation of particular measures advanced public opinion in Congress and the country, and prepared the way for a comprehensive amendment of the Constitution, while at the same time they insured beyond recall, as far as they went, the liberties and rights of the colored people. Speaking at the next session in favor of Wilson's bill freeing colored soldiers and their families, he replied to Sherman, who desired to have it wait for action on "the main proposition," — the constitutional amendment to abolish slavery, — "the main proposition is to strike slavery wherever you can hit it."[2]

William Lloyd Garrison wrote to Sumner from Boston, June 26, 1864: —

"My sojourn in Washington was much to see you and some others to the extent I desired; but I wish to express to you my thanks for your very kind attentions, and the great pleasure I felt on seeing you in your seat in the Senate chamber, — a seat which you have filled with so much personal and historic credit to yourself, and which can have no better successor in the long hereafter. The part you have taken in consummating those great Congressional measures, — the recognition of the independence of Hayti and Liberia, the anti-slave-trade treaty with Great Britain, the abolition of slavery in the District of Columbia, the consecration of all the Territories to freedom, the enrolment of negro soldiers for the suppression of the rebellion, the repeal of the fugitive-slave bill, etc., — has been as important to the country as honor-

[1] National Intelligencer, July 9, 1864.

[2] Jan. 5, 1865. Works, vol. ix. pp. 193-197. The bill became a law March 3, 1865.

able to yourself. A review of your senatorial career must at all times give you the deepest satisfaction, in that you have constantly endeavored to serve the cause of liberty and to extol the character of the republic in every possible way."

Sumner's devotion to questions concerning slavery seemed quite enough to fill his entire time; but his researches and labors in other lines of discussion and business were by themselves equal to those of senators who were deemed faithful and industrious. It was perhaps the most arduous session in which he served, and his friends feared that the excessive strain would bring back his old malady. The work of the two committees of which he was chairman fell wholly upon him, and he diverged from these specialties to take up many other topics which invited investigation. He wrote to Lieber, February 14: —

"I am tired. At this moment I have two important questions, — first, the capitalization of the duties paid by our commerce on the Scheldt, on which I expect to speak to-day in executive session; and secondly, a bill to pay five millions for French spoliations, on which I am now drawing a report. To these add business of all kinds, and the various questions of slavery and of England, and I wish for a day of rest."[1]

At this as also at the preceding session Sumner reported a bill for the payment of the "French Spoliation Claims," which had been pressed on Congress from the beginning of the century, — meeting generally the favor of committees, sometimes passing one House and failing in the other; twice passing both Houses, and then arrested by the Executive veto. He now took up the subject anew, making an exhaustive report, which traced the history and maintained the justice and equity of the claims.[2] The research and treatment of this subject alone would have been thought a good session's work for most public men.[3] It was, however, an investigation very congenial to Sumner. He wrote Lieber, March 17: "I go home to work at my report on French spoliations. I am struck by the scrubs of the French Directory; but especially by the magnificent ability of Talleyrand, whose reply to our commissioners is a masterpiece. He

1 Lord Lyons said to him at this time, "You do take good care of my treaties." One of them related to the Hudson Bay Company and Puget Sound.

2 April 4, 1864. Works, vol. viii. pp. 244–346.

3 It fills nearly one hundred and fifty pages of the report, and one hundred pages of Sumner's Works.

was then only a beginner." The report was strongly commended by Reverdy Johnson, who spoke in favor of the printing of extra copies. It called out letters of hearty approval from Edward Everett and Caleb Cushing, who when in Congress, as members of committees, had made reports in favor of the measure.[1] It stands to this day as the authoritative exposition of this case of long-deferred justice. The Senate committee on foreign relations adopted it twice afterwards (in 1867 and 1870), while Sumner was chairman; and again in 1882 and 1884 it was annexed for information to brief reports made in one or both Houses. The measure finally prevailed in 1885, and the payment of the claims began in 1891.

In a carefully prepared speech Sumner treated in the light of history and foreign examples the subject of coinage, with special reference to the question between one and several mints, and favored, on account of the extent of the country, a branch mint in Oregon.[2] The measure was carried in the Senate against the finance committee (Fessenden chairman) and advice from the departments.

At this session the national bank and currency system, established the year before and still hardly under way, underwent a radical transformation, and a new Act of Congress was substituted for the first one. There was a positive difference of opinion as to the propriety of allowing the States to tax their stock or shares, — some contending that it was unjust to the States to withdraw or "sequester" an immense amount of capital from liability to contribute to local revenues, and others contending that it was hazardous to subject the instruments and machinery of the national government to State control. The former were disposed also to a policy which would save the State banks; while the latter, for the sake of a uniform system, preferred that they should pass away. Henry Winter Davis, Samuel Hooper, and Justin S. Morrill, in the House, supported the Secretary of the Treasury in the policy of exempting the banks from State taxation and of subjecting them only to national taxation; but they failed to carry that body with them. Their view, however,

[1] The "National Intelligencer" of May 17, 1864, described the report as "very able and elaborate," and containing "a thorough and exhaustive discussion of the question." Among correspondents who expressed their satisfaction with it was James B. Murray, of New York, the last surviving member of a committee appointed in that city fifty years before to urge on Congress the payment of the claims.

[2] April 29, 1864. Works, vol. viii. pp. 437–451.

was that of persons who were conservative and experienced in financial matters. Fessenden, chairman of the Senate committee on finance, gave however his adhesion to the principle of State taxation in a proposition to allow the States to tax the market value of the shares. Sumner was very decided against subjecting the banks to State taxation, and proposed as a substitute a rate of taxation exclusively imposed by Congress. He entered earnestly into the debate on different days,[1] maintaining that the exemption of the national banks from local taxation and interference was essential to the working of the new system and to the support of the public credit at a critical period. His amendment[2] was lost; but he was supported by Chandler of Michigan, Conness, Howard, Lane of Indiana, Pomeroy, Ramsey, Sherman, Sprague, Wilkinson, and Wilson. Sumner received unstinted praise from Chandler, a banker by profession, who testified in debate to "the debt of gratitude which the country owed to the senator from Massachusetts for his patriotism and statesmanship," and pronounced his speech of May 5 to be "one of the ablest financial arguments ever delivered" in that body.

An incident of the debate cannot well be passed over, — a collision between Fessenden and Sumner, one of their early unpleasant encounters. Sumner's remarks had been strictly impersonal, and contained nothing to provoke temper, unless perhaps his assumption of the high ground that patriotism and nationality as opposed to State rights were on his side. Fessenden's temper was disturbed by ill-health.[3] He was naturally antipathetic to one like Sumner, who was so largely developed on the ideal side, and also took exception to the latter's "ex-cathedra" style, as he called it. He doubtless thought Sumner something like an intruder when he ventured into the field of finance. He was impatient, as senators are apt to be, with outsiders who take up their specialties; and his treatment of Chandler in the debate drew from the latter the retort that

1 April 26, 27, and 29; May 5 and 6. Works, vol. viii. pp. 419–436.

2 It was drawn by Mr. Chase.

3 Trumbull once told Fessenden that his ill-temper had left him no friends. (Nicolay and Hay's "Life of Lincoln," vol. ix. p. 100.) Its exhibitions were frequent, as in debate with Doolittle, July 26, 1866. (Congressional Globe, pp. 4167–4168.) The New York "Independent" in a discriminating tribute to Mr. Fessenden, Sept. 16, 1869, said: "Almost a king in dignity of demeanor, he was never safe against loss of temper; and there was scarce a senator whom sooner or later he did not sting. . . . He was a rare victim of personal antipathies."

"the senator from Maine had lectured the body about enough." Next he took Sumner to task for superfluous comments on a celebrated law case, for his style, particularly in the resort to poetry for illustrations, and for want of practical knowledge. Sumner tried to avoid a personal controversy, but Fessenden was persistent in his thrusts.[1] The unpleasant scene, lasting for some minutes, was closed by Sherman, who recalled the Senate to the question before it. Other encounters of the kind were in store, and the two senators, — both important to the public service, and of equal integrity and patriotism, — were not to be in cordial relations for some years.[2] Mutual respect, however, remained; and neither, it is believed, would have wished at any time to see the other dropped from public life.[3] In the end their reconcilement was complete.[4] Sumner as the survivor paid a heart-felt and discriminating tribute to Fessenden.[5]

The urgency of military matters did not exclude civil reforms from Sumner's attention. He had in early life expressed his disgust with "the patronage system," under which a new President paid off the political debts of his party and his own by the

1 The Boston "Commonwealth" replied, May 13, 1864, to Fessenden's imputation in debate that Sumner had instigated its criticisms of himself, and denied that Sumner had any complicity with them. Fessenden so far forgot himself at times as to talk audibly in the Senate while Sumner was speaking. This is stated by another senator, Mr. Conness, in an interview published in the Gold Hill (Colorado) "News," and sent by him in a note to Sumner, August 22, 1865. Mr. Conness said, "Mr. Fessenden was always snapping at Mr. Sumner in debate." Frederick Douglass, writing to Sumner, Sept. 9, 1869, the day after Mr. Fessenden's death, said: "He [Mr. Fessenden] was never just to you, and sometimes I fear intentionally offensive; but now that his chair is vacant, and his voice silent in the Senate, you must remember with satisfaction your forbearance towards him and your freedom from bitter retort when his words and bearing seemed to invite other treatment."

2 July 3, 5, 10, 1867. Works, vol. xi. pp. 369-396.

3 The writer passed two days in Portland, Me., in the summer of 1864, most of the time with Fessenden (then having Mr. Chase as his guest), and they spoke freely of Sumner, to whom Fessenden referred with entire respect.

4 In his later days Fessenden used to say to his neighbors in Portland that at first he misconceived Sumner, supposing him to be a mere idealist and theorist, but had afterwards found him to be a public man of various ability. In his last illness, hearing a report, which proved incorrect, that Sumner was very ill, he expressed his regret at the loss the country would suffer by Sumner's death, and his satisfaction that their differences had been settled and that they were now good friends. Sumner was touched by these expressions when they were communicated to him, and was sad to think that the happy intercourse and co-operation in the public service which he had looked forward to were terminated. A. L. Hobson to Sumner, Sept. 3, 1869, and in the Portland "Press," Nov. 20, 1876; New York "Independent," Sept. 16, 1869.

5 Dec. 14, 1869. Works, vol. xiii. pp. 189-194. Certain passages in Sumner's eulogy on Senator Collamer, Dec. 14, 1865, to which Fessenden listened, were supposed to refer to the latter (Works, vol. x. p. 40): "Though at times earnest, he was never bitter. He never dropped into the debate any poisoned ingredients."

displacement of faithful officials and the appointment in their stead of party workers or his own favorites.[1] He now made the first distinct and formal attempt ever made in Congress for the reform of the civil service,[2] anticipating by two years the effort of Mr. Jenckes in the same direction,[3] by introducing a bill, April 30, 1864, to provide a competitive system of examination for admission to and promotion in the civil service, — making merit and fitness the standard, to be determined by a board of examiners, and prohibiting removals except for good cause.[4] The bill was Sumner's own conception, drawn without conference with or suggestion from any one. It was not practicable to press it at the time, and at its author's suggestion it was laid on the table. His various labors kept him from calling it up. This earliest recognition of a needed reform, since a subject of agitation in Congress and among the people, found favor at the time with a few leading journals[5] and some advanced thinkers. Professor Joseph Henry, of the Smithsonian Institution, B. R. Wood, of Albany, and Dr. Lieber[6] wrote approving letters to the senator. Josiah Quincy, now at the age of ninety-two, within a few weeks of his death, and no longer able to use his pen, sent by his daughter's hand his hearty commendation of the measure. The Union League Club of New York appointed a committee to aid its passage. Generally, however, Sumner's correspondents and the newspapers were silent on this subject, which was destined later to come to the front. He was here, as often, a long way ahead of public sentiment.[7] He wrote to Lieber, January 31: —

"Did I write to you asking your opinion on introducing the system of competitive examinations for minor offices in our civil department? I have such a bill drawn; but I am not sure if public opinion will sustain me."

[1] *Ante*, vol. ii. p. 168; vol. iii. p. 149.

[2] He referred to it as the first effort in the direction, Dec. 4, 1871. Congressional Globe, p. 2.

[3] Sumner wrote of Jenckes at a later period: "When I think of Mr. Jenckes's work in Congress, I feel that he should not give place except to a superlative character."

[4] Works, vol. viii. pp. 452-457. He favored, Feb. 16, 1863, the "discarding personal and political favoritism" in the selection of midshipmen, and was one of only six senators who voted to limit the existing power of members of Congress to select them at will. (Works, vol. vii. pp. 301, 302.) Sumner took occasion, April 21, 1869 (Works, vol. xiii. pp. 94-97), to discredit any rule or practice for apportioning appointments among the States according to their population.

[5] National Intelligencer, May 10; New York Times, May 10; New York Evening Post, May 7; New York Independent, June 9.

[6] Lieber's "Life and Letters," pp. 339, 345.

[7] The Act of March 3, 1871, authorized a commission; and from that time the reform has held its place in the public attention.

Again, May 15 : —

"I am astonished at the echo to my little bill on civil service. I matured it alone, without consultation, and flung it on the table of the Senate as a way of drawing attention to the subject. Newspapers and letters show the interest it has caused. I do not doubt that the scale of business now and the immense interests involved will require some such system. We cannot transact our great concerns without serious loss unless we have trained men. 'Rotation in office' is proper enough in the political posts where political direction is determined, but absurd in the machinery of administration. A change in this respect would have a favorable influence doubtless on our national credit, and everywhere else. Such an influence as you propose to organize would be of great value; nor do I think the manner or form of much importance. Let those three 'Unions'[1] in any positive way — each perhaps in a different form — express an interest in the idea, and that will have a great effect on the country and on Congress too. This is a moment for changes. Our whole system is like molten wax, ready to receive an impression."

Other subjects on which Sumner spoke briefly were an appropriation for the training of pupils for the consular service;[2] the raising of the mission to Belgium to a first-class rank;[3] national academies for the promotion of literature, art, and of the moral and political sciences, — a project in relation to which Lieber, Agassiz, and R. W. Emerson were his correspondents,[4] all of whom entered heartily into it; the prohibition of sales of gold deliverable at a future day;[5] and several questions of internal taxation.[6]

Sumner pleaded two days before the final adjournment that the time for closing the session should be extended beyond July 4, insisting that further financial legislation was imperatively required; but the senators, weary and overcome with heat, were deaf to his entreaties.[7] He said : —

"Mr. President, it is natural that senators who have been engaged for months in the labors of an anxious session should be glad to escape from the confinement and heat of Washington. I sympathize with them. I wish to be away; I long to leave the capital. Did I allow myself to take counsel of personal advantage, I should be among the most earnest of those now crying for adjournment. Born on the seashore, accustomed to the sea air, I am less

1 Union League clubs.

2 March 15, 1864. Works, vol. viii. pp. 223–227.

3 March 15. Works, vol. viii. pp. 217–222. He wrote Lieber, March 17 : "I was badgered on all sides, but at last on ayes and noes carried it."

4 July 2. Works, vol. ix. pp. 51–54.

5 April 15. Congressional Globe, p. 1648.

6 July 4. Congressional Globe, pp. 3539, 3540.

7 Works, vol. ix. pp. 55–63.

prepared than many of my friends to endure the climate here. I feel sensibly its sultry heats, and I pant for the taste of salt in the atmosphere. Nor am I insensible to other influences: what little remains to me of home and friendship is far away from here, where I was born. But home, friendship, and seashore must not tempt me at this hour. Lord Bacon tells us, in striking and most suggestive phrase, 'The duties of life are more than life.' But if ever there was a time when the duties of a senator were supreme above all other things, so that temptation of all kinds should be trampled under foot, it is now."

He wrote to Lieber, May 4: —

"I think that Banks's military character has suffered very much, hardly more than he has suffered as a statesman by his proceedings for reconstruction.[1] The sentiment in Louisiana among the earnest antislavery men is very strong for Butler. The President some time ago sent for me to show me private letters from Banks on reconstruction; but I have not exchanged a word with him on Banks's military character, and considering that he is a Massachusetts man, I do not wish to interfere against him. For the present I stand aloof. . . . Tell me what you think of our duty now with regard to Mexico and France. You notice that the House resolution[2] has already caused an echo in Europe. I have kept it carefully in my committee room, where it still sleeps. My idea has been that we were not in a condition to give Louis Napoleon any excuse for hostility or recognition or breaking the blockade. At another time I shall be glad to speak plainly to France, or rather to its ruler; but I would not say anything now which cannot be maintained, nor which can add to our present embarrassments."

Again, May 17: —

"Winter Davis has just come to press me about his Mexican resolution. Goldwin Smith's pamphlet is excellent.[3] I doubt if it would interest the President, who reads very little. Seward said to me two days ago: 'There was a great cry last year on the question whether the President read despatches before they are sent; but I am sure he never reads one which we receive.'"

He wrote to Lieber, June 27, after referring to two measures he had succeeded in carrying that day, — the prohibition of the coastwise slave-trade, and the required admission of colored testimony in all national tribunals, —

"Meanwhile I keep Mexico in my committee, where I have the Arguelles case[4] and a joint resolution from the House of Representatives terminating the convention with Great Britain limiting ships and navy yards on the lakes.

[1] In Louisiana, under Mr. Lincoln's direction.

[2] *Ante*, p. 119. Lieber's "Life and Letters," p. 346.

[3] Letter to a Whig member of the Southern Independence Association. Lieber had asked Sumner to request the President to read it. Lieber's "Life and Letters," p. 345.

[4] Nicolay and Hay's "Life of Lincoln," vol. ix. pp. 44–47.

The latter if passed would be the first notice to England that war must come. I am not ready for any such step now. There is a dementia to adjourn and go home."

To the Duchess of Argyll, July 4: —

"Congress will disperse to-day, having done several good things: (1) All fugitive-slave acts have been repealed; (2) All acts sustaining the traffic in slaves on the coast from one domestic port to another have been repealed, so that now there is no support of slavery in our statute-book; (3) The railroads here in Washington have been required to admit colored persons into their carriages; (4) Greatest of all in practical importance, the rule of evidence excluding colored testimony in the United States courts has been abolished. All these measures are now the law of the land. They were all introduced and pressed by myself. I feel happy in this result; but I shrink from saying that anything can make me happy now.

"This war stretches on fearfully. The blood and treasure lavished to subdue belligerent slavery are beyond precedent. But so great and audacious a crime, sustained by European aid, resists with a natural diabolism. If it were left to itself, without foreign support, it would soon cease, under the assaults of the national government.

"The President, on his return from General Grant's headquarters, told me that the general, who is a man of very few words, said to him: 'I am as far off from Richmond now as I ever shall be. I shall take the place; but as the rebel papers say, it may require a long summer's day.' The President describes Grant as full of confidence, and as wanting nothing. His terrible losses have been promptly made up by reinforcements."

Mr. Lincoln was nominated in June, 1864, for re-election, at the Republican national convention in Baltimore, without open opposition except from the delegates from Missouri. There were times during the war when there was a lack of enthusiasm for Mr. Lincoln, and a distrust of his fitness for his place among public men who were associated with him. Visitors to Washington in 1863–1864 were struck with the want of personal loyalty to him.[1] They found few senators and representatives who would maintain cordially and positively that he combined the qualifications of a leader in the great crisis; and the larger number of them, as the national election approached, were dissatisfied with his candidacy.[2] An indifference towards him was noted in the commercial centres and among the most intelligent

[1] Adams's "Biography" of Dana, vol. ii. pp. 264, 265, 271, 274; Godwin's "Life of W. C. Bryant," vol. ii. pp. 175, 178; P. W. Chandler's "Memoir of John A. Andrew," pp. 111–114; Letter from Washington in Boston "Commonwealth," Nov. 12, 1864.

[2] Greeley's "American Conflict," vol. ii. p. 655; Wilson's "Rise and Fall of the Slave Power," vol. iii. p. 545; Julian's "Political Recollections," p. 243; New York "Tribune," July 2, 1889.

of the loyal people.[1] Historians and biographers have hesitated to reveal the state of opinion concerning him, but historical verity loses by the suppression. He was thought to be wanting in the style, in the gravity of manner and conversation, which are becoming in the chief of a nation. His habit of interrupting the consideration of grave matters with stories was attributed to levity, and offended sober-minded men who sought him on public business. A man of "infinite jest," the underlying seriousness of his nature was not readily observed. But the criticism did not stop here. He was felt to be too easy-going, to be disposed to give too much time to trifles; to be unbusinesslike in his methods, slow and hesitating where vigorous action was required;[2] and the objection in general was, that in capacity and temperament he was inadequate to the responsibilities of the head of a nation at such a momentous period. This estimate was honestly held by many clear-headed and patriotic men; nor can their sincerity be questioned, although the final judgment of mankind is that of all men he was the best fitted for the high place which he filled during the Civil War. This also is to be said, — that whatever those who came near him thought, the popular instinct was with him; and plain men — the masses of the people — did not admit the limitations apparent to those who were present at the seat of government. Indeed, the very qualities and ways which repelled public men brought the President near to the people. His retention of Montgomery Blair,[3] and particularly of Seward, in his Cabinet, weakened his position with that large body of loyal men who insisted on a direct and aggressive policy against slavery; and finally his treatment of reconstruction brought him into collision not only with radical leaders, but with wise and conservative men, who believed that it was a subject which belonged to Congress, and could not be safely intrusted to the exclusive discretion of the Executive.

In January, 1864, there was a conference in Washington of

1 Lieber to General Halleck, Sept. 1, 1864, in Lieber's "Life and Letters," pp. 350, 351.

2 Wilkinson in the Senate, March 10, 1864; Congressional Globe, p. 1027.

3 He removed Blair, September 23, yielding to the pressure. (Nicolay and Hay's "Life of Lincoln," vol. ix. pp. 339–342.) A resolution of the Republican national convention was intended to call for a change in his case as well as Seward's. (New York "Independent," June 20.) The President, in January, 1865, informed William Claflin, who had in 1864, as an active member of the Republican national committee, come into intimate relations with him, of his purpose to make a change in the office of Secretary of State during the coming summer. Governor Claflin, some years afterwards, gave an account of this conversation with Mr. Lincoln at a dinner of the Massachusetts Club in Boston.

members of Congress and citizens from different parts of the country to consult upon the nomination of Mr. Lincoln's successor, in which Mr. Chase appeared to be the favorite candidate. Two months later, March 10, Mr. Pomeroy, senator from Kansas, explained this movement in the Senate, and avowed his connection with it. Mr. Chase's candidacy, as well as the nomination of Fremont at Cleveland, came to no result; but the discontent remained during the summer, showing itself sometimes in a call for another candidate (as in the New York "Tribune"), or in a proposition, with a view to another candidate, for a postponement of the Republican convention, which was advocated in the New York "Evening Post"[1] and the New York "Independent."[2] The effort for another nomination did not end with the convention. Naturally B. F. Wade, senator, and Henry Winter Davis, representative, were earnest in it; but a large number of public men were in sympathy with them. Senator Grimes held their view of Mr. Lincoln's limitations.[3] Governor Andrew of Massachusetts, foremost among war governors, who had occasion to seek Mr. Lincoln from time to time on public business, was very active in the movement to displace him.[4] Greeley thought Mr. Lincoln already beaten, and that another ticket was necessary to save the cause from utter overthrow, naming three generals from whom a choice might be made, — Grant, Sherman, and Butler. Among others active in the movement were Richard Smith, the veteran editor, and Whitelaw Reid, both of Cincinnati.[5]

Republican conferences were held in the city of New York for the purpose of making a change: one at D. D. Field's house, August 14, where representative men were present, — Greeley, Parke Godwin of the "Evening Post," William Curtis Noyes, Henry Winter Davis, Dr. Lieber,[6] and twenty or more besides.

1 Both Mr. Greeley and Mr. Bryant joined with a committee to request the Republican national committee to postpone the convention. Nicolay and Hay's "Life of Lincoln," vol. ix. pp. 57, 58.

2 June 2. The same paper, June 16, gives its support to the nomination, but without enthusiasm.

3 Gurowski's diary, vol. iii. p. 358, where an extract from his letter is given. This is corroborated by his letter written after Mr. Lincoln's death. J. W. Grimes's "Life," p. 279.

4 P. W. Chandler's "Memoir and Reminiscences of Governor Andrew," pp. 111-114. Gurowski in his diary, vol. iii. pp. 69, 91, 358, names also Boutwell, Trumbull, Wilson, and W. D. Kelley as supporting the principles of the party rather than Mr. Lincoln.

5 A large number of letters of public men written at the time to John Austin Stevens, and published in the New York "Sun," June 30, 1889, throw light on the movement.

6 Lieber wrote Sumner, September 16, that he wished Lincoln could know that the people were to vote not for him but against McClellan.

It was agreed that a committee should request Mr. Lincoln to withdraw, and Grant was the name which found most favor as a substitute.[1] At this time Mr. Lincoln himself faced defeat as altogether probable.[2] The disaffection which then seemed so serious disappeared, however, immediately after the Democratic nomination of McClellan, August 31, at Chicago, upon a platform which declared the war to be "four years of failure," and called for "a cessation of hostilities."

Sumner shared in the opinion of Mr. Lincoln's limitations, which was common with public men in 1863–1864; but he took no part in the plans for putting another candidate in his stead. In correspondence he referred to the subject but slightly and incidentally, and was reserved in conversation at Washington, though less so in Boston, where he spoke more freely to personal friends of Mr. Lincoln's defects.[3] He thought a change of candidate desirable, but only with Mr. Lincoln's free and voluntary withdrawal; and he counselled against any action which might be construed as hostile to him.[4] This was also the position of Senator Collamer and John Jay. With Sumner, as with Bryant and Greeley and all other patriotic men, the question was settled by "the Chicago treason." The fear of an adverse decision of the people in November, felt by Mr. Lincoln himself as well as by others, vanished with the victories of our army in Georgia, which culminated in the evacuation of Atlanta by the rebels on the night of the day of McClellan's nomination. Mr. Lincoln carried the electoral vote of all the States except three,—Delaware, Kentucky, and New Jersey; but McClellan's vote was very large in some States, as New York, Pennsylvania, and Ohio. It is curious to observe how in a few months, when death had set its seal on a great character, Mr. Lincoln's honest critics became his sincere eulogists,—notably Bryant, Greeley, Bancroft, Andrew, and Sumner.[5]

1 Lieber to Sumner, August 15. According to Lieber, Davis stated at the conference that Mr. Lincoln had said in Corwin's presence that he should be beaten unless victories intervened.

2 Nicolay and Hay's "Life of Lincoln," vol. ix. pp. 249–251.

3 Life of Amos A. Lawrence, p. 195.

4 Nicolay and Hay ("Life of Lincoln," vol. ix. p. 367) are incorrect in saying that the New York movement had "the earnest support and eager instigation of Charles Sumner." Their statement is not supported by his letter cited by them of date Sept. 1, 1864, and printed in the New York "Sun," June 30, 1889, which is of similar tenor as his letter to Lieber, September 3.

5 Sumner read to the writer, in May, 1865, at his mother's house in Boston, some parts of his eulogy on Lincoln as he was preparing it. When reminded that he had sometimes

To Lieber, who had written, August 15, an account of the conference at D. D. Field's house in New York concerning a candidate for President, Sumner wrote from Boston, September 3:

"Your letter about the meeting was very interesting. I do not see how anything can be done except through Mr. Lincoln and with his good-will. If he could see that patriotism required his withdrawal, and would sincerely give his countenance and support to a new candidate, I am sure that the candidate of that convention, whoever he might be, could be chosen. But any adverse proceeding would disaffect him and his friends so as to destroy the unity of the party. This unity must be had at all hazards and at every sacrifice. If Mr. Lincoln does not withdraw, then all who now disincline to him must come into his support. I have declined to sign any paper or take any part in any action, because I was satisfied that nothing could be done except through Mr. Lincoln and with his good-will. To him the appeal must be made, and on him must be the final responsibility. But the Chicago platform will make it possible to elect him, if not easy. Indeed, I am prepared for an uprising against it. The country does not yet understand it; but its revolting character is too apparent. Like an overdose of arsenic, it will cure itself. Let me know what occurs. I was on the point of going to New York for counsel, and to find privacy with you; but I abandoned the idea."

The Republican national convention placed on the ticket with Mr. Lincoln, as candidate for Vice-President, Andrew Johnson of Tennessee. This nomination was assisted by some delegates from Massachusetts, who thought that a loyal Southern man would add more strength to the ticket than the present incumbent of the office, Mr. Hamlin. This was a reasonable view, although the history of the next four years proved the selection to have been an unfortunate one. In the change from Hamlin to Johnson, Sumner took no part whatever. While always ready for contests which concerned principles and policies, he had no taste for those which concerned only the individual or sectional claims of candidates. No urgency of persuasion would have moved him to leave his seat in the Senate in order to attend a national political convention.,

Sumner arrived at home, July 17. He passed a week early in August with Longfellow at Nahant, where "the air, the breeze, the sea were kindly," and where on the piazza they read together Tennyson's last volume, "Enoch Arden," enjoying it "more than air or breeze or sea." Later in the month he was

spoken of the President in a different tone, he answered: "Well, Mr. Lincoln was indeed the author of a new order of State papers." The study of the complete life evidently had withdrawn his attention from minor defects, and fixed it on the great qualities of his subject.

for a few days at Newport.[1] He attended the Saturday Club dinners, at one of which as a guest was Chase, just resigned from the Cabinet, and on his way to the White Mountains.[2] He dined with J. B. Smith when the latter entertained Auguste Laugel; he dined often at Mr. Hooper's, took tea at Mrs. J. E. Lodge's, and passed an evening at James T. Fields's. He began sittings with Milmore for his bust, which was finished late in the next year. In the autumn, as before, his visits to Longfellow at Cambridge were frequent.[3]

Sumner wrote to Mr. Cobden, September 18: —

"Bear witness that I have never been over-confident of sudden success. I am not now; but I am none the less sure of the great result. This struggle can have but one end. You must observe how we have constantly gained. The lines of the enemy have been drawn in, and their strong places have been taken; and this will continue to the end. . . . The capture of Atlanta is surely a great point in the war. I have had great confidence in Sherman; he is a consummate soldier, and I think military critics must confess that his campaign shows no ordinary ability. I agree with you in turning away from this bloodshed,[4] which I deplore always; but I have seen no alternative for us since the attack on Fort Sumter. Since then the national government has been acting in self-defence against belligerent slavery. General Grant is confident that he shall take Richmond, and he is no boaster. He gives great praise to Sherman, saying he is the best soldier on this continent, and ought to be in his place. . . . The hesitation in the support of Mr. Lincoln disappears at the promulgation of the Chicago treason. There was a meeting in New York of persons from different parts of the country to bring about a new convention to nominate a Union candidate. The 'Tribune,' 'Evening Post,' 'Independent,' and Cincinnati 'Gazette' were all represented in it; but as soon as they read the platform, they ranged in support of Mr. Lincoln. I declined to take any part in the meeting, for I could not but see that nothing could be done except with Mr. Lincoln's good-will. If he had patriotically withdrawn, and given his support to any nominee of a new convention, whoever he might be, — any one of a hundred names, — I was very sure the nominee would be elected. You understand that there is a strong feeling among those who have seen

[1] At a dinner at William Beach Lawrence's he met Lord Airlie, who recorded in his diary Sumner's remarks on the speeches of English statesmen, our Civil War, and other topics, — extracts from which, without Lord Airlie's authority, appeared in the "Scotsman," Jan. 7, 1865. Both Sumner and Lord Airlie were annoyed by the publication. Lord Airlie and his brother-in-law, E. Lyulph Stanley, who visited this country the same season, brought letters to Sumner from the Duchess of Argyll.

[2] William Curtis Noyes was another guest.

[3] Robert Ferguson, an Englishman, in his book, "America during and after the War" (p. 32), quoted in Longfellow's "Life" (vol. ii. pp. 414, 415), wrote his recollections of Craigie House: "Sumner, with the poet's little daughter nestling in his lap, — for he is a man to whom all children come, — calmly discussing some question of European literature, seeming to feel deeply the defection of certain of the old antislavery leaders of England from the Northern cause in the great crisis of the struggle."

[4] The battles in the Wilderness in Virginia.

Mr. Lincoln, in the way of business, that he lacks practical talent for his important place. It is thought that there should be more readiness, and also more capacity, for government. But these doubts are now abandoned, and all are united to prevent the election of McClellan; to my mind the election is already decided. . . . Chase for a long time hesitated in the support of Mr. Lincoln; he did not think him competent. But he finds that he has no alternative; as a patriot, he must oppose Chicago. The President made a great mistake in compelling him to resign. It was very much as when Louis XVI. threw overboard Necker, — and, by the way, I have often observed that Mr. Lincoln resembles Louis XVI. more than any other ruler in history. I once said to Chase that I should not be astonished if, like Necker, he was recalled; to which he replied, 'That might be if Mr. Lincoln were king and not politician.' Thus far the President has made no overture to him of any kind, although he has received him kindly.

"I have followed you through the last session, and especially enjoyed your very effective speech on the Danish question. But I am lost in wonder at the perseverance of Lord Russell as a prophet of evil to the United States. He has a *naïveté* in his avowals; witness that at the close of his speech of 27th of June. But we shall disappoint him. I thank you for your faith; but do not forget that we are fighting your battle here. Our triumph will help the liberal cause everywhere."

Sumner made several popular addresses in the autumn of 1864, — one at Faneuil Hall on the national victories;[1] another at the same place in support of Mr. Lincoln's re-election;[2] another at Cooper Institute on the issues of the election;[3] and the last at Faneuil Hall on the evening of the election.[4] He put forward on these occasions, as patriotic aims, the complete suppression of the rebellion and the complete extinction of slavery. "Never," said he, "was grander cause or sublimer conflict; never holier sacrifice." At Cooper Institute he was received with the same enthusiasm that had hitherto characterized his New York audiences. One incident of this address was a contrast between the mission of the "Mayflower" bound for Plymouth and that of the first slave-ship bound for Jamestown,[5] with an exposure of the pretension that Virginia was ennobled in her origin by cavalier colonists. He spoke in certain towns in Massachusetts, and also in Hartford and New London, Conn., where Mr. Winthrop made an address for McClellan, and in Newark, N. J.; but he declined calls from other States.

[1] September 6. Works, vol. ix. pp. 64-67.
[2] September 28. Works, vol. ix. pp. 68-82.
[3] November 5. Works, vol. ix. pp. 83-133.
[4] November 5. Works, vol. ix. pp. 134-136.
[5] This contrast appears in an earlier address. September 18, 1860. Works, vol. v. pp. 276-279.

The spirit and tone of his speeches in the autumn are indicated in these extracts from his letters to F. W. Ballard: —

October 25: "If I speak, it will be to put the cause of liberty for our country and all mankind in a new light, so that the pettifoggers and compromisers shall be silenced."

November 2: "I had last night [at New London] the largest audience known here of voters, — ladies excluded to make room. My aim is to exhibit the grandeur and dignity of our cause, and to lift people to their duties."

November 9: "I am indignant at the possible loss of New York State. It is because of the craven politics there, where intriguers and compromisers bear sway."

November 17, from Philadelphia: "The indications of an early organization of a Native American party to neutralize the Irish Roman Catholic vote are strong here; they voted against us almost to a man. At Burlington, N. J., the priest stood all day at the polls to see that his people voted for McClellan."

Sumner contributed two articles to a Boston journal on the seizure of the "Florida," a Confederate war vessel, in the neutral waters of Brazil, by the United States steamer "Wachusett." While not justifying the seizure, they were a reply in the nature of an *argumentum ad hominem* to British criticisms of the transaction, with a treatment of precedents similar to that which he had applied to the "Trent" case.[1]

During the war several of Sumner's friends, whom he had long cherished, were severed from him by death. Mr. Giddings died at Montreal, May 27, 1864, where he was serving as consul-general. He kept up a correspondence with Sumner on affairs in this country and our relations with Canada. He had visited Washington in January, when he and Sumner met for the last time. His last letter, written April 9, when a readjustment of reciprocity with Canada was contemplated, contained a postscript, which revealed his premonitions that the end was near, saying: "Should I live, I desire to be one of the commissioners to negotiate the new treaty." The bar of Ashtabula County, Ohio, of which he was a member, invited Sumner to deliver a

[1] Boston "Advertiser," Nov. 29, 1864, Jan. 17, 1865; Works, vol. ix. pp. 141–173. Other writers who took his view in the discussion were Theophilus Parsons, George Bemis, and C. F. Dunbar; but on the other side were Goldwin Smith and Prof. Henry W. Torrey, — the latter writing with the signature of "Privatus." Cobden, in the last letter but one which he wrote to Sumner, objected to his use of England's "old doings as an excuse for your present shortcomings;" and thought the vessel should have been promptly returned to Brazil. (Morley's "Life of Cobden," vol. ii. pp. 459, 460.) The vessel went to the bottom in Hampton Roads shortly after in a collision. Our government disavowed the acts of the American officers in making the seizure.

eulogy upon him, and his son-in-law, George W. Julian, urged an acceptance; but Sumner was obliged to decline.

Sumner paid, March 29, 1864, an affectionate tribute to Owen Lovejoy, a member of the House, from whom he had always received most cordial sympathy in his radical action against slavery. He used the opportunity, as was his custom, to urge the living to maintain the cause of freedom.[1]

Sumner wrote to Longfellow, May 21: —

"I have just seen in a paper the death of R. J. Mackintosh at London on the 26th of April. Is this so? It makes me unhappy. Tell me about it. Had he been ill? And what becomes of his family? I hear also that Hawthorne has gone. One by one, almost in twos, they seem to go. We shall be alone soon. I forget! *I* shall be alone; you have your children. Life is weary and dark, — full of pain and enmity. I am ready to go at once; but still I am left. Hawthorne was a genius. As a master of prose, he will come in the first class of all who have written the English language. He had not the grand style, but who has had a delicacy of touch superior to his?"

Josiah Quincy, president of Harvard College when Sumner was a student, died July 1, 1864, at the age of ninety-two. He was the friend of Sumner's father, and followed the son's career with constant interest. His eldest daughter, in communicating his death, wrote: "He was very fond of you, and took the greatest interest in your success." Sumner's reply to her was as follows: —

"On reaching home this morning, I make haste to assure you of the emotion with which I learned that my friend, your venerable father, had passed away. I had thought of him often during the late session of Congress, and hoped to see him again to talk with him of its events. I had hoped also that he might have lived to partake of the final triumph of our cause. It is with pain that I renounce all that I had hoped, — and especially that I think I shall never see him again. But few lives have been so completely filled and rounded as his; always industrious, faithful, true, and noble. He is an example to his country. Whether I think of him as patriot, as man, or as friend, I find in him the same enduring qualities. My recollection of Mr. Quincy goes back to my earliest childhood, when my father spoke of him in my hearing, and pointed him out to me in the street. From that time till I left Boston for Washington, last November, I have seen and known him, always looking up to him with reverence. It is hard to think that I shall not see and know him more on earth. I trust that his papers are in such condition that we can all have the benefit of them. It will be a rare pleasure to read the political reminiscences of a person who enjoyed such opportunities, and who was always so honest. You will be good enough to offer from me to his family the assurance of my sympathy."

[1] March 29, 1864. Works, vol. viii. pp. 228-235.

He wrote to Mrs. Nassau W. Senior, July 12, on the death of her husband: —

"Let me express to you the deep sympathy with which I have learned your recent bereavement. For more than a quarter of a century I have known Mr. Senior well, and had always found him kind, candid, considerate, and full of true friendship. A large circle will deplore his loss; and I pray you not to forget that it embraces many on this side of the ocean. But I wish to speak especially of myself; I shall always remember with pleasure and gratitude the relations it was my privilege to enjoy with him, and shall think of his loss with sorrow. Please to accept for Miss Senior[1] also my compliments and sympathies."

To Mr. and Mrs. Francis G. Shaw, October 28: —

"Again you are called to feel the calamity of this war. I sorrow with you most sincerely. There are very few persons of whom I have seen so little who interested me so much as Colonel Lowell.[2] He was beautiful in character as in countenance. He is another sacrifice to slavery. When at last our triumph is won, his name must be inscribed on that martyr list, without which slavery would have been supreme on the continent. I hope that his widowed wife, your noble daughter, may be comforted. She begins life where others end it; but she has a fountain of precious thoughts forever. Let her know, if you please, how truly I share her affliction."

[1] Afterwards Mrs. Simpson.

[2] Charles R. Lowell, killed Oct. 20, 1864, in battle in Virginia.

## CHAPTER L.

LAST MONTHS OF THE CIVIL WAR. — CHASE AND TANEY, CHIEF-JUSTICES. — THE FIRST COLORED ATTORNEY IN THE SUPREME COURT — RECIPROCITY WITH CANADA. — THE NEW JERSEY MONOPOLY. — RETALIATION IN WAR. — RECONSTRUCTION. — DEBATE ON LOUISIANA. — LINCOLN AND SUMNER. — VISIT TO RICHMOND. — THE PRESIDENT'S DEATH BY ASSASSINATION. — SUMNER'S EULOGY UPON HIM. — PRESIDENT JOHNSON; HIS METHOD OF RECONSTRUCTION. — SUMNER'S PROTESTS AGAINST RACE DISTINCTIONS. — DEATH OF FRIENDS. — FRENCH VISITORS AND CORRESPONDENTS. — 1864-1865.

LORD LYONS[1] left the British embassy at Washington at this time on account of ill health, and returned to England; afterwards he was ambassador for his country at Constantinople and at Paris. Sumner, who was much attached to him, wrote to him, Dec. 11, 1864: —

"I learn that you have already left us, and that you are unwell. I am very sorry on both accounts. Yours has been a most eventful service among us. Few ministers are called to perform in a whole life what you have been obliged to crowd into a brief term. It is well known that you have enjoyed in no common degree the confidence of your own government; while all on our side familiar with your conduct bear witness to the uniform kindness, courtesy, and forbearance by which it has been distinguished. To perform so successfully all the duties of your most difficult post in these terrible days, when strife and conflict seemed ready to embroil everything, was calculated to task the best powers of mind and body; and I am more pained than astonished to learn that your health has failed under the severe trial. But I trust that a vacation, and the welcome which awaits you from your own government, which you have served so well, will renew your strength, and that you will be disposed to come to us again. In any event, I can never forget the pleasant hours which it has been my fortune to have with you. My best wishes will follow you wherever you may be, and I pray you now to accept the expression of my friendship."

To Lieber, December 27: —

"What say you to Dix's order? There can be no question that any general on the frontier might follow invaders back into Canada if the Canadian government should fail in its duties; but a deliberate order in advance to invade neutral territory is a grave step.[2]

[1] 1817-1887. Sir Frederick Bruce was his successor at Washington.

[2] Sumner commented on the order in the Senate, Dec. 19, 1864. The President required General Dix to revoke it. Nicolay and Hay's "Life of Lincoln," vol. viii. p. 25.

"I have presented to the President the duty of harmony between Congress and the Executive. He is agreed. It is proposed to admit Louisiana (which ought not to be done), and at the same time pass the reconstruction bill for all the other States, giving the electoral franchise to 'all citizens' without distinction of color. If this arrangement is carried out, it will be an immense political act.

"I have great questions for the committee [on foreign relations]: (1) The termination of the reciprocity treaty; (2) Armaments on the lakes; (3) The Canadian complications; (4) Mexico; (5) Arguelles case; (6) Claims of England growing out of the war; (7) Florida case; (8) Question of belligerent rights. Anything on these matters will be welcome."

To Mr. Bright, February 15, 1865: —

"I am glad of your assurance, in harmony with Mr. Cobden's, that intervention is played out. I am glad also of your speech. It amuses me to read the criticisms, which I can appreciate at their value, as I have been exposed to the same. For years it was said I was governed by hatred for the slave-masters, and did not care at all for the slaves. Oh, no! not at all.

"You will read the report of the conferences.[1] It appears that the President was drawn into them by the assurances of General Grant, who was led to expect something.[2] Perhaps the country sees now more clearly than ever that the war must be pushed to the entire overthrow of the rebel armies. The interview was pleasant. Seward sent the commissioners on their arrival three bottles of choice whiskey, which it was reported they drank thirstily. As they were leaving, he gave them a couple of bottles of champagne for their dinner. Hunter, who is a very experienced politician, and had been all his life down to the rebellion, in Washington, said, after the discussions were closed, 'Governor, how is the Capitol? Is it finished?' This gave Seward an opportunity of picturing the present admired state of the works, with the dome completed, and the whole constituting one of the most magnificent edifices of the world. Campbell, formerly of the Supreme Court of the United States, and reputed the ablest lawyer in the slave States, began the conference by suggesting peace on the basis of a Zollverein, and continued free-trade between the two sections, which he thought might pave the way to something hereafter; but he could not promise anything. This was also the theory of the French minister here, M. Mercier, now at Madrid, who insisted that the war must end in that way. It was remarked that the men had nothing of the haughty and defiant way which they had in Washington formerly. Mr. Blair, who visited Richmond, still insists that peace is near. He says that the war cannot go on another month on their side unless they have help from Louis Napoleon. But here the question of a monarchical government may arise. Jefferson Davis, whom he describes as so emaciated and altered as not to be recognized, sets his face against it. He said to Mr. Blair that 'there was a Brutus who would brook the eternal devil as easily as a king in Rome;' and he was that Brutus in Richmond.

[1] At Hampton Roads, February 3, between Mr. Lincoln and Mr. Seward on the one side, and Stephens, Hunter, and Campbell on the other.

[2] Nicolay and Hay's "Life of Lincoln," vol. x. p. 127.

"Meanwhile the war goes on with converging forces. Mr. Stanton was with me yesterday, and gave me fully his expectations. He thinks that peace can be had only when Lee's army is beaten, captured, or dispersed; and there I agree with him. To that end all our military energies are now directed. Lee's army is sixty-five thousand men. Against him is Grant at Petersburg, a corps now demonstrating at Wilmington, and Sherman marching from Georgia. The latter will not turn aside for Augusta or Charleston, or any fortified place, but will traverse the Carolinas until he is able to co-operate with Grant. You will see from this statement something of the nature of the campaign. Mr. Stanton thinks it ought to be finished before May. I have for a long time been sanguine that after Lee's army is out of the way the whole rebellion will disappear. While that is in a fighting condition there is still a hope for the rebels, and the Unionists of the South are afraid to show themselves.

"I am sorry that so great and good a man as Goldwin Smith, who has done so much for us, should fall into what Mr. Canning would call 'cantanker.' He rushed too swiftly to his conclusion;[1] but I hope that we shall not lose his powerful support for the good cause. I have felt it my duty to say to the British *charge* here that nothing could be done to provide for British claims on our government arising out of the war, which are very numerous, until Lord Russell took a different course with regard to ours. He tosses ours aside haughtily. I am sorry, for my system is peace and good-will, which I shall try in my sphere to cultivate, but there must be reciprocity.

"P. S. Did I mention, as showing the good nature of the peace conferences, that after the serious discussions were over, including allusions on the part of the rebels to what was gently called 'the continental question,' Mr. Stephens asked the President to send back a nephew of his, a young lieutenant, who was a prisoner in the North? The President said at once, 'Stephens, I'll do it, if you will send back one of our young lieutenants.' It was agreed; and Mr. Stephens handed the President on a slip of paper the name of his nephew, and the President handed Mr. Stephens the name of an officer of corresponding rank. This was the only stipulation on that occasion; and the President tells me it has been carried out on each side. Mr. Schleiden, the new minister of the Hanse Towns to London, has been long in Washington, and knows us well. Few foreigners have ever studied us more. I commend him to you and Mr. Cobden."

To Lieber, February 18: —

"The President was exhausted a few days ago; but yesterday he made an appointment with me for eleven o'clock in the evening, and I did not leave him till some time after midnight. I hope you do not dislike the new judge[2] I made in Boston. What pleasure I should have had in placing Hillard in some post of comfort and honor, if he had not made it impossible!"[3]

[1] Reply of Goldwin Smith in Boston "Advertiser," January 26, to his critics, — Theophilus Parsons and George Bemis.

[2] John Lowell, appointed Judge of the United States District Court.

[3] A reference to George S. Hillard's political course. President Johnson a few months later appointed Mr. Hillard United States district attorney for the District of Massachusetts, and Sumner took pleasure in promoting his confirmation by the Senate.

The death of Chief-Justice Taney, which had been anticipated for some months, took place October 10, 1864. Sumner had regarded his friend and coadjutor, S. P. Chase, as the fittest person for the place, and had as early as the spring of the year urged the President to appoint him in the event of a vacancy. After that came the rupture between Mr. Lincoln and Mr. Chase, when the latter's resignation as Secretary of the Treasury was accepted, June 30. Other candidates were named on the death of the chief-justice, — namely, Judge Swayne, already a member of the court; W. M. Evarts, who was supported by E. R. Hoar and R. H. Dana, Jr., of Massachusetts; William Curtis Noyes, who was recommended by Governor Morgan and members of the New York bar; and Montgomery Blair, who claimed to have Mr. Seward's support. Sumner, while expressing the highest respect for the character, attainments, and abilities of Mr. Noyes, whom he thought fit for any place on the bench or in the Cabinet, adhered to his conviction that the public interests, particularly the new constitutional questions arising, clearly required that Mr. Chase should be called to this high office. He so wrote to the President as soon as the vacancy was reported;[1] and as there was delay in filling it, he renewed the recommendation as soon as he reached Washington.[2] Some thought that except for his insistence a different appointment would have been made; but this is uncertain, as the general judgment of the country was in harmony with the President's decision, which was made December 6. When the new chief-justice took his seat, Sumner was observed among the spectators, "leaning against the column at the right of the justices," being regarded after the chief-justice himself as "the most interesting figure in the group of celebrated persons there."[3]

Sumner wrote, October 12, to Lieber, who had urged him to visit Washington in order to press Chase's appointment: —

"Last spring, after a long conversation, Mr. Lincoln promised me to tender the chief-justiceship to Chase. He has referred to that promise since his break with Chase, and declared his willingness to nominate him. I wrote to him at once on hearing of the vacancy to urge the nomination, and I assigned some

[1] Schuckers's "Life of Chase," p. 512.

[2] Nicolay and Hay's "Life of Lincoln," vol. ix. p. 394. Sumner to F. W. Ballard, Dec. 7, 1864.

[3] D. W. Bartlett in the New York "Independent," Dec. 22, 1864.

reasons, insisting that from this time forward the Constitution must be interpreted for liberty, as it has been thus far for slavery. I presented also the importance of having our war measures sustained. I doubt if I could add anything by a personal interview, especially after what has already passed between us."

To a friend who had expressed to him the desire that he should succeed Taney, Sumner wrote, November 20: —

"I am not a candidate for the chief-justiceship, and never have been. In early days, when I still felt the 'fine frenzy' for law, I might have looked that way, despairingly of course, for I never supposed that I should hold an office of any kind; but that passed away long ago. I feel the grandeur of the judicial office, now that great questions of constitutional and public law are to be decided; but I am out of the question, and would not have it otherwise. Nothing has occurred to change my fixed conviction that Mr. Chase will be chief-justice. The President, in my opinion, errs by his delay. The appointment ought to have been made on the evening of Taney's funeral; but sooner or later Mr. Chase will be nominated."

The bill to place a bust of Taney in the Supreme Court room encountered the opposition of Sumner, Wilson, Hale, and Wade, in the Senate. It was reported by Trumbull from the judiciary committee, and he was the only Republican senator who spoke for it. As busts of official persons are historical emblems rather than testimonies to merit, such a controversy would occur only where the public feeling was intense. Taney's mind, as his Dred Scot opinion shows, was perverted on the slavery question, but otherwise he stood in high repute as a jurist. Sumner applied to him severe epithets for sustaining an unrighteous judgment by falsification of history, — a charge which was literally true.[1] Reverdy Johnson, the friend and fellow-citizen of the late chief-justice, became greatly excited, and lost the self-control which he usually maintained; and the contention between him and his four antagonists became bitter in personalities. A recess suspended the debate, and the bill did not come up again at this session. Nine years later, and only two months before Sumner's death, when illness kept him from his seat, a resolution for placing the busts of both Taney and Chase (the latter having recently died) in the Supreme Court room passed the Senate unanimously and without debate.[2]

[1] Feb. 23, 1865. Works, vol. ix. pp. 270, 310.

[2] Sumner showed his continued opposition to Taney's bust by his bill, Jan. 13, 1874, which provided one for Chase only; while Stevenson's, Dec. 8, 1873, included both chief-justices.

It was Sumner's felicity to move, February 1, 1865, in the Supreme Court, the admission as counsellor of J. S. Rock, a colored man, the first one of his race ever admitted there, — a race which was by Taney's decision excluded from citizenship, and therefore from admission to that tribunal.[1] Sumner had advised with the new chief-justice in advance, and was assured of a favorable result. The public journals and some of his correspondents — Mr. Cobden among them — took note of the event as connected with the senator's career, and as an important step in the enfranchisement of the colored people; and Sumner himself regarded it as preparing the way for the full recognition of their rights as citizens and voters.

Sumner reported from the committee on foreign relations, Dec. 20, 1864, a resolution for giving to Great Britain notice for the termination of the Canadian reciprocity treaty. His remarks in favor of the notice took into account chiefly the derangement to our war system of taxes, resulting from the treaty, and looked to a revision and suspension of the relation of reciprocity with Canada rather than to its final termination.[2] The resolution passed by a large majority, and the notice was given.[3] He also reported and advocated a resolution adopting and ratifying a notice already given by the President for terminating the treaty of 1817, by which the naval forces of the two powers on the lakes were limited.[4] He replied to Davis of Kentucky, who maintained that the President's act was void and incapable of ratification. A debate on the "St. Albans' Raid" drew from him some remarks against any acts on our side which would furnish any seeming apology for foreign intervention.[5]

Sumner argued in the Senate that rich and poor, when relieving themselves from a draft by paying a sum as commutation, should be put on an equality by requiring, in addition to a fixed sum required of all, a further sum, annually, proportionate to income; but his view did not prevail, though it obtained a respectable vote.[6] As the rebel debt was buoyed up in Europe

[1] Works, vol. ix. pp. 229-232.

[2] Letter to Mr. Bright, March 13 (in manuscript). Sumner supported earnestly a system of reciprocity with the Sandwich Islands, and received in 1868 a formal note of thanks from the king for his constant exertions in its behalf.

[3] Dec. 21, 1864, Jan. 11 and 12, 1865; Works, vol. ix. pp. 178-191. The treaty expired March 17, 1866; and though the subject has been kept alive by discussion, no new one has been made.

[4] Jan. 18, 1865. Works, vol. ix. pp. 201-205.

[5] Dec. 19, 1864. Works, vol. ix. pp. 174-177.

[6] Jan. 8, 12, June 20, 1864; Feb. 7, 1865. Works, vol. viii. pp. 42-50.

by the hope that it would finally be assumed by our government, he introduced and carried a resolution affirming that the United States would never recognize it in any way.[1]

Sumner attacked at different sessions the worst monopoly ever known in the country, which long resisted the spirit of the age, — the pretension of the State of New Jersey to levy exceptional tolls on passengers and freight passing through it, between New York and Philadelphia, which were not levied on passengers and freight passing from point to point within the State.[2] Its legislature also invested one corporation with the exclusive power of maintaining a railway within the State between those two cities. This corporation pushed its pretension to the extent of denying the right of the United States to transport between those cities soldiers and military stores over other railways. The monopoly sheltered itself behind State rights; it had at its command ample capital, and could always enlist able lawyers in the Senate, at the head of whom was Reverdy Johnson. The power of Congress "to regulate commerce between the States," since greatly developed, was then latent and untried. Nevertheless, Sumner was determined to make the issue, without calculating closely the chances of success. He called attention to the obstruction of travel and trade by resolutions in 1862 and 1863, and introduced in 1864 a resolution authorizing any railway company to carry the government's supplies and troops from State to State. Before it could be reached in the Senate, a bill of similar purport passed the House; but he could not, against the obstruction of interested parties, get his resolution or the House bill before the Senate.[3] The next session he made, February 14, 1865, an elaborate argument against the monopoly, exposing its character, and treating the constitutional points raised in its defence.[4]

1 Feb. 17, 1865. Works, vol. ix. p. 269.

2 June 9 and Dec. 5, 1862, Works, vol. vii. p. 121; Dec. 22, 1863, Congressional Globe, p. 76; April 25, 1864, Feb. 14, 18, 23, 24, and March 3, 1865, Globe, pp. 790, 889, 1008, 1009, 1059, 1064, 1339; May 29, 1866, Globe, p. 2870; Works, vol. ix. pp. 237-265; vol. x. pp. 469-471.

3 Horace Greeley in a letter to Sumner, June 26, 1864, approved this effort, and wished the bill pressed in the Senate; and a similar testimony came from James M. Scovil of New Jersey. On the other hand, the most eminent physician of Boston then living protested, June 10, 1864, in a letter to the senator, against any interference by Congress, stating that he was the owner of one thousand shares of the stock of the company which held the monopoly. Mr. Greeley attacked the monopoly in a leader printed in the New York "Tribune," July 31, 1865.

4 Works, vol. ix. pp. 238-265. The New York "Tribune," Feb. 21, 1865, called the speech a "concise, luminous, and masterly elucidation of the subject." George Bancroft,

The attempt was made at this session to establish a system of retaliation in kind on rebel prisoners of war, even to the extent of starvation and denial of clothing and medicines in return for like treatment inflicted on our soldiers in Southern prisons,— the retaliatory treatment to be inflicted by Union officers and soldiers who had suffered in such prisons. Sumner encountered the resolutions to that end, which had been reported by Howard of Michigan from the committee on military affairs, with a series of propositions, in which, while recognizing retaliation as an admitted right under the laws of war, he insisted that its methods must conform to the usages of civilized society, and that barbarous conduct in the enemy could not be imitated by the country without degrading the national character. His last resolution, while testifying the sympathy of the United States with their officers and soldiers in prison, "called upon all to bear witness that in this necessary warfare with barbarism, they renounce all vengeance and every evil example, and plant themselves firmly on the sacred landmarks of Christian civilization, under the protection of that God who is present with every prisoner, and enables heroic souls to suffer for their country." The committee's report found its most earnest support in the Western senators,—Wade, Chandler, Harlan, Howe, Lane, Wilkinson, and Brown,—the first two of whom forgot in this debate the requirements of good manners. When Sumner suggested on the first day that the resolutions came up that it was not best to go on with them then, Wade ejaculated, "You would if you were in prison." Chandler expressed surprise that Sumner thought it "inexpedient to protect our suffering prisoners," though expecting such conduct from those who desired the success of the rebellion, described the latter's substitute as "a sublimated specimen of humanitarianism that does not apply to these accursed rebels at this time," and, resorting to threats, proposed to hold Sumner and Wilson responsible before their constituents and the people of the United States for "the blood of every single man who is murdered by these barbarities."

wrote to Sumner that the speech was "masterly, practical, and statesmanlike." It was proposed to obtain votes for the Thirteenth Constitutional Amendment from Democratic members from New Jersey, who as counsel or otherwise were in close relations with the railway companies, by an agreement to postpone the bill. Sumner was not disposed to yield to the arrangement, not being in favor of such methods of obtaining votes, even for a good measure, and believing that the amendment would pass in any event. Nicolay and Hay's "Life of Lincoln," vol. x. p. 84. J. M. Ashley, whom those authors give as authority, has stated in a letter to the writer that neither Mr. Lincoln nor himself imputed Sumner's action to ambition or selfish motive.

Wilson, who took a middle course, resented their style of debate, and said that as he listened to them he thought "the old slave masters had come back again, . . . with all their insolence, and something more than their coarseness." Three Republican senators — Foster, Sprague, and Doolittle — joined with Sumner in opposition to the committee's report; but his allies were mostly Democrats, — two of them, Hendricks and Davis, usually his antagonists, warmly commending the stand he had taken. Sumner was never disturbed by finding himself in strange company when he held positions sustained by principles of humanity and public law. The brunt of Republican opposition to retaliation fell upon him. He spoke twice very earnestly, supporting himself with the citation of authorities and a letter from Dr. Lieber. Wade was driven to accept some amendments, and Sumner carried another against his resistance, which required "conformity with the laws and usages of war among civilized nations."[1] Henderson's amendment, requesting the President to procure a cartel which would allow commissioners of Union prisoners to visit them in their places of confinement, was carried against Wade's protest. The committee's resolutions, thus modified and reduced, passed the Senate without a division, but were not acted on in the House. In view of the profound feeling which was urging retaliation, Sumner's courage, breadth of view, and loyalty to great principles were never more conspicuous. His resolutions were commended by numerous correspondents, including Gen. Robert Anderson, the former commander at Fort Sumter, and General Donaldson of the Army of the Cumberland.

For continuity of narrative the proceedings for reconstruction, which belong to an earlier date, have been reserved for this chapter. The restoration of the revolted States to the Union — the time and manner of making it — had, from the beginning of the Civil War, been a subject of reflection with thoughtful citizens. The Constitution did not contemplate such an extraordinary rupture, — indeed, no government can contemplate its own dissolution, — and therefore no specific remedy or method of

[1] Jan. 24 and 29, 1865; Works, vol. ix. pp. 206-228. Among lawyers who wrote to him commending his course were John Lowell (afterwards United States circuit judge), P. W. Chandler, and Francis E. Parker of Boston, and Edwards Pierrepont of New York. Charles F. Adams, Jr., then an officer in the service, made some temperate criticisms on the senator's positions in letters to him, Feb. 1 and 7, 1865, and also contributed an article on "Retaliation" to the "Army and Navy Journal," January 28.

restoration was provided. In the absence of a prescribed process, the great function of re-establishing rightful government in one half of the country belonged to the people, acting through their representative body, — Congress. Clearly it was not one to be assumed by the President, acting as executive in civil matters, or as commander-in-chief. The trust is safer in the long run with the representatives of the people than with one man; for though the President for the time being may be wiser and better than Congress, he may be the reverse. The right of one President to do it in one way implies the right of another President to do it in another.

The question of reconstruction was not yet ripe for action at any time during the war. Even after the capture of Vicksburg in July, 1863, which broke up the military power of the Confederacy west of the Mississippi, the national troops held securely only sections of any of the revolted States, while other sections were still battle-grounds, or exposed to guerilla warfare; the larger part of the population lately in rebellion, though within our lines, was still hoping for the success of the Confederacy, and was in no mood to accept, in a genuinely loyal spirit, the obligations of citizens of the United States; and civil governments, if created on paper, would fail for want of respect and authority when resting, as they must rest at such a time, on a small fraction of the people. That part of the South which had been recovered, being still under military occupation and martial law, was too much a field of war to admit of the free action of citizens, or to allow civil authority to be more than nominal. Such governments if good for one purpose must be good for all, — for representation in Congress and in the electoral college, as well as for State autonomy. After all the struggle to create them, beginning in 1862, Congress and the President himself recognized that they had no substantial basis or title to respect by the joint resolution approved Feb. 8, 1865, which declared that the eleven rebel States, including Virginia, Louisiana, Arkansas, and Tennessee, were in such a condition at the time of the national election, Nov. 8, 1864, that no valid election for electors was held in them, and therefore no electoral votes from them should be received or counted. Clearly, therefore, they were not then, and had not been since the secession, in a condition to carry on State governments, or to be represented in Congress.

The premature attempts at reconstruction had, however, one justification. It was a common thought in Europe that though the Southern armies might be overcome, the Southern people, being united and determined in their hostility, could never be governed except as a subjugated people, and by arbitrary methods disowned by modern civilization.[1] That thought disturbed also some of our own people. The erection of almost any kind of local government, supported by a respectable portion of the inhabitants, and giving reasonable promise of accessions, would, as it was hoped, help to counteract that discouraging conviction or apprehension, whether existing abroad or at home, and thereby strengthen the government in its contest with the rebellion.[2]

The subject of reconstruction began at an early date in the war to occupy the President's thoughts. It was one for which he felt naturally a much greater aptitude than for the military operations then engrossing the public mind. In the spring of 1862 he appointed military governors for Tennessee, North Carolina, Arkansas, and Louisiana, only sections of each of which were as yet within our lines. Their commissions, while contemplating the restoration of civil order, conferred no authority for the initiation of State governments, or of representation in Congress. In the autumn, however, he began action in that direction by instructions to Shepley, colonel and military governor, which eventuated in the election, December 3, of Hahn and Flanders as members of Congress from Louisiana, when New Orleans and its suburbs only were within our lines, and these places were held under the protection of gunboats.[3] The time and manner of the election were fixed by military orders, and the commissions of the two candidates were signed by Shepley. Hahn and Flanders were admitted to seats in the House, but "not without contention and misgiving."[4] The Senate had no opportunity to pass upon the proceedings. The President resumed his active interest in the reconstruction of Louisiana in June, 1863, and from that time pressed it with great earnestness in his correspondence with the military officers of that department, — with

[1] Cairnes on "The Slave Power," p. 277.

[2] John Jay wrote to Sumner, Dec. 10, 1863: "I hope the President's plan meets your approval. I think the proclamation will have a happy effect on the public mind of the North, and that it will tend to demoralize the rebel army, and develop the Union sentiment of the South." He was, however, dissatisfied with the proceedings in Louisiana, as appears by his letter of March 8, 1864.

[3] Nicolas and Hay's "Life of Lincoln," vol. vi. pp. 349-353.

[4] Blaine's "Twenty Years of Congress," vol. ii. p. 36.

Banks, who had succeeded Butler in command, and Shepley, still military governor. He gave them clearly to understand that there must be no delay arising from conflict of jurisdiction or misconception of their instructions.[1] Meantime, in his annual message, December, 1863, and an accompanying proclamation, he defined a comprehensive scheme of reconstruction, which authorized the re-establishment of State governments on the basis of one-tenth at least of the number of votes cast at the last national election, requiring from the voters an oath to support the Constitution and laws and the proclamations concerning slaves.[2] The old basis of suffrage, excluding colored persons, was maintained. Under orders from General Banks, issued in January and February, 1864, which prescribed the conditions of suffrage (one limiting it to "male white citizens") and other details of the elections, State officers and delegates to a constitutional convention were chosen and a constitution adopted. Some of these orders were curious specimens of mixed civil and military pretensions, — one of them forbidding "open hostility" to the proceedings, and declaring that "indifference will be treated as crime, and faction as treason." The orders had no warrant in any Act of Congress, and did not conform even to the statutes and constitution of the State existing before the rebellion.[3] The vote was largely confined to the city of New Orleans; and out of sixty thousand voters in the State, less than eleven thousand and five hundred, including soldiers, voted for State officers, and only eight thousand and four hundred voted on the constitution, which was ratified September 5. Similar proceedings and elections took place contemporaneously in Arkansas under the lead and direction of military officers who received their orders immediately from the President.[4]

Sumner had from the first, even before the subject had enlisted the President's attention, insisted on the exclusive power of Congress to regulate and determine the restoration of the

[1] Nicolay and Hay's "Life of Lincoln," vol. viii. pp. 419-431.

[2] The President's statement in his speech, April 11, 1865, that this plan was approved by every member of the Cabinet at a meeting where he submitted it was at once corrected by Chase, then chief-justice, in a letter to Mr. Lincoln, April 12. Mr. Chase had at the meeting objected to the restriction of suffrage to the class qualified before the rebellion. Schuckers's "Life of Chase," pp. 516, 517.

[3] Senator Henderson said in debate, Feb. 24, 1865, while supporting a recognition of the Louisiana government, that he agreed that "General Banks had no legal authority to do a great many things that he did."

[4] Nicolay and Hay's "Life of Lincoln," vol. viii. pp. 408-418.

seceded States, and initiate the preliminary process.[1] He believed that the President's authority in the insurgent districts was purely military, derived from martial law, and did not include the power to appoint military governors,[2] — still less the power to regulate elections for members of Congress and State officers, to initiate constitutional conventions, and, above all, to prescribe the conditions of suffrage.[3] But he did not at once enter on a controversy, thinking it wiser to wait, and hopeful that the President's plan would go no further than the message.[4] He wrote to Mr. Bright, December 15: —

"The President's proclamation of reconstruction has two essential features, — (1) The irreversibility of emancipation, making it the corner-stone of the new order of things; (2) The reconstruction or revival of the States by preliminary process before they take their place in the Union. I doubt if the detail will be remembered a fortnight from now. Any plan which fastens emancipation beyond recall will suit me."

The President's proceedings for reconstruction did not meet with favor in Congress. A few days after his message in December, 1863, the subject was referred in the House to a select committee, of which Henry Winter Davis was appointed chairman. Their bill, which came under debate in March, 1864, authorized the appointment of provisional governors for each of the States in rebellion, and as soon as military resistance had been suppressed, and the people had sufficiently returned to their obedience to the Constitution and laws, the calling of constitutional conventions and the organization of State governments. It adopted the President's limitation of suffrage in the initiation of the State government to "white male citizens," and required the participation of one-half of the registered voters where he

1 Resolutions, Feb. 11, 1862; Works, vol. vi. pp. 301–306; letter to meeting in New York, March 6, 1862; ibid., pp. 381–384; article in the Atlantic Monthly, October, 1863; Works, vol. vii. pp. 493–546.

2 Resolutions, June 6, 1862; Works, vol. vii. p. 119; article in the Atlantic Monthly, October, 1863; Works, vol. vii. pp. 494–500.

3 It is likely that, looking to practical ends, he would have waived his constitutional objections to the initiation of reconstruction by the President, both by Mr. Lincoln and later by Mr. Johnson, if they had based the system on what he regarded as the essential condition, — namely, absolute equality of civil and political rights, irrespective of race or color.

4 Nicolay and Hay's statement, vol. ix. p. 109, that "Sumner was joyous, apparently forgetting for the moment his doctrine of State suicide," is contrary to the evidence, so far as the method of reconstruction was concerned. Sumner doubtless rejoiced at the President's renewed affirmation of the policy of emancipation, without at all sanctioning his plan for creating State governments.

had required only one-tenth. Its exclusions from voting and holding office on account of participation in the rebellion were substantially the same as those prescribed by the President. It required the constitutional convention in each State to prohibit slavery forever, and to guarantee the freedom of all persons therein; while the President's plan on this point only prescribed and made known that a provision "recognizing and declaring the permanent freedom of the freed people . . . would not be objected to by the national executive." The bill was in all respects as liberal as the President's scheme, carrying restrictions and disabilities no further;[1] while it was more conservative in requiring a larger proportion of the voters as the basis of the new governments, and wiser as well as juster in enforcing as a peremptory condition of restoration the perpetual prohibition of slavery in the constitutions of the restored States. In details it was more methodical and complete than the President's plan. Both schemes excluded the colored people from suffrage in the initiation of the new governments. In the House, May 4, a motion to strike out the word "white" was cut off by the previous question.[2] When the Senate had under consideration, July 1, the House bill, Wade, chairman of the committee which had reported the bill with an amendment striking out the word "white," declared against the amendment as likely to involve a sacrifice of the bill, and it received only five votes, — those of Brown, Lane of Kansas, Morgan, Pomeroy, and Sumner. Even Hale "waived his conscientious scruples and went for expediency," and Wilson also voted against the amendment. After the Senate had passed Brown's substitute, which omitted the emancipation clause of the House bill, Sumner moved an amendment confirming and enacting the President's proclamation of Jan. 1, 1863; but it was thought untimely, and was rejected,[3] and became unimportant by the Senate's action in receding. Sumner voted for the House bill, although dissatisfied with the basis of suffrage, waiving the point because it secured the abolition of slavery, and asserted the power of Congress over the seceded

[1] Mr. Schurz is in error when he says that this scheme of reconstruction was "much more stringent in its provisions" than the President's proclamation. "Abraham Lincoln: an Essay," p. 96.

[2] Boutwell in his speech, just before the vote was taken on the bill, expressed regret that the limitation of the elective franchise to white male citizens was required by the present judgment of the House and of the country.

[3] Works, vol. ix. p. 48.

States. The carrying of these points seemed to him so urgent then, that, strongly as he was for equality of suffrage, he waived it now and for the last time as a condition of reconstruction. The President neither vetoed nor signed the bill;[1] but under the provision of the Constitution allowing him ten days in which to approve or return a bill, he suffered it to fall with the session just expiring. Immediately after the adjournment of Congress he issued a proclamation stating as reasons for his action his unwillingness, "by a formal approval of the bill, to be inflexibly committed to any single plan of restoration," to set aside and hold for naught free State constitutions and governments already adopted and installed in Arkansas and Louisiana, "or to declare a constitutional competency in Congress to abolish slavery in States,"[2] — at the same time approving "the system of restoration contained in the bill as one very proper for the loyal people of any State choosing to adopt it." This explanatory proclamation called out an energetic protest from Wade of the Senate and Henry Winter Davis of the House, and the President's treatment of the bill encountered almost unanimous dissent among Republican members of Congress.[3] The result was, however, that he carried his point and kept the process of reconstruction in his own hands, to be worked out through the agency of military officers, without Congressional interference.

The President sincerely felt that one mind, and that his own, would reach a better or a speedier result than many minds, — those of senators and representatives, — with chances of disagreement, or of going wrong in the end. The key to his view is found in his instructions to military officers in Louisiana and Arkansas, charged by him with the proceedings for reconstruction, in which he expressed his intention that the officer was to be "the master," — adding, in a letter to one, "Some single mind must be master, else there will be no agreement in any-

[1] Sumner and other senators and representatives called at the President's room at the Capitol as he was signing bills on the last day of the session, to show their anxiety for the fate of this bill. Nicolay and Hay's "Life of Lincoln," vol. ix. pp. 120, 121.

[2] The President maintained his own right to abolish slavery in an emergency on military grounds, but denied such a power in Congress. (Nicolay and Hay's "Life of Lincoln," vol. ix. p. 120.) Congress, however, did not undertake to abolish slavery in States, but only to require each State which had joined the rebellion to abolish it as a condition of restoration to its place in the government.

[3] Blaine's "Twenty Years in Congress," vol. ii. p. 43; Wilson's "Rise and Fall of the Slave Power," vol. iii. pp. 525, 527, 528.

thing;"[1] and in each case he was himself the master of the officer. He was careful to reserve to each house full control over the admission of members from the State; but that power was already secured to those bodies by the Constitution. Its free exercise did not, however, prevent the President's action forestalling that of Congress, — as it would be an anomaly in our system, and greatly embarrass its working, to have State goverments in existence which were recognized by one department (the executive) and repudiated by another (the legislative).

Against Sumner and others, who insisted on grounds of policy and justice upon the inclusion of negroes in the voting body of the returning States, Mr. Lincoln contended that they were attempting "to change this government from its original form and make it a strong centralized power."[2] This contention, adverse to national power, was not in logical conformity with his own method; and it was afterwards altogether discarded by his party and by Congress. When he as well as his successor in their respective proclamations deviated, as each did radically, from the *ante bellum* statutes of Louisiana and the other States in question, making peremptory conditions and novel regulations, and excluding classes of voters, they thereby admitted the right and duty of the United States government to require of the returning States, in its discretion, any basis of suffrage, as well as all other securities which seemed necessary for the permanent peace and welfare of all their inhabitants and of the whole country.

No part of President Lincoln's entire official course was so open to exception as that which he pursued on this subject of reconstruction, where he seemed to assert power for himself, to the exclusion of the people of the United States and of Congress. His attempt, as the event showed, was premature, as no loyal population sufficient in number was found to exist in Louisiana where it was first made; and the history of that

[1] Nicolay and Hay's "Life of Lincoln," vol. viii. pp. 416, 427, 428. In his last Cabinet meeting, April 14, 1865, the President thought it providential that the end of the rebellion came when the question of reconstruction could be considered, as far as the Executive was concerned, without interference by Congress. Ibid., vol. x. p. 283; G. Welles in the "Galaxy," April, 1872, p. 526.

[2] Mr. Lincoln said this of Sumner, Jan. 18, 1865. (Nicolay and Hay's "Life of Lincoln," vol. x. pp. 84, 85.) He said at the Cabinet meeting on the last day of his life, "These humanitarians break down all State rights and constitutional rights. Had the Louisianians inserted the negro in their Constitution, and had that instrument been in all other respects the same, Mr. Sumner would never have excepted to that Constitution." G. Welles in the "Galaxy," April, 1872, p. 526.

people for the next ten years did not exhibit them as the most hopeful subjects of the first experiment. It proved to be a bad precedent, which, adopted by his successor, brought on a memorable conflict with Congress.

In view of the proceedings in Louisiana and Arkansas, and to prevent such exceptional and inconsiderate action as the House took in the admission of Hahn and Flanders from Louisiana, Sumner introduced a resolution, May 27, 1864, declaring that States pretending to secede, and still battling against the national government, must be regarded as rebel States, not to be readmitted to representation until after a vote of both houses,[1] — a precaution against hasty and exceptional action by one body without the other's concurrence, which Congress two years later found it wise to adopt.[2] A few days later the question came up directly on a resolution introduced by Lane of Kansas, to recognize the State government of Arkansas initiated under the President's direction, when Sumner addressed the Senate. He set forth as objections, that the proposed government was organized irregularly under a military order, and by only a small minority of the people, and within a territory still under military occupation, subject to hostile raids, and excluded by law from ordinary commercial intercourse; but the stress of his argument was on his chief proposition, that Congress alone — that is, the two houses (the President in this, as in other legislation, holding the veto power) — could readmit the revolted States.[3] The speech was a strong statement, briefer than most of his speeches on important topics, and it avoided any direct issue with the President. It was an appeal for caution and prudence in a first step of vast consequence, and for waiting on events. Both resolutions — Sumner's and Lane's — went to the judiciary committee, and were reported adversely by Trumbull its chairman; and the credentials of the persons claiming to be senators from the State met the same fate. This was equivalent to a decision

[1] Works, vol. viii. p. 470. He reaffirmed the same doctrine in resolutions, Feb. 23, 1865 (Works, vol. ix. p. 311); and again March 8, 1865 (Works, vol. ix. p. 340). Resolutions of a similar character were proposed by Garfield and Dawes in the House, June 13 and 22, 1864.

[2] The resolution passed the House Feb. 20, 1866, and the Senate March 2.

[3] June 13, 1864; Works, vol. ix. pp. 1-25. At the next session, Feb. 17, 1865, Sumner contended against the recognition of a State government set up in Virginia, on the ground that the Legislature was "little more than the Common Council of Alexandria," and that the greater part of the State was as yet in the possession of an armed rebellion. Works, vol. ix. pp. 266-268.

against the validity of the proceedings in Arkansas. The President, however, two days after the report was made, instructed the officer in command, notwithstanding the adverse action in Congress, to continue to support the State government which had been instituted under his direction.[1]

General Banks came to Washington in the autumn of 1864, and remained some months even after the session began, in order to press the recognition of the Louisiana State government.[2]

From the beginning of the session Sumner had personally urged the President to avoid controversy with Congress on reconstruction. He wrote to Mr. Bright, Jan. 1, 1865: —

> "Meanwhile the questions of statesmanship press for decision. The President is exerting every force to bring Congress to receive Louisiana under the Banks government. I do not believe Louisiana is strong enough in loyalty and freedom for an independent State. The evidence on this point seems overwhelming. I have discussed it with the President, and have tried to impress on him the necessity of having no break between him and Congress on such questions. Much as I am against the premature recognition of Louisiana, I will hold my peace if I can secure a rule for the other States, so that we may be saved from daily anxiety with regard to their condition."[3]

The narrative now reaches, so far as the Senate is concerned, the debate on Trumbull's resolution reported Feb. 18, 1865, from the committee on the judiciary, recognizing as the legitimate government of Louisiana the one formed under Mr. Lincoln's direction and supervision.[4] The manner in which the organization had been made was unsatisfactory to many Republican senators; but with the President earnestly enlisted in its behalf, opposition to the resolution put them in an embarrassing position, and most of them were disposed to overlook the illegal

[1] Nicolay and Hay's "Life of Lincoln," vol. viii. p. 418; vol. ix. p. 445.

[2] General Banks was not in favor with Mrs. Lincoln at this time. She wrote to Sumner notes, asking him to use his influence to prevent the general's appointment as a member of the Cabinet, which she feared might take place. Banks was "very sore" with Sumner on account of his opposition to the Louisiana plan. So the latter wrote to Lieber.

[3] There is other evidence that Sumner, to avoid a contest with the President, would have consented to the admission of Louisiana at this time, with a positive disclaimer that such admission was not to be a precedent, and with satisfactory conditions as to other States. Boston "Commonwealth," March 11, 1865; "Advertiser," Jan. 7, 1871; *ante*, p. 205.

[4] During the session Ashley's reconstruction bill, in different forms, was before the House (January 16, February 21 and 22), but it came to no result. Each draft confined suffrage to "white male citizens," except that in one colored soldiers were admitted to suffrage. Ashley was himself against this discrimination on account of race, but his committee overruled him. Dawes of Massachusetts, while expressing himself in his speech, Feb. 20, 1865, as in favor of suffrage irrespective of race, was opposed to requiring it as a condition in reconstruction.

and irregular origin of the movement. Trumbull's course was a surprise, as he had at the last session opposed the recognition of the Arkansas government, and had at the present session opposed the counting of the electoral votes of Louisiana, as well as of the other States in rebellion. His change of front was referred to in the debate.[1] The other Republican senators, who joined in resisting the recognition of Louisiana, put their opposition on the ground of the initiation of the government by executive and military orders, and an insufficient voting population. Sumner, while insisting on these objections, alone stood inexorable in his demand that all men, irrespective of color, should be equal as citizens in the reorganized States. In this stand, now and in later controversies, he would yield to no asserted urgency, no supposed adverse public opinion, no technical point of constitutional inability, no vote of caucus, no defeats in either house, not even to the pressure and prestige of the President himself. He made up his mind to stop the admission of rebellious States to the Union without absolute guaranties of freedom and equality, including the admission of the colored people to the right of suffrage upon precisely the same terms as were to be applied to white men. In effecting that purpose, the session being near its end, he was determined to avail himself of all the resources of parliamentary law to defeat the measure, even if, by its promoters refusing to yield, the revenue and appropriation bills should be lost. He believed that a first false step would be fatal; and with that conviction he did not hesitate to take the responsibility, cost what it might. As he said in the debate: "I think it [the measure] dangerous: and thinking it dangerous, I am justified in opposing it, and justified, too, in employing all the instruments that I can find in the arsenal of parliamentary warfare." [2]

The President was not, however, at any time personally opposed to the admission of the colored people to the elective franchise, and privately and publicly expressed his hope and desire that the very intelligent, and those who had served as soldiers, should be admitted to it; but he was firmly of opinion that the decision, as to whether they should have the right or not, must be left with the class of voters qualified before the war.[3]

[1] Trumbull had conferred personally with the President on the proceedings in Louisiana early in January. Nicolay and Hay's "Life of Lincoln," vol. ix. p. 453.

[2] February 25.

[3] Letter to Governor Hahn, March 13, 1864.

The struggle began Thursday, February 23, when Trumbull moved to take up the resolution concerning Louisiana, and Sumner urged instead the consideration of the interstate commerce bill, which, as he said, was a practical measure, unlike the Louisiana resolution, which would prove "merely a dance of debate." Trumbull reminded the Senate that "if a single negro is expelled from the cars in the District of Columbia the voice of the senator from Massachusetts is heard in this hall. He will repeal charters and take up the time of Congress about the rights of the negro," but he would not give a hearing to the ten thousand loyal men of Louisiana. Doolittle claimed that the vote of Louisiana was needed to ratify the thirteenth amendment to the Constitution; and Sumner replied that only nineteen loyal States were required to ratify it, rejecting from the whole number the States in rebellion,[1] at the same time charging Doolittle with "again setting himself upon the side of slavery, and by his interpretation seeking to arrest the great march of human freedom." Doolittle retorted that Sumner had opposed the thirteenth amendment, — a charge which the latter repelled with emphasis, declaring that he had given that measure his most ardent support. The Senate voted to take up the resolution; and Sumner moved a substitute, forbidding elections in any insurgent State until the President by proclamation shall have declared that armed hostility within it had ceased, and Congress shall have declared it entitled to representation; but it obtained only eight votes, — those of Brown, Conness, Grimes, Howard, Sprague, Stewart, Sumner, and Wade. On the 24th Sumner renewed his effort to displace the resolution with other business, but not with success. When asked not to waste time, and senators said from their seats, "Give up!" he replied, "That is not my habit." Conness said, "We know that," and there was laughter. The debate proceeded. Powell of Kentucky, from a Southern standpoint, opposed the resolution. A motion from Chandler to take up another bill, which was lost, called from Sumner the remark, "The measure that the senator from Michigan has in charge is a reality; the measure that the senator from Illinois has in charge is a shadow." Doolittle thought it unbecoming in Sumner, with all his professions for freedom and free States, to

[1] He maintained the same view in his letter to the New York "Evening Post," Sept. 28, 1865. (Works, vol. ix. pp. 489–492.) The same point was involved in his speech, July 12, 1862, on a constitutional quorum of the Senate. Works, vol. vii. pp. 169–175.

join hands with the Senator from Kentucky in undertaking to prevent the recognition of the free State of Louisiana. Henderson, speaking in irony, thought that the rebellion was about at an end, in view of "the close alliance and affiliation of the senators" from Massachusetts and Kentucky, and that "the lion and the lamb had lain down together." He reviewed at length the proceedings in Louisiana, and supported the resolution.

When the resolution came up at noon on Saturday, the 25th, Sumner sent to the chair, as a substitute, a series of propositions affirming the duty of the United States by Act of Congress to re-establish republican governments in place of those vacated by the rebellion, — denying that the power could be intrusted to any military commander or executive officer, and declaring that such new governments should not be founded on an "oligarchical class," with the disfranchisement of loyal people, and that the cause of human rights and of the Union needed the ballots as well as the muskets of colored men.[1] Another amendment which he offered imposed equal suffrage as a fundamental condition on the reconstructed States. Howard maintained the right of Congress to initiate the proceedings, and contended at length that the President's action was premature and illegal. Reverdy Johnson divided from his Southern associates and supported the resolution.[2] There was a colloquy between Sumner and Johnson as to the power of a State to establish slavery, — the former denying and the latter affirming it. The supporters of the resolution were determined to force a final vote on that day. Trumbull called upon senators, in order to dispose of the matter, to attend at a night session to hear all the senator from Massachusetts had to say, and then vote on his amendments. The principal debaters at the evening session, which began at seven, were the same as before, with the addition of Clark of New Hampshire, who came to the support of the committee. Henderson had denied that Congress had the right to impose conditions of suffrage on the returning States; and even Pomeroy, usually voting, as he said, for Sumner's antislavery propositions, took the same view. Sumner maintained stoutly and broadly that "Congress, when reconstructing rebel States, can stamp upon them freedom in all respects, and remove absolutely

[1] Works, vol. ix. pp. 329-336.

[2] Johnson and Sumner fell into an incidental controversy as to the meaning of the term, "the consolidation of the Union," in Washington's letter to Congress, Sept. 17, 1787. Congressional Globe, pp. 1068, 1098, 1103, 1104.

all disabilities on account of color." Motions by Wade, Chandler, Howard, and Sumner to adjourn or postpone or lay on the table were voted down, and even a motion from Wilson to adjourn met the same fate. The contest went on. Trumbull pushed personalities further than before, calling Sumner to account for "lecturing other senators" and "associating with those he had often denounced," for making obstructive motions and delaying the important business of the country, and for determining, in combination with other senators, to browbeat the Senate. Sumner repelled the charge of "browbeating" as more appropriate to Trumbull himself, declaring his purpose and maintaining his right to employ all the instruments of parliamentary warfare to defeat a measure which he believed to be dangerous. He counselled the senator from Illinois to look at the clock and note that it was twenty-five minutes to eleven, with Sunday morning near, and that efforts to force a vote would be fruitless, like "sowing salt in the sand by the seashore." He compared Trumbull's attempt "to cram the resolution down the throats of the Senate" to that of another senator from Illinois (Douglas), who brought in his Kansas-Nebraska bill in precisely the same manner, — "proudly, confidently, almost menacingly," with the declaration that it was to pass in twenty-four hours, "precisely as the senator from Illinois now speaks;" and he invoked the Senate to devote the remnant of the session to practical measures instead of consuming it with "a bantling not a week old." Doolittle called the American people to witness the scene in the Senate, and particularly the senator from Massachusetts, — one of five only among the Administration senators who had kept up a factious resistance, and usurped authority over their eighteen Republican associates, rebuking Sumner for "his arrogance and assumed superiority over his equals and his peers," and his attempt "to break down the right of every State to judge upon its own suffrage." Several passages took place between the two senators, in which each treated the other's position as hostile to freedom. Now and then a Democrat intervened briefly; and this time Hendricks, who said that "the senator from Massachusetts is determined that none of these States shall ever be heard in the halls of Congress until the men who speak from those States speak the voice of the negroes as well as of the white men." Trumbull admitted that a vote could not be reached against such "a factious opposition," and

Sumner replied, "I told you so some hours ago;" and finally, half an hour before midnight, the Senate adjourned. Five days only of the session remained, and the appropriation as well as revenue bills were to be debated. On Monday morning, with the first suggestion of taking a vote, Sumner assured the senator making it that it was "utterly impossible to take the vote." Trumbull renewed, with repetition, the charge of "factious opposition." Sherman now interposed with a plea for immediate attention to the revenue and appropriation bills, which required the remaining five days, disclaiming at the same time any censure on senators who had in the discussion of the Louisiana question been performing what they believed to be their conscientious duty; and he moved to take up a revenue bill. Wade, who with intense feeling on the subject had hitherto kept out of the debate, now entered on a fierce denunciation of the pretended State government as "a mockery,—a miserable mockery," like the Lecompton constitution for Kansas; taunted Trumbull for "his miraculous conversion" on the Louisiana question; protested against the President's claim of right, operating through his major-generals, to initiate a State government; repudiated the one formed as based on voters "drummed up from the riff-raff of New Orleans;" and denounced "the ten per cent principle as absurd, monarchical, and anti-American." Howard returned to the contest, and repelled "the unfounded, the ungentlemanly charges of the arrogant senator from Illinois," reminding him again of his sudden conversion to the measure. Grimes and Sprague briefly supported Sumner with statements as to the proceedings in Louisiana. The debate had gone on thus far since noon on Sherman's motion to take up a revenue bill, each senator, contrary to strict rule, discussing the main question. Sumner again rose and proceeded to denounce the pretended State government as "a mere seven months' abortion, begotten by the bayonet, in criminal conjunction with the spirit of caste, and born before its time, rickety, unformed, unfinished, whose continued existence will be a burden, a reproach, and a wrong." At the end of his next sentence, which was pointed at Trumbull, Sherman insisted on conforming the debate strictly to his motion to take up a revenue bill. Senators at last recognized the impossibility of reaching a vote on the pending resolution, and Sherman's motion was carried by a vote of thirty-four to twelve.[1]

1 Works, vol. ix. pp. 311-328, give extracts from the debate.

The five Republican senators (Brown, Chandler, Howard, Sumner, and Wade) and seven Democratic senators voted together on the dilatory motions against eighteen or twenty Republican senators who were in favor of recognizing the proposed State government of Louisiana. As many as twenty senators were silent on successive calls of the yeas and nays,[1] of whom a considerable majority were Republicans; and the larger number of the Republicans not answering were in sympathy with Sumner, though indisposed to an open stand against a measure which the President had greatly at heart.[2]

If the President's plan had prevailed for Louisiana and the other rebel States, it would have resulted in the permanent exclusion of the colored people from the suffrage in all the old slave States. It was clear to Sumner then that equal suffrage, without distinction of color or race, was to be established with reconstruction or not at all; and subsequent events — the stern contest under Johnson and all that has followed — have demonstrated his foresight. The white population, separated not only by the memories of the slave relation, but as well by the indelible brand of color, would never without national intervention have conferred the boon; and in this they would have been neither better nor worse than master races so separated have always been.

This was Sumner's hardest parliamentary contest, and he carried his point. He had earnest coadjutors in Howard and Wade; but it was admitted in unfriendly quarters that his masterful spirit alone defeated the recognition of the State government of Louisiana.[3] He stood alike for reconstruction by the people through Congress, and for the complete citizenship of a race; and on this last ground he stood alone. His resistance rallied the antislavery masses to his advanced position, to which

[1] Only four were recorded absent on the vote to take up the revenue bill, showing that as many as fifteen or sixteen were withholding their votes from want of sympathy with the resolution. The Senate contained only about ten Democratic members.

[2] Sumner referred to Collamer's views in his tribute to that senator, Dec. 14, 1865. Works, vol. x. p. 43.

[3] New York World, Feb. 28, 1865; New York Herald, March 1; Springfield Republican, March 1. R. H. Dana, Jr., passed a severe judgment on Sumner's bearing and positions in the contest; but he was not at the time in accord with Republican ideas of emancipation and reconstruction (being even opposed to Lincoln's proclamation), to which, however, he came a few months later; and he was not then, as at an earlier or later period, in political and personal sympathy with Sumner. Adams's "Biography of Dana," vol. ii. pp. 263, 276, 330–335. Sumner was strong in his language, but not stronger than his opponent Trumbull, or his supporters Howard and Wade.

after agitation and contention the people were yet to come. For weal or woe, whether it was well or not for the black man and the country, it is to Sumner's credit or discredit as a statesman that suffrage, irrespective of color or race, became fixed and universal in the American system.

The heated debate left some griefs behind. Sumner and Trumbull, though often co-operating, were not cordial for some years; but when Sumner was removed from the committee on foreign relations in 1871, one of his ablest defenders was the senator from Illinois; and when he left the Senate finally, Sumner parted from him with sincere regret.

The President had set his heart on the project, and was sorely disappointed at its failure. To friends, and even to strangers, he talked freely of Sumner's course, and some thought that the relations of confidence between them heretofore would now end; but those who thought thus did not understand Mr. Lincoln's largeness of soul. He was tolerant; and while tenacious of his rights as President, he respected the rights of a senator.[1] Besides, Sumner, while maintaining the sole right of Congress to initiate reconstruction, had avoided all direct reflection on the President's action. In the few weeks of life which remained to him, Mr. Lincoln bestowed more tokens of good-will on Sumner than on any senator.

The public attention was not diverted from the triumphs of the army by this contest in the Senate; nor had the masses of the people yet taken a practical interest in reconstruction. Sumner's chief congratulations came therefore from the distinctively antislavery men, — such as Wendell Phillips, Parker Pillsbury, F. W. Bird, F. B. Sanborn, Rev. George B. Cheever, and Frederick Douglass. A letter from the writer, March 4, who little thought then of his future connection with the memory of the statesman, said: —

"God bless you a thousand times for your indomitable resistance to the admission of Louisiana, with her caste system! This afternoon some forty gentlemen dined at Bird's room,[2] and all, *nemine dissentiente,* approved it, and with full praise."

[1] Works, vol. ix. p. 324. He is reported to have said, January 18, before the debate came on: "I can do nothing with Mr. Sumner in these matters. While Mr. Sumner is very cordial with me, he is making his history in an issue with me on this very point." Nicolay and Hay's "Life of Lincoln," vol. x. p. 85.

[2] A Republican club, composed mostly of radical antislavery men, which dined on Saturdays in Boston.

Frederick Douglass wrote from Rochester, April 29: —

"The friends of freedom all over the country have looked to you and confided in you, of all men in the United States Senate, during all this terrible war. They will look to you all the more now that peace dawns, and the final settlement of our national troubles is at hand. God grant you strength equal to your day and your duties, is my prayer and that of millions!"

Singularly enough, another Abolitionist (Garrison) failed to support the negro's cause at this initial stage of the struggle for his political enfranchisement, and heartily sustained the proceedings which excluded him.[1] Wendell Phillips, however, stood firmly against his old leader, and carried with him the mass of the Abolitionists.

Sumner wrote to Mr. Bright, March 13: —

"I have your good and most suggestive letter. I concur in it substantially. A practical difficulty is this: Can emancipation be carried out without using the lands of the slave-masters? We must see that the freedmen are established on the soil, and that they may become proprietors. From the beginning I have regarded confiscation only as ancillary to emancipation. The great plantations, which have been so many nurseries of the rebellion, must be broken up, and the freedmen must have the pieces. It looks as if we were on the eve of another agitation. I insist that the rebel States shall not come back except on the footing of the Declaration of Independence, with all persons equal before the law, and government founded on the consent of the governed. In other words, there shall be no discrimination on account of color. If all whites vote, then must all blacks; but there shall be no limitation of suffrage for one more than the other. It is sometimes said, 'What! let the freedman, yesterday a slave, vote?' I am inclined to think that there is more harm in refusing than in conceding the franchise. It is said that they are as intelligent as the Irish just arrived; but the question has become immensely practical in this respect. Without their votes we cannot establish stable governments in the rebel States. Their votes are as necessary as their muskets; of this I am satisfied. Without them, the old enemy will re-appear, and under the forms of law take possession of the governments, choose magistrates and officers, and in alliance with the Northern democracy, put us all in peril again, postpone the day of tranquillity, and menace the national credit by assailing the national debt. To my mind, the nation is now bound by self-interest — ay, self-defence — to be thoroughly just. The Declaration of Independence has pledges which have never been redeemed. We must redeem them, at least as regards the rebel States which have fallen under our jurisdiction. Mr. Lincoln is slow in accepting truths. I have reminded him that if he would say the word we might settle this question promptly and rightly. He hesitates. Meanwhile I felt it my duty to oppose his scheme of government in Louisiana, which for the present is defeated in Congress."

[1] W. L. Garrison's "Life," vol. iv. pp. 122, 123, 153, 154.

Mr. Lincoln was inaugurated, for his second term, March 4, and on that occasion delivered — save the one at Gettysburg — his most impressive address, closing it with the paragraph which began "with malice towards none, with charity for all." The same day the Vice-President elect, Andrew Johnson, appeared in the Senate chamber to take his oath, in a state of intoxication. Senators and citizens witnessed the strange scene with a sense of humiliation. This condition was prolonged for some days, during which he was taken from his hotel by Preston King, late senator from New York, and Montgomery Blair, to the house of Mr. Blair, Sr., at Silver Springs, near Washington. His unseemly exhibition of himself in the presence of the nation was the subject of discussion in a meeting of Republican senators held shortly after, in which Sumner, who was always sensitive to whatever concerned the dignity of high office, advised that he be waited upon with a request for his resignation. His consciousness that he had exposed himself in a disgusting plight, and that notice had been taken of it by leading Republicans, is thought to have had something to do with his speedy alienation from the best people of the country.[1]

These ceremonies, which took place on Saturday, were followed by the inauguration ball on Monday. On the intervening day Mr. Lincoln sent Sumner an autograph note,[2] as follows:

EXECUTIVE MANSION, WASHINGTON, March 5, 1865.

HON. C. SUMNER.

MY DEAR SIR, — I should be pleased for you to accompany us to-morrow evening, at ten o'clock, on a visit of half an hour to the Inaugural Ball. I enclose a ticket. Our carriage will call for you at half-past nine.

Yours truly, A. LINCOLN.

The President's carriage was at Sumner's lodgings at the time named. On entering the ball-room, Mr. Lincoln and Mr. Colfax (the Speaker) led; next followed Sumner escorting Mrs. Lincoln; and then Mr. Seward and daughter, Secretary Usher and wife, Senator Wilson and wife, and others.[3]

1 Wilson's "Rise and Fall of the Slave Power," vol. iii. p. 578; Julian's "Political Recollections," pp. 273-274.

2 The original note is preserved in the Harvard College Library.

3 The correspondent of the New York "Herald," March 8, remarked that "it was presumed that the President had indorsed his [Mr. Sumner's] reconstruction theories." The inference was not justified; but, as Sumner wrote subsequently, the President "recognized the right of Mr. Sumner to his individual judgment." Works, vol. ix. pp. 323, 324; Boston "Advertiser," Jan. 7, 1871.

Mrs. Lincoln had some time before conceived an admiration for Sumner's personal qualities and public work. It was shown not only in counsels with him on pending questions, but in friendly acts, — sometimes in flowers sent to his lodgings, and again in invitations to meet other guests informally at the White House. Notwithstanding her Southern origin, she had come, perhaps partly under Sumner's influence, to be in sympathy, more than her husband, with a radical antislavery policy. Before coming to Washington her social advantages had not been large, and her early training was not complete; but her education was beyond that of the people among whom she was born or had lived. She could read French fairly well, and was renewing the study of the language during her last days in Washington. Her notes to Sumner betoken a lady, kindly, refined, and of intellectual tastes.

The extra session of the Senate following the inauguration ended March 11. Sumner was again appointed chairman of the committee on foreign relations, and took also the second place on the committee on enrolled bills. The reconstruction of Arkansas and Louisiana was debated on propositions to receive credentials and pay mileage. Sumner spoke only briefly, but offered a resolution stating the conditions for the admission of senators from the rebel States; namely, the cessation of hostilities, the adoption of a republican form of government by the State, and an affirmative act of Congress recognizing its right to representation.[1] Lane of Kansas, who was the partisan of the senators seeking admission, referring to Sumner's opposition to the admission of the Louisiana senators, said he had a few days before worn out senators physically, and secured a postponement. Sumner kept out of the debate, and the credentials were referred, but no further action was taken.

He wrote to Mrs. L. M. Child, April 2: —

"I trust that the letter to the emperor of Brazil, with the excellent tract,[2] is already far on the way. I gave them to the Brazilian minister here, with the request that he would have the goodness to forward them. I count much upon the enlightened character of the emperor. Of course, slavery must cease everywhere when it ceases among us. Its neck is in our rebellion, which we are now sure to cut. Cuba, Porto Rico, and Brazil must do as we do, without our terrible war, I trust."

[1] March 8, 1865. Works, vol. ix. p. 340.

[2] Mrs. Child's pamphlet, "The Right Way the Safe Way."

Sumner remained in Washington two months longer. It was, as already seen, his custom to linger there after the close of a session in order to bring up arrears of business and correspondence, and to prosecute studies on questions pending or at hand; but he had a particular purpose now, when projects of reconstruction, in view of the approaching end of the rebellion, were rife. During these weeks he saw much of the President in friendly calls at the White House and in conference on business of different kinds. He accompanied Mr. and Mrs. Lincoln sometimes to the theatre or opera, — once on the President's visit next preceding the fatal one.[1]

Sumner had occasion soon after the adjournment of Congress to see the President with reference to the case of two Boston merchants, who had been prosecuted by the navy department on the charge of fraud, and after trial by court-martial, were sentenced to imprisonment and fine. He appealed directly to the President to annul the sentence, and at the latter's request prepared an Opinion[2] reviewing the report of the Secretary of the Navy, who had approved the proceedings of the court-martial. Sumner sought the President with his Opinion as soon as it was finished, Friday, March 17; and the next day the President, in a sententious indorsement on the papers characteristic in style, entirely annulled the proceedings. Sumner's account of what took place after he prepared his Opinion is interesting: —

"It was late in the afternoon, and the latter [the President] was about entering his carriage for a drive, when Mr. Sumner arrived with the papers in his hand. He at once mentioned the result he had reached, and added that it was a case for instant action. The President proposed that he should return the next day, when he would consider it with him. Mr. Sumner rejoined that in his opinion the President ought not to sleep on the case; that he should interfere promptly for the relief of innocent fellow-citizens, and urged that if Abraham Lincoln had suffered unjust imprisonment as a criminal, with degradation before his neighbors, an immense bill of expense, a trial by court-martial, and an unjust condemnation, he would cry out against any postponement of justice for a single day. The President, apparently impressed by Mr. Sumner's earnestness and his personal appeal, appointed eleven o'clock that evening, when he would go over the case and hear Mr. Sumner's Opinion. Accordingly, at eleven o'clock that evening, in the midst of a thunder-storm filling the streets with water and threatening chimneys, Mr. Sumner made his way to the Presidential mansion. At the very hour named he was received, and at the request of the President proceeded to read his Opinion.

[1] "Faust" at Grover's Theatre, Saturday evening, March 18.

[2] Works, vol. ix. pp. 341-360; vol. xv. p. 66.

The latter listened attentively, with occasional comments, and at the close showed his sympathy with the respondents. It was now twenty minutes after midnight, when the President said that he would write his conclusion at once, and that Mr. Sumner must come and hear it the next morning, — 'when I open shop,' said he. 'And when do you open shop?' Mr. Sumner inquired. 'At nine o'clock,' was the reply. At that hour Mr. Sumner was in the office he had left after midnight, when the President came running in, and read at once the indorsement in his own handwriting, as follows: —

I am unwilling for the sentence to stand and be executed, to any extent, in this case. In the absence of a more adequate motive than the evidence discloses, I am wholly unable to believe in the existence of criminal or fraudulent intent on the part of one of such well-established good character as the accused. If the evidence went as far toward establishing a guilty profit of one or two hundred thousand dollars, as it does of one or two hundred dollars, the case would, on the question of guilt, bear a far different aspect. That on this contract, involving from one million to twelve hundred thousand dollars, the contractors should attempt a fraud which at the most could profit them only one or two hundred, or even one thousand, dollars, is to my mind beyond the power of rational belief. That they did not, in such a case, strike for greater gains proves that they did not, with guilty or fraudulent intent, strike at all. The judgment and sentence are disapproved and declared null, and the accused ordered to be discharged.

A. LINCOLN.

March 18, 1865.

"Then followed an incident as original as anything in the life of Henry IV. of France, or of a Lacedæmonian king. As Mr. Sumner was making an abstract of the indorsement for communication by telegraph to the anxious parties, the President broke into quotation from Petroleum V. Nasby; and seeing that his visitor was less at home than himself in this patriotic literature, he said, 'I must initiate you,' and then repeated with enthusiasm the message he had sent to the author: 'For the genius to write these things I would gladly give up my office!' Then rising and turning to a standing-desk behind, he opened it, and took out a pamphlet collection of the letters already published, which he proceeded to read aloud, evidently enjoying it much. For the time he seemed to forget the case he had just decided, and Presidential duties. This continued more than twenty minutes, when Mr. Sumner, thinking there must be many at the door waiting to see the President on graver matters, took advantage of a pause, and, thanking him for the lesson of the morning, left. Some thirty persons, including senators and representatives, were in the anteroom as he passed out. Though with the President much during the intervening days before his death, this was the last business Mr. Sumner transacted with him."

The rebellion had now reached its last stage. The President left Washington by boat on the Potomac, Thursday, March 23, for City Point, the headquarters of the army of Virginia, and did not return to Washington till Sunday evening, April 9. Mrs. Lincoln, who went with him, expecting their return to be earlier than it proved to be, invited Sumner by note, as they were leaving, to accompany them the next Wednesday evening to the Italian opera, — at the same time promising to send him her copy of Louis Napoleon's "Cæsar," just received from Paris. She reached Washington from the headquarters on Sunday, April 2, leaving, however, Mr. Lincoln behind, and as soon as she arrived invited Sumner to join her on her return to City Point. The next morning she sent him from the Executive Mansion the tidings of the evacuation of Richmond, just received from the Secretary of War. She left Washington again, Wednesday, April 5, accompanied by Sumner, the Marquis de Chambrun (who was invited at the senator's suggestion), Secretary Harlan,[1] Mrs. and Miss Harlan, Mr. and Mrs. James Speed, and Judge Otto. At Fort Monroe, in the night or early morning, they heard by telegraph of Mr. Seward's serious injury received in a fall from his carriage. At City Point, where they arrived about noon on the 6th, they found Mr. Lincoln.[2] They visited him on board the "River Queen," where there was a pleasant conversation, in which the President indicated the places where the Confederate commissioners sat in the saloon of the steamer at the Hampton Roads conference, February 3, and with maps before him explained General Grant's present movements. The party, leaving Mr. Lincoln, went on to Richmond that afternoon (Thursday), and drove with an escort of cavalry to noted places, — among them the capitol, where Sumner sought for the ancient archives, and inquired about certain public men, particularly Hunter, formerly senator.[3] They returned to the boat, where they remained till morning.[4] The night was weird, with Manchester still burning, and the flames visible from the boat, but Richmond lying in darkness. The next morning (Friday) the party returned to City Point, and (the President joining them) they went to Petersburg, going and returning by

[1] Secretary of the Interior, with an appointment to take effect at a later date.

[2] This was the day when the President wrote to General Weitzel, and sent a despatch to General Grant concerning the Virginia Legislature. (Nicolay and Hay's "Life of Lincoln," vol. x. pp. 222–228.) His action in authorizing its members to meet was generally disapproved; and he himself, on reconsideration, recalled it April 12, — his last official act.

[3] The incident is related that Sumner's having obtained at Richmond the gavel of the Confederate Congress, which he proposed to give to Stanton, Mr. Lincoln said to Speaker Colfax that he ought to have it, adding, "Tell him [Sumner] from me to hand it over." This was the President's last pleasantry before going to the play on the fatal night. Boston "Journal," April 15; New York "Tribune," April 17.

[4] This was Sumner's first and only visit to Richmond; and it gave him an opportunity to see Crawford's statue of Washington, in which he had been greatly interested.

rail, and on Saturday visited the tent hospitals at City Point, where the President shook hands with five thousand sick and wounded soldiers, saying to Sumner that his arm was not tired.[1] Late that evening they left, the President with them, to return in the "River Queen" to Washington. The company was a small one; their meals were taken at one table, and they were thrown familiarly together.[2] Conversation flowed freely, and all were happy, full of rejoicing and hope. The recent successes, the sure and speedy end of the rebellion, and the coming of peace were the topics.[3] The President's mind was upon the subject of reconstruction; but he made no confidential communication to Sumner upon it, as each had fixed ideas not accepted by the other. In the course of the day the President read to the few friends about him, with a beautiful quarto copy of Shakspeare in his hands, the tribute to the murdered Duncan, — "Macbeth" being his favorite play, — and "impressed by the beauty of the words, or by some presentiment unuttered," he read the passage aloud a second time.[4] He repeated also from memory some lines from Longfellow's "Resignation."[5] It was probably the same day that Sumner asked him if he had ever had any doubt about his declaration made in 1858, when he opened his campaign with Douglas, — "A house divided against itself cannot stand;" and he answered, "Not in the least; it was clearly true, and time has justified me."[6]

The party arrived in Washington at six, P. M., Sunday, the 9th, and the President at once sought Mr. Seward, who had been kept in bed by his injury. It is not certain that Sumner saw the President again until he stood at his bedside on the night of the 14th. On the 10th a message from the White House, accompanied with a bunch of flowers, communicated to Sumner the surrender of Lee's army. On Tuesday evening, the 11th, the

1 Works, vol. ix. p. 410; New York "Tribune," April 11; Boston "Journal," April 15. The correspondent of the "Journal," April 10, probably obtained the details of his account from Sumner.

2 "Breakfasting, lunching, and dining in one small family party," etc. Sumner to the Duchess of Argyll, April 24 (manuscript).

3 Probably it was while coming up the Potomac that Mr. Lincoln replied to one "privileged to address him familiarly [Mrs. Lincoln], who had adjured him to see that Jefferson Davis suffered the extreme penalty, "Judge not, that ye be not judged," repeating the same answer when further pressed. Sumner's Eulogy on Lincoln, June 1, 1865; Works, vol. ix. p. 416.

4 Works, vol. ix. pp. 407, 408.

5 Mrs. Lincoln's letter to Sumner, July 5, 1865 (manuscript).

6 Works, vol. ix. p. 379.

city was illuminated in honor of the final victory. A note from Mrs. Lincoln invited Sumner to come to the White House, bringing his friend the marquis to witness the spectacle, and mentioned that "a little speech" from Mr. Lincoln was expected.[1] It was the President's last public utterance; and the subject of reconstruction was absorbing his thoughts. He defended at length what had been done in Louisiana, apparently with Sumner's opposition in mind.[2] As in his letter to Hahn, a year before, he signified his own personal desire to have the suffrage conferred on some of the colored people, "on the very intelligent, and on those who serve our cause as soldiers," but he preferred (such was the tenor of his speech) to have that question left to events, and not to insist on their admission at the outset, and thereby arrest the process of reconstruction.[3] Sumner was called for by the crowd, but he was not present. The speech was not in keeping with what was in men's minds. The people had gathered, from an instinctive impulse, to rejoice over a great and final victory; and they listened with respect, but with no expressions of enthusiasm, except that the quaint simile of "the egg" drew applause.[4] The more serious among them felt that the President's utterances on the subject were untimely, and that his insistence at such an hour on his favorite plan was not the harbinger of peace among the loyal supporters of the government. Sumner was thoughtful and sad when the speech was reported to him; for he saw at hand another painful contest with a President whom he respected, on a question where he felt it his duty to stand firm, whatever might be the odds against him.[5] He wrote at once to Lieber: "The President's speech and other things augur confusion and uncertainty in the future, with hot controversy. Alas! alas!"

[1] The Marquis de Chambrun's "Personal Recollections" of Lincoln and Sumner, particularly in the visit to Richmond, have been published posthumously in Scribner's Magazine for January and February, 1893, since these pages were in type. While the marquis was living, the writer had access to the manuscript, as prepared in French, which has been enlarged in the translation.

[2] Nicolay and Hay's "Life of Lincoln," vol. ix. pp. 457-463.

[3] The New York "Tribune's" correspondent, April 12, wrote that "the speech fell dead, wholly without effect on the audience," and that "it caused a great disappointment and left a painful impression." The correspondent of the Boston "Journal," April 12, notes applause at other passages of the speech, but says that this part was "listened to with attention and silence."

[4] "We shall sooner have the fowl by hatching the egg than by smashing it." Sumner, in his tribute to Senator Collamer, Dec. 14, 1865 (Works, vol. x. p. 44), said: "The eggs of crocodiles can produce only crocodiles; and it is not easy to see how eggs laid by military power can be hatched into an American State."

[5] Dr. George B. Loring, who had heard the speech, called on Sumner the next morning and found him much grieved by it.

Mrs. Lincoln invited Sumner to witness from the White House, on Thursday evening, the illuminations, in company with General Grant, who was expected to arrive that evening; but it is not known that he accepted. The next day (Friday, the 14th, ever memorable in American annals), at a meeting of the Cabinet, the President resumed the question of reconstruction, repeating the views he had already expressed, mentioning Sumner's opposite view, and adjourning the discussion to a day of the next week, when he was not to meet them.[1] On the evening of that Friday, at or about twenty minutes past ten, he was assassinated at Ford's Theatre by John Wilkes Booth. He became instantly senseless, and did not recover consciousness. Sumner was at the time at the house of Senator Conness, in company with him and Senator Stewart; and being told what had occurred by some one rushing in from the street, they went quickly to the White House, and then to the theatre, reaching Mr. Lincoln, who was already in the house opposite, about half an hour after the fatal shot had been fired. There Sumner remained till the President's last breath, at twenty-two minutes past seven, the next morning.[2] A bystander, at one in the night, wrote: "Senator Sumner was seated on the right of the President's couch, near the head, holding the right hand of the President in his own. He was sobbing like a woman, with his head bowed down almost on the pillow of the bed on which the President was lying."[3] A witness, in describing the last moment of the scene, said: "Senator Sumner, General Todd, Robert Lincoln, and Rufus Andrews stood leaning over the headboard, watching every motion of the beating heart of the dying President. Robert Lincoln was resting on the arm of Senator Sumner."[4] At the moment of death Sumner was at the head of the bed, by the side of Robert Lincoln.[5] As soon as Mr.

[1] Nicolay and Hay's "Life of Lincoln," vol. x. pp. 282–285; G. Welles in "The Galaxy," April, 1872, p. 526. Speed, the attorney-general, reported to Chief-Justice Chase that the President came nearer at this meeting than before to those who were in favor of equal suffrage, and admitted that he "had perhaps been too fast in his desire for early reconstruction." Schuckers's "Life of Chase," p. 519. But this does not appear in Welles's account of the meeting.

[2] Sumner's movements that evening are detailed by A. B. Johnson in Scribner's Magazine, October, 1874, p. 224, in the correspondence of the Boston "Journal," April 15, and in Chaplin's "Life of Sumner," pp. 413–417, which contains a statement furnished by Moorfield Storey. These accounts, like most of the accounts of that night, are likely to contain inaccuracies and discrepancies.

[3] New York Herald, April 15; Tribune, April 15.

[4] New York Herald, April 16.

[5] Nicolay and Hay's "Life of Lincoln," vol. x. p. 300.

Lincoln breathed his last, Sumner drove with General Halleck to Mr. Seward's, whose murder had been attempted by another assassin, an accomplice of Booth. He spoke words of consolation to Mrs. Seward, whom he was not to meet again, and then went to his lodgings, which he reached at eight o'clock, — finding them guarded by soldiers under orders from the Secretary of War, in consequence of rumors of meditated violence on him as well as others.[1] His friend and former secretary, A. B. Johnson, has described his manner and conversation at this time, while "he sat stern and haggard over his untasted breakfast," but "steady in mind and unshaken in courage," as he contemplated "the rebellion defeated and degraded to assassination."[2]

The senators and representatives who were in Washington met at noon on Monday, the 17th, and after the choice of a chairman and secretary, and a statement by Senator Foot of Vermont, Sumner moved a committee of five to report at four in the afternoon the action proper for the meeting. The committee (Sumner chairman) reported a list of pall-bearers, and a committee of one from each State to accompany the remains to Illinois, and resolutions, and the report was agreed to without dissent. The resolutions (drawn by Sumner), confessing "the dependence of those present upon Almighty God, who rules all that is done for human good," bore "testimony of their veneration and affection for the illustrious dead," and recognized in his life "an example of purity, simplicity, and virtue which should be a lesson to mankind," and in his death "a martyr whose memory will become more precious as men learn to prize those principles of constitutional order, and those rights, civil, political, and human, for which he was made a sacrifice." They proposed also a day to be named by the President (Andrew Johnson) for commemorating the deceased.[3]

Sumner called on Mrs. Lincoln several times to give her his sympathies in her terrible sorrow. She sent him, before she left Washington, two souvenirs of the late President, — one a likeness of John Bright, which Mr. Lincoln had prized "as representing so noble and so good a friend of our cause," and the

[1] Scribner's Magazine, October, 1874, p. 224.

[2] Sumner chafed under the presence of the guard, which he thought useless; but Stanton decided it to be a necessary precaution. Lieber, in a letter, April 23, enjoined on Sumner to be careful, believing him to be one of those who had been "spotted."

[3] Works, vol. ix. pp. 361, 362.

other the President's cane. This last gift was accompanied with this note: —

EXECUTIVE MANSION, Tuesday Morning, May 9, 1865.

MY DEAR MR. SUMNER, — Your unwavering kindness to my idolized husband, and the great regard he entertained for you, prompts me to offer for your acceptance this simple relic, which being connected with his blessed memory I am sure you will prize. I am endeavoring to regain my strength sufficiently to be able to leave here in a few days. I go hence broken-hearted, with every hope almost in life crushed. Notwithstanding my utter desolation through life, the memory of the cherished friend of my husband and myself will always be most gratefully remembered.

With kindest regards, I remain always

Yours very truly, MARY LINCOLN.

Sumner wrote to Mr. Bright, April 18: —

"Not even the tragedy here can make me indifferent to the death of Richard Cobden, who was my personal friend and the friend of my country. I felt with you entirely in the touching words which you uttered in Parliament. I wish he could have lived to enjoy our triumph and to continue his counsels. His name will be cherished here as in England. History will be for him more than Westminster Abbey. You will be shocked by the crime in which belligerent slavery, crushed in arms, has sought to revenge itself; but your confidence in the people and popular institutions will not, I am sure, be shaken for a moment. Our government will continue tranquilly, according to the requirements of fundamental law. It is probable that the policy towards leading rebels will be modified. President Lincoln was so essentially humane and gentle that he could not make up his mind to any severity, even to Jefferson Davis. I was with him for four days, shortly before his death, on an excursion to the front; and during all this period he was not for a moment tempted into any remark indicating any desire to punish even Jefferson Davis. When a person of his family said, 'He must be hanged,' the President repeated again and again, 'Judge not, that ye be not judged.' President Johnson is in a different mood. My own line, so far as I can now see the true course, would be between the two. I confess my desire that our terrible rebellion should close without a capital punishment. Of course, I do not allude to military courts; but the men who have made so many tombs and vacant chairs must not be allowed to govern us again, and the colored people must be protected. To this end we must drive all the leaders out of the country.[1] President Lincoln's policy with regard to foreign powers was fixed; that of his successor is less certain. But I trust that the sense of responsibility and trust will make him wise; and there can be no wisdom in war. There are some who have supposed that Congress would be convened at once. I hope not. President Lincoln had determined not to convene it. We are not ready for the discussions on domestic policy; while on foreign policy, I think it probable the House of Representatives would, by resolutions passed without debate, call at once for the withdrawal of Maximilian from Mexico, and the payment of our claims

[1] It was a prevailing idea at the time that the leaders of the rebellion were to be punished in some way, and the more humane preferred exile for them to severer penalties.

by England. . . . Mr. Seward is better daily. His escape is a marvel. No less than six persons were wounded in his house by a single assassin. His son, the assistant secretary, has been insensible till last evening, when he asked for something to eat. His skull is fractured in two places, and his case is critical, but there is hope now that he will recover. The new President has asked the late Cabinet to remain. This was natural and proper. Of course, his first policy must be to secure public confidence; but there is an impression that sooner or later there will be a change. Among the aspirants is General Butler. He cannot be expected to succeed so long as Mr. Adams is in London, as they are both from Massachusetts. Our people continue to be moved. They are now thronging the streets to visit the remains of the late President, at the Executive Mansion."

This letter, written as soon as tidings of the assassination reached England, was received from Mr. Bright: —

ROCHDALE, April 29, 1865.

DEAR MR. SUMNER, — How can I write to you, and what can I say? For fifty years, I think, no other event has created such a sensation in this country as the great crime which has robbed you of your President. The whole people positively mourn, and it would seem as if again we were one nation with you, so universal is the grief and the horror at the deed of which Washington has been the scene. I have had a month of extraordinary suffering, — the death of Mr. Cobden; then the death of my brother-in-law, Mr. Lucas, of the "Morning Star;" then this new and inconceivable calamity. I feel as if all was unstable, and that nothing can stand.

When I read that the President had gone to Richmond without a guard, I felt that he ran a risk to which he ought not to have subjected himself. In times of great excitement dangerous men become more dangerous, partly vicious and partly mad; and men of great mark become the objects of their hate and passion. The deed is done, and it is now too late to take precautions. It is easy to kill a President, but it is not easy to destroy a nation.

We await the arrival of the boat with great anxiety; she was expected yesterday. I hope she may tell us that no other victim has fallen, and that Mr. Seward is recovering. If you have an opportunity of doing so, tell him how much I long to hear that he is safe; and if it be proper, convey to Mrs. Lincoln the assurance that we all grieve for her, and mourn for the noble life that has been cruelly taken from her and from the nation. In this great sorrow I hope that the two nations may forget what is irritating and evil in the past.

Forgive this short and hurried note. I feel unable to write what I wish and what I feel.

Always with much sympathy,

Your sincere friend, JOHN BRIGHT.

Sumner wrote to the Duchess of Argyll, April 24: —

"The Sewards, father and son, have rallied to-day, and seem to be doing well. The conspirators will be caught. Perhaps you will not be offended if I let you know that I showed the late President, at his request, your letter of March 2, in which you express the confidence in him and speak of the distrust of me.[1] I was at the theatre with him the last time he had been there before his assassination. I mentioned to him the purport of your letter. He at once said, 'I wish you would show me that letter.' I sent it to him, and he returned it in an envelope on which he had written your name and under cover to my address, with his frank in the upper right-hand corner, where with us the frank is written. I send them as autographs, which may interest some of your friends."

To F. W. Bird, April 25: —

"I have seen a good deal of the new President, and have conversed on questions of business and of general policy. His manner has been excellent, and even sympathetic, without any uncomfortable reticence. On Saturday the chief-justice and myself visited him in the evening, especially with the view of conversing on negro suffrage. Suffice it to say that he is well disposed, and sees the rights and necessities of the case, all of which I urged earnestly. Both of us left him light-hearted. Wade has also seen a good deal of him. He tells me that the President does not disguise his hostility to the Louisiana scheme. I am confident that our ideas will prevail; therefore, be not disheartened, nor in any way relax your energies. Forward!"

To Mr. Bright, May 1: —

"Just this moment I have read your letter of April 14, sent to me at Boston, in which you tell me something of the last hours of our good friend. Now that he is gone, we long for his voice and his thoughts more than ever before. I wish he could have spoken on the Canada question, and touched again the chords of justice. I do not doubt that Richard Cobden will be placed very soon among England's greatest men. He will be known now better than ever, as the prejudices of life will be hushed. Your letter is dated the very day when our President was assassinated. Now while I write you we are filled with the emotion which that transcendent event is calculated to excite. Family and friends may mourn; but his death will do more for the cause than any human life, for it will fix the sentiments of the country, perhaps of mankind. In my mind, few have been happier. You will note the tranquillity with which the vast power he held passed to his successor. Mr. Johnson was at the bedside of the dying President only two minutes, about two o'clock in the morning. The heart of Mr. Lincoln ceased to beat at twenty-two minutes after seven o'clock in the morning. I left the bedside at once, and going to the door in the gray of a drizzling morning found General Halleck just getting into his carriage, which had been within call all night. I got in with him, and asked him to set me down at Mr. Seward's. He said that he must first stop at Mr. Johnson's. Here the general went in to tell the new President that he 'must not go out without a guard;' and this was the way he first knew of the post he then occupied. A few hours later he took the oath before the chief-justice.

[1] The reference is to the feeling among English people that Sumner had become unfriendly to their country.

In the evening I had an interview with him on public business;[1] this was in the common room of the hotel where he was staying. I mention these things to illustrate the simplicity with which his accession was marked. Since then I have seen him repeatedly. Last evening I had a long conversation with him, mainly on the rebel States and how they shall be tranquillized. Of course my theme is justice to the colored race. He accepted this idea completely, and indeed went so far as to say 'that there is no difference between us.' You understand that the question whether rebel States shall be treated as military provinces or territories is simply one of form, with a view to the great result. It is the result that I aim at; and I shall never stickle on any intermediate question if that is secured. He deprecates haste; is unwilling that States should be precipitated back; thinks there must be a period of probation, but that meanwhile all loyal people, without distinction of color, must be treated as citizens, and must take part in any proceedings for reorganization. He doubts at present the expediency of announcing this from Washington lest it should give a handle to party, but is willing it should be made known to the people in the rebel States. The chief-justice started yesterday on a visit to North Carolina, South Carolina, Florida, and New Orleans, and will on his way touch the necessary strings, so far as he can. I anticipate much from this journey. His opinions are fixed, and he is well informed with regard to those of the President. I would not be too sanguine, but I should not be surprised if we had this great question settled before the next meeting of Congress, — I mean by this that we had such expressions of opinion and acts as will forever conclude it. My confidence is founded in part upon the essential justice of our aims and the necessity of the case. With the President as well disposed as he shows himself, and the chief-justice as positive, we must prevail. Will not all this sanctify our war beyond any in history? The President has not yet approached foreign questions. Last evening he said to me with reference to our claims on England, that he thought the time had come when we could insist on having them settled on correct principles."

To R. Schleiden, May 1:[2] —

"At last the military power of the rebellion is broken, and we are dismissing our troops. But, say the doubters, you cannot establish peace and tranquillity. This is the second line of diplomacy. Here again I reply confidently, as I once replied on the other question, We can. This will be by calling the colored population to the elective franchise. You know that for some time this has been my demand, so that all shall be equal before the law. Our late President accepted the principle, but hesitated in the application. You may remember the same hesitation with regard to emancipation, to which he finally consented. Our new President accepts the principle and the application. Our excellent chief-justice is, of course, very ardent and decided. I feel that at last I can see the end, when this terrible war will be justified.

"I am much interested to note in Europe the *contre-coup* of the great events of the last month, with the tragic death of the President. I trust that

1 With regard to receiving Sir Frederick Bruce, the newly arrived British minister.

2 Mr. Schleiden was now minister of the Hanse Towns in London.

in England that perverse spirit, which has caused so much mischief, will be crushed, and that Lord Russell will become amiable and just. Alas! alas! You know my opinion of his course. I cannot see it except in the most painful light. Congress is not in session, so that the House of Representatives will not make a demand for the instant payment of our claims; but I trust this question will in some way be put in train of settlement before the next session.

"Mr. Seward shows considerable vitality. The broken jaw is now the troublesome part of his case. Poor Frederick is well for one who has been so low; but his case is still doubtful. He speaks very little, and of course the extent of his injuries cannot be measured. Cruel devil, — that assassin!"

To Lieber, May 2: —

"I read to President Johnson Colonel Baker's letter,[1] with your introduction. He said at once that he accepted every word of it; that colored persons are to have the right of suffrage; that no State can be precipitated into the Union; that rebel States must go through a term of probation. All this he had said to me before. Ten days ago the chief-justice and myself visited him in the evening to speak of these things. I was charmed by his sympathy, which was entirely different from his predecessor's. The chief-justice is authorized to say wherever he is what the President desires, and to do everything he can to promote organization without distinction of color. The President desires that the movement should appear to proceed from the people. This is in conformity with his general ideas; but he thinks it will disarm party at home. I told him that while I doubted if the work could be effectively done without federal authority, I regarded the *modus operandi* as an inferior question; and that I should be content, provided equality before the law was secured for all without distinction of color. I said during this winter that the rebel States could not come back, except on the footing of the Declaration of Independence and the complete recognition of human rights. I feel more than ever confident that all this will be fulfilled. And then what a regenerated land! I had looked for a bitter contest on this question; but with the President on our side, it will be carried by simple avoirdupois."

To Mr. Bright, May 16: —

"Just before starting for Boston, I acknowledge yours of April 29. The feeling in England is not greater than I anticipated. I hope it will make your government see the crime with which for four years it has fraternized. Mr. Seward's disability causes a suspension of our diplomatic discussions, which I think he is anxious to resume. He was aroused to great indignation when he heard that the British authorities at Nassau had been receiving the pirate 'Stonewall.' A proclamation was sent to him yesterday, in the draft which concluded with something about the 'peace and safety of the United States.' He speaks with difficulty, but he stammered forth not 'safety,' but 'dignity; the United States are safe enough.' I have been pained by seeing him, as he shows so many signs of the terrible hazards he has passed. I am sorry that Jeff. Davis is caught; if not shot in pursuit, I wish he had escaped. Grant was anxious to keep him out of Mexico."

[1] Of North Carolina, late a Confederate officer.

At the meeting of the Cabinet with Mr. Lincoln on the last day of his life, Friday, April 14, Mr. Stanton submitted the draft of an ordinance for the restoration of order and the establishment of governments in the States lately in rebellion, — the draft applying expressly to two States, but intended as a model for the others. The President suggested a revision, and the subject went over to be resumed the next Tuesday, the 18th.[1] On Sunday, the 16th (Andrew Johnson now being President), Stanton read his draft at the war department to Sumner and other gentlemen, members of the House, and to Mr. Welles. Sumner interrupted the reading with the inquiry "whether any provision was made for enfranchising the colored man," saying, also, that "unless the black man is given the right to vote his freedom is mockery." Stanton deprecated the agitation of the subject on account of differences among the supporters of the Administration, but Sumner insisted that the black man's right to vote was "the essence, — the great essential." Stanton's draft, now confined to North Carolina, was considered in the Cabinet May 9, when it appeared with a provision for suffrage in the election of members of a constitutional convention for the State. It included "the loyal citizens of the United States residing within the State." This paragraph, it appears, Stanton had accepted April 16, as an amendment from Sumner and Colfax. Being now questioned as to its purport, he admitted that it was intended to include negroes as well as white men. He objected to a discussion, but invited an expression of opinion; and the members (Seward absent) were equally divided, — Stanton, Dennison, and Speed for the inclusion, and McCulloch, Welles, and Usher against it. The President took the papers without expressing an opinion. Sumner was quickly informed of what had transpired in the Cabinet, — as appears by his interview the next day with Welles, — and he counted at this time on the President's decision in favor of equal suffrage, irrespective of race.[2]

1 Nicolay and Hay's "Life of Lincoln," vol. x. pp. 283-285. According to Mr. Welles, the President said, "There were men in Congress who if their motives were good were nevertheless impracticable, and who possessed feelings of hate and vindictiveness in which he did not sympathize and could not participate." This remark may have been intended to apply to Wade, Davis, Stevens, and Sumner; but certainly it did not justly apply to Sumner, who was not influenced by those passions.

2 This statement as to Stanton's draft and Sumner's relation to it rests on Welles's articles in the "Galaxy," April and May, 1872, pp. 525-531, 666,667. Welles in Hartford "Times," March 19, 1872; Sumner's Works, vol. ix. p. 479.

Mr. Johnson was, during the weeks following his accession, waited upon by delegations to express their sympathy and confidence. To these he talked with a certain vigor, but with looseness, declaring, with repetition, that "treason is a crime" and ought to be punished. His apparent ardor in this direction caused apprehension among thoughtful men, even among those who favored radical measures of reconstruction, but who dreaded a period of vengeance and retaliation as a sequel of the Civil War. A marked feature of these wordy addresses, as well as of his conversation, was the inordinate vanity with which he dwelt upon his own career. Chase and Sumner were impressed with the exhibition of this quality, and the former said, "Let us see the President, and try to give him another topic." The President's first strong expressions against treason led some earnest men to believe that the reconstruction of the Southern States was now in safer hands than it would have been in Mr. Lincoln's; but in a few weeks they were to be undeceived.

Sumner remained in Washington till the middle of May. The President, since Mr. Lincoln's death, had been lodging in Mr. Hooper's house, and occupying temporarily as his office a room in the treasury department. Sumner had waited on him almost daily, calling often on public business, and had at several of these interviews pressed his views of reconstruction, particularly as to the justice and policy of suffrage for the colored people. On the evening of Saturday, April 22, just a week after he took his oath, Chase (the chief-justice) and Sumner had an interview with him, in which they urged him to say something for the equal rights of the colored people. He was sympathetic in manner, and while reserved, was no more so than his position justified.[1] Both left him "light-hearted." A few days later, when the President and senator were alone together, the former said to the latter, "On this question [that of suffrage] there is no difference between us; you and I are alike." Sumner expressed his joy and gratitude that the President had taken this position, and that as a consequence there would be no division in the Union party; and the President replied, "I mean to keep you all together." As he walked away that evening, Sumner felt that the battle of his own life was ended. In another interview the President's unwillingness to interfere in Tennessee for impartial suffrage — saying that he would do so if he were at

[1] Works, vol. ix. p. 478.

Nashville — disturbed Sumner; but the senator suspected no change of front, attributing the hesitation to unnecessary caution rather than to infidelity.[1] Just before leaving Washington, Sumner had a final interview with the President, in which the latter's manner and expressions remained the same. The senator apologizing for his repetition of views expressed in former meetings, Mr. Johnson said pleasantly, and with a smile, "Have I not always listened to you?" Before he went home, as well as for a week after, the senator assured his friends and correspondents that the cause he had at heart was safe with the new President.[2]

On June 1, the day appointed by President Johnson to be observed throughout the country in commemoration of Mr. Lincoln, Sumner, by invitation of the municipal authorities, delivered the eulogy upon him in Boston.[3] The services were held in the Music Hall. A colored clergyman, by the expressed preference of the orator, served as one of the chaplains.[4] The delivery began late in the afternoon, and occupied nearly two hours. The tone of the eulogy was solemn, beginning, "In the universe of God there are no accidents," and recognizing the divine Providence[5] which had watched over the nation and the career of him who had been so lately its chief. The style was calm and restrained. The life of Lincoln from lowly condition to exalted place was drawn with happy touches of comparison and contrast. He was fitly placed in history among the noblest characters, with no stint of tribute, and yet with discrimination, — the orator bearing testimony to his great qualities, most of all to his essential integrity of purpose, and his freedom from all envy and malice and unworthy ambition. The only limitation suggested was a certain slowness and hesitation in taking positions, — compensated, however, by firmness in maintaining them. In no study of Mr. Lincoln is there so fine a statement

1 Sumner's Address, Oct. 2, 1866. Works, vol. xi. p. 21.

2 There were, however, not wanting some disturbing signs. Carl Schurz wrote Sumner, May 9, warning against the schemes of Southern leaders in Mississippi, Georgia, and North Carolina. Thaddeus Stevens wrote, May 10, with alarm at the President's proclamation of the day before, recognizing the Pierpont government of Virginia. A caucus was held in the National Hotel in Washington, May 12, with a view of preventing the Administration from falling under adverse influences; but confidence was reassured by Wade and Sumner, who said the President was in no danger, and that he was in favor of negro suffrage. Julian's "Political Recollections," p. 263.

3 Works, vol. ix. pp. 369-428.

4 Chaplin's "Life of Sumner," p. 422.

5 Such recognitions were frequent in Sumner's addresses. Works, vol. ix. p. 407.

of his simplicity in character and habit, — carried, as with Saint Louis of France,[1] into public business, — or of the qualities of his style, suggesting Bacon as well as Franklin, and distinguishing his state papers, as well as his conversation and speeches, — "argumentative, logical, and spirited, with quaint humor and sinewy sententiousness." Sumner's personal intercourse with the late President, particularly in his last days, gave a color to the most impressive passages.

The oration was, however, wanting in artistic unity. In parts a sense of due proportion was disregarded; and at the end there was a digression which seriously marred the effect. Suffrage for the freedmen had been for some months a burden on Sumner's mind, now all the heavier on account of proceedings just instituted by the new President; and he was determined to improve the opportunity to make his appeal to the country. With him a moral purpose always overrode artistic limitations. He found at hand Mr. Lincoln's constant insistence, in debates with Douglas and in later speeches and papers, upon the equal rights of all men, without exception of race; and he read a number of extracts from them, some quite long, where one, with a mere reference to the others, would have sufficed. Pregnant as the quoted sentences were, the orator, in applying them to political rights, gave them a significance which was not in the mind of their author. He dwelt longer on Great Britain's recognition of rebel belligerency than was fitting on a commemorative occasion;[2] but he could not forego the opportunity to renew his protest against an act which signified to him moral obliquity as well as indifference to the claims of national good fellowship. When he had reached the natural end of the eulogy, he began, with an abrupt transition, an argument for colored suffrage, which he continued for some minutes. Even those in the audience who were altogether sympathetic with him on this subject were quite disturbed at the incongruity. About one fourth of the oration was in this way a departure from the main subject, arising from an earnest desire to give a right direction to public opinion at a critical moment.

[1] Montalembert, in a letter to Sumner, referred to this comparison as felicitous.

[2] Mr. Bancroft's eulogy on Mr. Lincoln before Congress in February, 1866, set forth the shortcomings of England, France, and the Pope, to the discomfort of the diplomatists present.

It was noted on that day that something of the former fascination of Sumner's oratory had gone.[1] His voice was still resonant, but no longer so rich and varied; and there was a certain heaviness in his manner. He read from his manuscript, and many times paused to adjust his glasses, which kept falling. Once with some effort he read the President's address at Gettysburg, which, printed in large letters, hung in front across the hall. He seemed to take little interest in the audience before him, being in this respect quite unlike Mr. Everett, who to the last was intent on oratorical effect. As observed in a previous chapter, he had for some years cared chiefly in speaking to reach through the press the American people, and had become to a degree indifferent to the impression on his hearers.[2]

Mrs. Lincoln wrote from the neighborhood of Chicago, whither she had gone, a letter of gratitude for the truthful and eloquent eulogy on her "lamented husband by a friend so cherished as you were by the great and good man who has been called away. Your words as testimonials in his praise are very welcomely received."

Robert T. Lincoln wrote, July 5: —

"I desire to assure you that I have been deeply gratified by your oration. I have seen no eulogy out of all that have been delivered that has so well expressed what all who knew my father feel, but cannot say."

Isaac N. Arnold, the biographer of Mr. Lincoln, wrote, June 8: —

"I have just finished reading your most comprehensive, appreciative, and grand eulogy upon our great and good Lincoln. As one of his humble friends, — one who, while reverencing him as one of the greatest of men, loved him as a brother, — I desire to thank you for this noble effort of genius."

Sumner had not been ten days at home before all his hopes for a just and speedy reconstruction on the basis of equal rights were dashed by the President's proclamations, May 29, — one of amnesty, with various exceptions, and the other prescribing in detail a method of reconstruction for North Carolina, including a constitutional convention, and confining suffrage to the class of voters qualified by the Constitution and laws of that State

[1] Springfield Republican, June 5.

[2] This change had been noted two years before by an acute observer of public speakers. W. S. Robinson's ("Warrington's") "Pen Portraits," pp. 517, 518.

before secession; thus excluding, as Mr. Lincoln had done, the colored people from the qualified body. Similar proclamations were shortly issued for reconstructing the other Southern States, and affirming the validity of the proceedings which had been taken in Tennessee, Louisiana, and Arkansas.

The change of mind which the President underwent during the last ten days of May has been attributed to his egotism, which was plied by the flatteries of Southern leaders;[1] to the notice that was taken of his condition in the Senate when he took his oath;[2] to the plausible counsels of persons who had screened him at the time of this exposure of himself, — Preston King and the Blairs, always irrepressible and indefatigable in political scheming; and above all to Mr. Seward, who, partly recovered from his wounds, had resumed his official work.[3]

Carl Schurz, to whom the President showed his proclamation for North Carolina before it was issued, urged him to modify it so as to include the colored people as voters. In July General Schurz visited, by commission from the President, the Southern States to examine their condition; but when he returned in October he was received by the President without welcome, hardly with civility. His report is an important historical document, giving a truthful survey of the South at that time. During his absence in that section, and after his return, he was in frequent communication with Sumner.

While at home in the summer the burden of this question was all the time on Sumner's mind. Wherever he met citizens, — on the street, at club dinners, or in society, — he let slip no opportunity to urge them to action. A large edition of a pamphlet, containing his article in the Atlantic Monthly, already referred to, as well as several resolutions introduced by him in Congress, and his speeches on the proceedings in Arkansas and Louisiana, was distributed among the people. In Boston there was a quick response in a meeting held June 21, 1865, to maintain equal suffrage, at which Theophilus Parsons was in the chair, and Richard H. Dana, Jr., made the principal speech.[4]

[1] Carl Schurz in two letters, June 27 and July 8, urged Sumner to go to Washington in order to counteract the efforts of the Southern leaders.

[2] *Ante*, p. 230.

[3] Sumner's Address, Oct. 2, 1866; Works, vol. xi. p. 18; Blaine's "Twenty Years of Congress," vol. ii. pp. 63, 67, 68, 83, 108.

[4] Mr. Dana, who had been Sumner's critic, now came substantially to his position. Adams's "Biography" of Dana, vol. ii. p. 333.

Authentic reports from the South were in the mean time arriving, which verified the worst apprehensions concerning the President's policy, showing that it had revived the old slaveholding spirit, and was pressing heavily on Unionists, white and black.

Sumner wrote very earnest letters to members of the Cabinet, urging them to arrest the President's course; but none of them in their replies gave him any satisfaction.[1] The President was doing what Seward had advised, and what Welles and McCulloch cordially approved. Stanton was friendly enough to the principle of equal suffrage, without regard to color, but, as already seen, was unwilling to bring it to the front and make it an issue which would divide Republicans. Speed also was friendly to it, but was opposed to dictating conditions of suffrage to the returning States. Harlan thought the triumph of the President's plan inevitable, and counselled trust "in an overruling Providence," adding, "I know the potency of your great idea of the duty of a statesman to create rather than to be controlled by circumstances; but this creation requires time." Three members of the Cabinet, — Speed, Harlan, and Dennison, — who were then deaf to Sumner's entreaties, retired from it in a twelvemonth, unwilling to compromise themselves by further association with the Administration.

Sumner wrote to Lieber, August 11: —

"The attorney-general (Speed) is the best of the Cabinet; but they are all courtiers, unhappily, as if they were the counsellors of a king. Preston King and Mr. Blair went to the President when he was intoxicated, and took him away from the hotel and sheltered him at the house of Mr. Blair. *Hinc amicitia!*"

Sumner's correspondence at the time discloses little sympathy with his steadfast support of colored suffrage against the President's plan. Members of Congress were confused by events. Conness did not see how impartial suffrage, although he believed in it, could be imposed by Congress. Wilson,[2] E. D. Morgan, Morrill of Maine, and Howard of Michigan were disposed to hope for the best, and to make the best of the situation, and advised a conciliatory treatment of the President.

[1] The replies from members of the Cabinet and of Congress are valuable for political history; but in this connection their tenor only can be indicated.

[2] Fessenden, who had an interview with the President early in September, expressed the same view to Wilson.

Thaddeus Stevens, Henry Winter Davis, and Wade[1] took a cheerless view of the political prospect, and saw small chance of success against Executive influence and patronage on a question where there was so much popular indifference and opposition among Republicans. Howard and Davis were averse to any direct issue with the President on negro suffrage, confident that the public mind was not ready for it, and thinking it wiser to make it on the right of Congress to control the reconstruction. B. Gratz Brown alone responded without qualification to Sumner's appeal. Of the members of the House, Boutwell[2] of Massachusetts, Julian[3] of Indiana, and Garfield of Ohio,[4] each addressed the people of his State in favor of admitting freedmen to the suffrage.[5] But on the other hand Dawes of Massachusetts, already a leader in that body, in an address to his neighbors, which was widely read, came earnestly to the support of the President's action, and contested as unconstitutional any attempt of Congress to make suffrage for the colored people a condition precedent in the restoration of the rebel States.[6]

Among public men not in Congress, journalists and other leaders of public opinion, Sumner's cause found little support. Governor Morton of Indiana denounced it before the people, and took issue directly with the senator.[7] Governor Andrew of Massachusetts felt assured of the President's honesty of purpose, and advised co-operation with him.[8] The editors of the New York "Evening Post," Bryant and Godwin, usually radical in their views, contended against compulsory action by Congress in the matter of suffrage, treating it as "a prodigious and overwhelm-

1 Howard and Wade ascribed the present difficulty to President Lincoln's course on the reconstruction bill in 1864, and thought that his action was in substance the same as his successor's.

2 At Weymouth, July 4.

3 Julian's "Political Recollections," p. 268.

4 At Ravenna, O., July 4. Works of J. A. Garfield, vol. i. p. 85.

5 Sherman, speaking at Circleville, O., June 10, showed himself friendly to negro suffrage (New York "Tribune," June 14); and Morrill of Vermont spoke in favor of it before the Republican convention of that State.

6 July 4, at Pittsfield. (Springfield "Republican," July 19.) This journal agreed fully with Mr. Dawes's view, and sustained President Johnson, June 12. Mr. Dawes had taken the same position in a speech in the House, Feb. 20, 1865.

7 Julian's "Political Recollections," pp. 260–268. George W. Julian at once replied to Morton in the Indiana "True Republican," and also in speeches.

8 Letter to Sumner, November 21. At the Union Club in Boston, November 7, the Governor and Henry Ward Beecher had a spirited encounter with Sumner when Governor Parsons of Alabama was present to solicit a loan for that State. (Boston "Commonwealth," November 25.) Governor Andrew, as his valedictory message in January, 1866, shows, was not in entire accord with Republican methods of reconstruction.

ing centralism," and involving "the danger of dangers."[1] From this time they were often at issue with Sumner on measures of reconstruction.[2] The New York "Times," in successive leaders, took positive ground against negro suffrage as any part of the reconstruction.[3] Charles A. Dana, then an editor in Chicago, wrote to Sumner that it was advisable to keep with the President as far as possible in order to prevent "the Democrats coming into power through any unnecessary quarrel among ourselves."[4] John W. Forney of the Philadelphia "Press," a partisan of the President, who had come also to be an admirer of Sumner, begged him, in view of all he had accomplished, to yield something of his present judgment for the sake of harmony with the vast political army of which he had "been a conscientious and courageous leader." Sumner's chief sympathizers at this time were the old Abolitionists and Free Soilers, with here and there men of radical ways of thinking, like Wayne MacVeagh and Horace Greeley. The latter advocated during the summer and autumn in the "Tribune," in able and earnest leaders,[5] the admission of the negroes to suffrage as a just and politic measure, though disclaiming the purpose to make such admission an inexorable condition in reconstruction, and avoiding any reflection on the President's proceedings.[6]

Not overlooking voices in different directions which avowed the duty or expediency of admitting the emancipated race to full citizenship as a part of the reconstruction, this may be said of

[1] Parke Godwin to Sumner, September 18 (manuscript). New York "Evening Post," September 26. That journal contended that more States were needed to ratify the thirteenth Constitutional amendment, and Sumner replied that it had already been ratified by a quorum of States. New York "Evening Post," September 29, Works, vol. ix. pp. 489–492.

[2] Godwin's "Life of Bryant," vol. ii. pp. 238–242. The "Evening Post," March 1, 1866, contains a rather cynical notice of Sumner's speech of February 5 and 6, 1866. While retaining its Republican connection, it regarded (November 6, 7, and 8, 1867) the reconstruction measures of Congress, except the fourteenth amendment, as "needless, violent, unstatesmanlike, and fanatical."

[3] March 2; June 3, 19, 21, 23, 24, 26, 28, 29. The Cincinnati "Commercial" printed eleven years later letters found in Andrew Johnson's office at Greenville, Tenn., after his death, which approved his policy of reconstruction at the outset. Among them were letters and telegrams from George Bancroft, James Gordon Bennett, Henry J. Raymond, Simon Cameron, and W. H. Seward.

[4] His journal, the Chicago "Republican," justified President Johnson's exclusion of the colored people from his plan of reconstruction.

[5] June 14, 15, 20, 22, 23, 26, 27, 28, 29; July 8, 10, 11, 31; August 1, 26; September 18, 20, 30; October 7, 19.

[6] George L. Stearns, of Massachusetts, distinguished for his services for the colored people, who had while raising negro troops in Tennessee become acquainted with Mr. Johnson, was at this time his apologist. New York "Tribune," October 23.

Sumner (a repetition by way of emphasis of what has already been said in substance), that among public men and leaders of opinion at this time he was the only one who resolutely held the position — alike against one President and then another, against also resistance, hostile votes, and attempts within his own party to shift the issue — that the reconstruction should make that people finally and irrevocably citizens and voters on the same terms as white men, or it should not go on.[1] Whatever at last may be the judgment of mankind on the act itself, the honor or discredit of that great enfranchisement must ever remain with him.

He wrote to Mr. Bright, June 5: —

"I thank you for your letter pleading so wisely and well for the humane course towards our traitors. I agree with you entirely, and have already enforced the same views. There has been a perceptible change in the public feeling, and I do not despair to see it right if time is allowed. It was Stanton who wished to hang three or four in a State; I think that even he is more moderate now.

"There has been immense disappointment in Johnson's proclamation for the reorganization of North Carolina, excluding the colored persons. This is madness. But it is also inconsistent with his sayings to the chief-justice and myself. . . . There is great tranquillity in the public mind with regard to our foreign relations, and a disposition to peace. But knowing as I do the sentiment of leading politicians, I wish to get every pending question out of the way; I mean by this that it should be put in such train of settlement as to be taken out of the sphere of congressional action, if that be possible. Therefore, Lord Russell's letter repelling our claims must be reconsidered. A resolution calling upon the government to demand the settlement of our claims and to follow the British precedent in the case of the 'Trent,' would pass the House of Representatives almost unanimously. But the House is not in session, and when I left Washington the President had no idea of calling it together. Sherman[2] has one of his paroxysms arising from his excitable organization, and is ruining himself by wild talk. Seward wishes to stay in the Cabinet long enough 'to finish his work;' but he is very feeble. The centres of life have not been touched; but he speaks only a few words, and with great difficulty. There is a pressure against Stanton, in which the Blairs and the ring of cotton speculators are very active. When I left Washington there was not the least sign that the President would listen to them. There are but two questions now that interest the public: (1) The question of reconstruction, including of course the question of the suffrage; and (2) The execution of Jeff. Davis. I notice the cry for Jeff. Davis in England. This is the

[1] Even in 1866, according to Mr. Blaine, "the great mass of the Republicans stopped short of the demand for the conferment of suffrage on the negro." "Twenty Years of Congress," vol. ii. p. 92.

[2] General W. T. Sherman, who was indignant at the way Stanton and Halleck had treated his convention with General J. E. Johnston.

present form of sympathy for the rebellion. He does not deserve it. And yet I wish that his life should not be touched. It was painful to read what was said in Parliament on the President's death, except by Disraeli. Derby was wicked. Russell was drivel. It was a beautiful and masterly speech which Stansfeld[1] made at the public meeting. That speech, if made by Russell, would have been as good as the payment of our claims. I have not the pleasure of knowing him; but I wished to thank him as I read it. The case was stated admirably."

To R. Schleiden, June 27:—

"You will be pained to hear that poor Seward has been called to bear another blow. His wife, who is now dead, was a lady of rare talent and character.[2] She was nothing of a politician. I last saw her in the gray of the morning after the assassination, when she spoke of 'Henry' and of her son 'Fred' as 'both murdered.' I have always admired her, and have been sure of her sympathy. How Seward can travel I do not understand, or how he can converse. He still wears in his mouth that machine like a Spanish bit, which serves as a splint to the broken jaw-bone. He seemed to rally something of his old force when he wrote that brief note to Lord Russell. I think he is determined to persevere in that way. I see that the correspondent of the 'Times' says that as soon as the elections are over the 'Alabama' claims will be paid. The lawyers here all side with Mr. Bemis, and think he has shown the shifts and pretensions of the British government, and that the idea of the blockade is an afterthought.

"On the suffrage question the President has changed. Shortly after I left Washington, Southern influences proved too strong. The ascendency is with the Blairs. I have a letter from a member of the Cabinet, telling me of a strong pressure on the President to enforce the Monroe doctrine as a safety-valve now, and to divert attention from domestic questions. You will see at once that this comes from the Blairs. They presented it to Mr. Lincoln shortly before his death, and he spoke with me about it, although he never inclined to it for a moment.

"I have always been an admirer of Lord Russell, and read his speeches with constant interest, except when he speaks of my country; and then he is so full of mistakes, and is so unjust, that he offends me. I think Seward wishes to finish the controversies growing out of the rebellion, which of course include the question of belligerency. 'His work will be done,' as he expresses it, when these questions are over. He thinks Adams should stay 'to finish his work.' So do I. The newspapers are all at fault about Chase. His visit to the South was not political. It was, after conference with the President, to promote the colored suffrage."

Again, August 8:—

"I wish I were with you in Germany, away from these heats of weather and these cares. Your pleasant letter forgets to tell me how you like London,

[1] James Stansfeld, who entered Parliament in 1859, and is still (1893) a member.

[2] She died June 21, at the age of sixty. Sumner's affectionate tribute to her memory is printed in Seward's "Life," vol. iii. pp. 286, 287.

its society, its politicians, its cabinet ministers. I imagine you already surrounded by choice spirits. But pray tell me something of the scene.

"The mission to Spain was offered first to Montgomery Blair, who was indignant, saying that he had refused the post when he was a young man during the administration of Polk, and he complained to Seward that he had not pushed him for the chief-justiceship against Chase. Seward said that he had 'presented his papers,' and that Blair was 'his candidate.' Blair thought that if Seward had been much in earnest he could have prevented Chase's nomination. President Lincoln selected Hale [for the mission to Spain] out of general kindness and good-will to the 'lame ducks.' Hale had lost his seat in the Senate, and the President wished to break his fall. He had been urged for Paris. He brought a paper to me recommending him, and wished me to sign it. I said at once, 'I am your friend, and shall speak to you frankly. You ought not to desire the mission to Paris.' Fifteen or twenty senators signed it. President Lincoln afterwards read to me the list of names with comments. I then pressed Mr. Everett for Paris. It was at a later day that he let me know of the treaty with Bennett of the 'Herald.'"[1]

To Mr. Bright, August 8:—

"My early prophecy in 1862 will be fulfilled, and nobody hanged for treason. . . . Meanwhile the day of tranquillity and reconciliation is still further postponed. Some of our friends are in great despair; I am not. The good cause cannot be lost. My counsel has been to put off the question. Neither party is ready to accept in proper spirit any final settlement. The former masters are as little ready for equality as the freedmen; but the latter are the better prepared. I think Congress will be disposed to settle the great question on proper principles. Thus far there is more agreement among us than I have ever known at any other stage of our protracted controversies.

"General Grant was here last week. He told me that he had mustered out eight hundred thousand men, leaving two hundred thousand still on the rolls, of whom one hundred and thirty thousand were ready for the field. On our foreign policy he was very positive. He regarded the French invasion of Mexico as 'a part of the rebellion,' which ought now to cease. He kept twenty-five thousand men in Texas beyond police necessities on this account, making an annual cost of twenty-five millions of dollars, which we must charge to Louis Napoleon. He cared little whether England paid 'our little bill' or not; upon the whole, he would rather she should not, as that would leave the precedent of her conduct in full force for us to follow, and he wished it understood that we should follow it. He thought that we should make more out of 'the precedent' than out of 'the bill,' and that Boston especially would gain. Of course, General Grant has no official connection with our foreign relations, but his weight in the country gives value to his opinion. I need not say that I dissented from his policy most resolutely. I told him that our true object should be to bring the two countries into relations of harmony and good-will;

1 On Mr. Dayton's death, Mr. Lincoln offered the French mission to Mr. Bennett as a grateful recognition of the "Herald's" change from a disloyal to a loyal journal in 1861,—the change taking place after a call from Thurlow Weed, which was made at the President's instance. Weed's "Life," vol. i. pp. 615–619.

that this could not be done if one nation was watching an opportunity to strike, and the other was standing on guard; that the truest statesmanship was to remove all questions, and to that end I wished the precedent rejected. But I do not see how this can be done with Lord Russell in his declared moods. Thank God! he is less supercilious. His last letter had a tone which I hail as a harbinger of better days."

To Lieber, August 14: —

"All my first impressions were for the writing and reading qualification; but on reflection it seemed to me impracticable. Of course, any rule must apply to the whites as well as to the blacks. Now, you cannot get votes of Congress to disfranchise, which you must do in imposing this qualification. Providence has so arranged it that the work shall be done completely, because it must be done. Besides, there are very intelligent persons, especially among the freedmen, who cannot read or write. But we need the votes of all, and cannot afford to wait."

To the Duchess of Argyll, August 15: —

"I have yours of the 4th of July, as you were about to flee to Inverary, where I trust my tree has not ceased to flourish, although I am 'hostile to England.' Lady Drogheda had heard the same story. You had better judge me by what you know and by my letters. You know, my dear duchess, I have never disguised my feelings at the unexpected course of England when slavery assumed the privileges of war. I thought that at that time England was bound by all the logic of her history, and by every consideration of duty, — moral, political, and religious, — to say to the representatives of rebel slavery, 'Get out of my sight!' Here was a sad and terrible failure. I cannot see it otherwise. I have tried to see it as you see it; I cannot. To my mind it was direct complicity with slavery in its last diabolical struggle. Now, at home, I have denounced Administration after Administration; I have criticised friends who entered into this complicity. Should I be more lenient to England, which was doing more for slavery than any American Administration, or any friend of mine, had ever done? I know you say that the United States, under military necessity, and to soften the rigors of war, had recognized the representatives of rebel slavery as belligerents. Belligerents to a certain extent! But this cannot justify England in an act which opened work-shops and ports, and unleashed ships to be employed in the support of rebel slavery. Morally the act is utterly indefensible, and history will so write it down."

To Lieber, August 21: —

"The true policy of the Administration is as plain as noonday. No path was ever clearer; and how they could get away from it is astonishing. (1) Refer the whole question of reconstruction to Congress, where it belongs. What right has the President to reorganize States? (2) Meanwhile, by good government through military officers, to lead public opinion in the right direction. (3) To obey the existing laws of Congress, which expressly exclude from public service any person who has sustained the rebellion. (4) To obey the Constitution, which refuses to make any distinction of color. (5) To redeem the promises of the Declaration of Independence instead of openly setting them at defiance. Why the Cabinet have not insisted upon these plain rules is very strange. I have been invited to preside at the coming Republican State convention for Massachusetts. At any other time I should not do it; but I shall now, in order to speak the voice of Massachusetts."

Sumner had already made an appeal to the public in his eulogy upon Mr. Lincoln, which immediately followed the President's proclamation for North Carolina. Another opportunity occurred September 14, when he took the chair as president of the Republican State convention at Worcester.[1] His presence and his speech on that day were greeted with applause as cordial and demonstrative as any which had ever greeted him in such meetings with his constituents. There was a popular craving for guidance on the pending question, and the Republican leaders had hitherto been generally reticent. As he began, he paid a tribute to "the intelligence, the heart, and the conscience of Massachusetts, — God bless her!" He had hoped the year before that he had made his last antislavery speech; but the work of liberation was not yet completed, nor would it be "until the equal rights of every one once claimed as a slave are placed under the safeguard of irreversible guaranties." The key-note of the address was the right of the colored race to equality in suffrage as in other things, both for its own protection and for the safety of the country, — to be maintained by Congress as a condition in the restoration of the rebel States, and irrevocably secured by an amendment of the Constitution forbidding any exclusion on account of race or color.[2] He rebuked haste in reconstruction, and laid emphasis on *time* as a helper in the process. Recognizing the reluctance among Republicans to break with the President, he avoided a direct criticism of his course, but plainly showed his opposition to it.

In conclusion, he said: —

"For myself, fellow-citizens, pardon me if I say that my course is fixed. Many may hesitate; many may turn away from those great truths which make the far-reaching brightness of the republic; many may seek a temporary favor by untimely surrender. I shall not. . . . A righteous government cannot be founded on any exclusion of race. This is not the first time that I

[1] Works, vol. ix. pp. 437–477.

[2] This was a very early suggestion, perhaps the earliest, in any high quarter of the fifteenth Amendment.

have battled with the barbarism of slavery. I battle still, as the bloody monster retreats to its last citadel; and, God willing, I mean to hold on if it takes what remains to me of life."

The reception which the address met with showed clearly that whatever might be the current of opinion elsewhere, the people of Massachusetts were with Sumner. Fortunate the senator who had such a constituency!

The convention approved the admission of negroes to suffrage as a part and condition of reconstruction.[1] A similar ground was taken by the Republicans of Vermont, Iowa, and Minnesota; but generally Republican State conventions shrank from an explicit declaration. Notwithstanding the prudent reserve of politicians, there was however, during the recess of Congress, a growing conviction among the Northern people that governments at once loyal, stable, and securing the rights of all, white and black, could not be established in the rebel States without admitting the freedmen to a share in them. It was Sumner who took the lead in spreading and organizing that conviction. He wrote to Lieber, September 18: —

"As to reconstruction, I know, of course, the difficulties of detail, tasking patience; but the general principles are found in national security and national faith. If the President had from the beginning seen these duties clearly, and headed that way in all that he said and did, the whole North would have been with him, and the South would not have been recalcitrant. As it is, all for the present is uncertain. Controversy is certain; division probable. But I still trust to that good Providence which has conducted us thus far safely. Meanwhile we must work. My speech [September 14] was received with perfect harmony and assent. Perhaps I never before stated better the precise opinions of Massachusetts. Stanton is here; he thanked me very cordially for my address to him in the speech, and said that I asked him to do only what he wanted to do. I am glad that they have got over the nonsense of trying Jefferson Davis by a jury. The whole idea has been weak and impossible from the beginning."

Again, October 12: —

"Send me the reference to your article on 'Republican Government;' also any other references to history or discussion explaining its meaning. Words receive expansion and elevation with time. Our fathers builded wiser than they knew. Did they simply mean a guarantee against a king? Something more, I believe, — all of which was not fully revealed to themselves, but which we must now declare in the light of our institutions. We know more than

[1] The Republican State committee had already in July issued an Address for equal suffrage in reconstruction. New York "Tribune," July 25.

Montesquieu on this question. The time has come to fix a meaning upon those words. We cannot avoid it. Let us affix a meaning which will make us an example and will elevate mankind. To this end I spoke in my eulogy of Mr. Lincoln, and I find from all parts of the country an echo. If the President had not set himself the other way, there would have been one universal voice. What one man in the same time ever did so much to arrest a great cause? My point is that liberty, equality before the law, and the consent of the governed are essential elements of a republican government."

To Mr. Bright, November 14: —

"I enclose letters just received from my correspondent, Dr. Lieber, our most learned publicist, a Prussian by birth, but for forty years a citizen here, having with us something of the position which Panizzi obtained with you. I think you will be interested in what he says about arbitration. The President's 'experiment' appears to be breaking down; but at what fearful cost! The rebels have once more been put on their legs; the freedmen and the Unionists are down. This is very sad. I cannot be otherwise than unhappy as I think of it. Our session is uncertain. Nobody can tell certainly what pressure the President will bring to bear on Congress; and how Congress can stand it. I think that Congress will insist upon time, — this will be our first demand; and then generally upon adequate guarantees. There are unpleasant stories from Washington; but we must persevere to the end."

To Mrs. Waterston, November 19: —

"Tempted to an article in the last Atlantic[1] by its title, I read it with delight, enjoying its elegance of style, its sympathy with books, and its knowledge; and marvelling at the allusions to my small possessions, I could not imagine who wrote it. At last I saw in a newspaper that it was by you, and then I understood. Style, knowledge, sympathy with books, and kindness to me were all explained. I hope that you will write more. Such a pen ought not to be idle."

While at home Sumner prepared an article for a magazine, entitled "Clemency and Common Sense," the subject of which was a curiosity of literature: two lines from the Latin,[2] — the first connecting clemency with stability in the State, and the second warning against extremes, — which, doubtful in origin and running into variations, have obtained a remarkable currency among proverbs.[3] It was packed with bibliographical research,

[1] "The Visible and Invisible in Libraries," Atlantic Monthly, November, 1865, pp. 525-535.

[2] "Instabile est regnum quod non clementia firmat."
"Incidis in Scyllam, cupiens vitare Charybdim."

[3] Atlantic Monthly, December, 1865; Works, vol. ix. pp. 503-544. The classical explanations at the beginning drew some criticisms from James A. Garfield, then a member of Congress, which found their way into the New York "Evening Post," and were sent as printed by Garfield to Sumner, Dec. 28, 1865.

which was enlivened by a pleasant commentary on authors and editions, — largely upon Philip Gaulthier's poem on Alexander the Great, a copy of which, once owned by John Mitford, had come into Sumner's possession. The moral at the end, for enforcing which the paper was written, was that while applying a wise clemency there must be no weak surrender of essential rights, no neglect of sacred obligations to loyal men of every race. "There must be no vengeance on enemies; but there must be no sacrifice of friends." Follow common-sense; and while escaping from the dangers of civil war, centralism, government by military power, and distrust of fellow-citizens, do not drive upon opposite perils, — concessions to slavery or its spirit, or a premature restoration of the disarmed insurgents to political power without the surest guaranty of the rights of loyal persons, whether white or black, and especially the freedmen.

Between the time of Mr. Lincoln's death and the beginning of the session of Congress in December, 1865, Sumner wrote several brief letters and communications with a view to promote the cause of equal suffrage, which found their way to the public, — some to colored people in the South who sought his counsel and sympathy,[1] one to the mayor of Boston,[2] and another to the editor of the New York "Independent."[3]

At this period death severed Sumner's relations with several friends with whom he had been more or less intimate. Edward Everett, whom he had known from youth, died Jan. 15, 1865. Their correspondence began as early as 1833; and while they had differed in domestic politics, they were sympathetic on literary and foreign questions.[4] Mr. Everett supported steadily the government during the Civil War, and gave his vote as citizen and member of the electoral college to Mr. Lincoln in 1864. Shortly before Mr. Everett's death Sumner recommended his appointment as minister to Paris. On account of his duties as senator, he was obliged to decline the invitation of the Legislature of Massachusetts to deliver a eulogy upon one whom he regarded as "a great example of genius, learning, and eloquence, consecrated to patriotic service."[5]

[1] May 13 (Works, vol. ix. p. 364); May (Ibid., p. 366); July 8 (Ibid., p. 430); August 16 (Ibid., p. 432).

[2] July 4. Works, vol. ix. p. 429.

[3] October 29. Works, vol. ix. pp. 500-502.

[4] Some of Mr. Everett's later letters to Sumner concerned questions with England.

[5] Works, vol. ix. p. 200.

Sumner had enjoyed a long friendship with George Livermore, a Boston merchant resident in Cambridge, a lover of books, a collector of manuscripts and rare pamphlets, and interested in historical research. He was conservative by temperament; and while withholding approval at times of Sumner's radical action against slavery, he always followed him with personal sympathy. He was an invalid at home when Sumner returned from Washington, and the latter sought his bedside, bearing to him books and pamphlets most likely to interest him. Mr. Livermore's last note to him, dated June 7, was grateful and affectionate. He died in August. Sumner at once published a tribute to his friend, in which he commemorated his refined tastes, generous sympathies, and enthusiasm in bibliography.[1]

Sumner's early friend, the seventh Earl of Carlisle,[2] died Dec. 5, 1864, at Castle Howard, Yorkshire. His disease was paralysis, which had disabled him in the summer. His niece, the Duchess of Argyll, kept Sumner informed of the progress of his malady, and his brother, Charles Howard,[3] communicated the tidings of his death. The portraits of Prescott and Sumner hung in his chamber to the last. Sumner wrote to the duchess, December 27, when, by telegram from Cape Race, he heard of the earl's death: —

"I do not think justice is done to his powers. His moral nature was so beautiful that people forget the rest; or perhaps he was to blame for not entering with more activity and directness into government. I have lost a friend; but there is no good cause which does not suffer by his death. I should like to know who was with him at Castle Howard during his last days. While I was there he took me to the tomb where he was to lie, and spoke calmly and beautifully of death."

To Charles Howard, M. P., December 27: —

"I was prepared for the sad intelligence which the telegraph flashed a thousand miles from Cape Race, and which your kind letter now confirms. I had feared from the first moment when I learned the character of his illness that it could have but one end; but I hoped by every packet to hear of some favorable change, — at least that he had been able to communicate freely with those about him whom he loved so well. But his nature was so gentle, his heart so warm, and his faith so perfect, that I do not doubt his

1 Boston "Advertiser," Sept. 2, 1865; Works, vol. ix. pp. 433-436.

2 *Ante*, vol. ii. p. 71.

3 Younger brother of the seventh earl and son-in-law of Lord Wensleydale (Baron Parke). His only son George, who married a daughter of the second Lord Stanley of Alderley, succeeded to the earldom in 1889 by the death of his uncle, William George, eighth earl.

entire submission to the painful decree under which he suffered, or his grateful sense of all the blessings by which he was surrounded. It will be for us to imitate his example. But in life, as in death, he is an example. He was one of the best of men; I have never seen a better. Clarendon said of Falkland 'that he was a person of inimitable sweetness and delight in conversation, of flowing and obliging humanity and goodness to mankind, and of primitive simplicity and integrity of life;' but I do not believe that the hero of King Charles deserved this praise more than him whom I now honor. I always looked for him to take a more active part in government, and to bring his beautiful nature to bear directly on the times. I do not doubt his powers had he been so disposed. Perhaps his hesitation may be attributed to that refined artistic sense which sought to finish whatever he touched. Many of his speeches were 'gems.' I think they have been so called by others; and I remember well that Mr. Webster spoke with admiration of that made to the electors of the West Riding when he was defeated, saying that it was by far the best at that general election. It was a beautiful effort. While in the United States he mingled much with people, and I was always struck by his singular sagacity or intuition with regard to character. He seemed to know men after a brief interview, as if he had seen them habitually. He took most to the simple and retiring, and especially liked the Abolitionists; this was when Abolitionists were in very little favor. I am touched by his recollection of me, and shall cherish it always. Let me confess that from the beginning I felt for him a peculiar friendship, and he seemed to feel the same for me. While I was an invalid his sympathy was complete and constant. I cannot forget his letters then. For more than a quarter of a century this friendship has been to me a treasure and a solace. It is gone now; and England, with which he was so much associated in my mind, seems to me less England than before. I know how his family loved and cherished him, and therefore I can appreciate your sorrow. To lose his companionship is much; but on the other hand it is much to have had him so long, and still to have his example.

"You are now with my venerated friend Lord Wensleydale. Pray let him know that I think of him and Lady Wensleydale, and remember me also to your son, of whose marriage I hear."

Richard Cobden died April 2, 1865. The intelligence was received in the United States immediately after the assassination of President Lincoln; and the public journals, in the same numbers which recounted the last scene in the life of Mr. Lincoln, gave their tributes to the English statesman who had befriended our cause. Sumner communicated officially to Mrs. Cobden the tribute to her husband's memory in the resolutions of the Republican convention of Massachusetts, adding the expression of his individual grief.[1] A friend of Cobden, who had introduced Sumner to him many years before (Joseph Parkes), died a few months later. His last letter to Sumner, April 5 of the same

[1] Works, vol. ix. pp. 498, 499.

year, gave an account of Cobden's last days and an estimate of his character.

Cobden's last letter[1] to Sumner was written March 2, just one month before his death. He wrote: —

"I feel it a pleasant duty to give you my best congratulations on the recent proceedings within and without your halls of Congress. The vote on the amendment of the Constitution was a memorable and glorious event in your history. Another incident — that of your introduction of a colored man to the Supreme Court — was hardly less interesting. In all these proceedings at Washington *you* ought to be allowed to indulge the feelings of a triumphant general.[2] You served as a volunteer in the forlorn hope when the battle of emancipation seemed a hopeless struggle. *Your* position within the walls of Congress was very different from that of the agitators out of doors, meritorious as were their labors. I have served in both capacities, and know the difference between addressing an audience of partisans at a public meeting and a hostile Parliamentary assembly. The rapid progress of events and the sudden transformation of opinion must impart a constant excitement to your life; it must be something like the movements of the kaleidoscope! I heartily congratulate you, and wish I could shake hands and have a chat with you on all that is passing. Looking on from this distance, I cannot doubt that your great military operations are drawing to a close. The war is being driven into a corner. A few months must decide the fate of the armies in the field. . . .

"It is nothing but your great power that has kept the hands of Europe off you. . . . There is no denying the fact that your great struggle has demonstrated an amount of hostility on the part of the ruling class here, and the ruling powers of Europe generally, towards your democratic institutions for which none of us were prepared. Still, it must not be forgotten that the common people of England were true to the cause of freedom. It has never been possible to call a public open meeting, with notice, to pass a resolution in favor of the rebellion. It would have been voted down by the workingmen. I know you are greatly and justly angered at the conduct of our upper classes; but do not forget the attitude of the workers."

Sumner's French correspondents during the war — Circourt, Henri Martin, Laboulaye, Augustin Cochin, Laugel, Montalembert, the Count of Paris, and his old friends at Montpellier, the family Martins-Gordon — were all friendly to our country as well as opponents of the second empire.[3] There was hardly any public opinion in France, and the action of the government was the

[1] Extracts from the two letters preceding the last from Mr. Cobden, dated Aug. 18, 1864, and Jan. 11, 1865, may be found in Morley's "Life of Cobden," vol. ii. pp. 446, 459.

[2] Cobden wrote, Aug. 18, 1864: "I heartily congratulate you on every step you have gained in your struggle for human rights and freedom. Whatever may be the fate of the war, *your* triumphs will be a permanent gain to humanity."

[3] Circourt, Martin, and Cochin were friends of George Sumner, whose death drew from them sympathetic letters to his brother. M. Chevalier wrote July 2, 1865, but his letters were infrequent.

expression of the emperor's will. Montalembert, whom Sumner had met on his later visits to Paris, rejoiced in our successes, and expressed in his letters his admiration of Sumner's career. The Count of Paris,[1] whose connection with our army led to his History of the Civil War, wrote frequently and at length. Writing from Claremont, Nov. 8, 1863, he testified his sympathy for "the liberal and national cause," and counted his conversations with the senator as among the most valued recollections of his sojourn in America. Sumner wrote to Richard Gordon, April 9, 1863: —

"I am sad to think of your poor father's death. I was hoping soon for another letter from him, when your communication told the melancholy tidings. And so another of my Montpellier friends has dropped away. I took a great interest, you may remember, in M. Renouvier; but I have heard only of his death, and nothing more. He had several works in hand, — one of them, Engraving in the Revolution; another, something mediæval, — which I fear are stopped. We used to talk of them when I visited him. But your father was my constant ally, and I cannot reconcile myself to the blow which we all feel. I wish you would have the goodness to write me about him and his last illness. I trust that he passed away without much suffering. And tell me also of your own family, and of the excellent professor,[2] who I see by the 'Moniteur' now on my table has been elected a corresponding member of the section of rural economy in the Academy. And how is M. Taillandier, whom I read occasionally in the 'Revue,'[3] and wish I could hear again? But those tranquil days of convalescence will never be mine again. My life at Montpellier was an episode in contrast with all before and after. As I think of myself on those benches, a listener, it seems like a fable. But I should like a day for Montpellier, to visit again its library, its collection of pictures, its walks, its streets, and especially a few friends. It seems to me I should enjoy it now more than ever. Its streets alone, especially that street[4] from the hotel by the market to your father's home, haunt me now. Tell me something about it.

"I was not surprised to hear of M. Abauzit's marriage. You will remember that I foretold it, to the incredulous amusement of the professor.[5] I hope that he and madame are well. Pray, is that *Serre*[6] constructed which was promised to the Jardin? And how is M. Nevet, my host?"

The young Ernest Duvergier de Hauranne came with letters to Sumner in 1864 from the Count of Paris and M. Cochin. He was with the senator familiarly in Washington and Boston,

[1] The count, who wrote English as perfectly as French, wrote to Sumner in French, saying that he did so because of Sumner's thorough knowledge of the language.

[2] Professor Martins.

[3] Revue des Deux Mondes.

[4] Now all changed by a new and wide street or avenue.

[5] *Ante*, vol. iii. p. 577.

[6] The *Serre* (hot-house) in the Jardin des Plantes, which was constructed afterwards.

and seems to have made a study of his personal qualities and position as a public man.[1] He quotes Sumner's remark, "L'homme d'État doit se guider par la lumière immuable des principes comme le marinier par l'étoile du matin," adding that "this solemn language fell naturally from his lips as the intimate and familiar expression of his thoughts, in itself sufficient to describe him."

Auguste Laugel, between whom and Sumner relations of confidence had subsisted since their meeting in Paris in 1857, visited the United States in 1864–1865. Their familiar intercourse was renewed at that time both in Boston and Washington. Sumner introduced M. Laugel and Madame Laugel, an American lady, at the White House a few days before the great tragedy.[2]

The Marquis de Chambrun arrived early in 1865, commended to Sumner by his father-in-law, Baron de Corcelle,[3] — friend of Tocqueville, and at one time French ambassador at Rome, whose acquaintance Sumner had made in Paris. The marquis was from that time a frequent visitor at Sumner's lodgings, and he continued for many years to live in Washington.[4]

[1] Huit Mois en Amérique, vol. i. pp. 49, 50, 359–361; vol. ii. pp. 81, 94, 253; first published in the "Revue des deux Mondes." M. de Hauranne, who was twenty-one at the time of his visit, became a member of the Chamber of Deputies, and died in 1877, his distinguished father surviving him.

[2] Laugel gave to the public the recollections of his intercourse with Sumner at this time, and his impressions of his personal and public character, in the "Revue des Deux Mondes," June, 1874, pp. 721–749. His summing-up was as follows: —

"Le trait le plus frappant de son caractère était un respect sincère, instinctif et plein pour l'intelligence; ses amis les plus chers étaient des poètes, des historiens, des penseurs. Il ornait sans cesse son esprit par la lecture des grands écrivains de tous les pays. La collection de ses discours, qui sera bientôt publiée, formera plus de dix volumes; on y trouvera, au milieu des matières souvent les plus arides, des échappées fréquentes sur le monde heureux des muses. Il y avait par momens une grâce singulière mêlée à son éloquence, d'ordinaire un peu lourde, à sa logique écrasante, à sa science trop exubérante. Dans un pays à la fois avide et prodigue, enflé de sa force et de sa richesse, Sumner restait comme un type des anciens temps; simple de moeurs, désintéressé, délicat et raffiné dans ses goûts, vivant sur les bords du fleuve que charriait les ambitions et les convoitises vulgaires, les yeux toujours fixés sur quelque chose de noble et de grand. On peut dire enfin de lui qu'il sut servir à la fois, ce qui est parfois malaisé, son pays et l'humanité, qu'il défendit toute sa vie les intérêts des États-Unis et ceux d'une race opprimée, et réussit à confondre les deux causes qui lui étaient les plus chères, celle de l'émancipation et celle de l'Union."

[3] The baron sent Sumner, July 14, 1866, a lamp from the Roman catacombs, on which was the figure of a shepherd caring for one of his flock, the giver thinking it appropriate to the senator as protector of the blacks. Upon Sumner's death, the lamp came into the possession of his friend, F. W. Bird.

[4] Sumner, in his testimony in 1872 in the French arms investigation, as also in his speech February 28 of that year (Works, vol. xv. p. 9), spoke of the studies and eminent connections of the marquis. He died in New York in 1891.

Agassiz sailed in April, 1865, on his expedition to Brazil and the Amazon. Sumner entered heartily into the plans of the great naturalist. He wrote to him a God-speed[1] just before he sailed, and received letters in return in which Agassiz gave an account of his researches.[2]

In the summer of 1865, Mr. and Mrs. William W. Story, long residents in Rome, were visiting relatives in Boston. It was pleasant for Sumner to meet again his old friends. He saw much of Story at dinners at the Saturday Club and on other days, and in drives in the suburbs of the city. Sumner always reverted with tenderness to old fellowships, and in intercourse with the son he revived the memories of the father. He kept up his interest in Story's work as a sculptor, and art as well as life in Italy were refreshing topics of conversation.

In the summer and autumn Sumner had his usual reunions with Longfellow at Nahant and Cambridge. One was a dinner at the Craigie House, where Burlingame, Palfrey, and Dana, "all original Free-Soilers," assisted.[3]

[1] March 20, 1865. "Life of Agassiz," by E. C. Agassiz, vol. ii. p. 634.

[2] June 21, 1865, and Dec. 26, 1865, the latter printed in Agassiz's "Life," p. 635.

[3] Longfellow's "Life," vol. ii. pp. 424, 425. 429.

## CHAPTER LI.

RECONSTRUCTION UNDER JOHNSON'S POLICY. — THE FOURTEENTH AMENDMENT TO THE CONSTITUTION. — DEFEAT OF EQUAL SUFFRAGE FOR THE DISTRICT OF COLUMBIA, AND FOR COLORADO, NEBRASKA, AND TENNESSEE. — FUNDAMENTAL CONDITIONS. — PROPOSED TRIAL OF JEFFERSON DAVIS. — THE NEUTRALITY ACTS. — STOCKTON'S CLAIM AS A SENATOR. — TRIBUTES TO PUBLIC MEN. — CONSOLIDATION OF THE STATUTES. — EXCESSIVE LABOR. — ADDRESS ON JOHNSON'S POLICY. — HIS MOTHER'S DEATH. — HIS MARRIAGE. — 1865-1866.

THE constitutional conventions and legislatures organized under President Johnson's policy in the summer and autumn of 1865 and the following winter annulled the ordinances of secession, repudiated the rebel debt, and accepted the Thirteenth Amendment. They uniformly rejected colored suffrage, although the President advised them to confer it to a limited extent, in order (giving as a sinister reason) that "the radicals, who are wild upon negro franchise, should be completely foiled in their attempt to keep the Southern States from renewing their relations to the Union by not accepting their senators and representatives." [1] They passed acts of apprenticeship and vagrancy, and other statutes, which reduced the freedmen to a condition of peonage, punished their breaches of contract as crimes, denied to them the power to acquire real estate or to carry arms, and excluded them from other privileges and rights enjoyed by white persons. This legislation represented the spirit of the people at the time, which was shown in persecutions of various kinds and in acts of violence, which finally culminated in massacres at Norfolk, Memphis, New Orleans, and Mobile.

Immediately after the autumn election, Sumner sent to the President an appeal against his policy in a long telegraphic despatch.[2] On arriving in Washington the Saturday evening before the session began, he sought the President at once, and passed two and a half hours with him.[3] He found him "changed

[1] Letter to W. L. Sharkey, Aug. 15, 1866.
[2] Nov. 12, 1865. Address, Oct. 2, 1866; Works, vol. xi. p. 24.
[3] Works, vol. xi. pp. 24, 25.

in temper and purpose, . . . no longer sympathetic, or even kindly," but "harsh, petulant, and unreasonable." Near the end of the interview there was a colloquy, in which the President reminded the senator of murders in Massachusetts and assaults in Boston as an offset to outrages visited at the South on negroes and white Union men under the inspiration of political or race animosity. The two parted that evening not to meet again, — the senator leaving "with the painful conviction that the President's whole soul was set as a flint against the good cause, and that by the assassination of Abraham Lincoln the rebellion had vaulted into the Presidential chair."

The Thirty-ninth Congress met Dec. 4, 1865. Its members had been mostly chosen at the time of Mr. Lincoln's second election, and the Republicans held each branch by a more than two-thirds majority; but it was not yet known how far the President's course might divide them. His message was moderate and plausible so far as language was concerned.[1] A large body of Republicans, who subsequently went against him, still adhered to him, and the message gave them hope of a change in his policy.

Before the message was received, and as soon as he could get the floor on the first day, Sumner offered a series (ten in number) of resolutions covering the whole subject of reconstruction.[2] Some of them were mere declarations of Congressional duty and power under the Constitution, without being intended for enactment as laws. The senator was in the habit of presenting such general statements with the view of leading public opinion.[3] Others were shaped with reference to legislation, and all were in open conflict with the President's scheme. The purport of the entire series was to affirm as fundamental conditions in reconstruction the absolute equality, as well in political as in civil rights, of the enfranchised blacks with all other citizens, to be maintained by the United States (through Congress) under its constitutional duty "to guarantee to every State a republican form of government."

[1] It was praised as a state paper in the New York "Nation," December 14, and "Harper's Weeekly," Dec. 23, 1865, and Jan. 20, 1866.

[2] Works, vol. x. pp. 1-37. For similar resolutions on reconstruction at later sessions compare those of Dec. 5, 1866. Works, vol. xi. pp. 44-46; March 7, 1867, Ibid., p. 124; July 3, 1867, Ibid., p. 368.

[3] In the Senate, March 11, 1867 (Works, vol. xi. p. 126), he instanced precedents in justification of such a course.

Sumner wrote to Lieber, December 3, 1865:—

"I was sorry to miss you, as I wished much to confer with you quietly on history and philosophy. Of course, Holland was called a republic. Bodin,[1] whom I have just read, calls the government of Nimrod a republic. I have been through everything on this question, and see my way clearly, — never before more clearly. The debate which approaches on the meaning of a 'republican government' will be the greatest in our history. I shall launch it to-morrow.

"On my arrival last evening I went at once to the President, with whom I was two and one-half hours. He began the interview warmly and antagonistically; but at the close thanked me for my visit. He does not understand the case. Much that he said was painful, from its prejudice, ignorance, and perversity.

"You ask about my relations with Mr. Welles. I am on excellent terms with every member of the Cabinet. With him I had special relations, so that he was in the habit of appealing to me to carry some things with President Lincoln. He has latterly written me, complaining that I exercised on one occasion too much influence with the latter against something which the department had at heart. I have been disgusted with his course on reconstruction; and we have had considerable correspondence on the subject, which was always amiable in manner. This is my answer to your inquiry."

To George Bemis, Christmas Day, 1865:—

"I have too long failed to acknowledge your last article, which produced a marked impression.[2] Baron Gerolt, our excellent dean, spoke of it as decisive; so did the Danish minister. But where is the Artigas[3] article? Sir F. Bruce, at dinner Saturday evening, said to me that England would fight before she would pay a dollar, or consent to arbitration; and then added, the Portuguese precedent had settled opinion in England, and that until that was answered we had no case; that Adams was worsted in the controversy. Of course I do not give any reply to all this, as my object is simply to let you see the importance of showing the true character of that Portuguese precedent. Mr. Hunter has had a search at the state department, and then at the treasury, without finding any trace of the paper you desire. He has sent to the New York custom-house, where it may be. The treasury papers were all destroyed by fire in 1830, or thereabout. Perhaps this paper perished then. But finish your article, and then gather all your sheaves together in a big pamphlet. Remember me kindly to Judge Fletcher when you see him."

To Mr. Bright, Jan. 1, 1866:—

"I have just read your magnificent speech,[4] I need not say, with perfect sympathy. I wish I had good news from our side. The President is per-

[1] A French writer, 1530–1596.

[2] Hasty Recognition of Rebel Belligerency.

[3] The South American general. "Memoirs of J. Q. Adams," vol. iv. p. 133.

[4] At Birmingham, Dec. 14, 1865, chiefly on the enlargement of the franchise.

verse, and not well-informed. He is also fired with the idea of carrying through his 'experiment,' which thus far is a terrible failure. It is very hard that we should have this new controversy. But I have no doubt with regard to my course; the way was never clearer. Affairs with France are very tender, but the Marquis de Montholon [1] thinks that with 'time' the question can be arranged. He expects that the emperor will make some statement in his address to the Chambers which will open the way to a good understanding; I hope so. Sir F. Bruce is very amiable and excellent; but he can do nothing. Lord Russell has sent him on an impossible mission. It is time that your ministry should consider the old rule, that 'whoso would have equity must do equity.' I write in great haste, and merely to wish you a Happy New Year. Seward assures me that his voyage [2] is solely for health and to avoid holidays."

To Bemis, March 15: —

"As to Bancroft's eulogy,[3] I felt at the time that there was something wrong in such a speech when the diplomatic corps were official guests. Of course I objected to his adhesion to Mr. Johnson's absurd scheme of reconstruction. But the chief error was in addressing such a speech to guests. Either they should not have been invited, or the speech should have been what could be said in their presence without giving offence."

To Lieber, March 21: —

"Consider carefully, and answer promptly. The committee of the Senate on foreign relations has before it the question, Shall the national government be represented at the French Exhibition? A bill authorizing a certain representation there has already passed the House. Its provision, as you have doubtless observed, is grossly inadequate. I have been considering how to add to the appropriations, and to make our position at the Exhibition respectable. There is something very captivating in such an occasion.

"Meanwhile comes the decree of the emperor, by which he appoints the princeling of his house 'Président d'Honneur,' — that is, the actual head and chief of the exhibition, conference, and congress. The functions of president are to be performed by a minister, but the princeling is left as head and chief. Can the United States send commissioners to be presided over by a boy nine years old? You will remember the scene when Louis XIV., only five years of age, attended Parliament, held a *lit de justice*, and gave his royal assent to Acts of Parliament. Louis XV. did the same thing. Now, if the French choose to tolerate such a folly we cannot complain; but can the great republic participate in such an occasion, and send its bearded men to bow to this boy? The more I think of it the less disposed I am to sanction it. Shall I report that on this account we decline? Of course this would be a *coup de foudre*. But must we not do so?"

[1] The French minister at Washington.
[2] To the West Indies.
[3] On President Lincoln before Congress, in which foreign nations were arraigned for their treatment of this country during the Civil War.

A joint committee of the two houses on reconstruction was appointed in the second week of the session, with Fessenden chairman on the part of the Senate, and Stevens on the part of the House. Stevens opened the debate, December 18, with a speech on the duties and powers of Congress in relation to the States lately in rebellion, taking positions in direct opposition to the President, and going as far as Sumner's most radical propositions. He was answered by Henry J. Raymond, a Republican, but now the President's supporter. The House gave a sign of its temper just after the holiday recess by referring to a committee, instead of passing, a resolution approving the President's policy. In the Senate there was equal alertness on the part of those who were opposed to his proceedings. Wilson pressed, in the second week of the session, his bill to annul statutes of the late rebel States which established inequality of civil rights on account of color, race, or former condition of servitude, — calling attention to recent legislation of this character. Johnson of Maryland replied to him.

The President, in answer to a call of the Senate made on Sumner's motion, sent to the Senate, December 19, the reports of Generals Grant and Schurz on the condition of the States lately in rebellion. The latter's report, containing a full description, and made after a careful inspection lasting for three months, did not meet the changed views of the President; and he sought to counteract it by the report of General Grant, who had passed only four days in a similar inspection as incidental to a military tour. The two reports were in conflict. General Schurz discovered in the South, with exceptions, "an entire absence of that national spirit which forms the basis of true loyalty and patriotism," and for a remedy he contended for negro suffrage as a condition in the readmission of those States to political power. General Grant's brief report, on the other hand, found that "the mass of thinking men of the South accept the present situation of affairs in good faith." The general's political relations were at that time undefined, and he appeared then as likely to associate himself with one party as with the other. It is also probable that, being as yet unused to civil affairs, he had in mind rather submission to military authority than that active loyalty which is essential to good citizenship. The President in communicating the reports called attention to General Grant's, but avoided a like mention of General Schurz's, and avowed his own "belief that sectional animosity is surely and rapidly merging itself into a spirit of nationality" in the late rebel States. The message and General Grant's report having been read from the desk, Sumner called for the reading of General Schurz's report, but this was found to be impracticable on account of its length. Sumner, in brief remarks, said that the message was "like the whitewashing message of Franklin Pierce with regard to the enormities in Kansas," and referred to Schurz's report as "accurate, authentic, and most authoritative," and to Grant's visit as "hasty." [1]

The epithet "whitewashing" drew at once protests from Reverdy Johnson and from two Republican supporters of the President, Doolittle and Dixon; and Sumner, while declining to retract or modify his language, disclaimed having made, as charged, "any reflection on the patriotism or the truth of the President." Sumner's treatment of the message became the occasion of widespread comment in the press. It was deprecated by Republican journals, which expressed confidence in the President's good intentions, and regarded as disastrous to the party any premature conflict with him; [2] but the greater part of these critics came to the senator's position a few months later.[3] There was the same hesitation among senators, all others holding back from comments on the message. Sumner, who had watched Mr. Johnson closely ever since he came to Washington to be inaugurated as Vice-President, was satisfied that he had taken an irrevocable step in antagonism to just measures of reconstruction, — a conviction in which he proved wiser than his associates, — and he felt that time should not be lost in making an appeal to the country.[4]

The day after the message came in, Sumner took the floor on Wilson's bill for the protection of freedmen, and proceeded to refute the President's argument, calling to mind at the outset

[1] Works, vol. x. pp. 47-54.

[2] Harper's Weekly, March 10, 1866. The New York "Nation," Dec. 28, 1865, defended, against Sumner's imputation, the President's sincerity, truthfulness, frankness, and candor.

[3] A change of feeling took place just two months later, February 9, when the President vetoed the Freedmen's Bureau bill.

[4] Two years later Whitelaw Reid ("Agate"), in a letter to the Cincinnati "Gazette," dated March 3, 1868, referring to the scene in the Senate, recalled the profound surprise and even bitterness of feeling with which Sumner's remarks were received by senators who not long after led in hostile action against the President. According to the same writer, the sentiments of these senators prevailed at the time among Republican journals and leaders who were "within the inner circles of the party."

"the attempt to whitewash the unhappy condition of the Southern States;" and then taking the States one by one, he read at great length extracts concerning the state of things in each from letters received by himself, from Southern journals and from other documents, showing a spirit hostile to the government and to the rights of the freedmen.[1] He closed thus:—

> "Insist upon guaranties. Pass the bill under consideration, — pass any bill, — but do not let this crying injustice rage any longer. An avenging God cannot sleep while such things find countenance. If you are not ready to be the Moses[2] of an oppressed people, do not become its Pharaoh."

The array of testimony confounded the President's partisans. The only reply came from Cowan, a Republican, who treated Sumner's evidence as relating to exceptional instances, and not to any general features of society at the South; and he as well as the President made much of General Grant's report. He asked why, if Sumner and others thinking with him desired suffrage for the negroes, they did not say so broadly, and Sumner answered promptly from his seat, "I do say so." A few days later Sumner called for full information concerning the provisional governors appointed by the President and the action of the Southern conventions and legislatures. Soon after he drew attention to the illegal appointments at the South of persons unable to take the required oath of loyalty.[3]

The protests against the President's policy came from the people more tardily than otherwise, on account of certain conditions in the public mind which are not revealed in the debates in Congress. The country sought repose after the war, and was not in the mood for a severe civil conflict. Wise men feared the effects on our polity of a prolonged military administration at the South, and were anxious for a speedy restoration of civil governments. Capitalists desired an immediate pacification of the Southern territory as opening a market which had been closed for four years; as a mass, they could not treat critically schemes of reconstruction, and they inclined to the one which promised the

[1] Works, vol. x. pp. 55-97. In another speech, Jan. 19, 1866 (Works, vol. x. pp. 109, 110), when the credentials of a senator from Florida were presented, he added evidence as to the condition of things in that State. His reading a letter from Texas in the Senate without giving the signature, Dec. 5, 1866, was made a point of order, which was overruled. (Works, vol. xi. p. 46.) Senator Nye, Jan. 12, 1871 (Congressional Globe, p. 452), referred to Sumner's habit of reading letters in the Senate in support of his positions.

[2] President Johnson had spoken of himself as the "Moses" of the colored people.

[3] January 5, 11; February 2; Congressional Globe, pp. 129, 184, 185, 593.

quickest results. Political considerations were superadded. The Republicans held some of the largest States at the North by narrow majorities, and were fearful of any division which would throw the balance against them. It was felt that any imprudent step might be followed by the return of the Democratic party to power, — a party composed, at the North, largely of adherents whose loyalty had been uncertain, and, at the South, of the mass of the supporters of the rebellion. With that dreaded event would, as was believed, come the repudiation of the public debt, the oppression of the freedmen, and a loss of most that had been gained in the war. The objections to the President's course would not, it was felt, be apparent to the popular intelligence, and a conflict with him would be fatal to the party. Office-holders, anxious to retain their places, were loath to have a break with him, as also were candidates for elective offices, who shrank from the uncertain issue of a conflict with the head of the party. Besides such complexities, the problem of reconstruction, especially in view of the changed condition of the colored race, was itself a novel and strange one, involving a chaos of opinions and plans.

One of Sumner's friends, P. W. Chandler, writing Feb. 12, 1866, expressed the public feeling as follows: —

> "There is a very feverish dread in Boston, and I find the same here,[1] of any breach with the President. It would be a terrible misfortune at this crisis to have a divided North, and especially to have the influence of the President thrown into the Democratic party. There was never a time when prudence and sagacity were so needed. If we cannot have all we need, we must take what we can get."

The conflict between Congress and the President, which Sumner had foreseen for several months to be inevitable, came finally, February 19, when he vetoed the bill to enlarge the powers of the Freedmen's Bureau, following it three days later with a ribald speech to a crowd gathered at the White House, in which he put the Republican leaders opposed to him (Sumner among them) on a footing with Davis, Toombs, and Slidell, and exalted, as was his habit, his own personal career. The veto and the harangue marked a distinct step in his departure from the Republican party. Then came his veto, March 27, of the Civil Rights bill, and July 16, of the second Freedmen's Bureau bill, — the

[1] At Philadelphia.

last two vetoes being overcome by a two-thirds vote of both houses. Trumbull showed consummate ability in the drafting, management, and advocacy of these measures. As they were well handled in debate, — not only by Trumbull, but by Howard, Morrill of Maine, Fessenden, and Wilson, — Sumner, although he had prepared himself on the Civil Rights bill, did not speak; but he watched the measure closely and with deep interest, approving it altogether, and recognizing it as a precedent for his own bill for equal political rights in the reconstructed States.[1] He wrote to the Duchess of Argyll, April 3: —

"These are trying days for us. I am more anxious now than during the war. The animal passions of the nation aided the rally then. Now the appeal is to the intelligence, and to the moral and religious sentiments. How strangely we are misrepresented in the 'Times.' I read it always, and find nothing true in its portraiture of our affairs. Believe me, the people are with Congress. When it is considered that the President has such an amazing power, it is extraordinary to see how the conscience of the masses has stood firm. Congress is misrepresented in England. I speak of the lower House now. In my opinion it is the best that has ever been since the beginning of our government. It is full of talent, and is governed by patriotic purpose. There is no personal or party ambition which prompts its course. It is to save the country that it takes its present responsibilities.

"You say, 'Why not urge the abolition of the black codes?' This I have done from the beginning. There are several speeches of mine which you have never seen, three years ago, against any exclusion of witnesses on account of color; also an elaborate report. A partial measure I carried. Since the cessation of hostilities this subject has occupied me constantly. In my speech at Worcester I dwelt on the black codes; then again in a speech early this session. At last we passed a bill, known as the Civil Rights bill; it went through both houses by unprecedented majorities. The President refuses to sign it. By our Constitution it requires a vote of two thirds to pass it over his veto. It is still uncertain if we can command this large vote; the division will be very close. The loss of this bill will be a terrible calamity. It leaves the new crop of black laws in full force, and gives to the old masters a new letter of license to do anything with the freedman short of making him a chattel. A new serfdom may be substituted, and this is their cruel purpose. But after most careful consideration I see no substantial protection for the freedman except in the franchise. He must have this — (1) For his own protection; (2) For the protection of the white Unionist; and (3) For the peace of the country. We put the musket in his hands because it was necessary; for the same reason we must give him the franchise. Unionists from the South tell me that unless this is done they will be defenceless. And here is the necessity for the universality of the suffrage: every vote is needed to counterbalance the rebels.

[1] Feb. 7, 1866; Congressional Globe, p. 707. Feb. 9, 1866; Globe, pp. 765-767. Works, vol. x. pp. 271-279.

"It is very sad that we should be tried in this way. For our country it is an incalculable calamity. Nobody can yet see the end. Congress will not yield. The President is angry and brutal. Seward is the marplot. In the Cabinet, on the question of the last veto, there were four against it to three for it; so even there, among his immediate advisers, the President is left in a minority. Stanton reviewed at length the bill, section by section, in the Cabinet, and pronounced it an excellent and safe bill every way from beginning to end. But the veto message was already prepared, and an hour later was sent to Congress.

"You hear that I do not bear contradiction. Perhaps not. I try to bear everything. But my conscience and feelings are sometimes moved, so that I may show impatience. It is hard to meet all these exigencies with calmness. I hope not to fail.

"I despair of the President. He is no Moses, but a Pharaoh to the colored race, and they now regard him so. He has all the narrowness and ignorance of a certain class of whites, who have always looked upon the colored race as out of the pale of humanity.

"Fenianism is to us only a noisy shadow, without reality. I never saw a Fenian. My excellent friend, Mr. Schleiden, is much mistaken in his present views of our affairs. He follows the London 'Times.'"

The fourteenth amendment of the Constitution passed both houses at this session. It defined citizenship; prohibited the States from abridging the privileges or immunities of citizens; excluded persons from national and State offices who, having held certain offices under the nation or the States, engaged in the rebellion, until Congress by a two-thirds vote removed the disability; affirmed the validity of the public debt, and forbade the national or State governments from assuming the rebel debt. Another section which gave rise to controversy among Republicans, in determining the basis of representation in Congress, prescribed that when the right to vote was denied to any of the male inhabitants of a State, being twenty-one years of age and citizens, or was in any way abridged except for participation in rebellion or other crime, "the basis of representation therein shall be reduced in the proportion which the number of such male citizens shall bear to the whole number of male citizens twenty-one years of age in such State." This provision, with some variations, was the same as was proposed by Stevens at the beginning of the session, and later offered with some change of phraseology by Spalding, Blaine, Conkling, and Schenck, and was at last reported by the reconstruction committee.[1] It failed in the

[1] Sumner referred, Feb. 8, 1869 (Congressional Globe, p. 1003), to the different forms of the proposed amendment, and his objections to them.

Senate, but finally prevailed after it had been recast by the committee. The idea of the provision in its different forms was to make it for the interest of the former slave States to confer suffrage on the colored people by diminishing their representation in Congress to the extent to which they should withhold the right. The effect of the entire exclusion of the colored people in those States was stated to be the reduction of their representation from eighty-three to thirty-five. The attractions of political power were assumed to be so great as to be altogether likely to overcome the antagonism of race, notwithstanding the fact that such a temptation had had no effect in promoting the abolition of slavery. The amendment, however, drew out sincere enthusiasm. Stevens saw in it the speedy regeneration of the South. Wilson approved it with his heart, his conscience, and his judgment, and was ready to go to the scaffold joyfully in order to put it into the Constitution! Many who would gladly have gone further were deterred by the fear that a prohibition of race discrimination in suffrage would fail in the Northern States, in the larger number of which the negro was still excluded from the elective franchise by stubborn prejudice, — as in Connecticut and Wisconsin, where the exclusion had recently been reaffirmed.

Sumner had no sympathy, or even patience, with the proposed amendment so far as it concerned representation, regarding it as "another compromise with human rights," and, in the form in which it was first submitted to the Senate, as an express recognition of the right of the State to make an unrepublican discrimination "on account of race or color," hitherto kept out of the Constitution;[1] and in its offer of a larger representation as the price of political equality, he saw only "a delusion and a snare," — a bribe offered that would not tempt.[2]

The amendment as it first passed the House on the last day of January and was laid before the Senate provided "that whenever the elective franchise shall be denied or abridged in any State on account of race or color, the persons therein of such race or color shall be excluded from the basis of representation."

[1] The partisans of the amendment claimed that it was "punitive" in intent, and did not sanction any exclusion on account of race or color; but Sumner rejected this theory. Works, vol. x. p. 293.

[2] G. W. Julian, then a member of the House and voting for the amendment, has since, in his "Political Recollections," p. 272, denounced it as "a scheme of cold-blooded treachery and ingratitude" to the colored people.

A few Republican votes were thrown against it in the House; and some Republican leaders who voted for it showed in their speeches a distrust of its efficacy.

As ill health prevented Mr. Fessenden from opening the debate in the Senate, February 5, he gave his place to Sumner, who took the opportunity to review the whole subject of reconstruction in a speech of four hours, divided between two successive days.[1] The public interest in it was as great on the second as on the first day. The seats of the senators were filled; members of the House occupied the sofas or were standing in the lobbies; the galleries were densely crowded. Looking down on the scene as spectators most interested were a considerable number of the race for whom he was pleading, among them Frederick Douglass and Rev. H. H. Garnett. Before the senator was the friendly face of Mr. Pomeroy, who was filling the chair of the Vice-President. The audience listened to a discourse rather than a speech; but the solemn earnestness of the speaker and his fascinations of style, voice, and presence held them to the end. Rarely, if ever, did he make a deeper impression in the Senate or awaken a wider interest in the country. At the outset he subjected the proposed amendment to criticism, being strictly impersonal and making no reflection on its authors or advocates; but the main body of the speech took a broader range, covering all the propositions concerning reconstruction which he offered on the first day of the session. As in previous speeches and papers, Sumner argued that all power was in Congress to establish the political as well as the civil rights of the freedmen, reasoning from the necessity growing out of the Civil War, from the power under the thirteenth amendment to enforce emancipation by appropriate legislation, and above all, from the duty of the United States to guarantee to every State a republican form of government. He dwelt at almost wearisome length on the meaning of the constitutional phrase, "a republican form of government," and rejecting various definitions, maintained as his main thesis that no government was within the guaranty which was founded on caste and excluded great masses of citizens from a share in it solely because of conditions of color and race which were beyond their control.[2] His quotations, gath-

1 Works, vol. x. pp. 119-237.

2 T. W. Higginson, writing February 18, noted with admiration the thoroughness and exhaustiveness of the speech, finding nothing in contemporary statesmanship, here or abroad, to equal it.

ered from a wide research in books on morals and politics (some from French sources), were in some instances given a broader meaning than their authors intended.[1] The latter part of the speech laid stress on the advantages of the ballot in establishing free institutions at the South, educating the freedmen and giving them the capacity to defend themselves. The conclusion was a plea for "liberty and equality as the God-given birthright of all men," against the opposite assumption, which he pronounced "false in religion, false in statesmanship, and false in economy." "Show me," said he in an appeal which recalls those of Curran and Brougham, "a creature with lifted countenance looking to heaven, made in the image of God, and I show you a MAN, who of whatever country or race, whether bronzed by equatorial sun or blanched by northern cold, is with you a child of the Heavenly Father, and equal with you in all the rights of human nature." The audience broke out with applause as he took his seat.

Sumner's argument was that of a moralist, not that of a lawyer. He declared that "whatever is required for the national safety is constitutional," — a doctrine to be confined strictly to the exigencies of war. His test of "a republican form of government" was rather one that on the highest view of political society ought to be applied, than one which the framers of the Constitution had in mind when they founded the nation, or the one which has been accepted by the common judgment of the American people. With perfect confidence in his positions, he maintained that Congress could by mere statute impose conditions as to suffrage on the rebel States from which they could not rid themselves after their complete restoration;[2] and while he did not go so far in the debate, it was his deliberate opinion, as shown by a resolution moved by him, that Congress could dictate equal suffrage to all the States.[3] A few senators — for instance, Pomeroy and Yates — appeared to favor his opinion; and pending bills for protecting civil rights were an apt analogy, of which he took advantage later in the debate, saying, "If Congress can decree equality in civil rights, by the same reason, if not *a fortiori*, it can decree equality in political rights." Even, however, on his own view of the power of Congress there was an element of uncertainty in legislation which

[1] Compare Lieber's letter to Sumner. in his "Life and Letters," pp. 360, 361.
[2] Works, vol. x. pp. 14, 113.
[3] Works, vol. x. pp. 123, 239.

was subject to repeal, or might fail to pass the ordeal of judicial revision; and this uncertainty, as was maintained in reply to him, was sufficient to justify the precaution of a constitutional amendment. But Sumner had come to the conviction that for the protection of human rights the power of Congress was supreme; that the decision for equality of rights could be made at once, and that the people could be trusted to maintain it. He distrusted the fate of a constitutional amendment, which would have to run the gauntlet of the States, and was averse to the admission implied in it that Congress was incompetent to establish the equality; therefore he moved, in the course of his speech, as a substitute for the House resolution, a bill prohibiting the denial of civil or political rights on account of race or color, — which as first offered was to apply to all the States, but later was modified by him so as to apply only to the States lately in rebellion.

Sumner's speech had an effect on his associates, even on those who did not assent to his theory of the Constitution. He had held up in a glaring light the distinction of caste, as offensive to the moral sense and repugnant to the principles and pledges of the nation. No Republican senator had the hardihood from that time to vindicate the justice of the discrimination which the proposed amendment allowed the States to continue, and the argument for it became largely apologetic. It was admitted to come short of what was best, while no more was thought attainable in the existing conditions of public sentiment. One senator,[1] though withholding assent from Sumner's advanced position, confessed his profound admiration of the speech, pronouncing it "worthy of the subject, worthy of the occasion, worthy of the author," and predicted that "when those who heard it shall be forgotten, the echoes of its lofty and majestic periods will linger and repeat themselves among the corridors of history." It was the text of a wide discussion in the country, and it received commendation from public journals and a large number of approving correspondents.[2]

Most cordial testimonies came from the antislavery leaders. Garrison wrote of "the eloquent and unanswerable speech," "based as it is upon absolute justice and eternal right," and bore witness to the assiduity and perseverance, the courage and determination, the devotion and inflexible purpose of its author,

1 Williams of Oregon. 2 Works, vol. x. pp. 247-266.

through fiery trials and at the risk of martyrdom. Wendell Phillips wrote of the speech with equal enthusiasm and gratitude. Whittier thought the argument "irresistible, iron-linked throughout," and "sure to live as long as the country has a history." Henry Ward Beecher, who did not agree with the senator's objection to the language of the amendment, recognized the merit of the speech as "rising far above the occasion and object for which it was uttered, and covering a ground which will abide after all temporary questions of special legislation have passed away." Others, of more conservative temperament, were not less emphatic in their approval. The response to the speech was made, however, rather to its general scope and spirit, — its ideal of national duty, — than to its particular treatment of the pending measure or of questions of constitutional law.

The President was greatly incensed at certain passages of the speech. The next day, in an interview with the colored people, he referred to its "rounded periods," and intimated that its doctrines would bring on "a contest between the races." Later on (February 22), he broke out, in the harangue at the White House already referred to, into unseemly language, and associated Sumner with the chiefs of the rebellion. Sumner took no notice of the outburst; but the Massachusetts Legislature, by a resolution passed almost unanimously, pronounced it without "the shadow of justification or defence," and other public bodies took similar action.[1] The President's language found an echo in threats of violence against the senator, originating with the partisans of the former's policy.[2]

The debate continued for more than a month, Fessenden being the leader in favor of the amendment, and Henderson, Yates, and Pomeroy among Republicans opposing it. Sumner spoke twice after his first speech, on March 7 and on the 9th, when the vote was taken.[3] Some of the epithets applied by him to the committee's proposition, which, though short-sighted, was well meant, exceeded the measure of the occasion. He was perhaps led to make them the stronger by the treatment he received from Fessenden, who without any due provocation descended into personalities, and pursued Sumner with unconcealed bitterness.[4] Sumner followed with a reply which was made in

1 Works, vol. x. p. 268.
2 Works, vol. x. p. 269.
3 Works, vol. x. pp. 282–337, 338–345.
4 March 9. Congressional Globe, pp. 1277–1280.

the best of temper. Unlike the Maine senator, Williams, Howe, Henderson, and Yates referred to Sumner in very complimentary terms.

Sumner's substitute received eight votes, — his own and those of Brown, Chandler, Howe, Pomeroy, Wade, and Wilson. Henderson's proposition of an amendment to the Constitution, forbidding the States in prescribing the qualifications of electors to discriminate against any person on account of race or color, received the votes of the same senators with Henderson and Clark added, making only ten votes in the Senate at that time in favor of the principle afterwards adopted in the fifteenth amendment. The committee's proposition was then rejected by a vote of twenty-five yeas to twenty-two nays, — not two-thirds in favor of it. The Republicans voting against it were Brown, Dixon, Henderson, Lane of Kansas, Pomeroy, Stewart, Sumner, and Yates.[1]

The result was a disappointment in political quarters, and Sumner was held responsible for it. Stevens said in the House that the amendment had "been slaughtered by a puerile and pedantic criticism," and "by the united forces of self-righteous Republicans and unrighteous copperheads."[2] There was a feeling among Republicans that the party would lose prestige with the people unless it carried through Congress some constitutional amendment concerning representation, and that it would enter at a disadvantage into a contest with the President in the autumn elections unless it presented a definite and positive policy as the alternative of the one on which he had appealed to the country.[3] Sumner himself may have felt the force of the political consideration when, after the defeat of the committee's proposition, he offered, March 12, a form for a constitutional amendment which as to representation was in substance the same as finally prevailed.[4] The rejected proposition concerned

[1] Sprague of Rhode Island had intended to vote against the amendment, but informed Sumner the day before by note that he should support it. Chief-Justice Chase wrote Sumner, on the morning of the day when the vote was taken, a brief and confidential note, expressing the earnest hope that the amendment would not be defeated by his vote.

[2] The Boston "Advertiser," February 27 and March 9, 10, 12, disapproved Sumner's opposition to the amendment. Sumner replied in its columns to its article of March 12 (Works, vol. x. pp. 375, 376). C. E. Norton in the New England Publication Society's paper. March 16, also took exception to the senator's course.

[3] Sumner in the Senate, May 2, 1866, referred to "voices from without insisting that there must be a political issue presented to the country." Works, vol. x. p. 429.

[4] This form, as offered by Sumner, encountered criticism in letters to him from Parker Pillsbury, Wendell Phillips, and Gerrit Smith. "Antislavery Standard," March 31 and April 21.

only representation; but the second one, proposed by the committee on reconstruction after the defeat of the first, and revised in both houses, concerned not only representation but also citizenship, exclusion from office-holding of certain persons who had engaged in the rebellion until the disability should be removed by Congress, the sanctity of the national debt, and a prohibition against the assumption or payment of the Confederate debt. It did not recognize expressly the right of the States to deny or abridge the elective franchise on account of race or color, but it recognized their general right to deny and abridge suffrage at their discretion without specifying any particular form of discrimination. Finally the amendment in its new form passed both houses in June, receiving the entire Republican vote in each house, — a result which was promoted by a caucus. Sumner, though voting for the amendment in its new form, took no part in the debate and suggested no changes. The speeches were largely apologetic. The contest had become, so far as representation was concerned, a trial of party strength rather than a vital issue involving the rights and well-being of a race.[1]

The history of this representation clause of the fourteenth amendment is a curious one. Stevens's and Wilson's extravagant hopes of its efficacy have been noted. Several members of the House, anxious for fame, were rivals for the honor of its paternity. It consumed the time of Congress, divided the Republicans into factions, and made patriotic senators and representatives for a while think very ill of one another. Yet with all this, so far as voting and representation were concerned, it never bore the slightest fruit. The power to discriminate as to suffrage on account of race, color, or former condition of servitude, which it permitted to the States, with the penalty of a reduced representation, was taken away from them by the fifteenth amendment, which became a part of the Constitution in 1870. After that, it could only operate — where those who prompted it did not desire to have it operate — on limitations of suffrage founded on insufficient education, as in Massachusetts and Mississippi; or insufficient property, as in Rhode Island.[2]

[1] The ratification of the amendment by a sufficient number of States was officially announced July 28, 1868. The Democratic Legislature of Ohio undertook to revoke the assent of the State, which had been given by a Republican Legislature. Sumner in a speech, Jan. 31, 1868, denied the right of a State to withdraw its assent. Works, vol. xii. pp. 253-256.

[2] This discrimination in Rhode Island, affecting only naturalized citizens, has been removed.

The census of 1870 provided statistics to meet such discriminations, but Congress ignored them; and such exclusions, though clearly within the amendment, have not been taken into account in determining the basis of representation. The provision proved unworkable with a limited application, as it would probably have proved with a larger scope.[1] The amendment concerned only legal exclusions, and therefore is no remedy for illegal counts, or the prevention of voting by intimidation. It proved to be one of the cases where statesmen look far but see little. Fortunately, the perversity of the Southern people soon demonstrated the inadequacy of the fourteenth amendment. They rejected it when it was presented to them as a test of the fitness of their States for restoration, and their stubbornness showed the necessity of a compulsory provision.[2]

Sumner proposed at a meeting of the nominating committee appointed by the caucus of Republican senators that the committee on the District of Columbia should be constituted so as to secure suffrage in the District without distinction of color. Sherman at once said, "Then you must go on it." Notwithstanding he was already fully occupied by the duties of the foreign relations committee, Sumner accepted this additional service, and remained on the committee until December, 1872. His motion in the committee for reporting a bill to prohibit exclusion from suffrage in the District on account of race or color was adopted. The bill underwent debate, but did not reach a vote at this session.[3] The reading and writing qualification was moved as an amendment, but it was rejected by a vote of fifteen to nineteen. Sumner's vote is among the nays.[4] In declining to admit the restriction into this bill as a precedent, he had in view the political necessity which required the entire voting force of the colored people in the disorganized States as the support of the national cause.

Sumner was determined that hereafter equality of suffrage should be required of new States on their admission, as well as of rebel States on their readmission. The Territory of Colorado,

[1] The judiciary committee of the House reported, Feb. 26, 1891, that the restrictive provisions of the constitutions of Massachusetts and Mississippi required a reduction in the representation of those States.

[2] Julian's "Political Recollections," p. 304.

[3] Works, vol. x. p. 7. He spoke briefly for equal suffrage, December 21, on presenting a petition. Ibid., p. 98.

[4] Speech, Dec. 13, 1866 (Works, vol. xi. pp. 48–51), when he voted against the same amendment.

seeking admission at this time, contained less than one hundred colored inhabitants. Its entire population was very small, and the proceedings for forming a constitution had been quite irregular. Sumner in several speeches opposed the application on the ground of irregularity and insufficient numbers, but chiefly because the constitution of the proposed State expressly confined suffrage to "white male citizens."[1] He proposed as a fundamental condition, framed after the model of the Missouri restriction of slavery, that there should be no denial of the elective franchise, or of any other rights, on account of race or color in the proposed State; and in his view the condition when accepted would be perpetually obligatory.[2] Western senators from sectional sympathy pressed the admission; and some senators, like Wilson, acting from political considerations, — which, unhappily, are apt to enter into such questions, — were desirous of making another Republican State. Sumner was charged with inconsistency in having waived in previous instances the point on which he now insisted; but he explained the distinction between the former cases and the present. He refused to take into account a similar discrimination in existing States as barring a prohibition in the case of new States. Nor did it matter to him, a principle being at stake, that there were only ninety colored persons already in the Territory; it would be all the same if there were but one. The debate went on at intervals; and meantime, after it began, Edmunds of Vermont took his seat for the first time as senator, and made his first considerable speech against the bill. As he finished, Sumner thanked him for his noble utterance. The amendment imposing the conditions received only seven votes, — those of Edmunds, Foster, Grimes, Howe, Morgan, Poland, and Sumner.[3] The bill passed, — Sumner and five other Republicans and some Democrats voting against it.

An amendment moved by E. B. Washburne in the House, requiring the people of Colorado as a condition of admission to

[1] March 12 and 13, April 17, 19, and 24, May 21, 1866. Works, vol. x. pp. 346–374.

[2] Sumner proposed, Feb. 25, 1865, to apply the same fundamental condition to Louisiana, following the Missouri Compromise precedent. (Works, vol. ix. p. 317.) The validity of such conditions was treated by him and other senators in debates, Jan. 14 and Feb. 17, 1870. Works, vol. xiii. pp. 216–221, 331–335.

[3] Wendell Phillips wrote to Mrs. Child as to Sumner's failure to obtain support from his colleague in this instance: "How superbly Sumner does! How foolish Wilson, with such a leader at hand, to go so absurdly astray!" New England Magazine, February, 1892, p. 734.

strike out from the constitution the word "white" as a qualification of voters, was defeated, receiving only thirty-seven votes; but among them were those of well-known public men, — Blaine, Boutwell, Garfield, Jenckes, Julian, Kasson, Morrill, and Stevens. The President vetoed the bill chiefly on the ground of an insufficient population in the Territory. When the question came up at the next session, Sumner's amendment prevailed; but the President again vetoed the bill.

Sumner, just before the close of the session, made an ineffectual effort to incorporate the same condition in the bill to admit Nebraska, the constitution of which had expressly confined suffrage to "white male citizens;" but only four senators voted with him, two of whom were Edmunds and Fessenden. Nye was facetious at Sumner's expense, saying that his "conscientious friend mistook twinges of dyspepsia for constitutional scruples;" and Sumner replied that he had "never had the dyspepsia in his life." Wade thought that Sumner "had a certain one idea that covered the whole ground." The bill not receiving the President's signature failed to become a law; and the fundamental condition, which was lost at this session, was to be carried at the next, the bill containing it being passed over the President's veto.[1]

Sumner likewise failed to impose his fundamental condition of equal suffrage on Tennessee, one of the reconstructed States. The House by ordering the previous question cut off Boutwell's amendment for equal suffrage, and under the fervor inspired by the stubborn loyalty of a large portion of the inhabitants passed almost unanimously the resolution for the admission. Sumner contended in the Senate that the admission would be premature, as the rebel spirit was still controlling large districts; and further, that the denial of equal suffrage to the colored people made the constitution unrepublican.[2] The Senate yielded to his criticisms of the preamble, but only three senators — Brown, Pomeroy, and Wade — joined him in insisting on equal suffrage as a condition. His earnestness did not bring his own colleague

[1] July 27, Dec. 14 and 19, 1866; Jan. 8, 1867: Works, vol. x. pp. 504-523. When the bill first passed the House, July 27, 1866, Kelley of Pennsylvania objected to the exclusion of colored men from the suffrage, and among the minority who voted against the bill were distinguished Republicans, — Allison, Boutwell, Eliot, Garfield, Jenckes, Julian, Morrill, Stevens, and E. B. Washburne.

[2] July 21, 1866; Works, vol. x. pp. 490-494. He insisted on an inquiry into the loyalty of D. T. Patterson when his credentials as senator from Tennessee were presented, July 26. Works, vol. x. pp. 502, 503.

to his side.[1] Brown closed the debate, declaring his conviction against discrimination of race or color in the groundwork of reconstruction. Singularly enough, the only senator who stood uniformly with Sumner in his contest for equal suffrage was to be in 1872 the Democratic candidate for Vice-President. The President signed the resolution, though under protest against the preamble.

Sumner, though failing to apply his condition of equal suffrage to Colorado, Nebraska, and Tennessee, or to establish the equality in any statute or constitutional amendment, had by his constant insistence on the principle materially advanced the cause. He had brought the question to the front; he had educated public sentiment, and driven his Republican opponents to the attitude of apologists. He had been almost alone in the contest, with only one or two constant supporters in the Senate; but his spirit was undaunted, and his triumph was to come.[2]

Two years later he argued at length in favor of the validity and necessity of such conditions, of their perpetual force and obligation after the admission of the State, so as to be forever beyond its power to repeal,[3] — when he was supported by the entire Republican vote; and the bill applying the condition to North Carolina, South Carolina, Louisiana, Georgia, and Alabama became a law notwithstanding President Johnson's veto.[4]

The partisans of woman suffrage made an effort without success to enlist Sumner in their movement. Withholding an opinion as to its essential merits, he dismissed it as unseasonable at a period when it was likely to embarrass the pressing issue of the equality of the races as to the franchise.[5] This reserve was

[1] Wilson gave his reasons, Dec. 19, 1866 (Congressional Globe, p. 192), for his vote.

[2] His other efforts for equal suffrage at this session need only be noted here. Remarks, Feb. 15, 1866, on a petition of colored men, January 19, in relation to the credentials of W. Marvin, senator from Florida (Works, vol. x. pp. 109, 110); proposed amendment to the reconstruction bill, May 29, 1866 (Works, vol. x. p. 468); remarks on time and reconstruction, May 2, 1866 (Works, vol. x. pp. 428–431); letter to a committee of the District of Columbia, April 14, 1866 (Works, vol. x. pp. 417, 418); letter to the American Antislavery Society, May, 1866 (Works, vol. x. p. 427). Other references by him to the condition of the South are a letter on delay in the removal of disabilities, May, 1866 (Works, vol. x. p. 461), and remarks on the interruption of the right of petition, May 24, 1866 (Works, vol. x. pp. 462, 463).

[3] June 10, 1868; Works, vol. xii. pp. 414–438. He expressed himself, May 28, in favor of applying the condition to Arkansas. (Congressional Globe, p. 2628.) His argument did not satisfy some of his friends, particularly E. L. Pierce, who wrote, June 23, doubting the validity of such conditions after the admission of the State, and regarding a constitutional prohibition as the only perfect and effective remedy.

[4] It passed the Senate June 25, 1868.

[5] Feb. 14 and 21, 1866. Congressional Globe, pp. 829, 952.

not satisfactory to Mrs. E. C. Stanton and Miss Susan B. Anthony, who took occasion in letters to him to express their discontent with his apologetic manner in presenting their petition. At the next session he voted and spoke, on the ground of untimeliness, against woman suffrage in the District of Columbia, remarking that suffrage for that sex was "one of the great questions of the future," which would "be easily settled whenever the women in any considerable proportion insist that it shall be settled."[1]

He wrote to William Claflin, May 4: —

"If Massachusetts speaks, it must be for those principles which are essential to the peace and stability of the republic.[2] . . . It is said the President will veto the Colorado bill. What madness to pass such a bill, and brave such a veto, where Congress is in the wrong! Fessenden, Grimes, and myself, to say nothing of others, will sustain the veto when it comes. Thus the politicians who engineered Colorado will fail in their purposes, while they injure their influence inconceivably in sustaining the just course with regard to the rebel States. How can they insist upon impartial suffrage in any rebel State when they refused to require it in a State over which at the moment they had jurisdiction?"

To Mr. Bright, May 21: —

"I was very glad to hear from you, and to find you so cheerful. Of course, I note day by day all that you say and do. I see how you are the selected mark; that will not hurt. I speak from a little experience of my own. I am sure that there can be no tranquillity or security here until complete justice is rendered to the negro. Perhaps your question is not so urgent, yet I confess I can see nothing but 'agitate and convert' until the franchise is extended. It seems to me that you consent to accept a very small instalment. Our deadlock continues, with no chance of relief. The people sustain Congress, which stands firm. But there is no hint that the President will give way; he is indocile, obstinate, perverse, impenetrable, and hates the education and civilization of New England. Seward encourages him; McCulloch is bitterly with him; Dennison sometimes with him, and sometimes against him; Welles is with him; Stanton, Harlan, and Speed are against his policy, — so that his Cabinet is nearly equally divided. When I speak of the opinions of these men I speak according to my personal knowledge, from conversation with each of them. I do not think that they are always frank with the President. Seward is rash and visionary, with a most wonderful want of common-sense. For instance, only a week ago he told me that he had drawn a message for the President, asking for proceedings against Ecuador, because this puny republic had failed to pay the first instalment on an award of our claims, and that he has had a

[1] Dec. 13, 1866; Works, vol. xi. pp. 48–51. Mrs. L. M. Child plied him with arguments on the subject. See her "Letters," p. 207.

[2] A reference to a proposed public meeting for the support of Congress which was held at Faneuil Hall, May 31, 1866. Governor Bullock and Mr. Boutwell were among the speakers.

bill drawn, which he hoped I would report, giving to the President the authority to make reprisals. I made a mild protest at the time, shrugged my shoulders, and said, 'If we must do this thing, let us take one of our size.' Since then the message has been received, and is now before my committee, where it is safe enough. Meanwhile I have ascertained the sum for which war was to be waged. The award was for $94,799, payable in nine instalments, — the first instalment, due Feb. 17, 1866, being $10,533, for which we were to launch the bolt! Was there ever an enterprise more ridiculous? Your Don Pacifico case was nothing to it.

"On protection and free-trade there does not seem to be any general feeling. This question will be settled for some time by the necessities of our position, without much reference to principles. My own people, originally strong protectionists, are silent now. It is Pennsylvania which is clamorous, and the balance of parties in this important State makes the question one of political power.

"I read the 'Times' constantly. The perversions of its correspondent about our affairs are as great now as during the war, only in a different way; nothing he says is true. I never see my own name without saying, 'What falsehood!' The correspondent writes like a Presidential hireling. I am pained to see that you are not well; I hope you will tell me that you are better. Curiously, I too have fallen into the doctor's hands. He finds my brain and nervous system overtasked, and suffering from my original injuries as a predisposing cause. I long for rest, and yet every day I grind in my mill."

Popular feeling at the time favored a trial of Jefferson Davis for treason, making him an exception among the leaders of the rebellion, whom it was thought best not to bring to trial. A great trial like that of Warren Hastings was in the public mind. The judiciary committee of the Senate, in order to facilitate the proceedings, reported a bill to remove objections to jurors on account of "opinions founded upon public rumor, statements in public journals, or common notoriety." Sumner, who was opposed altogether to the trial of Davis, questioned such a retroactive provision intended for a case of unprecedented historical importance, which, as he said, "should be approached carefully, most discreetly," and "with absolute reference to the existing law of the land."[1] Davis of Kentucky, rarely in accord with Sumner, made a hearty response to his view.

[1] January 22; Works, vol. x. pp. 111, 112. Harlan recalled in the Senate, July 12, 1870 (Congressional Globe, p. 5508), in presence of Sumner, who by his silence assented to the statement, that very soon after the close of the war, when he (Harlan) expressed the opinion that a few of the rebel leaders ought to be hung, Sumner "looked grave, as he often does under such circumstances, and said he had come to the conclusion that it would be wrong to inflict capital punishment on any of them. He thought that we ought to be able to close up that fearful contest without the shedding of any more blood." W. B. Lawrence wrote, Dec. 2, 1871, that on the day of Jefferson Davis's arrest, Sumner said to him that

The course of Great Britain towards the United States during the Civil War had left a deep sense of wrong in the minds of our people. The British government still maintained that it had done nothing which it had not a right to do, and left undone nothing which it was bound to do, in the matter of the rebel cruisers issuing from its ports; and there were as yet no signs of its receding from its position. There was a disposition among our people to make our power felt against England in any war in which she might hereafter be engaged; and this disposition led to a movement in Congress for an essential modification and "scaling down" of our neutrality laws, which were of long standing, and in some provisions coeval with the government itself. Banks, the chairman, and a majority of the House committee on foreign affairs were in sympathy with the recent Fenian raids into Canada. The committee reported a bill recasting the neutrality acts,[1] and among the changes authorized the dispensing with the requirement of a bond not to use ships in hostilities against a friendly foreign power; permitted the sale of ships by American citizens to either belligerent in a foreign war, the United States not being a party thereto; and repealed the provisions against the fitting out of military expeditions in this country against foreign governments with which we were at peace.[2] Banks, in his report and speech, disparaged the American system of neutrality as wanting in principle, and established at the behest of a foreign power, — a necessity at a period of national weakness, but out of place in a condition of national strength.[3] Conkling and Orth supported Banks, and

the war having terminated successfully, he desired two measures, — universal suffrage and universal amnesty.

1 H. J. Raymond of New York, and J. W. Patterson of New Hampshire, members of the committee, proposed, instead of the bill, a commission to revise the neutrality laws.

2 Chandler in the Senate, Jan. 15, 1866 (Congressional Globe, p. 226), had proposed a resolution of non-intercourse with Great Britain on account of her refusal to entertain the "Alabama" claims; but it was laid on the table (Globe, p. 243) on Reverdy Johnson's motion, Sumner voting for it.

3 George Bemis (1816-1878), the eminent lawyer and publicist, in a pamphlet entitled "American Neutrality, its Honorable Past, its Expedient Future," subjected this report and speech to the tests of international law and duty, saying at the outset, "I conceive that the country is under great obligations to Senator Sumner for sturdily standing in the way of this ill-digested and revolutionary legislation, and preventing its passage through the Senate by storm, amid the excitement of the closing hours of the session." Mr. Bemis was distinguished as a lawyer for his critical and scientific treatment of criminal law; but for twenty years after his retirement from practice the study of public and international law was his favorite pursuit. His will contained a legacy to Sumner, which, as he was the survivor, lapsed; it contained also a tribute to the senator as a public man and personal friend.

the bill passed the House unanimously, — a large proportion of the members refraining from voting.

Sumner's convictions were as strong as those of any one against the justice and legality of British conduct in our Civil War; but he was in this as in other cases opposed to retaliation as a principle. He meant to maintain our right and pursue our remedy according to just and honorable methods, and he was determined always to keep the United States strictly within the lines of international law and duty. At this session he carried against opposition a bill to indemnify the owners of a British vessel illegally seized by one of our ships of war, — expressing his earnest desire, when defending it, that notwithstanding Great Britain still denied compensation for our just claims, "our own country should be kept firm and constant in the attitude of justice." [1]

The Banks bill passed July 26, two days before the session closed, and was sent at once to the Senate, where Chandler undertook to force its passage, but in vain.[2] What took place was related by Sumner some months later, in answer to an inquiry from Lieber: —

"I thought that I had told you the fate of the neutrality bill of Banks, which Bemis has so thoroughly riddled. It passed the House unanimously and came to the Senate Friday afternoon, when the end of the session had been fixed for four o'clock Saturday afternoon. It was at once referred to the committee of foreign relations. I made up my mind to let it sleep there without calling the committee together for its consideration. Of course this was a grave responsibility for me to take, but I felt justified in it. In the afternoon a plan was formed among the heated heads to discharge the committee by special vote, and to pass the bill in the Senate, as in the House. Taking advantage of the recess from five till seven o'clock in the evening, I got together the old statutes on the subject and examined the new bill. At seven o'clock I came to my desk with an armful of books, and announced to all about me that I was 'good for five hours at least,' if the neutrality bill were called up. Very soon Wade tried to move it, but did not succeed. From seven o'clock in the evening till seven o'clock in the morning I kept my seat, on the watch. At last, at eleven o'clock in the forenoon of Saturday, Chandler actually made the motion to take up the bill. I gave notice that I should speak all the

[1] June 26. Works, vol. x. pp. 472–474.

[2] Chandler, at the next session, undertook to carry a similar bill in the Senate, but was defeated in the attempt by Sumner, who was now assisted by Morton. (March 23 and 25, 1867, Congressional Globe, pp. 290, 328.) Sumner wrote to George Bemis, Dec. 12, 1866: "You noticed the allusion to the neutrality laws in the President's message; bad enough. He seemed to invite the repeal. To-day I laid the subject before my committee. The feeling was strong to stand on the ancient ways. The prevailing idea was that we had better bury the bill in the committee room, and not call attention to it by a report."

remainder of the session, if necessary, to defeat it. This was the end of the effort, and the bill now sleeps the sleep of death in my committee room. Such is the fate of a measure which began so loftily."

But for Sumner's resolute opposition this bill would have undoubtedly passed the Senate, pressed as it was by the anti-English feeling and Irish-American sympathy with Fenianism.[1] It is one of the many illustrations of his serenity of mind and fidelity to principle in the midst of popular frenzy.[2]

Bright wrote to Sumner, Aug. 16, 1866: —

"I am sorry to see an attempt made to lessen the force of your neutrality laws. You should, as heretofore, set us an example of something better, instead of coming down to our level. You as a nation are so great and so secure that you can do what is great and noble, and help the world onward as no other nation can."

In the case of Mr. Stockton, who had been elected senator from New Jersey by a plurality which it had been agreed in joint convention of the two houses of the State should be decisive, and whose vote in the Senate made the majority by which his title was affirmed, Sumner made the test motions on which the decision was finally against his right to vote, and in debate reviewed at length the power of a State legislature or joint convention to establish a plurality as a sufficient vote to elect, and also the right of a senator to vote on his own title.[3] Trumbull, of the judiciary committee, supported the validity of Stockton's election; but Fessenden and Sumner were in agreement against it. This contested case led to a bill passed by this Congress for regulating the election of senators; in the debate upon it Sumner defended its provision for open voting, and distinguished between legislative and popular elections.[4]

Tributes to three public men came from Sumner at this time, — two in eulogies upon his deceased associates, the two senators

1 At the next session, March 27, 1867 (Congressional Globe, pp. 393, 394), Banks carried through the House unanimously a resolution of sympathy with the Fenian movement for Irish independence, but Sumner retained it with his committee. He also required a similar resolution of Senator Nye to lie over. March 12, 1867, Globe, p. 68.

2 An American writer for the "Pall Mall Gazette," Dec. 26, 1866, by no means an admirer of Sumner, wrote that his influence on foreign questions was far beyond that of any other American, having in several instances prevailed over Seward. Referring to his interposition at this time, he said that "no other man could have arrested by his single voice a measure unanimously passed by the House as Mr. Sumner did, as in the case of the late measure abolishing the American neutrality laws."

3 March 23 and 26. Works, vol. x. pp. 377-390, 391-405.

4 July 11. Works, vol. x. pp. 481-485.

from Vermont, Collamer[1] and Foot;[2] and the third in an "In Memoriam" on Henry Winter Davis,[3] of the House. The character of each of the two senators was cast in a different mould from his own, but he dwelt with a generous appreciation on their qualities and services, — particularly on Foot's aptitude for the chair, and Collamer's skill in drawing bills and his remarkable facility in committee work.[4] To Davis, esteemed by many associates the most brilliant man in public life, he paid a still warmer tribute, placing him foremost among all the sons of his State, and regarding his death as a national calamity.

At this session Congress passed the bill for the revision and consolidation of the statutes of the United States, — a measure which Sumner was the first to propose, making the effort at his first session, and keeping it alive by successive resolutions.[5] His interest in it continued, but he did not live to see it consummated. Caleb Cushing, appointed at his instance as one of the commissioners to execute the work, sought his counsels as to the best plan, and wrote to him: —

"I desire at the outset to express my admiration of the catholic and elevated spirit you have manifested in the whole matter, not less than my profound and sincere gratitude for your consideration toward me personally. . . . This being said, I have once for all to request of you the favor of being permitted to consult you as to any general plan of operations now and hereafter as to matters of detail, from time to time, as the work proceeds."

Sumner was from his youth the supporter of an international copyright, putting himself on record in its favor as early as 1836.[6] His view was that "if authors should have a copyright anywhere, they should have it everywhere within the limits of civilization;"[7] and he was induced to think that their rights could be better advanced under the treaty-making power than by an attempt at legislation. At different times, beginning with his first session, he commended the subject as deserving the

1 Dec. 14, 1865. Works, vol. x. pp. 38–46.

2 April 12, 1866. Works, vol. x. pp. 409–416.

3 New York "Independent," Jan. 11, 1866. Works, vol. x. pp. 104–108.

4 Both in the speech on Collamer and the article on Davis, emphasis was put on their independence of Executive influence on the question of reconstruction. One passage in the tribute to Davis (Works, vol. x. p. 105) may have been a self-vindication for the use of severe language in the contest with slavery.

5 *Ante*, vol. iii. p. 275; Boston "Advertiser," July 9, 1874. Sumner spoke briefly on the codification of the customs laws, July 16, 1866. Congressional Globe, p. 3828.

6 *Ante*, vol. i. p. 186; vol. ii. pp. 47, 212, 271.

7 Letter to a committee, Feb. 17, 1868. Works, vol. xii. pp. 270, 271.

speedy action of Congress;[1] but none took place till 1891. As usual, Sumner was on this subject a long way in advance of public opinion, or at least of public action. He wrote to Lieber, March 11, 1866:—

"When Mr. Everett was secretary of state he did me the honor to consult me on a copyright treaty. I encouraged him to negotiate it. He did so, but the treaty was never acted on by the Senate. Last spring, when Sir Frederick Bruce arrived, I opened the subject with him, and he said that he should be glad to take it up; he would be delighted; it would be to him the God-send of his diplomatic life, for it would save his mission from being an absolute failure. Then came Lord Russell's refusal of all reciprocity with us, when like a bull in a china shop he broke all our wares. Since then we have had no negotiation with England on any subject. I have had several letters this session on copyright, and more on our Canadian relations. To all I have been obliged to reply, 'We have no negotiations with England.' Seward would be glad to suppress, if he could, the Puget Sound joint commission; but this had commenced its session under a treaty before Lord Russell sundered our relations. As to legislation about books, if you will look at the Globe you will see that all the motions against the tax on them have been made by me. I shall continue to watch this interest,—of this be assured; I know nobody else in Congress who takes any care of it. You said in your note the other day that I am out evenings. Very rarely. I dine between six and seven;[2] but after that am always at home, except in rare cases. I abjure parties."

Sumner introduced a resolution of inquiry as to the kidnapping of freedmen on the southern coast for transportation to Cuba and Brazil; and in consequence a statute for punishing it was enacted.[3] He spoke in favor of raising the rank of our diplomatic representatives abroad, with the view of insuring them due consideration, carrying his point against the opposition of Fessenden and Grimes.[4] He took part in the debate on a bill for relieving the Supreme Court of excessive business, stating his conviction that the true remedy was to confine that tribunal exclusively to appeals, and relieve the judges of *nisi prius* duties.[5] He called attention to the ill-construction of the Capitol, particularly to that of the Senate chamber, now excessive in size, and secluded from light and air.[6] He resisted the resolution authorizing a contract with Vinnie Ream for a statue of Mr. Lincoln;

1 *Ante*, vol. iii. p. 275. March 2, 1866, Congressional Globe, p. 1131. Lieber took an active interest in the question, as will be seen in his "Life and Letters," pp. 169, 380, 410.

2 Usually at Wormley's restaurant.

3 Jan. 9, 1866. Works, vol. x. pp. 101-103.

4 May 16 and 17. Works, vol. x. pp. 450-457.

5 April 2. Works, vol. x. pp. 406-408.

6 July 23. Works, vol. x. pp. 495-499. July 24, Congressional Globe, p. 4072.

but her fascinations with Western senators persuaded a majority to approve a commission, which ended in a caricature. He took this opportunity to dwell at some length on Art in the national Capitol,[1] and his remarks brought an approving note from Mr. Winthrop. He had taken a special interest in the metric system from the beginning of his public life, and had obtained rare publications concerning it from Europe through his brother George. At this session he explained it to the Senate at some length, reviewing its history, and carried bills and resolutions to bring it into favor.[2] Notwithstanding his political separation from Mr. Seward, their cordial personal relations continued, and they were in almost daily communication on public business. The senator promoted with such zeal the secretary's wishes as to clerical force, the contingent fund, and office arrangements, even during the heats of the impeachment contest, that he brought on himself the criticism of being too partial to Mr. Seward's department.[3] The circumstance is worthy of note, as showing Sumner's fairness in dealing with public officers with whom he was not in political sympathy. He advocated a new building for the state department, since erected.[4] He paid a deserved tribute to Mr. Hunter, who had served in the department for more than thirty years, and carried a provision for the appointment of a second assistant secretary of state, a place intended for that officer.[5] Sumner's addiction to the discussion of ques-

[1] July 27, 1866. Works, vol. x. pp. 540-556. He commented on the statue, March 2, 1869; Congressional Globe, pp. 1782, 1784.

[2] July 27, 1866; Works, vol. x. pp. 524-539. He brought the subject to the attention of the Senate, Feb. 6, 1854. Congressional Globe, p. 335; and Dec. 21, 1868, Globe, p. 165.

[3] May 16 and 17, 1866, Congressional Globe, pp. 2622, 2623, 2645, 2646; June 30; July 23; Globe, pp. 3504, 4029, 4030, 4143, 4146, 4176, 4178, 4180. He received the formal thanks of the clerks of the state department for the increase of their salaries, which he had promoted. His interest in the details of the business of the department and his co-operation with its head appear in the debates of the next Congress. Jan. 30 and 31; Feb. 4, 7, 8, 9; March 9; June 2, 22, 23, 1868; Globe, pp. 846, 878, 951, 952, 960, 964, 1026-1029, 1749-1758, 2772, 3355, 3356, 3360, 3389-3391.

[4] May 3, Congressional Globe, p. 2355.

[5] May 16 and 17: Works, vol. x. pp. 458-460. Other topics to which Sumner gave attention was a resolution on the attempted assassination of Alexander, Emperor of Russia, May 8, 1866 (Works, vol. x. pp. 432-434); the power of Congress to provide against the introduction of cholera into the country, May 9, 11, and 15 (Works, vol. x. pp. 435-449); the representation of the United States at the Paris Exhibition in 1867. Jan. 10 and 11 (Congressional Globe, pp. 160, 161), — Feb. 22, 1867 (Globe, pp. 1720-1722); March 7, 1867 (Globe, p. 15), — at the international maritime exhibition at Havre, Jan 24, 27, 30, and Feb. 6, 1868 (Globe, pp. 731, 767, 848, 1006-1011), and at the international health congress at Constantinople, April 11, 1866 (Globe, p. 1883); a survey of the Isthmus of Darien with a view to a ship canal, July 25, 1866 (Works, vol. x. pp. 500, 501); a ship canal at Niagara,

tions of general policy did not keep him from the closest attention to the humblest details of official business which properly belonged to him.

It was a most laborious session, lasting far into the heats of summer, and ending only on July 28. Sumner's speeches, with notes, fill an entire volume of his Works, making five hundred and fifty pages, covering a great variety of topics, and requiring a severe toil in investigation. This excessive labor seriously affected his health, and brought back early in 1866 the symptoms of the malady which came with the assault ten years before. He had recourse in the spring to medical treatment for cerebral and nervous troubles, which was applied by Dr. Brown-Séquard, then sojourning in the United States. Longfellow wrote to a common friend, G. W. Greene: "This relapse is a warning that he can no longer work day and night."[1] His friends counselled rest and absence from the Senate; but his interest in exigent questions did not allow him this relief. He did not spare himself even in the recess, but went to work on a lecture, — when Longfellow wrote again to Greene: "What confidence Sumner has in Sumner! I would not trust H. W. L. to that amount, nor would you G. W. G."

In August, Sumner made a visit to the White Mountains, his only excursion after he entered the Senate to that attractive resort of tourists. He made brief pauses at Centre Harbor, at the Glen, and at Crawford's, and ascended Mt. Washington, — on

independent of State assent, June 28 (Works, vol. x. pp. 475–478); a submarine cable at Behring Strait, February 21 (Globe, p. 953); more intimate relations with the Sandwich Islands by a direct mail service, July 17 (Works, vol. x. pp. 486–489); exclusion of criminals pardoned by foreign governments on condition of emigrating to the United States, March 19 (Globe. pp. 1492, 1493); claims or compensation of persons connected with the foreign service of the government, March 15 and 16, May 16, July 2 and 3 (Globe, pp. 1421, 1439, 1443, 2615, 2621, 3523, 3549): the mission to Portugal, July 20 (Globe, pp. 3952–3954); the editing of the Confederate archives, May 24 (Works, vol. x. pp. 464–467); the purchase of land for the navy yard at Charlestown, Mass., March 16 (Globe, p. 1446); the publication of the annual report of the National Academy of Sciences, March 15 (Globe, pp. 1418, 1419); the purchase of the law library of James L. Petigru, the intrepid Unionist of South Carolina, July 3 (Works, vol. x. pp. 479, 480); the power of Congress to take measures against the cattle plague, April 25 (Works, vol. x. pp. 425, 426); the relief of certain contractors in the construction of war vessels, April 17 (Works, vol. x. pp. 419–424); appeals in patent cases, April 2 (Globe, p. 1715); burden of proof in seizures under revenue laws, May 14 and 15 (Globe, pp. 2564, 2565, 2590); the conditions making "a vacancy" which the President can fill during a recess of Congress, April 23, 30, May 8 (Globe, pp. 2117, 2276, 2449); the limit of time for receiving a minority report, in this case one concerning reconstruction, July 7 (Globe, p. 3648); salaries of clerks of committees, July 25 (Globe, pp. 4132, 4133); the extension of Hyatt's patent for vault lights, July 9 (Globe, pp. 3665, 3666); a general bankrupt law, July 23 (Globe, p. 4025).

[1] Longfellow's Life, vol. iii. pp. 85, 87.

the summit of which a photographer insisted on taking him and Judge Clifford of the United States Supreme Court in one picture, which combined two public men about as opposite in character and career as they could be, and never standing so long together before or after. During this excursion Sumner and George Bemis casually met, — two friends who were always in unison.

Sumner wrote to Henry Woods, Paris, August 15: —

"I am glad to believe that our relations with France are to be excellent. I have insisted throughout the session that has closed that there should be no offensive declaration; in other words, that Congress should be quiet. My desire was that there should be nothing to leave behind any heart-burning in the French people; but I have in a proper way always insisted that the French troops should be withdrawn from Mexico."

To Mr. Bright, August 17: —

"I am your debtor for an excellent letter. Meanwhile on both sides of the water affairs have moved rapidly. I am glad that England keeps out of Continental war. She is wise in this, and will increase in means for any future emergency. If I could admire battle, I should confess the singular brilliancy of that victory by which Austria has been driven from the German Confederation.[1] Of course I rejoice in the result. It seems as if German unity must be established; and as this is normal and natural, I am sure that it must be for the welfare of mankind. Two days ago I was much disturbed by the cable news that France insisted upon going to the Rhine. In this claim I saw nothing but terrible war. All Germany would rise as in 1813. I am glad to learn to-day that the claim is abandoned.

"Our President goes on from bad to worse. He is another James II., with Seward for his Sunderland. His apostasy is complete. People now see that I was right at the beginning of the late session when I declared the breach irreparable. I had seen him under such circumstances as to draw him out, so that I knew his system. The Philadelphia convention, now in session, has no constituency behind it except the Democracy. The Republican party stands unmoved, losing very few here and there, but I think not weakened materially. The West is very firm. I think the autumn elections will vindicate Congress. I repeat now what I have said constantly, that I see small chance of peace or security so long as the freedmen are denied equality of rights. I have insisted upon impartial, not universal, suffrage; in other words, there must be only one rule for the two colors. All this might have been easily established had the President gone with Congress. Now we have before us terrible strife, and perhaps war again. Among the practical measures of the last Congress was one for the revision and consolidation of our statutes, which I have long had at heart; also another, following British example, with regard to the metric system. On the main question of equal rights Congress did much, but

1 The war between Prussia and Austria terminated in July, 1866, creating the North German Confederation, and forcing the cession of Venice to Italy.

not all it ought to do. Your new ministry seems softening towards us; is it not? I was glad to arrest in the Senate that mad vote of the House upsetting the neutrality system. I gave notice that if they attempted to pass it I should speak till the close of the session, so that nothing else could be done. It was then abandoned."

To R. Schleiden, August 17:—

"What great events are passing in Europe? I rejoice in the prospect of a united Germany. If I had the honor to be a German, that would be my passion. I trust it will be soon accomplished. But where are you now? I imagine you in some German retreat, which is to you pleasure-house and watch-tower."

To F. W. Bird, August 17:—

"I cannot comprehend those spirits who seek to misrepresent me with Andrew. What do they seek to accomplish? I have known Andrew[1] for years, and have never thought of him except with affection and respect. I was one of the earliest and most determined to press him for governor, and I have ever since sought to serve him. The speech which you say was attributed to me was impossible. I never said it or thought it. I have often said that whenever Andrew desires my place I shall not be in his way. There are reasons why I might be glad to exchange it for another service; and yet there are two objects which I should like to see accomplished before I quit. One is the establishment of our government on the principles of the Declaration of Independence, and the other is the revision of international maritime law. But I would give up readily opportunities which I value if I could in this way gratify an old friend and a valuable public character like Andrew. I mention these things that you may see the absurdity and wickedness of those who seem so constantly attributing to me something which is not in me. Should I quit the national service, I should find employment with my pen or as lecturer, after a visit to Europe."

To Mr. Bright, September 3:—

"In my last letter I anticipated several of your inquiries in the letter just received. Before the adjournment of Congress many persons were satisfied that the President contemplated a *coup d'état*. This was discussed in one of our confidential caucuses. Several senators wished to make some provision against it. I did not see how it could occur without revolution and another civil war, and I did not think the President would dare to commence such proceedings. But there is a painful uncertainty with regard to the future. He is perverse, distempered, ignorant, and thoroughly wrong. You may judge him by the terrible massacre at New Orleans. Stanton confessed to me that he [the President] was its author. I think this recent journey, not yet finished,

[1] John A. Andrew, formerly governor of Massachusetts, now retired from office and engaged in the practice of the law. There was a general feeling in the State that he ought to be called again into public life. Some persons without his privity were busy in pitting his name against Sumner. Governor Andrew died in October, 1867.

and the speeches of the President and of Seward, have done them no good. People are disgusted. Seward seems to have lost his wits as well as principles. The President, of course, is driven into close relations with the latter; but it is only a short time ago that he said of him to a member of the Cabinet, 'Mr. Seward seems to have no cardinals.' The French minister was with me last evening. I am satisfied that he expects the substantial withdrawal of the French troops from Mexico before next winter. It was on this assurance, given by me in my committee, that Congress was kept still, and I have let M. Drouyn de l'Huys know this. I agree with you about our neutrality statutes. I think that in my last I let you know something of what passed on that head. Mr. Bemis is preparing an elaborate article on our statutes and Mr. Banks's madness. Meanwhile peace seems to be prevailing in Europe. I thank God for this; but I am also grateful for the changes brought by the war. I am for German unity, as well as Italian unity; indeed, I see little chance of permanent peace until these nations are established in their natural relations. Austria is an abnormal, unreal nation, and ought to cease. I follow your excitements in England, and look forward to the next session of Parliament as of great importance. New York is the only State where we have anxiety as to the elections. It remains to be seen what Seward and Weed can accomplish."

To George Bancroft, November 8: —

"Just as I am leaving Newport I make haste to acknowledge your ninth volume, which I brought with me here, and which has been one of my companions. The work is full of thoroughness and unprecedented research. I know not where I see these the most, whether in the home chapters or the foreign chapters. The White Plains battle, the surrender of Fort Washington, and the Jersey campaign are very vividly presented. The name of Reed suffers from your narrative, and it seems to me deservedly. I am glad to recognize on every page a constant sympathy with those great principles which make our country one of time's landmarks.

"I enjoyed with another[1] the flowers you so kindly sent. Carefully tended for several days, they filled our room with their beauty. Remember me kindly to Mrs. Bancroft."

The separation between the President and the Republicans was constantly widening during the session and the recess which followed. The offensive and almost revolutionary style in which he spoke of Congress deepened the alienation between him and the Republican majority, which had followed his vetoes. In a message, June 22, he raised (by formally waiving it) the question whether Congress was a constitutional body, for the reason given by him that it represented only a fraction of the country, — a reference to its exclusion of members who claimed elections under his proceedings for reconstruction. In a speech, August 18.

1 The senator's wife.

he treated it as a rump Congress, as "hanging upon the verge of the government, as it were; a body called, or which assumes to be, the Congress of the United States, while in fact it is a Congress of only a part of the States." Then followed in September his political tour, his "swinging round the circle," with Mr. Seward and General Grant and others as companions, in which his addresses were all marked by personalities, egotism, ribaldry, contempt of Congress, and want of respect for himself and his office.

Shortly before the autumn election for State officers and members of Congress, Sumner delivered a political address, or lecture, at the Music Hall, in Boston, to which he gave the title of "The One Man Power *vs*. Congress." [1] It was an arraignment of President Johnson, whom he charged with having done more mischief in the same space of time than any ruler in all history. He contrasted the South as it was at the close of the rebellion, — ready to accept the situation, to do justice to the emancipated slaves, — with what it had now become, heated with political and sectional controversy, hostile to the government, proscriptive of loyal men, persecuting the freedmen, and breaking out in massacres at Memphis and New Orleans; a revolution for which he held Mr. Johnson altogether responsible. He exposed the President's proscription of office-holders who refused to support his policy, — "kicking them out," as the latter had described his own course on the stump. He set forth the President's change of sentiment and policy within a few weeks after he entered on his office, and related his own interviews with him before and after it took place, attributing the change to Mr. Johnson's character. as shown in his conduct and utterances, notably on the day he took his oath as Vice-President. The change, as he said, began under the lead of the Blairs, father and son; of Preston King, late senator from New York; and above all of Mr. Seward, "not a wise counsellor," who had "failed to comprehend the rebellion, while in nature he is abnormal and eccentric, jumping like the knight on the chess-board rather than moving on straight lines." As in speeches in the Senate, he insisted again that Congress, clothed with ample powers and taught by historical examples and warnings, should not deliver over the freedmen to the control of their old masters without the surest guaranties of equal political as well as civil rights, including suffrage

[1] Oct. 2, 1866. Works, vol. xi. pp. 3–39.

and homesteads; and in demanding these safeguards he declared himself undisturbed by any clamors which came in the shape of cries against "centralization," "consolidation," and "imperialism."

The autumn elections resulted in an entire defeat of the President and in the return of a large Republican majority altogether opposed to his policy.[1] Meantime, during the summer and autumn public opinion in favor of suffrage for the negroes had advanced greatly, its progress in that direction being promoted by the alarming condition of the South.

It is necessary now to turn aside from the current of public affairs to relate two domestic events in Sumner's life, both occurring during the session of Congress which has been described, — the sundering of one family relation, and the beginning of another.

In the summer and autumn of 1865 it was evident that Sumner's mother would not long survive.[2] She had reached fourscore years, and her physical powers were waning. Her physician, from the beginning of the session in December, sent Charles (now the only surviving son), by his directions, weekly statements of her condition, while other reports came from Dr. Howe and other friends, and also from Miss Ford, a constant attendant and for many years living at intervals with the family. He had been looking for a summons during the session, which was to come before its close. The mother kept up to the last her interest in his career. He had been to her a good son; and she had lived, as she often said, in him and in what he was doing. In her last days her eyes brightened at the mention of his name and of his work. While at home, though his own tastes had been changed by his larger life, he never jarred on her simple ways of living, but conformed cheerfully to them; and she had nothing to recall of him but uniform dutifulness. His last note to her, written May 26, in part to quiet her fears on account of reports of his ill health, began with "My dearest mother," and ended "Good-by. God bless you always! Ever your affectionate Charles." It bade her not be concerned for him, as there was nothing serious in his case, being only overworked; and he hoped for the best as to her illness. It was read to her, and she

[1] This was the Congress which, in 1868, attempted the impeachment of the President.

[2] The mother's character is given, *ante*, vol. i. pp. 30, 31.

said to the one who was answering it, "Give him my love," and then lapsed into the partial unconsciousness of an aged invalid whose days were nearly numbered.

Summoned by telegram, he left Washington, June 10, for her bedside, — his first absence from his seat since his public life began, except during the disability which followed the assault in 1856. She died June 15. Large as the family had been, he was the only relative present, — the one surviving daughter, Mrs. Hastings, being at her home in San Francisco. The funeral service was conducted at the house by Rev. Henry W. Foote, who afterwards performed the same service for the son. Before returning to Washington, Sumner accepted an invitation to drive with his friend, E. L. Pierce, in the suburb of Milton, — a diversion which he had been accustomed to take once during each recess of Congress. During the drive around the Blue Hills, the conversation turning upon the conditions which inclined people to marriage, he said that for the first time in his life he had now the means to support a family, and if he should meet some one who inspired him, he felt at liberty to marry; but checking himself, he enjoined silence as to this revelation of his thought.

Shortly after his return to Washington he became engaged to the widowed daughter-in-law of Samuel Hooper, who was the mother of one child, a daughter of eight years. They had met in a friendly way for several years at Mr. Hooper's house in Washington, and for some months those who observed them closely had thought a nearer relation probable. Rumors of the new connection were rife late in August, and it was finally acknowledged in September, when Sumner communicated it in notes. Warm congratulations came to him from a wide circle, — from companions of his youth, Howe, Longfellow, Greene, Phillips, Lieber, Agassiz, Palfrey, Whittier, the Waterstons, the Lodges, the Wadsworths, Mrs. R. B. Forbes, and Mrs. Charles Francis Adams; from later associates of his public life, Chief-Justice Chase, Hamilton Fish, Governor Morgan, and Mrs. President Lincoln; from friends across the ocean who had kept up a constant interest in his welfare and followed closely his career, the Duchess of Sutherland, the Argylls, the Cranworths, Robert Ingham, the Count of Paris, and the Laugels. From Washington, the diplomatic corps, particularly Baron Gerolt, its dean, saluted him cordially. The congratulations expressed only one regret, — that he had delayed the step so long.

At last he was to enter on a life for which he had expressed a longing more than twenty years before; indeed, earlier than that he had failed in a suit in which his whole heart was enlisted. In a letter to Howe, August 16, 1844, already partly given,[1] after referring to his recent illness and a former unhappiness which had unmanned him, he wrote: "If I had been called away, it would have been with the regret that I never had enjoyed the choicest experience of life, — that no lips responsive to my own had ever said to me, 'I love you.'" With what sentiments and expectations he entered on the new relation appears in the notes announcing his engagement or accepting congratulations. He wrote to Lieber, September 22: —

"I wish you to know directly from myself that I am engaged to be married. I am not sure if you have ever met the beautiful lady of twenty-eight, who sometime this latter season presided at Mr. Hooper's house in Washington. I hope you will meet her this winter, if not before, at mine. Tell this to Mrs. Lieber from me. I write this gayly, and yet I cannot withhold from an early friend the solicitude which I feel at this great change in my life. I am an idealist, and I now hope to live my idea; but I cannot forget that I am on the earth, where there is so much of disappointment and sorrow. But I have said enough. Good-by!"

The following correspondence was with the eminent historian:

NEWPORT, Sept. 15, 1866.

MY DEAR SUMNER, — Though you may think I come tardily, like the lame son of the Israelitish king, yet you must receive with a true welcome my heartfelt congratulations on the impending change which is to make of the rest of your life a romance of untold happiness. Love in very young folks is so natural that it is no more observable than the blending of two drops of dew into one, or the mixing of two tears, or the junction of two tiny brooks, or anything else that may be charming but is commonplace and not noteworthy; but when a man of mature years, of high endowments, of the most varied culture, a robust nature, hardened by conflicts, treading the paths of ambition with energy and daring, is touched by the tender passion, love gains majesty as well as gentleness. To feel the passion of love in its full force, the subject of it needs to have the ripened experience of an active and unblemished character, the strength of a powerful, complete, and undecaying manhood.

To the lady in whom your affections have found a home I had the pleasure of being presented a few years ago; but I do not know her well enough to justify my writing to her directly; so I must claim of you to be the bearer of my regard, and to charge her to include me henceforward among her friends, having so many years been included among yours. I hope your marriage will prove not only fraught with blessings for you and for her, but an omen

[1] *Ante*, vol. ii. pp. 311, 312; vol. iii. pp. 51, 52.

of peace to the country, in whose history you have gained yourself so lasting a name. Mrs. Bancroft joins in all I have written, and more.

I am ever, dear Sumner, most faithfully yours,

GEORGE BANCROFT.

BOSTON, Sept. 19, 1866

MY DEAR BANCROFT, — Your beautiful note has gratified and touched me much. It revives the past and it opens the future. Most sincerely do I trust that I may fulfil all your pleasant auguries. You shall be my soothsayer. I am an idealist, and now I hope to live my idea. Mrs. Bancroft may perhaps recall conversations many years ago in which I expressed my longings and aspirations. She will surely remember something that was said when I was at your house last December while on my way to Washington.

Let me confess that I am not without solicitude. I tremble sometimes at the responsibility I assume. I am to make another happy; for unless I do this there can be no happiness *for me*, and my idea will be quenched in darkness. But the good God that gave me this new life will, I trust, protect it. If you knew how little of design or will there was in what has occurred, you would see the Providence which has ruled.

I have sent your note to her whom it so much concerns. Thank Mrs. Bancroft and Mr. Bliss, whom I should be glad to see, and believe me gratefully and sincerely yours,

CHARLES SUMNER.

To Whittier he wrote, October 17: —

"To-day, at three o'clock, I shall be married, and at the age of fifty-five begin to live. Your good wishes are precious to me."

The unhappy sequel may as well be given here. After a few weeks in Newport and at the family home in Boston, Mr. and Mrs. Sumner began to occupy, just before the session in December, 1866, a house in Washington, — 322 I Street. The various preparations for housekeeping were made; a French teacher engaged for the child; a pew in the Church of the Epiphany rented; a span of horses, which had been Lord Lyons's, bought, to be sold a year later, — the only beasts that Sumner ever owned. During the winter he and his wife participated in the social life of Washington, entertaining and being entertained by senators, diplomatists, and friends, and occasionally attending balls.[1] Remaining at the capital for some weeks after the close of the session, they were again in the house in Hancock Street, Boston, at the beginning of June, 1867. Late in the same month she went to Lenox, and they parted not to meet again. The final break, however, did not take place till Septem-

[1] They declined President Johnson's invitation to dine, Jan. 30, 1867.

ber; and in the mean time it was doubtful, so far as others knew, if they were to live together again. Late in September the domestic disaster was no longer a secret, and was noted in the public journals. Sumner retained the sympathy and support of all his friends, who were grieved at the blasting of the bright hopes with which in less than a twelvemonth he had entered on the relation.[1] One brief note may be given as expressing the sentiments of all: —

CAMBRIDGE, Oct. 2, 1867.

MY DEAR SUMNER, — You have my deepest and truest silent sympathy.

Ever truly your friend,

L. AGASSIZ.

Mr. Hooper, who stood in very close relation to the wife, as grandfather of her only child, did what he could to avert the catastrophe, and expressing his faith in Sumner's "manly strength and magnanimity," hoped for a while for a reconciliation, and remained his constant friend, full of tender regard, performing all good offices, and faithful unto death. Neither he nor any of his family in their correspondence with Sumner (still preserved) ever complained or hinted to him that he was not in every respect, in conduct and otherwise, all that a husband should be. Some years later there was a divorce procured at Sumner's instance, but without controversy, — the counsel of both parties arranging it, and the cause alleged being intended to keep out of sight the real cause or causes of the separation.

Beyond this brief account of a relation which could not be ignored altogether in a complete narrative, the biographer does not feel called upon to dwell on an event which shadowed the last years of the statesman's life.

[1] Longfellow's feelings are given in Adams's "Biography" of Dana, vol. ii. p. 339.

## CHAPTER LII.

TENURE-OF-OFFICE ACT. — EQUAL SUFFRAGE IN THE DISTRICT OF COLUMBIA, IN NEW STATES, IN TERRITORIES, AND IN RECONSTRUCTED STATES. — SCHOOLS AND HOMESTEADS FOR THE FREEDMEN. — PURCHASE OF ALASKA AND OF ST. THOMAS. — DEATH OF SIR FREDERICK BRUCE. — SUMNER ON FESSENDEN AND EDMUNDS. — "THE PROPHETIC VOICES." — LECTURE TOUR IN THE WEST. — "ARE WE A NATION?" — 1866-1867.

THE Republican party, now united against President Johnson, entered on measures to restrict his power, going in that direction as far as the Constitution admitted. At the second session of the Thirty-ninth Congress, beginning Dec. 3, 1866, it passed the Tenure-of-Office bill over his veto. This measure, intended to restrict his use of patronage for carrying out his policy, required the consent of the Senate to removals of all officers (except members of the Cabinet) whose appointment required confirmation by the Senate, giving him a power to suspend officers during a recess of the Senate, who were to be restored if the Senate at its next meeting failed to concur. A motion to include members of the Cabinet, for which Sumner voted, was at first rejected, though later the Senate yielded to the insistence of the House that they should, with a certain limitation, be included. He attempted an extension of the measure by requiring, where it had not before been required, a confirmation by the Senate in the appointment of a large class of officers; but though supported by a majority of the Republicans, his amendment was lost.[1] Edmunds and Fessenden contested his proposition as involving too great a departure from the existing system, and putting too great a burden on the Senate; and his reply related to these points. The bill became a

1 January 15, 17, and 18 (Works, vol. xi. pp. 59-81); January 11 (Congressional Globe, p. 405). Sumner made a similar effort to protect pension agents, January 14 (Globe, p. 432). In another debate he called attention to the use of patronage by the Secretary of the Treasury to promote the President's policy, Feb. 7, 1867 (Globe, p. 1051), and by the Secretary of the Navy, March 1, 1867 (Globe, pp. 1944-1948). He was opposed to repealing the Act at the close of Mr. Johnson's term, and so voted in caucus.

law, notwithstanding the President's veto.[1] In the debate Sumner set aside, as he always did, the objection that a measure would impose labor and vexation on his associates and himself. He said: —

"I am willing to act on an inspector or a night watchman; and if I could, I would save him from Executive tyranny. The senator would leave him a prey, so far as I can understand, for no other reason than that he is an inspector, an officer of inferior dignity, and because if we embrace all inspectors we shall have too much to do. Sir, we are sent to the Senate for work, and especially to surround the citizen with all possible safeguards. Let us not, then, be deterred even by the humble rank of these officers or by their number, but whether humble or numerous, embrace them within the protecting arms of the Senate."

In the debate on the Tenure-of-office bill and in other debates the impeachment of the President was foreshadowed.[2] Sumner spoke of him as "the enemy of his country,"[3] "the successor of Jefferson Davis, in the spirit by which he is governed and in the mischief he is inflicting on his country."[4] Reverdy Johnson, anticipating the course of events, thought that such remarks put Sumner out of the pale of the President's judges, and Howe answered that Johnson's partisanship for the President would impose a similar disability on him.[5] The current of feeling in Congress during this session and the first session of the Fortieth Congress in the following summer was running in favor of the impeachment; but the country was as yet opposed to a resort to this extraordinary remedy for Executive misdoing.[6]

Sumner wrote to W. W. Story, Dec. 16, 1866: —

"I wish you might make a statue of Lincoln. He is an historic character, worthy of bronze and marble. I do not give up the Shaw statue.

"Congress is doing pretty well; every step is forward. The next Congress, which will probably meet on the 4th of March, will be still better inspired. All that is possible will be done to limit the Executive power. It is possible that the President may be impeached. If we go forward and supersede the sham governments set up in the rebel States, we encounter the

1 Sumner called, April 11, 1867 (Works, vol. xi. pp. 350, 351), for legal opinions given to the President on the construction of the Act.

2 A resolution for impeachment was offered in the House, Jan. 14, 1867. Congressional Globe, p. 443.

3 January 17 (Congressional Globe, pp. He was called to order by McDougall, but sustained by a vote of the Senate.

4 January 18 (Congressional Globe, p. 542).

5 Sumner recurred to the question of a senator's right to speak freely of the President's conduct, notwithstanding his possible duty as a judge, July 19, 1867 (Works, vol. xi. p. 421), and offered resolutions affirming the right, July 20 (Globe, pp. 429, 430).

6 C. G. Loring and E. L. Pierce so wrote to Sumner in the winter and spring.

appointing power of the President, who would put in office men who sympathize with him. It is this consideration which makes ardent representatives say that he must be removed. Should this be attempted, a new question will be presented.

"I sorrow for Seward, who seems to be more than usually perverse; but he lost his head when he lost the nomination at Chicago, and has done nothing but blunder since. He never understood our war, and he does not now understand how peace is to be secured. Remember me kindly to your wife, and to Edith, now a beautiful young lady."

To George Bemis, December 23: —

"I wish you a Merry Christmas; and you deserve it after your good work, for such I call your recent book on neutrality. I have not written to you before about this remarkable production, because I wished to read it wholly before I wrote. Reading it carefully, I have finished it to-day. This is your *opus magnum*. I do not think you can have any answer. Perhaps the first impression from it is its thoroughness; you seem to take up everything. My next impression is the high and just tone which you adopt, especially in the suggestions at the close. When you propose to reform our practice about transports, do you consider that every such transport by admitted law is liable to seizure and condemnation? By the treaty of Utrecht neutral ships were not allowed to carry soldiers, and this exception has been continued in our treaties. I have had at heart for years a revision of maritime international law, — indeed, of the whole code. If our domestic questions ever give me leisure, I shall take this up next."

Again, December 24: —

"Sir Frederick Bruce has been to see me several times on the present relations with our country. He tells me that he has left with Mr. Seward informally, for his perusal, without giving him an official copy, a despatch from Lord Stanley, accepting arbitration in the 'Alabama' case. As he has not left any official copy, Mr. Seward has nothing as yet to answer. Sir Frederick wishes to know of me whether, if the 'Alabama' case is put in train of settlement, we will then proceed to a general settlement of reciprocity, fisheries, and everything else. He thinks that one motive for advances on the 'Alabama' claims would be that there was to be a sincere restoration of good relations. Talking with Seward, I find him watching the signs of public opinion, and to this end, he says, he reads the 'Herald.' I think I have already complained to you that our diplomatic relations with England are merely formal; no questions are discussed between us, and no negotiation is opened. Lord Russell's refusal of our offer in the 'Alabama' case is the reason. I should like to put an end to this abnormal condition if possible. .

"There are claims of Prussia, which my excellent friend Baron Gerolt is pushing with ardor. He hoped to sign a convention for a joint commission; but Mr. Seward retreated after the convention had been drawn up and ready for signature. The baron feels sore; the secretary says he must leave it to Congress. Of course this adds to my work.

"General Baez,[1] the deposed president of Dominica, has been here to obtain help of some kind. Seward would not see him. I listened to his bad French by the hour. There is also the Cretan question, which is becoming interesting. Seward wishes us to sanction a minister to Greece; but I fear a political job."

Again, December 30: —

"Sir Frederick Bruce tells me confidentially that Seward does not wish him to present his letter on the claims officially for the present, so that he can continue to say that he has received no such proposition. I pray you, therefore, to give no hint beyond what you may already have done for counsel."

Congress, recognizing the popular will, accepted at this session the principle of equal suffrage, irrespective of race,[2] — first establishing it in the District of Columbia. Sumner urged the consideration of the bill on the first day of the session. It came up on December 10, when Morrill of Maine, who had charge of it, opened the debate. It passed after four days' debate by a vote of thirty-two to thirteen, Sumner speaking for it on the 13th.[3] The next day it passed the House, and Jan. 7, 1867, became a law, by a two-thirds vote, notwithstanding the President's veto.

The bill for the admission of Nebraska as a State, with a constitution limiting suffrage to white citizens, which failed at the previous session, was again pressed at the beginning of this session, — and now as before by Wade, chairman of the committee on territories. His impetuous and careless way of speaking led him, in his endeavor to impute inconsistency to Sumner, into misstatements, which he was obliged to withdraw. The Senate, prompted largely by the desire to increase the Republican majority in that body, voted to take up the bill against Sumner's opposition. Brown moved the amendment for equal suffrage, irrespective of race or color, to be assented to by a majority of the voters, which Sumner had moved at the previous session. Wade and Sherman resisted it, urging that there were but few colored people in the Territory; that it was not just to forbid a discrimination in Nebraska, which was established in many of the existing States; that the condition imposed by the amendment should be confined to the rebel States; and that even as to them there was an implied pledge not to impose it on such

1 This first interview with the Dominican adventurer is referred to in Sumner's speech, March 27, 1871. Works, vol. xiv. p. 187.

2 Works, vol. x. pp. 8, 9.

3 Works, vol. xi. pp. 48-51.

of those States as adopted the fourteenth amendment. Wade thought Sumner's objection to the Nebraska constitution "a little miserable technicality," and reproached him for not being "practical." Sumner reminded the senator from Ohio that there had been times (in the contest over Louisiana) when he had more clearly seen the importance of a question of human rights, and had not belittled it as trivial and as only a "technicality." He denied also emphatically that he was bound by any understanding, such as Wade recognized, to readmit rebel States which, while ratifying that amendment, denied equality of rights in their constitutions. He called upon senators not to create another "white man's government," and set aside human rights after having honored them the day before by establishing them in the District of Columbia. Kirkwood of Iowa assumed to take offence because, though his State was not mentioned, its constitution contained the same clause of exclusion which Sumner had characterized as "odious and offensive" in that of Nebraska.[1] Sumner reminded him that, being a new senator, he did not know that almost his own first effort in the Senate was for the promotion of the interests of the people of that State in a donation of public lands. The debate, after going on for five days, was interrupted by the holiday season, and came on again Jan. 8, 1867. Sumner was busy in the mean time in stirring up by letters[2] an agitation against the proposed inequality. The same field of controversy was traversed again. The binding force of fundamental conditions after the State's admission was treated at length. Howard thought he had made a good point on Sumner by offsetting the Massachusetts exclusion of ignorant voters against the Nebraska exclusion of colored persons.[3] On the 9th, just as the vote was being taken, Wade called on the friends of the bill to vote down Brown's amendment, and Sumner called on all "the friends of human freedom" to support it; it received only eight votes. Edmunds's amendment, which imposed impartial suffrage as a condition, without requiring a popular or legislative acceptance, and therefore interposing no delay in the admission, was lost only by a tie vote in committee

1 Dec. 14, 19, 1866; Jan. 8, 1867. Works, vol. x. pp. 504-523.

2 To Frederick Douglass, G. T. Downing, Gerrit Smith, F. W. Bird, and C. W. Slack.

3 Cowan dismissed with levity the idea of political equality, — resorting to physical analogies, and comparing his own height, six feet and three inches, and his weight, as one hundred and ninety pounds, with Sumner's height as the same, and thirty pounds greater weight.

of the whole; but when renewed a few minutes later, it prevailed by two majority, and the bill then passed. The condition not requiring any acceptance was thought imperfect, and the House, on Boutwell's motion, required the assent of the State Legislature. Sumner was content with this result, though preferring and voting for the requirement of a popular acceptance of the condition. The bill became a law, notwithstanding the President's veto. Thus Sumner's stubborn resistance to discrimination on account of race or color in new States which had not taken part in the rebellion was at last successful.

On the day (January 9) that the Nebraska bill passed the Senate, and immediately after, the same condition was inserted in the Colorado bill, and being recast for one bill was made to correspond in the other. The admission was carried in both Houses; but it was thought premature by some senators, and failed, after the President's veto, to obtain a two-thirds vote.

The same day (January 9) that the Senate voted impartial suffrage as a fundamental condition in the admission of Nebraska and Colorado, it took up the House bill, which prohibited the denial of the elective franchise in the Territories on account of race or color. On the suggestion being made that it would be debated, Sumner said, "Oh, no, I think not! Let us pass it through now. Let us crown what we have done to-day with that." The bill passed the next day without dissent from the Republican side. The President did not approve, or return the bill with objections, and it became a law without his action upon it.

Sumner wrote to F. W. Bird, Jan. 10, 1867: —

"I think it best to adopt the amendment;[1] but since a question has been made as to its character as an offer to the rebel States, I would in a report or resolution declare that it is in no respect an offer which, if accepted by them, will bind Congress to receive them back. In one word, it is only an instalment, and not a finality.

"I think you will be satisfied with the result on Nebraska and Colorado. The declaration that there shall be no exclusion from the elective franchise on account of color is not in the form which I preferred; but you have the declaration, which to my mind is a great gain. Is it not? And thus ends a long contest, where at first I was alone. Mr. Stewart of Nevada, who is sitting near me, says that 'it cannot be said now that the Republican party is not committed to negro suffrage.' You have (1) The District bill; (2) The Ne-

[1] The fourteenth amendment, pending before the Massachusetts Legislature.

braska bill; (3) The Colorado bill; and (4) The Territorial bill passed to-day, declaring that in the territories there shall be no exclusion from the suffrage on account of color."

To Mr. Bemis, January 13: —

"There are difficulties in the way of finding an arbitrator. What power would dare to decide against England? What power would dare to decide against the United States? Whom will England accept that we will accept? On another occasion Lord Lyons told me that England would accept Switzerland, and I drew up and reported a resolution authorizing the submission. But the war soon diverted attention, and that resolution was never acted on. It was on the San Juan difficulty; but there England was anxious simply for a settlement. What say you to a commission of wise men? Who shall they be? Will the country be contented with such a submission? Seward thinks not. Give my best regards to my good friend, the judge,[1] with best wishes for his health."

There was an understanding among Republican senators and representatives that if the legislatures of the rebel States organized under President Johnson's scheme of reconstruction accepted the fourteenth amendment, those States would be admitted to representation.[2] Sumner had, as already seen, no part in this understanding; and whatever their action on that amendment, he was determined to insist on equal political rights, irrespective of race or color, as the basis of their suffrage.[3] But if they had accepted that amendment, it is not at all likely that he could have brought his Republican associates to his position. The Southern States, however, were his best coadjutors. All the States which had engaged in the rebellion, except Tennessee, rejected unanimously, or nearly so, the amendment. This contumacy, in connection with the injustice which the freedmen were suffering in those States from oppressive legislation and popular violence, brought Congress at last to the most "thorough" measure known in our history. The House, under Stevens's lead, carried a bill which divided those States into military districts, put them under military authority,

[1] Richard Fletcher, an early friend. *Ante*, vol. i. p. 199.

[2] Garfield in the House, Feb. 8, 1867 (Congressional Globe, p. 1104); Norton in the Senate, Feb. 16, 1867 (Globe, p. 1463); Wade in the Senate, Dec. 14, 1866 (Globe, p. 124). Sherman said, March 11, 1867 (Globe, p. 55): "A year ago I was not in favor of extending enforced negro suffrage upon the Southern States;" and he gave their rejection of the fourteenth amendment as the reason why he had come to support the condition.

[3] Dec. 14, 19, 1866; Jan. 8, 1867; Works, vol. x. pp. 508, 509. Howard and Wilson also denied any obligation to admit the rebel States to representation on their acceptance of the fourteenth amendment. Dec. 19, 1866, Congressional Globe, pp. 185, 186, 192.

set up military tribunals, and forbade all interference with proceedings under the Act by "the pretended State governments" organized by the President. The purely military character of the measure, opening no way to the restoration of civil authority, was unsatisfactory to many members, but the previous question shut off amendments. One of these members was Mr. Blaine, who sought to put into the bill a provision admitting to representation any of the States which accepted the fourteenth amendment and established impartial suffrage.[1] The Senate, which began to consider the bill February 15, passed most of the night in an earnest debate, not adjourning till 3 A. M.[2] There was even a greater indisposition than in the House to carry a measure so purely military in its features without relieving it by provisions looking towards the initiation of civil government; but what such provisions should be, brought back an old question always fruitful in stubborn contention. The House had passed Eliot's bill for civil government in Louisiana, providing a full method, and establishing suffrage "without distinction of race or color,"[3] which Sumner wished to be taken as a model, it being similar in tenor to one already offered by himself at the beginning of the previous session,[4] though going more into detail. The situation was complicated by the question of the precedence to be given to bills. In the emergency resort was had, as is common in such cases, to a party caucus. After the session, which closed at 3 A. M., the Republican senators met at 11 A. M., when a committee, consisting of Sherman, Fessenden, Howard, Harris,[5] Frelinghuysen, Trumbull, and Sumner, was appointed to consider the whole subject. They at once proceeded to their business, and remained in session the greater part of the afternoon, during which they revised the House bill, and added conditions on which the rebel States should be admitted to representation. Sumner made an earnest effort for equal suffrage, but it found no favor with his associates, only one supporting him;[6] and he gave notice that he should appeal to the caucus. At 5 P. M. the caucus met, and Sumner, warmly

1 Feb. 12, 13, 1867. Congressional Globe, pp. 1182, 1213.

2 J. S. Pike in the New York "Tribune," Feb. 21, 1867, gives an account of the differences between the two houses.

3 Feb. 11, 12, 1867. Congressional Globe, pp. 1129, 1175.

4 Dec. 4, 1865. Works, vol. x. pp. 21–29.

5 Howe is likely to have served instead of Harris; Sherman, Feb. 10, 1870. Congressional Globe, p. 1182.

6 Howard probably.

encouraged by his colleague Wilson, renewed his proposition excluding discriminations of race and color in the basis of suffrage for those States; and it was declared to be carried. Fessenden doubted the decision, and Anthony, the chairman, calling on senators to stand, the result was fifteen in favor to thirteen (or perhaps fourteen) against.[1] This action committed the Republicans to the requirement of suffrage, irrespective of race or color, in the election of delegates to constitutional conventions, and as the basis of suffrage in the constitutions of the rebel States. Wilson expressed supreme satisfaction at the result, saying that "then and there, in that small room, in that caucus, was decided the greatest pending question on the North American continent." [2] It was generally accepted, loyally and in good faith.[3] Sherman, hitherto averse to it, maintained it in the Senate. The bill passed after a night session, at 6.22 Sunday morning, February 17. Sumner was not present to give his vote, having left the Senate at midnight, not deeming it important to remain merely "to swell the large and ascertained majority which the bill was destined to receive." His absence was a subject of comment in subsequent debates.[4] He was ill and worn out. and the result had been determined by a caucus of senators, who comprehended a large majority of the Senate. The bill passed the House with slight modifications, and was vetoed by the President. It was carried over the veto, and at this stage Sumner's vote was recorded in its favor.

An entire race, recently in slavery, was thus at one stroke admitted to the suffrage in the reconstructed States. Afterwards there was a constitutional guaranty, but it was this legislation which settled the policy beyond chance of retreat. Whether Sumner who led, or the statesmen who followed, in this wholesale inclusion of the colored people within the electoral body,

[1] Fifteen to fourteen are the figures of Mr. Conness, and also of the New York "Tribune," February 18. Sumner, in a note to his Works (vol. xi. p. 104), gives the vote as fifteen to thirteen, and in a letter to Mr. Bright as seventeen to fifteen. Sherman gave his recollections of the committee's action, Feb. 10, 1870. Congressional Globe, pp. 1181, 1182.

[2] Sumner's speech, Feb. 10, 1870. Works, vol. xiii. p. 329.

[3] Mr. Fessenden, however, was greatly displeased with the adoption of the proposition. He left the caucus at once. and sought to defeat it by personal appeals to members of the House. His action in this respect led to an acrimonious debate in the Senate, in which Wade took him severely to task; and Conness also made reflections on the senator from Maine. (Feb. 19, 1867, Congressional Globe, pp. 1555-1560.) The griefs of this debate were thought to have had an effect on the impeachment trial of the next year.

[4] Feb. 19, 1867, Congressional Globe, p. 1563; Jan. 21 and Feb. 10, 1870, Globe, pp. 638. 640, 1182-1184; Works, vol. xi. p. 105; vol. xiii. pp. 303-330.

without respect to education or training in citizenship, were wise in their generation has been doubted by very intelligent thinkers, and scepticism on this point is entitled to respect. Their action, it is to be observed, was not with many of them voluntary, being forced by the oppression and abuse of power practised under the Johnson governments. But aside from this political consideration, which was only a secondary motive with Sumner, it would not have been, indeed, a complete consummation if the national struggle, exceeding all other civil conflicts in history, had closed without uprooting all distinctions of race, and planting firmly in the American system the absolute civil and political equality of all men.

This extraordinary enfranchisement of a people, in mass and without restriction, was followed by derangements which, bad as they have been, are likely to prove transitory. In the bewilderment of their strange circumstances the new electors did not at first use wisely their power, left as they were without the guidance of superior intelligence by the abstention of the old population who were discontented with the conditions imposed by Congress. The chief impediment to the restoration of a normal state of things has been, all along, that they have been massed in one party, under (it is complained) too much pressure from the North; but this difficulty will pass away with time and that better view of their rights and capacities which is slowly but surely making its way among the white people of the South. One may hazard the prediction that the final judgment of mankind will accord the merits of courage and foresight to the statesmen of the reconstruction period who did thoroughly, and with equal justice to all, the work of rebuilding States which Providence had committed to them.

Although rejoicing that equal suffrage had thus been established as a part of reconstruction, Sumner was disappointed that Congress would go no further at this time, by providing a complete method for the initiation of new governments, taking further precautions against disloyalty, and securing to the freedmen the benefits of homesteads and free schools.[1] He foresaw that without education, and land for their homes, the enfranchised blacks would be exposed to an adverse fortune hardly less than

[1] Feb. 14, 19, and 20, 1867; Works, vol. xi. pp. 102–116. March 7 and 11, 1867: Ibid., pp. 124–136; March 15 and 16, 1867; Ibid., pp. 141–163. Sumner reviewed his own course on the subject, Jan. 21 and Feb. 10, 1870. Works, vol. xiii. pp. 303–330.

that from which they had escaped. Other senators, however (Sherman for instance), thought that they must stop somewhere in imposing conditions, and that with the ballot established the other ameliorations would gradually follow.[1]

At the close of the session Wade was chosen president of the Senate.[2] The Thirty-ninth Congress came to an end March 4, 1867; but it had provided, with the view of holding the President in check, that the Fortieth Congress should assemble on the expiration of the Thirty-ninth. Three days after the session of the Fortieth began, Sumner, convinced of the inadequacy of the Act of the last Congress, being chiefly a military measure, offered, according to his habit, a series of resolutions setting forth the measures necessary to complete the process of reconstruction,—among which were the entire vacating of the Johnson governments, the creation of provisional governments, and provisions for schools and homesteads for the freedmen,[3] which he defended in debate.[4] They were opposed by Sherman and Frelinghuysen on the ground that such supplementary demands on the Southern people, following so closely on the recent Act, were discouraging and distracting, and they encountered the objection of being mere declarations of opinion, and not legislation. Morton spoke in favor of the provision for education, and Howe sustained the resolutions generally, and both contested the idea that the recent legislation was in any respect a finality. The resolutions did not come to a vote.[5] Congress found it necessary to cure the deficiencies of the reconstruction Act of the last session, particularly as to the registration of voters, by two supplementary acts,—those of March 22 and July 19, both carried over the President's veto. Sumner endeavored to engraft on this legislation the requirement of free schools, open to all without distinction

[1] Sumner went further than Sherman in favoring the exclusion of rebels from voting, though saying, "I do not seek their punishment. Never has one word fallen from my lips asking for their punishment, for any punishment of the South." March 11, 1867; Works, vol. xi. p. 133.

[2] Wade received twenty-two out of twenty-six votes in the Republican caucus.

[3] He offered, July 3, 1867 (Works, vol. xi. p. 368, Congressional Globe, p. 467), another resolution for creating homesteads for the former slaves of a master from his land, and proposed again his former series of resolutions. He spoke, Feb. 26, 1867 (Works, vol. xi. pp. 117, 118), in favor of a bureau of education, with special reference to the Southern States.

[4] March 11; Works, vol. xi. pp. 124-136. He defended the plan proposed by the resolutions at a later date, March 16; Ibid., pp. 143-163. Address, Oct. 29, 1868; Works, vol. xii. pp. 526, 527.

[5] Sumner made an effort to bring the resolutions up July 3, 1867; Congressional Globe, p. 467.

of race or color; but though he found new allies in Morton and Cole, this effort failed by a tie vote, a majority of the Republican senators, however, sustaining him.[1] He again declared his regret that military rather than civil methods and agents had been adopted in reconstruction, saying, "I would not see new States born of the bayonet," — a declaration which called out protests from Frelinghuysen and Stewart. He agreed with Conkling, who had just then become a senator, in making a majority of the registered voters, instead of a mere majority of those voting, necessary for the calling of a convention.

Sumner was sorely grieved that he was unable to embody in the reconstruction acts further provisions which would secure to the freedmen the means of education and a practicable method of becoming landholders. His disappointment had something to do with his absence from the vote on the bill which first granted them suffrage, although spite of weariness and illness he would have remained at his post if his presence had been required.[2] His failure to do more at this time, to supplement the great work with what he deemed to be essential securities, remained with him a permanent regret. A few days before his death, when a member of the House, George F. Hoar (since senator), suggested to him in a friendly way that he had seemed to give a disproportionate share of effort to the suffrage question, without giving a due place to provisions for education, his answer was that on the contrary he had from the beginning put the latter on a level with the former, and that his disappointment at his failure in 1867 to secure schools and homes for the freedmen was so keen that he left the Senate chamber, and when he reached his house his grief found vent in tears.

Already before the fifteenth amendment was seriously contemplated, Sumner was endeavoring to bring to pass equality of suffrage in all the States, whether ever engaged in the rebellion or not;[3] and he desired also the election of colored men to Congress, believing that their presence there would be "a constant testimony and argument" for equal rights.[4]

[1] March 16; Works, vol. xi. pp. 146-163. He made another like effort July 11 and 13; Ibid., pp. 397-408.

[2] Remarks in the Senate, Jan. 21, 1870. Congressional Globe, p. 640.

[3] In the Senate, July 12, 1867; Works, vol. xi. pp. 409-413. Dec. 11, 1867; March 9 and 20, 1868; Congressional Globe, pp. 123, 1742, 1743, 2007. Letters, Sept. 8, 1867, and Oct. 3, 1868; Works, vol. xii. pp. 184, 515, 516.

[4] Letters, June 22 and July 3, 1868; Works, vol. xii. pp. 439, 441, 442.

In the debates on reconstruction, as in those on slavery, it was noted in the Senate how often Sumner's Republican associates, first rejecting his views, afterwards accepted them; and though disagreeing with him in a body when he announced these views, they all came later, even within two years, if not at heart concurring with him, to act and vote with him.[1] Buckalew called him "the pioneer of agitation in the Senate," whose propositions when made were "criticised by all his colleagues as extreme, inappropriate, and untimely," but were supported by them the next year with a zeal and vehemence even greater than his.[2] The Democratic senators were apt to harass their Republican opponents with thrusts of this kind.[3]

During the debates on reconstruction and suffrage, Sumner's style of treating his Republican opponents was not altogether agreeable to them. He had an insight into the rebellion which they had not had, and he saw what Johnson was before they did. Tardily they came to his positions, forced by circumstances and popular pressure. When in pressing forward he encountered their resistance, he was apt to remind them how they had from time to time changed their course, and come at last to accept doctrines which they had before repudiated.[4] When confronted by a large majority, almost a unanimous opposition of Republican senators, he recalled old days when he had confronted almost alone an equally solid pro-slavery body. This was not agreeable to the self-love of public men, and would not be read, as they knew, to their advantage by their constituents. Senators affected to resent his "didactic style," or his "lecturing,"[5] as they called it,—a term which they are apt to apply to remarks savoring of reproof. There is a temptation to administer such correction, but there is a want of tact in doing it. Laggards do not take kindly to "the cracking of the whip."

Sumner wrote to Mr. Bright, April 16:—

"The Russian treaty tried me severely; abstractedly I am against further accessions of territory, unless by the free choice of the inhabitants. But this

1 Dixon in the Senate, March 11, 1867; Congressional Globe, pp. 51, 52.

2 March 16; Congressional Globe, p. 170.

3 Hendricks said (Jan. 30, 1868, Congressional Globe, p. 860): "I said in the Senate a year or two ago that the course of things is this: the senator from Massachusetts steps out boldly, declares his doctrine, and then he is approached [reproached?], and finally he governs." He referred probably to his remarks, June 24, 1864. Doolittle's remarks (June 6, 1868, Globe, p. 2898, and Feb. 9, 1869, Globe, p. 1031) were to the same effect.

4 March 15, 1867; Works, vol. xi. p. 133.

5 "Warrington" (W. S. Robinson) in the Springfield "Republican," Sept. 7, 1867.

question was perplexed by considerations of politics and comity and the engagements already entered into by the government. I hesitated to take the responsibility of defeating it. I think you will like a recent Act of Congress declaring that our foreign ministers shall not wear any uniform 'unless previously authorized by Congress.' Of course Congress will not authorize any; our ministers must appear in plain clothes, to the dismay of some who are afraid of being taken for 'upper servants.'"

Again, May 27: —

"Your reform discussions are a perpetual mystification. You seem to be splitting hairs instead of asserting principles. It cannot be that so important a question as whether a citizen shall have a voice in the government can depend on such narrow considerations and technicalities of property. Who but the learned can ever know how to define a 'compound householder'? It seems to me that the present success of Disraeli will drive you to place the suffrage on absolute principles, where I am sure it belongs. For a long time I was perplexed by the subtlety so often presented that the suffrage was a 'privilege' and not a 'right,' and being a 'privilege' it was subject to such limitations as the policy or good-will of the legislature chose to impose. The more I think of it, the more it seems to me an essential right, which government can only regulate and guard, but cannot abridge. All just government stands on 'the consent of the governed.' Starting with this principle from our Declaration of Independence, I see no other conclusion than that every citizen having a proper residence must be a voter. If it be said that, then, the ignorant man has the same electoral weight as the intelligent, I reply: 'No; each has the same vote; but the other exercises an influence over the result, — in other words, over other votes, — in proportion to his intelligence.' In the vote itself all are equal. This is another instance of equality before the law. I cannot but think that you will be driven in England to discuss the question on higher grounds; parties will then arrange themselves anew. Until then there will be no response; nothing short of this will be hard pan. As our discussion has proceeded here, the hard pan has prevailed. In Massachusetts we have what is equivalent to a small rating; every voter, before his name can be registered, must pay a poll-tax, which is usually $1.50, or about six shillings. Thus far, our great change at the South promises well. Without the colored vote the white Unionists would have been left in the hands of the rebels; loyal governments could not be organized. The colored vote was a necessity; this I saw at the beginning, and insisted pertinaciously that it should be secured. It was on this ground, rather than principle, that I relied most; but the argument of principle was like a reinforcement. I do not know that I have mentioned to you how the requirements of universal suffrage in the new constitutions came to be readjusted in our reconstruction bill. The bill, as it came from the House, was simply a military bill. In the Senate several amendments were moved in the nature of conditions of restoration. I did not take much interest in them, as I preferred delay, and therefore was content with anything that secured this, believing that Congress must ultimately come to the true ground. In the confusion which ensued, a caucus of Republican senators was called. Then Mr. Sherman moved that all the pending propositions be referred to a committee of seven. Of this committee he was chairman; I was a member. In the committee I insisted that the existing governments should be declared invalid: adopted. Then that the States in question be designated simply 'rebel States': adopted. Then that in the new constitutions there should be no exclusion from suffrage on account of color. This was voted down; only one other member of the committee sustaining me, Mr. Sherman being strongly averse. When the committee reported their bill to the caucus, I stated my objections and moved my amendment in an enlarged form, to the effect that in the new constitutions all citizens with a proper residence should be voters. In moving it, I simply said that it was in our power to decide this question, and to supersede its discussion in the Southern States; that if we did not decide it, every State and village between here and the Rio Grande would be agitated by it. It was dinner-time, and there was impatience for a vote, which was by the ayes standing and being counted, and then the noes. There were two counts, seventeen ayes to fifteen noes; so this important requirement was adopted. Mr. Sherman, as chairman of the committee, was directed to move the amended bill as a substitute for the pending measure, and it was passed by the usual Republican majorities. That evening in caucus some few saw the magnitude of the act, and there was corresponding exultation. Wilson wished to dance with somebody. I have given you this narrative because it concerns an important event, and will show you how business with us is sometimes conducted. Could my way have prevailed, I would have provided provisional governments of a civil character, which should have shaped the rebel States into their new political forms and superintended the transition. I am entirely satisfied now that this would have been the better course; but we were obliged to sacrifice to the impatience of politicians, who thought that the President could be met only by the promptest reconstruction. It is in politics as in life, — we rarely obtain precisely what we desire.

"I have just perused the correspondence between Mr. Seward and Lord Stanley on the 'Alabama' claims. There is a deadlock, the legacy of Lord Russell. The British government offers arbitration, but insists upon excluding the fundamental question on which our claims rest, — namely, the right, morally and legally, of the recognition of the rebels as belligerents on the ocean. We are willing to arbitrate, provided the whole case is submitted. I think that the correspondence, when published, will rally the whole country. . . . Thus far have I avoided saying anything on this question in the Senate, because I was anxious to secure time for an amicable adjustment. The next Congress will debate it fully, unless meanwhile in some way it is settled. I was glad that Lord Derby was able to speak as confidently as he did about the future. I fear that on this question we may not have the sympathy of some of our good friends in England. Mr. Stansfeld's speech on the duties of England to the United States was a model of completeness and elegance. I know nothing in the same space which at the time struck me so favorably."

To the Count of Paris, May 28: —

"I am always interested in what you so kindly write. I regret that my constant duties leave me so little time for any proper reply. You always open so many questions, American and European, as to be encyclopædic, and therefore instructive. These latter days must have been anxious enough with you and all good Frenchmen. For a while war seemed inevitable. I rejoice that peace is assured for the moment, at least. Meanwhile our affairs here have marched swiftly. Not only slavery, but all civil and political distinctions on account of color, have disappeared in the rebel States, never to return. Thus did the rebels become instruments of Providence for the establishment of human rights. Thus far the colored people have done well, showing gentleness and intelligence. At their public meetings some of them are orators. The mass of rebels are very slightly converted ; but the most offensive resistance comes from the women, who are perverse and bitter. Add to these the parsons. But our President has the bad qualities of both. Without his support the rebel spirit would have yielded long ago.

"The question of the President's impeachment is still pending before the judiciary committee of the House. Out of nine, there are six Republicans and three Democrats. Of these, four Republicans are for the impeachment; two Republicans and three Democrats are against it. Perhaps the two Republicans may change; but should the report of the committee be as they stand now, the impeachment will be defeated in committee by Democratic votes. It is probable that the Republican minority of the committee will appeal to the House, where they expect a different result. All the Republican leaders in the House, with one exception, are in favor of impeachment. I state these facts without expressing any opinion upon them.

"We have a new French minister, Monsieur Berthémy, who is discreet and clever. As he is still young, I doubt not he will have a brilliant career. Mr. Seward is singularly well, and completely restored from injuries and wounds of all kinds, talking as much as ever. Let me thank you sincerely for your kind words on my marriage, and remember me, if you please, to the Prince de Joinville."

Congress was in session from March 4 to the 30th, from July 3 to the 20th, and from November 21 to the 30th ; and the Senate held a special session from April 1 to the 20th.[1] Sumner pressed for a continuous or almost continuous session, with the view of checking the President and defeating his plans ; but others did not see the necessity for the constant presence of Congress at the Capitol.[2] While at home, in June, he attended a municipal festival at Arlington, formerly West Cambridge,

[1] The resolution for adjourning from March 20 to July 3 limited the power of senators not making a quorum to voting an adjournment, — a limitation which Sumner did not think constitutional. July 3, 1867 ; Works, vol. xi. pp. 365–367.

[2] March 23, 26, 28, and 29, 1867 ; Works, vol. xi. pp. 168–177. April 11 and 12 ; Ibid., pp. 352, 353. July 19 ; Ibid., pp. 420–425. November 26 ; Works, vol. xii. pp. 250–252. He desired the Senate to remain so as to pass, with other measures, Boutwell's resolution to prevent the President removing district commanders without the consent of the Senate, or the recommendation of the commanding general, instancing Sheridan as likely to be removed from Louisiana. (July 19 ; Works, vol. xi. p. 424.) The President, as the bill was not acted upon, removed Sheridan ten days later.

where he spoke briefly on the historical associations of the place.[1]

At the session in July the Republican senators, in a caucus, agreed to limit the business of legislation to the removal of obstructions to the execution of the acts of reconstruction; and this agreement was carried out by the adoption of a rule to that effect in the Senate. Sumner, believing that legislation for the protection of the freedmen and on other subjects was imperatively required, resisted the passage of the rule; and when reminded of caucus obligations, he maintained that senators were to look to the Constitution and not to a caucus for rules of honor and duty. The rule was adopted, and Sumner was very restive under the restriction.[2] This debate, which called out much feeling, is one of the few in Congress which has raised the question of the obligations of a party caucus.[3]

Sumner was unsuccessful in an effort to strike the word "white" from the naturalization laws.[4] He sought to establish equal suffrage in all the States by statute, but the restrictive rule shut out its consideration.[5] Immediately after, Conkling, a partisan of the rule, endeavored to introduce a resolution to enable a young man to enter the Naval Academy, when Sumner, to the amusement of the Senate, reminded that senator that while he had insisted on the rule against a bill to confer rights upon a whole race, he now asked to have it set aside for a bill to confer a right upon one young man.[6] Sumner carried at this time a bill to prevent exclusions from office and juries in the District of Columbia on account of race or color.[7] It passed the House, but did not become a law for want of the President's sig-

1 June 17, 1867; Works, vol. xi. pp. 361-364.

2 July 3, 5, 10, 1867; Works, vol. xi. pp. 369-396. Some of his amendments to the third reconstruction bill, offered July 11, were ruled out under the restriction; but two of them were held not to be excluded, and were carried, July 11 and 13. Works, vol. xi. pp. 397-408.

3 In a debate Dec. 18, 1871 (Congressional Globe, p. 190), Sumner treated senatorial caucuses as only "a convenience," and denied their binding force.

4 July 19, 1867; Works, vol. xi. pp. 418, 419. He said: "I do not wish that it [the bill] should go over to December. I do not wish that any wrong should go over to December." The fear of Chinese emigrants stood in the way of this measure. See debate in the Senate, Feb. 9, 1869, Congressional Globe, pp. 1031-1035.

5 July 12, 1867: Works, vol. xi. pp. 409-413. He advised a popular agitation for this measure. Letter to the New York "Independent," May 2, 1867. Works, vol. xi. pp. 356-360.

6 July 12. Congressional Globe, p. 615. Sumner aided Conkling's bill a few days later. July 17, Globe, p. 701.

7 Works, vol. xi. pp. 414-417.

nature. Twice, at the next session, when carried at his instance, it met the same fate;[1] but his fourth effort at the beginning of President Grant's administration was successful. This is an illustration of his pertinacity.

Sumner carried through at this time a resolution of sympathy with Crete in her struggle against Turkey,[2] another denouncing the Coolie trade,[3] and another prohibiting persons in our diplomatic service from wearing a uniform or official costume.[4] He moved the expulsion of Saulsbury, a senator, for appearing repeatedly in the Senate in a state of intoxication, but let the resolution lie on the table upon that senator's promising amendment.[5] He received the thanks of temperance societies for this effort in behalf of sobriety and decency, — one which few senators would have had the courage to make in the case of an associate. He was no cynic; but exhibitions of drunkenness excited his disgust, and he had always a keen sense of the dignity and decorum becoming to the Senate.

The Secretary of the Treasury, Mr. McCulloch, a stout supporter of Johnson's policy, had appointed, contrary to the statute, officers in Southern States who could not take the required oath of loyalty, — justifying the illegal appointments on the ground that by the universal participation of the people in the rebellion no discrimination was possible.[6] Sumner had at the time they were made in 1865 protested, in correspon-

1 Dec. 5, 12, 1867; Jan. 7, 24; Feb. 24, 1868: Congressional Globe, pp. 38, 151, 344–346, 720, 1373; Feb. 11, 1869, Globe, p. 1080. He had a prohibition of the discrimination inserted in a bill amending the charter of the city of Washington, April 7, 1868; Globe, pp. 2260–2267.

2 July 19, 1867; Works, vol. xi. pp. 426. Later he carried other resolutions of sympathy with Crete. July 21, 1868; Works, vol. xi. pp. 427, 428.

3 Jan. 16, 1867; Works, vol. xi. p. 82.

4 March 20, 1867; Works, vol. xi. pp. 164–167. Other subjects in which Sumner took an interest were the reconstruction of the levees of the Mississippi, which he thought should be postponed until the restoration to the Union of the States in which they were situated, March 29, 1867 (Works, vol. xi. pp. 178–180); cenotaphs in the Congressional burial-ground for senators dying in Washington and buried elsewhere, a measure which he disapproved, Feb. 27, 1867 (Works, vol. xi. pp. 119, 120); the completion of the Atlantic cable, which drew from him a tribute to Cyrus W. Field, March 2, 1867 (Works, vol. xi. pp. 121–123), and a letter to a banquet committee, Nov. 14, 1866 (Ibid., pp. 40–41); George Peabody's munificent gift for education in the Southern States, for which he introduced a resolution of thanks, afterwards adopted by a vote of both houses, — both Mr. Peabody and Mr. Winthrop acknowledging gratefully his speech and action, — March 8, 1867 (Works, vol. xi. pp. 137–140).

5 April 5, 1867, Congressional Globe, p. 825; Boston "Journal," April 6; New York "Independent," April 25.

6 Feb. 7, 1867, Congressional Globe, pp. 1051–1053; February 28, Globe, pp. 1899, 1911.

dence with the secretary, against his setting aside legal prohibitions on the plea of convenience or necessity. The disqualified persons were, however, kept in office, and Fessenden reported a bill for paying them, which passed the Senate, but was lost in the House. Sumner's opposition to the bill provoked Fessenden to some bitter reflections, of which Gillette, formerly a senator, wrote from Hartford: "I have just read with unutterable disgust Mr. Fessenden's gross and wanton outrage upon you. . . . I congratulate you upon the dignity of your noble bearing under so great provocation."[1] Three years later the compensation was voted, notwithstanding Sumner's persevering opposition.[2] When the heats of the contest had passed, the senator and the secretary had, in 1872, a cordial meeting in London.[3]

The cession of Russian America to the United States, a territory of 570,000 square miles, took place at this time,—an acquisition with which the names of Seward and Sumner will always be associated. Late on Friday evening, March 29, 1867, Sumner received a note from Seward asking for an immediate call at his house on a matter of public business. He went at once, but too late to meet the secretary, who had left for the state department. His son the assistant secretary, and M. de Stoeckl the Russian minister, who soon came in, explained the proposed cession which was the occasion of the summons, and indicated the boundary as traced by the Archduke Constantine in a personal interview with that minister who had just arrived from St. Petersburg. All then went to the department, where the treaty was being copied.[4] Sumner listened, but gave no opinion, and the conference ended at midnight. Four hours later, the morning of March 30, the treaty was signed; it was sent to the Senate the same day, and referred at once to the foreign relations committee. It was the day appointed for the adjournment of Congress, but the Senate convened April 1 for the consideration of executive business.

The question was not without difficulty. There had been no opinion developed in the country for the acquisition, except to a

1 After this session Sumner had no reason to complain of Fessenden, and they came better to understand each other.

2 July 12, 1870, Congressional Globe, pp. 5497, 5502, 5508.

3 "Men and Measures of Half a Century," pp. 232-234, by Hugh McCulloch. Mr. McCulloch suggests that Sumner had a personal grievance which prompted his opposition, — a suggestion which is without proof, and contrary to the presumptions.

4 Leutze painted the scene when the treaty was explained. A photograph of the picture is given in Seward's "Life," vol. iii. p. 349.

small extent on the Pacific coast. The territory was separated from our empire by intervening British possessions. The war debt was still pressing, with a clamor for repudiation in certain quarters, and every effort was being made to put the finances of the country on a firm footing. The purchase-money, $7,200,000, equal to $10,000,000 of our currency as then depreciated, would add to existing embarrassments. A mere enlargement of boundaries, unless sought with an inspiring idea, had no charm for Sumner; and the cant phrase, "the extension of the area of freedom," which had helped to precipitate our country into an unjust war with Mexico for the support of slavery, had happily lost its spell on the American mind. Aside from the commercial attractions of the acquisition, other considerations had a certain influence on the senator. The negotiation needed only the action of the Senate to consummate it, and a breaking off at this stage would be a disappointment to Russia, whose government had been exceptionally friendly to our own during the Civil War, — not, however, from any sympathy with our republican polity or with liberal ideas. Such were their friendly relations that the senator was glad of an opportunity to please the secretary when he could do so without injury to the public interests. The committee was also composed, with two exceptions, of Eastern senators, and there was a desire to avoid even an appearance of indifference to Western interests.[1] It was something in favor of the acquisition that, unlike some others which had preceded, it was not promoted with a view to extend and strengthen slavery. Sumner's vision, as his "Prophetic Voices" shows, was at the time of a republic coextensive with the continent, and he looked kindly on the expansion, believing it to be "a visible step in the occupation of the whole North American continent," and "unwilling to miss the opportunity of dismissing another European sovereign from our continent, predestined, as he believed, to become the broad, undivided home of the American people." Senators were at first somewhat surprised to find him co-operating in such a novel enterprise with an Administration which he and they were now steadily opposing.

After the treaty had been considered by the committee from day to day for a week, Sumner reported in favor of a ratification, Fessenden alone dissenting. The pendency of the treaty becom-

[1] Sumner gave to the writer, on his return from Washington, the reasons stated in the text why he was disposed to consider the treaty favorably.

ing known, the expediency of the purchase, though admitted by some intelligent persons, was questioned by the greater number. The New York "Tribune" took ground against the acquisition.[1] Sumner's correspondence shows the conflicting opinions, — the purchase being approved by Professor Spencer Baird of the Smithsonian Institution, G. V. Fox, Commander John Rodgers, M. C. Meigs, Louis Agassiz,[2] Thaddeus Stevens, W. Beach Lawrence, and John M. Forbes, but disapproved by George S. Boutwell, B. R. Wood of Albany, and Moses Pierce of Norwich, Conn. With rare exceptions, generally those of officers of the navy and of the coast survey, incredulity as to the value of the territory prevailed in the eastern and middle sections of the country. To them it was an unknown land, as yet without a name, except that of "Russian America." Sumner occupied in executive session, April 9, three hours in the explanation and defence of the treaty, speaking with a single sheet of notes before him;[3] and the ratification was carried by thirty-seven yeas to two nays, the negative votes being those of Fessenden and Morrill of Vermont. At the request of the senators, Sumner wrote out his speech for publication, and the injunction of secrecy was removed. The work of amplifying his original speech with details and authorities consumed six weeks, — the greater part of his time until his return to Boston in the last of May. He was assisted in obtaining materials by Professor Baird, Julius E. Hilgard[4] of the coast survey, George Gibbs,[5] an old friend of his student days, and C. C. Beaman, his secretary. No description of the territory both modern and complete existed. Sumner was obliged to grope among books and pamphlets, largely in foreign languages, some in the Russian, which were translated for him; and all these materials needed to be classified and arranged, as well as enlivened with comments which would attract public interest. The result was a marvel, — an essay or book rather than a speech, which sets out all that was then known of "Russian America;" its fisheries, furs, timber, minerals, physical features,

[1] April 1, 8, 10, 11. The New York "Independent," April 18, opposed the purchase. The opposite opinions were brought out in the debate in 1868 in the House, on the bill appropriating the purchase-money. Sumner reported the bill in the Senate, and was chairman of the committee of conference on a difference between the houses. July 17, 22, 24, 1868, Congressional Globe, pp. 4159, 4321, 4404.

[2] Agassiz wrote (April 6) of the immense natural resources of the country in fisheries, furs, and timber, and the space unoccupied by population opening before our race.

[3] Works, vol. xi. pp. 181-349.

[4] 1825-1891; a native of Bavaria.

[5] *Ante*, vol. i. p. 92, *note*.

climate, commerce, history, and inhabitants, as also its possibilities in its new character as a possession of the United States.[1] This was the first exposition of a vast territory now a part of our domain, and it set public opinion in favor of the purchase. Sumner applied the name of a promontory to the whole territory, and it was his choice which placed Alaska in the nomenclature of American States and Territories.[2]

The speech was widely distributed as a pamphlet in this country.[3] An edition was published in St. Petersburg, with an introduction which noted Sumner's constant interest in the emancipation of the serfs, as well as his leadership in the kindred movement in the United States. From associates in public life, from scientific men, and from intelligent persons in different parts of the country he received many letters of approval, often with an expression of wonder at his capacity for labor and his ability to command the time for such toil, pressed as he was in other directions. Agassiz sent him full comments on the speech. Cochin, in one of his books, mentioned it as "erudite, eloquent, and poetic." Allibone thought it "an admirable topographical monograph in every point of view," and urged its author to put his speeches into a handsome and permanent edition, with full index, and "to compose some great work which posterity will not let die." This vast country, then a *terra incognita* to our people, is now annually visited by throngs of tourists; it is a frequent theme for descriptions in books, magazines, and newspapers; it has become the theatre of American enterprise; it has been widely explored, and its capabilities ascertained; and after the quarter of a century which has passed since the acquisition, Sumner's original exposition remains a singularly accurate and complete statement of its character and resources.[4] He wrote to Agassiz, June 4: —

"I am glad to know that you have read my speech, or disquisition. You will observe the multiplicity of topics which I was obliged to treat. I hope

[1] Works, vol. ii. pp. 186–349. Seward subscribed for copies from the funds of the state department, to be distributed for the information of the public and of Congress. Seward's "Life," vol. iii. p. 392.

[2] Letter of Sumner to Hiram Barney, and of Mr. Hilgard to Sumner (Works, vol. xi. p. 348, *note*). It was Seward's decision, however, which determined the name (Seward's "Life," vol. iii. p. 369).

[3] It exceeded ordinary newspaper limits, but the Boston "Journal" printed it, making nineteen and a half columns.

[4] Sumner's prophetic instinct and faithful description are the topic of a leader in the Boston "Advertiser," Aug. 25, 1888.

that I have not made any very great blunders. I have referred only to the authorities which I examined or used. I know the debt to Berghaus; but I had before me Keith Johnston's vulgarization in English with Rogers's additions. I hope you will examine the pen-and-ink copy of the map of 1566 with the *stretto di Anian,* which is my most curious discovery in all this research. This you will find at the Coast Survey. I had two works of Kittlitz, — one in German and the other in English."

Sumner put into his speech an intimation that the Senate should have been consulted in advance as to the treaty,[1] and also a protest against its being made "a precedent for a system of indiscriminate and costly annexion," — adding his hope that subsequent expansions would come solely by the attraction of republican institutions without war, and even without purchase. This *caveat* proved to be opportune; for Seward, though it was not then known, was already embarked in a wild enterprise,[2] — a negotiation with Denmark for the purchase of St. Thomas at the price of $7,500,000, which was submitted to the Senate in December, 1867, though not ripe for action till a year later than that time. It is a worthless island, remarkable for hurricanes, earthquakes, and droughts, destitute of productions, and inhabited by a miserable population. The treaty was the beginning of a system of insular and extra-continental acquisitions, contrary hitherto to the policy of our government. The ministry of Denmark was anxious to dispose of what was valueless to that country for a sum of money which was sorely needed by its empty treasury. Their tenure of office depended on the success of the negotiation, principally conducted by one of their number, General Raasloff, who having been at one time consul-general in New York, and later Danish minister at Washington, came to the country at this time to press the treaty, and remained in Washington during the winter of 1868–1869, covering the last of Johnson's and the first month of Grant's Administration. Raasloff, to whom Sumner seems to have been personally attracted, was allowed every opportunity to press the treaty. He was heard before the committee on foreign relations, — an unusual proceeding; he employed counsel, distributed a plea for the

[1] Mr. Seward submitted in 1862 to the Senate the draught of a convention with Mexico for the assumption in part of her debt, and the Senate advising against it, the negotiation went no further. President Polk asked the advice of the Senate before concluding the treaty with Great Britain on the Oregon boundary.

[2] Seward had visions of indefinite extension to the South. He said once at Sumner's table, in 1868, that "in thirty years the City of Mexico would be the capital of the United States." He sought to annex the Sandwich Islands. Seward's "Life," vol. iii. p. 372.

purchase in a pamphlet written by James Parton, gave dinners, called on Sumner almost daily, and made himself agreeable in the society of the capital. But all this was of no avail; he made no converts. None of the members of the committee, — Sumner, Fessenden, Cameron, Harlan, Morton, Patterson, or Casserly, — no senator, no one else in Washington, save Mr. Seward alone, saw anything to be gained by the purchase. The House of Representatives having learned what was going on passed, Nov. 25, 1867, a resolution by more than a two-thirds vote against any further purchases of territory, which was intended, as the debate shows, as a protest against the negotiation. President Grant, when he came into office in March, 1869, dismissed the scheme summarily, saying it was one of Seward's, and he would have nothing to do with it. The Senate committee, anxious not to embarrass Raasloff at home, kept the matter alive, — refraining from final adverse action at his written request to Mr. Fish, the new Secretary of State, — and finally, on March 30, after he had been heard and left Washington, laid the treaty on the table, recording on its minutes the words, "The understanding being that this was equivalent to a rejection, and was a gentler method of effecting it." A year later it cleared its docket by a report adverse to a ratification. Raasloff returned to Copenhagen, where, by public speech and private letter to Sumner, though not claiming him as a supporter of the ratification, he bore witness to his good offices in securing for it fair treatment. He also showed his estimate of the senator's discretion and influence, and his confidence in his kindly sentiments, by soliciting his friendly intervention in the embarrassed relations between Prussia and Denmark. The treaty then slept a long sleep, from which it has never waked. The unhappy negotiator, Raasloff, went out of office with his ministry, which was discredited by the failure, and leaving his country, soured with disappointment, passed the remainder of his life in France, Italy, and Germany, dying at Passy in 1883. Later Administrations have not been tempted to renew a negotiation which in Mr. Seward's hands proved to be a diplomatic fiasco.[1]

[1] In Scribner's "Magazine," November, 1887 (pp. 587-602), a lady, not of kin to Mr. Seward, but adopting his name, published an article entitled "A Diplomatic Episode," full of insinuations which had no basis of fact, and of untrue statements as to the action of the Senate and of its committee, as shown by the records and Raasloff's own letters. The article appeared while the Senate records and files were under the injunction of secrecy; but on that being removed, Jan. 5, 1888, it was found that not one of the entries she had

Sir Frederick Bruce,[1] the successor of Lord Lyons as British minister at Washington, was of a family with whom Sumner had long maintained cordial relations. He was the brother of the Earl of Elgin, former governor-general of Canada, and of Lady Augusta, wife of Dean Stanley. Sumner had also been kindly received in Paris in 1858–1859 by their mother, the Dowager Lady Elizabeth Bruce. Sir Frederick came to Washington just before Mr. Lincoln's death, and from his arrival was on terms of intimacy with Sumner. Coming North in the summer, he arrived in Boston from Narragansett Pier at 9 P. M., Sept. 18, 1867, suffering, as he reached the city, with a throat affection, which skilful physicians, — Dr. Bigelow being one of them, — who were called to his lodgings at the Tremont House, saw at once would prove fatal. Sumner, his only friend in the city, being sent for, arrived at eleven, and was recognized by the sufferer. Sumner was with him till his death, at two the next morning, holding his hand and closing his eyes at the last moment. He superintended the arrangements for the funeral, was the first pall-bearer, and saw the remains deposited for temporary interment in the mortuary vault under Trinity Church. Seward wrote an affectionate letter to Sumner, who had communicated to him the tidings, thanking him with a full heart for "giving him the last that was and is to be on earth of our noble, loyal, genial friend, Sir Frederick." From the family and the British Legation Sumner received grateful acknowledgments. Lady Augusta Stanley, her husband, and Thomas Charles Bruce wrote letters in tender recognition of his offices, grateful that one whom they had long known and honored was with their brother in his last hours. The dean, when the remains had been deposited in the ancient burial-place of the Bruces in Scotland, sent Sumner a picture of the Abbey Church at Dunfermline, where, as he said, on the day of interment, "the eye rested on the Frith of Forth, the distant hills, and the Castle

stated to have been made were upon them. A reply was made to her article by E. L. Pierce, published in pamphlet in Boston, 1889, and in the Boston "Herald," Nov. 10, 1889. It contained the testimonies of the only surviving members of the committee — Cameron, Patterson, and Harlan — to Sumner's fair and honorable dealing with the business, and to the universal conviction that the purchase would be a bad investment. Harlan answered the inquiry as to Sumner's acting fairly in the transaction thus: "None who ever knew Mr. Sumner could have any doubt on that point; he was the soul of candor and frankness." See Appendix.

[1] 1814–1867. Mr. Choate said of him when he was one of Lord Ashburton's suite in 1841, referring to his attractive person, "He is the Corinthian part of the British legation."

of Edinburgh, — all radiant with the sunshine in which he [Sir Frederick] so delighted, and of which he was so full."[1]

"The interviewer" was at this time beginning his visits, and Sumner was one of his early victims. James Redpath published in a Boston newspaper Sumner's free comments on his associates in the Senate, — the chief interest of which attached to what he said of Edmunds and Fessenden.[2] He thought the former "a prodigy of obstructiveness and technicality," — terms which he was apt to apply to those who set up constitutional objections to his fixed belief in the supremacy of human rights. The Vermont senator was not disturbed by the character Sumner drew of him, and referred to it pleasantly in a letter written to Sumner shortly after; but the Maine senator was not so well pleased with the description of his qualities. Sumner, in the interview, could not account for Fessenden's unkindness to himself, having always treated him with respect. He thought his "peculiar talent to be controversy, and his *forte* personality," — being always quarrelsome in debates on the appropriation bills, in contrast with Sherman, who was always amiable. Further, he said of the Maine senator, "He is accurate in speech and logical in form. As a lawyer, he is of the *nisi prius* order. There is nothing of the jurist in his attainments or nature." His report on reconstruction, being free from personality, Sumner thought his best production. One sentence of the description was prophetic: "If any person takes the side of the President, it will be Fessenden." We have not in similar form Fessenden's estimate of Sumner at this time; but it would have been no more complimentary. Those who knew and admired both, wished that each could have appropriated some of the mental qualities of the other.

Sumner's monograph, entitled "Prophetic Voices concerning America,"[3] appeared in the Atlantic Monthly for September, 1867, — a collection of the predictions in relation to our country and continent, mostly from foreigners, gathered from time to time in a wide range of reading, beginning with those which antedated the discovery by Columbus, and ending with those of

[1] In 1879 Dean Stanley went with the writer about Westminster Abbey, and taking him to the chapel where Lady Augusta had been laid in 1876, pointed to some carvings on the wall commemorative of the Bruce family, saying, "You will see a ship there; it is bearing home from Boston the body of Sir Frederick Bruce."

[2] "Berwick," in Boston Advertiser, Sept. 4, 1867.

[3] Works, vol. xii. pp. 1-183.

Tocqueville and Cobden, each one accompanied with a sketch of its author. He was led to the research by his conception of a republic with limits as wide as the continent. His love of books — always a passion with him — drew him to such diversions from public anxieties. He delighted not only in fresh volumes, but also in old and rare and forgotten books, and in tracing out those who gave them to the world. This habit, contracted in youth, began with his "Characters of Lawyers and Judges,"[1] and appears in later papers,[2] which required toilsome research. John Sherman, writing, September 6, from Mansfield, Ohio, said: —

"Aside from its elegance as a literary composition and its romantic interest, it has a political significance of very great importance. I have felt that after reconstruction is settled, we must have some grand idea as the centre of our political policy. What can be better than the gradual extension of our republican system over the continent?"

George F. Edmunds wrote from Burlington, Vt.: —

"It ought to have a place in every school-room and in every library of the land. Give me leave to hope, however, that you will not hasten the closing prophecy of irresistible attraction, and that you bring a little of your potent 'obstructiveness and technicality' to bear against the hasty purchase of the Danish islands or Cuba. You see I do not include British Columbia."

Schuyler Colfax wrote from South Bend, Indiana: —

"I write this hurried note to tell you how much I was interested and instructed by your article in the last 'Atlantic.' How you find time for so much research I cannot imagine; but the results are always valuable to your friends, among whom allow me to count as one."

James Dixon, late senator from Connecticut, wrote, September 11: —

"The fertility of your mind seems exhaustless. The speech on the Russian treaty would have seemed labor enough for the season. It was admirable as delivered, and as elaborated really a great performance. Thus I speak my mind freely to you, who think me so entirely wrong in my politics. Yet you have never coarsely denounced me as wilfully wrong, as some of my old friends in the Senate have done. Knowing that I am right, I can smile at abuse. You are now on the topmost wave of popularity. If the radicals are just, they will make you their chief leader in the coming battle. . . . How severe you were upon Fessenden, etc., in your talk with Redpath! Did you know how your words stung? But you have a right to talk, for you have been a prophet indeed."

1 *Ante*, vol. i. p. 124.

2 "Benjamin Franklin and John Slidell at Paris" (Works, vol. viii. pp. 1–38); "Clemency and Common Sense, a Curiosity of Literature." Works, vol. ix. pp. 503–544.

This monograph has a pathetic interest, the revision of which occupied the author's last thoughts. In the winter of 1873–1874 he was at work on a new edition, greatly enlarged, to be issued as a volume in commemoration of the centenary of American Independence, which was to take place a year later. Most of it was in type and the proof read, when in March, 1874, the work was arrested by his final illness. In the side-pocket of his coat which he had worn for the day was found the conclusion as it appeared in the magazine,[1] with one or two verbal changes, but without the amplification which he had probably intended to give it.

He wrote to Lieber, September, 1867 : —

"I am glad that you are interested in my article. Some of these 'voices' are curious enough. I did not introduce the Greenlanders, because their record is of discovery and not prophecy. Humboldt, in his first volume on the 'Discovery of America,' discusses at great length the verses of Seneca, which had an influence on Columbus. The Italian verses of Pulci are remarkable. I am most interested by the later 'voices,' where statesmanship is the inspiration. Aranda's counsels are memorable; so is the prophetic humor of that rare character the Abbé Galiani. I know nothing in all history more touching than that page from Alaman, the Mexican historian, pronouncing the doom of his own country, and pointing the way to us. It is now ten years since I first read these words, and they have haunted me ever since. Recent events have given them more than their original significance.

"What did Calhoun say about a national name? Let me know. Is there anything about a national name in any early writing or speech? There is a tradition that Columbia was spoken of, but I do not remember any debate on this point. Did not David Dudley Field propose a national name some eight or ten years ago?

"I am here in Boston, having just sold this old family house; and now comes the trouble and responsibility of dismantling it, abandoning some things, preserving others, packing papers and books. The task is painful, and I have no heart to write a lecture. Chase is on a tour, which has an electioneering color. Stanton is still with Hooper on the southern shore of Massachusetts; they were to be in Nantucket to-day."

Sumner had only once (in 1855) visited the West, and though often urged to do so had never been before a Western audience. In the autumn of 1867 — partly to impress his favorite idea on the country, and partly to meet his increased expenses as a householder — he accepted invitations to deliver a lecture at different points in the Western States, taking for its title and subject,

[1] Works, vol. xii. pp. 179–183.

"The Nation."[1] The journey, beginning the first week of October, occupied that month and the first week of the next, — a time when the thought of his domestic calamity, which had just become known to the public, was pressing on his mind. He spoke first at Pontiac, Mich., where he mentioned, as he began, that just as he left home a friend had put in his hand Tocqueville's "A Fortnight in the Wilderness," — an account of the Frenchman's visit to Pontiac in 1831, whither he had gone to find the limits of civilization, and to see how it shaded off into savage life.[2] His lecturing tour extended as far west as St. Louis and Dubuque, and as far north as Milwaukee.[3] A severe cold, accompanied with hoarseness and exhaustion, obliged him to give up his engagements in Iowa (except at Dubuque), and to rest a few days in Chicago. At Dubuque his welcome was from Hon. William B. Allison, then a member of the House, and since for a long period a senator, who made the arrangements for the lecture at that place. During the day of his last appointment, at Elkhart, a station between La Porte and Toledo, he met with an accident while stepping from a train in motion, without knowing that it had started. He fell prostrate, and was for some minutes insensible; and a worse fate might have befallen him but for a stiff hat, which in a measure lessened the shock. Though bruised in his face, he stood before his audience at Toledo the same evening for the two hours which the reading of the entire lecture required. He reached Boston November 9, weary, and still showing the effects of his injury. He repeated the lecture in Boston, Providence, Portland, and finally at Cooper Institute in New York, where Dr. Lieber was in the chair. On the later occasions of its delivery he dispensed with his notes.[4]

[1] "Are We a Nation?" Works, vol. xii. pp. 187–249.

[2] None of the audience knew before of Tocqueville's visit; but the daughter of the landlord, at whose hotel the French visitor had lodged, speaking to Sumner after the lecture, recalled the strangers whose coming was a mystery. Beaumont was probably with Tocqueville.

[3] The appointments which he filled were as follows: Pontiac, Mich., October 7; Grand Rapids, October 8; Lansing, October 9; Detroit, October 10; Ann Arbor, October 11; Battle Creek, October 12; Milwaukee, Wis., October 14; Ripon, October 15; Janesville, October 16; Belvidere, Ill., October 17; Rockford, October 18; Dubuque, Ia., October 19; Bloomington, Ill., October 21; Peoria, October 22; Galesburg, October 25; Chicago, October 29; St. Louis, Mo., November 1; Jacksonville, Ill., November 2; Quincy, November 4; Aurora, November 5; La Porte, Ind., November 6; Toledo, O., November 7.

[4] The New York "Tribune" and Boston "Journal" published, November 20, the lecture in full.

The style of the lecture is stately and finished, and at the end are lines of which his father was the author.[1] In intent and idea it was the sequel of the senator's speeches on reconstruction. It upheld the power and duty of the national government to establish through the whole country absolute equality of civil and political rights beyond any possibility of abridgment by the States acting under false traditions or prejudices of race. Rejecting the term "federal," which had been improperly substituted for "national,"[2] he developed the idea of "a nation," — namely, a people united, though perhaps of different races, under one government; and that unity symbolized by a common name and common emblems, and including as an essential element the protection of the rights of all, — one sovereignty, one citizenship, and one people. To illustrate his theme, he traced the process of unification in history, whereby great nations had risen by the absorption of petty States, their power and glory being in proportion to their triumph over local pretensions to sovereignty; and he then followed the course of American nationality, beginning with colonies which sought from time to time a closer fellowship, encountering the distractions of the Confederation, and finally attaining a complete expression in the Constitution of the United States. Thoughtful students of the American system recognized, even at that period when national power was being pressed to its utmost verge in the interest of freedom, that Sumner's conception was one-sided.[3] He admitted indeed the place of States in our system, as supplying opportunities for education and meeting local wants:[4] but he treated them as conveniences rather than essential organs of national life, and his conception reduced them

[1] Senator Anthony took Sumner and the writer, after the lecture at Providence, to a restaurant, where Anthony asked Sumner the name of the poet from whom he had quoted. The latter apparently pleased at his friend's curiosity, answered, "My father."

[2] B. J. Lossing, in a letter, Nov. 9, 1868, approved the preference which Sumner gave to the term "national."

[3] His colleague Wilson, as we were coming away from the hall in Boston on the evening of the lecture, said in the tone of criticism, "The States are something, still." E. L. Pierce wrote to Sumner, November 19: "People are much pleased, particularly average people, with the Address. It perhaps declares a somewhat higher Cæsarism than some minds would assent to; but tone, thought, sweep, general principles, and aspirations are all right." The New York "Evening Post," Nov. 20, 1867, the day after the lecture in New York, controverted its main idea, and November 25 replied to exceptions which Sumner had taken to its first article. Parke Godwin was in the hall when the lecture was being delivered, but did not, as in other days, come to the platform at its close. The editor and the senator were not in agreement on measures of reconstruction.

[4] Works, vol. xii. pp. 197, 243, 244.

almost to the level of counties and towns, — as if States, with equal representation in the Senate and with jurisdictions guarded by the Constitution against national interference, bore any real analogy to the municipal divisions of a State, which are useful for local administration but absolutely subject, as to their sphere and even as to their existence, to legislative power.[1]

[1] Before the Civil War Sumner and other Antislavery leaders contended for the restriction of the powers of the national government to certain specified functions, and guarded jealously the autonomy of the States. *Ante*, vol. iii. p. 296.

## CHAPTER LIII.

NEW HOME IN WASHINGTON. — RETALIATION AGAIN. — A NEW YORK SENATOR. — IMPEACHMENT OF THE PRESIDENT. — SACREDNESS OF THE PUBLIC DEBT. — RESUMPTION OF SPECIE PAYMENTS. — THE NATIONAL ELECTION OF 1868. — FOURTH ELECTION TO THE SENATE. — THE FIFTEENTH AMENDMENT. — THE SENATOR'S "WORKS." — 1867–1869.

AS Sumner left for Washington in November, 1867, he bade a final adieu to the paternal home in Boston, 20 Hancock Street, where he had lived since its purchase by his father in 1830. During the last weeks he was engaged in sorting family papers and clearing the house for its new proprietor. This was not a cheery task; and as he went through it, his thoughts were on his recent domestic calamity. To Longfellow he said: "I have buried from this house my father, my mother, a brother and sister; and now I am leaving it, the deadest of them all."[1] From that time, when in the city, his lodgings were at the Coolidge House, Bowdoin Square, — two rooms of quite moderate size on the third floor in the rear. His breakfast was served there, but he dined at the Union Club or with friends. By the death of his mother, whose estate was equally divided between him and his sister Mrs. Hastings, his property, already about forty thousand dollars, chiefly derived from inheritance, was increased to one hundred thousand dollars. He bought a house in Washington in the spring of 1867 for thirty thousand dollars; he had fifty thousand dollars invested in securities and yielding an income, and the residue consisted of pictures, bric-à-brac, and furniture. He made no considerable addition to his estate for the remainder of his life, except in the increased value of his house and his investments in pictures, partly paid for by his fees as a lecturer.

[1] Adams's "Biography" of Dana, vol. ii. p. 339. Mr. Dana did not report him accurately, for he had buried three sisters from it. Longfellow wrote in his diary, October 2: "Dine with Sumner for the last time in the old house. At sunset walk across the bridge with him, and take leave of him at the end of it."

The senator's house in Washington[1] was for the remainder of his life to be his home. The site was then the most attractive in the city. It stood on a corner, well exposed to sunlight, looking out on Lafayette Park, and across the park to the Executive Mansion, convenient for reaching the departments and the foreign legations. Just before Christmas, 1867, he moved into it,—taking the step with some hesitation, partly related to his domestic trouble and partly to the expense of housekeeping, which he feared was beyond his means, but yielding to advice from Mr. Hooper, who was very desirous that he should occupy it. He wrote, December 13, to his friend J. B. Smith: "It is a large house for a solitary person. I am now in the midst of preparation. This is something of a job for one inexperienced in such things. I am to examine carpets to-day." Smith in Boston and Wormley in Washington, both of the race which he had served, assisted him in purchases of stores, the hire of servants, and other arrangements. Some furniture came from the old family house, and later arrived from Boston his personal souvenirs, marbles, bronzes, engravings, and books,—"household companions," as he called them. Gradually the rooms became homelike; but it was some months before the furnishing was completed. The dining-room, library, and drawing-room were below, but he and his guests remained in this story only at meals or for a few moments after. His time was passed chiefly on the second floor, in a large room in the centre taken for his study,—opening into his bedroom at one end, whence the Executive Mansion was visible, and into the guest chamber at the other. The walls of each room—even the doors and the hall as well—were covered with paintings, engravings, and photographs, many of them having a personal or historical interest. Bronzes and vases, with here and there a piece of sculpture, filled each nook and niche. In the study, tables, chairs, shelves, and floor were piled with books and documents, which it was necessary to disturb in order to find a seat for a visitor.[2] In one corner, the

[1] Now a part of the Arlington Hotel, and let to families.

[2] Photographs were taken of the rooms on the first and second story after the senator's death, in 1874. Pictures of some of them may be found in "Frank Leslie's Illustrated Newspaper," April 22, 1871, March 28, 1874, and in Harper's Weekly, April 4, 1874. The interior of the house, the pictures, rare books, and autographs, as well as Sumner's manners and style of living and conversation, have been often described. "Recollections of Charles Sumner," by A. B. Johnson, Scribner's Magazine, August, 1874, pp. 475-490; November, 1874, pp. 101-114; June, 1875, pp. 224-229; July, 1875, pp. 297-304; J. W. Forney's "Anecdotes of Public Men," vol. ii. pp. 259, 260; "Christian Union," April 1,

one farthest from his chamber, was his desk, above which, on a shelf, were kept five books, — Harvey's Shakespeare and Hazlitt's Select British Poets (both bought with college prize-money), Roget's Thesaurus, Hickey's Constitution, and the Rules and Usages of the Senate. On his desk, always littered with papers, lay a Bible, the gift of Mr. Seward's daughter.[1] In a movable bookcase within reach were Webster's and Worcester's dictionaries, Allibone's Dictionary of Authors, and Smith's Classical dictionaries. Near the door of his bedroom, against the wall, was his secretary's desk.

During his visit to Europe in 1858–1859 he had secured for himself a costly collection of books, often richly bound, missals, manuscripts and autographs of celebrated persons, and authors' copies of their own works with corrections by themselves for a new edition.[2] Among these were Madame de Pompadour's copy of Cicero's Letters to Atticus; Milton's Pindar; Melancthon's Aulus Gellius; Erasmus's St. Luke, with original pen-and-ink designs by Holbein on the margins; Bunyan's Bible; Dryden's Greek exercise-book studied by the poet when a boy at the Westminster School; Voltaire's tragedy of Mahomet, with his corrections; Pope's Essay on Man, with his revision in ink for a new edition; a gift copy of Thomson's Spring, with verses in the author's handwriting on the titlepage; Dr. Parr's Hobbes;[3] and books which had belonged to Anne Boleyn, Queen Elizabeth, a doge of Venice, Ben Jonson, Wordsworth, Turgot, and Napoleon. With these were autographs of reformers, popes, kings, statesmen, poets; and choicest of all to Sumner was the Album kept at Geneva, 1608–1640, in which Milton had recorded his name, an extract from Comus, and a line of Horace.[4]

1874, Springfield "Republican," March 17, 1874, by Miss A. L. Dawes ("Haigha"); Philadelphia "Press," Sept. 5, 1871, by Mrs. A. M. Howard; New York "Independent," June 1, 1871, and March 26, 1874, and "Outlines of Men, Women, and Things," pp. 43–45, by Mrs. M. C. Ames; New York "World," Dec. 11, 1869: Boston "Journal," March 23, 1874, by B. P. Poore; Boston "Commonwealth," April 4. 1868, by C. W. Slack; San Francisco "Post," March 24, 1874, by R. J. Hinton; Chicago "Tribune," March 20, 1871, and March, 1874, by G. A. Townsend ("Gath"); New York "Tribune," April 5, 1891, by Mrs. Janet Chase Hoyt; Chaplin's "Life of Sumner," pp. 471-479.

[1] This book, as well as the "Shakespeare" and the "Select British Poets," were found on his desk on the day of his death. *Ante*, vol. i. p. 57.

[2] The books, manuscripts, and autographs were bequeathed to Harvard College, and the most important are given with titles and explanations in the bulletins of the Library. They are also described by Miss A. B. Harris in letters to the New York "Evening Post," June 11, July 17, 1875; Jan. 22, 1876.

[3] The gift of Sir William Molesworth.

[4] *Ante*, vol. ii. pp. 124, *note*; p. 351, *note*.

Quaritch and other dealers in curiosities in London and Paris, as well as Sypher in New York, found in him a customer who rarely questioned their prices. He bought a large number of oil paintings, chiefly in Washington and Boston, — some well done and others quite indifferent, paying extravagant prices, and being easily imposed upon as to value and artist.[1] He had a large number of engravings, — for these he had a better eye than for paintings, — many of them from the old French masters.[2] His bronzes were from the well-known Paris house of Barbedienne. His fancy led him to clocks, vases, and porcelain. His gratification of his tastes in the way of rare books, autographs, and works of art must have cost him twenty thousand dollars, — a fifth of all he had.

Lonely as he was, without wife or sister as companion, he nevertheless found satisfaction in his new mode of living. At the age of fifty-seven he was now for the first time dwelling in his own house, arranged just as he would have it. There came to him a sense of freedom as well as of proprietorship in his surroundings. He enjoyed the ample space, the opportunity to reciprocate hospitality, the companionship of pictures, books, and souvenirs which met his eye at every glance. He delighted to escort visitors, friends or strangers, through his rooms, pointing out his treasures, naming artist and period, reticent however as to cost and pedigree. If connoisseurs, they sympathized too much with his pride of possession to question the authenticity of any painting which was attributed to some famous Dutch or Italian artist. Among his callers to whom he showed his treasures were Dr. Holmes and Mr. Winthrop; but the larger number were undistinguished or quite young persons, who will ever recall his kindly welcome and his enthusiasm as he passed from one picture or old book or autograph to another.

A few friends occupied his guest chamber, — Dr. Palfrey, E. L. Pierce, Dr. S. G. Howe, G. W. Greene, J. B. Smith, and M. Mil-

[1] His paintings and engravings were bequeathed to the Art Museum of Boston. The latter are still in the Museum, but the paintings, except about a dozen, were sold. The experts, of whom the late Charles C. Perkins was one, decided that the grade of those which were sold was not high enough for permanent exhibition. The fund derived from the sale was applied to the purchase of casts, which are marked "Sumner's bequest."

[2] The City (a New York magazine), January, 1872, containing his article on "The Best Portraits in Engravings," shows his genuine interest in the art, and reproduces in photographs some of his engravings (Works, vol. xiv. pp. 327–354). His taste was developed while he was withdrawn from the Senate by his injury in 1856 (*ante*, vol. iii. pp. 559. 560, 594).

more, — while Emerson, Whittier, Agassiz, Bemis, G. W. Curtis, and James A. Hamilton received invitations which they were unable to accept. To Whittier he wrote: "It will be a delight and a solace to me if I know that you are under my roof." He kept aloof from parties, but he could now return the courtesies which he had been receiving as a bachelor.[1] Members of the diplomatic corps were often at his round table. He was catholic in his relations with men, and his guests were of no one political class. Caleb Cushing was perhaps oftener with him than any one, and William Beach Lawrence, whenever he was in Washington, was invited. In February of his first winter in the house, Charles Dickens, whom he had first known in 1842, dined with him in company with Stanton, when one of the topics was the experience of Sumner and Stanton on the night of Mr. Lincoln's assassination.[2] Ladies were very rarely at his table, — only Mrs. Charles Eames, widow of his early friend, Mrs. J. E. Lodge, and Mrs. Claflin, who came with her husband. The Marquis de Chambrun dined often with him, and few foreigners of distinction came to Washington without partaking of his hospitality. He would say to Schurz, who entered the Senate in 1869, "Come and dine with me to-day, and I will show you another Englishman."

Those who sat at his table recall his "cordial greeting and genial smile, with conversation embroidered with both wisdom and mirth, when he exhibited the full and varied attractions of his head and heart."[3] He sought to make all happy, and avoided everything that could give pain. One who was fixed in opposition to his most cherished ideas said of him: "I never knew him in a mixed company to introduce any topic that might prove disagreeable to any one present; and when by inadvertence or otherwise such a topic was introduced by others, he was always

1 Among those known to have dined with him are Seward, Motley, Fish, Conkling, Hooper, Reverdy Johnson, John Sherman, Carl Schurz, Morrill of Vermont, General Sickles, General Webb, W. M. Evarts, Edmund Quincy, Agassiz, Ex-President Roberts of Liberia, Berthémy the French minister, Sir Edward Thornton the English minister, Gerolt the Prussian minister, and Blacque Bey the Turkish minister. George William Curtis, while at Washington as chairman of the Civil Service Commission, in June, 1871, though not accepting Sumner's invitation to occupy a room at his house, dined with him every day, joining him afterwards in his drive, and the next winter was also almost daily at his house.

2 Feb. 2, 1868. Forster's "Life of Dickens," vol. iii. p. 386; Dickens's Letters, vol. ii. pp. 407, 410, 411. Mr. Storey's account of the conversation will be found in Chaplin's "Life of Sumner," pp. 413–416.

3 Morrill of Vermont, in the Senate, April 27, 1874. Congressional Globe, p. 3402.

one of the first to divert the conversation to some other subject."[1] Though not a humorist himself, he enjoyed humor as it flowed from others, and often greeted it with a ringing laugh.[2]

His ordinary hours for meals were 8.30 A. M. for breakfast and 5.30 P. M. for dinner, and he took food only at these meals.[3] He seldom dined alone, and was in the habit of bringing from the Capitol one or two friends to take "pot-luck" with him,—as Ben Perley Poore, the journalist, or Henry L. Pierce, an old friend who entered the House in 1873, or any constituent who happened to be in Washington.

Sumner had most cordial relations with his secretaries; they were clerks of the foreign relations committee while he was chairman, being, according to the practice, designated by him. As early as 1855, A. B. Johnson assisted him in clerical and kindred services, and though engaged afterwards in professional or official work, came to his aid at intervals and was a devoted friend to the end. Other secretaries in succession, from 1863 to 1872, were Francis V. Balch, Charles C. Beaman, Moorfield Storey, and Edward J. Holmes, all graduates of Harvard College. The last, son of Dr. Oliver Wendell Holmes, died in 1884; the other three hold an honorable place in the legal profession. Sumner's interest in them was personal and affectionate. He gave always a welcome to Johnson, and from time to time remembered his children with gifts. When Balch resigned to enter on his profession, the senator made him the custodian and manager of his funds, and afterwards the sole executor of his will. He was earnest in assisting Storey to an appointment, which was the latter's first start in his profession. This secretary writes: "He showed me a side of his character that few except his intimate friends saw,—a paternal, personal kindliness, of which I have a very grateful remembrance." He entered heartily into the connections for life which his young friends made, giving a dinner to Storey and his *fiancée*, a Washington lady, and writing to Beaman, Sept. 10, 1873, when the latter became engaged to Mr. Evarts's daughter, as follows: "It is as it should be, and I wish

1 Thurman of Ohio, in the Senate, April 27, 1874. Congressional Globe, p. 3400.

2 W. S. Robinson's (Warrington's) "Pen Portraits," p. 519. A. B. Muzzey's "Reminiscences and Memorials," p. 225. E. P. Whipple's "Recollections," Harper's Magazine, May, 1879, pp. 279–280.

3 At first he had a housekeeper: but this arrangement not working satisfactorily, he carried on the house afterwards only with servants, aided in daily needs as well as emergencies by Mr. Wormley.

a great deal of happiness to both of you. I remember Miss Evarts well. Lafayette would have said of you, 'Lucky dog!' and knowing you, I say of her, 'Happy maiden!'"[1]

At a meeting in Boston, April 7, 1888, commemorative of Sumner, Mr. Balch gave the following estimate of the senator's character: —

"I was intimately acquainted with Mr. Sumner during two of the war years. I was then just out of college and beginning work at the bar, immature and inexperienced. Although a stranger to him, he treated me as if I were his tried friend. My belief is that he had absolutely no secrets from me. He received his visitors in the room where my desk stood. I cannot recall that I was once asked to leave the room, or that there ever were asides. His whole correspondence was, as I believe, submitted to me. Such letters as I could answer I was expected to draft a reply to for his signature; as to the rest, I had to take his instructions. Then there were authorities to be hunted up, and material to be prepared for speeches or reports, — perhaps reciprocity, perhaps the French spoliation claims. Soon I was expected to sign his name on the outside of letters, to frank them. The relation was most confidential and close. Never was he impatient or inconsiderate. Working himself to an extent to me before unimagined, sitting at his desk till late in the night, and sometimes till the morning, so that a change of linen stood to him in place of the night's rest, he was careful not to overwork those about him. He was never arrogant, but always ready to listen to objections or suggestions, however crude, and most generous in his appreciation of honest effort, however ineffective.

"I was brought up a conservative Whig, and of course was far from agreement with Mr. Sumner's views; but again and again I found myself pulling up my conservative stakes and planting them nearer his position, until it came to seem to me only a question of time when I should be brought into entire agreement with him.

"I wish I could reproduce the impression he made upon me when I first knew him. He was to me strikingly handsome, large-framed, majestic, though somewhat ungainly. His familiarity with history, with letters, with society, with art, was to me simply astonishing. Of his style I am not an admirer.

"He stands in my mind a picture of manly vigor, of absolute integrity of character, of purity without stain. It may be a small matter, but it seemed to me characteristic that he never appeared to enjoy the so-called 'broad' stories which some visitors might retail. He was magnanimous. He had warm friendships and warm antagonisms, but he was not revengeful.

"Mr. Sumner was a man not ready to yield to his equals. 'Domineering' is a strong word; but he felt a superiority which really existed, and his manner asserted it. To his subordinates no one could be more considerate, more generous.

[1] The story is that Lafayette, on his visit to this country, was accustomed to inquire of persons presented to him whether they were married or not. To those answering one way he was wont to say, "Happy man!" and to those answering the other, "Lucky dog!"

"He was not religious, in the sense that religious ordinances entered much into his life, but he had the essence of the matter. I never knew a man with a firmer grasp upon the faith in the good God. He once said to a friend in my presence that he would not turn over his hand to know whether he should consciously live again or not, so sure was he that all was for the best. He was a man to inspire devotion. Perhaps I am a *laudator temporis acti* in so saying; but he seems to my memory a giant, and I see no more of his kind."

Sumner wrote to Mr. Bemis, Jan. 5, 1868: —

"I would not press you to any exertion inconsistent with health. But cannot you undertake a direction and supervision of the proposed compilation without applying yourself injuriously? If you turn away, I do not know where to look for this work. You are, as the Germans said of Goethe, 'The only one.' You have fitted yourself for it, and have obtained all the needful information. Of some matters you are the sole depositary.

"I am anxious that you should complete your own articles on this subject, and then collect them in a volume, to take an honorable place on the shelves of libraries, after having exercised an immediate influence over your own generation. This has been my desire, often communicated to you. I have it now as strong as ever; but meanwhile the interests of the country must not suffer. You must take the field, not for a protracted campaign, but long enough to drill the undisciplined squads of the state department. I am sanguine that in a fortnight you might do enough to obtain an honorable discharge. I have a chamber for a friend, opening from my own study, which shall be at any desired temperature, according to the exigencies of your case. Come and make yourself at home with me. I have seen Mr. Seward, who is anxious as ever that you should carry on the proposed compilation."[1]

To Lieber, March 28: —

"I think you will like the German treaty. To my mind it is essentially just.[2] It embodies the claim originally made by Cass, and for a long time denied by Prussia. His claim represented 'high-water mark' on this question in our country, and now Germany reaches this point. The treaty was carried, after debate, by thirty-nine to eight."

The House passed at this session a bill concerning the rights of naturalized citizens. It came up for consideration late in January, and was voted upon April 20, 1868. N. P. Banks, chairman of the committee on foreign affairs, reported it, and led in the debate. He had been a conspicuous "Know-Nothing," and was elected to Congress in 1854 by that secret order. He

[1] Sumner had, after consultation with Seward, called in the Senate for the correspondence with Great Britain concerning the recognition of rebel belligerency and depredations by the "Alabama" and other cruisers fitted out in that country. Both Seward and Sumner were desirous that Mr. Bemis should arrange the papers.

[2] Concerning naturalized citizens emigrating from Germany.

made a speech the next winter in the House in favor of its methods of secrecy and against foreigners and Catholics.[1] He continued that connection until the "Know-Nothing" or "American" party lost its power, and he had now swung to the opposite extreme. He seemed bent, in order to suit what he thought the passion of the hour, on breaking down our neutrality system, provoking collisions with foreign powers, and imposing on the country practices which had been disowned by civilized States. Sumner was obliged in the Senate to watch and counteract the House committee acting under Banks's leadership. The bill itself maintained very properly the right of individuals to dissolve their native allegiance and assume a new citizenship, thus settling a long controverted question; and this right was at the time, through diplomacy, being acknowledged by Great Britain and Germany. The bill, however, added a provision, which was stimulated by the Fenian party, that in case an American citizen was arrested and detained by a foreign government in contravention of its intents and purposes, the President was empowered to suspend commercial intercourse with such government, and to order the arrest and detention of any subject or citizen of such government found within our jurisdiction. Contrary to all modern ideas, it undertook to hold an innocent person responsible for acts with which he had no connection; indeed, to punish the innocent for the guilty. It violated the rights of hospitality to travellers which civilized nations have been careful to respect. It was condemned in debate as setting up a policy of retaliation and revenge of a most personal kind, exacting "an eye for an eye, and a tooth for a tooth;" putting into the hands of the President, whoever he might be, the power to seize and imprison persons (a traveller like John Bright), — an arbitrary power to be exercised without judicial warrant, without indictment by grand jury or trial by jury, with no right of appeal by the arrested person to the writ of *habeas corpus*. The bill disregarded moral distinctions, the safeguards of public law, and the traditions of the government. The provision for stopping commercial intercourse came from General Butler; but the

[1] Dec. 18, 1854, Congressional Globe, App. p. 48. Sumner had maintained the rights of foreign-born citizens against the Know-Nothing or American party. Speech in Faneuil Hall, Nov. 2, 1855; Works, vol. iv. pp. 74-80; *ante*, vol. iii. pp. 421-423. When accused in the debate, July 18 and 22, 1868, of being less sensitive to the rights of naturalized citizens than to those of the colored people, he referred to his speech in Faneuil Hall, and read extracts from it. Globe, pp. 4208, 4331, 4332.

manager of the bill, while resisting all attempts to conform it to just principles, made no opposition to this or other provisions which only extended the principle of retaliation.

The retaliatory provisions of the bill encountered earnest remonstrance in the House from its foremost members,— Jenckes of Rhode Island, Eliot and Dawes of Massachusetts, Woodbridge of Vermont, Baker and Judd of Illinois, and Schofield of Pennsylvania. The first three did their best in debate to eliminate the obnoxious feature from the measure. Garfield read, as in conflict with it, the thirteenth amendment to the Constitution; but Banks could not see the point. At last, when the vote was taken, there occurred one of those scenes which illustrate the pusillanimity of public men when serving for short terms. The yeas were one hundred and four, and the nays four only. Baker and Jenckes gave two of the negative votes; Eliot, Garfield, and Judd voted for the bill; while Dawes and Woodbridge and seventy-nine more did not vote.[1]

Attempts were made in the Senate to force the committee on foreign relations to prompt action on the House bill, and also on resolutions of kindred purport.[2] After holding the bill two months, Sumner reported it (all the members of his committee agreeing) with an amendment, substituting for the retaliatory clauses a provision requiring the President to report to Congress cases of the arrest and detention of American citizens by foreign governments, with the purpose of having prompt action taken to secure their rights. He opened the debate, July 18, with a brief speech, and continued the discussion the next day.[3] He maintained that our government had been strenuous and steadfast in the maintenance of the rights of our citizens, whether native-born or naturalized, and that foreign powers — Prussia, for instance — had met us fairly in controversies concerning them, particularly in negotiations concerning the right of expatriation. He denounced the retaliatory clauses of the House bill as "nothing less than monstrous, and utterly unworthy of a generous republic hoping to give an example to mankind;" as "an

[1] Some members voted for the bill, though opposed to it, trusting to Sumner to defeat it in the Senate. When the writer asked his own representative how he could vote for such a monstrous perversion of justice, his answer was, "It was of no account; I knew Sumner would put his foot on it."

[2] Dec. 19, 1867, Congressional Globe, pp. 268-270; Feb. 12, 1868, Globe, pp. 1121, 1122; June 22, Globe, p. 3347.

[3] Works, vol. xii. pp. 481-501.

outrage to the stranger within our gates;" as "conferring on the President prodigious powers never lavished before in our history;" "without precedent," and "inconsistent with the requirements of modern civilization;" as holding, against all sense of justice, a private individual responsible for the acts of his government. He was equally emphatic in rejecting the suspension of commercial intercourse[1] and the arrest of private individuals for public wrongs as peaceful remedies, denying that either proceeding was in accord with just principles or the practice of enlightened States. He said: —

> "Suppose the law is passed, and the authority conferred upon the President. Whom shall he seize? What innocent foreigner, what trustful traveller, what honored guest? It may be Mr. Dickens or Mr. Trollope or Rev. Newman Hall; or it may be some merchant here on business, guiltless of any wrong and under the constant safeguard of the public faith. Permit me to say, sir, that the moment you do this, you will cover the country with shame, of which the present bill will be the painful prelude. You will be guilty of a barbarism kindred to that of the Abyssinian king Theodorus; you will degrade the national name, and make it a byword of reproach. Sir, now is the time to arrest this dishonor. See to it by your votes that it is impossible forever."

The Senate rejected the House retaliatory provisions by a vote of thirty yeas to seven nays, but yielded to clamor far enough to insert Williams's amendment requiring the President, "whenever an American citizen was unjustly deprived of his liberty by a foreign government, to use such means, not amounting to acts of war, as he may think necessary and proper to obtain or effectuate a release." Sumner opposed this amendment as conferring undefined powers, even those of reprisal.[2] He approved the definition in the bill of the rights of citizenship growing out of expatriation, but Williams's amendment left the measure in such an unsatisfactory shape that he did not vote upon it. The bill passed with only five negative votes.[3]

[1] Congress was led by popular excitement, but perhaps more by a rivalry of parties, at the time of the dispute concerning the fisheries with Great Britain, to pass a resolution in 1887 authorizing the President to suspend commercial intercourse with that power; but President Cleveland did not exercise the power conferred.

[2] July 23. Congressional Globe, pp. 4359, 4360. His colleague Wilson, once a member, like Banks, of the Know-Nothing order, supported the bill, even voting for Williams's amendment.

[3] Speaker Colfax urged Sumner, in an interview, July 23, and by letter the next day, to support the bill for political reasons. On the other hand, letters approving his course came from E. R. Hoar, P. W. Chandler, Marshall O. Roberts, and George Wilkes.

Agassiz, referring in a letter, July 21, 1868, to talks with Sumner at Washington on the progress of culture in the United States, which he wished to renew, said: —

"Your last speeches, especially the two on the funding bill and protection to American citizens abroad, have given me so much pleasure; they are so high-toned and truly human in the elevated sense, and honorable, of that kind of honor which nothing can tarnish, — that I want to make an opportunity for thanking you for my part of the good I trust they may do in every direction."

Dixon, late senator from Connecticut, wrote to Sumner concerning his resistance to the retaliation bill: "It is a noble and brave utterance. You never lack the nerve to say what you think right in the face of present apparent unpopularity. If I have differed from you, it has not been without pain."

Roscoe Conkling of New York entered the Senate March 4, 1867. He had on well known occasions turned the House into a bear-garden, finally provoking Mr. Blaine to speak of his "cheap swagger," his "haughty disdain, his grandiloquent swell, his majestic, super-eminent, overpowering turkey-gobbler strut." [1] His subsequent quarrels with three Presidents (Hayes, Garfield, and Arthur), his melodramatic resignation as senator, and his abortive effort to obtain a re-election, have given him a place in the history of the times out of proportion to any record of his public work.[2] His career was marked by a jealousy of associates who had rendered meritorious service or gained a position in the public esteem unattainable by himself. He had no respect for age or high service or the common feelings of men. The more sensitive they were to reproach or insult, the more they felt bound by the limitations of decent speech, — the more his nature prompted him to say offensive things of them. He was not happy without some one at hand whom he could make uncomfortable. The condition of good-fellowship with him was that one should pay court to him and minister to his arrogance. Rather than encounter his insolence, his associates generally were inclined to let him have his way. But his party grew

[1] Debate, April 24, 25, and 30, 1866, Congressional Globe, pp. 2152, 2180, 2299. Mr. Blaine in his speech refers to want of courage shown by Conkling in the Thirty-seventh Congress. It is not known to what occasion the reference is made; but it may have been to a scene in the lobby of the House and at his seat, when Conkling received, without reply, from E. B. Washburne a severe imputation on his honor. Conkling's expeditious retreat from Narragansett Pier is of a later date than that of this chapter.

[2] For an estimate of Conkling's character as a public man, see New York "Times," Jan. 18, 1879, and New York "Nation," Jan. 23, 1879.

restive under the domination which he acquired by the use of patronage during General Grant's two terms; and the resistance to a third term for the Ex-President in 1880 was partly due to the fear that it would restore the New York senator to the power which he had lost under Hayes's Administration. At last, when he had resigned his seat abruptly to obtain a popular approval of himself and a condemnation of President Garfield, the Republicans of New York felt a sense of relief, and seized the occasion to bar his entrance from that time to public life. His last interference in politics was after the election of 1884, when he received a large fee as counsel for Mr. Cleveland's supporters on the count of the electoral vote of New York against his old antagonist in the House, Mr. Blaine.

Conkling was antipathetic to Sumner, as any one who knew the two men might expect he would be. He had sat in the Senate scarcely thirty days before he made some offensive remarks concerning Sumner, to which the latter paid no attention.[1] At the next session, in June, 1868, he returned to the same kind of treatment, when the question was one of a mere order of business or some clerical provision for the state department, and set upon Sumner very much in the style of a terrier.[2] Sumner at first ignored the malice; but Conkling was not to be put aside in that way, and kept up his hectoring from day to day. In putting a question to Sumner, he called him, in irony, "a fountain of light," and the latter returned a civil answer; notwithstanding this, Conkling went on with his offensive thrusts and imputations. His perseverance had such an air of puerility that it reminded one of school-days, when a coarse-grained boy would pick continuously on a sensitive youth. He imputed to Sumner an assumption of infallibility, the expression of opinions *ex cathedra*, and the uttering of "stately phrases, which the senator employs with a view to convincing the Senate that he knows more about this matter than anybody else;" described him as "the great orb of the state department who rises periodically in his effulgence," — continuing further in this style of stilted rhetoric. Sumner bore it all without retort, never failing to answer civilly Conkling's questions; till finally, when the latter had been four or five times on his feet with no apparent purpose other than to annoy and provoke, Sumner took notice of these

1 July 12, 1867, Congressional Globe, p. 611.

2 June 17, 22, and 23, 1868, Congressional Globe, pp. 3249, 3358, 3360, 3391–3394.

personal thrusts, and replied with dignity and calmness, although Mr. Blaine's style of treating such an antagonist would have been more effective. He said: —

"Mr. President, the senator from New York has a passion for misunderstanding me at least, and he has a manner of expressing it imported from the other end of the Capitol, to which we have been less accustomed, I believe, in this chamber than others have been in the House of Representatives. I am sorry. I wish it were otherwise. I have tried to make a frank statement; I have no personal interest; I am seeking nothing but the public interest. I do not doubt that the senator from New York is also seeking the public interest; I make no suggestion to the contrary, though I do not see that the public interest requires the peculiar line of argument and cross-examination, and the manner which the senator has chosen to adopt; but that is for him to choose, and not for me."[1]

Sumner then went on to restate his positions. Conkling did not rise again, and Sumner was sustained on the contested point (not an important one) by a vote of twenty-two to fourteen. The incident is of some importance as bearing on later controversies.[2] From other senators, like Anthony, Frelinghuysen, Sherman, and Dixon, though often or generally voting against him on measures which he had greatly at heart, Sumner received most friendly treatment.

The impeachment of President Johnson consumed the attention of Congress during the larger part of this session. The House, after refusing, Dec. 7, 1867, by a decisive vote, to order it (the Republicans being divided), voted it, Feb. 24, 1868, by a large majority, — a strict party vote. Between the two votes the Senate voted, January 13, not to concur with the President's suspension of Secretary Stanton, which took place the preceding August; but the President, notwithstanding the refusal to concur, removed Mr. Stanton, February 21, in violation, as alleged, of the Tenure-of-Office Act.[3] The Senate began its session, March 5, for the trial of the impeachment, Chief-Justice Chase

[1] June 23, Congressional Globe, p. 3394. A passage in Sumner's tribute to Thaddeus Stevens, Dec. 18, 1869. Works, vol. xiii. p. 5, is likely to refer to Conkling.

[2] Another debate shows Conkling's favorite style, in which his treatment of Sumner was of the same kind. Jan. 14 and 17, Feb. 9, July 4, 1870, Congressional Globe, pp. 459, 506, 1143-1145, 5166. After his failure of election to the Senate, Conkling found that his bullying style did not avail him at the bar of New York city in contests with Joseph H. Choate and other leaders, and his manner sensibly changed for the better.

[3] Sumner wrote in pencil, February 2, from his seat to Stanton a note with the single word "stick" in the body of it, which for a while had currency in political discussions. The note came into the possession of Ben Perley Poore, and was sold in 1888 at an auction in Boston to a New York dealer in autographs.

presiding; and the vote was taken May 11, resulting in an acquittal,— thirty-five declaring the President guilty, and eighteen declaring him not guilty, which was not the two-thirds required. Among the nays were six Republicans, including Fessenden, Grimes, Henderson, and Trumbull. The change of a single vote would have effected the President's deposition from office. As often occurs in such contests, the personal element had a part in the result. Some of the senators had been in controversies with Wade, president of the Senate, who would have succeeded an impeached President; and his style and temperament were more or less publicly referred to as objections to his becoming Mr. Johnson's successor. The chief-justice bore himself with dignity and impartiality, but his undisguised sympathy with the defence, Republican as he had been, weakened the support of the prosecution in public opinion. Nor was the case against the President strengthened with the Senate or the people by the fact that the manager who was most in the public eye was General Butler.

Sumner wrote to Lieber in May, 1868: —

> "I take it that the whole story in the 'Sun' is a quiz. Wade assures me that he has not spoken with a human being about appointments, and that every story to the contrary was an invention. He has spoken with me on some possibilities of the future, telling me that I was the only person he had spoken with on the matter. I advised him at the proper moment, and before taking any decisive step, to see General Grant. The latter is earnest for the condemnation of the President."

The strictly legal charge against the President was the removal of Stanton; but the weight of argument, though verbal and technical, was with those who insisted that the Tenure-of Office Act did not protect an officer appointed, as Stanton was, before the President came into office. Other charges set up "his intemperate, inflammatory, and scandalous harangues," and his denial in speeches that Congress was a legal and constitutional body. The moral justification of the proceeding was aside from these formal averments, and must be found, if anywhere, in Johnson's conduct and methods, which had obstructed the pacification of the States lately in rebellion, brought on bloody conflicts of race, and renewed in that vast region the spirit of civil war. His acts in this respect would have justified and insured a judgment of removal if a transcendent necessity had existed for so extraordinary a remedy. But it is plain now that no such necessity then existed. He had been hampered by successive acts of Congress. The Republicans held both houses firmly by a two-thirds vote in each, and could pass over his veto any measure they were agreed upon. They retained in the Senate control over the appointments. They held the military power of the government through the sympathy of General Grant, its chief, and most of its generals of high rank. Only eight months of the President's term remained when the vote was taken on the articles of impeachment; and though he had wrought mischief, it was not in his power to aggravate it materially. During the whole proceeding a large number of Republicans in the country, while not openly opposing it, dreaded an event which was for the first time to break the continuity of the government; with these added to the Democrats, probably at no stage would the proceeding have been sanctioned by a popular vote. Congress rather than the people were behind it. After the national election in the autumn, the great trial soon dropped out of sight, with no one wishing there had been a different verdict. The Republicans have never counted the attempted impeachment among their achievements.[1] The spectacle, so profoundly interesting at the time, excites now only an academic interest. One who lived through the contest can hardly bring back to mind at a distance of twenty or more years the hopes and fears which he then felt profoundly, and readers not then living will have all the greater difficulty in comprehending the spirit of the actors.

Sumner was among the first to favor the impeachment, being impressed with the infinite harm which the President had done. He regarded it as a political rather than a judicial proceeding, as it involved expulsion from office without punishment of any kind, to be conducted without technicality in procedure or in the admission of evidence, — a remedy which, though extraordinary, was not to be shrunk from in a great emergency; one which, without confining attention minutely to each act or word of offence, was intended to rid the government of an officer who had destroyed the public peace, and had brought the country to the verge of civil war. If the time had been 1861-1865 instead of 1868, this view would have prevailed. No nation would, in a struggle for life, have spared a President on the fine points which upon the record secured the acquittal.

[1] Mr. Blaine, who as a member of the House voted for the proceeding, has treated it as unwise in his "Twenty Years of Congress."

Sumner, taking the view that the proceeding was political and not judicial, did not consider that a senator was bound beforehand to reserve his opinion in comments upon the conduct of the President, or that he was exempt afterwards from public criticism and disapproval for his action or final vote.[1] His Opinion, one of several given by senators, reviewed the case at length. He dwelt upon the political character of the proceeding, the true construction of the Act concerning the tenure of office, the various offences of the President standing by themselves and as illustrated by his general character, speeches, and conduct; and he rebuked, after the manner of Burke in the Hastings trial, the professional dialectics which had been the reliance of his defenders at the bar and among senators.[2]

Early in the proceedings he argued for the right of Senator Wade, the president *pro tem.* of the Senate, to vote on all questions during the trial, notwithstanding he would become the President's successor if the impeachment should be carried. He also made an argument in which, with a complete survey of the authorities, he contended that the chief-justice, not being a senator, was not entitled, in performing his limited duty to "preside," to decide or vote upon any question interlocutory or final.[3] Sumner made a reluctant protest against the decision of the chief-justice that he had the power to decide on interlocutory questions, in which he referred to their fellowship for long years, and acknowledged his old friend's fidelity and services.[4]

The idea of a practical repudiation of the public debt, which three years after the war amounted to twenty-five hundred millions of dollars, had seized on large masses of voters, especially in the Western States. The burden seemed heavy, heavier than it proved to be; it was a choice opportunity for demagogues, and they improved it well. Very few openly advocated repudiation, but generally the scheme was put forward in the more plausible shape of a payment of the national bonds, known as the "five-

1 Resolutions, June 3, 1868. Works, vol. xii. p. 411.

2 May 26, 1868; Works, vol. xii. pp. 318–410. What he said about lawyers at this time corresponds to his criticisms of judges in connection with the fugitive-slave cases. *Ante*, vol. iii. p. 396.

3 March 31, 1868, Works, vol. xii. pp. 282–317. Gerrit Smith published a friendly criticism on Sumner's view, thinking that his learning had misled him, and repeated his dissent also in a letter, April 21, 1868.

4 Sumner, in a letter to T. W. Higginson, April 11, repelled the charge of unworthy motives which had been imputed to the chief-justice, and declared his confidence that the latter would prove true to the principles he had supported through life.

twenties," by legal-tender notes, or greenbacks, either already issued or to be issued, which were not redeemable in gold, and were at the time greatly depreciated from the gold standard. Another scheme was the taxation of the bonds. The Democratic party under Pendleton's leadership espoused this plan, which became known with its friends as "the Ohio idea," and with its opponents as the "rag baby." Republicans in the West were carried away by the frenzy, but they came out of it sooner than the Democrats;[1] and some Republican leaders in that section, notably Hayes and Garfield, remained always steadfast in favor of an honest payment of the public debt.[2] Sherman, chairman of the Senate finance committee, made a speech, Feb. 27, 1868, in which, taking ground against Edmunds and New England senators generally, he maintained the right of the government to redeem the principal of the debt in existing depreciated currency, although, by a nice distinction, denying the right to make a new issue of currency for the purpose. The speech caused general alarm for the safety of the national honor. Edward Atkinson, of Boston, wrote to Sumner, February 29: "Sherman's speech has created more distrust here than anything that has yet taken place."[3] William Endicott, Jr., of the same city, wrote the same day, invoking Sumner "to remonstrate against the national perfidy proposed by Mr. Sherman."[4] These correspondents, and also George B. Blake, the Boston banker, were very anxious that Sumner should at this session expose the financial heresies. His colleague had little taste for such discussions; and General Butler, of Massachusetts, a champion of "the Ohio idea" in the House, had encountered no reply from any colleague. Sumner had indeed no aptitude for abstruse questions of finance; but he was ready to

[1] The general sentiment of Pennsylvania corresponded with that of the West. Henry C. Carey wrote Sumner, Dec. 9, 1868, in opposition to a contraction of the currency; and the last words of Thaddeus Stevens in the House, within a month before his death, were for the payment of the "five-twenties" in paper currency.

[2] Garfield spoke, July 15 and 21, maintaining the national obligation to pay the five-twenties in coin, and replying to Butler of Massachusetts, and Pike of Maine, who had advocated the taxation of the national bonds. His position at this time, though against the apparent sentiment of his section of the country, led more than anything else to his selection for the Presidency in 1880.

[3] Mr. Atkinson contributed a series of papers to the New York "Evening Post," which were published in a pamphlet, with the title "Senator Sherman's Fallacies."

[4] The country will always be grateful to Mr. Sherman for his later services, both in the Senate and in the Cabinet, in promoting the resumption of specie payments, and in resisting the scheme for silver inflation.

set himself to any task, however uncongenial, where national honor and safety were concerned.[1] On technical points he had excellent advisers in Atkinson and Endicott, both experts in finance, and distinguished for disinterested patriotism. It was a characteristic of Sumner, that on subjects on which he did not claim to be a specialist he knew by instinct whom it was safe to follow.

He wrote to Mr. Bright,[2] February 4: —

"I wish I could answer your inquiry directly and without explanation. Evidently the idea of paying the five-twenties in greenbacks has made an impression, especially at the West, destined to predominate in the approaching Presidential election. I say this of the West, and not of the idea, for I trust that this will never predominate. But I do not disguise my anxieties at times. And yet, as I reflect upon the question and confer with my associates, I am encouraged to believe that the public faith will not be tarnished. There can be no declaration of Congress that the five-twenties must be paid in coin;[3] but I do not think there can be any declaration that they shall be paid in greenbacks. The question will be postponed, or, if dealt with, settled without deciding the meaning of the original obligation. It may be settled by the arrival of specie payments, when every obligation will be payable in coin. Another solution, which is now under the consideration of our financial committee, is the creation of a new stock, principal and interest declared to be payable in coin, probably at five per cent, into which the five-twenties will be convertible as they become due, at the option of the holder. In other words, the holder of the five-twenties can have these coin bonds if he will take them, even if specie payments have not arrived. The more I reflect upon the situation, the more I feel the impossibility of any act of repudiation. And yet anything short of payment in coin is, I fear, in the nature of repudiation. I wish I could write more positively: you will see that I write frankly. So much do I trust to the public faith, that, although sometimes disturbed by adverse menaces, I cannot bring myself to believe that there is any real danger. My only sister, who is in California, has all her small means in five-twenties, but I have not counselled any change. I fear that this is a very unsatisfactory letter. Mr. Thornton[4] has arrived. We have exchanged calls without meeting. I hear him called amiable and interesting. I cannot cease to deplore the blow dealt at arbitration by the English government, through whose rep-

[1] He replied to a correspondent from Cleveland, Ohio, who had written to him in favor of a complete repudiation of the national debt: "The faith of the nation is solemnly pledged to the payment of all our obligations in full, and with our abundant resources it would be an inexcusable perfidy should we break this solemn engagement."

[2] Mr. Bright had written to Sumner, in behalf of a relative who had invested in United States bonds, as to the probable effect of the agitation in favor of paying them in depreciated paper currency.

[3] The first act of President Grant's Administration was the approval, March 18, 1869, of an Act declaring the faith of the United States pledged to pay in coin all the national obligations, unless otherwise expressed in them.

[4] Sir Edward Thornton, British minister.

resentative it was recognized at the Congress of Paris as the proper mode of deciding questions between nations."

Sumner made an elaborate speech in favor of a return to specie payments, in which he reprobated various schemes for tampering with the public debt, — such as State taxation of the national bonds, or their payment in a depreciated currency, or in anything less than coin;[1] and he further advocated a simplification of the system of taxation, confining it chiefly to whiskey and tobacco, and the funding of the public debt at long terms, without attempting the strain of a rapid payment. He dwelt on the evils of a continued suspension of specie payments, and contended for a reduction of the paper currency as essential to that end. Foremost, recurring to it again and again, he put the supreme importance of maintaining the public faith.[2] This speech on finance greatly strengthened Sumner's position with the commercial and conservative classes, who, though approving his prudent course on foreign relations, were rarely in accord with his action on questions growing out of slavery and reconstruction.[3] Mr. William Amory, a worthy representative of the Boston merchants of the old type, who had been accustomed to regard Sumner as an enthusiast of dangerous ability, and had been severe in his strictures on the senator, thus expressed the opinion of his class at this time: —

"But this is no reason why I should not feel and express to you my great admiration for the cogent, simple, but masterly manner in which you have treated the practical question of financial reconstruction, in language eloquent with truth, sound sense, and comprehensible simplicity. The country is largely indebted to you for such outspoken truth, so forcibly, plainly, and irresistibly set forth, by one whose influence is so great, if not always exerted in the right direction. Let me add, as some amends for my freedom, — which I am sure you will excuse, — that I have generally with equal approval and admiration watched your course and read your speeches as chairman of the com-

1 "Coin" and "gold" were then synonymous: the "silver question" was to come after Sumner's time.

2 July 11, 1868; Works, vol. xii. pp. 443-480. The Boston "Advertiser" printed the speech; and a pamphlet edition was widely distributed in the State. Sumner spoke briefly, July 14 (Congressional Globe, p. 4046), in favor of allowing the conversion of United States notes into bonds, in order to promote a return to specie payments. He kept up during his life his interest in financial questions. He maintained the validity of contracts payable in coin, March 11, 1869 (Globe, pp. 48, 51). The right of localities to their share of banking facilities engaged his attention, March 25, 1869 (Globe, pp. 274-276). In the session of 1873-1874 he was meditating a speech on the return to specie payments, but death prevented his carrying out his purpose.

3 Letters approving his speech and action on financial questions came from A. A. Lawrence, T. M. Brewer, R. H. Dana, Jr., P. W. Chandler, and William Whiting.

mittee on foreign relations through the critical period of the war and since, and am at a loss to reconcile your eminent and sound statesmanship in that department with the errors of your reconstruction and impeachment policy upon any other theory than that I am wrong myself, — which, of course, can't be!"

In his autumn address to his constituents Sumner advanced another step, and called for the resumption of specie payments in eight months, — July 4, 1869, — thus anticipating an event which did not take place till ten years later.[1] His proposition alarmed those of his constituents on whose wisdom in finance he had relied, — Atkinson, Endicott, J. M. Forbes, Amasa Walker, and J. S. Ropes, — all insisting that the measure was premature, and would derange business without a previous reduction of the currency.[2] But Sumner, who always assigned to moral forces (in this case confidence and a fixed purpose) a larger share in a desired consummation than others could admit, adhered to his view; and the event proved his faith to be well founded. The final resumption came without a further reduction of the currency, which, under McCulloch's wise administration, had been already withdrawn to the extent of $160,000,000, and brought down to $580,000,000 before his power to contract it further was taken away by Congress in January, 1868. After this no further reduction took place before the resumption, but rather an increase by $26,000,000 in 1873–1874. Other causes were at work which rendered resumption safe without so great a contraction of the currency as conservative financiers thought necessary. The great West, hitherto limited to the line of States bordering on the western shore of the Mississippi, was now, by the opening of the Pacific Railway and kindred enterprises, to develop commercial needs sufficient to absorb the full amount of the existing currency.

During the last year of the Civil War it became evident that General Grant would, if he chose, be a candidate for the Presidency in 1868, with the chances altogether in favor of his election; but it was quite uncertain whether he was to be the Republican or the Democratic candidate. His last vote at a

[1] He introduced at the beginning of the next session a bill for resuming at that date. E. G. Spaulding's "History of Legal Tender Paper Money" (p. 28) contains a letter from the senator expressing his impatience at the continued postponement of resumption.

[2] On the other hand, the conservative jurist, R. A. Chapman, Chief-Justice of the Supreme Court of Massachusetts, in a letter to Sumner, October 30, commended the speech fully, and particularly the naming of the date of resumption.

national election had been for Buchanan. His report read in Congress in December, 1865, on the state of the South, his accompanying of President Johnson on the latter's political tour in 1866, and his acceptance of the portfolio of the war department upon Mr. Stanton's removal were interpreted as showing leanings towards the party with which he had acted before the war. But his later misunderstandings with President Johnson, growing out of the manner of his leaving the war department in January, 1868, led to a bitter antagonism between them; and henceforth the general was in close relations with the Republicans, and an earnest supporter of the impeachment. His nomination by them, notwithstanding the disadvantage to which they had been put by the impeachment proceedings, insured their success in the national election of 1868. The only hope of the Democrats was in presenting a candidate of undoubted loyalty in the Civil War, — which at one time was thought likely in the person of Chief-Justice Chase, now parted from his old associates; but that hope they threw away when they nominated Horatio Seymour.

One with Sumner's ideas of what a statesman should be would not, if the choice had been left solely with him, have selected for President a military officer, however meritorious his services, who had had no civil experience. Sumner probably accepted General Grant's candidacy rather as a necessity than as a fortunate event. He is, however, not on record as objecting to it in any letter or public way; and, as far as known, he acquiesced without protest in the final decision of his party.[1] He took the best view of the General's qualities, — writing to Lieber, November 1: "Grant will be our President, with infinite opportunities. I hope and believe he will be true to them."

[1] The Cincinnati "Commercial," July 19, 1891, published D. C. Forney's statement concerning a private meeting at the rooms of John W. Forney in Washington, D. C., Nov. 6, 1867, for conference on the political situation, where were present Senators Wade, Chandler, and Sumner, John W. and D. C. Forney, D. K. Cartter, General Rawlins, O. E. Babcock, and others. All present were in favor of nominating General Grant, except Sumner, who, while recognizing his merits as a soldier, and making no personal points against him, earnestly protested against his nomination. He believed in the strength of the party, saw no necessity for a step which was a confession of its weakness and a reflection on its civil administrative patriotism, and predicted that such a programme, if carried out, would bring about its gradual disintegration. D. C. Forney, the narrator, believes that General Grant's knowledge of what took place, — probably obtained through Babcock, — planted in his mind a permanent dislike of the senator, which was revealed some years later in the San Domingo controversy. This account, which seems to be truthful, was, however, not given to the public till twenty-four years after the transaction, and is not corroborated by any other statements known to the writer.

Sumner wrote to the Duchess of Argyll, July 28: —

"The duke's letter came to sustain the reports by the cable and the press of the reception of Longfellow. I am charmed to know this; he deserves it all. He is too modest for a lion, and has too little sympathy with public dinners and meetings. But you seem to have made him docile; I imagine him now like that saintly lion of Jerome.

"The cable this morning tells us that Lord Cranworth is dead. He was not a great man, but of a sweet and gentle nature, who seemed to do everything well and kindly. I liked him always from my first visit to England thirty years ago, and am sad to think that he has gone. I am not satisfied that Lord Brougham is not buried in Westminster Abbey. The next generation will often ask where he lies, and will wonder that there was not room for him in the Abbey. I know something of his eccentricities, moral and political; but he did fight a good fight, and has left one of the foremost names in English history. Some of his speeches will be read always. I am inclined to think that there are two or three sentences from him which are among the best in the English language. Dr. Johnson used to give the palm to that famous sentence of Hooker on law; but I think that Brougham has matched it. And yet he lies obscurely in a village burial-ground far away in the south of France!

"You approach your election as we approach ours. With you it is Gladstone; with us it is Grant, — two G's. I do not doubt the success of each.

"Mr. Reverdy Johnson came to see me last evening. He will begin on the naturalization question, and has every reason to believe that it will be settled harmoniously. He is more truly a lawyer than any person ever sent by the United States, except, perhaps, Pinkney. He is essentially pacific, and detests the idea of war or wrangle with England. On this account I am sorry to lose him from my committee in the Senate.

"The suffering at the South is great, through the misconduct of the President. His course has kept the rebel spirit alive, and depressed the loyal, white and black. It makes me very sad to see this. Considering the difficulties of their position, the blacks have done wonderfully well. They should have had a Moses as President; but they have found a Pharaoh, as I have often said. Reconstruction should have had sympathy and support, with gentle breezes always in the right direction, while it has had enmity and opposition, with adverse gales and storms. I hope that we can save it under the next Administration. I read the duke's speech with great interest, and the bishop's, and am glad Longfellow was there."

To Mr. Bright, August 11: —

"It is long since we have exchanged letters, and I now employ my last moments before leaving for Boston to keep alive our correspondence. Events have been more active than any pens, whether in England or the United States. I watch with constant interest the increasing strength of the liberal cause, and look forward to its accession to power with you as home secretary, at least, if you choose to enter a cabinet.[1] I remember Mr. Cobden thought

[1] Mr. Bright became in December, 1868, President of the Board of Trade in Mr. Gladstone's Cabinet.

that you and he ought never to take a cabinet place; but this opinion was founded on the public sentiment of his day. Would that he were now alive to enjoy the prodigious change! Meanwhile, we too have had our vicissitudes. The President is still in office, but checked and humbled. His removal seemed inevitable; he was saved by the delays of the trial. Grant will be his successor; of this I cannot doubt. I am happy to be able to assure you that repudiation is dead in all its forms and aliases. Long before the five-twenties can mature, specie payments will be the law of the land, and meanwhile the repudiators will be powerless. Had the President been removed, we might have had specie payments just so much sooner. I do not see why it should not follow the election of Grant.

"Our new minister at London is more a lawyer than a diplomatist. The lawyers ought to make much of him, for he is one of them. He is easy, affable, and naturally courteous, and disposed to peace. For several years he has been on my committee, and I believe has uniformly harmonized with me, except on party questions and nominations. He hopes to settle all outstanding questions. I think he will be successful on the naturalization question. But I do not see signs of accord on the other question. Our recent bill on naturalization, with all its abominations, was Seward's work. He desires to be known as its author. It passed the House of Representatives by a large vote, and on coming to the Senate was referred to the committee of foreign relations. The committee was unanimous for postponing it till the next session. Meanwhile, the Fenians and their sympathizers of both parties came on by committees to press it. The Presidential election was at hand, and the committee did not feel authorized to stand in the way. I reported the bill with amendments, taking out its worst features, and these were adopted. I thought it better to settle the question by a treaty. The Fenians pressed it, as furnishing possibilities of embroilment with England. I hope to hear from you soon, invigorated with salmon fishing."

Again, August 13: —

"I have been detained here by the death of Mr. Stevens. He was a hero, but no financier. On slavery and the suppression of the rebellion he was always austere and fixed. His death will make no essential change except on the financial question, where his activity and authority will no longer perplex. Here he erred; but in all else he was a great leader, to whom be all gratitude and honor! It is hard that the United States should be so misrepresented by the London press. The 'Times' has a correspondent who sees through rebel spectacles and writes with a rebel pen. I doubt if my name is ever mentioned without a misrepresentation. But it is harder to bear the pretentious liberalism of the 'News' correspondent, who is more mischievous than the other from his pretences. It is strange that the 'News' will tolerate such hostile perversion. I wish you well through your great election."

Congress took a recess July 27.[1] Sumner lingered at the capital, as was his custom, attending there the funeral of Thad-

[1] Sumner was in his seat, September 21, when Congress sat only for the day.

deus Stevens,[1] at which he served as pall-bearer, and arriving in Boston in the middle of August. Just before leaving Washington, he wrote to E. L. Pierce: "I am hot and weary, with many things to trouble me. You cannot enter into the depths of my sorrows, which revive at every stage. To think that in Boston I am homeless is very bitter."

To Dr. Howe he had already written: —

"I hear much of a new hotel in Boston, — the St. James. Is this the place for me? And how are its charges? Nothing perhaps can show how entirely homeless I am in Boston better than this inquiry. The old house belongs to another, and there is no roof for me in the city of my birth. I had thought of Parker's, but this will be hot and crowded. Better still would be a couple of good rooms, which I might occupy permanently, in some private house. I have put so much money into house and pictures here, to say nothing of trees and shrubs and green grass, that I must economize elsewhere. I hope you are well, and your children. When will Flossy be married?"

Shortly after arriving, Sumner attended in Boston the municipal banquet given to his old Free-Soil coadjutor, Anson Burlingame, who was now the head of an imperial embassy from China, — a festivity remarkable for the distinction of its guests. Sumner had carried the treaty with China unanimously in the Senate, and had recently taken the lead in a formal reception to the Chinese embassy by that body. In his remarks at the dinner the senator compared the romantic career of Burlingame with that of Marco Polo.[2]

To Bemis, September 22, from Washington: —

"There seems to be a new and favorable turn. Seward is sanguine, and Johnson writes that he shall settle everything. Nothing just yet, but everything very soon. The naturalization treaty comes first. Seward then expects a commission to hear and determine everything; therefore, the time is at hand for your work. I wish I could lend you my physical strength and power of work, everything but my hoarse voice. But with your knowledge, — of which you have a monopoly, — is there not a patriotic duty which you cannot avoid?"

An obstinate throat trouble, for which Sumner sought the advice of an eminent specialist, Dr. H. I. Bowditch, withdrew him from any general participation in the political canvass of the

[1] He delivered at the next session, Dec. 18, 1869 (Works, vol. xiii. pp. 2–9), a eulogy on Mr. Stevens, in which he described the latter's remarkable qualities as a parliamentary leader.

[2] August 21; Works, vol. xii. pp. 502–509. Before completing his mission, Burlingame died at St. Petersburg, Feb. 23, 1870. Our government afterwards sought and obtained a modification of the treaty, sending a special commission to China for the purpose.

autumn. General Grant's candidacy had settled in advance the result of the national election. Sumner's third term as senator was expiring, but his return was altogether unopposed. The Republican State convention, meeting at Worcester, nominated him for re-election by a resolution [1] passed unanimously, which was drawn by E. L. Pierce, and presented by R. H. Dana, Jr., the latter having been the opponent six years before of a similar declaration. Sumner declined invitations from other States,—among them those of H. C. Bowen, Woodstock, Conn., and W. B. Allison of Iowa. He spoke only twice during the canvass, once briefly at a flag-raising in his own ward,[2] and again at Cambridge shortly before the election,—where, after a brief reference to his own public activity, covering as he maintained the various interests of the country, he defended the reconstruction acts, and renewed the discussion of financial questions, urging the speedy resumption of specie payments.[3] He had hoped to deliver some lectures to meet what he called his "extravagances in house and pictures," but he reconsidered this purpose under the orders of his physician.

He missed during this vacation his communings with Longfellow, now making his last journey in Europe. Other friends, however, were thoughtful. Amos A. Lawrence offered him, shortly after he arrived in Boston, a room in his house at Longwood; but this welcome was declined. In the autumn Mr. Lawrence brought guests together whom he thought would be most agreeable for the senator to meet at dinner, saying, in his note of invitation, "The company shall not exceed the Muses in number; and though they may not be distinguished, they shall be 'all honest men.'" Rev. Samuel K. Lothrop, always liberal in thought and genial in personal relations, invited him to meet the Wednesday Club at his house. His colored friend, J. B. Smith, gave him a dinner, with Rev. Dr. Potter of New York, Moses Kimball, and Edward Atkinson among the guests.

Sumner wrote to Whittier, November 13:—

"Last evening I was told that you were in Boston, and to be found at the Marlboro' House. I hurried there at once, and was pained to learn that you had left for home. This was hard for me, for I longed to see you. Why did you not let me know of your visit? It would have been pleasant to review

[1] September 9; Works, vol. xii. p. 518.

[2] September 14; Works, vol. xii. pp. 510-514.

[3] October 29; Works, vol. xii. pp. 519-548. This speech had a wide circulation by publication in the leading New York journals.

our days and note the great progression of events; and I wished also to look with you at the future, and compare the destinies as we each see them. I confess my anguish when I think of the rebel States, and the brutalities to which good people are exposed. Opportunity has been sacrificed during the last four years. I hope we can recover it. Under proper influences, those States could have been moulded into republican commonwealths, where every man should enjoy equal rights. But they have been hardened and bedevilled.

"I hope you are well, dear Whittier, and happy. Except in my throat, I am reasonably well; but there is very little happiness for me. This is my lot, and I try to bear it. I am very sorry to have missed you. Good-by."

The Legislature of Massachusetts, meeting in January, 1869, promptly re-elected Sumner for his fourth and last term, with a unanimity rare in the election of senators, and contrasting with the long and close contest which first sent him to the Senate, — his vote in the State Senate being thirty-seven out of thirty-nine votes cast, and in the House, two hundred and sixteen out of two hundred and thirty-two. He was now to be the senator of longest continuous service in the distinguished body which he entered in 1851,[1] and he had been since 1861 its most conspicuous presence. The strength of his position was generally recognized through the country in tributes from the public journals.[2] He was treated, even by those who did not agree with him, as an historical figure, always maintaining the dignity of his high office, laborious and faithful, specially discreet and highly informed by studies and correspondence, in matters of an international character.

In a letter at this time, Mr. Garrison thus bore testimony to Sumner's career: —

"I take up my pen to congratulate you and the Commonwealth of Massachusetts and the whole country upon your re-election to the Senate of the United States by an almost unanimous vote of the State legislature, in accordance with the all-prevailing sentiment of the people. This fresh expression

[1] Wade entered the Senate at the same time with Sumner, but his term was to expire March 4, 1869. Cameron and Hamlin entered the Senate earlier than Sumner, but their service had been broken by intervals. The New York "Tribune," March 4, 1869, comments on Wade's retirement.

[2] Washington Chronicle, Jan. 20, 1869. Henry B. Anthony, senator from Rhode Island, a conservative by temperament and associations, contributed as editor to the Providence "Journal," Sept. 19, 1868, an estimate of Sumner's position as a public man, saying that his service for freedom "had overshadowed his services in other departments which would alone make the reputation of a public man;" describing him as "careful, cautious, and deliberate in the conduct of that most important branch of the public service that is especially committed to him," with "qualifications of the highest character" for the position of chairman of the Senate committee on foreign relations; and adding, as to the grave questions of public law arising during and after the Civil War, "Their settlement to the advantage and honor of the country has been largely due to the information and ability which he has brought to them."

of popular confidence and appreciation must be extremely gratifying to your feelings, — not on the ground of personal exaltation, but because it is another remarkable proof of the marvellous and substantial change which has taken place in public opinion, pertaining to the cause of impartial freedom, since you espoused that cause as one of its most eloquent advocates, and one of its most successful defenders; when there was a heavy cross to be borne, and for the praises of men you had their bitterest reproaches. Your senatorial career covers the most important portion of American history. For a long period you were in an almost hopeless minority, misunderstood, grossly caricatured, shamefully traduced, in constant peril of your life while discharging the official duties of your position at Washington. In view of the deadly enmity engendered against you at the South, as the most prominent and efficient political opponent of her nefarious slave system, it is a marvel that you are at this day a living man, even aside from the murderous assault made upon you by Preston S. Brooks, himself long since gone to the shades, and his memory as detestable as he hoped to make your own. It was a dark hour when you were beaten down by his merciless blows; but out of that darkness what light has sprung, and out of that humiliation what fame and exaltation have followed! Your blood, staining the floor of the Senate Chamber, was the blood of a martyr; now it is given to you to wear a martyr's crown! This is no human, but a divine triumph; this is not in the wisdom of man, but in the power of God. His is the glory, yours the reward. But the work which you have had so much at heart, though astonishingly advanced, is not yet fully consummated; and you will assuredly continue to bring to it the same unquenchable zeal, the same heroic devotion, the same unfaltering determination, the same sleepless vigilance, the same transcendent ability, that have characterized your public labors from the beginning. Whether you will be assigned to a position in the new Cabinet under President Grant, and if so, whether you will deem it advisable to accept of it, I do not know, and presume not to conjecture. Though no one could fill your place in the Senate, yet I confess it would give me, as I believe it would your constituents generally, great satisfaction to see you in the office of Secretary of State, or as minister plenipotentiary to the Court of St. James. In either case, it would be 'the right man in the right place.' But you will not seek the office; it must seek you."

Three of Sumner's English friends died at this period, — Lord Cranworth, Lord Wensleydale, and the Duchess of Sutherland. He had become intimate with the two former on his visit to England as a youth, and with the duchess on his two later visits. Writing to the Duchess of Argyll, he referred to the many tombs which had opened for those to whom he had been attached. Among English travellers calling on him in this or the preceding year were John Morley, G. Shaw Lefevre, and Leslie Stephen. From his French acquaintance, M. Chevalier, came the expression of the wish that he would take the mission to France.[1]

[1] Chevalier wrote concerning the proposed canal between the Atlantic and the Pacific, expressing his belief that the Nicaragua route was the only practicable one.

The chief Act of the third session of the Fortieth Congress, Dec. 7, 1868, to March 4, 1869, was the passage of the fifteenth amendment to the Constitution, which ordained that "the right of citizens of the United States to vote shall not be denied or abridged by the United States, or by any State, on account of race, color, or previous condition of servitude." This form was only reached after disagreements between the two houses, shifting votes in each, and serious differences among the supporters of the measure; and, in the end, the terms adopted were not satisfactory to many Republicans, because the prohibition did not extend to discriminations in the holding of office or exclude other tests, like those of education and property, which might be used to effect indirectly the practical disfranchisement of the colored people.

Sumner thought that if such an amendment were to be adopted it should cover all civil and political rights;[1] but his chief insistence was that the amendment was unnecessary, Congress having already the power to forbid such discriminations; and he feared to admit, by the submission of the amendment to the States, that they had already the power to disfranchise on account of race and color, and that they would retain it in the event that the amendment failed to be approved by three fourths of the States. He therefore took no part in the votes, preliminary or final, upon the proposition. He moved as a substitute a bill[2] establishing the right to vote and hold office without discrimination as to race or color, in all national, State, territorial, and municipal elections, which received only nine votes, including those of Edmunds, Wade, and Wilson. In a speech he traversed familiar ground, in which he maintained that disabilities of race and color, at once irrational and beyond the power of any individual to remove, were not "qualifications" or "regulations" of suffrage which the States could prescribe.[3] He affirmed, as the supreme rule of interpretation, "Anything for human rights is constitutional. . . . Whatever you enact for human rights is constitutional. There can be no State rights against

[1] Feb. 8 and 17, 1869, Congressional Globe, pp. 1008, 1298. He proposed a form which senators from the Pacific coast objected to as including the Chinese. (February 9, Globe, pp. 1030, 1033–1035.) Doolittle, in this as in former debates, called attention to Sumner's success in carrying his measures by agitation and persistence against opposition which it seemed at first impossible to overcome.

[2] Introduced by him the first day of the session.

[3] Feb. 5, 1869; Works, vol. xiii. pp. 34–52. He made further remarks, February 8 and 9 (Congressional Globe, pp. 986, 1041).

human rights." To him it was incomprehensible that all publicists, all reasonable men, should not see the question as he saw it, and he had full faith in the efficacy of a statute. Somewhat unfairly he treated those who held to the existing power of the States to maintain the discrimination of race which still prevailed in many of the States, even at the North, as partisans of "State rights," in the sense that those rights had been heretofore set up in defence of slavery; and those to whom this imputation was applied could not be expected to do otherwise than resent it. He failed, as many others failed at this time who were seeking the means to meet novel exigencies, to recognize the permanent distinction between the unconstitutional pretensions of secession and the constitutional autonomy of the States.[1]

Few of the radical Antislavery men agreed with Sumner in his preference for an Act of Congress as an effective remedy against discriminations of race as to suffrage. Wendell Phillips expressed his doubts upon this point, and in a letter urged Sumner, on personal as well as public grounds, to support the amendment. He wrote:

> "I know you will pardon this private hint from one who loves your fame, and is jealous for it. Give us all your weight for the amendment; and if it fails, rally the ranks on the next best line, — your bill. Dispute the ground, as you have always done, inch by inch. 'Before you've gone over all Judea, the Lord will come.'"

The fifteenth amendment failed to attract the public interest which had been connected with the two preceding amendments. The New York "Evening Post," still a Republican journal, did not mention it in its leaders, and hardly any journals of wide influence gave it special attention. Sumner's failure to support it and his preference for an Act of Congress did not provoke criticism in the newspapers or among his constituents; but senators opposed to him in later debates did not forego the opportunity to recall his peculiar action at this time. He however yielded a ready assent to the amendment after it had passed, promoted its adoption by the States,[2] and joined in congratulations when it was proclaimed a part of the Constitution.[3]

[1] Sumner had full faith that his bill would be sustained by the Supreme Court; but its subsequent decision against national legislation for the protection of civil rights shows that he was mistaken.

[2] He wrote to the governor of Nebraska in favor of his convening the Legislature in order to act upon its adoption.

[3] April 1, 1870. Works, vol. xiii. pp. 350-352.

Shortly after the close of the war, claims for injury by our army to private property situated in the rebel States and belonging to persons domiciled there (loyal, or pretending to be so) were urged on Congress, often with the assertion of special merit and hardship and an appeal to good nature rather than to sober judgment. Sumner, treating the question, as was his habit, under the light of history and international law, insisted that such petitions should be entertained with caution, and only upon some well-defined principle, — maintaining, with a citation of the authorities, that under the rules of public law the appeal could be made, not to any legal right, but only to favor and charity.[1]

There was a spirited debate in the Senate on the question whether Massachusetts, having already in 1859 received the principal, was entitled to the interest on her advances to the United States in 1812 in the war with Great Britain. The claim was historically connected with Governor Strong's refusal to comply with President Madison's call for the State militia. Maine, as a part of Massachusetts in 1812, was entitled to a share in the amount to be recovered; and Massachusetts had in advance appropriated her own share to the aid of the European and North American Railway, in which Maine was greatly interested. Sumner took the lead in supporting the claim,[2] and showed to good advantage his capacity for a running debate, which would have been always conceded but for his too great proneness to prepare himself with elaborate speeches.[3] The debate brought together in pleasant relations Sumner and Fessenden in their encounter with the Western senators, who were led by Sherman and supported by Frelinghuysen and Conkling. The measure failed at this time, but was carried at a later session.[4]

Other subjects to which Sumner gave attention during this session were the death of Mr. Hinds of Missouri, a member of the House, to whom he paid a tribute;[5] a resolution of sym-

[1] Jan. 12 and 15, 1869 (Works, vol. xiii. pp. 10-31). He spoke briefly on the same question July 14, 1870 (Congressional Globe, pp. 5552, 5564, 5566), and April 8, 1872 (Globe, p. 2252).

[2] Feb. 24 and 25, March 1, 2, and 3. Congressional Globe, pp. 1518, 1519, 1579, 1585, 1718-1722, 1732- 1734, 1840, 1854.

[3] C. W. Slack in the Boston "Commonwealth," March 6, 1869.

[4] Sumner made a full report on the subject April 1, 1869, and pressed the claim in the session of 1869-1870. June 6, July 6, 1870 (Congressional Globe, pp. 4146, 5293).

[5] Jan. 23, 1869. Works, vol. xiii. pp. 32, 33.

pathy with Spain in her effort for liberal institutions, with an appeal for the abolition of slavery;[1] the maintenance of mixed courts in Africa for the suppression of the slave-trade under the treaty with Great Britain, and the payment of salaries to the judges.[2]

He wrote to Dr. Howe, Jan. 1869: —

"It is difficult to understand the precise position of Crete. Can the late telegraphic news be true? I suspect it as an invention of the Turk. I regret that there is no good sympathetic Russian minister here with whom I could confer. Stoeckl has gone home; and even he was little better than an old Democrat, with a Massachusetts wife steeped in Webster whiggery; so, we fight our great battle generally with little support or sympathy."

To Mr. Bright, January 17: —

"Of course I read carefully all that you say, whether to the public, or better still, to myself. Your last letter was full of interest. All the treaties[3] have been sent to the Senate in copy. They would have been ratified at any time last year almost unanimously. I fear that time will be needed to smooth the way now. Our minister has advertised the questions by his numerous speeches, so that he has provoked the public attention if not opposition. The Senate is not removed from popular influence; and I doubt if it will act until it begins to hear the public voice. Thus far nothing has been said on the question in the Senate or in my committee, but I have heard loose talk from senators to the effect that our minister has made it impossible to adopt anything he has done. I mention this, not to vindicate it, but only to give you a glimpse of floating impressions. All this troubles me. I think that never at any time have I felt so powerless over the question. This may change; but I think time will be needed. You are aware, of course, that the feeling towards Mr. Seward will not help the treaties. At this moment I do not know well enough the views of General Grant, which will necessarily exercise great influence. It is some time since I spoke with him on the subject. He was then very exacting.

"*Tuesday, January 19.* I finish this letter at my seat in the Senate. Last evening I met General Grant at dinner, and conversed with him briefly on the new treaties. I would not commit him, and do not think that he has any very precise policy. He did not seem to object to the naturalization and San Juan negotiations, but I think he had a different feeling with regard to the Claims convention. He asked why this could not be allowed to go over to the next Administration? This morning I called up the subject in my com-

[1] Dec. 17 and 19, 1868 (Congressional Globe, pp. 122, 145). He reported against the resolution after the House had added a recognition of the independence of Cuba, — one of Mr. Banks's projects, — March 2 and 3, 1669 (Globe, pp. 1819, 1828, 1864).

[2] Feb. 1, 2, and 3 (Congressional Globe, pp. 765-767, 783-786, 818). The New York "World," with reference to this debate, referred, February 5, to "his dictatorship" in the Senate.

[3] The Johnson-Clarendon treaties.

mittee. There was nothing but general conversation, in the course of which it was remarked that Great Britain had never appreciated the wrong, the terrible wrong, done to us, not only in the cases of ships destroyed, but also in driving our commerce from the ocean. You know that I have never disguised the opinion that the concession of belligerent rights was wrongful; that there can be no ocean belligerency in a power without the capacity of administering justice on the ocean, — in other words, without prize-courts and ports. Of course, therefore, such a concession to pretenders without this capacity must be at the cost of the power which makes it. As a principle of law and justice I cannot see how this can be doubted. Denied or questioned, it must ultimately be adopted as essential to the safeguard of the seas. To what extent it will enter into our settlement I cannot now say. I wish I could write more fully and carefully, and see the future more clearly; but I write as well as I can under pressure and with business going on about me. There are topics in your letter of great interest."

To R. H. Dana, Jr., January 26: —

"The Claims question with England will go over to the next Administration, and will probably become one of the greatest international litigations in history."

To Whittier, February 26: —

"Last evening I received your note, which saddened me. I was sorry to know that you are not well, besides being disappointed in not having you under my roof; the time will come, I trust. I shall write to Emerson, who likes the experience of life, and hope to have him. I am sorry to know that Stanton has not seen Grant since the election. He has been too ill to call; and Grant has called only once, when Stanton was too ill to see him. Stanton says that he hears of declarations by Grant in favor of economy, retrenchment, and the collection of the revenue, but nothing about the rights of man to be maintained in all their fulness; but I hope for the best."

Early in 1869 a plan was brought to a head which Sumner had long had in mind, — a complete edition of his speeches and writings, revised and annotated by himself. Literary friends counselled him to undertake it; and he was prompted also by calls for copies of speeches long out of print, from different parts of the country. S. Austin Allibone wrote, Jan. 9, 1868: "I have it much in my heart that there should be a handsome octavo edition (like Everett's) of your orations, etc. They should have a copious index; and do prepare autobiographical memoranda, with notices of your eminent friends in Europe and America." The senator had a statesman's ambition to place what he had done in permanent volumes, accessible for all time; and the American edition of Burke's works furnished the model. He had an instinct that it would not do to defer longer the cherished plan. To Dr. Howe he wrote: —

"I wish to be the executor of my own will in this respect. . . . Latterly I have been led to think more than ever of the uncertainty of life. Perhaps the little interest I have in it has made me notice symptoms that in a gayer mood I might have neglected. Suffice it to say that I have now but one solicitude, — it is to print a revised edition of my speeches before I die. If this were done I should be ready to go. These speeches are my life. As a connected series they will illustrate the progress of the great battle with slavery, and what I have done in it. I hope it is not unpardonable in me to desire to see them together, especially as I have nothing else. Sometimes I think of giving up my house, or cutting off expenditures, in order to devote my means to this object; but I am so comfortable in my surroundings, and at my time of life and in my public position feel their necessity so much, that I hesitate."

As the printing was beginning, he wrote to Longfellow: —

"The revision tempts me to great work, beyond my anticipation. I have filed and amended those two early volumes so that it would have been as easy to re-write. If I could throw them into the fire I would, and have an end of them; but since this is impossible, next to their destruction is a good edition revised and amended before I die."

The enterprise was undertaken by Messrs. Lee and Shepard, of Boston. The preparation of the volumes occupied the senator's spare time for the remainder of his life; and it was unfinished at his death. His work comprehended changes of the text, — mostly verbal, but sometimes modifying the substance, — verification of authorities, notes explanatory of the occasion and circumstances, and extracts from public journals and his correspondence, sometimes, as in the case of the speech which preceded the assault in 1856, extended to great length. The edition was to be comprised in ten volumes, one or two of which were to be reserved for a biography to be prepared by another; but the notes and later speeches lengthened it to fifteen, even without a biography. The senator was assisted in verbal criticisms and verifying references by an accomplished proof-reader, George Nichols, of Cambridge. The printing began in July, 1869; and the first volume, beginning with the oration (July 4, 1845) on "The True Grandeur of Nations," came out in May, 1870. Ten volumes were printed under the author's eye,[1] and he supplied notes for the eleventh; but with the exception of

[1] At the time of his death he had read and returned the proof as far as page 467 of Vol. X.

the "Prophetic Voices concerning America," which at the time of his death he was enlarging for a separate publication, it fell to his literary executors to complete the enterprise, with the assistance of proof-readers, acting under Mr. Longfellow's immediate direction. The last two volumes, the proofs of which were read by Mr. A. W. Stevens, did not appear till May, 1883, on account of a suspension of the work, the completion of which Mr. Longfellow and Mr. Nichols did not live to see. The announcement of the proposed complete edition of his Works called out a large number of notices, which dwelt at length on his habits of mind, his style, and his position as a statesman. The one contributed to the New York "Independent," May 12, 1870, was from the distinguished scholar, Moses Coit Tyler.

Sumner's name had at different times been mentioned for Secretary of State and for the missions to England and France. Mr. Lincoln, at the time he called for the resignation of Mr. Blair, Postmaster-general, in 1864, contemplated a change in the state department after the election in 1864;[1] and in that event it is likely that he would have invited Sumner to be Seward's successor. Sumner's name was mentioned in connection with the Cabinet which Wade might have formed if Johnson had been removed by impeachment; and it was now again, after General Grant's election, canvassed in connection with the state department. It is not likely that Sumner would have consented to pass from the Senate to the Cabinet except at an exigent call; certainly he never indicated any wish to make the change, or any disappointment that he had not been called to make it. The duties of the place he had long held were congenial to him; its tenure was secure, and work remained to be done in it on the completion of which he had set his heart. His friends also, who took the most interest in his personal fortunes, were averse to his leaving the Senate. E. L. Pierce wrote to him, Jan. 20, 1869: "By your service in the Senate you are to live in the history of the country. Is it not best to remain there? With it there is fixedness and independence; beyond, there is uncertainty of tenure and a measure of subordination."[2] Sumner was reticent when his name was mentioned for the Cabinet as among the probabilities. The most that he said was in a letter

[1] *Ante*, p. 195, *note*.

[2] William Endicott, Jr., of Boston, and W. M. Dickson, of Cincinnati, took the same view in letters; and the Boston "Commonwealth," Nov. 21, 1868, concurred in it.

to Lieber, written the day after the election in November in reply to the latter's suggestions on the subject: —

"The headship of the first committee of the Senate is equal in position to anything in our government under the President; and it leaves to the senator great opportunities. Had Mr. Lincoln lived, I think I should have been obliged to determine then if I would supersede Mr. Seward. The thought troubled me at the time; for how could I leave reconstruction and equal rights unsettled in the Senate? Nobody has ever heard me say that I would accept any place out of the Senate, if it were offered to me. I admit, however, that my country has a right to determine where I can work best."

## CHAPTER LIV.

PRESIDENT GRANT'S CABINET. — A. T. STEWART'S DISABILITY. — MR. FISH, SECRETARY OF STATE. — MOTLEY, MINISTER TO ENGLAND. — THE "ALABAMA" CLAIMS. — THE JOHNSON-CLARENDON CONVENTION. — THE SENATOR'S SPEECH: ITS RECEPTION IN THIS COUNTRY AND IN ENGLAND. — THE BRITISH PROCLAMATION OF BELLIGERENCY. — NATIONAL CLAIMS. — INSTRUCTIONS TO MOTLEY. — CONSULTATIONS WITH FISH. — POLITICAL ADDRESS IN THE AUTUMN. — LECTURE ON CASTE. — 1869.

PRESIDENT GRANT, as was to be expected from one whose career had been hitherto exclusively military, selected his Cabinet very much as a general selects his staff officers.[1] Their names when announced suggested in most instances personal choice rather than public considerations. Two exceptions, however, were E. R. Hoar, who was called from the Supreme Court of Massachusetts to become Attorney-General; and Governor J. D. Cox of Ohio, who was appointed Secretary of the Interior. The selection of Cresswell of Maryland for Postmaster-General was well received by the country. Senators and Representatives were not consulted in these arrangements; and as all were treated alike none could take offence.[2] The Cabinet, made up as it was, underwent from necessity rapid and even immediate reconstruction. The President was least fortunate in his personal surroundings. He chose for his secretaries four of his staff officers (O. E. Babcock, Adam Badeau, Horace Porter, and F. T. Dent),[3] who, holding commissions in the army and drawing salaries

[1] Badeau's "Grant in Peace," p. 163. This writer is cited only where his statements are intrinsically very probable, or he is corroborated by trustworthy evidence.

[2] Sumner by habit kept aloof from President-making and Cabinet-making. The following statements of Adam Badeau are fictions; they have no support in trustworthy evidence: (1) That Sumner hoped to be Secretary of State in the Cabinet of President Grant; (2) That his friends with his consent pressed his name on Grant for the place; (3) That it had been arranged that Sumner should be Secretary of State in the event of President Johnson's impeachment being effected; (4) That Sumner came tardily in 1868 to the support of the Republican nominations. (Badeau's "Grant in Peace," pp. 210, 211.) Another fiction for which another writer is responsible is that Sumner expected to be the Republican candidate for President in 1868, and expressed surprise that his name was passed by.

[3] Also two more who rendered temporary service.

as army officers, were misplaced when assigned to civil duties. They continued to display army titles in civil correspondence. The Executive Mansion had never before, and has never since, assumed such a military aspect. Another staff officer (John A. Rawlins) became Secretary of War.

The appointment of A. T. Stewart as Secretary of the Treasury was found to be in contravention of the Act of Sept. 2, 1789, drawn by Alexander Hamilton, which provided that "no person appointed to any office instituted by this Act shall directly or indirectly be concerned in carrying on the business of trade or commerce." In order to qualify Mr. Stewart, Patterson and Sherman urged the instant repeal of this disabling provision. Sumner, when the measure was about to pass, interposed, and insisted on a preliminary consideration by a committee. A few moments later a message was received from the President, in which he asked that Mr. Stewart be exempted from the Act. When Sherman sought to have a bill at once carried to that effect, Sumner again interposed an objection to such summary action, saying that "the bill ought to be most profoundly considered before it is acted upon by the Senate."[1] As senators were found after reflection to be averse to making a discrimination in Mr. Stewart's favor, the President withdrew his request, and nominated Mr. Boutwell of the House to the place. The Cabinet now had two members from Massachusetts, — a circumstance which led to the retirement of Judge Hoar a few months later.

E. B. Washburne, who had sought and received his place in the Cabinet as a compliment, held it only a week, and the President was in the mean time looking for his successor.[2] Hamilton Fish was in Washington on the day of the inauguration. That evening he dined at Sumner's in company with John Lothrop Motley, each little thinking how their names were afterwards to

[1] Mr. Fish, in an interview with Sumner in June, 1870, instanced Sumner's action in the proposed repeal of the Tenure-of-Office Act as one of his acts in opposition to the President (Works, vol. xiv. p. 259); but all the senator did in relation to the repeal was to object to action, March 9, without deliberation. He kept out of the debate and contention altogether, and voted with the mass of senators of his party. It is more likely that the President was displeased by his objection to summary and exceptional legislation which would relieve Mr. Stewart from disability. The New York "Tribune," March 21, 1872, said that Sumner's "sonorous voice" arrested the proposed exemption, and that the senators after reflection were generally found to be against it.

[2] Fessenden, when the temporary character of the appointment became known, is reported to have said to senators, "Who ever heard before of a Cabinet officer being appointed as a *compliment*?"

figure in a bitter controversy. The next evening Mr. Fish left a "good-by" note, as he was to return home the morning after, in which he expressed the wish to see Sumner in New York for a talk. But he was soon called back by the offer of the vacancy in the state department. His appointment was not expected by himself or the public. He had served one term as governor of New York, and one term in each house of Congress, where his service was altogether without note, and in neither case ratified by a re-election. All he had to say in the Senate was usually comprised in a dozen lines or so, — only once or twice equalling half a column of the Congressional Globe; and this brevity was accompanied by neither wisdom nor felicity of speech. No service of a senator was ever more undistinguished; and while it continued, the representation of New York fell almost wholly on his colleague, Seward. During six years — a memorable period though it was — he did not develop a single subject, or throw on any the light of experience or study. He never rose even to the celebrity of "a single speech." He is quite unknown to the Globe's "Appendix," where the well-considered arguments made in either house appear. What he did and said in the Senate was to answer calls for the yeas and nays, present petitions, offer a few resolutions, report one or two bills, reply now and then to questions from his associates, make an inquiry, or explain some interlocutory matter, — and this was all. Not a word came from him, even during the struggle on the repeal of the Missouri Compromise, or the invasions and violence which followed in Kansas, — an historic contest in which every man who had any earnest feeling for or against slavery took part.

Outwardly Mr. Fish maintained relations with his colleague; but at heart he was antipathetic to him,[1] — very hostile to his antislavery position, and to his candidacy for President.[2] He was utterly out of sympathy with the antislavery movement which resulted in the Republican party. He was opposed to the efforts in the State of New York in 1855 to form a Republican party, in which Preston King, John A. King, and Edwin D. Morgan co-operated; and he rejoiced over its defeat by the union of pro-slavery "Americans" and "Silver Gray" Whigs,

[1] Seward made a generous defence of Fish in the Senate, Feb. 20, 1855, when the latter was assailed by some New York ship-owners.

[2] This appears in letters in manuscript from Fish to Sumner. Some of them apply coarse epithets to Seward, to which it is not worth while to give publicity.

as likely to effect Seward's exclusion from public life. He wrote to Sumner, Nov. 8, 1855: —

"'Fusion,' I believe and hope, is soundly beaten in New York; with it Seward is beaten. I cannot find tears to shed on either account. The 'Republican' vote embraced all the Seward men, the bulk of the Abolitionists, and a large number of Whigs (anti-Sewardites), who, in 'the noise and confusion' of the breaking up of an old organization, found themselves in the predicament of your illustrious predecessor, and did not know 'where to go,' and from habit and association followed old leaders. The defeat of the 'Fusion' ticket in New York means just exactly the rejection of Seward's abolitionism, — *et id omne genus*, all the isms which he and his tribe of hangers-on have endeavored to make subservient to his advancement and their opportunities of speculation and money-making."

Further on in this lengthy letter, in which he reprobates antislavery agitation and "the abolition platform" of the "Fusion" (Republican) convention, and objects to the denial of "property in slaves," he reviews the political distractions among the opponents of slavery, and adds: —

"But to my dull comprehension the recent results suggest the deep-seated predominance of a strong, conservative, Union-loving, anti-agitation feeling, and that the cause of emancipation cannot be promoted, but has been, is, and ever will be retarded, by antislavery agitation in the free States."

Mr. Fish, hardly knowing "where to go," came, in the national election of the next year, tardily, and after "much embarrassment in determining the course which duty required," to the support of the Republican candidates, still calling himself a Whig (the name of an extinct party), and revealing his dissatisfaction with his new connection by hoping for some future organization which would "assume broader and more catholic grounds."[1] Naturally he did not ask for a re-election to the Senate, and was not asked to accept one; and the most representative Republican journal of the State wrote at the time that if he had desired another term he could not have expected the suffrages of a Republican legislature.[2] He was thus dropped from public life with general accord, and Preston King succeeded to his seat. He went abroad shortly after his term expired, and remained in Europe the next two years. He voted with the Republicans in 1860, but was at no time prominent among them. While absent from the country, and after his

1 Mr. Fish's letter, Sept. 12, 1856, in New York "Tribune," Sept. 26, 1856.
2 New York Tribune, Jan. 28, 1857.

return, his attitude towards the Republican party and its administration was critical rather than sympathetic; in 1860 he dreaded the probability of Seward being the candidate for President, and during the Civil War he indulged rather in complaint than in praise of the Administration; and his tone as to public affairs — alike as to the action of President, Cabinet, and Congress — was uniformly querulous and pessimistic.[1] He wrote to Sumner, March 19, 1861: —

"Do you think that the government of the United States, under which we have lived, will ever again send abroad another batch of representatives? Soberly and candidly, *I do not*."

In urging Sumner to take ground publicly against the foreign appointments, he wrote, Jan. 27, 1863: —

"I write as a friend who has loved you long and much. I trust that I do not offend. But I see country and government and nationality fading and passing away amid the riot of vulgarity, violence, and corruption, and under the rule of imbecility and vacillation. For God's sake, give us an eloquent outburst of honest, patriotic indignation and rebuke of the gross wrongs to which our poor country is subjected. Then, if we are to perish, let us have at least one protest in favor of honesty, of decency, and of national virtue; then history may say that the appreciation of something noble had not been wholly lost."

Such is Mr. Fish's public record from his taking his seat as a Whig in the Senate at the same time with Sumner in December, 1851, to 1869, a period of eighteen years, including the period of his severance from public affairs for twelve years. He had hitherto done nothing to give him a line in our history, and he was out of sympathy with the spirit of the time. Nothing but the accident of personal association with General Grant and their relation as host and guest during the latter's visits or residence in New York brought him again into public life.

Sumner and Fish entered the Senate together in December, 1851, and though the latter had no sympathy with the former's antislavery views, their relations became most cordial and intimate.[2] There was no friend's house in Washington where

[1] The writer has had at hand one hundred letters of Mr. and Mrs. Fish to Sumner, — much the larger number being from Mr. Fish.

[2] When Mr. Fish was assailed publicly by Moses Grinnell and the merchants of New York city, on account of his bill concerning emigrant passengers (Congressional Globe, Feb. 20, 1855, p. 825), he received Sumner's sympathies, which he gratefully acknowledged in a letter from Havana, March 11, 1855, saying: "Thanks, my good friend, for your kind letter. Like a drop of water in a dry desert is a kind word in a moment of pain."

Sumner ever enjoyed so much as at Mr. Fish's, and no one was for many years so welcome a guest there. The latter's home in New York and his seat on the Hudson were always open to the senator. Letters of host and hostess, and of younger members of the family, still preserved, show that he was admitted to a confidence seldom given to any but kinsfolk. If an interesting relation was to be formed, his congratulations were among the first to be sought. The fascination of refined hospitality was always strong with him, and he found it in perfection under that roof. These relations, established at Washington, continued after Mr. Fish had passed out of public life, apparently not to return to it. The two were henceforth in correspondence and met from time to time, as well in Europe when Sumner was an invalid, as afterwards in New York.

When Mr. Fish and his family visited England in 1858, they carried introductions from Sumner to the Sutherlands, Argylls, Carlisles, and Hathertons. It was Sumner's letters — favors charily given by him — which opened to them the hospitalities of Stafford House and Chiswick House.[1] Mr. and Mrs. Fish expressed their thanks for his attentions to their daughters, then school girls in Paris, whom he called upon when his wounds from the application of the moxa compelled abstinence from society. Some weeks later, on their visit to that city, when he was still under Dr. Brown-Séquard's treatment, they made a call of sympathy upon him; and meeting again in Paris the same year, he was their guest at their family Thanksgiving dinner. Letters were passing between them and him while he was at Montpellier and in Italy; and one of his warmest welcomes on his return home, with health restored, was from them. These incidents have been noted here, to be recalled when it will be pertinent to remark what is due to a friendship, even after it is broken.

Mr. Fish's appointment was most agreeable to Sumner; none could have been more so either on personal or public grounds. His equipment for his post was indeed meagre; he had little knowledge of public law; he was not a ready or even a correct writer; and the result was that the drawing of his official papers fell during his term mostly, if not wholly, into the hands of others. But he had enjoyed large relations with society; he was

[1] Here Mr. Fish met Motley the historian. Correspondence of J. L. Motley, vol. i. p. 261.

esteemed in the great city where he lived; he was pledged by his conservative instincts and associations to a prudent and honorable policy; and one of his position and character seemed at the time needed to counteract certain influences likely to manifest themselves in the Cabinet. He hesitated to accept the President's invitation; and Sumner's expected counsels and co-operation were an important element in his decision. The following is his letter communicating to the senator his acceptance: —

(*Confidential.*)

NEW YORK, March 13, 1869.

MY DEAR SUMNER, — Very much against my own wishes, and after a very positive refusal, I am going to Washington to undertake duties for which I have little taste and less fitness. In yielding, I hoped that I could rely upon your friendship and your experience and ability, for your support and aid to supply my manifold deficiencies. My name was sent to the Senate without my knowledge. I had declined by telegraph to a letter tendering the place. This is some way accounted for; when I see you I can state more particulars. I expect to be in Washington on Tuesday morning, but go with a heavy heart, and with unnumbered misgivings, and at the sacrifice of personal ease and comfort, without my family, and without any reasonable prospect of my wife being able to join me. I make this sacrifice on the most earnest appeal "not to allow another break," etc. I hesitated long to reverse my decision; and if I was wrong in yielding, God knows that I did it reluctantly, and because the reasons presented seemed to me to affect high interests.

I want to see you. I expect to be at the Ebbitt House on Tuesday morning. Possibly I may be expected to be present at a Cabinet meeting on that day. Can you come to see me before it may be necessary to go?

Very faithfully yours,

HAMILTON FISH.

From that time until the San Domingo controversy the relations of the senator and the secretary were confidential to a remarkable degree, in many respects to an extent without precedent in such intercourse. Sumner was consulted about appointments and all difficult questions which came up in the department. The assistant secretary, Mr. Hunter, long familiar with its practices, in sending, July 8, to Sumner, then in Boston, a copy of a despatch from one of our ministers, took occasion to explain that he had never known such a thing "to be done in any other instance, even of a gentleman whose personal, political, and official relations towards the secretary were like yours." [1] At first Mr. Fish found his duties irksome. In the summer he wrote to

[1] Mr. Fish quoted this remark of Hunter in a pleasant way in a letter to Sumner.

Sumner from his seat on the Hudson: "I do not wish to go back to Washington, and most sincerely wish I were out of the department."

The relations of the President and of the senator were, up to the time of the San Domingo controversy, altogether agreeable. An associate of the senator on the committee on foreign relations states that the chairman, as well as other members, chafed at times under nominations for foreign posts which seemed below the correct standard;[1] but anxious to preserve harmony, they approved most of them. Fish and Sumner were naturally in accord as to the attainments and character required of our representatives abroad; but the former, from facility of nature, was not disposed to stand in the way of the President's inclinations.

Mr. Motley was nominated, April 12, as minister to England.[2] The selection was the President's, without pressure from any quarter, and it was very agreeable to Mr. Fish. Motley, returning from Europe in the summer of 1868, made an address in the campaign, which with brilliant rhetoric maintained the Republican cause, and described the qualities and achievements of General Grant. Naturally this praise was grateful to the general, coming from the historian who had set forth the character of William the Silent.[3] In the early part of the winter Motley delivered an historical address in New York, when he was introduced to the audience by Mr. Fish with a very complimentary tribute. During the month preceding the inauguration he was in Washington, where he frequently met in society the President elect, and after dinner there were genial smokes and talks. The address he had made in the campaign, of which the President was well informed, their agreeable intercourse in Washington, the general feeling that injustice was done to him by the last Administration, as well as his accomplishments, — all these put him in the foreground as a candidate for the English mission.[4] Sumner altogether approved the appointment, but his part in making it was a minor one; and so far as appearances go, it

[1] One of these was J. R. Jones of Chicago, for Belgium. Works, vol. xiv. p. 260.

[2] He was confirmed the 13th, the same day that the Johnson-Clarendon convention was rejected.

[3] According to Badeau, the President was impressed by this speech. "Grant in Peace," p. 153.

[4] The public took note of the favor with which he was regarded at the Executive Mansion, and even associated his name with the state department.

would have been made without a word from him. He spoke to the President once casually in favor of Motley on the stairs of the Executive Mansion, and then again in a formal interview, when he named him for London as one of five whom he thought should be sent to or kept in diplomatic posts, — the other four being Marsh in Italy, Morris at Constantinople, Bancroft at Berlin, and Dr. S. G. Howe in Greece. Mr. Fish was prompt to place Motley on his list. It was afterwards represented, but not truly, that the appointment was due to Sumner's "influence and urgency,"[1] with the intimation that otherwise it would not have been made, and the Administration would not have been misled. It was, however, clearly the President's prepossession and Mr. Fish's friendly interest and popular favor that gave Motley the place. The minister, although knowing that he had the senator's good wishes, never supposed himself indebted to him for the appointment. Sumner, however, while not the chief promoter of Motley's success, urged another appointment without avail. His friend from youth, Dr. Howe, desired greatly, and had long desired, the mission to Greece, the scene of his early adventures. Sumner had intervened for him before while Mr. Seward was secretary, and had waited for the present opportunity. In long and intimate conversations with Mr. Fish, beginning within two weeks after the latter took office, Sumner pressed Dr. Howe's appointment, requesting it, as he did no other, as a personal favor. The secretary, while willing to make other provision for Dr. Howe, declined to recommend him for Greece, to the displacement of a gentleman with whose family he was in friendly relations. Sumner thought Dr. Howe specially fitted for that one mission by early and constant connection with the country, and declined to name him for any other. He was sorely disappointed; but he saw the force of the secretary's reasons, and did no injustice to his motives.[2] His failure to obtain what he had most at heart in the line of appointments makes it doubly improbable that Motley's selection was due to his potency.

Unfortunately for Motley, he was required by the President to take with him as secretary of legation Adam Badeau, whose tales of public life are compounded of gossip and fiction, and who has followed hungrily the fortunes of public men, and been faithful

[1] Fish to Moran, Dec. 30, 1870.

[2] Luigi Monti was displaced from the consulship at Palermo, but Mr. Fish restored him at Sumner's request.

in the pursuit so long as it has proved thrifty to himself. His courage has been displayed, not in attacking them while living, but in the attempt to blast their memories when dead. He insinuated himself into Motley's confidence, and then betrayed him, — accepting hospitality, and afterwards doing his best to deride his host. His false statements concerning Sumner were preceded by correspondence in which he assumed to be a friend. He wrote from London to the senator, July 8, 1869, offering advice and soliciting confidence, saying at the end: "I should be very glad if you could find time to say anything to me, whether to repeat or not, as you choose, either on this subject or any other. With great respect, yours very faithfully." He worried Grant for favors, sinecures, emoluments, and suretyships [1] (a list numbering thirty and more [2] has been published, but these are not all); and finally he brought a suit against the general's executors when he was safe from the contradiction and withering eye of one who had long befriended him. His benefactor in his last days found out the true quality of the man he had nursed in his camp and home, and closed by formal notice all business relations with him, — rebuking his pretensions to the authorship of his own writings, describing his unbearable traits and manners, as well as his addiction to quarrels, and expressing in quaint and emphatic phrase the belief, that, with a contract for service at one thousand dollars a month, Badeau would not after the other party's death ever finish the job.[3] Ingratitude to Grant and disrespect to his memory were the fitting sequel to slanders on Sumner and treachery to Motley. The mention of this person in this connection is justified only by the circumstance that for a time his narrations carried a factitious credit with uncritical readers, on account of the confidence which General Grant

1 A suit was brought by the United States in the U. S. Circuit Court for the Southern District of New York against Badeau, charging him with converting to his own use funds received by him as consul-general at Havana. His sureties were General Grant and Horace Porter, who were discharged in May, 1892, from liability by the payment of a certain sum which was agreed upon as a compromise. New York "Evening Post," June 16, 1892.

2 New York Herald, March 21, 1888.

3 The details of Badeau's exposure before the country in his treatment of General Grant are found in the journals of the day (New York "Tribune," March 18, 1888; New York "Evening Post," March 19, 21; New York "Herald," March 21). Badeau's persistence in claiming two salaries at the same time, one in civil and the other in military service, has found a record in the reports of the United States Supreme Court, vol. cxxx. p. 439. General Butler's description of Badeau in his "Book," p. 860, *note*, has the double merit of truth and piquancy.

placed in him at one time, and was supposed to place in him for a longer period.

Reverdy Johnson while a senator was nominated by President Johnson in the summer of 1868, during the pendency of the national election, minister to England, and was unanimously confirmed by a Republican Senate. He was thought to be a better person for the post than any other the President was likely to name; he had shown himself on the foreign relations committee uniformly conservative and wise; he had risen above his surroundings in his support of the thirteenth constitutional amendment;[1] he was very amiable with his associates of both parties in the Senate; and there was a general disposition to give him the compliment of the brief term of service which remained under the present Administration. Sumner, however, was of another opinion, believing that our interests in England were too important to be hazarded on a compliment, and preferring to leave the post vacant, with its current business intrusted to the secretary of legation. Finding, however, by conversation, that senators were not inclined to this view, he thought the next best thing was to have no contest on the nomination, so that the minister would feel his obligation to the Republican majority. The day after his confirmation, Mr. Johnson sought Sumner's house and thanked him warmly for the unanimous action of the Senate.

It was not supposed that the new minister would undertake a negotiation concerning the "Alabama" claims. Both he and Seward, in interviews with Sumner, instanced naturalization and the San Juan boundary as subjects to be considered, but neither referred to the vexed question which, it was generally believed, would go over to the next Administration. Sumner did not see the minister's instructions, and was not consulted concerning them. In letters to English friends, Mr. Bright among them,[2] he mentioned Mr. Johnson's genial qualities, his remarkable position at the bar, and his pacific and conservative position, without any suggestion that he represented the American view on the "Alabama" question, or was expected to present it; and he gave the new minister no letters of introduction. He did not do, what

1 Mr. Johnson escaped the madness of his section at the time of the assault on Sumner. *Ante*, vol. iii. p. 496, *note*.

2 These letters (*ante*, pp. 359, 360) became the subject of controversy in the New York "Nation," September 9 and 23, where their purport was erroneously stated.

would have been quite unbecoming, warn his English correspondents not to respect Mr. Johnson's commission; but he kept himself entirely free from any pledge in advance to accept Mr. Johnson's work, whatever it might be. Mr. Johnson did not, while in England, retain the good opinion of his countrymen with which he entered on his mission. He cheapened his office by an inordinate love of speech-making, and offended the patriotic masses at home by his convivial and apparently sympathetic association with the bitterest English partisans of the rebellion. His imprudence did not end here. Notwithstanding the repudiation of the Administration he represented by the election of General Grant as President in November, he proceeded with the negotiation of a treaty for the settlement of the "Alabama" claims, and signed, Jan. 14, 1869, what became known as the Johnson-Clarendon convention. It is remarkable that the English ministry did not itself see the hazards of a negotiation carried on under such circumstances. It was a dead treaty as soon as it was signed. At some earlier period Mr. Johnson's settlement, imperfect as it was, might have been accepted.[1] The good nature of the American people is indisposed to a long controversy. Individual sufferers had been pressing their claims for indemnity at Washington, through Mr. Evarts and other counsel, and such private pressure often gives a turn to a negotiation. But the time for an incomplete adjustment had now passed. The subject belonged properly to a new Administration, which was supported by the confidence of the people. The President elect expressed himself freely in conversation against the Johnson treaty, and his first annual message, as well as the instructions to Motley, indicate the general discredit with which it was received in this country. When it was first taken up in the committee on foreign relations, in February, 1869, all the members were found to be opposed to a ratification. Sumner said, when action was about to be taken: "Before putting the question, I wish the committee to understand fully the responsibility of the vote. We begin to-day an international debate, the greatest of our history, and before it is finished, in all probability the greatest of all history."

[1] Sumner wrote to Motley, July 6: "There was a time when we would have accepted very little, as when Mr. Adams made his first proposition, and even on the proposition of 1866. During this time I said nothing, although my feelings have been from the beginning so strong on this question."

Sumner had refrained for six years — since his address in September, 1863 — from the public discussion of the "Alabama" question, and he had hoped not to be obliged to enter on it again. While at the outset, before a rebel cruiser was upon the sea, he gave repeated warnings in his correspondence with English friends, high in public position, against the acts of their government which brought on the controversy, and had set forth the dangers of keeping the controversy open, he had meanwhile been most assiduous in the Senate in maintaining pacific relations with Great Britain, and preventing measures likely to produce irritation, — as in his speech in 1862 on the "Trent" case; his opposition in 1863 to letters of marque and reprisal; his resistance in 1864 to the attempt to embroil us with that country on account of the St. Albans raid; his defeat of the attempt in 1866 to scale down the neutrality acts; his opposition in 1868 to the retaliation bill; and his constant suppression of Mr. Chandler's bills and resolutions aimed against Great Britain.[1]

It became now his duty, as chairman of the committee on foreign relations, in reporting adversely upon the convention, to state the reasons for its rejection when it was under consideration at the special session of the Senate, April 13. This he did in a speech somewhat brief for him, — occupying, perhaps, an hour in delivery.[2] He avoided matters of aggravation, like the "Trent" case and the St. Albans raid, and maintained a tone as conciliatory as his statement admitted. He showed the inadequacy of the convention; how it belittled the work to be done by its very form, in taking for a model the claims-convention of 1853, which was for the settlement of purely individual claims, and in choosing in a certain event an arbitrator by lot; how it ignored the greater national grievance; and how it settled no rule of international duty as to the past, and what was of most concern, none as to the future; and expressed not a word of regret for the injuries we had suffered, — an expression which the senator greatly desired. The speech then developed generally our case against Great Britain, — laying stress on the swift concession of ocean belligerency, which was proclaimed the day of Mr. Adams's arrival in England, when as yet the

[1] The New York "Tribune," April 21, 1869, contrasts Sumner and Chandler in their treatment of international questions.

[2] Works, vol. xiii. pp. 53–93.

rebels had not a ship on the ocean; the fitting out of the "Alabama" and other rebel cruisers in England; the hospitality accorded to them in British ports, and their destruction of American ships. He stated our individual and then our national losses, — the last arising from the destruction of our commerce, the transfer of commercial marine from American to foreign flags, the rise of insurance on American vessels, the expense of the blockade, and the prolongation of the war caused by British intervention. The speech, while declaring England "justly responsible for the additional expenditure to which our country was doomed," and referring to the war expenses caused by the cruisers, stated no sum or ultimatum, presented no bill, and made no pecuniary demands. It was necessary, in seeking the full and complete adjustment of the great questions of international law and duty which he sought, to declare her just responsibility according to "the judgment in any chancery which consults the simple equity of the case;" but with this he contented himself. The speech was kindly and pacific in tone, frankly stating our grievances, but making no threats. He spoke "in the interest of peace, which every one should have at heart," against "a treaty which, instead of removing an existing grievance, left it for heart-burning and rancor. . . . In the interest of peace it is the duty of both sides to find a remedy complete, just, and conciliatory, so that the deep sense of wrong and the detriment to the republic may be forgotten in that proper satisfaction which a nation loving justice cannot hesitate to offer." He rebuked the suggestion of some of our countrymen that the claims should remain unsettled, "so as to furnish a precedent in kind should England find herself at war." He said: —

"Be the claims more or less, they are honestly presented, with the conviction that they are just; and they should be considered candidly, so that they shall no longer lower like a cloud ready to burst upon two nations, which, according to their inclinations, can do each other such infinite injury or such infinite good. I know it is sometimes said that war between us must come sooner or later; I do not believe it. But if it must come, let it be later, and then I am sure it will never come. Meanwhile, good men must unite to make it impossible."

And again: —

"Mr. President, in concluding these remarks, I desire to say that I am no volunteer. For several years I have carefully avoided saying anything on this most irritating question, being anxious that negotiations should be left undisturbed to secure a settlement which could be accepted by a deeply injured nation. The submission of the pending treaty to the judgment of the Senate left me no alternative. It became my duty to consider it carefully in committee, and to review the whole subject. If I failed to find what we had a right to expect, and if the just claims of our country assumed unexpected proportions, it was not because I would bear hard on England, but because I wish most sincerely to remove all possibility of strife between our two countries; and it is evident that this can be done only by first ascertaining the nature and extent of difference. In this spirit I have spoken to-day. If the case against England is strong, and if our claims are unprecedented in magnitude, it is only because the conduct of this power at a trying period was most unfriendly, and the injurious consequences of this conduct were on a scale corresponding to the theatre of action. Life and property were both swallowed up, leaving behind a deep-seated sense of enormous wrong, as yet unatoned and even unacknowledged, which is one of the chief factors in the problem now presented to the statesmen of both countries. The attempt to close this great international debate without a complete settlement is little short of puerile. . . . Again, I say, this debate is not of my seeking. It is not tempting, for it compels criticism of a foreign power with which I would have more than peace, — more even than concord. But it cannot be avoided; the truth must be told, not in anger, but in sadness. England has done to the United States an injury most difficult to measure. Considering when it was done, and in what complicity, it is truly unaccountable. . . . Like every departure from the rule of justice and good neighborhood, her conduct was pernicious in proportion to the scale of operations, affecting individuals, corporations, communities, and the nation itself; and yet down to this day there is no acknowledgment of this wrong, — not a single word. Such a generous expression would be the beginning of a just settlement, and the best assurance of that harmony between two great and kindred nations which all must desire."

This was the conclusion of a speech pacific in tone and moderate in statement. What he sought by the speech was, not to obtain a heavy assessment of damages, but to establish a principle, — the duty of a friendly nation towards another engaged in suppressing a pro-slavery insurrection. As Mr. Schurz well said :[1] —

"What he desired to accomplish was, not to extort from England a large sum of money, but to put our grievance in the strongest light; to convince England of the great wrong she had inflicted upon us, and thus to prepare a composition which, consisting more in the settlement of great principles and rules of international law to govern the future intercourse of nations than in the payment of large damages, would remove all questions of difference, and serve to restore and confirm a friendship which ought never to have been interrupted."

[1] Eulogy, April 29, 1874.

Sumner wrote to Lieber, May 30: —

"I have made no demand, not a word of apology, not a dollar; nor have I menaced, suggested, or thought of 'war.'[1] . . . My object was simply to expose our wrongs as plainly but as gently as possible, with illustrations of how reparation has been made in other cases when England expressed regret or paid money. . . . To my mind our first duty is to make England see what she has done to us. How the case shall be settled, whether by money more or less, by territorial compensation, by apology, or by an amendment of the law of nations, is still an open question; all may be combined."

The tone of the speech is as moderate as that of Mr. Adams's correspondence on the subject, — milder to a considerable degree than that of Mr. Fish's letter to Motley, Sept. 25, 1869, and in entire contrast with that of our "Case" at Geneva, prepared, under Mr. Fish's immediate direction, by his assistant secretary, J. C. B. Davis, which charges the British government with "insincerity," — the most odious epithet which the representatives of one nation can apply to another.

It will appear at a later date that the Treaty of Washington was modelled with reference to Sumner's speech, following closely its points and meeting his objections. The speech met with unusual favor with senators from both parties, particularly with those most conservative and pacific. There was no word of dissent or qualification from any quarter. Anthony, who was in the chair, sent at once to Sumner a bit of paper with these words and his initials: "That was a great speech."[2] Fessenden was the first to approve; and he was followed by Sherman, Howard, Morton, Scott, Thurman, Casserly, Stockton, Chandler, and Warner. Fessenden and other senators, in personal congratulations and in public remarks, commended particularly its moderation and conciliatory spirit.[3] The treaty was then rejected by a vote of fifty-four to one. The Senate of its own motion, without prompt-

[1] R. H. Dana, Jr., who thought that our government should not have put forward the national or indirect damages for pecuniary assessment before the tribunal at Geneva, wrote to Sumner, May 22, 1872: "I ought to say, however, that I had not understood you to favor the submission of the indirect damages for pecuniary adjustment at the arbitration, but only to hold that they were actual national grievances, and traceable to the whole course of Great Britain, — not as assessable, by the week and month, on specific cruisers."

[2] The leader in the Providence "Journal," April 20, 1869, was presumably written by Senator Anthony, who was its editor as well as chief proprietor. It approved the speech as free from the spirit of hostility and revenge, and representing the views of the senators as well as public opinion.

[3] New York "Tribune," April 14; New York "Times," April 14; New York "Herald," April 14. The last-named journal, May 3, reports an interview with the senator, in which he stated some incidents connected with the speech.

ing from Sumner, removed before opening its doors the injunction of secrecy from the speech.[1] Two days later it appeared in all the leading journals of the principal cities of the country. It was notable that conservative public men were positive in their approval of the speech. Among those who wrote to Sumner in terms of unstinted praise were H. B. Anthony, senator; F. T. Frelinghuysen, ex-senator; E. D. Morgan, former governor of New York; John H. Clifford, former governor of Massachusetts; John M. Read, the jurist of Pennsylvania; and James Russell Lowell. The current of opinion was the same in the press. The leaders of the New York journals laid stress on the senator's judicial treatment of the question, his calm and friendly tone, and his pacific spirit.[2] The British minister communicated to his government the fact that "the speech had been received with vehement applause by the whole of the Republican press;" but there was no division growing out of political differences. Sumner stood then as the representative of American sentiment as rarely any statesman has stood. It was remarked at a later period that this was "the most popular speech that he ever delivered."[3]

The President and the Secretary of State expressed themselves as in accord with Sumner at the time. The senator wrote, May 25, to George Bemis, then in Europe: "For you I say that I conversed with the President before I spoke, and found his views to be in strict conformity with mine. Since the speech, he has thanked and congratulated me."[4] General Cushing, in a note to Sumner, June 26, more fully quoted later, wrote that Mr. Fish had stated "in more general but in explicit terms the accordance of the Administration with yourself in opinion and purpose on the points of controversy with England."

The speech met with a reception of an unexpected kind in

1 Mr. Grimes, senator from Iowa, wrote to the London "Times," May 12 ("An American Citizen") that the injunction was removed at Sumner's request. Sumner denied this in a letter to Grimes, but the latter did not retract or reply. James W. Grimes's "Life," by W. Salter, p. 369.

2 New York "Times," April 16, 1869; New York "Tribune," April 15; New York "Evening Post," April 14 and 15, and May 12. W. L. Garrison, in the New York "Independent," April 22, while making some points of criticism, wrote that the speech was "delivered in the interest of peace, and for the promotion of justice and good-will."

3 Harper's Weekly, March 16, 1872.

4 Sumner's letter of the same date to Longfellow, and his letter to Bemis, July 7 (*post*, p. 410), are to the same effect.

England. The London press is able, or was then able, to throw the English people into a frenzy, — having a power in this respect which does not belong to metropolitan journals in this country; and it used effectively its opportunity at this time. It did not publish the speech, — as is the habit of American journals with foreign matter affecting the United States, — but made it the topic of inflammatory harangues.[1] Not one of them, not even the "Times," with its enormous space, admitted it to its columns, but only culled extracts to suit a purpose.[2]

The English people were very sensitive at the time; and the sensitiveness was natural. The ministry, in which were Gladstone, Bright, Argyll, Forster, and Stansfeld, — all except the first our friends in the Civil War, — had been very desirous of settling the question, and sincerely thought they had done so. They as well as the English people were at first puzzled by the unanimous rejection of the treaty; and when Sumner's speech came to hand, they attributed the rejection wholly to him. They did not understand that its fate was sealed before he had said a word upon it, and that even his support would not have saved it.[3] It is not, however, difficult to account for their

[1] G. W. Smalley reviewed in the New York "Tribune," May 12, 1869, the notices of Sumner's speech which appeared in the London journals. The "Spectator," always friendly to the United States in the Civil War, stated its objections to the speech in a fair and temperate way. Its chief points were that expressions of regret from the British government could not be expected, and that the senator had "confounded legal considerations of the first importance with totally distinct moral considerations." Goldwin Smith, then in the United States, wrote from Boston, April 18, to a workingmen's paper in England, that after the speech English emigration to the United States could not be encouraged, and that English residents might soon have to leave this country! This letter was copied generally by the English press, and was effective in spreading alarm in that country. It was the subject of kindly but trenchant criticism in two Boston journals, May 21, — the "Advertiser" and the "Journal." Mr. Smith also replied to Sumner in a speech at Ithaca, May 19.

[2] That journal contained, May 1, twenty columns of debates in Parliament, while Sumner's speech just received would have filled only five. It was more moderate that day in its estimate of the speech than in later issues, — allowing it then "the merit of an argumentative and dispassionate manner;" and the day before it said that "its prevailing tone is rather that of passionate remonstrance than of menace." A few days later, however (May 5), it began its leader: "Mr. Sumner had the questionable honor of contributing more than any other man to the war which broke up the Union, and to the differences which keep the breach still open."

[3] Mr. Bright expressed the view in conversations, without sufficient reflection, that Sumner, by joining in Mr. Johnson's confirmation, and commending in private letters his personal qualities, had committed himself in favor of the minister's work. W. E. Forster complained that the senator condemned what "the fashionable people" of England had done, without taking into account the sympathies of "the working people" for our cause; but Sumner's reply was that he had dealt with the government, and not with divisions of the people. His correspondence with Mr. Forster is printed in the latter's life by T. W.

misconception of his temper and purpose. The mass of men, even of intelligent men, are not critical readers; and they did not take note that he had spoken in the line of all the diplomatic statements of our grievances.[1] They had put aside with indifference what others had written, and now Sumner's position and authority brought the American case for the first time directly before them. In this way he seemed to them the principal accuser, — almost if not quite an enemy. They were all the more aggravated because of his familiarity with English life, his intimacy with English public men, and his well-known prepossession in favor of their country. Of all Americans, he seemed the last one from whom such an indictment was to be expected. From that time — and he felt keenly the change of feeling — he lost largely the favor with the English people which he had before held. Those who knew him best were considerate in their judgments, and time cured the soreness of others; but some — Lord Houghton among them — continued to regard him as "an enemy of England." The Duchess of Argyll wrote sadly, May 1: "Your speech is a grievous disappointment. . . . Alas! that I should think so sadly of any speech of yours. For the first time I am silenced when you are spoken about. I understood you through the war; I do not now." A month later she reminded him of one truth which did not always impress him as it should: "Do you remember that you never can be engaged in a cause again where right and wrong stand face to face as they did in the Antislavery fight? In most human struggles, they are much mixed together." Nevertheless her friendship was unbroken, and she wrote late in the year: "May I tell you my wish for you?

Reid (vol. ii. pp. 15-21). Mr. Forster, in an address to his constituents at Bradford, May 21, made a reply, in a friendly tone, to the senator's speech.

[1] In a few instances the conformity of the speech to the preceding statements of the American case was recognized. The Pall Mall "Gazette," April 29, wrote: "Though Mr. Sumner is more outspoken than Mr. Seward or Mr. Adams, he says nothing which was not contained implicitly in their despatches." Sir Charles Dilke said in a speech, Jan. 6, 1870 (New York "Tribune," January 22), that Sumner had only stated the American case almost in the same words in which it had often been stated before; and he took note that the senator had said nothing about claiming two hundred million pounds sterling, or required an abject apology, but that what he said was that England's action had in some measure been the occasion of an enormous loss, and that there had never been on her part any expression of national regret. F. W. Newman, writing to the London "Morning Star," May 11, 1869, found nothing in the speech not in principle found in the senator's address in September, 1863, which, as he thought, was "more excited and exciting." (F. W. Newman's "Miscellanies," vol. iii. pp. 195-197.) A pamphlet edition of the speech, with a special view to its circulation in England, was published at the instance of John M. Forbes, the eminent merchant of Boston.

Is not what Dr. Chalmers called your 'Sabbath of Life' come when you feel that you may give up the strife of politics and have time for still better things? It has been a very full day of work, and I wish you may see when resting time comes. God bless that evening, and give hope of a glad morning!"

The speech, however, had in the end a wholesome influence on English opinion. It ended the indifference which had come from Earl Russell's levity. The English people for the first time recognized the gravity of the American case, and were anxious for a complete settlement. From that date the foreign office, through Sir Edward Thornton, minister at Washington, and Sir John Rose, an unofficial envoy, kept plying our government to learn our terms of settlement.[1] The purpose of the speech was to insure a permanent peace, and such too was its effect. On this point there is the indisputable authority of Sir Stafford Northcote, who, while serving at Washington on the Joint High Commission, wrote as follows: —

1311 K Street, April 27, 1871.

My dear Mr. Sumner, — I have to thank you for sending me your speech on the Johnson-Clarendon treaty. It is one which I am glad to possess for many reasons, not the least of which is that it marks an epoch, perhaps the turning point, in the great controversy which I am sanguine enough to think is now approaching its termination. I cannot tell you how cordially I sympathize with what seems to me the governing idea of the speech. Great international differences are not to be disposed of by huddling them up and pretending not to look at them, nor to be treated as a man treats a bad shilling, by trying to pass it among a handful of half-pence. It is worth while to make concessions on both sides and to agree upon honorable compromises for the sake of peace and friendship between two such nations as ours. It is still better worth while to make such concessions and compromises if we can evoke out of our present settlement rules that will be of use for all nations and for all times. But whatever we do should be done frankly; and though I must own your speech was somewhat sharp, I verily believe that it taught us a valuable lesson in that respect, and that we may say of it, *Fidelia vulnera amantis.*

Believe me, yours very faithfully,

Stafford H. Northcote.

Sir Stafford wrote to Sumner, Aug. 9, 1871: —

"I think almost every one agrees with him [Sir R. Palmer] that we have come to a much better settlement than would have been afforded by the Johnson-Clarendon convention."

[1] Earl Russell and Lord Clarendon, by letters to Mr. Adams (Nov. 2 and Dec. 2, 1865), formally closed the discussion by refusing to entertain further the consideration of our claims. Lord Stanley modified this position (Nov. 30, 1866, March 9 and Nov. 10, 1867), only to the extent of expressing a willingness to consent to "a limited reference."

Sumner wrote, May 25, to Mr. Bemis then in Italy: —

"I wish you were at home to resume your pen. This is the time. The country is interested, and will read. You have seen the fate of the treaty. Though grossly inadequate, yet such was the oblivious good-nature of our people that before Reverdy Johnson had aroused them they would have accepted anything. When it was determined to reject it, I was obliged to state the reasons, and it seemed proper then that I should present our case, being an exhibition of our wrongs. I entered upon this with infinite reluctance, but it was my duty. I was thanked and congratulated by persons like Fessenden for the moderation and pacific tone of my speech, and it was by a unanimous vote given to the country. You will observe that while stating our case I make no demand, not an apology, or a dollar. All this I left to the diplomacy of the future."

To Motley, May 27: —

"Last evening I dined in company with the President. Before dinner I had considerable talk on the English storm, which I hoped had not disturbed him. 'Not in the least,' he said, grimly; 'let it go on.' After speaking of the necessity of firmness in the Administration, I told him what you wrote me just as you were leaving New York; and I mentioned some of the letters I have received from Europe during the last few days, the best being by Laugel, who writes in admirable spirit. The President then turned to the course of England during our war, which he said could not be overstated in its mischief. He regarded her then as 'an enemy.'"

Notwithstanding the false light in which for a time he was regarded, Sumner had then in his heart and kept to the end the love of England, which was his youthful enthusiasm. Of all the public men of his time, not one would have resisted, as he would have resisted, any attempt to bring the two nations into conflict. He scorned that demagogism, conspicuous in American politics, which seeks votes by playing on national or race hatreds.

Nine years after the speech was made, and four years after Sumner's death, Mr. J. C. B. Davis, in an attempt to cover up the real cause of the senator's removal from the head of the committee on foreign relations in 1871, set up that this speech two years before was "the beginning of the differences" between him and the Administration; that it was "a surprise" to the President and the Secretary of State; that the senator in making it "must have intended to put a stop to all negotiations;" and the two positions of the speech, to which such reference is made, were those upon the British proclamation of belligerency and our national claims. All this is pure fiction. The President and his secretary, instead of expressing surprise or disapproval, were in accord with the senator, and commended the speech, as Sumner's contemporaneous letters show. Mr. Fish continued to repose a confidence in Sumner such as no secretary ever reposed in a senator, and such as no secretary would have continued to repose in a senator who had embarrassed his position on so important a question. The President and the secretary sent out contemporaneously as minister to England Sumner's friend, whose appointment they afterwards attributed to his "influence and urgency." On one of the points, — that of belligerency, — Sumner said no more than he had said six years before in a celebrated address,[1] when he pronounced the proclamation "inconsiderate, . . . a moral absurdity, offensive to reason, . . . a precipitate, unfriendly, and immoral concession, . . . an overflowing fountain of mischief and bloodshed, . . . a direct encouragement and overture to the Rebellion, . . . the first stage to independence, . . . a half-way house to recognition," a "blunder" as well as a "crime,"[2] — a proceeding altogether unjustifiable and illegal in establishing ocean belligerency when (a point on which Sumner always laid great stress) the Confederates had no ports from which their ships could issue, and no courts before which their prizes could be brought. A repetition in 1869 of what was said in 1863 could be no "surprise."

Sumner's positions in his speech, April 13, 1869, were in conformity with the American contention from the beginning of the controversy to its end at Geneva in 1872. Neither as to the British proclamation of belligerency, nor as to the national, as distinct from individual claims, did he go beyond what those who stood for our government — whether presidents, secretaries, ministers, commissioners, and counsel — steadily maintained. It may be remarked that he uniformly spoke of "national" injuries and claims, never of "indirect," though the two terms were in popular use synonymous.

Sumner in the speech treated the proclamation as unfriendly in precipitancy and in substance, "the first stage in the depredations on our commerce," [3] compromising the British government "in the concession of ocean belligerency on which all

[1] At New York, Sept. 10, 1863; Works, vol. vii. pp. 338–341, 450–464.

[2] Later he called it "the first stage of evidence." March, 1871; Works, vol. xiv. p. 273.

[3] Adams in his letter, April 7, 1865, calls it "the first step taken," and in his letter of May 20, 1865, "an extraordinary step."

depended," one of "the three different acts which lighted the torch;" and thus, in his view, "to England must be traced also all the widespread consequences which ensued." The same import was given to the proclamation by all the complaints and statements made by our government. From Mr. Adams's first arrival in England the proclamation was treated by him and Mr. Seward in their correspondence as precipitate, unprecedented, unnecessary, unfriendly, injurious, and in derogation of the sovereignty of the United States. They maintained that the depredations of the Confederate cruisers were "its fruits," and they "traced all the evils" to it as "one cause;"[1] they affirmed it to be "the first unfriendly or wrongful proceeding of which they [losses by the depredations] are but the consequences, . . . a violation of neutrality," and a "national wrong and injury."[2] Adams contended in his letter of May 20, 1865, that "the nation that recognizes a power as a belligerent before it had built a vessel, and became itself the sole source of all the belligerent character it has ever possessed on the ocean, must be regarded as responsible for all the damage that has ensued from that cause to the commerce of a power with which it was under the most sacred of obligations to preserve amity and peace." Our counsel at Geneva maintained that "a portion of these claims had been throughout the discussions of Mr. Seward and Mr. Adams *grounded* on the unnecessary proclamation recognizing the insurgents as belligerents; the remainder rested on the acts of the cruisers." Reverdy Johnson, the successor of Mr. Adams, maintained that "the recognition of belligerent rights" was included in his treaty as one of the grounds of Great Britain's liability.[3]

Mr. Fish in no respect waived the claim of our government founded on the premature recognition of rebel belligerency, and he put it in the foreground as much as ever Sumner did. In the instructions to Motley, May 15, 1869, a month after Sumner's speech was made, he treated the concession as "the beginning and the animus of that course of conduct which resulted so disastrously to the United States;" as "important in that it foreshadowed subsequent events," — embodying Sumner's point that,

1 Seward to Adams, Oct. 20, 1862; Oct. 5 and Nov. 17, 1863; Jan. 6, 1864. Adams to Russell, April 7, May 20, 1865. Mr. Adams contended in this last cited letter against the right of the Confederates to be recognized as belligerents on the ocean, on the same grounds that Sumner took in 1863, and later in 1869.

2 Seward to Adams, May 22, 1867, and Jan. 13, 1868.

3 Reverdy Johnson to Seward, Feb. 17, 1869.

unlike the French proclamation, it was "supplemented by acts causing direct damage to the United States." Then followed the instructions to the same minister, Sept. 25, 1869, which heap epithets on the proclamation, declaring that "Great Britain alone had founded on that recognition a systematic maritime war against the United States," and charging it to be "an act of unfriendliness, . . . the sign of a purpose of unfriendliness to the United States and of friendliness to the insurgents," one of "the various causes of injury, . . . a virtual act of war," by which Great Britain "became, and to the end continued to be, the arsenal, the navy yard, and the treasury of the insurgent confederates."

The American "Case" at Geneva, drawn by J. C. B. Davis, assigned to the proclamation all the prominence that Sumner ever gave to it, adding imputations of insincerity (which the senator would not indulge in, and which he expressly condemned), calling it "a precipitate and unfriendly act," issued "*with a conscious unfriendly purpose*," showing "*an insincere neutrality*," and being "the beginning and animus of that course of conduct which resulted so disastrously to the United States."[1] Our counsel at Geneva, — Cushing, Evarts, and Waite, — in their argument, call the proclamation "the first step taken by Great Britain in her relations to the conflict," and an "intervention" leading to injurious results.

These various terms by which the representatives of our government as well as Sumner describe the proclamation are the same in purport. None but a schoolman or a casuist of the Sorbonne could draw a distinction between them. The English foreign office treated them all alike, repudiating them indifferently, whether used to charge a hostile animus or a substantive offence. Its contention was that the issue of the proclamation was made in the exercise of a sovereign right, not open to question by any other power. Our complaint of untimeliness and precipitancy was met by two considerations: (1) That the proclamation was inevitable, and a week sooner or later was immaterial; and (2) That our government was recognizing in-

1 The British arbitrator, Sir Alexander Cockburn, in his "Opinion" at Geneva, deeming the "Case" intentionally offensive in this and other respects, resented "the hostile and insulting tone thus offensively and unnecessarily adopted towards Great Britain, her statesmen, and her institutions." Earl Russell, in his "Recollections and Suggestions," wrote: "In fact Mr. Fish, who succeeded Mr. Seward as Secretary of State, did not scruple to allege that Lord Palmerston and I, the prime minister and Secretary of State, Sir Roundell Palmer, and the law officers of the crown, Sir Thomas Freemantle and the commissioners of customs, were all guilty of falsehood and hypocrisy."

surgents as belligerents, by declaring a blockade of Southern ports and treating captured rebels as prisoners of war.

Sumner's position as to the national claims was the same as our government maintained from the beginning until the spontaneous decision of the tribunal at Geneva, June 19, 1872, that they did not constitute a good foundation for an award of compensation or computation of damages. As early as Nov. 20, 1862, Mr. Adams, under instructions, "solicited redress for the national and private injuries." In his important communications to Earl Russell, April 7 and May 20, 1865, he based a valid claim for reparation and indemnification against Great Britain on the expulsion of our commercial marine from the ocean and the rise of the rates of insurance, as an indirect effect of the proclamation, and of the sailing of the Confederate cruisers from English ports, — an injury which he put as a greater grievance than the actual losses of individuals; and Earl Russell in his replies (May 4 and Aug. 30, 1865), recognized the full import of this language as an attempt to hold Great Britain "responsible for the whole damages of the war." "Allow me to observe in the first place," wrote the earl, May 4, "that I can never admit that the duties of Great Britain towards the United States are to be measured by the losses which the trade and commerce of the United States may have sustained." Reverdy Johnson, who had first put aside the national claims, brought them forward under instructions in his letters to Lord Clarendon, March 25 and April 9, 1869. All this was written before Sumner's speech in April, 1869, which in no respect advanced beyond the positions of our government. Later there was no variance in official communications.

The instructions to Motley, Sept. 25, 1869, were in striking conformity with Sumner's speech on this point as well as on others. They made the objections to the Johnson-Clarendon convention which he made; they set up, as he had set up, the pro-slavery origin of the rebellion, the inability of the Confederates, being without ports or prize courts, to be belligerents on the ocean; they treated the proclamation as he had treated it; distinguished, as he had distinguished, between the English concession with damage and the French concession without damage; quoted English speeches which he quoted; arrayed the same class of statistics of loss of tonnage which he had arrayed; left the statement without a demand, just as he had left it and advised it should be left; and finally near the end they brought to the front, as he had done, not only the indemnities due to individual citizens, but "the larger account of the vast national injuries" arising from "various causes," in which "the untimely recognition of belligerency" was included during a war in which Great Britain "became the military, naval, and financial basis of insurgent warfare against the United States." Mr. Fish understood at the time that this despatch was fully up to Sumner's positions, and wrote him, Oct. 15, 1869, that "the despatch is a calm, full review of our entire case, making no demand, no valuation of damages, but I believe covering all the ground and all the points that have been made on our side. I hope that it will meet your views; I think you will like it." Sumner wrote in 1871 that it did meet his views, particularly "where it arraigned so strongly that fatal concession of belligerent rights on the ocean, which will always be the first stage of evidence."

President Grant in his message of December, 1869, brought forward the national claims, enumerating increased rates of insurance, diminution of exports and imports, decrease and transfer of our commercial marine, the prolongation of the war and the increased cost, both in treasure and lives, of its suppression; and he emphasized in that connection the inadequacy of the Johnson-Clarendon convention, repeating the senator's objections. Placed in parallel lines, the passages from the President's message and the senator's speech would seem to have come from the same hand. The American members of the Joint High Commission,—Fish, Schenck, E. R. Hoar, Nelson, and Williams,—in their protocol of March 8, 1871, repeated these national claims, following closely the President's enumeration, adding the cost of pursuing the cruisers, and including the losses "in the prolongation of the war and in the addition of a large sum to the cost of the war and the suppression of the rebellion."

The American "Case,"[1] prepared by Davis under Fish's direction, and approved by President Grant,[2] enumerated these na-

[1] The "Case" as a whole lacks the legal spirit; its style is highly wrought, not to say sensational. Its statement of the national claims is peculiarly Davis's, as he did not submit it, as he did the other parts of the "Case," to publicists for revision. Davis to Fish, Sept. 21, 1872.

[2] J. Russell Young ("Around the World with General Grant," vol. ii. pp. 279, 280) reports General Grant as stating that he consented, against his belief, to the inclusion of

tional claims under four heads, — (1) National expenditures in the pursuit of cruisers; (2) Transfer of the American commercial marine to the British flag; (3) Enhanced payments of insurance; and (4) "The prolongation of the war, and the addition of a large sum to the cost of the war and the suppression of the rebellion." It undertook computations under some of these heads; and, without naming a sum but reciting military events, put on England the responsibility of the war after July 4, 1863 (the day of the battle of Gettysburg), leaving to the tribunal "to determine whether Great Britain ought not in equity to reimburse to the United States the expenses thereby entailed upon them," with interest at seven per cent from July 1, 1863. Lord Granville[1] thought this "an incredible demand," involving a "magnitude of damages" which might be "enormous;" and undertaking to compute such a claim from official tables published by our government, found it to amount, without interest, to more than four thousand five hundred millions of dollars![2] Davis afterwards charged Sumner with putting forth doctrines and figures which "would have shut the door against future negotiation;" but it was left for him and Mr. Fish to mount far higher in their basis of calculation. It was their "Case," not any speech from a senator, which came near breaking up the arbitration at Geneva and a peaceful settlement of the controversy.

Our counsel at Geneva in their printed argument maintained with fulness and earnestness and reiteration these national claims, classifying them as in the "Case," tracing their history

the indirect claims in the American "Case," — doing so at Mr. Fish's request, who thought it necessary to consider Mr. Sumner, then at the head of the committee on foreign relations. If General Grant talked, as he is reported, he committed an anachronism, as the senator ceased to be a member of that committee March 10. 1871, two months even before the treaty was made. The "Case" was handed to the secretary November 13, eight months after Sumner ceased to be chairman of the foreign relations committee. The next day Mr. Fish wrote to Davis, "The President approves of your presentation of the Case." It was not presented to the arbitrators till December 15. The respective dates of the termination of Sumner's connection with the committee and of the preparation and filing of the "Case" make it clear that General Grant did not include the indirect claims in the "Case" for the reason he is reported to have given. The New York "Tribune," May 23, 1880, in commenting on Young's narrative, wrote that the pressing of claims by the President which he did not believe in would be "deceiving both the country and England," and that "it seems impossible that the Ex-President should be unconscious of the immorality and indecency of such a course."

[1] Letter to Schenck, March 30, 1872.

[2] Or more than half of $9,095,000,000. "Memorandum" to Granville's letter to Schenck.

in the diplomatic correspondence, and treating them as based on direct injuries by one government to another, as capable of estimation and pecuniary indemnity, and entitling the injured one to a substantial compensation; and they laid altogether greater stress upon them than Sumner did in his speech. They rebuked with spirit and emphasis Lord Granville's assumption that they had been put forth for the first time in that speech.

When the American "Case" became known, the English people were again thrown into a frenzy by the London press. There was a clamor for a withdrawal from the arbitration in view of the demand of the American "Case." Lord Granville sought by correspondence to obtain the exclusion of the national claims from consideration by the tribunal, contending that they were not within the terms of the submission. A voluminous correspondence ensued between Granville and our minister, Schenck, and between Schenck and Fish. Mr. Fish's two letters of February 27 and April 16, 1872, maintained, on a full review of the controversy, that the national claims had been insisted upon from the beginning, — that they were included in the treaty of Washington, — and declined to withdraw them, leaving the arbitrators to make such a disposition of them as they should think just. He said, Feb. 27, 1872: "What are called the indirect losses and claims are not now put forward for the first time. For years they have been prominently and historically part of the 'Alabama claims.'" Referring to passages which, as he said, it would be superfluous to quote, but indicating the state papers which contained them, he said: "Incidental or consequential damages were often mentioned as included in the accountability." Again, April 16, 1872: "At no time during the occurrence of the events which gave rise to the differences between the two governments did the United States fail to present ample and frequent notice of the nature of the indirect injuries, or of their inclusion in the accountability of Great Britain." He recalled that in his instructions to Motley, both in May and in September, 1869, he "presented the vast national injuries so that Lord Clarendon in his reply manifested no difficulty in discerning that the United States did expect and would demand the consideration of national, indirect, or consequential losses." In setting forth the history of the national claims he referred to the successive representatives of the government, making no mention of Sumner, to whose speech Lord

Clarendon had called attention, — showing that in his judgment he did not then consider the senator to have any particular responsibility for them. The stubborn insistence on the inclusion of the national claims on the one side and on their exclusion on the other was terminated, as already suggested, by the voluntary action of the tribunal. As it was Davis's "Case" — his portentous exhibition of the national injuries — which brought that tribunal almost to the point of premature dissolution, he was not the accuser qualified to call the senator or any other advocate of the national claims into judgment.

This digression into diplomatic history became necessary on account of a controversy which subsequently arose. Sumner's position as to the proclamation of belligerency and the national claims, whether well founded or not, was, as the above citations show, the position of the United States from 1861 to 1872, maintained by Seward, Adams, Fish, Schenck, Grant, the American members of the Joint High Commission, the eminent counsel at Geneva, — Cushing, Evarts, and Waite, — and the author of the "Case," J. C. B. Davis.

Whether the national claims ought on a final view to have been the subject of pecuniary indemnity, or whether they deserved recognition by a cession of territory, the adoption of new and better rules of international law for the future, or a simple expression of regret, was settled by the decision at Geneva; but it was not unpatriotic or unstatesmanlike to urge them in the forum of nations and before a tribunal of arbitration. They may have added strength to strictly legal grounds, and brought the government and people we were dealing with to realize the full import of our cause. It does not detract from the character or wisdom of statesmen that they have pushed the pretensions of their country when founded, as they believed, on morals and equity, beyond the impartial judgment of arbitrators, — beyond what in the end they themselves accepted as a reasonable adjustment. If a severer standard is to be applied, a list of distinguished publicists must come under condemnation.

An insurrection in Cuba was in progress when the President entered on his term, and Spain was engaged in the effort to suppress it. It had a considerable support in this country, particularly in the city of New York. Rawlins, Secretary of War, became an active partisan of the insurgents, and made every effort to embroil the country in intervention in their behalf. His complicity with them brought him under suspicion of being affected by other than public motives.[1] His close relations with the President almost gave him success. The latter was disposed to recognize Cuban belligerency, as a step to the recognition of Cuban independence; and his subsequent urgency for the acquisition of San Domingo gives reason to suppose that the acquisition of Cuba was in his mind as an ultimate result.

Sumner was sympathetic with the idea that the age of colonial empire in America had passed, and regarded the independence of the island as a final solution to which he hoped the parent country would eventually yield. He was, however, clearly of opinion that the insurgents had not established a title to recognition as belligerents. Two other considerations had influence with his mind: (1) They had not declared in favor of the abolition of slavery in the island; (2) Moral assistance to them would be a hindrance to the liberal cause in Spain, from which country the royal family had recently been expelled.[2] He thought it most important too, at this time, that the United States should not weaken its position in its controversy with Great Britain by a waiver of its complaint against the rightfulness of the queen's proclamation. He was therefore urgent with Mr. Fish that the Administration should not compromise itself by premature action on the Cuban question; and his persuasions came at the time when his influence with the secretary was greater than that of any one. He was supported by Judge Hoar and also by General Cushing, who though not an official person, carried weight with public men. Mr. Fish's pressure on the President was effective; and it would have been well for his reputation and to the advantage of the Administration if in the later case of San Domingo he had proved as sturdy in the maintenance of his convictions.

Sumner wrote to Cushing, July 10, from Boston: —

"I am obliged by your note of July 8. My desire is to act so that our example may give new force to international law and help future peace. For a republic to give this example is much. It is plain that there is nothing to justify this great concession to insurgent Cubans, unless you discard all rule and follow simply your own passions or desires. They have not reached that

[1] Badeau states that "men high in position and public estimation accepted these bonds [of the Cuban insurgents], and afterwards advocated the recognition of Cuban independence." "Grant in Peace," p. 234.

[2] Sumner's views on the Cuban question are given further, *post*, pp. 425, 426.

point of reasonable certainty for the present and future which alone can justify such a step on our part, unless we accept the hazard of war with Spain. Two things I wish for Cuba: (1) Independence, and (2) emancipation; and both are certain to come very soon. But why should we assume needless responsibilities of money or arms?"

Again, July 19: —

"The best chance for Cuba is through a kindly policy with Spain. With a thoroughly upright system we can obtain all we desire."

Judge Hoar wrote to Sumner, June 28: —

"You would make no apology for your Cuban sermon if you knew how zealous a member of the same church you were addressing. My wish and first impulse was to inclose your note to the President, but I forbore for two reasons: (1) I had not your permission to do so; and (2) I was afraid he would suspect you of plagiarism, as he must be reasonably familiar with that train of remark if he keeps up any recollection of my discourses. I shall not be back at Washington till next Monday, and I do not think that anything can happen before then; but there is need of all the steadiness that anybody can contribute."

Sumner wrote to Motley, June 29, from Boston: —

"Hoar, who is now here, tells me that at the last Cabinet meeting he went into the belligerency question, and against the concession to the Cubans. This is our present trouble."

Mr. Fish consulted Sumner as to the instructions to Motley, specially asking his help on that part relating to the concession of belligerent rights. The consultation, which took place about a month after Sumner's speech, shows that no difference existed between them as to the basis of our claims or the mode of presenting them. When the two were dining at Mr. Hooper's[1] Sumner suggested to the secretary that Motley be invited to prepare a "memoir" or sketch of his views on the questions with England, and the latter readily assented. Subsequently there was a difference of memory between them as to whether the senator was to give the invitation in the secretary's name; but this was immaterial, the main fact being that Mr. Fish sanctioned the drawing of the proposed paper. Mr. Fish wrote, more than a year later, to Sumner: —

"My recollection is not in precise accord with yours as to the suggestion to him to write a paper being authorized to be made in my name. The proposition was made by you to me that he should write or furnish a paper; to

1 Compare Boston "Journal," July 22, 1870.

which I certainly and readily assented, without however understanding that I was placing my duties on him, or doing else than assent to his doing what from the source or manner of the suggestion I supposed he was desirous of undertaking." [1]

Motley prepared the paper, and Mr. Fish after receiving it sent it to Sumner.[2] It was laid aside without adverse comment by Mr. Fish on its substance, or objection by Sumner or feeling by Motley; and it seemed to play no part in the business until it was revived the next year by controversy. Sumner thought well of it, regarding it afterwards as followed in substance by Mr. Fish's letter to Motley of Sept. 25, 1869;[3] but he and Mr. Fish had no difference as to the propriety of laying it aside.[4] The latter wrote to the senator, July 19, 1870: —

"I enclose the copy of Motley's memoir. Until Sunday last it had not been out of the drawer in which I deposited it a year ago last May or June. You may remember my comment upon it, in which you partially, if not wholly, oined."

The President's earnest interest in Cuban belligerency, and his purpose to avoid the statement of any principle adverse to its recognition, compelled Mr. Fish to exclude from his first draft of the instructions to Motley, altogether or substantially, the proclamation of belligerency as a point of our case against England. When the draft was submitted to Sumner he took strong ground against its waiver of the position on this point which our government had all along steadily held. Anxious, however, to keep the Administration from a fatal step, he submitted a sketch of a statement less distinct and positive than he wished. This, after reflection and a conference with Cushing (the two being in agreement on the question of belligerency), he recalled, withdrawing it May 17, as inadequate and doing injustice to the national cause, and wishing to keep himself free on a question which must necessarily come before Congress. He did not mean, if he could help it, that the greatest international controversy in our history — with its issue altogether in obscurity — should be

[1] Strangely enough, in the debate in the Senate, July 15, 1870, on Frelinghuysen's confirmation as minister to England, it was treated as an offence on Motley's part that he had "volunteered to write his instructions." This accusation must have come from the state department.

[2] Badeau says ("Grant in Peace," p. 199) that "this was doubtless in part drawn up by Sumner," — another fiction of that writer.

[3] Works, vol. xiv. pp. 273, 274.

[4] Badeau states that Sumner was "very indignant, and almost offensive in behavior," because the "memoir" was not adopted, — another fiction of that writer.

deflected by a band of Cuban insurgents supported by American adventurers. At heart Mr. Fish was doubtless with him, and grateful to him for help in saving him from the sacrifice of the American position on the duties of a neutral power. He saw well enough, too, that it would not be safe for the Administration at that time to make an issue before the people with the senator on the propriety of compromising our case against England by taking part in one of the periodically recurring disturbances in Cuba.

On the 16th (Sunday), Sumner, anxious to keep the Administration right, asked General Cushing — always ready with good offices — to intervene. He wrote that day to Motley, then in Boston: —

"Your instructions cannot reach you before Tuesday. I have called in C. C., who has just come from the secretary. The first draft was fatal, — very. I protested, and wrote a substitute. Last evening I dined at Fish's."

Mr. Fish was troubled, — being anxious to maintain the position of the country as Sumner stated it, and at the same time to meet the President's wishes. He wrote to Sumner on the morning of the 17th: —

MY DEAR SUMNER, — General Cushing called on me yesterday, as I understood on your suggestion, and was to have called again in the evening. I waited for him until near midnight. I had determined to ask to introduce your suggestions, almost *in totidem verbis.* I am sorry to receive your note this morning. I think that you are scarcely doing justice either to me or to the Administration. We have but one object, and differ only as to some incidents, — they may be of more importance than I suppose, or of less than you think, but can hardly be of sufficient importance to break up an effort at negotiation or to break down an Administration. I trust, therefore, you will reconsider the intimations of your letter.

Faithfully your friend,

HAMILTON FISH.

Cushing's skilful hand adjusted the difficulty. Sumner was content with the result. The instructions, while recognizing the right of a power to define its relations to the parties in a civil conflict in another country, did not admit the propriety of the concession of belligerency, and treated it as "the beginning and the animus of that course of conduct which resulted so disastrously to the United States," and as "foreshadowing future events." As the senator afterwards wrote: —

"I have here the first draft of this important passage in pencil and in my own handwriting, varying in no essential particular from that adopted. Here will be found the distinction on which I have always insisted, — that while other powers conceded belligerent rights to our rebels, it was in England only that the concession was supplemented by acts causing direct damage to the United States." [1]

He wrote to Motley the same day a letter which shows how satisfied he was with the result finally reached: —

"At last the document is finished. Caleb Cushing dined here last evening, and we discussed the points thoroughly, there being no difference between us. He had reperused my speech and examined the books, and was prepared to stand by my text as in complete conformity with the law of nations. He thought the paragraph I drew as a mode of settlement toned down the true doctrine and inadequately stated our case. I knew it was so, but I did it in order to harmonize the ideas of the Administration with our case. On reflection this morning, I wrote a note to Fish withdrawing my draft, and at the same time expressing my dissent from the draft he proposed. My purpose was to leave him to make his own statement, for which I should be in no respect responsible. Shortly after breakfast Cushing called, and went from me to the state department. After four hours he has just returned, saying that it is all settled to his satisfaction; that the clause abandoning our position on belligerency is given up, and that the rest of the paragraph is very much as I wrote it.

"Fish is going to give you a consular convention to negotiate, which has long been desired, but which England has always hesitated about, owing to the difficulty of reconciling some of the ordinary consular prerogatives with the common law.

"The President is desirous to have it known that he recognizes as a right of sovereignty the concession of belligerency, as he may wish to use it with regard to Cuba. It was the effort to state this principle that caused the embarrassment. Of course there is no doubt that a nation may do this thing precisely as it may make war; but if it does it without good reason it is an unfriendly act. Fish was also very desirous to separate England from France, and I drew a clause to meet this point. Obviously the two cases are different. Both did wrong in the concession of belligerency, but it was only in England that the concession was followed by blockade-runners and pirate ships. In France there was *damnum absque injuria;* in England, *damnum cum injuria.* And yet the English are busy over this alleged inconsistency of my speech in arraigning England and not arraigning France. But (1) There was no French treaty under discussion; and (2) There were no damages from France. All this is plain enough. I feel very grateful to Cushing, who has brought his authority to bear on Fish. I say to you for your encouragement that he agrees with me on all the points. To my mind, his opinion is the best we can have."

[1] Works, vol. xiv. p. 272. It is possible that Sumner made two drafts for Mr. Fish, — the first expressing his own views, and the second, which he withdrew, being a less positive statement, made with a view to conform to the President's wishes. As Cushing, who settled the instructions to suit Sumner, thought that one draft went too far in the way of toning down our case, it is probably the senator's first draft (if there were two) which was adopted substantially in the end.

J. C. B. Davis misapplies Sumner's protest, which was against Fish's first draft of the instructions, and not against the document as finally settled under Cushing's lead. The senator continued his friendly intercourse with the President while he remained in Washington, and during the summer his relations with the secretary were cordial, intimate, and confidential. All the trustworthy evidence shows that the three were at the time in entire agreement on the English question.

Mr. Fish, as well as others who were anxious for a settlement of the claims, was disturbed by the clamor in England which followed Sumner's speech, and which, it was feared, might interfere with the negotiation.[1] Correspondents started the rumor that there were differences between Fish and the senator,[2] and the latter wrote to Cushing, June 16: —

"I saw Fish last evening, and found him as always with me most friendly. We spoke of the attempt to make it appear that there were differences between us; and I ventured to remark that, whatever might be the effect of such efforts on my position, I feared more the influence on our case in England and the position of our legation. There should be union at home. He agreed, and, I think, would be glad to make a statement on the point. I write this for your information, as I am about to leave for Boston."

Three days after this letter, a special despatch, dictated by Mr. Fish, appeared in a leading newspaper of New York,[3] which, referring to the report of differences between the senator and the President and secretary, growing out of the instructions to Motley, said: —

"Nothing could possibly be further from the truth than this. Mr. Sumner, as chairman of the Senate committee on foreign relations, was consulted constantly during the preparation of these instructions; and when they were completed he not only expressed his entire approval of the course Mr. Motley was instructed to pursue, but signified that the policy thus marked out was as firm and vigorous as our foreign relations would now justify. In fact, at no time has Mr. Sumner been in closer accord or in more direct sympathy with the policy of President Grant than at present, and rumors of disagreement are entirely unfounded."

The despatch then states that Motley's instructions differed from Sumner's views only as to the question of "the amount of

1 The New York "Times," which approved both the substance and tone of the speech, April 16, changed its position after the report of its reception in England was received, May 13, 18, 19, 22, 23, 26; June 12, 18.

2 New York Times, June 14.

3 Evening Post, June 19.

damages," and added that "both President Grant and Secretary Fish signified their approval of Mr. Sumner's speech as an expression of our grievances against Great Britain for her unfriendly course towards us." Cushing wrote to Sumner, June 26: —

"Mr. Fish dictated to a correspondent of the 'Evening Post' the article which you doubtless read in that journal on the 19th, and which was copied or commented on by many other journals. He also sent for Mr. Gobright,[1] and stated to him in more general but in explicit terms the accordance of the Administration with yourself in opinion and purpose on the points of controversy with England. You will have perceived that all newspaper discussion of this question has now ceased in consequence apparently of these representations on the part of the United States. The reservation on the point of belligerency, or qualification rather, contained in the article in the 'Evening Post,' is, I conjecture, attributable to the desire of the President to feel uncommitted on this subject in the matter of Cuba, — as to which, however, I trust there will be no premature or indiscreet action calculated to be inconvenient to the United States or unjust to Spain." [2]

Sumner wrote to Cushing, June 28, from Boston: —

"The statement to which you refer has perhaps tranquillized the press; but I question if it does not contain expressions which weaken our case at home and abroad. I would never have said that the policy 'was as firm and vigorous as our foreign relations would now justify.' Our policy should always be firm and vigorous. These qualities are sometimes silent, as we are disposed to be now. Nor do I understand that there should be any question as to amount. If we would succeed with England, we must show confidence in our case. *Crede ut possis et potes.*"

Mr. Fish is thus the author of a statement, dictated for the "Evening Post," that Sumner entirely approved the instructions to Motley; and Sumner impliedly sanctions that statement by not taking exception to it, although questioning certain other expressions of the newspaper despatch.

Contrary to representations made at a later date by Mr. Fish, or on his behalf, Motley left for Europe with the unimpaired confidence of the President and the secretary. Nothing in the "Memoir," which was set up as an afterthought, had weakened him.[3] That confidence continued. Davis's statement that on receiving, June 23, Motley's report of his first interview with Lord Clarendon, "the President's first impulse on reading the

1 Agent of the Associated Press.

2 The general mistook the *caveat*, which was as stated above.

3 New York "Herald," Jan. 14, 1878. Badeau's "Grant in Peace," p. 202.

despatch was to recall him" on account of departure from his instructions, is disproved by the President's letter to Badeau, July 14, three weeks after the report was received, in which he writes: [1] —

"So far I have been pleased with Mr. Motley's utterances abroad, and I have no doubt he will prove the very best man that could have been selected for the English mission. It is not half so important that the 'Alabama' claims be settled as it is that when settled it should be on terms creditable to this nation. I do not see that any harm is to arise from the matter standing in an unsettled state."

This letter corresponds strictly with Sumner's contemporaneous statement of the President's expressions to him, June 7. Motley's appointment was still the President's, expressive of his own choice, and not of "the influence and urgency" of another. Sumner wrote Motley, June 8: —

"Yesterday I saw the President alone for more than an hour. He has reconsidered the propriety of allowing Mr. Curtin to make a pronunciamento against England next Saturday, and I think him right. It would hardly be decent. He volunteered to say very kind things of you, especially that he is satisfied that you are the best man for England now."

Again, June 11: —

"The President left for West Point day before yesterday. I was with him for an hour before he left, during which we discussed belligerency, and England and Cuba. He asked how it would do to issue a proclamation with regard to Cuba identical with that issued by Spain with regard to us. I advised against it. He is very confident that the Cubans will succeed. On the same day I had a call from two Cubans, — one of whom was Aldama, the richest man of the island and an old friend of mine, — who had come to solicit the concession of belligerency, saying that with it success was certain, and that without it the island would become a desert. I gave them no encouragement.

"In the evening I had a prolonged talk with Fish, whom Thornton had visited that day. Fish said to him that our claims were too large to be settled pecuniarily, and sounded him about Canada, to which he replied that England did not wish to keep Canada, but could not part with it without the consent of the population. Fish desired to know of me how to state the amount of claims

1 "Grant in Peace," p. 468. Motley, on arriving at Liverpool, made brief replies to deputations from two chambers of commerce, in which he confined himself to platitudes about the duty of peace between two kindred nations. These were altogether harmless, and seemed well adapted to calm the disturbed English mind. It would have been thought churlish in him to have said less. But the President, reading the report by cable, was not, it has been stated, at first pleased that he had made the replies, thinking, doubtless, that after Reverdy Johnson's too much speaking, silence was better than any words, however well chosen. His dissatisfaction, whatever it was, was short-lived, for he told the senator within a week that he considered Motley the best man for the mission.

to England, to which I replied that I should make no 'claim' or 'demand' for the present, nor was I disposed to speak of 'claim' or 'demand.'"

Again, June 15: —

"I had at dinner here last evening the attorney-general (E. R. Hoar), Cushing, and Mr. Hunter, etc. There was but one opinion among them expressed, — most kindly to you. I mention this now for your information, and as a guide in the future. . . . All feel that your position is as historic as any described by your pen. England must listen, and at last yield. I do not despair seeing the debate end — (1) In the withdrawal of England from this hemisphere; (2) In remodelling maritime international law. Such a consummation would place our republic at the head of the civilized world."

Again, June 20: —

"The late statements from Washington that there was no difference between Fish and myself have had a tranquillizing effect. With more experience at Washington, our front would have been more perfect.

"P. S. Paul Forbes arrived here three days ago directly from Madrid, with overtures from Prim about Cuba. The language of the latter was, 'When a family is in distress, it sells its jewels.' The idea seemed to be that the United States should mediate between Spain and the insurgents, the latter paying for their independence. The President is disposed to undertake the mediation if any representative of the insurgents can give assurances that the idea can be carried through. The President told me that he was entirely satisfied that England made the concession of belligerency 'to injure us.'"

Sumner wrote to Bemis, July 7: —

"The President, Secretary of State, minister to England, and chairman of Senate committee, are all of one mind;[1] and you will see that Reverdy Johnson in his despatch vindicating his treaty has taken our ground on belligerency."

The general discussion of the question of the "Alabama" claims was withdrawn from Motley, to be resumed only in Washington. Mr. Fish gave as the reason of the withdrawal, at the time of Sumner's visit to him in the summer, that the Senate was accessible for advice at Washington; and in a letter, Oct. 9, 1869, "*because* [the italics being Mr. Fish's] we think that when reversed it can be carried on here with a better prospect of settlement than where the late attempt at a convention resulted so disastrously." Mr. Fish, however, in his letter to Mr. Moran, Dec. 30, 1870, gave a different and inconsistent reason for the withdrawal, putting it then on the ground of the minister's disobedience to instructions, — manifestly an afterthought.

[1] Sumner gave the same assurance to Longfellow, then in Europe, by letter, July 8.

It is not proposed in this narrative to review the controversy between Fish and Motley as to the latter's departure from or conformity to his instructions. That duty properly belongs to his biographer and his representatives.[1] It will only be referred to incidentally in these pages when it comes into connection with Sumner's relations to the Administration. He wrote to Cushing, July 19: —

"There is a lull in our relations with England, which, I suppose, will continue until broken by Congress. *Mihi multum cogitanti*, it seems best that our case, in length and breadth, with all details, should be stated to England without any demand of any kind.[2] England must know our grievances before any demand can be presented. When this is comprehended, a settlement will be easy."

Sumner came home from Washington shortly after the middle of June, in time to follow his old friend, Richard Fletcher, to his grave at Mt. Auburn. During the recess of Congress, he was several times with the Saturday Club. At the end of August he was glad to welcome Longfellow home from Europe. Late in the autumn Mr. Winthrop invited him to meet at his house Père Hyacinthe, but he was unable to accept. In August he was the guest of Mr. and Mrs. J. V. L. Pruyn, at Albany,[3] and there dined with Mrs. Pruyn's father, Judge Amasa Parker. Thence he went to Henry Winthrop Sargent's, at Fishkill-on-the-Hudson, where he amused himself with studying his classmate's experiments in horticulture. Next he visited Mr. Fish, who wrote from Glenclyffe, on the Hudson River, August 3: "We shall be very glad to see you; you will always find a welcome under my roof. Let me know by what train you are coming. The President and family will be with us on Thursday, to remain a few days. . . . I telegraph to Boston, and send this to Albany."

Sumner in his visit to Mr. Fish in August advised him to renew the discussion with the British government by a fresh and vigorous statement of our case. He thought the time favorable, as there was a lull in the demonstrations of English feeling; and he feared, after some hints from General Butler, that

1 Dr. O. W. Holmes treats the controversy in his "Memoir of Motley," pp. 155–190. John Jay reviews it in his "Motley's Appeal to History" ("International Review," November, 1877, pp. 838–854). Sumner touches certain points concerning it in his statement, March, 1871; Works, vol. xiv. pp. 251–276. New York "Tribune," April 6, 1874.

2 This was done by Sumner's advice in the letter of Fish to Motley, Sept. 25, 1869.

3 Sumner's acquaintance with Mr. Pruyn began when the latter (a Democrat) was a member of the House of Representatives.

unless something were done Congress might take action unfavorable to a peaceful settlement. Mr. Fish invited Sumner to prepare the paper, but the latter declined, thinking that it should be drawn by another, and being himself already overworked, recommended General Cushing in his place. Mr. Fish adopted his view, and the result was the despatch to Mr. Motley, Sept. 25, 1869, — a remarkably able and forcible statement, drawn by Cushing, of which the leading points have already been given. The waning fortunes of the Cuban insurgents and the death of Rawlins,[1] Secretary of War, September 9, removed or greatly diminished the obstruction to a statement of our complaint as to the English proclamation of belligerency. This despatch was said by Lord Clarendon to be "Mr. Sumner's speech over again," and by another Englishman to have "out-Sumnered Sumner." Mr. Fish, as already seen, anticipated Sumner's full approval, and he received it. Judge Hoar also wrote Sumner the day before it was signed, probably after it had been read in the Cabinet: "I think matters with England are going to your mind, and that your speech and our acts will not trouble each other." Sumner wrote to Motley, August 17:

"I talked over our question with Fish, and advised him strongly to present our case before the meeting of Congress, in length and breadth, with all its aggravations, so as to show our grievance; and at the same time to say that this was done to enable the British government to understand the feelings of our people; that we should rest without any demand of any kind, but that the British government should be invited to take it into candid consideration, to prepare the way for some equitable adjustment with a view to peace and reconciliation. I insisted that something of this nature must be done before the meeting of Congress, or there would be dissatisfaction. I think that I made an impression upon him, for he invited me to prepare such a paper. This I declined, saying that I was too much occupied otherwise, and besides I had

[1] Rawlins's successor, W. W. Belknap, proved to be a corrupt official. Within about a year after he took office he sold a post-tradership, and continued for nearly six years (1870–1876) to receive large payments on account of the transaction. His malfeasance being discovered, the House of Representatives unanimously voted articles of impeachment against him. He anticipated this action, as soon as he saw that it was contemplated, by an instant resignation, asking, with a view to his defence, for an immediate acceptance, which the President at once gave. This resignation and acceptance were the basis of his plea to the jurisdiction set up by his counsel, M. H. Carpenter, former senator, which contended that the proceeding could not be maintained against a person not holding office at the time it was instituted. Though a majority of the senators voted for conviction, a number sufficient to prevent the necessary two-thirds vote (most of them supporters of the Administration) justified their refusal to join with the majority, on the ground of want of jurisdiction. The most distinguished of the managers, George F. Hoar, closed his argument against Belknap's plea with a passage descriptive of the official degeneracy of the period, which has become famous.

made my statement. . . . There was a room kept for me at Fish's while the President was there, but I did not think it best to be there. I arrived immediately afterwards. Fish was kind and confidential. I think he is weary of official life. He did not intend to remain after the meeting of Congress, but his purpose now is to stay for a year. I am pained at the attacks which I fear he must encounter. A vigorous presentment of our case will take from critics one of their weapons. . . . Fish thought that any negotiation on the claims should be at Washington, where the Senate can be consulted, as nothing can be done without the consent of that body. He had talked with John Rose of Canada, who had sounded him about sending out the Duke of Argyll. The duke must not come unless to be successful. The case must not be embittered by another rejection."

Sumner delivered an address, September 22, before the Republican State convention on national affairs at home and abroad, in which he maintained the sacredness of the public debt, then assailed by various schemes of repudiation, and treated our relations with Spain growing out of the Cuban insurrection, and our relations with England growing out of our Civil War.[1] In connection with the last subject he replied to some of the points which had been made by English critics, and restated his views of the circumstances which justify a recognition of belligerency in a conflict between an established government and revolted sections or bodies. The most interesting passage of the speech related to Canada, — the cession of which had been suggested as a compensation for our claims.[2] While regarding the future union of Canada with the United States as an appointed destiny, it must come, such was his thought, by a peaceful process, with the consent of her people. He closed with a description of the republic as it was to be with this continental extension. The speech found great favor, and was widely read, as published and commended in leading journals outside the State. It was approved for its decisive support of the public credit, its temperate discussion of foreign relations, and its lifting the public mind above local questions, — as prohibition, then a disturbing force in political calculations. Ex-Governor John H. Clifford, whose habit of mind was conservative, wrote with complete approval of its magnificent and unanswerable defence of the public credit,

1 Works, vol. xiii. pp. 98–130.

2 New York "Herald," Feb. 13, 1869; New York "Tribune," Feb. 22 and April 7. Joseph Medill, of the Chicago "Tribune," in a letter to Sumner, Dec. 2, 1868, urged that the acquisition was the only adequate solution, — suggesting also the payment of one or two hundred millions of dollars to Great Britain, in order to save the point of pride on her part.

the clear and decisive direction it gave to the public conscience, and to the duty of the Administration in respect to foreign relations, especially on the Cuban question.[1] Similar testimonies came from Mr. Hooper, R. H. Dana, Jr., General Cushing, E. R. Hoar, E. G. Spaulding, Ira Harris, E. B. Washburne (from Paris), and A. G. Curtin (from St. Petersburg). Mr. Fish was pleased with the speech, particularly with its treatment of the Cuban question. He wrote, October 9, to the senator: "Plumb writes from Havana that your speech seemed so timely and admirable, and in accord with what he had heard of views of the department, that he brought it officially to the attention of the authorities."

The British Cabinet was uneasy under the suspension of negotiations, and through Sir Edward Thornton sounded our government as to what terms of settlement would be satisfactory to it. The following letter, given in full, shows the diplomatic condition, and also the intimate relations between the secretary and the senator, and the confidence the former continued to repose in the latter:[2] —

WASHINGTON, Nov. 6, 1869.

MY DEAR SUMNER, — On two or three occasions within the last few months Mr. Thornton has, in conversation, casually expressed the wish that I would intimate to him the views of this government as to the basis on which the "Alabama" claims may be settled. The day before yesterday he mentioned that a private letter from Lord Clarendon informed him of Mr. Motley having read a despatch from this department, of which a copy was also furnished, and which he should submit to the British Cabinet; he professed to feel regret on account of the tone of the paper. I told him that it was intended to be a calm presentation of our views of the grievances we had sustained; that we thought they had not allowed themselves to appreciate the depth and the earnestness of our feelings; and that until they would or could fully appreciate these, I feared that we could not arrive at an agreement; that we make no claim or demand in the paper referred to, but do endeavor strongly and forcibly to present our case, — not with a view or expectation to reopen a discussion on these points, but for their calm consideration. He asked whether I wished an answer to it. I replied, "No, I certainly do not wish one; but of course if the British government think one necessary, it is for them to decide. My own judgment would be that it were better not to reply; that we were anxious to have the questions settled, and the case disposed of." He said his government were also anxious for a settlement; but that having once accepted all

[1] The New York "Nation," usually critical in its treatment of Sumner, in its leader, Sept. 30, 1869, approved the speech, with emphasis on the part relating to Cuba. The Boston "Advertiser," September 23, was equally emphatic in its approval.

[2] The whole tone of the letter discredits Davis's account of differences between Mr. Fish and Sumner in April and May preceding.

that this government had asked, and the treaty being "somewhat contumeliously" rejected, they were under difficulties as to a renewal of negotiations. We agreed that it would be very unwise to attempt any new negotiation, unless with reasonable assurance of an agreement that would be accepted by both governments; and he asked me with much earnestness to give him an intimation of what would be accepted by our government. I answered somewhat vaguely; but he evidently wished (and as I thought had been instructed) to obtain something more definite, — which I was not willing to give until I could have the opportunity of consulting with you to know what your committee and the Senate will agree to. When will you be here? Will you either note what you think will be sufficient to meet the views of the Senate and of the country, or will you formulate such proposition? Let me hear from you as soon as you can, and I should like to confer with you at the earliest convenient time.

Faithfully yours, HAMILTON FISH.

When the vacation of 1869 ended, Sumner was in full accord with the Administration on all questions. The state department, in its original and later instructions to our minister to England, had met fully his views as given in his speech in April.[1] His relations with the President were those of confidence and cordiality. There was no one in public life on whose counsels the Secretary of State then rested so securely as on those of the senator from Massachusetts.

Sumner's uppermost thought at this time, so far as domestic affairs were concerned, was to establish absolute political and civil equality through the land. As the sentiment or prejudice of race stood in the way, he prepared an elaborate discourse on "Caste,"[2] which he delivered as a lecture before lyceums during the autumn, — first in Boston, October 21, and afterwards in other places in Massachusetts, as also in Maine, Vermont, Rhode Island, New Jersey, New York, Delaware, and Pennsylvania, and finally in the cities of Brooklyn and New York. Its preparation seemed like a full six months' work. It abounded in historical and ethnological learning; it pleaded for the essential unity of the race, and most of all for the full recognition of the African as man and citizen. He sought not only the political enfranchisement of the colored people, but the opening to them of all the opportunities of civilization. It was an effort quite

[1] This statement, which is justified by the correspondence given in this chapter, is supported by a letter from Washington in the New York "Herald," Dec. 29, 1869, — which shows also that Sumner was satisfied with the instructions to Motley.

[2] Works, vol. xiii. pp. 131–183.

characteristic of its author, but not altogether welcome with audiences that had expected entertainment on some literary theme.

Sumner longed to have emancipation in the United States followed by the extinction of slavery everywhere. He wrote, September 8, to Joseph Cooper, Walthamston, England, concerning slavery in Brazil: —

"I send you the letter of Senator Nabuco, of Brazil, on emancipation, forwarded to me by the Brazilian legation, at the request of the senator. In acknowledging it, I felt it my duty to say that the senator himself did not go far enough; that the longer continuance of slavery is inconsistent with the civilization of the age, besides being essentially wrong, and that it ought to be terminated at once. Of this I have no doubt. Slavery will end very soon in Cuba; it cannot remain much longer in Brazil. The earth will be fairer when this terrible blot is erased."

The senator considered a year later the propriety of a resolution of Congress suspending diplomatic intercourse with nations maintaining slavery. He thought the example of the United States should be brought to bear for the promotion of that great end. Lieber, whom he consulted, did not second his thought, and he did not carry it out.

## CHAPTER LV.

FESSENDEN'S DEATH. — THE PUBLIC DEBT. — REDUCTION OF POSTAGE. — MRS. LINCOLN'S PENSION. — END OF RECONSTRUCTION. — RACE DISCRIMINATIONS IN NATURALIZATION. — THE CHINESE. — THE SENATOR'S RECORD. — THE CUBAN CIVIL WAR. — ANNEXATION OF SAN DOMINGO. — THE TREATIES. — THE USE OF THE NAVY. — INTERVIEW WITH THE PRESIDENT. — OPPOSITION TO THE ANNEXATION; ITS DEFEAT. — MR. FISH. — REMOVAL OF MOTLEY. — LECTURE ON FRANCO-PRUSSIAN WAR. — 1869-1870.

THE chair of Fessenden was vacant when the Senate convened, Dec. 6, 1869, he having died September 8. Sumner paid a tribute to his memory[1] which drew grateful letters from the friends and admirers of the deceased senator, — among whom were James S. Pike, the journalist, Mr. Clifford, former governor, and Mr. Rockwell, late senator. The time was not far ahead when Sumner was to be in need of the Maine senator's courage and sense of honor. Whittier wrote, March 8: —

> "I was especially delighted with thy remarks on the death of Senator Fessenden. Viewed in connection with the circumstances, I know of nothing finer, truer, and more magnanimous. It is such things that bring thee nearer to the hearts of the people."

Carl Schurz, who had taken his seat in March, 1869, was, at Sumner's instance, put in Fessenden's place on the committee on foreign relations, the other members being Cameron, Harlan, Morton, Patterson, and Casserly. Sumner was also a member of two other committees, — on the District of Columbia, and on the revision of the laws. The session, which lasted till the middle of July, 1870, was, with him, like all his sessions since 1861, a laborious one, during which he dealt with a great variety of subjects, both in running debates and elaborate speeches.[2]

1 Dec. 14, 1869, Works, vol. xiii. pp. 189-194.

2 Among the subjects to which he gave attention in debate were the following: Telegraphic communication between the United States and foreign countries by ocean cables, Dec. 17 and 21, 1869 (Congressional Globe, pp. 198, 199, 269, 273), — recurring again to this subject at the next session, Jan. 11, 13, 24. Feb. 14, and March 13, 1871 (Globe, pp. 424, 450, 451, 477, 478, 689, 1217, 1944), and taking part, March 17, 1869 (Globe, p. 103), in a

Sumner's facility in dealing with financial questions increased with the thought and research he applied to them, as well for current debates as for prepared efforts. He had come to them late, and he developed unexpected power in treating them. Sherman said of him in 1874, that he had of late years carefully studied these questions, and had contributed to their solution.[1] He continued his active interest in the treatment of the public debt and currency, and in the working out of a scheme for the restoration of specie payments. He was in favor of reducing taxation; and in that view was disposed to extend the payment of the national debt over a considerable period, when the larger resources of the future would be available, — differing in this respect from the Secretary of the Treasury, Mr. Boutwell.[2] He was especially earnest in opposing the continuance of the income-tax.[3] As a means for the restoration of specie payments, he proposed by bill and advocated in debate the substitution of national bank-notes for the legal-tender United States notes, known as "greenbacks."[4] He lost no opportunity to re-

debate concerning a particular cable company; the schedules and methods for taking the census, Feb. 7 and 8, 1870 (Globe, pp. 1083, 1103, 1108); the apportionment of members of the House, the number of whom he thought should be limited to two hundred, June 13 (Globe, p. 4392), — treating this subject again Jan. 29, 1872 (Works, vol. xv. pp. 1-4), *ante*, iii. 37; the transportation, in bond, of imported goods to inland cities, July 5, 1870 (Globe, p. 5218); the defence of General Fremont, whose connection with a railway was a subject of controversy, June 23 (Globe, pp. 4774); the right of the United States to the free use of patented inventions in the public service, April 27 and June 24 (Globe, pp. 3026, 3027, 4827); a new building for the state department, May 10 (Globe, p. 3339); the needs of that department and of foreign missions and consulates, May 6, June 14, 21 (Globe, pp. 3285, 3288, 4419, 4659, 4660); salaries in the treasury department, May 6, 1870 (Globe, p. 3287); the character and services of General Nathaniel Greene, to whom he paid a tribute on the presentation of his statue to be placed in the Capitol, Jan. 20, 1870 (Works, vol. xiii. pp. 299-302); the admission of Mr. Revels, the first colored senator, Feb. 25, 1870 (Works, vol. xiii. pp. 336-338); the residence of a senator as affecting his eligibility, April 1, 1870 (Works, vol. xiii. pp. 341-349); the proposed exclusion of retired army officers from civil offices, which he opposed, May 12, 1870 (Works, vol. xiii. pp. 381-383); a bureau of education, and an expedition for Arctic explorations, both of which he favored, May 9, 27, 1870 (Works, vol. xiii. pp. 377-380; Ibid., pp. 384-386), — advocating the bureau again, March 13, 1872 (Globe, p. 1637); the return of the surplus of the Chinese indemnity fund remaining after payment of all just claims, for which he made an elaborate report, June 24, 1870 (Works, vol. xiii. pp. 445-470), and April 26 (Globe, p. 2977).

[1] April 27, 1874, Congressional Globe, p. 3405.

[2] Jan. 12, 1870, Works, vol. xiii. pp. 237-241; July 1, Congressional Globe, pp. 5095, 5100.

[3] April 7, 1870, Works, vol. xiii. pp. 370-374; June 22, Congressional Globe, p. 4709; July 1, Globe, p. 5100.

[4] One of his last speeches was Dec. 11, 1873 (Congressional Globe, pp. 142, 143), for his bill to substitute compound interest notes for the United States legal-tender notes. He had introduced a bill for the purpose, Dec. 4, 1871 (Globe, p. 3), with a brief statement of the effect of such a measure in restoring specie payments, which was approved by the Boston Board of Trade, Feb. 20, 1872.

buke the spirit of repudiation which was rife at the time. He opposed all devices calculated to impair the national good faith, among which were propositions to tax the interest on the national bonds by a deduction from payments or otherwise.[1] He embodied his views on financial reconstruction and specie payments in bills which he introduced at the beginning of the session,[2] and maintained them in a series of instructive speeches.[3] Except Sherman, no senator at this session contributed so much to the debate on the refunding and consolidation of the public debt. He succeeded in modifying in some points the committee's bill, but in his insistence on definite measures of resumption he was in advance of his associates.

Sumner had from his first entrance into the Senate taken a constant interest in the reduction of postage, both on foreign and domestic letters.[4] Ocean postage had been recently reduced from thirty and twenty-four cents a letter to fifteen and twelve, and the domestic rate was three cents. Sumner's desire was to reduce the foreign rate to three cents, and the domestic to one cent,—the lowest monetary unit. He put aside the idea that the postal system should be self-supporting, and treated it as a humane and civilizing agent, advocating the lowest charge which would prevent imposition and abuse. He had no sympathy with the current of opinion then running against the franking privilege (or "system," as he preferred to call it) then held by members of Congress, regarding it as an educating force, which gave freedom of communication between the people and those who were participating in the government at Washington. He took advantage of a pending bill for the abolition of the franking privilege to press amendments embodying his views, and made a speech on the whole subject of rates of postage and the principles which should govern them,[5] intervening often in the debate.[6] He also urged a reduction and simplification of rates

[1] July 1, 1870, Congressional Globe, p. 5080.

[2] Dec. 7, 1869, Works, vol. xiii. pp. 184, 185; Jan. 12, 1870, Ibid., pp. 234–236. The New York "Evening Post," in its leader (January 13), wrote approvingly of his scheme.

[3] Jan. 12, 26, Feb. 1, March 2, 10, 11, 1870, Works, vol. xiii. pp. 237–298; January 31, Congressional Globe, p. 908; March 2, Globe, p. 1634; March 3, Globe, pp. 1660, 1663, 1664; March 9, Globe, p. 1795; March 10, Globe, pp. 1839, 1841; March 11, Globe, pp. 1861, 1871.

[4] *Ante*, vol. iii. p. 274.

[5] June 10, 1870, Works, vol. xiii. pp. 387–444. The speech was reviewed and commended in the New York "Independent," June 23.

[6] June 17, 18, and 20, Congressional Globe, pp. 4554–4557, 4562–4565, 4573, 4577–4579, 4624–4626.

for carrying newspapers and other printed matter.[1] He obtained a considerable but not a sufficient vote for his proposition for a one cent, and afterwards for a two cent, rate for domestic postage.[2]

The passage of the bill, July 14, at this session, giving Mrs. Lincoln a pension of three thousand dollars, illustrated the senator's personal loyalty as well as his perseverance. There was a studied effort to defeat it by indirect and dilatory action, but overcoming obstruction was with Sumner only a question of time. She was the choice of the martyr President, and had been his loyal wife. She had gone from Washington, not to return. Sumner, though never seeing her again, remembered her kindness to himself. Perhaps he thought she might have been wiser and more reserved at times; but he knew little of, and cared nothing for, the small talk of lobbies and drawing-rooms. Above all, he believed it to be a sacred duty of the nation to care for one who bore the name of its great chief during the rebellion.

It came to the senator's knowledge in January, 1869, that Mrs. Lincoln was living in Frankfort-on-the-Main in straitened circumstances, and he at once made an effort to secure for her a pension of five thousand dollars;[3] but his motions on different days to take up the bill failed, and the one made on the last day of the session was defeated by a vote of twenty-three to twenty-seven. He introduced it at the session which immediately followed, in March, 1869, when the Senate, against his protest, referred it by a small majority to the committee on pensions. Mr. Edmunds, the chairman, who was adverse to the pension, held the bill for a year without action. Twice Sumner in open Senate inquired when a report might be expected, but without obtaining a satisfactory answer. At length, a House bill granting three thousand dollars reached the Senate, and Sumner insisted on action. Now the chairman presented an adverse report from a unanimous committee. Sumner for the last two or three months of this session kept up his pressure by successive motions for the consideration of the bill, even declining to listen to appeals for postponement on

[1] June 17 and 20, Congressional Globe, pp. 4554, 4555.

[2] He recurred to the subject Feb. 4, 1871, Congressional Globe, p. 961.

[3] The bill with a blank for the sum was introduced by Mr. Morton, and Sumner moved to fill it with the sum named.

account of the chairman's absence. All efforts to avoid a vote were found to be hopeless against such pertinacity, and the bill finally passed by eight majority. Mr. Arnold, the biographer of the President, attributes to Sumner the favorable result.[1] Mrs. Lincoln wrote to him grateful letters from Frankfort and London. In the first she expressed her satisfaction that those who most urgently pressed the pension were the men whom her husband most highly regarded and loved as if they were brothers; and she closed the second with this sentence: "Words are inadequate to express my thanks for all your goodness to me."

The condition of affairs in the Southern States still required the attention of Congress. Three of the States — Virginia, Mississippi, and Texas — had not hitherto complied with the Acts of reconstruction so as to be admitted to representation in Congress, but applications for such admission were now pending. A spirit hostile to Unionists, white and black, was still, however, dominant in large sections of the South, and the rebel spirit was organized in Ku Klux clans. The Legislature of Georgia — one of the States which had been recognized as having complied with those Acts and entitled to representation — had afterwards expelled all its colored members, while admitting to seats persons who were ineligible on account of former disloyalty under the fourteenth amendment. The first Act of this session of Congress was a thorough measure for reforming the Legislature of Georgia; and the State having complied with its terms, one of which was the ratification of the fifteenth amendment, was admitted to representation on the last day of the session. The other three States were also admitted, — with, however, "fundamental conditions" imposed, the same in each case, which prohibited changes in the State constitutions allowing exclusions from suffrage or office or school rights based on race, color, or former condition of servitude.[2] The conditions as to suffrage and office were deemed important, as the fate of the fifteenth amendment was still uncertain. That amendment, however, soon received the approval of a sufficient number of States, and was

[1] The correspondent of the New York "Tribune," June 18, 1870, wrote that the senator's efforts for the bill were indefatigable; that he had appealed to senators personally in its behalf, and had given the Senate no rest for eighteen months on the subject.

[2] These conditions went beyond the fifteenth amendment by prohibiting discriminations as to holding office. They have been thought to go further as to suffrage by securing it to "the class of citizens" already entitled to vote.

promulgated as a part of the Constitution, March 30. Two months later, Congress passed an Act providing means and penalties for enforcing it.

Sumner was in full accord with his Republican associates in promoting these final measures of reconstruction. He was emphatic in insisting on the necessity and validity of the conditions and on the duty of Congress to continue its protecting supervision over the reconstructed States, even after their formal admission to representation.[1] A few of the Republican senators (Trumbull, Stewart, and M. H. Carpenter) did not recognize the propriety of "the fundamental conditions,"[2] or the competency of Congress to impose them. At different stages of the discussion there were collisions between the three senators and Sumner.[3] Carpenter was a new senator, succeeding Doolittle of Wisconsin.[4] During the controversy Trumbull and Stewart challenged Sumner's action on the fifteenth amendment, and held him to account for his absence on the night of the passage of the Act of March, 1867, which first secured suffrage to the colored people of the reconstructed States. Sumner in reply reviewed his own record in detail, maintaining by citations and extracts from speeches his early espousal of the cause of equal suffrage and his constant loyalty to it.[5] Sherman, who regretted the waste of time in such controversies, said that the senator from Massachusetts needed no defender on this question; that he had from the very first advocated and maintained with repetition, early and late, the necessity of giving to the colored

[1] Jan. 10, 11, 12, 13, 14, 19, 21, 1870, Works, vol. xiii. pp. 204-233; Feb. 10 and 17, 1870 Ibid., pp. 331-335; April 5, Ibid., pp. 353-369; April 19, Congressional Globe, p. 2828.

[2] *Ante*, pp. 284-287, 309-311.

[3] April 18, Congressional Globe, pp. 2746-2753.

[4] Carpenter, by letter (July 29, 1868), applied to Sumner to write a letter, intended for publication, in favor of his candidacy for senator, and added the assurance: "I am aware this is asking a great favor; but if you will grant it, I pledge myself that whenever you shall say to me that I have disappointed your expectations or falsified your friendly predictions, I will resign." Sumner declined to write the letter, thinking such interference improper. Carpenter professed to be quite satisfied, but it is not unlikely that he was piqued by the refusal.

[5] Jan. 21 and Feb. 10, 1870, Works, vol. xiii. pp. 303-330; Congressional Globe, pp. 640-642; National Antislavery Standard, February 5; letter from Grace Greenwood in the New York "Tribune," January 24. In the debate, Drake of Missouri and Fowler of Tennessee disapproved the attacks made on Sumner. (February 11, Globe, p. 1216.) Forney wrote to Sumner, January 22: "I hope you will excuse me for adding the expression of my deep regret at the controversy into which you have been forced by the discourteous conduct of Mr. Trumbull." The correspondent of the New York "Times," February 11, wrote of the controversy: "With all his faults there is hardly a better-natured man in the Senate than Mr. Sumner."

people of the Southern States the right to vote as the basis of reconstruction, and was justified in stating that he was the first to propose it. He added: "In my judgment it would be just as well for George Washington to defend himself against the charge of disloyalty to the American colonies, for whom he was fighting, as for the honorable senator to defend his record on this question." [1]

Sumner spoke briefly on the Georgia bill, maintaining the necessity and validity of the fundamental conditions as justified by necessity, essential equity, and the "guaranty" provision of the Constitution, and protesting against the technicalities and "State-rights" assumptions set up against them. Carpenter made an elaborate reply to Sumner, Morton, and Edmunds. He thought Sumner a "vaulting logician," and asked him "to descend from his tripod, to emerge from his oracular and profane mysteries, and meet the precise questions." [2] He chafed under the charge made by Morton and Yates in the earlier debate on Mississippi as well as now by Sumner, that he was maintaining "State rights" in the Calhoun sense.[3] He was very impatient with Sumner's habit of referring to the Declaration of Independence as a source of power; and after the manner of Rufus Choate, whose pupil he had been, he spoke of "the generalities of that revolutionary pronunciamento." [4] Sumner replied a few days later,[5] and a running debate [6] followed, in which he maintained that the Declaration, though not a grant of power to Congress, was a commanding guide in interpreting the Constitution. Carpenter's ill-will is of little account in estimating the position of a public man whom he disliked; but it must be said that Sumner's way of dismissing reasonable points of law by an appeal to the supremacy of human rights grated on the ears of associates whose training was chiefly that of the bar. Nor was it fair in him to treat the maintenance of constitutional limitations on the powers of Congress as a revival of the odious pretensions of nullifiers and secessionists.

1 February 10, Congressional Globe, p. 1181; *ante*, p. 318.

2 April 5. Congressional Globe, pp. 2425, 2426.

3 Feb. 14, 1870. Congressional Globe, pp. 1257, 1258.

4 April 5, 1870; Congressional Globe, p. 2425. Carpenter was not satisfied with his own phrase, and in a later contention with Sumner withdrew it, saying it was an unfortunate expression, and "uttered in the heat of an *extempore* debate" (Feb. 1, 1872, Globe, p. 760).

5 April 18. Congressional Globe, pp. 2747-2749.

6 April 18. Congressional Globe, pp. 2749-2753.

By such a course he weakened his authority in the treatment of these questions.

When a bill to amend the naturalization laws with a view to prevent frauds in elections was pending, Sumner moved as an amendment a section striking out the word "white" from those laws wherever it occurred, so as to remove all distinctions of race or color in admitting to naturalization.[1] The proposition had been embodied in a bill introduced by him and reported by the judiciary committee. Some senators who favored it thought it untimely, as imperilling a measure immediately needed to prevent frauds, while those from the Pacific coast saw in it the introduction of the Chinese to citizenship. Sumner, unlike his colleague Wilson, was not daunted by fears of an Oriental invasion; and again (it was the Fourth of July) he stood on the Declaration of Independence, fortifying himself also with Scripture and Lincoln's argument against Douglas.[2] His amendment was lost when he moved it at one stage, and was carried when he moved it at another; but it was finally rejected by the combined votes of the Democratic senators, senators from the Pacific coast, and Republican senators who thought it untimely; an amendment, however, admitting aliens of African nativity or descent was carried, and became a part of the Act as passed. The differences between Trumbull and Sumner on "fundamental conditions" did not prevent their hearty co-operation on this question. A few days later, Sumner, when a bill to prohibit contracts for servile labor was pending, renewed his motion for the exclusion of the word "white" from the naturalization laws, again standing on the Declaration of Independence and protesting against the imposition of disabilities on Chinese emigrants to this country;[3] but his proposition did not come to a vote. He said in the debate: —

"We send missionaries to the distant heathen, and there are annual contributions for that purpose, — wise contributions; but now the heathen come to us. Will you drive them back? Rather do them all the good you can, — convert them here on our own soil; but you cannot do this by any lesson of exclusion and inequality. The senator from Kansas very properly suggests

[1] July 2. Congressional Globe, pp. 5121-5124.

[2] July 2 and 4. Works, vol. xiii. pp. 474-498.

[3] July 8; Congressional Globe, pp. 5387, 5388. Longfellow wrote to G. W. Greene, July 10: "I wish this *fainéant* Congress would rise and let Sumner loose. I agree with him about the Chinese, and about striking the word 'white' out of every law of the land; of course you do."

that a returned Chinaman is worth a dozen missionaries; but while he is here, —if he does not return, — he comes under our influences, he shares the good, of our churches, of our schools, and if you will let him he will grow up in the glory and the beauty of our citizenship. Senators say no; shut him out from citizenship; let him have nothing of this great privilege. Here I differ. I claim for him all that you accord to others, — nor more, nor less. There can be but one rule for all. Because the Almighty made him of a color slightly different from my friend the senator from Oregon, I know not why he should not be equal to that senator in rights, — I know not why he should not enter into the same citizenship."

In the debate on the naturalization laws, as also in other debates during the session, Conkling was offensive to Sumner, being uniformly the aggressor.[1] It aggravated him that Sumner ignored him and let his thrusts pass in silence. Finally, when interrupting as if he had been referred to, Sumner said, "I ask a thousand pardons of the senator from New York; he is the last person that I would refer to." Conkling was at a loss for a retort, and could only reply, "I am very much obliged to the senator."[2]

The Cuban insurgents were still pressing for the recognition of their status as belligerents, and for partisans in Congress they had Carpenter in the Senate and Banks in the House. Sumner did not consider that they had established a government *de facto* so as to entitle them to recognition; but he drew and reported resolutions condemning the barbarities of the civil war on the island, expressing regret that slavery was still maintained upon it, and declaring sympathy with fellow-Americans in Cuba who were struggling for independence,[3] — which, however, did not come to a vote. Dr. Howe, who had a passion for revolutions and civil disturbances of all kinds, and had no respect for the restrictions of international law or comity, was

1 Jan. 14, 17, Feb. 10, 1870. Congressional Globe, pp. 459, 506, 1143–1146.

2 July 5. Congressional Globe, p. 5236.

3 June 23 and 24; Congressional Globe, pp. 4753, 4754, 4806. The House had rejected Banks's resolutions acknowledging the Cuban insurgents as belligerents, and passed a single resolution of remonstrance against the barbarous manner in which the war was being conducted. Sumner spoke briefly on the subject at other times in the session (Dec. 15, 1869, Works, vol. xiii. pp. 195–203; Feb. 3, 1870, Globe, pp. 1003, 1007, 1008). His resolutions were approved by the press (New York "Evening Post," June 24; New York "Herald," June 24 and 25; Harper's Weekly, July 9). They were in accord with the President's message, June 13 (Globe, p. 4400). Interviews with the senator on the Cuban question are reported in the New York "Herald," May 7, 1869; New York "Times," Jan. 10, 1870; New York "World," Dec. 11, 1869. The last-named journal contains (Feb. 10, 1870) the senator's views given at length. *Ante*, pp. 401–403.

vexed with Sumner for not promoting the intervention of the United States in behalf of the insurgent Cubans.[1] Sumner replied to him, March 16: —

"As to Cuba, I am obliged to say that I have never seen any evidence that brings her insurgents within any rule of law, reason, or humanity justifying our concession to them of a flag on the ocean. No nation can concede to insurgents a flag on the ocean — which is the present question — unless it bounds on the ocean, has ports and the means of administering justice on the ocean. Such is the requirement of civilization in the interest of peace, and to prevent the burning of ships on the ocean. Every captured ship must be carried into port and condemned as prize; and unless this can be done, the captors are no better than pirates. . . . I have no doubt that the concession of a flag on the ocean to Cuban insurgents would be a wrong to Spain; therefore I cannot consent to it. But beyond my judgment of its wrongful character is the positive peril of war which it must create. . . . If we must have war, I prefer that the United States should declare at once openly that it sides with the insurgents, and accepts war with Spain; but let it not begin by telling a lie, — in other words, by declaring what is notoriously untrue. . . . For myself, I desire her [Cuba's] independence, and I see what seems to me the best way of obtaining it. Among these ways I discard (1) Bribery of United States officials who are implicated on a large scale; and (2) War by the United States. Both these agencies I repel. I have reason to believe that the people will be indignant at the dishonest efforts made to compromise our country. At any rate, when I am dead there is nothing which I would have remembered about me more than the tenacity with which I have clung to the duty and policy of peace when pressed as I have been for months. I believe in peace, and I am against any act or declaration that will thwart or imperil civilization. . . . I look to annexation at the North. I wish to have that whole zone from Newfoundland to Vancouver; but a war with Spain would postpone this triumph indefinitely."

A controversy began at this session which was to throw Sumner out of relations with his party, and to sadden the remaining years of his life. It related to the proposed acquisition of San Domingo by the United States.[2]

Hayti and San Domingo — the French and Spanish divisions of the same island — were under one government from 1822 to 1844. Then followed a civil war of four years, which ended

[1] Mrs. Howe also subjected Sumner to public criticism for his refusal to have the United States make common cause with the Cuban insurgents.

[2] For authorities on the subject see documents communicated by the President, Feb. 7, 1871, on a call of the Senate moved by Sumner (Executive documents, Forty-first Congress, third session, 1870-1871, Senate No. 34; Executive documents, Forty-first Congress, third session, Senate No. 17; Report on D. Hatch's case, Forty-first Congress, second session, 1869-1870, Senate No. 234; Sumner's speeches, Dec. 21, 1870, and March 27, 1871, Works, vol. xiv. pp. 89-131, 168-249). Seward entered into negotiations for the gulf and peninsula of Samana (Seward's "Life," vol. iii. pp. 344, 372).

with the latter becoming a separate republic. Its independence was, however, precarious, — threatened by Hayti, where ambition for the former unity prevailed. San Domingo occupied two-thirds of the island, but had only one-fifth of its population, and was far inferior in resources to its French rival. Both divisions of the island have ever since their separation been subject to frequent revolutions; and the disturbances in one have almost always found support in the other.[1]

Cabral and Baez had for some years alternately held power in San Domingo, each obtaining it with violence. It is hazardous to weigh the comparative merits of these two chiefs of a semi-barbarous society. Cabral was the better patriot, in the sense that he adhered to the independence of his country; while Baez, with his more complete training and greater craft, knew better how to trade on her fortunes or misfortunes. After all, it was not safe to stake much on the disinterestedness of either. In 1868 Baez took his turn as chief of the republic, succeeding this time as before by revolution; while Cabral, who had been dislodged by his partisans, held out with a certain armed force against the usurper, and bided his time for recovering power. Baez had no troops at command sufficient to disperse those of his rival, who was hovering on the Haytian frontier; his treasury was empty, and he lived in constant dread of being driven away, — a fate which befell him twice afterwards. A temporary ruler, with so precarious an authority, was incompetent to contract for the sale of his country;[2] and the inhabitants were in too distracted a condition to express their genuine wishes. The national spirit was at all times against a sale, and the revival of the project led to the final downfall of Baez and his party in 1878. The acquisition of the territory by a power like the United States could, under the circumstances, whatever form it might assume, be in fact nothing else than a conquest. While Baez was out of power (1866–1868), he came to Wash-

1 The history of both Hayti and San Domingo is a history of revolutions. Two have taken place in the former country as late as 1888 and 1891, and others have been attempted later still.

2 Baez's tenure continued to be uncertain. He was overthrown early in 1874 by Gonzales, and came to the United States; he was recalled in 1876, and again driven out in 1878. From that time he lived in retirement in Mayaguez, Porto Rico, where he died in 1884. Cabral retired to his home in San Juan, province of Azua, and was living there in 1889. It is difficult to obtain trustworthy accounts of the recent history of San Domingo, but the best is found in the Boston "Transcript," Aug. 12, 1889, written by an American resident in the island.

ington seeking intervention against Cabral, who was then president by a popular vote. Seward referred him to Sumner, who gave him no countenance. In the winter of 1868–1869 he sent to Washington a confidential envoy (Louis Paul Argenard), and also an American resident of the island (J. W. Fabens). They plied members of Congress by personal solicitation, and distributed freely a pamphlet which they had prepared. The result appeared in Banks's resolution for a protectorate over Hayti and San Domingo, which after debate was laid on the table by a large majority.[1] A few weeks later Banks and Orth attempted without success to bring forward for debate a resolution for annexing San Domingo.[2]

Public opinion in the United States was at this time averse to tropical extension, and to the acquisition of islands occupied by a population alien to our own, who could be governed only by methods unknown to the American system. This is seen in the unanimous disfavor which the St. Thomas treaty, negotiated by Mr. Seward, encountered in the Senate in 1868–1869, and the resolution of the House, Nov. 25, 1867, against such purchases; as also in the action of the last-named body in January and February, 1869, already referred to. President Johnson's last annual message, in a passage doubtless drawn by Mr. Seward, suggested the annexation of the whole island, including San Domingo and Hayti; but he as well as his secretary were at the time without popular support. President Grant, from the beginning of his term, had additions of territory in mind. His first thought was of Cuba; but the scheme for the acquisition of that island did not prosper. Next he turned to San Domingo, which was brought to his attention soon after his inauguration by that indefatigable trader Baez, followed shortly by "a second gentleman"[3] from that country, whose name does not appear. The President lent a ready ear, desirous to extend the national area, and also, as he afterwards said, to open a refuge for the colored people of the United States.[4] Wise or unwise, his purpose appears to have been simple and honorable; but around him were adventurers who had ends of their own. His estimate of the resources of the territory was from the first fanciful. The negotiation properly

[1] Jan. 12 and 13, 1869. Congressional Globe, pp. 317, 333.

[2] Feb. 1 and 8, 1869. Congressional Globe, pp. 769, 972.

[3] Probably Fabens.

[4] Personal Memoirs, vol. ii. p. 550.

belonged to the state department, but the President kept it in his own hands. Mr. Fish, who is supposed not to have been in sympathy with it, took at first only a perfunctory part. The original orders went no further than to justify inquiry; but as more was done, and what was done was ratified, it is evident that the President himself in conversation supplemented the written directions with further authority. The person on whom he put the responsible business, involving wide discretion and dangerous powers, was his secretary, Orville E. Babcock; and a more unfit agent could not have been selected.[1] He not only was not in the diplomatic service, but his character disqualified him for a delicate and responsible trust.

On May 17, 1869, Mr. Fish communicated to Robeson, Secretary of the Navy, the President's desire to have a man-of-war "ordered to visit the several ports of the Dominican republic, and to report upon the condition of affairs in that quarter," with the addition: "It is also important that we should have full and accurate information in regard to the views of the Dominican people of all parties in regard to annexation to the country, or the sale or lease of the Bay of Samana, or of territory adjacent thereto."

The President despatched Babcock in July, under instructions dated the 13th, and signed by Mr. Fish, which so far as printed limited his errand to one of full inquiry into the population and

[1] Babcock was tried in the United States court at St. Louis in February, 1876, on an indictment for conspiring to defraud the government in the collection of revenue on distilled spirits. His acquittal was attributed by some to defects in the chain of evidence which was strongly inculpatory, and by others to the moral support which he received from President Grant, who declared in a deposition entire confidence in his character. The prosecutions were embarrassed by the President's summary dismissal of John B. Henderson, former senator from Missouri, who was serving the government as special counsel, — the cause of the dismissal being certain language of General Henderson, used by him in court, which the President deemed disrespectful to himself, though an offensive purpose was disavowed by the counsel. General Henderson has continued to hold a high place in his party, serving as president of the Republican national convention in 1884, and of the Pan-American Congress.

An unfavorable view of Babcock is given by H. C. Boynton in the North American Review, October, 1876 (pp. 283–327), and by Whitelaw Reid in the New York "Tribune," Feb. 17 and 23, 1876. (Compare the numbers of this journal for February 13, 14, 15, 16, 18, 21, 22, 24, 25, and 28.) These writers reflect on the President's support of Babcock, and his want of sympathy with the prosecution, — the "Tribune" saying, "He is better fitted to rule an Asiatic kingdom than a free American people." Babcock was again indicted, April 16, 1876, in the District of Columbia, and this time on the charge of complicity with certain safe burglaries (New York "Tribune," April 17, 1876); but this case did not come to a trial. His transactions were the subject of investigation by committees of Congress, — Forty-third Congress, first session, No. 785, concerning safe burglaries; Forty-fourth Congress, first session, No. 799, concerning sale of post-traderships.

resources of the island, and other like points. But while directions for inquiry only appeared on Mr. Fish's papers, Robeson was issuing orders which contemplated force. On the 13th, the day the instructions were dated, he ordered one war vessel to give Babcock not only "every attention and facility in the execution of his present duty," but also "the moral support of its guns;" and by telegram, August 23, he ordered another to proceed from Key West and to be placed at Babcock's disposal while he was on that coast. Though only authorized, so far as written instructions showed, to inquire and report, Babcock executed, September 4, with the Dominican authorities a protocol which stipulated for the annexation of Dominica to the United States, with the payment by the United States of $1,500,000 for the extinction of the Dominican debt; and two days later he started on his return to Washington. He assumed in the body of the protocol the ambitious title of "Aide-de-camp to his Excellency, Ulysses S. Grant, President of the United States of America," and added to the terms of cession and payment the strange pledge that "his Excellency, General Grant, President of the United States, promises privately to use all his influence in order that the idea of annexing the Dominican republic to the United States may acquire such a degree of popularity among members of Congress as will be necessary for its accomplishment." [1] Here was a military agent assuming to conduct civil business with military forms, and making the extraordinary pledge that the President would exert personal pressure on Congress!

Though Babcock's written commission was confined to inquiry, his transgression of its limits was afterwards publicly approved by the President, who certified that he had done his duty, and had not exceeded his instructions.[2] After conferences at Washington he returned in November to San Domingo, bearing instructions from Mr. Fish, and having a naval force placed at his disposal with directions "to conform to all his wishes and orders, and to convey him to such points as he may desire to visit." On arriving at his destination he concluded, December 3,

1 This protocol, not communicated to the Senate with the treaty, came out casually in the investigation of Hatch's case. New York "Times," June 28, 1870.

2 The President's letter to Senator Nye, June 27, 1870, closed with the words, "General Babcock's conduct throughout merits my entire approval." Washington "Republican," Dec. 23, 1870.

two treaties, — one for the annexation of San Domingo, and another for the lease of the Bay of Samana; giving the President's guaranty to the Dominican republic against all foreign interposition until the treaties were submitted to the Dominican people, — a pledge which was beyond Executive authority before the treaty was ratified by the Senate. With three armed vessels, which the Secretary of the Navy had put under his directions, — two to remain at San Domingo, and one to return with him, — he forthwith announced formally his purpose to take possession of the bay and peninsula of Samana in the name of the United States, to raise the United States flag on the shore, and place a guard with it; and he further directed the commander of a man-of-war to use all his force to carry out to the letter the guaranty against intervention, particularly with reference to any which might come from Hayti. This formidable show of war-power was continued for many months. During 1870 twelve different ships of the navy — some of them monitors — were kept in the waters of San Domingo with positive orders to repel any attack from Hayti, or any other power, and to aid in suppressing any domestic revolt against Baez. The tenor of their commissions appears in the orders given by Secretary Robeson to Admiral Poor, Jan. 29, 1870: —

"Proceed at once with the 'Severn' and 'Dictator' to Port-au-Prince; communicate with our consul there, and inform the present Haytian authorities that this government is determined to protect the present Dominican government with all its power. You will then proceed to Dominica, and use your force to give the most ample protection to the Dominican government against any power attempting to interfere with it. Visit Samana Bay and the capital, and see the United States power and authority secure there. There must be no failure in this matter. If the Haytians attack the Dominicans with their ships, destroy or capture them. See that there is a proper force at both San Domingo City and Samana."

A succession of orders from Robeson directed the support of Baez against his enemies, or any revolutionary force, and against attacks from abroad, and the recapture of any places taken from Baez. The ships were sent from place to place, as Baez requested, to protect him against his rival Cabral, to transport himself and his staff and troops from one port to another in the island, and to carry his despatches. For the time being the navy of the United States was the navy of Baez. So precarious was his power at the time that it appeared in the official correspondence that without the support of our ships of war he could not have maintained himself against his own people, and would have been obliged to leave the island.[1]

Admiral Poor in February, 1870, in pursuance of his orders, made a formal demonstration at the Haytian capital. Arriving at Port-au-Prince with his flag-ship, both by written communication and in a personal interview, he announced to the President of the republic the determination of the government at Washington to prevent any interference with the Baez government during the negotiations, and to treat any attack upon it as an act of hostility to the United States which would provoke hostility in return. As significant of his capacity to make his declaration effective, he pointed to his fleet in the harbor, and stated that other ships were to arrive. The Haytian president and secretary of state, in whose presence this threat was made, though "displeased with what they regarded as a menace on the part of the United States accompanied with force," answered with dignity and reserve, expressing the hope that the friendly relations now so happily existing between the two countries would not be interrupted, and saying that while "they were aware of their weakness, they knew their rights, and would maintain them and their dignity as far as they were able, and that they must be allowed to be the judges of their own policy." The white admiral must have blushed for himself and his country at this rebuke from the negro statesmen. His conduct was without diplomatic formality, and was wanting in decent respect for the Haytian government; but it was not disavowed.

These movements of our ships were war, which was alike threatened in the instructions to their commanders and in the final notice to Hayti; and only the weakness of that government and of Cabral's party prevented an actual collision. Such Executive measures violated the principle of non-intervention in foreign or civil wars prescribed by international law, as well as the Constitution, which invests Congress only with the power to declare war, — a provision which would be idle words if the Executive were left at liberty to make war before it was thus declared.[2] But by such action our government was actually put

1 Commodore Green's despatch, July 21, 1870.

2 In Congress these proceedings were justified by Polk's military movements against Mexico, which were the beginning of an unjust war for the extension of slavery; but generally they were disapproved, even by those who justified the President's good intentions. Senator Harlan, who supported the treaty, admitted them to have been "irregular." Harper's Weekly wrote, April 15, 1871: "There has unquestionably been a misconcep-

in the position of assuming dominion in San Domingo, at least for the time being. British dominion in Egypt, with the khedive as a puppet corresponding to Baez, is not more complete than was ours at that time in San Domingo. These war demonstrations were without any previous sanction of Congress under its war-declaring power, or even of the Senate under its treaty-making power; and they were continued many months, a year even, after Babcock's treaty had, by its deliberate rejection, become a dead letter. These events and State papers were not known at their dates, but came to light from time to time by call of Congress and otherwise. Babcock having completed his business, Dec. 3, 1869, returned shortly after to Washington, bringing his treaties. The narrative has now reached the date of Sumner's connection with and knowledge of the transactions.

At the beginning of January, 1870,[1] one evening when Sumner was at dinner at his own house, with J. W. Forney and B. P. Poore as guests, the President called. The servant informed him that the senator was at dinner, but his voice being recognized in the dining-room, the senator went himself to the door and returned with the President, who took a seat at the table, beckoning the two guests, who were about to leave, to remain. The four shortly adjourned to the library, the adjoining room. The President began the formal part of the interview with a reference to some treaties relating to San Domingo. So untutored was he at the time in civil business that he addressed the senator several times as "chairman of the judiciary committee," saying that as they were to come before that committee, he wished to speak with the senator concerning them. Sumner, partly to divert attention from the treaties (as to which he did not care to commit himself in advance), and partly to take advantage of an opportunity to say a word for his friend J. M. Ashley, recently removed from the governorship of Montana, turned the conversation to Ashley's case. After this interruption, the President recurred to the treaties, but gave no definite idea as to what they were, the senator even supposing that they might provide only for a protectorate in the Gulf, always a

tion of the limits of Executive power, and a consequent action which is constitutionally indefensible."

[1] B. P. Poore, in a letter to the Boston "Journal," puts the day as Sunday, Jan. 2, 1870, while J. C. B. Davis puts it as Dec. 31, 1869; but the precise day is immaterial.

favorite idea of his own.[1] The interview closed by his saying: "Mr. President, I am an Administration man, and whatever you do will always find in me the most careful and candid consideration."[2] He affirmed afterwards that his reply was precise, and that the language was fixed in his memory. He never spoke at random, and his uniform habit in conversation was to speak in well formed and deliberate sentences. On public business he was specially careful not to commit himself in advance. As yet he had no information as to the provisions of the treaties or the manner of their negotiation. He meant to withhold his judgment, awaiting fuller knowledge, and supposed the President understood him as withholding it.[3] This is what any thoughtful man with a sense of responsibility would have done. The President, however, afterwards maintained that the senator assured him that he would support the treaties, and complained bitterly of his bad faith in not doing so.[4] Colonel Forney also, being invited by Babcock to make a statement, wrote that he understood the senator to say that he would cheerfully support the

[1] In the Senate, Dec. 21, 1870; Congressional Globe, p. 253. New York "Tribune," April 5, 1871.

[2] Sumner's account may be found in his speeches, Dec. 21, 1870, Works, vol. xiv. pp. 125, 126; Congressional Globe, p. 253; March 28, 1871, Globe, App. p. 45. Letter to Speaker Blaine, Aug. 5, 1872, Works, vol. xv. p. 200. Address, Sept. 3, 1872, Ibid., p. 218.

[3] The absurdity of the senator's being supposed to have given a promise to support the treaties is evident from what Harlan, another member of the committee, who finally supported the treaty, said in debate, Dec. 21, 1870 (Congressional Globe, p. 266), when he mentioned the difficulty the committee had experienced for several weeks in obtaining the requisite information for action, during which search was made in books, maps, and public documents.

[4] The President was an inaccurate narrator of civil affairs. Thus, in his "Personal Memoirs," vol. ii. pp. 505, 506, he gives as an instance of Stanton's characteristic of "never questioning his own authority," that he revoked at Washington, while Mr. Lincoln was at or near Richmond, the latter's order for the meeting of the rebel Legislature of Virginia; whereas the revocation — a fact always well known — was made by Mr. Lincoln himself at Washington two days before his death. (Nicolay and Hay's "Life of Lincoln," vol. x. pp. 227-228.) Gideon Welles in the "Galaxy" (April and May, 1872, pp. 531, 532, 666) disagrees with the general's memory of what took place in the Cabinet, April 14, 1865. General Grant also stated to George William Curtis that Sumner had neglected to report several treaties; but when Harper's Weekly of Dec. 8, 1877, was shown to him, which gave the record of the Senate proving that he had reported them with due promptness, the general continued to assume in an extended conversation that the senator had not reported them. (New York "Herald," Feb. 22, 1878, containing letter from Cairo, January 17.) His anachronism in his comments on the "Alabama" claims has already been pointed out. (*Ante*, p. 398, *note*.) General Grant's accuracy as a narrator of military affairs has been contested by several authors. "Misunderstandings: Halleck and Grant;" by J. B. Fry, Magazine of American History, vol. xvi. p. 561. "The Mistakes of Grant;" by W. S. Rosecrans, North American Review, December, 1885, pp. 580-599. "Grant *versus* The Record;" by Carswell McClellan.

treaties; but he was unable to recall the exact words.[1] The words, however, as recalled by him later, do not contain a promise to support them, but only an assurance that the senator would give his best thought to them.[2] Forney, as appears from his own report, drew at first a hasty inference which was not justified by the language as he reported it. He says further that he told General Grant more than once that he ought to receive Sumner's explanation as sufficient, and adds his solemn belief that "there never lived a purer, better, or more truthful man than Charles Sumner." The other guest, Major Poore, states that the President dwelt on Babcock's expenditure of money, and while meaning to secure favor for the treaties gave the senator the impression that reimbursement was the main question.[3] Sumner said in his speech, Dec. 21, 1870:

> "I have heard it said that I assured the President that I would support the Administration in this measure. Never! He may have formed this opinion, but never did I say anything to justify it; nor did I suppose he could have failed to appreciate the reserve with which I spoke. My language, I repeat, was precise, well considered, and chosen in advance; 'I am an Administration man, and whatever you do will always find in me the most careful and candid consideration.' In this statement I am positive. It was early fixed in my mind, and I know that I am right."

Sumner mentioned the interview the next day to Mr. Schurz, who, being by conviction against tropical acquisitions, asked anxiously what his reply was, and Sumner stated it then as he uniformly stated it afterwards. According equal veracity to all who were present, Sumner's statement of his own language is the best evidence, and it corresponds to natural presumptions. A pledge without knowledge is what no man fit to be senator would give, and what no man fit to be President would expect.

Sumner's language to the President expressed his sincere feelings. He was in full agreement with the Administration on

[1] Letter to Babcock, June 6, 1870, Congressional Globe, Dec. 21, 1870, p. 242.

[2] Philadelphia Press, Oct. 3, 1877; New York Herald, Oct. 5, 1877. Forney in this second statement gives Sumner's answer to the President as follows: "Well, Mr. President, I am a Republican and an Administration man, and I will do all I can to make your Administration a success. I will give the subject my best thought, and will do all I can rightly and consistently to aid you." This report of Forney does not differ substantially from Sumner's, though naturally the recollection of one who spoke the words is more precise than that of one who only heard them casually without being a party to the conversation.

[3] Boston Journal, Oct. 24, 1877. Babcock claimed that the senator told him when he took the treaties to him that he would support them; but his statements, in view of his character and career, are worthless.

foreign and domestic questions. His personal relations with the President and all the members of the Cabinet were cordial, and with Mr. Fish still intimate and confidential. He found in the President one who went as far as he did in removing the relics of slavery and protecting the freedmen. He had no personal grievance of any kind against his party or its representative leaders.[1] All was peace at the close of 1869; but a dark cloud was coming on the horizon.

The day after the President's call, Babcock called on the senator and exhibited the treaties to him. They were shortly sent to the Senate, and being referred, Sumner laid them, January 18, before the committee on foreign relations. The conversation in the committee was at that time preliminary and general. Sumner withheld his own opinion, waiting for the other members to express theirs. The general opinion as far as indicated was against them, one senator only (Morton) saying anything in their favor. Sumner then expressed the hope that "the conversation would be regarded as informal, and that there would be no immediate vote, or any course taken which could be interpreted as otherwise than friendly to the Administration; too prompt action might be misconstrued." Harlan, a member of the committee, who finally voted for annexation and remained the President's steadfast friend, bore witness in the debate, Dec. 21, 1870, that he was not able to understand what Sumner's judgment was (though he might have formed one) for several weeks after the treaties went to the committee, — doing him the justice to say that he might have withheld it from a sense of duty so as not to influence unduly the judgment of his associates, and that he aided them in the investigation by bringing to the subject all his great learning and ripe experience.[2] No member of the committee ever charged him with haste or partisanship in the business; all recognized his fairness. He did with the treaties just as he told the President that he would do. Afterwards in open Senate he challenged scrutiny of his record in this respect, and met no contradiction.[3] He said: —

[1] Mr. Blaine states erroneously, but without specifying, that Sumner had some personal grievance against General Grant ("Twenty Years of Congress," vol. ii. p. 461); but the senator's private correspondence and public speeches disprove the suggestion.

[2] Harlan's uncontested statement made openly in the Senate disposes of the fiction that Sumner showed disrespect to the President by violently opposing the treaty from the beginning.

[3] Dec. 21, 1870, Works, vol. xiv. p. 127.

"My desire was to proceed with utmost delicacy. I did not know then, what I have learned since, how the President had set his heart upon the project of annexion. With my experience of treaties, familiar as I have been with them in the Senate, I supposed that I was pursuing the course most agreeable to him, and, should the report be adverse, most respectful and considerate. This I state, sir, on my conscience, as my solemn judgment at the time, and my motive of conduct I wished to be careful and candid. It was easy to see from the beginning that annexion had small chance in the committee, whatever might be its fate in the Senate; but I was determined to say and do nothing by which the result should in any way be aggravated. Again I appeal to every one of my colleagues on that committee for their testimony in this behalf. I know that I am above criticism. I know that I have pursued a patriotic course, always just and considerate to the President."

Sumner had no prejudices against territorial extension, but kept an open mind whenever any particular acquisition was in question. Considerations of race, climate, and insular position, affecting decisively other minds, had their weight with him, but less so than with most public men. He preferred, however, extension northward rather than southward. From the first he was not impressed with the advantages to the United States which the acquisition of San Domingo promised; but when he came to the serious consideration of the project, he was most concerned as to its relations to the future of the African race. He thought it all important to that race that a republic created by it should be maintained in this hemisphere as an example and inspiration, and that the extinction of San Domingo was sure to involve at the next step the extinction of the other black republic occupying a part of the same island. It was according to history and reason that the island could not long be occupied by two powers, — one strong like our own, and the other weak. Indeed, some of the promoters of the annexation confessed to far-reaching schemes which comprehended not only the entire island, but all the Antilles. Sumner had always taken a more than common interest in Hayti. As a youth he had listened to the tales of his father's visit to the island, made at the end of the last century; and as a senator he had carried the bill giving that republic diplomatic representation, which had hitherto been unjustly denied. He believed it to be the high duty of the United States, as a strong power, to foster and protect the weaker powers in this hemisphere, instead of plotting to absorb them.[1]

Such reflections were on the senator's mind before he had

[1] New York Tribune, April 5, 1871.

been admitted to knowledge of the circumstances of the negotiation. One day the assistant secretary of state (Davis) brought him some despatches from San Domingo, which revealed to him that Baez was maintained in power by our navy. "I confess now," he said afterwards, "my emotion as I read this painful revelation. Until then I had supposed the proceeding blameless, although precipitate. I had not imagined any such indefensible transgressions." He at once visited the navy department, and found that its instructions to commanders and their reports corresponded to what he had discovered in the papers of the state department. It then appeared clearly to him that "the treaty was a contract which, according to our own witnesses, was obtained through a ruler owing power to our war ships," and that "we were engaged in forcing upon a weak people the sacrifice of their country." These disclosures, only a part of what came out during the controversy, settled him in his decision to oppose the ratification. When he came to this conclusion, the better course for him — the President having called on him first — would have been to notify the latter that he could not support the treaties. It is not at all likely that he would by so doing have changed the President's purpose,[1] but he might possibly by such a recognition have mitigated the heated controversy which ensued. Sumner afterwards explained why he did not go to the President and state the grounds of his opposition.[2] He said:

"I will tell you, sir, where perhaps I erred. It was in not going to the President and telling him frankly my opinion of the treaties. Knowing his present interest in annexation, it is easy to imagine that had I seen him on the subject and exposed its true character, some misapprehension would have been avoided; but on careful reflection at the time, I did not regard it as expedient. I thought it more gentle and considerate to avoid discussions with him, being assured that he would ascertain the judgment on annexation through the expression of public sentiment in the newspapers and various report. If in this respect I erred, it was an honest mistake, believing at the time that I was pursuing the more delicate course. Here let me add that I acted also according to my experience with treaties. I am told of a boast by Mr. Seward that he has negotiated half of the treaties of this government. I know not how this is; but if it be true, then have I had the responsibility of carrying half the treaties

1 According to one of the President's secretaries, he was at this time affected by adulation and not disposed to consult others. (Badeau's "Grant in Peace," pp. 156-158, 159, 160.) This may be true, but it is not the more credible because Badeau states it. This writer implies, though he has not the hardihood to say so explicitly, that the senator could have been brought to support the treaty by an appointment being given to J. M. Ashley. Ibid., pp. 214, 215.

2 In Senate, Dec. 21, 1870. Congressional Globe, p. 253.

of this government through the committee on foreign relations and the Senate. Never before have I known a President take any such interest in a treaty. Never have I been approached by a President on a treaty. I had no reason from any communication outside to suppose at that time that the interest of the President was what I now know it to have been. Had I imagined it, my course might have been different. Probably I should have seen and conferred with him when I was satisfied that the treaty could not receive my support. If I erred in this respect, I erred honestly and with a sincere desire to act gently and considerately."

The President had expected the easy ratification of the treaties, and was impatient with the opposition which developed.[1] As the prospect of a favorable report receded, he became more determined in his course. It was hard for one whose will in camp had been law to be thwarted in civil affairs, in which a constitutional system requires concurrence of opinion and action in different departments. It soon appeared that he held the chairman of the committee on foreign relations responsible for its indisposition to approve the proposed annexation.[2] Mr. Forney, recently clerk of the Senate and editor of republican journals in Washington and Philadelphia, and also in close relations with the Administration, wrote to Sumner from the latter city, Feb. 22, 1870, a month before the matter came before the Senate: —

"The President has evidently determined to stand by the Republican party and to strike down the Republican statesmen. The idea has got abroad here that he has marked you out for sacrifice, and it excites much feeling. I have in all cases discouraged it, because I cannot think the President madman enough to follow the example of Andrew Johnson."

The President's active interest in the treaty was manifested in various ways. He sent two messages to the Senate (March 14 and May 31) concerning the extension of the time of ratification, in which he set forth the benefits of the annexation. But he did not content himself with official communications. He addressed himself personally to members of the committee. He held conferences at the Executive Mansion with senators whom he sent for. He went to the President's room at the Capitol, which Presidents hitherto had occupied only on the last day of the

1 Badeau says: "I believe it was the heat of the contest that made him so eager for success at last; for he had the soldier's instinct, even in civil affairs. When he was once engaged in battle, he was always anxious to win."

2 Outside of the Senate Sumner was regarded as an obstacle to the treaty. The New York "Herald," March 24, 1870, called him "the old man of the sea." Its leader, Dec. 23, 1870, gave him the same prominence.

session for signing bills, and there sent for senators to meet him. He was there a day or two before the committee began the deliberate consideration of the treaties. Two days after the adverse report he was there again, and sent for as many as fourteen senators; and he was reported as making another similar visit three days before the final rejection. This unprecedented activity was the occasion of considerable comment at the time.[1]

The treaties lay with the committee till March 11, when Babcock was present at its meeting to explain them. Four days later it made a report adverse to a ratification, in which Sumner, Patterson, Schurz, Cameron, and Casserly joined. Cameron, however, explained at the time that under some circumstances he might hereafter vote for annexation. The minority, who were in favor of ratification, were Morton and Harlan. Ferry moved, with Sumner supporting him, that the treaties be considered in open session of the Senate; but the motion did not prevail. The debate began on the 24th.

The tenor of debates in secret session is obtained by correspondents, who ply the senators with inquiries and receive answers more or less full; and generally they obtain the chief points with considerable correctness. In this instance they described Sumner's speech, lasting four hours, which opened the debate, as "very able, exhaustive, and scholarly, . . . the finest effort he ever made, . . . covering all the points likely to arise in connection with the subject," and "holding the attention of the Senate throughout its entire delivery." The correspondents do not state that he referred to the irregularity of the negotiation and the use of the war ships; he appears to have made that point briefly at a later day, but not in a way to provoke an issue with the Administration.[2] He is reported to have expressed confidence in the President's entire honesty in the transaction, and no account attributes to him any different expression.[3] All

1 See the New York journals in March, 1870. Under an ancient but disused rule the President can meet the Senate when in executive session. Washington met the Senate before any regular system of intercourse was established.

2 Remarks in Senate, March 28, 1871, Congressional Globe, App. p. 45. The Washington "Chronicle," March 26, 1870, said that he made no attack on the negotiations, and said nothing on this head, while he spoke "with great courtesy of the President." He was less informed at this time as to the use of the navy and Babcock's proceedings than at a later date.

3 There was a good deal of speculation in the scheme, and the President did not look keenly into his surroundings; but Sumner uniformly disclaimed imputations on the President's personal integrity, and invoked his associates to bear witness to the truth of his disclaimer, saying: "I have never alluded to the President in executive session except in most

question is settled on this point by a letter from Senator Howe, always the President's partisan, who heard the speech, and who in a letter to Sumner the next summer, August 23, contended that Motley's removal was not aimed at him, — adding that "the President had no cause of complaint against you, and therefore the pretence that he was influenced by any such cause to remove Motley must be groundless." Stewart — a supporter of the treaty, devoted to the President but not friendly to Sumner — told Forney that the speech was "magnificent." The main points of the speech as given by correspondents were as follows:[1] 1. The proposed annexation likely to encourage further acquisitions in the same direction, bringing to the United States a population difficult to assimilate, involving large expense and complications with other powers, particularly with Hayti, which asserted claims against San Domingo. 2. The half island not heretofore tempting to, and not likely to tempt, European powers. 3. The uncertainty as to the amount of the Dominican debt, which was probably much greater than had been represented. 4. The chronic condition of civil war in San Domingo, and the fresh crop of rebellions which would come from the annexation. 5. The injustice of impairing the predominance of the colored race in the West Indies. "To the African," he is reported to have said, "belongs the equatorial belt, and he should enjoy it undisturbed."

Caleb Cushing wrote, March 25: —

"You must be gratified to find that all the journals commend your speech on Dominica, especially seeing that these outside opinions are, of course, but the echo of the judgments of senators."

J. R. Hawley, late governor of Connecticut, and afterwards senator, wrote from Hartford, March 23: —

"What little I see concerning your speech on San Domingo greatly pleases me. The course of the government for several years in these matters is demoralizing and dangerous. I would not have an Administration negotiate an acquisition in time of peace without the previous consent of Congress. We

respectful kindness, and I challenge anybody to say the contrary." (In Senate, Dec. 21, 1870, Congressional Globe, pp. 217, 218, 247. Statement, March, 1871, Works, vol. xiv. p. 257.) The President, however, assumed otherwise in communicating to Congress the report of the commissioners to San Domingo.

[1] New York Herald, March 25, 26, 28, 31. New York Times, March 25. New York Tribune, March 25. New York World, March 25. Boston Advertiser, March 26. Boston Journal, March 28. Chicago Republican, March 25. The correspondent of the New York Times, March 14, stated the senator's expected opposition to the annexation on grounds like those he took in the debate.

**don't want any of those islands just yet, with their mongrel, cut-throat races and foreign languages and religion."**

Sumner completed his speech on the second day, and was followed by Morton, who maintained that the acquisition was desirable as the key to the West Indies; and that if not made by the United States, England or France would shortly have the prize. This is a familiar argument in such cases; but an interval now of more than twenty years has shown it in this instance to have been misapplied. The ratification was then supported by Cole, Nye, and Stewart, and opposed by Schurz, Patterson, and Casserly. After a few weeks' debate the Senate laid the subject aside, and did not take it up again till late in June.

There was no popular demand for the annexation outside of a ring of speculators and adventurers. Here and there a journal, which was under their influence, or was quick to respond to the President's wishes, favored it.[1] Sumner's colleague voted for it finally, confessing that nine-tenths of his constituents were opposed to it; and he was governed in his vote only by fear of a rupture with the President. A popular demonstration in its favor was attempted at Cooper Institute in New York, evidently stimulated from Washington. Moses H. Grinnell, collector of the port, took the chair, and the speakers were two members of Congress, — Banks of Massachusetts, and Fitch of Nevada. Fabens, the speculator, already mentioned, was on the platform. The conservative patriotism of the city kept aloof from the affair.

One of the incidents of the San Domingo controversy was the investigation by the Senate of the imprisonment by the Baez government of Davis Hatch of Connecticut, described by Senator Ferry from that State to be "as high-toned and honorable a gentleman as any in the Senate." The charge against him was that he was a partisan of Cabral; but the real purpose of his illegal confinement was to prevent his coming to the United States, where he was likely to exert influence against the annexation. Babcock, who was the chief support of Baez's power, and two speculators who were co-operating with him (W. L. Cazneau and Fabens), were charged with being privy to the illegal detention. Senator Ferry brought Hatch's petition to

**[1] New York "Evening Post," July 1, 1870, wrote that the scheme had no sympathy or favor with the people, and that the journals which supported it had not been able to give good or plausible reasons for it.**

the attention of the Senate June 8, and remarked of Babcock that such a person no longer deserved to be an officer of the United States. Sumner at once said, from his seat, "He ought to be cashiered at once!"[1] Regularly the petition should have gone to the committee on foreign relations; but Nye and Carpenter made the point that Sumner's remark disqualified him from sitting on the case. Sumner, while maintaining the fairness of his committee, accepted Sherman's friendly suggestion that the petition be referred to a special committee. The special committee was, however, a partial one, as its chairman was Nye, who in the debate had said that Babcock was "as pure as the waters of the mountain from melted snow." The committee by one majority justified Babcock and the Dominican authorities;[2] but the minority report had the signature of Ferry, who was unquestioned in his devotion to the Republican party, and who in character and position carried greater weight than Nye.

Mr. Fish, as might have been expected from one of his conservative temperament, was at first no better affected towards the annexation than Sumner;[3] but under the President's pressure he became its partisan, and at Sumner's house pleaded with the senator to support the treaty, — not on the ground that it was a good thing, but on the ground that the President desired it. Sumner pointed out to him the unlawful use of the war ships; but the secretary did not regard those transactions as the senator regarded them. Sumner told him that he ought to resign rather than be a party to them; but he answered that he was the President's friend, and had taken office as such.[4] At last, two weeks before the final vote in the Senate, the secretary was at the senator's house from nine in the evening till midnight. He pressed Sumner to forego his opposition, urging that the wishes of the President, who had carried the election for his party, were entitled to especial attention.[5] He continued his pressure in

1 This was explained by the senator in debate, Dec. 21, 1870 (Congressional Globe, p. 247), as being said on the basis that the facts alleged were true.

2 The majority were Nye, Howard, Williams, and Warner; and the minority, Ferry, Schurz, and Vickers.

3 Sumner's Statement, March, 1871, p. 259; H. B. Adams in North American Review, July, 1870, p. 57. Badeau says for once what was doubtless true: "Even when Grant determined on a course that Fish would not perhaps have advised, the secretary stanchly supported his chief." "Grant in Peace," p. 233.

4 Statement. Works, vol. xiv. p. 259. In Senate, March 28, 1871. Congressional Globe, App. p. 45.

5 In the same interview Mr. Fish mentioned other projects of the President which Sumner had opposed, — instancing as one of them the appointment of J. R. Jones as minister to

various forms, and at last said to Sumner, as the latter states: "Why not go to London? I offer you the English mission; it is yours." The senator regarded this as an attempt to silence him by an inducement; but suppressing his indignation, and remembering that the secretary was an old friend and in his own house, he replied: "We have a minister there who cannot be bettered." This offer was made, according to the senator, without a word on his part leading to such an overture, which was as unexpected as it was undesired. Mr. Fish afterwards admitted that he did make the suggestion of the English mission to the senator, but claimed that he made it inconsiderately, and with no view to influence the senator's action, being led to it by the senator's reference to his own unhappy state of mind, growing out of a former domestic trouble.[1] On the whole, Mr. Fish's statement of his own motives in this matter is to be accepted. He knew the senator's official integrity, as he stated afterwards, too well to suppose him liable to be tempted in that way; and besides, the office itself could be no temptation to a senator who had recently begun a new term, and was quite sure of as many re-elections as he desired. If the offer was serious, — and surely Sumner was justified in so regarding it, — the suggestion of the mission which the secretary might think would promote at the same time a friend's happiness and the peace of the Administration does not appear dishonorable. Mr. Fish states truly that it was not until months after this conversation that the friendly and intimate relations between the senator and himself were interrupted.

The debate on the treaty of annexation was not resumed till June 29.[2] Morrill of Vermont at this time alone made any considerable remarks, beginning on the 29th, and finishing the next day. Sumner was silent, showing no disposition for controversy, and not doubting the result. The vote was taken on the second day of the debate, and resulted in a tie, —

Belgium. If the senator disapproved it, he was in agreement with all who knew Mr. Jones, except the President.

[1] Letter in the Boston Transcript, Oct. 31, 1877.

[2] Badeau states absurdly as well as untruthfully that Sumner kept back the Senate from considering the treaty against Mr. Fish's pressure for a vote. ("Grant in Peace," p. 215.) The treaty was before the Senate, and its friends — Morton or Harlan, or any other — could have moved to take it up. Neither they nor any member of the committee ever complained that Sumner was an obstruction to a report. Fish did not press for a vote, and makes no statement that he did in his account of the interview printed in the Boston "Transcript," Oct. 31, 1877. The delay was quite agreeable to the President, who was hoping for a favorable turn.

twenty-eight to twenty-eight, not the two-thirds required.[1] The composition of the Senate was such at this time and for four years after that it was open to Executive pressure as at no other period of our history. The Administration majority was still large. The Southern States were represented to a great extent by Northern men who were sojourning in them temporarily for what they could make, or by Southern men who had not the support of the Southern people. Such men did not expect a re-election, but they looked for Executive favor. This accounts for the large vote — one-half of the body — given for a measure which had no considerable popular support.

The day after the rejection of the treaty, Motley was removed from his post as minister to England;[2] and the public, as well as Sumner, connected the two events as cause and effect.[3] The President's friends at times attempted to disconnect them by giving reasons to show that the minister was already weak in his hold upon the place; but they have substantially admitted that the time chosen for the removal had reference to the rejection.[4]

[1] The vote was reported as follows (Democrats in italics): For the treaty — Abbott (N. C.), Brownlow (Tenn.), Cameron (Penn.), Cattell (N. J.), Chandler (Mich.), Cole (Cal.), Conkling (N. Y.), Corbett (Oregon), Drake (Mo.), Fenton (N. Y.), Hamlin (Me.), Harlan (Iowa), Howard (Mich.), Howell (Iowa), McDonald (Ark.), Morton (Ind.), Nye (Nev.), Osborn (Fla.), Pratt (Ind.), Ramsey (Minn.), Revels (Miss.), Rice (Ark.), Spencer (Ala.), Stewart (Nev.), Thayer (Neb.), Warner (Ala.), Williams (Oregon), Wilson (Mass.). Against the treaty, — Boreman (W. Va.), *Casserly* (Cal.), Cragin (N. H.), *Davis* (Ky.), Edmunds (Vt.), Ferry (Conn.), Fowler (Tenn.), *Hamilton* (Md.), Harris (La.), *Johnston* (Va.), *McCreery* (Ky.), Morrill (Me.), Morrill (Vt.), Patterson (N. H.), Pool (N. C.), Robertson (S. C.), Ross (Kan.), *Saulsbury* (Del.), Sawyer (S. C.), Schurz (Mo.), Scott (Penn.), Sprague (R. I.), *Stockton* (N. J.), Sumner (Mass.), *Thurman* (O.), Tipton (Neb.), *Vickers* (Md.), Willey (W. Va.). Pairs for the treaty, — Ames (Miss.), Anthony (R. I.), Carpenter (Wis.), Gilbert (Fla.), Hamilton (Tex.), Howe (Wis.), and Pomeroy (Kan.). Pairs against the treaty, — *Bayard* (Del.), Buckingham (Conn.), Kellogg (La.), and Yates (Ill.). Sherman, though in his seat, did not vote. The Senate records might show a slight variation from the above lists.

[2] Motley's resignation was called for, but as he refused to give it he remained some months at his post. Mr. Fish, in calling for his resignation, wrote him a private letter expressing regret that the change was to be made, and that he had to be the agent in communicating it.

[3] This was the inference in England as well as in the United States. London "Times," Jan. 24, 1871; Harper's Weekly, Jan. 7, 1871.

[4] J. C. B. Davis in New York "Herald," Jan. 4, 1878; Badeau's "Grant in Peace," p. 216. In order to escape just indignation at an act of revenge, Lord Clarendon's death, June 27, was set up as determining the time of removal, — that being claimed to be an event auspicious for renewing negotiations. This pretext was absurd, as the contemplated removal was reported in the Boston papers June 24, and telegraphed to the London "Times" June 25, in which journal the telegram appeared on the 27th, — dates when Lord Clarendon's death was not expected. The anachronism was noticed in the London "Times," Jan. 24, 1871. The two events were claimed to have no connection, because

Senator Howe, who had supported the treaty, as soon as the removal was reported, called on the President and endeavored to avert it, but without avail. Morrill of Vermont also took the opportunity to protest against any blow at Sumner on account of his conscientious action on the Dominican treaty. Wilson, who had voted for it, wrote, July 5, from his seat in the Senate to the President, urging him to reconsider the step: —

"I fear you will make a sad mistake if you remove him [Motley], and I beg of you to consider the case carefully before acting. His removal is believed to be aimed at Mr. Sumner. Right or wrong, this is the construction that will be put upon it. Can you, my dear sir, afford to have such an imputation rest upon your Administration? . . . I assure you, my dear sir, that the men of Massachusetts, who gave you more than seventy-five thousand majority, are proud to number Mr. Motley among their most loved and honored sons. I need not say that they are surprised at the rumor that he is to be removed. They are pained to have it said that his removal is on account of Mr. Sumner's opposition to the San Domingo treaty. His removal will be regarded by the Republicans of Massachusetts as a blow not only at him, but at Mr. Sumner."

Forney had anticipated that Sumner would be held responsible for the rejection of the treaty. He wrote, June 14, to the senator, "I am glad to meet you; but my heart bleeds over the future. But come what may, I am yours."

On the last day of the session, July 15, the President nominated Mr. Frelinghuysen as Motley's successor, and he was confirmed. Sumner withheld his vote, but spoke in defence of Motley, — sketching his career, and laying emphasis on his thoroughly American sentiments (a supposed allusion to one of the President's reported criticisms on the minister).[1] He rose again, after further debate, to reply to what he called "the war of pretexts."

History cannot take account of what may have been brought to the President's ears by eavesdroppers and parasites (and of these there were many about him); but this can be said with confidence, that up to the time of Motley's removal Sumner had said nothing of the President in speech or writing which was want-

the defeat of the San Domingo treaty had been assured for months. This is not so, as Mr. Fish the same month in which it was rejected did all he could to dissuade Sumner from opposing it. Not till that interview, at least, was all hope of success given up. Mr. Blaine states that the rejection was to the President's "utter surprise." ("Twenty Years in Congress," vol. ii. p. 459.)

1 Boston "Journal," July 16. He read as a part of his speech Senator Wilson's letter to the President in disapproval of Motley's removal.

ing in respect for his character and services, but had treated him throughout with perfect deference and courtesy. He had kept strictly within his right and duty as a senator in resisting the San Domingo scheme, — a right and duty equal to the President's in promoting it. The President might be disappointed at the rejection of his favorite measure; but the senator, by the testimony of his associates, was blameless. The removal of Motley was the first act which gave a personal direction to a public question. Sumner regarded it, as the common judgment of men regarded it, as an attempt to punish a senator for the just exercise of his right and the honest performance of his duty; and his indignation was natural and human. He, however, kept his feelings from the public, not referring to them in any speech or open letter, expressing them chiefly to senators and friends having a special connection with Motley, but repressing them in his general correspondence. What he wrote related to the injustice to Motley, and not to himself. Strong as these feelings were, the controversy would have ended here if the President had not revived it at the session in December.

Sumner wrote a note June 26, marked "private," to J. L. Stackpole of Boston, nephew of Motley, who had written to him of the report in that city, on the 24th, of the minister's intended removal: —

"I fear that there is ground for the rumor to which you refer; but I shall not believe the thing possible until it is done. I say to you confidentially that I have reason to believe that Mr. Grinnell, collector of New York, has been thought of as the successor. This would settle New York difficulties; but the whole thing is beyond the line of ordinary credence. The President has become much excited in his attempt to introduce San Domingo into the Union, and uses all his influence and his appointing power to advance his plan. This is supposed to have a bearing on the appointment at London. I beg you to believe that all this is to me most painful and intolerable.

"P. S. Since writing you this morning I learn that the President tendered the place of Mr. Bancroft to Mr. Grinnell, who refused it. It is said that he will accept the naval agency. But the President avows his determination to remove Mr. Motley. My colleague conversed with him on the subject this morning. The President wished somebody 'more American;' but my colleague thought San Domingo was at the bottom. 'More American!' Where is he? Show him! Of course this is an excuse."

To Mrs. L. M. Child, July 7: —

"Your letters are always interesting and encouraging. I feel stronger when I think of two friends so kind and sympathetic. It is painful to me that I am still pursued by controversy. I long for repose, and am now tried as much as ever. On the Chinese, I was left to do battle alone. On the annexation of the West India islands, I began alone. The heats have been great. The President has spared no pains to carry out his ill-considered plan. I insisted that these islands by climate, occupation, and destiny under Providence belonged to the colored race, and that we should not take them away. No greed of land should prevail against the rights of this people.

"I knew Mrs. Lincoln well during the presidency of her husband, and am sure that the stories of disloyalty are without foundation. She was his companion, and sat by his side in his afternoon drives and at his assassination. She is needy and unpopular. I was the friend of the President, and therefore I exert myself for her. I wish you could see this case as I do. Ever sincerely yours and your husband's."

To Longfellow, July 16: —

"At last the bolt has fallen on Motley. I am unhappy at the thought of the unhappiness in his house. Wilson tells me that there is a talk of removing Monti also.[1] When I see you on that piazza, I will tell you this story of — 'Revenge!'"

To Mr. Bemis, then in Europe, July 22: —

"The removal of Motley is simply brutal. This is the only word to describe it; add also heartless and cruel. I hope you will see him and strengthen him. The tragical death of Prévost Paradol[2] adds to the gloom. He was with me half an hour three days before his suicide, speaking of the war and his surprise at it, but saying that it was necessary; also of literature and Guizot, Thiers, and Saint Beuve. He evidently was a great admirer of Thiers."

The senator and the secretary kept up correspondence during the recess of Congress, in which they continued to address each other as "My dear Fish" and "My dear Sumner." They wrote familiarly of various matters, — disagreeing of course upon one. This correspondence continued during October, and the senator was during the next month on his journey. Sumner wrote plainly, even reproachfully, to his old friend, who, as he thought, had failed to stand by Motley as he should, and who seemed to be the source of insinuations against the minister recently made in executive session. Fish replied at length, endeavoring to remove what he regarded as the senator's misapprehension concerning himself, and still professing a warm and strong friend-

[1] This took place shortly after.
[2] 1829-1870; French minister at Washington.

ship for him. He referred to some newspaper criticisms on Motley's removal which had been supposed to be the echo of the senator's conversations; but the latter disavowed having prompted them. The secretary's letters were written in good temper, and personally he was without doubt disinclined to the rupture to which the exigencies of his official relations were hurrying him. Sumner, when the session opened in December, 1870, had given no occasion for a disturbance of the old friendship. Mr. Fish wrote years afterwards:[1] "I declare positively and emphatically that Mr. Sumner never but once spoke an unkind word to me, and never a discourteous one; and on the one occasion referred to[2] (in the Senate chamber in July, 1870) he instantly withdrew his hasty expression, and warmly seized my hand in friendship, as he expressed himself, in order to remove the impression of his quick word." Nor up to this time had Mr. Fish done aught inconsistent with his friendship for the senator. His weak compliance with a scheme to which, unless he is misjudged, he was opposed stands to his discredit as a public man; but it does not up to this time impeach his honor and fidelity as a friend.

As usual in the summer Sumner passed some days with Longfellow at Nahant;[3] and he made a brief visit to a friend in Beverly. In September he was Mr. Hooper's guest at Cotuit. He had promised a visit to the poet Bryant at Cummington, but the burden of a lecture on his mind compelled him to forego it. He was glad to greet Bemis, fresh from foreign journeys. It always pleased him to meet in Boston his associates in the Senate of either party; and this summer he was able to take Mr. Hendricks of Indiana to the interesting points of the city.

Sumner took the chair at a Republican meeting in Faneuil Hall, October 15, to ratify nominations for members of Congress and State officers. His presence was greeted with the enthusiasm which it always called out in Massachusetts. He mentioned, as worthy of all support, Mr. Hooper, the member from Boston; Governor Claflin, candidate for re-election; and his col-

1 Letter to Boston Transcript, Oct. 31, 1877.

2 Probably with reference to Motley's removal.

3 "Sumner lying all the morning in a hammock reading Lothair. Dine with him and T. at George James's." (Longfellow's Journal, August 1.) Longfellow's letter of July 18 welcomed him to the sea-shore, and said of Motley's removal, "It is a gross insult to him, and a very disreputable act to all concerned in it."

league Wilson, whose term in the Senate was near its expiration. He spoke good words for the integrity of the national debt and the work of reconstruction. "Stand by the Republican party" was his exhortation. He introduced, with a warm tribute, as principal speaker, Governor Hawley of Connecticut. In what he said there was no hint of differences with the President.[1]

Immediately after the meeting he started on a lecturing tour, which filled the interval until the session in December. After the labors and vexations of the last session, almost any one else would have insisted on repose; but he was anxious to meet expenses in Washington without incurring debt or diminishing his capital. He appeared thirty-eight times before audiences in the States of Massachusetts, Rhode Island, New Jersey, New York, Pennsylvania, Michigan, and Illinois. He spoke twice in each of the three cities, — Philadelphia, Brooklyn, and Chicago. His fees ranged from two hundred dollars to four hundred dollars an evening, and the net result above expenses exceeded seven thousand dollars. He used sometimes, with his audiences, his address on "Lafayette," which he had delivered ten years before; but generally he gave a lecture prepared in the autumn on the war between France and Prussia, in which he treated the opening events, and passed a heavy judgment on Louis Napoleon, with a plea for sympathy for France now that her usurper was overthrown, and a protest against her dismemberment.[2] The address pointed as its moral that the war-system should be discarded, and the nations should disarm themselves.[3] In 1870 he was still enforcing the truths which he announced twenty-five years before, in his celebrated oration of July 4, 1845. On his route he enjoyed the hospitality of friends, — of Judge Harris at Albany, Gerrit Smith at Peterborough, and Senator Fenton at Jamestown. While at a hotel in Chicago, during a call from Mr. Arnold, biographer of Lincoln, a newspaper reporter, without disclosing his purpose, happened to be present, and the next day gave to a journal of the city what purported to be an account of Sumner's conversation on the President and on

[1] October 15. Works, vol. xiv. pp. 1-5.

[2] "The Duel between France and Germany, with its Lesson to Civilization." (Works, vol. xiv. pp. 9-85.) The lecture was the subject of a review, by M. Chevalier, in the "Journal des Debats."

[3] The New York "Herald," Dec. 2, 1870, took exception to the idealism of the lecture.

Motley.[1] The senator read it with great regret, and repudiated it as a whole,—calling it afterwards in the Senate "a stolen, surreptitious, and false report, . . . with a mixture of truth, of falsehood, and of exaggeration, producing in the main the effect of falsehood."[2]

1 Chicago Republican, November 19; New York Herald, November 21; Boston Journal, December 5.

2 Dec. 21, 1870. Congressional Globe, pp. 247, 253, 254.

## CHAPTER LVI.

SAN DOMINGO AGAIN. — THE SENATOR'S FIRST SPEECH. — RETURN OF THE ANGINA PECTORIS. — FISH'S INSULT IN THE MOTLEY PAPERS. — THE SENATOR'S REMOVAL FROM THE FOREIGN RELATIONS COMMITTEE. — PRETEXTS FOR THE REMOVAL. — SECOND SPEECH AGAINST THE SAN DOMINGO SCHEME. — THE TREATY OF WASHINGTON. — SUMNER AND WILSON AGAINST BUTLER FOR GOVERNOR. — 1870-1871.

SUMNER, it may be repeated, had kept hitherto strictly within the line of his right and duty as a senator in his discussions of the San Domingo scheme. He had given the President by word or act no just cause of offence, the latter's friends as well as the record being witnesses. He felt — and in this he was justified by common belief — that Motley's removal was a blow struck at him personally; but that wound would have healed with time, explanations, or the intervening of other questions. He was still a Republican, loyal to his party, and so avowed himself. The scheme which had divided the party was wanting in public favor, and had been rejected by the decisive vote of the Senate. Without its further agitation there would be harmony; its revival was sure to bring discord.

The President, however, acting wholly on his own motion or more or less by the instigation of others, decided to bring the disturbing question again to the front. His decision was deeply regretted by the mass of the members of his party in Congress and in the country, and it was fraught only with mischief. In his annual message, in December, 1870, he earnestly urged upon Congress early action for acquiring "the island of San Domingo."[1] His estimates of the capacities of the territory were wildly extravagant.[2] Its acquisition would in his view reduce our imports by one hundred millions of dollars, turn the balance of foreign trade in our favor, stimulate enormously commerce and industry, open a market for the products of our farms and

[1] The Haytian minister at Washington asked an explanation of the proposition to acquire "the island," which included Hayti; but Mr. Fish declined to give it.

[2] Blaine's "Twenty Years in Congress," vol. ii. p. 459.

factories, give remunerative wages to tens of thousands of laborers not already on the island, cheapen the cost of living, and (he even went so far as to say) open the way — and the only way he found it easy to see — for the extinguishment of our national debt, then amounting to nearly two billion five hundred million dollars: all this was to be accomplished by a territory only twenty thousand square miles in extent, and having a population imperfectly civilized, and numbering only one hundred and twenty thousand! He avowed his conviction that the moment the project was entirely abandoned, European nations would negotiate for a free port in the Bay of Samana, and that then would be seen "the folly of our rejecting so great a prize," — a prediction of the fulfilment of which no signs have appeared during the succeeding period. He proposed, as one mode for making the acquisition, the joint action of the two houses of Congress by a resolution of annexation, as in the case of the acquisition of Texas. This mode would, of course, overcome the obstruction of a two-thirds vote of the Senate required in the exercise of the treaty-making power; but it was an extraordinary proposition to be made by a Republican President. Its only precedent was the one named, — that made by Tyler, after the Texas treaty had been rejected by the Senate, for the annexation of that territory, being the resort of the propagandists of slavery for the purpose of extending and perpetuating their institution. The friends of liberty had fought it to the end as revolutionary, unconstitutional, and wicked; and their resistance was almost the beginning of the political movement against slavery, out of which the Republican party was born.[1] This idea of recurring to an act which had been repudiated as a precedent in the change of American opinion on the extension of slavery came from General Butler, who at the last session, when the approval of the treaty by the Senate seemed improbable, tried on nine different days[2] without success to introduce a joint resolution for the acquisition of San Domingo. Such a measure from such a quarter was no occasion of surprise, as its author was in full accord with the pro-slavery

[1] The plea made for the Texas resolution that it came under the power "to admit States" did not apply to San Domingo, which it was not proposed to admit as a State. In Senate, Dec. 20 and 21, 1870. Thurman, Congressional Globe, pp. 193, 250; Davis, Ibid., p. 195; Bayard, Ibid., p. 226.

[2] April 6, 7, 9, 11, 13, 20; May 12; June 1, 14. The New York "Herald" approved the method, April 8 and July 1, 1870.

policy of the Democratic party at the time of the annexation of Texas, and had so recently as 1860 supported the nomination of Jefferson Davis and the candidacy of Breckinridge.

During the recess of Congress, busybodies of low or high degree, hoping to gain advantage thereby to themselves, had been doing their best to inflame the President's mind against the senator; and then as always he lent a too ready ear to suggestions unfriendly to those who had thwarted his will. Sumner on arriving in Washington, in December, was assured from various quarters that the President was angry with him, and had even said that but for the dignity of his office as President he would call the senator to account.[1] Threats also had been uttered by Babcock, which at one time he denied, and at another admitted.

Attempts at reconcilement between the President and the senator were made, most likely by Wilson, who was always a peacemaker; but according to the report, the President, manifesting a good deal of feeling, refused to give his consent to any movement having in view a reconciliation. At length, in the third week of the session there came out in a newspaper a statement which appeared to have the sanction of the President or of those very near him. It represented him to have stated that the senator "had attacked him in executive sessions of the Senate; that he had spoken bitterly of him publicly in street cars and other public conveyances, and that he had grossly abused him in Boston and during his recent journey West;" and the President added, "that on some of these occasions Mr. Sumner had attributed dishonest motives to him." The same day Sumner had the passage read in the Senate, when he at once denied the President's charges, calling senators around him, and particularly Morton, to witness that never in executive sessions had he alluded to the President except in most respectful kindness, — asking Morton to repeat to the President what he (Morton) had said the day before to him (Sumner) as to this allegation.[2] He challenged senators and every one else to witness that he had never attributed dishonest motives to the President,[3] declaring that the strongest things he had ever said of him and his acts had been said to Mr. Fish and Mr. Boutwell, whom he summoned

1 Works, vol. xiv. p. 256; Harper's Weekly, Jan. 7, 1871; Boston Journal, Dec. 21, 1870.

2 Dec. 20, 1870, Congressional Globe, pp. 217, 218.

3 He repeated this disclaimer, Works, vol. xiv. p. 257; also in letter to Gerrit Smith, Aug. 20, 1871; Frothingham's "Life of Gerrit Smith," p. 329.

to bear witness to the truth of his assertions. When he took his seat no senator questioned his statement. It was made by one who knew the integrity of his own mind, who always said what he meant, who spoke openly and not in whispers, and who never smote men with hints and insinuations. This public denial drew no disclaimer from the President of the language attributed to him.

There was doubtless free talk at the senator's house as well as at the Executive Mansion and at Mr. Fish's; and the President's military secretaries, with assistance from the state department, were diligent in carrying to him all they heard, and some things which they did not hear. But the official tenure would be fragile indeed if such tales told by such men were, without personal confronting or the scrutiny of cross-examination, to determine the position of statesmen, and their opportunity to serve their country. A truly great man has no ears for them. After Chase had left Lincoln's Cabinet, in 1864, reports were carried to the President of what the late secretary had said of him; but he turned away from the tale-bearers, saying he could not as President take such things into account; and spite of all he heard, he made Chase chief-justice.

The measure on which Sumner had put his foot was not to rise again, but in the contest it had brought on he was to be worsted. The Northern masses as well as their leaders took then, as they take now, but a languid interest in the fate of populations, African or Asiatic, which cannot be counted in the political forces of the country. Patriotic people, who dreaded any distracting issue which might restore the South and the Democratic party to power, held back from coming to his support. There was then as always a widespread sentiment, partisan rather than patriotic, which rebuked dissent within the party when carried to a point likely to break its column at an election. It was a period of low ambitions, — lower than before or since, — when public men, especially senators, were compacted into a body submissive to the Executive will, while their followers were fed from their hands by the booty of patronage. Sumner, idealist as he was, did not comprehend at the outset what powers he had challenged.

When the session began, a plan for the reconstruction of the Senate committee on foreign relations was presented in the Republican caucus. It was proposed, with a view of obtaining favorable action on the San Domingo question, to drop Sumner, Schurz, or Patterson; but it was not found practicable at that time to dislodge either of the first two. A committee (Chandler chairman) in offering a new list in caucus dropped the name of Patterson, placing him elsewhere without consulting him, and substituting Conkling in his stead. Sumner objected to parting with Patterson without the latter's consent, and, Wilson coming to his aid, was able to keep the committee as before. The fact that the change was agitated found its way into the public journals and the debates in the Senate.[1]

The President in his message had asked for "a commission to negotiate a treaty with the authorities of San Domingo for the acquisition of that island." Congress was not deemed to be in a mood to go so far, and Morton introduced a resolution on the sixth day of the session for a commission to investigate and report concerning the condition of the people and various points affecting the question of annexation. Its consideration was pressed to the exclusion of Sumner's earlier call for documents and information,[2] "anterior in time and essentially preliminary in substance," as he said. A reference to a committee was refused, and the debate beginning December 20, a vote was forced the next day. The vote to take up the resolution disclosed the fact that Republican senators generally, even though opposed to the annexation, thought it well to go thus far with the President, hoping that he would be content with this recognition of his wishes and let the matter rest with a report. Morrill and Patterson, however, as well as Sumner and Schurz, voted against taking up the resolution. Edmunds, though still declaring himself opposed to the annexation, supported the resolution as a means for obtaining useful information without committing any one; but his colleague Morrill believed that it was the wise way for an experienced legislator to meet such questions at the threshold, and he considered that the President could not be expected to do otherwise than appoint "a partisan commission."

The main contest was on the second day, when, after brief remarks from Tipton (Republican) and Bayard (Democrat) in opposition, Sumner took the floor.[3] He had before him only

[1] Dec. 21, 1870, Congressional Globe, pp. 230, 241; March 10, 1871, Globe, pp. 39, 42, 47; New York Herald, Dec. 9, 1870; New York Evening Post, December 29.

[2] The call was not voted till Jan. 4, 1871.

[3] Works, vol. xiv. pp. 89-131.

notes in pencil. His self-restraint in manner did not conceal his intensity of feeling, which was hardly ever so great, not even in the debates on Kansas. All the fire of youth came back again, as those who had often heard him felt as they now listened to him.[1] He began by saying that the resolution, though nominally one of inquiry, committed Congress to "a dance of blood," and further on pronounced it "another stage in a drama of blood," — expressions which drew the retort that no blood had been shed, and on account of the superior power of the United States was not likely to be. He gave to Baez, Cazneau, and Fabens the character of "political jockeys,"[2] and described Babcock as a young officer who, acting without known instructions, had assumed in the protocol a lofty title. The stress of his speech was in support of the allegation, based on documents, that Baez had been maintained in power by our navy, and that the President had in his message menaced the independence of Hayti; that attempts at jurisdiction in those waters made by our navy were a usurpation and acts of violence and war, contrary to the Constitution and to international law.[3] The waters of a weak power, he said, were as sacred as those of France or England. He found a parallel to the proposed scheme and the spirit with which it was pressed in the repeal of the Missouri Compromise, and in the Lecompton constitution by which it was sought to subjugate Kansas to slavery. He likened the President's attempt to interfere with the committee on foreign relations to Buchanan's insistence on Douglas's removal in 1868 from the committee on territories in order to carry the Lecompton constitution, and he referred to the menace of personal assault filling the air. He called on Colfax, the Vice-President, to counsel the President "to shun all approach to the example of Franklin Pierce, James Buchanan, and Andrew Johnson." At the end he insisted on the title of the colored race to the island, — "theirs by right of possession, by their sweat and blood mingling with the soil, by tropical position, by its burning sun, and by unalterable laws of climate." The passages in the senator's speech which provoked criticism among Republicans were those in which a comparison was suggested between the

[1] Boston Advertiser, Dec. 22, 1870. "Perley" (B. P. Poore) called it "the most remarkable speech of his life." Boston Journal, Dec. 22, 1870.

[2] Davis Hatch, who knew Baez well, wrote that the term "jockey" was fitly applied to him. New York "Evening Post," Feb. 10, 1871.

[3] This use of the ships was condemned in Harper's Weekly, Feb. 11 and April 15, 1871.

President and his Democratic predecessors, and in which he was charged with menacing the independence of Hayti. He was felt to have treated with disrespect the head of his own party, whose errors, in view of his eminent military services, ought not to be held up as offences against patriotism and humanity. He disclaimed in the debate any charge of corruption against the President and any imputation on his good faith or integrity. Afterwards, he denied with emphasis the charge that he had been influenced by personal hostility to the President, maintaining that he had abstained from any word of personality, and had been simply in earnest on a question of public duty where he felt profoundly that he was right.[1] The Senate took a recess till half-past seven in the evening, when Morton replied to Sumner. He repelled the charge of usurpation and the comparison of the President with Buchanan and Pierce, but passed lightly over the use of our ships in the Haytian and Dominican waters. Though predicting the annexation of San Domingo and also of Cuba and Porto Rico at some future time, he as well as the other supporters of the resolution put aside the ultimate question, and contended that the proposed commission would result in useful information. Morton's speech was the strongest on his side, and it kept within the limits of parliamentary law and good breeding. Nye justified the President, but paid a tribute to Sumner's character "as the boldest among the bold of the champions of human freedom, . . . as spotless as the mountain snow," and spoke of "the glory clustering around him, and the triumphs that he has won." Harlan, who supported annexation, nevertheless testified that the senator from Massachusetts "always acts from the purest motives, and is sustained by the largest intelligence and the most exalted patriotism."

All night long the Massachusetts senator was the target, sometimes of fair argument, but often of unseemly epithets. With some of his associates coarseness of speech and bitter personalities were congenial. Conspicuous in this class was Chandler of Michigan, who on this occasion gave vent to his natural feelings. His charge that Sumner pledged himself to support the treaties in a personal interview with the President called out a positive denial from Sumner, and a statement of what occurred

[1] This appears in his letters at this time, one written to Mrs. J. T. Furness, Jan. 13, 1871. J. W. Forney's "Anecdotes of Public Men," vol. ii. p. 263. See also letter to Gerrit Smith, Aug. 20, 1871, in the latter's "Life," by Frothingham, p. 329.

at the time. Conkling brought into the debate a characteristic speech, and disclosed the scheme, already determined upon, of removing Sumner from the committee on foreign relations. Thurman from the opposite side of the chamber reminded Republican senators that the senator they were now dismissing from their party stood alone in that body in 1852 without a single follower, but sixty had come, including the senator from Michigan, to follow implicitly in his footsteps. Edmunds went at least to the extreme limits of honorable debate. He accused Sumner of private resentment and animosity to the President, and of forgetting, in the indulgence of private griefs, his duty as a senator, going so far as to impute to him an equivocal answer to the President's request for his support of the treaties. He also brought up the Chicago interview, already referred to, which Sumner again repudiated. For an hour the contest between Sumner and Edmunds went on, the latter closing his part of it by saying that the former "had demonstrated to the Senate and his own friends that the worst enemy he has in North America to-day is himself." Sumner repelled his accusations as "an unfounded, vindictive, personal assault." He justified himself against Howe's censure for having charged the President with menacing Hayti; but he dismissed Carpenter as "a jester," when he joined in the attack. Sumner maintained in the contest the dignity and decorum becoming a senator. His opponents were restless and noisy, gathering in a group about Morton's chair, so that once he took his seat, remarking that he should not proceed till order was restored. He bore throughout the brunt of the debate. His knowledge of the methods of the negotiation and of the use of the war ships — points on which the supporters of the resolution were most sensitive — had been obtained from sources not yet open to the public. The Republican senators who agreed with him confined themselves to the impolicy of the acquisition and the futility of the inquiry.

The majority was inexorable in its determination to force the measure to a vote before another day's session, and after midnight voted down motions to adjourn as well as amendments, one of which was for removing the ships from the waters of San Domingo while the commission was at work. Finally, at 6.37 in the morning, with thirty senators absent, the resolution was carried by a vote of thirty-two to nine.[1]

[1] The Senate consisted at this time of sixty-one Republicans and ten Democrats.

In the House, the committee on foreign affairs (Mr. Banks, chairman) reported the resolution, which was taken up January 9 under a suspension of the rules, the Republicans having a two-thirds majority, and it passed on the 10th by a vote of one hundred and twenty-three to sixty-three. Speeches were limited to ten minutes, and the majority, under General Butler's lead, allowed only a two-hours debate. One of the members who spoke and voted against the resolution was George F. Hoar. Butler had a passage-at-arms with Garfield; the latter, taking note of the former's objection to his motion for a brief extension of the debate, said, "Listen to the man who cracks the whip!" and Butler retorted, "Listen to the man whose back smarts!" The House, while concurring in the inquiry, recorded its opposition to the project which lay behind it, by voting an amendment — one hundred and eight yeas to seventy-six nays — to the effect that the resolution should not be understood as committing Congress to the policy of annexing San Domingo. This declaration, showing the judgment of that body, was the decisive influence which ended the agitation of the project after the inquiry had been concluded; it showed that the joint resolution for annexation could not be carried in the House. Among Republicans voting for the amendment were G. F. Hoar, H. L. Dawes, Eugene Hale, and James A. Garfield; and among those voting against it were B. F. Butler and N. P. Banks. The resolution was sent the same day to the Senate, where it was at once taken up. Sumner read from the newspapers accounts of civil war in San Domingo, and said that "the whole scheme was nothing less than the buying of a bloody law-suit." The next day, after speeches from Stewart, Yates, and Wilson for the resolution, and from Schurz against it, the Senate concurred unanimously in the House amendment (Sumner voting for it), and rejected eight amendments offered by the senator.

The removal of Sumner from the committee on foreign relations, which had been threatened by Conkling in the debate, was now fully determined upon, to be effected at the next election in March. The purpose to remove him was freely avowed by senators who assumed to be the President's special friends, and was a subject of comment in the public journals. This, it may be noted, was some weeks before the conferences resulting in the treaty of Washington were entered upon.

The President appointed as commissioners Benjamin F. Wade

of Ohio, Andrew D. White of New York, and Samuel G. Howe of Massachusetts. Professor Agassiz declined an appointment, not wishing to take a place which might involve any semblance of antagonism to his friend the senator; but Dr. Howe was less considerate in this respect. The commission sailed Jan. 18, 1871, accompanied by Frederick Douglass, General Sigel, and several editors. They remained in San Domingo or its waters from January 23 to February 28, being engaged about five weeks in their observations. The character of their report was assured from the beginning.

William L. Garrison wrote,[1] December 26: —

"I want to thank you for your recent speech in the Senate in opposition to the undesirable and uncalled-for scheme of President Grant for the annexation of San Domingo. With all my understanding, heart, and soul I am with you, both in the letter and the spirit. The assaults made upon you by Morton, Conkling, and Chandler excite equal disgust and indignation, and will certainly recoil heavily upon themselves, doing you in the end no harm. You will not allow yourself to be browbeaten or intimidated by the outpouring of any phial of rhetorical abuse, or by any menace of personal malice, or by any presidential overbearing. Maintain your personal and senatorial independence in all matters of profound judgment and conscientious dissent, and the whole country will be indebted to you for the example, and will profit by it. If a servile or compliant endorsement of whatever the President chooses to submit to Congress is to be made the test of fidelity to the Republican party, then the sooner the party is dissolved the better. It is apparent that President Grant means to coerce Congress into an approval of his scheme, whether or no; but I trust that body will steadfastly resist anything like dictation from that quarter. I am sorry that commissioners are to be appointed, because as the President is to appoint them, and he is mad on annexation, they will surely report in conformity with his wishes. To me it is utterly incredible that the people of San Domingo wish to part with their independence, and to become a fractional part of our republic. I regard it as a mercenary, land-grabbing speculation of the worst type. Yours for sturdy uprightness."

Frederick Douglass, writing Jan. 6, 1871, while he objected to Sumner's direct references to the President, paid a tribute to the senator for what he had done to his oppressed race as higher than the highest, better than the best of our statesmen. Of the delivery of the speech he said: —

"I heard every word of it, and would go many miles to hear a similar effort. It has been many years since I have seen you so roused and so terribly effective. Your printed speech, grand and powerful as it is, falls short of the speech as heard from the gallery, where voice, manner, and action united to give it force and effect."

[1] Sumner's letter to Garrison is printed in the latter's "Life," vol. iv. p. 259.

It was a surprise at the time, and the mystery has never been explained, how Mr. Douglass was afterwards brought to the support of a scheme involving the extinction of one, if not two, republics founded by his race. The mystery is all the greater, since during the long period which has followed he has not again pressed it upon the attention of the country, or in any way signified that he continued to regard it with favor.

G. W. Curtis admitted the reasons for Sumner's warmth found in the printed documents, but objected that he "criticised the Administration as a relentless enemy and not as a friend," at a time when it was "of the utmost possible importance to criticise without weakening it," and asking if he could not have substituted private remonstrance with the President.

The strain of the San Domingo contest had a serious effect on the senator's health. During a good part of the winter he suffered from an affection of the throat or lungs. He had come regretfully to the controversy, and the bitterness which it brought out made him unhappy. He wrote, February 5, to Dr. Brown-Séquard, who had just arrived in the country: "I am weary and old, and much disheartened by the course of our President, who is not the man we supposed." On the 14th and 15th he pressed a mass of business on the Senate from his committee, and on the 18th was seized with a severe illness, during which he suffered a violent attack of the *angina pectoris*, — a paroxysm on the chest, embracing heart and left arm, — the revival of his old disease, which had been dormant since 1859.[1] His illness, which kept him from his seat a week, drew cordial tributes from journals and private correspondents, even from many who had dissented from his style of treating the San Domingo proceedings of the Administration. Wendell Phillips's extract from Burke expressed the feeling of many who differed from him on this point, — "At this exigent moment the loss of a finished man is not easily supplied." Widespread sympathy was felt in Massachusetts and elsewhere.[2] Many cautions enjoining rest and abstinence from excitement came to him. Amos A. Lawrence wrote: "After this last illness you must have become satisfied that your enemies are all died

[1] Except some symptoms in 1866.

[2] New York Evening "Post," March 6, 1871; New York "Herald," February 19; Boston "Journal," February 20; Harper's Weekly, March 11, containing not only an expression of sympathy with the senator in his illness, but a tribute to his high character as a public man, and to the integrity of his motives in the San Domingo controversy.

out." Richard Yates of Illinois on leaving the Senate wrote a tender letter to Sumner, which closed thus: "Pardon me if I say that the remembrance of your kind demeanor towards me inspires me with many a pleasing emotion, and that through life I shall cherish for you the liveliest gratitude and the deepest affection." One who had no sympathy with the San Domingo scheme or the methods by which it was being promoted, not finding him at home, left this note in pencil at his door: —

Sunday, Feb. 19, 1871.

DEAR MR. SUMNER, — I called to inquire after your health, and am rejoiced to learn you are better. "Serus in cœlum redeas."

Your friend,

J. A. GARFIELD.

Wendell Phillips, who was Sumner's guest, wrote to Lydia Maria Child,[1] March 4, 1871: —

"I spent two days with Sumner. His illness is some heart disease, probably the remote effect of his old blow. The doctors say the only policy is rest; the more he'll take, the better health, and the better chance of life prolonged. I argued and prayed; so did we all. How would it do for you to drop him one line beseeching the same course? I told him any harm to him would be greater evil than the stealing of all the west shores.[2] Sometime I'll tell you lots of good things. The Russian minister said to me: 'Make him rest, — he must. No man in Washington can fill his place, — *no man*, NO MAN. We foreigners all know he is honest. We do not think that of many.'"

Notwithstanding the controversy in which he was engaged, Sumner kept up his interest in ordinary matters of legislation, and was never more active in the details of the business of his committee, which he was about to leave.[3] His article on New Year's Day in the New York "Independent" touched upon various

1 New England Magazine, February, 1892, p. 732.

2 An allusion to the measures for acquiring San Domingo.

3 As to committee or other work, see Congressional Globe for January 19; February 4, 7, 8, 14, 15 (pp. 592, 953, 1013, 1049, 1208-1211, 1253-1255). Among subjects which he treated in debate were the proposed removal of the remains of soldiers from the Arlington cemetery, Dec. 13, 1870 (Works, vol. xiv. pp. 86-88), which he opposed (for this effort Nast sent with his autograph to the senator his picture in Harper's Weekly, Jan. 14, 1871); transportation of supplies in national vessels to France and Germany for the relief of those who had been impoverished in the war between the two countries, Feb. 4, 1871 (Works, vol. xiv. pp. 151, 152); abolition of the discrimination of color in the public schools of the District of Columbia, Feb. 8, 1871 (Works, vol. xiv. pp. 153-163), — Dec. 5 and 8, 1870, and Jan. 24, 1871 (Globe, pp. 2, 3, 39, 687); emblems on coins, Jan. 10, 1871 (Globe, p. 399); the death of John Covode, member of Congress, to whom he paid a tribute, commending his opposition to "outside and disturbing questions calculated to distract and divide," Feb. 10, 1871 (Works, vol. xiv. pp. 164-166).

political topics, — Ku-Klux violence at the South, amnesty, specie payments, and the San Domingo question; and it pleaded for the unity of the Republican party, with a protest against the forcing of distracting questions into its councils.[1] He was a guest at a complimentary dinner given in Washington to John W. Forney,[2] and a few days later addressed the graduating class of colored law-students at Howard University.[3] He introduced Anna Dickinson to the audience on the occasion of her lecture at Lincoln Hall in Washington.[4]

He was always earnest for Italian unity, and was glad now to join in commemorating the occupation of Rome by the Italian government.[5] Appropriately in this connection may be given his letter to Lieber, May 7, 1869: —

"At the beginning of Mr. Lincoln's Administration I counselled earnestly against a mission to Rome, but in vain. Seward wished it as a 'preserve' for one of his friends. At last, two years ago, I was able to stop this appropriation, and I have refused to allow it since. My reason was that it was to fortify the Italian government at Florence, and not to strengthen the temporal power of the Pope. Within a few weeks I have received a communication from M. Menabrea, thanking me in the name of the Italian government. I am glad that you agree with me."

He closed, Sept. 15, 1870, a letter to W. W. Story thus: —

"Meanwhile Italy ascends in her career, and Rome is at last the capital. Is not the Church falling gradually, never to rise? Clearly it is a wide-spread anachronism."

He wrote to Bemis, Jan. 18, 1871: —

"Sir John Rose is here with proposals, or rather to sound our government. The English pray for settlement as never before. Mr. Fish has asked my judgment. I have sent him a memorandum, in which I have said: 'A discrimination in favor of claims arising from the depredations of any particular ship will dishonor the claims arising from the depredations of other ships, which the American government cannot afford to do; nor should the English government expect it, if they would sincerely remove all occasions of difference.' If you will not write for the public, then write for me. General Cushing was with me this morning, and agreed against allowing any discrimination in favor of a particular ship. Nothing would please the English more."

Sumner was in friendly personal relations with Mr. Fish from the beginning of the session till Jan. 9, 1871. On December 21,

1 January 5, 1871. Works, vol. xiv. pp. 132-138.
2 January 28. Works, vol. xiv. pp. 142-145; Washington "Star," January 30.
3 February 3. Works, vol. xiv. pp. 146-150.
4 January 26.
5 January 10. Works, vol. xiv. pp. 139-141. February 21, 1871. Ibid., p. 167.

1870, he referred in the Senate to the secretary as his distinguished friend. Even after the heated debate of December 21, he dined on the 23d at Mr. Fish's in company with Senator Morton. The day before, he had cordially assisted in the confirmation of Mr. Schenck as Motley's successor, when he asked for the Senate's immediate action with a waiver of a reference to the committee on foreign relations. On the 27th Mr. Fish was before the committee to explain the business of his department. Sumner wrote afterwards: "Within a brief fortnight [before January 9] I had been in conference with him [Mr. Fish] at the state department, and had dined at his house, besides about the same time making a call there." They were meeting in this way in agreeable personal intercourse through the greater part of December, and so far as Sumner knew might have continued thus to meet up to January 9, when the President sent to the Senate the papers concerning Motley's recall.

The reader who has followed this narrative will recall that up to this time, by the testimony of both of them, their relations had not been disturbed. They were still friends, — differing widely on one question or some of its incidents, but still friends as they had been for twenty years. With these ties and under these circumstances, without provocation or any reason or even pretext ever given, Mr. Fish proceeded on December 30 to put on record the grossest insult against Sumner, — a senator and a friend. On that day he signed the letter to Moran, intended as an answer to Motley's letter of December 7. This is not the place to dwell on the ribaldry and insolence of office exhibited towards that minister in this extraordinary paper, and it will be noted in this connection only so far as it concerns Sumner. Motley in his letter of defence had referred to the rumor of his removal on account of Sumner's opposition to the San Domingo treaty. Fish in his reply said that the rumor had its origin in Washington, "in a source bitterly, personally, and vindictively hostile to the President." He designated Sumner in this way as the author of a view of Motley's removal which was taken on both sides of the Atlantic, in journals and common belief. Sumner was spoken of as "the venerable senator," although he was then only fifty-nine, while Fish was sixty-two, — a reference to age which indicated that a younger hand than the secretary's was holding the pen. Then follows the gross insult to the senator which has been referred to: —

"Mr. Motley must know — or if he does not know it he stands alone in his ignorance of the fact — that many senators opposed the San Domingo treaty openly, generously, and with as much efficiency as did the distinguished senator to whom he refers, and have nevertheless continued to enjoy the undiminished confidence and the friendship of the President, — than whom no man living is more tolerant of honest and manly differences of opinion, is more single or sincere in his desire for the public welfare, or more disinterested or regardless of what concerns himself, is more frank and confiding in his own dealings, *is more sensitive to a betrayal of confidence*, or *would look with more scorn and contempt upon one who uses the words and the assurances of friendship to cover a secret and determined purpose of hostility*."

These terms imply a charge against some one — and the connection shows that Sumner was meant as the object — of falseness of nature and hypocrisy. They were written by Mr. Fish of one who for twenty years had been his confidential friend,[1] often his guest, for a year or more his closest adviser, a week or two before sitting at his table, — written without quarrel or provocation; not naturally coming into the argument, but forced into it; written in cool blood, and placed there to remain forever on the public records, — words containing an imputation which would have broken any friendship. How Mr. Fish could do this thing it is difficult to see; but it is more difficult to explain how he could write seven years later:[2] "The cessation and interruption of that intimacy [with Sumner] were to me the cause of deep and continuing regret. I am not conscious of any just cause for the discontinuing of the relations which had existed between us."[3] The interval may have worked confusion in his memory, but what follows will show that at the time he did know the cause, and a "just cause" too. He knew when he sealed the despatch that the senator he had libelled could not as a man of honor have anything to do with him thereafter except purely in an official way. Sumner wrote afterwards: —

"If beyond paying court to the President, even at the expense of making him praise himself, the concluding sentence of this elaborate passage, so full of gall from beginning to end, had any object; if it were anything but a mountain of words, — it was an open attempt to make an official document the vehicle of personal insult to me; and this insult was signed 'Hamilton Fish.' As I became aware of it, and found also that it was regarded by oth-

[1] *Ante*, pp. 377-379.

[2] Letter in Boston Transcript, Oct. 31, 1877.

[3] Mr. Fish's partisans, as well as himself, uniformly ignore the insult to Sumner in the letter to Moran. Badeau says that Fish's letter to Moran "in no way reflected on Sumner." "Grant in Peace," p. 218.

ers in the same light, I was distressed and perplexed. I could not comprehend it. I knew not why the secretary should step so far out of his way, in a manner absolutely without precedent, to treat me with ostentatious indignity, — especially when I thought that for years I had been his friend; that I had never spoken of him except with kindness; and that constantly, since assuming his present duties, he had turned to me for help. This was more incomprehensible when I considered how utterly groundless were all his imputations. I have lived in vain if such an attempt on me can fail to rebound on its author." [1]

Sumner did not read the Motley papers for some days, but being informed of the offensive passage in Fish's letter, he recognized that the insult was aimed at himself. It was incomprehensible to him that the secretary should have written it, in view of past relations. He talked with some intimate friends about it, who interpreted it as he did, but said nothing publicly, hoping for some explanation. Sir John Rose was in Washington at this time for the purpose of sounding the Administration as to what would be acceptable for the disposition of the "Alabama" claims, and it became important for the secretary to consult the senator. But for the studied insult in the despatch to Moran the secretary might have gone at once to Sumner, and would have done so without any one's mediation; but knowing what he had done, and knowing or supposing that Sumner knew what he had done, he asked Mr. Patterson of the foreign relations committee, three days after the Motley correspondence had gone in, to ascertain for him what his relations with the senator were, and how he would be received. Sumner answered Patterson that — "Should the secretary come to my house he would be received as an old friend, and that at any time I should be at his service for consultation on public business; but that I could not conceal my deep sense of personal wrong received from him, absolutely and without excuse." Patterson communicated the answer to Fish, and the latter called on the senator on the 15th. There was a frank interchange of views on the pending question, but the conversation was confined exclusively to public business.[2] There is no claim from any quarter that in this interview the senator was reserved, or

[1] Works, vol. xiv. pp. 263–264.

[2] Sumner did not fail to deny positively the statement, when coming from any responsible quarter, that he had declined to hold any intercourse, official or otherwise, with Mr. Fish. William Whiting of Boston, former solicitor of the war department, having repeated the statement as he had heard it from others, and being called to account by the senator, admitted after a careful inquiry that he had been misinformed. He closed his letter of

in any way wanting in courtesy or duty. Sumner had made up his mind, however, that until the secretary retracted the insult, his relations with him could be only official. Two days after, he communicated to Mr. Fish his views on the subject of their interview in writing. Then as always he held himself ready to confer and co-operate officially with the secretary; but no man with any sense of honor could keep up friendly or personal relations with one who had imputed to him the baseness charged in the letter to Moran. After this meeting Sumner declined to recognize Mr. Fish at a dinner at Mr. Schenck's house. Sumner, in reply to a note from Edward Eggleston of Brooklyn, wrote from the Senate chamber while Schurz was speaking on his proposed removal, March 10, the following note: —

"The President has such relations with me as he chooses. I have never declined to see him or confer with him. If there is a quarrel, it is all on his side. The secretary of state sent to me through Senator Patterson to know if I would receive him if he came to my house on business. I replied that I had a deep sense of wrong from him, but that I should receive him at any time, or confer with him, on public business. Accordingly, he came to my house, and I received him kindly. Afterwards, when meeting him socially, I gave him the cold shoulder. . . . Mr. Fish insulted me personally in his despatch to Motley."[1]

Sumner wrote afterwards: —

"On careful reflection, it seemed to me plain that while meeting the secretary officially, it would not be consistent with self-respect for me to continue personal relations with one who had put his name to a document which, after protracted fury toward another [Motley], contained a studied insult to me, where the fury was intensified rather than tempered by too obvious premeditation. Public business must not suffer, but in such a case personal relations naturally cease; and this rule I have followed since. Is there any senator who would have done less? Are there not many who would have done more? I am at a loss to understand how the secretary could expect anything beyond those official relations which I declared my readiness at all times to maintain, and which, even after his assault on me, he was willing to seek at my own house. To expect more shows on his part grievous insensibility to the thing he had done. Whatever one signs he makes his own; and the secretary, when he signed this document, adopted a libel upon his friend; and when he communicated it to the Senate he published the libel. Nothing like it can be

May 7, 1872, thus: "It is hardly necessary for me to say that these facts change the whole aspect of the matter in my view; and as it is my duty to you, it is also a great pleasure to myself, frankly to say so."

[1] Meaning the letter to Moran, intended as a reply to Motley.

shown in the history of our government. It stands alone. The secretary is alone. Like Jean Paul in German literature his just title will be, 'The only one.' For years I have known secretaries of state, and often differed from them; but never before did I receive from one anything but kindness. Never before did a secretary of state sign a document libelling an associate in the public service, and publish it to the world. Never before did a secretary of state so entirely set at defiance every sentiment of friendship. It is impossible to explain this strange aberration except from the disturbing influence of San Domingo. But whatever its origin, its true character is beyond question." [1]

Hypocrisy and duplicity were never before attributed to Sumner, even by most unfriendly critics. His characteristics, his defects and limitations, as well as his excellencies, were thought to lie in a different direction,— in remarkable openness and sincerity, and in want of tact. What Fish meant in his offensive passage he never explained; but the allusion was supposed to be to Sumner's interview with Grant concerning San Domingo, during which the senator did not mislead the President, or fail to do what he said he would do. But even if Fish adopted the President's version of the conversation, it was not for him after twenty years of intimacy, in which he had professed to love Sumner "long and much," [2] to accept a construction which imputed insincerity and baseness. That is not the way of fair-minded men, least of all of old friends, in interpreting each other's acts and words. Something is due to a friendship, even after it is broken. The common instincts of men enjoin reserve on divided friends as well as parted kinsmen; and this reserve Sumner kept. If he spoke, as he rarely did, of his old friend, now his slanderer, it was in strict self-defence, and in the tone of sorrow, not of anger. Fish, on the other hand, even after Sumner's death, accused him of gross neglect of official duty in the non-reporting of treaties; and when the accusation was disproved by the opening of the secret records of the Senate, he never withdrew his libel, or explained how he came to utter it. Sumner in his day, like all public men of strong natures dealing with vital questions, had his controversies, as with Winthrop, Adams, Seward, Fessenden, Trumbull, Edmunds; but *they* were all honorable men, and they respected the grave.

The new Congress (the Forty-second) met March 4, immediately on the expiration of the preceding one, and continued its session till May 27. The Republican caucus for arranging the committees met on the morning of March 9. The chairman,

[1] Works, vol. xiv. pp. 265–266.

[2] *Ante*, p. 377.

Anthony, appointed as the committee to present a list Sherman, Morrill of Vermont, Howe, Nye, and Pool. Anthony was friendly to Sumner, and if in naming the committee he had in mind the proposed exclusion of Sumner, he supposed at least the first three favorable to his retention, as Sherman and Morrill proved to be. Howe had, however, as it appeared, taken a position against Sumner.[1] Two gentlemen, anxious for harmony in the party, — Horace White of the Chicago "Tribune," and W. B. Allison, member of Congress from Iowa, — without Sumner's knowledge, called on Howe before the committee reported, and endeavored to dissuade him from recommending Sumner's removal; but they found him inflexible. The ground, and the only ground, he then took was that the senator had made himself offensive to the President by the kind of his opposition to the San Domingo treaty, making no reference to his relations to Fish, whose name was not even mentioned. The pretext of "personal relations" was adopted later as the best for forensic use. The committee (its majority being Howe, Nye, and Pool) placed Cameron instead of Sumner at the head of the foreign relations committee, and put Sumner at the head of a new committee, — that of privileges and elections. Sumner said, when the report of the committee came up, March 9, in the caucus: —

"It is now twelve years since I became a member of the committee on foreign relations, and ten years since I became its chairman. I began as chairman with Mr. Lincoln's Administration in 1861, and entered at once upon the important questions by which our country was then tried. During this period I have had as associates able and eminent senators, some of whom have passed away. Wherever they may be, I am willing to be judged by them. I would summon the dead, — Douglas, Collamer, Fessenden. I would leave all these to testify if I have ever failed in any duty of labor or patriotism."

The senator then declined the place on the new committee, and retired from the caucus. A debate followed, in which the change was justified on the ground that the senator was not on speaking terms with the President and the Secretary of State. This was manifestly a pretext, as the removal had been agitated three months before, when the senator's and the secretary's

[1] Howe had been Sumner's eulogist, speaking of him in the Senate, Jan. 26, 1866 (Congressional Globe, p. 441), as the author of a great number of living sentiments destined to live long after his colleague (Doolittle) and himself should have passed from this stage of existence. See also *ante*, p. 163 *note*.

relations were as yet undisturbed. Howe gave also as a reason that the majority of the Senate being in favor of the annexation of San Domingo (a fact which had not appeared by any vote), it was proper to constitute the committee so that it should represent the majority. Wilson expressed the general belief in saying that the real cause was the San Domingo business. A motion was made to recommit, with instructions to report the list as it was at the last session. This was the test vote, those opposed to Sumner's removal voting for the recommitment. It failed by a vote of twenty-one to twenty-six.[1] The caucus met again the next morning, when a motion to reconsider the vote by which the report was adopted failed by a vote of twenty-one to twenty-three, — a falling off of three from the opposition to the senator. Sumner was present when the caucus met, but left as soon as this motion was made, anticipating correctly that its consideration would involve a debate concerning himself.

On the 10th Howe moved in the Senate the adoption of the list, with Cameron at the head of the committee on foreign relations, and Sumner at the head of that on privileges and elections. Sumner asked to be excused from taking the place assigned him, saying that after twenty years of service he felt that a new class of duties which were not welcome should not be imposed upon him; and his request was granted. Schurz moved a postponement of the vote on the list, hoping to have differences reconciled; but his motion was rejected. He then referred to Sumner's long service and rare fitness for a post which he had filled "with great credit to himself and to the committee, and with great satisfaction to the American people," and called on Howe to give the reasons for the change. There was an indisposition on

[1] The yeas for recommitment were as follows: Cragin (N. H.), Morrill (Maine), Morrill (Vt.), Ferry (Conn.), Wilson (Mass.), Sprague (R. I.), Fenton (N. Y.), Sherman (Ohio), Windom (Minn.), Wright (Iowa), Logan (Ill.), Trumbull (Ill.), Tipton (Neb.), Hitchcock (Neb.), Caldwell (Kan.), Corbett (Oregon), Schurz (Mo.), Boreman (W. Va.), Robertson (S. C.), Spencer (Ala.), Gilbert (Fla.). The nays were Hamlin (Maine), Edmunds (Vt.), Conkling (N. Y.), Frelinghuysen (N. J.), Scott (Penn.), J. Hill (Ga.), Morton (Ind.), Harlan (Iowa) Howe (Wis.), Carpenter (Wis.), Chandler (Mich.), Ferry (Mich.), Pomeroy (Kan.), Nye (Nev.), Stewart (Nev.), Ramsey (Minn.), Lewis (Va.), Brownlow (Tenn.), Pool (N. C.), Sawyer (S. C.), Osborn (Fla.), West (La.), Kellogg (La.), Ames (Miss.), Flanagan (Texas), Cole (Col.). Some reports put Hamilton (Texas) in place of Flanagan (Texas), and Pratt (Ind.) in place of J. Hill (Ga.); but Pratt's eulogy on Sumner, April 27, 1874, makes it improbable that he favored Sumner's removal. Those reported as speaking in the caucus for the removal were Nye, Hamlin, Stewart, Conkling, Howe, Edmunds, and Carpenter, — the last named making the longest speech. Those reported as speaking against the removal were Wilson, Schurz, Fenton, Sherman, Ferry (Conn.), Trumbull, Corbett, and Morrill (Vt.).

the part of the Republican majority to have a debate on the question, but they found that it could not well be avoided. Howe admitted Sumner's ability to fill the place, even better than any one, and gave as the only reason for the change that there were no personal and social relations between the senator and the President and the head of the state department; or in other words, that the senator was not in personal intercourse or on speaking terms with them. He did not claim that there was any exclusion of official intercourse, and when pressed as to details, said that Sumner had refused in presence of official characters to answer some question from Fish; [1] but he was unable to state what the question was, and he did not claim that it referred to official business. Sumner from his seat denied at once the allegation that he had refused to answer any question. Howe bore this tribute: "Eloquent as my friends are, powerful as they are in description, they cannot employ any terms which will give me a livelier idea of the manner in which the senator from Massachusetts has discharged his duties than I have while I stand here now. He is not arraigned for any misconduct in his management of the affairs of that committee in the years that have passed." And again: "If senators insist upon it, I will admit that the senator from Massachusetts could under happier circumstances fill it [the place of chairman] better than anybody else." Stewart, Nye, and other supporters of the senator's displacement sought to avoid the real issue by assuming the change to be an ordinary matter, occurring at each session, and arranged by the majority party, the decision of which was not to be questioned outside of the caucus; but Trumbull pointed out that the proposed action was extraordinary, and that according to the established usages of the body chairmen were not changed contrary to their expressed wishes. From Nye came the admission: "When anybody says that the honorable senator has been faithful in his chairmanship, no voice will deny it." This was the case of the promoters of the removal, as they put it on record, — non-speaking with the President and secretary in social life; and this was all of it. No suggestion or hint was made that he had failed in any public duty, or was in any way an obstruction to public business.

The propriety of the removal was earnestly contested. Schurz maintained that "the San Domingo scheme was at the bottom

[1] Supposed to be a reference to what occurred at Mr. Schenck's dinner-table.

of the whole difficulty," attributed the proposed removal to the President's instance, and stigmatized the justification based on absence of personal relations as "a flimsy pretext." He produced the offensive passage contained in Fish's despatch to Moran, and justified the senator for acting upon the instincts of a man and a gentleman in refusing, after he knew of the insult, friendly recognition.[1] He mentioned, too, that in spite of the insult the senator had still expressed his readiness to confer freely with the secretary on public business, — a statement which Howe did not contest. Wilson earnestly protested against the removal, ascribing it wholly to the San Domingo controversy. He said: —

> "Sir, the truth is, and everybody knows it, and it is useless for the senator from Wisconsin, or any other senator, to deny it, that this proposition to remove my colleague grows out of the San Domingo question. If there never had been an effort to annex San Domingo, we should have had no attempt to change the chairmanship of the committee on foreign relations, or to remove members from that committee. . . . The people of the country, say what you may about it, will come to the conclusion that at the bottom of it all lies this San Domingo annexation question."

He denied that it was the business of the Senate to entertain questions of personal and social relations between senators and the President and members of his Cabinet. He pleaded against distraction in the party, and against the counsels of certain senators "whose only trophies are the scalps of their political friends." He said: —

> "Sir, why should the Senate of the United States to-day undertake to strike down a senator who has been twenty years in this body; a senator who has stood for ten years at the head of the committee on foreign relations; a senator who, you all admit, understands by his education, his foreign travel, the studies of his life, and his ripe experience here our foreign affairs better than any other member of either house of Congress? Why is this senator disrated before the country? Because he held certain views on San Domingo; because he opposed its acquisition; because with all the earnestness of his soul he opposed it; because he had a difference with the President and the Secretary of State. Sir, a senator has the right to differ with the President and Secretary of State as well as with any other public officers. Senators are nobody's servants."

Tipton maintained that Sumner's disclaimer of any refusal of conference on official business should be accepted, saying: "No man ever doubted his word, and no man ever doubted his fidel-

1 Howe did not know until this mention by Schurz that the passage was intended for Sumner. Howe was in error in stating that the unhappy relation between Fish and Sumner did not arise till sometime after those words saw the light.

ity, and no man ever doubted his high honor." Logan was hearty in declaring the injustice of displacing, at the beck of a Secretary of State, a senator as chairman who had done his duty, and maintained that it involved a surrender of the independence of the Senate to any Cabinet officer who saw fit to object to a senator as chairman. He spoke of Sumner as one whom, when himself entering Congress as a Democrat, he recognized as "a man of great ability and of sterling integrity and worth," and "leading the army of liberty in this country." Trumbull said: "I stood by him [Sumner] when he was stricken down in his seat by a hostile party, by the powers of slavery. I stand by him to-day when the blow comes, not from those who would perpetuate slavery, and make a slave of every man that was for freedom, but comes from those who have been brought into power as much through the instrumentality of the senator from Massachusetts as of any other individual in the country." Sherman felt bound by the action of the caucus; but he recorded his deliberate conviction that it was an unwise proceeding, made without sufficient cause. He said: "But, sir, as we have been drawn into this debate, in justice to myself,—and I call other senators to witness the truth of it,—I do here repeat what I have said in other places, that I regard this change as unjustifiable, as impolitic, as unnecessary, and that no reason has been given which ought to weigh, in my judgment, to induce the change." There was no senator on that floor whose opinion, in view of his constant interest in public business and his judicial temperament, was worth so much as that of the senator from Ohio. Indeed, hardly any senator in our history has kept his balance so perfectly in the midst of controversy. He spoke without partiality, not being an intimate friend of Sumner, or of the same type of public men. Wilson closed the debate, affirming "that what had been resolved upon by a small majority of a caucus, by a minority of the Republican members of the Senate, is not right in itself, is not expedient, is a political blunder, wrong in itself, and had better be abandoned instead of being consummated." Logan and Wilson reminded the majority that the one precedent for a change at the instance of the Executive was the removal of Douglas from the head of the committee on territories at Buchanan's dictation on account of that senator's opposition to the Lecompton constitution. It was recalled in the debate that

Henry Clay was chairman of the committee on foreign affairs at a time when there were no personal relations between him and President Jackson, and that senators held their chairmanships under President Johnson, with whom they had no intercourse.[1] The majority did not claim that the senator was an aggressor in his trouble with the secretary, and it was implied that their action would have been the same, no matter what provocation he might have had for discontinuing social or personal intercourse with Mr. Fish. On the theory of personal relations, which they assumed as their justification, it would always be practicable for any Secretary of State to provoke a quarrel with the chairman of the Senate committee on foreign relations, and by his own wrongful act create an occasion for that chairman's dismissal. It should be considered, too, that if there were to be a change on account of broken personal relations, without inquiry as to the cause, then it was for the secretary to leave a post which he had held for less than two years rather than for the senator to leave a post he had held for ten years.

Argument and protest were, however, of no avail against an inexorable majority. Motions to adjourn and postpone for a day were lost. Several senators, who regarded the change as a calamity, and had opposed it in caucus, felt bound to acquiesce at this stage. Sumner and his Republican friends withheld their votes, and the negative vote was composed of the nine Democrats who had kept out of the debate. Garrett Davis said at the end that the foregone conclusion had originated at the White House, and there alone, — a statement repeated by Thurman. Bayard moved that the title of the committee be changed from "foreign" to "personal" relations. Sumner took no part in the debate, only making one or two remarks from his seat. The audience (a large one) was in sympathy with him, and applauded points made in his behalf.

The same influences which swayed Southern Republican senators on the San Domingo question — weak at home in their positions, and expectants of Executive favor — controlled them now.[2] Chandler, Conkling, and Edmunds were, as Wilson intimated, on the war-path for another scalp. The last named, at

[1] Later, Conkling had no personal relations with President Hayes, and was bitterly hostile to President Garfield; but there was no attempt to remove him from the chairmanship of committees.

[2] One of these, convicted of official malversation, was serving a term of imprisonment in the Washington jail in 1877.

a later day, succeeded in defeating the confirmation of E. Rockwood Hoar as a justice of the Supreme Court, — an accomplished jurist, eminently fitted to adorn that tribunal. Mr. Edmunds has won deserved distinction for his wisdom and fidelity as a legislator; but his treatment of these two New England public men will never be placed among his meritorious services. Unlike the Vermont senator, Trumbull forgot the heats of former conflicts, and stood manfully by his old antagonist. One who had formerly led in that body, ever high-minded and jealous of the dignity of the Senate, impatient indeed with Sumner when their peculiarities clashed, but having full faith in his fidelity and honor, was no longer there. Had Fessenden lived, the removal of Sumner would not have been carried, — indeed, would not have been attempted.[1]

Cameron, who succeeded Sumner, was by general opinion unfitted for the duties of the chairman; hardly a senator was less fitted. It is to his credit that he did not seek the place, and came to it with regret. He took no part in the struggle, which, as he said, was painful to him. Once, when he was absent in Russia, Sumner had defended him in executive session; and whatever were Cameron's faults, he never forgot a favor, and was never false to a friend. Their relations continued most friendly, and on Sumner's last day in the Senate they parted with a mutual "God bless you!"[2] Cameron lived to a great age, and to the end was always ready to testify to Sumner's fidelity and honor.

There was joy at the Executive Mansion and the state department, and the San Domingo adventurers were in ecstasies. To Conkling and Carpenter had come the opportunity for which they had long been waiting, and to Edmunds one which he had been craving since the debate on the San Domingo commission. But other senators, who had been reluctant instruments of injustice, were not content with what they had done. They knew how their subserviency would be regarded by living men, and

[1] Fessenden's most intimate friend in the Senate (Grimes of Iowa) wrote from Switzerland to F. A. Pike, Jan. 10, 1871: "Was there ever anything so absurd, so wicked indeed, as the attempt to force the country to accept San Domingo against its will? I have no great admiration for Sumner, but I glory in his pluck, and I wish I were able to be in Washington to fight by his side." (Salter's "Life of J. W. Grimes," pp. 382, 383.) Mr. Grimes died in February, 1872; but he signified by a letter, afterwards published, his opposition to the President's re-election. Another public man, though while in office altogether unfriendly to Sumner, condemned the removal. Hugh McCulloch's "Men and Measures of Half a Century," p. 353.

[2] Cameron in the Senate, April 28, 1874. Congressional Globe, p. 3434.

they anticipated already the judgment of history. Fortune did not favor some of the leading prosecutors. Carpenter and Chandler failed of re-elections to the Senate. Conkling chafed during Hayes's Administration, when he was no longer master of patronage, and affronted at like neglect by Garfield, resigned his seat. Appealing to the legislature of his State to approve his conduct by another election, he met with an ignominious refusal, and then passed forever out of public life. Outside the circle of partisans holding office, or in direct relations with the President, there was almost universal condemnation of the removal as unjust or impolitic,[1] while the tone of its defenders was apologetic. Forney telegraphed to Sumner from Philadelphia, March 9: "The indignation here over your removal extends to men of all parties. I have not heard one Republican approving it. I shall denounce it without stint to-morrow." His despatch the next day was as follows: "The leading evening Republican papers follow the morning Republicans in stern denunciation of the course of the senatorial caucus." Among letters received by Sumner which condemned strongly the action of the Senate were those from Ira Harris, former senator from New York, M. S. Wilkinson, former senator from Minnesota, William Lloyd Garrison, Gerrit Smith, Governor Claflin of Massachusetts, and A. H. Bullock, former governor of that State. This correspondence noted the popular disapproval and indignation with which the removal had been received. Within a week came an election in New Hampshire, a State hitherto steadily Republican, and the result was a Democratic success, which was attributed to the action of the Senate. Gerrit Smith wrote to Sumner, March 17: "The New Hampshire election! What do they who expelled you from your committee think of this first response to their deed of shame?"

A leader of the party, destined to be its foremost leader, Mr. Blaine, then Speaker of the House, on a careful review of the debate and the reasons assigned, put on record at a later period his conviction of the injustice and folly of the Republican members of the Senate in the displacement of Sumner,[2] as follows:

"The removal of Mr. Sumner from his place had been determined in a caucus of Republican senators; and never was the power of the caucus more

[1] Garfield, afterwards President, called the removal "the greatest act of folly." Lieber's letter to Sumner, March 15, 1871.

[2] "Twenty Years in Congress," vol. ii. pp. 503–506.

wrongfully applied. Many senators were compelled, from their sense of obedience to the decision of the majority, to commit an act against their conceptions of right, against what they believed to be justice to a political associate, against what they believed to be sound public policy, against what they believed to be the interest of the Republican party. . . . For his fidelity to principle and his boldness in asserting the truth at an earlier day, Mr. Sumner was struck down in the Senate chamber by a weapon in the hands of a political foe. It was impossible to anticipate that fifteen years later he would be even more cruelly struck down in the Senate by the members of the party he had done so much to establish. . . . In both instances his bearing was distinguished by dignity and magnanimity. He gave utterance to no complaints, and silently submitted to the unjustifiable wrong of which he was a victim."

The popular judgment agreed with Wilson and other senators, that the San Domingo contest was at the bottom of the scheme to remove the senator from the post which he had long held to the satisfaction of his associates and the country, and in which by established usage he would but for that contest have been continued. It was also the common belief that the President's hand as well as the secretary's was in the scheme.[1] It did not matter, as was claimed in their behalf, that other senators who voted as Sumner voted were not subjected to like discipline ; he was the antagonist who kept up the spirit of the opposition ; his was the leadership which secured the rejection of the treaty, and his humiliation was felt to be victory enough.

The partisans of the removal in the Senate maintained a prudent reserve as to the real reason for the removal, which was the senator's effective opposition to the annexation of San Domingo, and his exposure of the methods by which it was promoted. They put forth, however, a succession of pretexts, and as each failed, they substituted another in its place. The attempt has been made to assist them by alleged conversations with the senator, prudently withheld by Mr. Fish and his assistant while he lived, and coming from a storehouse which perhaps is not yet exhausted. The pretexts were as follows : —

I. The only reason given in the Senate (all others being disclaimed)[2] was the senator's want of personal relations with the President and secretary, particularly the latter. The invalidity of this reason was, as already seen, exposed in the debate.

[1] Compare New York "Tribune," March 9; New York "Herald," March 9, 10, 15; New York "Evening Post," March 9, 10, 11; Boston "Journal," March 9 and 10; Chicago "Tribune," March 11 and 13.

[2] Howe said in the Senate, April 24, 1874, that "it became his duty to assign the reasons for the change," thus again excluding all others.

II. Four years after the senator's death and six years after his removal, Mr. Fish set up his default in not reporting treaties referred to the committee, — first naming the number as from eight to eleven, and afterwards on a call for a specification enumerating nine, — and in leaving them unreported at the time of his removal,[1] a charge which the secretary had already privately communicated to General Grant, and which the general on his authority continued to repeat.[2] In the debate, it will be remembered, the senator's fidelity was as cheerfully affirmed by those who supported the removal as by those who opposed it.[3] Mr. Fish made his accusation when the Senate records, though open to him, were not accessible to the public, and as he supposed never would be. Nevertheless, Sumner's friends having procured the removal of the seal of secrecy, it appeared that the senator had reported all but one of the treaties, reporting the eight with remarkable promptness, keeping five of them only about a month, and one of them only a single day; and the one unreported had been with the committee but three months, and was held back presumably for good reasons.[4] He was busy with its work to the last, reporting two treaties March 1, two days before his connection with it ended. Yet, after this disclosure and vindication, Mr. Fish did not regard it a duty to recall his libel on a dead man. His gravest charge being thus shown by the record to have been

[1] Fish's interview and letter in Boston "Transcript," Oct. 19, 1877; Oct. 31, 1877.

[2] Letter of Mr. Copeland from Edinburgh to the New York "Herald," Sept. 25, 1877. According to this writer, General Grant stated that Sumner "had hampered the business of the state department by pigeon-holing treaties for months," and further, in mentioning to George William Curtis that he had left a clean docket when leaving the committee, "had not told Mr. Curtis the facts, and had made these statements knowing them to be falsehoods." The general offered, as he said at the time to Mr. Curtis, to prove his assertion by the records of the state department, and afterwards gave Mr. Curtis a list which he had procured from it (G. W. Curtis in the New York "Herald," Nov. 13, 1877; Harper's Weekly, Dec. 8, 1877, March 16, 1878). General Grant, however, in an interview at Cairo, reported in the New York "Herald," Feb. 22, 1878, disclaimed so much of the interview in Scotland as made him impute intentional falsehood to Sumner. It is, however, curious to note that the main subject of this interview was the leader in Harper's Weekly, Dec. 8, 1877, which explicitly stated that, as now shown by the divulged records of the Senate Sumner had done his full duty as to the treaties; and the list, therefore, of unreported treaties sent by the general to Mr. Curtis was not a true one. Nevertheless, the general kept on in the interview repeating in detail his original charge as if it had not been entirely disproved. The only explanation for his ignoring the substance of the article on which he was making his comments is that when an idea became once fixed in his mind concerning a public man whom he disliked it could not be dislodged by any evidence.

[3] The only reason given for the removal, in the Senate, April 28, 1874, when Cameron, Howe, and Anthony recurred to the subject, was the "non-speaking" one. The same reason, and no other, was given by Howe in his letter printed in the "Golden Age," April 10, 1871.

[4] E. L. Pierce in the Boston "Transcript," Nov. 28, 1877, and in the North American Review, July–August, 1878, pp. 61–80. See Appendix.

false, all other charges and insinuations against the senator dependent on his testimony, whether coming directly from him or prompted by him, deserve no credit.

III. The charge of not reporting the treaties being thus disposed of, and Mr. Fish retiring without confession or explanation, his former assistant, J. C. B. Davis, — also not explaining how the false charge of not reporting came to be made, — alleged that the senator did not "move forward" the treaties in the Senate and "secure its action upon them." This charge, which was as baseless as the other, at once encountered conclusive answers: (1) It is the custom of the Senate while Congress is in session, when no urgency appears, to defer action on treaties till its special session immediately following the regular session, when (the House not being in session) it is not encumbered with the duties of ordinary legislation.[1] (2) It does not appear that the Secretary of State ever asked the senator to obtain earlier action on any one of the treaties. (3) The treaties when reported were in the hands of the Senate, and could be called up by any senator. (4) Surviving associates of the senator, — Patterson, Schurz, Casserly, Morrill of Vermont, Trumbull, Fenton, Thurman, Bayard, Morrill of Maine, Logan, Anthony, Windom, and Spencer, — when their opinions were requested, all cordially testified to Sumner's remarkable fidelity to public business, particularly that of his committee, at all its stages. (5) Neglect of duty, if it had existed, would have been charged in the Senate March 10, 1871, when Sumner's adversaries were hard pressed for reasons justifying their action.

IV. The three preceding pretexts failing, it was at last claimed that Sumner was an expected obstacle to the negotiations for the Treaty of Washington; and by way of specification it was stated that in a memorandum sent to Mr. Fish two days after their conference, Jan. 15, 1871, he set forth as a condition or preliminary of settlement the withdrawal of Great Britain from her possessions on this continent.[2] This final pretext or after-

[1] Mr. Cameron secured action on all but one of the treaties at the session of Congress meeting March 4, 1871, when general legislation, except as to the condition of affairs in the Southern States, was excluded by rule; so that there was ample time for the consideration of treaties, as there is at special sessions of the Senate when the House is not in session. The Darien Canal treaty, which Sumner reported July 13, 1870, is still (1893) pending in the Senate; and, according to Davis's method of accusing Sumner, not only he but all his successors in the chairmanship have been, during a period of twenty-three years, culpable for not "moving forward" this treaty and "securing the Senate's action upon it"!

[2] J. C. B. Davis, in the New York "Herald," Jan. 4, 1878. See reply of Wendell Phillips to Davis's letter (New York "Herald," Jan. 9, 1878; Boston "Herald," Jan. 13, 1878).

thought came out seven years after the date of the memorandum and four years after the senator's death. It was said to have been communicated to senators at the time; but this could not be,[1] as they did not then give it as a reason for their action, or at a later day when the subject was again mooted.[2] In all their justifications, contemporary or subsequent, the non-speaking reason was the only one given.

Sumner would have had no right — it may be remarked in this connection — to make the cession of Canada an absolute condition of a settlement; and he did not do so. Other language of the memorandum and his vote for the Treaty of Washington, without making any point that it did not provide for such a cession, without moving any amendment concerning it though moving other amendments, show that he held no obstructive or impracticable position. His address of Sept. 22, 1869, pointed to such a union as an American aspiration, to be realized, however, only "in the fulness of time, with the good-will of the mother country and the accord of both parties." It was his permanent conviction that without the union of North America under one dominion disputes as to fisheries and jurisdiction would perpetually recur. He believed with Cobden and Bright that that union was a certain destiny, and was to come without war, with the assent of both countries and of the colonists themselves. The event proved not to be so near as he thought; but it seemed to him that the time had come to test the disposition of all concerned in what he regarded as a great consummation. That was his idea, and that was all of it.[3]

[1] It did not occur to Mr. Davis, who is the authority for this statement, that it would be an unmanly thing to communicate privately such a reason to senators without giving Sumner an opportunity to reply or explain.

[2] Davis, after stating what does not appear except on his authority, — that this memorandum was communicated to senators (not named), — says it was not referred to openly in the Senate, as such a revelation would have been "the height of indiscretion" while the Joint High Commission was in session. This theory fails, because the non-speaking relation with Mr. Fish was alone given in the debate, April 28, 1874, in the Senate, three years after the session of the Commission, when the reasons for the removal were again canvassed. Mr. Fish in his statements by interviews and letters in October, 1877, gave the non-speaking and the non-reporting as the only reasons for the removal; and there would have been no "height of indiscretion" in revealing then the Canada reason if it had existed.

[3] This is the substance of the explanation of his position as given by him to "Perley" (B. P. Poore) and printed in the Boston "Journal," Feb. 27, 1871. A fuller account is given in the same journal, Jan. 8 and 14, 1878. According to these reports he declared it a "pure invention" that he wished to dictate terms to England, or to require a cession of the British provinces as a condition of a settlement; and he referred, for a statement of his position, to his address Sept. 22, 1869 (Works, vol. xiii. pp. 127, 128; compare Springfield "Republican," March 25-27, 1871). The senator's letter to Bemis, Jan. 18, 1871 (*ante*,

The indignity of the removal was aggravated by the time chosen for effecting it. The Joint High Commission for the settlement of all questions between Great Britain and the United States was in session in Washington, and had taken up the "Alabama" claims March 8, the day preceding the action of the caucus.[1] The American commissioners were Fish, Schenck, E. R. Hoar, Judge Nelson, and G. H. Williams; the British commissioners were Earl de Grey (afterwards Marquis of Ripon), Sir Stafford Northcote (afterwards Lord Iddlesleigh), Professor Mountague Bernard, Sir Edward Thornton, and Sir John Macdonald. Just then came the dismissal from the post he had long held of the statesman who had studied the questions at issue more than any one of his countrymen, and whose treatment of them in his speech in 1869 had led the British Cabinet to see the necessity of an early settlement. Sumner said nothing; but it would not have been human in him not to feel a pang at being left out of the historic debate at its final stage.

In view of the statements made in debate March 10, apparently on Mr. Fish's authority as to their personal relations, the senator prepared a statement concerning them shortly after. It was intended as a speech to be made in the Senate; but friends, who believed that its delivery would aggravate a controversy which they still thought it possible to bring to a friendly conclusion, persuaded him to withhold it from the Senate.[2] It was, however, put in type and copies were sent by him to certain friends, marked in each case, "unpublished, private and confidential, — not to go out of Mr. ——'s hands." After his death one of those who had received a copy caused it to be published.[3]

Sumner showed shortly after his removal his sympathetic adherence to the Republican party in his support of one of its measures for enforcing the fourteenth amendment and the suppression of the Ku Klux clans.[4] He renewed also the effort to

p. 464), asks counsel as to another part of the memorandum, but does not mention the clause concerning Canada. The omission is proof that he did not regard the cession of that province as a peremptory condition of a settlement. See Appendix.

[1] The Commission began its sessions February 27, and ended them May 8.

[2] Anthony in the Senate, April 28, 1874 (Congressional Globe, p. 3435). Wilson in a letter to Sumner, June 6, 1871, advised against giving the statement publicity.

[3] It was sent by F. W. Bird to the New York "Tribune," in which it appeared April 6, 1874. Works, vol. xiv. pp. 251-276.

[4] April 13, 1871 (Works, vol. xiv. pp. 277-282). The New York "Evening Post," April 19, 1871, took exception to the centralizing drift of this speech.

bring forward his civil rights bill.[1] His contention against the right of the Senate to hold in confinement recusant witnesses after final adjournment called out a grateful recognition from Whitelaw Reid and other journalists.[2]

Since the debate in December on San Domingo, important documents relating to the negotiations and the use of war ships had, on calls moved by Sumner, been sent to the Senate. With the facts revealed by them being now before the public, he was ready to speak again on the subject later in the same session, but his illness in February prevented.[3] Some friends advised him to await the report of the commissioners; but he was not impressed with the suggestion of delay, as his positions were quite independent of any investigations and conclusions they might bring back. In his effort to be heard again he encountered a restrictive rule in the Senate, adopted for the session, excluding general legislation, and limiting the subjects for consideration to a few specially designated. This obstruction he overcame by a decision of the Vice-President in his favor against Conkling's prolonged resistance;[4] and on Friday, March 24, he obtained the floor for the next Monday.

At nine o'clock on that day the people began to gather in the galleries of the Senate chamber, and by eleven had filled them. Thousands sought entrance in vain, and a throng lingered outside during the afternoon, awaiting any vacant space. Ladies by special privilege were admitted to the cloak-rooms and corridors, and later on they pressed into the body of the chamber. Sumner, entering just before noon, was greeted with applause. Rarely if ever had an audience so remarkable in numbers and character filled the chamber. Two thousand persons were within sight or hearing. Diplomatists, judges, members of the Cabinet, and army

[1] March 9 and 17, 1871. Congressional Globe, pp. 21, 144.

[2] May 18 and 27 (Works, vol. xiv. pp. 284-305). In this case Messrs. White and Ramsdell, having obtained and published a copy of the Treaty of Washington before its promulgation, refused to disclose by what means it was obtained. Other subjects to which the senator gave attention at this session were a bill for the relief of N. P. Trist, negotiator of the Treaty of Guadaloupe Hidalgo, which he succeeded in carrying, Feb. 3, 14 (Congressional Globe, pp. 923, 1212, 1216, 1217), and March 13 and April 19 (Globe, pp. 69, 74, 809); representation at an international penitentiary congress, March 7 (Globe, p. 13); the removal of the distinction in legislation between acts and resolutions, March 15 (Globe, pp. 113, 120); and the payment of claims for French spoliations, to which he invoked the attention of his successor, Mr. Cameron, March 13 (Globe, p. 66). At this as at the previous session, being the oldest senator in continuous service, he moved the appointment of Senator Anthony as President *pro tem.* of the Senate.

[3] March 24, 1871. Congressional Globe, p. 255.

[4] March 23 and 24. Congressional Globe, pp. 233-235, 250-256.

officers (including General Sherman) were present. The House having adjourned in expectation of the speech, its members thronged the aisles; and its Speaker, Mr. Blaine, sat by the side of the Vice-President.[1] As no morning business was on hand, Sumner's elaborate and comprehensive resolutions, which summarized his views, were first read, and he then took the floor, using printed slips, and speaking three and a half hours. His manner throughout was solemn and earnest; but emotion, so far as could be, was repressed. He put aside, as he began as well as at the end, the question of policy involved in the annexation, touching on it only as it concerned the future of the African race, and confined himself to the methods employed to accomplish the end. He reviewed, as in the earlier debate but with fuller knowledge, the character and proceedings of the negotiators (Baez, Cazneau, Fabens, and Babcock), the orders of the navy department, and the conduct of the officers of the ships, which were a menace to Hayti as well as the sole support of Baez. He upheld by citations from international law the equality of States, denying the right to do aught against Hayti which would be unlawful if attempted against the most puissant nations. While condemning in sober language the President's belligerent intervention in Dominica and Hayti, and his usurpation of war powers, as well as his unusual pressure on senators for a ratification of the treaty, and his calling its rejection "a folly," he abstained from epithets and invective, — and this to the surprise of spectators, who led by a false rumor had come expecting an exposure of the President's delinquencies in the way of nepotism and otherwise. As to his own recent dismissal from his committee or the part which the President or others had taken in it, he was silent. He carried with him until he reached the conclusion the sympathy of the great mass of those who heard him.[2] One passage near the end was not in harmony with the spirit of his effort, and that was inserted in his manuscript on the morning of the day he spoke. It was a comparison, or the suggestion of a comparison, between the President's proceedings with the

[1] For descriptions of the scene see New York "Tribune," March 31; New York "Herald," March 28; New York "Sun," March 28; Washington "Patriot," March 28; Boston "Journal," March 28; Boston "Advertiser," March 28; New York "Independent," April 6; London "Telegraph," April 12.

[2] The New York "Evening Post," Chicago "Tribune," and New York "Herald," March 28, approved the speech, particularly in its timeliness. It found general approval except in its last passage (Boston "Journal," March 28 and 29).

ships and the Ku-Klux outrages at the South, with an intimation that the time and effort applied to schemes of annexation would, if properly directed, have saved Southern Unionists from harm. The comparison was not just or pertinent. The President had gone as far as any Republican could ask in suppressing violence at the South. He might not have paid due respect to the limitations of international law in his support of a pretender in San Domingo; he might, consciously or unconsciously, through the navy have menaced the sovereignty of Hayti; but personal injury to any one, least of all the assassinations and midnight outrages practised by the Ku-Klux clan, were furthest from his thought. This reference to the President drew applause from the galleries; but Sumner's best friends, who were satisfied with the speech up to this point, withheld their approval of this passage, which he had without proper weighing inserted at the last.[1]

While the audience in the galleries listened with profound interest, there was restlessness among a certain division of the senators. At first they affected to be busily occupied at their desks in correspondence, but later on they engaged in audible conversation. Sumner paused once when annoyed in this way by Conkling and Hamlin, and again when interrupted by a conference between Edmunds and Carpenter, saying at the second interruption that his voice was worn and lacked the strength it had once. A direction from the chair brought a forced apology and silence.[2]

The San Domingo senators arranged at first that the speech should be received without reply, but they did not adhere to this understanding. Morton commented on its untimeliness, coming on the very day that the commissioners were to arrive from San Domingo. Howe compared Sumner to statesmen, ancient and modern, who had fallen from their first estate;[3] upbraided him for the injustice he had done to the President, the savior of his country, and strangely enough reproached him for not having promptly protested against the alleged wrongs. Frelinghuysen and Harlan followed in the same line, and justified the

[1] Schurz, who had read the speech before delivery, was greatly surprised when he heard this passage. It was not in the copy sent before delivery to the leading journals.

[2] New York Herald, March 28; Brooklyn Union, March 28; Boston Advertiser, March 28.

[6] Howe withdrew (April 14), after Sumner's speech on the Ku-Klux bill, his insinuation that Sumner had become a Democrat in disguise. Congressional Globe, p. 686.

use of naval power, chiefly relying on the action of Tyler and Polk in the acquisition of Texas, — pro-slavery Presidents carrying out pro-slavery purposes. Schurz supported Sumner in a speech begun on one day and ending on the other, in which he dealt at length with the President's use of military power without authority from Congress. On the third day the subject was laid on the table on Harlan's motion.

The President communicated to Congress, April 5, the report of the commissioners, which, as was expected, was altogether favorable to his view.[1] His message contained passages understood to be intended for Sumner. He alluded to "acrimonious debates in Congress" and "unjust aspersions elsewhere;" to "the censure of disappointed men;" to "the hostility of those who deem their opinions and wishes treated with insufficient consideration;" and to charges of corruption against himself. Sumner had, however, made no charges of corruption against him, but had again and again disclaimed making them.[2] The President was, however, not a careful reader, and accepted as true what his military secretaries told him. Sumner took no notice of these allusions pointed at himself. Morrill of Vermont at once sought the opportunity to reply to the argument of the message; and though the attempt was made to shut him off, he obtained (Sumner and others supporting him) his right to be heard at length. A few days afterwards Cole of California spoke briefly on the other side; and this was the end of the discussion in Congress. It had been found impossible to obtain a two-thirds vote in the Senate for a treaty, or a majority vote in the House for a joint resolution. Outside of speculators and adventurers the measure had no popular support,[3] and the vote it received in the Senate was due almost wholly to a desire to please the President on a matter in which his feelings were warmly enlisted. During the succeeding interval of more than twenty years there has been no attempt to revive the scheme, even among those who were its intolerant partisans in 1870–1871. The President, however, adhered to his conviction, and in his last annual message, when the senator who had accomplished its defeat was no longer living,

[1] The report was reviewed and its positions contested by W. L. Garrison in the New York "Independent," April 13, 1871.

[2] Mr. Blaine says in his history that Sumner "had not imputed, as General Grant assumed, any personal corruption to him." "Twenty Years of Congress," vol. ii. p. 462.

[3] Isaac N. Arnold wrote Sumner from Chicago, March 28, 1871: "I know not one man in the Northwest in favor of this annexation scheme."

avowed his belief that Congress had made a fatal mistake in rejecting the measure.

Mr. Garrison wrote Sumner, March 28, in earnest approval of his speech,[1] saying: —

"It is a judicial decision rather than a speech, — dispassionate, grave, dignified, exhaustive, admitting of no appeal. To my mind, the legitimate corollary is the impeachment of the President, if not of the Secretary of the Navy, as guilty of high crimes and misdemeanors within the meaning of section 4, article 11, of the U. S. Constitution; and were I a member of the Senate, I am not sure that I would not propose such impeachment, even if I stood alone. The case is much worse than I had supposed, and characterized by the most flagrant usurpation. . . . The manner in which you were replied to by Senators Morton and Howe was worthy of that side of the matter in the controversy."

Sumner's relations with Morton, the leader of the San Domingo party, remained cordial; and the following correspondence between them took place in the summer: —

WASHINGTON, August 8, 1871.

MY DEAR GOVERNOR, — As I am leaving Washington for Boston, it occurs to me that I ought not to close my doings here without correcting in formal terms a misapprehension under which you labored with regard to me. Already I have corrected it in conversation, but I hope you will pardon me if I put my correction in writing.

I understood you to say, or allege, that I had prepared my speech on San Domingo in advance, and that this was before my sudden illness at the end of February; that I had announced that it would be very bitter on the President, embracing various topics, among them inattention to business and nepotism, and that I had actually read specimens to visitors. Of course, in making this allegation you evidently believed it true; nor was I much astonished, for there was an evident disposition in certain quarters to believe anything about me. At all events, you seemed incredulous when I denied it. Returning to the allegation, you quoted my colleague as authority, at least in part. Now, this whole story in gross and detail is an invention, without one word of truth. I write now to deny it in every particular. At the time of my sudden illness the speech was in contemplation only, and there was no specimen to read if I had any such disposition. None such ever was read, repeated, or described. Never did I say anything to anybody giving the idea that the speech would be very bitter on the President, least of all that it would touch on the topics to which you referred, — never even to my colleague. To him and the few others with whom I conversed I simply expressed my strong desire for a hearing on the violations of international law and of the Constitution in the employment of the naval forces at San Domingo. In the course of preparation I submitted

[1] In a later letter Mr. Garrison expressed his regret at the "Ku-Klux" passage of the speech, as "it made a recoil to a certain extent which would not otherwise have been felt."

certain questions to W. Beach Lawrence, Richard H. Dana, W. Whiting, and Dr. Lieber, four distinguished publicists, with whom I have been in the habit of conferring on questions of international law; but I never communicated to either of them my own conclusions, or anything I proposed to say, — except that in conversation I stated to Mr. Whiting the propositions of law which I intended to maintain. Allow me to add that the story — to which you give credence to the extent at least of quoting it — first appeared in a newspaper much under an influence very little scrupulous with regard to me. In making this correction I do not intend to revive controversy, but to correct a story which in every respect comes within the sphere of my own knowledge, so that if it were true I should know it; and as it is not true, I know this also.

I hope you are not suffering from these heats.

Faithfully yours,

CHARLES SUMNER.

INDIANAPOLIS, Aug. 20, 1871.

MY DEAR SENATOR, — Returning yesterday, I found your letter, and hasten to reply. The subject to which it refers is among the things of the past, the memory of which I would not willingly revive. It refers to a controversy which will ever be among my most disagreeable experiences in the Senate, for it was a controversy among friends. I am, as I have been for years, your friend and admirer, and an earnest well-wisher for your continued health and happiness. In the course I took I believed I was doing right, and what was best for my country and party; and I give you credit for equal purity of purpose and patriotism. My earnest wish is now for the harmony of the Republican party for the sake of the country. I send you a copy of my late speech at St. Louis. It was badly reported and was not revised; I did not say what I am reported as saying about Chase. Some of the mistakes in the report you can correct from the context.

Yours very truly,

O. P. MORTON.

While the Joint High Commission was in session, Sumner, though his connection with the treaty was to be only that of a senator, was in frequent conference with its English members. They recognized that he retained his hold on the American people, and that it was very important to have his co-operation in the final result. Two of them — Earl de Grey and Sir Stafford Northcote — had brought letters to him, the former from the Duke of Argyll, and the latter from Thomas Baring. The senator and Professor Bernard were already in sympathy by common studies in international law. Sumner was invited by Sir Edward Thornton to meet them at his table without other guests. Once he dined with the commissioners, and several times he breakfasted with Earl de Grey. Late in April the senator gave all the members, including Lord Tenterden their secretary, a dinner, when were also present Lady Thornton and Lady Macdonald, Cushing, Thurman, and Hunter, the assistant secretary of state. The next day he gave a quiet dinner to the commissioners only, which allowed a free conference on the pending business. Two weeks later, and perhaps on other days, he had them to dine. He was in communication with the American commissioners through Judge Hoar, to whom he made suggestions from time to time. Finally, when the treaty had been signed, May 8, taking the first copy available at the department of state, the judge went at once to the senator, delivering it enclosed in an envelope addressed to him, on which was written: "The result of long and earnest labor is presented and dedicated with respect and confidence by his friend, E. R. Hoar." He commended the treaty to the senator as meeting on all substantial points the objections he had so well urged against the Johnson-Clarendon convention.

Sumner made the principal speech upon the treaty, May 19, entering fully into all the points of the negotiation, stating in what respects it met the objections to the rejected convention, explaining the rules to be such as we had heretofore insisted upon, and while not thinking the result as complete as it should be, regarded the treaty as promising substantial good, and supported it by his vote.[1] He expressed the opinion that it would "be hailed with joy by the thinking men of Great Britain and the United States."[2] He moved some amendments, though not pressing them, with these ends: (1) The security of private property at sea, not contraband of war, in conformity with the amendment proposed by the United States to the Declaration of Paris; (2) The abolition of commercial blockades, a measure which had been greatly desired by Mr. Cobden; (3) The denial of a national or belligerent character to vessels not holding a commission given at a port in the actual occupation of the commissioning government, — a provision which was in accordance with his view of ocean belligerency, and to which the British commissioners had been specially authorized in their instructions to assent; (4) The treatment as pirates of vessels employed in

[1] Sumner, on May 20 and 22, denied in the Senate the truth of reports of his speech on the treaty, calling that in the New York "Herald," May 20, "a pure invention" (Congressional Globe, pp. 889, 890); and the one in the "Washington Chronicle," May 25, "a fabrication" (Globe, p. 891). Sumner appears to have spoken in executive session, May 10, in favor of the publication of the treaty (Boston "Journal," May 11).

[2] Boston Journal. Jan. 14, 1878.

burning prizes at sea; (5) The substitution of a stronger and more definite term than "due diligence" in the statement of the duty of neutral powers to prevent the fitting out of ships in their ports for the aid or service of either belligerent.[1] He thought too that the controversy had better be ended at Washington by a final settlement than prolonged by the cumbrous proceeding of a debate at Geneva, where, as it proved, a fatal rupture was barely escaped.[2] Cameron also moved amendments; but the Senate as well as the British commissioners did not think it prudent to open anew the negotiations, and the treaty was ratified without change.

The "Alabama" claims came before the Senate again in 1872, when the British government indicated its purpose to withdraw from the hearing at Geneva on account of the claim for "indirect losses" set up in the American case. A supplemental article providing for their exclusion was proposed by that government, and with a modification was approved, as was supposed, by the Senate by a vote of forty-two to nine. Sumner took part in the debate. In his view there had been a want of candor on our side, and of caution and diligence on the English, in not making the terms such as to avoid controversy; he thought our "Case" had been badly drawn and was "harsh;" and at this stage he was for leaving the difficulty to the discretion of the Executive.[3]

It is instructive to note the points of Sumner's speech of April, 1869,[4] which were taken account of in the negotiations at Washington. This appears first in the protocol of the American commissioners, March 8, which specified in detail the national claims as they were enumerated in the speech. It appears also in the treaty itself. (1) The senator had complained that the Johnson-Clarendon convention belittled our cause by making it "a bundle of individual claims," and providing in a certain event for the choice of an arbitrator by lot. The Washington treaty, in its first words, dealt with the controversy as one of differences be-

[1] The scope and meaning of the terms "due diligence" was a subject of contention at Geneva.

[2] The senator's relations to the treaty and his desire to include other improved rules of international law are stated in G. W. Smalley's letters to the London "Times," Feb. 14 and 15, 1872.

[3] Brief minutes of his remarks are preserved. The New York "Times" assumed (May 24, 1872) to give a report of what he said in executive session, which the next day he pronounced "a fabrication" at once "absurd and ridiculous," and called senators to witness the truth of his statement, May 25, 1872. Congressional Globe, p. 3864.

[4] *Ante*, pp. 385-388.

tween nations, and allowed nothing to depend on lot. (2) The convention was limited, as he objected, to individual claims, while the treaty comprehended "all complaints and claims" of the United States, — thus covering national claims, though not, as it proved, so explicitly as to avoid the controversy (perilous to the proceedings) which came later. (3) The convention contained "no word of regret" for the injuries, "no acknowledgment of the wrong." The senator's mention of this defect had been treated by some American as well as British critics as pure sentimentalism, as asking for a confession that no nation could be expected to make. The treaty, however, expressed "in a friendly spirit the regret felt by her Majesty's government for the escape of the 'Alabama' and other vessels from British ports, and for the depredations committed by those vessels." This was a statement which did honor to the country on whose behalf it was made; and in Sumner's view it was, as a guaranty of peace and good-will, worth more than any pecuniary penalty. (4) The convention, as the senator objected, contained no rule of international duty for the future. The treaty declared the rule of "due diligence" binding on a neutral power to prevent the fitting out or assisting of belligerent vessels in its ports, and to prevent its ports being made a base of naval operations by one belligerent against the other; and these rules were accepted as binding, both in the pending contention and for the future. (5) The senator found in the convention a possible construction which would admit the claims of Confederate bondholders against the United States; but the treaty clearly excluded them by limiting the submission to the "Alabama" claims.

Sumner took satisfaction in the result. He wrote to Lieber in August: "I know not if I told you that Lord de Grey told me that without my speech the treaty could not have been made, and that he had worked by it as a chart.[1] Every point I made against the Johnson convention is met in the treaty. Of course the amount of damages belongs to the evidence, and will be considered at Geneva."

Sumner had pleasant letters from Northcote and Earl de Grey

1 Sir Stafford Northcote's letter to Sumner stating that the latter's speech in April, 1869, was "the turning point," has been given. (*Ante*, p. 392.) Harper's Weekly, June 15, 1872, compares the two treaties with reference to the way the second treaty met the senator's objections to the first, and reports Earl de Grey as saying that the senator "made" the Washington treaty, — the earl meaning thereby "that the suggestions of Mr. Sumner's speech had been substantially adopted."

after their return, both of whom would have been glad to go further in making new and better rules, if it could have been done without putting the whole work in danger. Sir Stafford wrote: "Though I should individually have preferred a broader measure, I am not dissatisfied with what we have got. The matter cannot rest where it is, and we shall see by and by a development of our principles in the direction of a further improvement and ascertainment of the rules of international law." Earl de Grey wrote from London, June 17: —

"The day may come when your views as to the immunity of private property at sea will prevail; but at present they would meet with much opposition on both sides of the Atlantic, and I am glad therefore that you did not press the insertion of the amendment in the treaty. . . . I found that people here fully believed in the accuracy of the sham report of your speech,[1] but I have, I think, dispelled the illusion and placed your position on the question in its true light. It has been a great satisfaction to me and to my colleagues that you were able to give your vote in favor of our work."

Again, August 4, after recurring to the pleasant evenings passed at the senator's house, "with all their attractive memories of art and literature," De Grey, now Marquis of Ripon, wrote: —

"The result of our labors there may not have been perfect, or rather, I should say, were not perfect (for what work of man can be?); but it was a result worth attaining. And if it left something undone in the direction to which you point, it does not follow that through your effort and that of those who think with you on these questions the two nations may not advance yet farther, hand in hand, in the path upon which they have entered, of limiting and restricting the evils of war by the application of improved principles of international law."

Sumner lingered in Washington (the Senate adjourning May 27) till the second week of August. He passed his time in studies, relieving them by afternoon drives, during which George William Curtis, then in Washington as chairman of the civil service commission, was often his companion, and they ended the day by dining at the senator's house. Mr. Curtis was a stanch supporter of the President, though not agreeing with his San Domingo scheme. He wrote from Ashfield, Mass., July 28: "My summer days in Washington were a delightful episode in my life. Our long talks, our drives, our dinners, our

[1] New York "Herald's" report, May 20, on a copy of which the senator wrote "a fabrication."

differences, our debates, linger happily in my memory, my only regret being that I could not quite bring you to see the truth as it really is."

Sumner on his way from Washington stopped at Philadelphia to call upon Mr. Forney and Thomas Fitzgerald,[1] and in New York, where he dined with Lieber. As soon as he reached Boston he went to Nahant, where he divided his time between Longfellow and Mr. George Abbot James. One day in August, in company with Longfellow and son, Agassiz, James, and a young Japanese prince, he went by invitation of Judge Russell, collector of the port, on a revenue cutter to Minot's Ledge, where they were hoisted up in a chair into the light-house.[2] The poet saw in his friend traces of the attack of *angina pectoris* in the winter, and wrote to G. W. Greene: "He complains that I walk too fast, and is averse to walking at all." Sumner made a brief visit to Mr. Hooper at Cotuit, and was for a day with B. P. Poore at Newbury. On September 23 he assisted at the Bird Club in commemorating the Whig State convention of 1846, in which he was a leader of the Conscience Whigs at the opening of his career. One evening in the autumn he was at Mrs. Sargent's Radical Club, where M. Coquerel, the French clergyman, was received, and where were also Wendell Phillips and James Freeman Clarke. He was glad to entertain with a dinner and a drive Forney and Daniel Dougherty [3] on their visit to Boston. The former wrote, after his return to Philadelphia: "It was a never-to-be-forgotten evening, — one which it would give me rare satisfaction to be permitted to describe in my own volumes;" and he communicated Dougherty's enthusiasm in recalling the meeting of the three friends in Boston. Sumner appeared twice in the autumn before the people of Boston, — once at the Music Hall to introduce as a lecturer M. Coquerel,[4] and again at Faneuil Hall, where he spoke briefly for aid to the sufferers by the great fire in Chicago.[5] The President and people of Hayti recognized his services for their country by the gift of a medal, which, as it was declined in deference to the spirit of a constitutional in-

1 Proprietor and editor of the Philadelphia "Item." He died in 1891 at the age of seventy-one.

2 Longfellow's "Life," vol. iii. p. 170.

3 He had introduced Mr. Dougherty at a lecture, February 7, at Lincoln Hall in Washington.

4 October 9. Works, vol. xiv. pp. 311, 312.

5 October 10. Ibid., pp. 313-315.

hibition, was given to the State of Massachusetts, and placed in the library of its capitol.[1] In the autumn he prepared a paper on "The Best Portraits in Engraving," which appeared, with photographs of several engravings of his own collection, in a magazine. It contained biographical sketches of eminent engravers, with comments on the qualities of their work.[2] This was the revival of old studies which he had pursued with zeal during the period of disability which followed the Brooks assault.

Notwithstanding Republican senators had disowned Sumner, his standing in his party at home was as firm as ever. His controversy with the President had not weakened him in the least. General Butler in the autumn made a canvass for the Republican nomination for governor, during which he assailed the Republican administration of the State for a considerable period. He sought also to procure a majority of delegates by bringing into the primary meetings large masses of voters, chiefly of foreign nativity, who had uniformly voted as Democrats. Aside from the objections made to him personally, his extraordinary methods provoked the most determined opposition from the great body of Republicans who were interested in maintaining the integrity of the party. At one time his prospect of success was imminent, and Republican leaders, editors of newspapers and others, sought the intervention of the two senators to prevent what they deemed a calamity. Sumner, whose personal relations with Butler had been uniformly cordial, and who by habit had abstained from participating in any contests within the party for nominations, yielded with some hesitation to the pressure, which was put on the ground that his influence was absolutely necessary to save the Republican cause from discredit and defeat. He drew a paper, assented to also by his colleague, which was as follows: —

"The question is often asked, 'Where are the two Massachusetts senators, and what are their opinions on the present crisis in Massachusetts?' Nobody knowing them has doubted; but we are able to set this matter at rest by their authority. We have seen Senator Sumner and Senator Wilson personally, and are authorized by them to say that they deeply regret and deplore the extraordinary canvass which General Butler has precipitated upon the Com-

[1] Works, vol. xiv. pp. 306–309.

[2] "The City," January, 1872. No other copy of the magazine was published. Works, vol. xiv. pp. 327–354.

monwealth, and especially the attacks which he has volunteered against the existing State government and the Republican party of Massachusetts; and that in their opinion his nomination as governor would be hostile to the best interests of the Commonwealth and of the Republican party."

At the convention General Butler lost the nomination by only a small adverse majority, and the result was attributed to the interposition of the senators. The general shortly after sent Sumner a newspaper paragraph which reflected on the two senators for not doing more, accompanying it with the introduction: "In memory of a former friendship I send you an extract from your late friend, Samuel Bowles, of the Springfield 'Republican,' at whose behest you threw away the kindly feelings of twenty years."[1] Wilson joined reluctantly in the declaration of the senators. It was with reference particularly to his assent to it that General Butler used to say of him that Sumner "dominated" him. General Butler's "Book," published twenty years afterwards, showed in his estimate of Sumner that he had not forgotten this political incident of the autumn of 1871.

It was feared by many Republicans that Sumner's earnest opposition to the President on the San Domingo question would lead him into association with the Democrats; but they had been reassured by his support of legislation against the Ku-Klux outrages at the last session. Another national election was, however, to come the next year, and the question anxiously considered by his Republican supporters was, what would be his decision in case of the President's renomination, — an event altogether likely to take place. Not only partisans, but others like Mr. Garrison, Gerrit Smith, and George William Curtis, who were in sympathy with Sumner on the San Domingo issue, attributed the President's methods in that business to mistaken judgment, and thought that such errors should be overlooked in view of party necessities and his eminent services in the Civil War. They felt, too, that the senator was brooding too much over the President's gift-taking and nepotism, — defects which, if existing, seemed to them altogether exaggerated. Sober-minded men also dreaded at that time the success of the Demo-

[1] General Butler called on Sumner on the day the statement of the senators appeared in the newspapers, September 19, and found him and his colleague together at the Coolidge House in Boston. An account of the interview was given by "Warrington" (W. S. Robinson) in the Atlantic Monthly, December, 1871, pp. 747, 748. Boston "Journal," September 19, 20.

cratic party, fearing that it would bring disorder and violence at the South, and commercial derangement over the whole country. But Sumner could not accept the prospect of a prolongation of what he regarded as a period of misrule and usurpation, and was determined to spare no effort to effect a change of candidate.

## CHAPTER LVII.

ATTEMPTS TO RECONCILE THE PRESIDENT AND THE SENATOR. — INELIGIBILITY OF THE PRESIDENT FOR A SECOND TERM. — THE CIVIL-RIGHTS BILL. — SALE OF ARMS TO FRANCE. — THE LIBERAL REPUBLICAN PARTY: HORACE GREELEY ITS CANDIDATE ADOPTED BY THE DEMOCRATS. — SUMNER'S RESERVE. — HIS RELATIONS WITH REPUBLICAN FRIENDS AND HIS COLLEAGUE. — SPEECH AGAINST THE PRESIDENT. — SUPPORT OF GREELEY. — LAST JOURNEY TO EUROPE. — A MEETING WITH MOTLEY. — A NIGHT WITH JOHN BRIGHT. — THE PRESIDENT'S RE-ELECTION. — 1871–1872.

THE hope of reconciling the President and the senator was not given up by their common friends; and with that view Wilson, at the beginning of this session, made more than one visit to the White House, accompanied on one occasion by another senator. A similar controversy with Mr. Lincoln might readily have been adjusted; but the two Presidents were constituted differently.[1] Wilson found his errand bootless; and when he gave up the effort he applied a term to the President which it is not worth while to perpetuate. He desired his colleague's restoration to the leadership of the foreign relations committee, now called for in public journals of large influence; but he encountered obstructions in the state department, as well as in the Executive Mansion, which could not be overcome.

With another type of public men the President was more easily reconciled. General Butler having been relieved (unjustly as he thought) by General Grant from command after the affair at Fort Fisher issued a farewell address to his troops which was almost mutinous; and in that address, and also in one made at Lowell shortly after, he charged, by certain implication, on his chief a wanton or wasteful sacrifice of human life. His conversations, guarded with no privacy, abounded in still more offensive imputations; and he went so far as to prepare a bulky manuscript

[1] Cameron in the Senate, Feb. 29, 1872, noted this difference (Congressional Globe. p. 1289): "Grant, however, has a good deal of my own spirit. If a man smites him in the face he smites back; and that I hold to be the better policy."

to exhibit the incapacity of the head of the army.[1] He carried his resentment still further; and having intimated to Judge D. K. Cartter, a friend of General Grant, that an invitation to the general's party in Washington would be agreeable to him, after having received one he returned it to the sender. Nevertheless the two generals, now both in public life as civilians, were brought into friendly relations by the mediation of George Wilkes, the editor; and General Butler came to have an influence with the President, at least in appointments to office, greater than that of any public man, or indeed of all public men, in Massachusetts.[2]

Sumner renewed at this session his proposition, made in 1867,[3] for an amendment to the Constitution, establishing the ineligibility of the President for a second term, expressly excepting, however, the next election.[4] The President's special friends saw fit to regard the measure as aimed at him, and opposed it in a body. Conkling, calling it up while advocating the President's re-election, attempted some sarcasms on Sumner. The latter in a brief reply declined to follow "the insinuations and innuendoes which the senator had so freely strown in his path." Carpenter, in an elaborate speech against civil service reform[5] (this speech showing to what class of public men he belonged), took occasion to dissent from the proposition. Later in the session Sumner introduced a resolution for substituting a popular vote for President in place of the electoral colleges.[6]

[1] This manuscript, which the author freely spoke of, was prepared shortly after the war, but was not published.

[2] General Butler has said: "I can say without fear of contradiction that few men possessed a greater share of his confidence, or had more personal influence with General Grant upon public questions, than I had." Butler's "Book," p. 855.

[3] Feb. 11, 1867; Works, vol. xi. pp. 98-101. His effort at this time also corresponds with a conviction of his early manhood. *Ante*, vol. ii. p. 159.

[4] Dec. 21, 1871, Works, vol. xiv. pp. 320-326; Jan. 11, 1872, Congressional Globe, p. 358. The resolution (which was referred at the next session to the judiciary committee) was introduced by an argumentative recital of opinions and historical facts. Sumner had a fancy for preambles, once saying: "Some preambles are eloquent morsels of history and style." Feb. 27, 1874; Globe, p. 1831.

[5] Chandler and Logan of the Senate, and Butler of the House, were also opposed to civil service reform.

[6] May 30, 1872; Congressional Globe, p. 4036. Among subjects which he treated briefly in debate this session were the preservation of the park at Washington from railway encroachments, May 15, 1872 (Works, vol. xv. pp. 72-78: his interest in the city, and particularly in the grounds about the Capitol, appears also in a later debate, Jan. 22, 1874, Globe, p. 832); the acceptance of gifts from foreign powers by our diplomatic agents, which he was opposed to allowing, May 2, 1872 (Works, vol. xv. pp. 70, 71), — a subject treated by him in a later debate, Jan. 6, 1874 (Globe, p. 390); the limitation of a day's labor to eight hours in national work-shops, — a measure not favored by him at first, but which he thought should now have a fair trial, — Dec. 12, 14, 1871, and April 26, 1872 (Globe, pp. 69, 70, 124,

Sumner made at this session an earnest and determined effort to carry his civil-rights bill, — a measure securing equality of civil rights to the colored people, and prohibiting discriminations against them by common carriers of passengers, by proprietors of theatres and inns, managers of schools, of cemeteries, and of churches, or as to service as jurors in any courts, State or national. His association with the Democrats in opposing the San Domingo scheme had not, as was observed, affected his loyalty to the colored people. He continued to present from the beginning of the session petitions for the bill, usually pressing them in brief remarks; and he endeavored to make action on the bill a condition of final adjournment.[1] He sought to make the pressure for reconciliation serve his purpose. He moved his bill as an amendment to the amnesty bill which had come from the House, maintaining it at some length; but he encountered the objection that his bill, which required only a majority vote, could not be moved as an amendment to a bill which required a two-thirds vote.[2] The Vice-President, however, sustained by the Senate, overruled the objection. Sumner doubtless obtained some votes for his proposition from senators who were opposed to the amnesty bill, and who were sure that the adoption of the amendment, by repelling the Democratic senators, would defeat it. He thought the two measures should be associated in history, — the one an act of justice, and the other an act of generosity; and it was his opinion, not, however, justified by the result, that the desire for amnesty was so strong that when once his civil-rights measure had been incorporated in it the bill thus amended would pass by a two-thirds vote. His amendment was lost in committee of the whole by a single vote;[3] and moving it again after the bill was reported,

2804–2806; Works, vol. xv. p. 79); and the discontinuance of the internal revenue bureau, with "the tribe of officeholders" which it imposed on the country, — introducing a bill for the purpose, Dec. 11, 1871, March 21, 26, and June 4, 1872 (Globe, pp. 45, 46, 1856, 1857, 1977, 4217). This effort was approved by the New York "Herald," Dec. 11, 1871, and the New York "World," December 12. He pushed his measure at his two remaining sessions, Dec. 12, 1872 (Globe, pp. 144, 145), Dec. 17, 1873, Jan. 6, 1874 (Globe, pp. 249, 390). He wrote at this time, at the request of the publishers and the author, an introduction to an edition of Nasby's letters, April 1, 1872; Works, vol. xv. pp. 65–67.

1 Dec. 4, 7, 12, 13, 1871, Jan. 24, 1872; Congressional Globe, pp. 2, 36, 69, 84, 546.

2 Dec. 21, 1871; Congressional Globe, pp. 263, 265, 271–274; Works, vol. xiv. pp. 366–368.

3 Some senators explained that they voted for the principle of the bill without committing themselves on its details, Jan. 23, 1872. (Congressional Globe, p. 531.) The President did not approve the union of the two measures in the same bill. Boston "Journal," Jan. 11, 1872.

he said: "I entreat senators over the way [the Democrats] who really seek reconciliation now to unite in this honest effort. Give me an opportunity to vote for this bill; I long to do it. Gladly would I reach out the olive branch; but I know no way in which that can be done unless you begin by justice to the colored race."[1] No further action was taken till after the holiday recess. The colored people held meetings to advance the measure; but beyond them and old Abolitionists there was no great popular interest in it.[2]

After the recess Sumner made his most elaborate speech on the subject, in which he reviewed the arguments against caste distinctions, and traversed ground already familiar to him.[3] His final appeal was characteristic in style: —

"I make this appeal also for the sake of peace, so that at last there shall be an end of slavery, and the rights of the citizen shall be everywhere under the equal safeguard of national law. There is beauty in art, in literature, in science, and in every triumph of intelligence, all of which I covet for my country; but there is a higher beauty still, — in relieving the poor, in elevating the down-trodden, and being a succor to the oppressed. There is true grandeur in an example of justice, making the rights of all the same as our own, and beating down prejudice, like Satan, under our feet. Humbly do I pray that the republic may not lose this great prize, or postpone its enjoyment."

When the debate was resumed, two days later, the senator read at length documents, letters, and extracts from newspapers, showing the necessity of his bill.[4] The galleries were filled on the first day, — mostly with colored people, — but the subject did not interest the public generally. Letters of congratulation came from Gerrit Smith, Garrison, S. E. Sewall, Whittier, and D. H. Chamberlain, then attorney-general of South Carolina; but political leaders were silent. Whittier wrote: "Thanks for thy noble speech. Some of our politicians are half afraid to commend it, but depend upon it the heart of Massachusetts is with thee. Amnesty for rebels and a guaranty of safety to the freedmen should go together." Morrill of Maine and Ferry of Connecticut opposed Sumner's measure as attempting to deal

[1] There was a colloquy between Sumner and Hill of Georgia on the social aspects of the question, in which both were amiable, Dec. 20, 1871. Congressional Globe, pp. 241-244; Works, vol. xiv. pp. 358-364.

[2] A delegation of colored people waited on the senator New Year's Day; and an account of the interview is given in the Boston "Journal," Jan. 3, 1872.

[3] Jan. 15, 1872, Works, vol. xiv. pp. 369-413.

[4] Works, vol. xiv. pp. 413-415.

with matters which were purely of State concern. Schurz did not sympathize with his friend's pressure for national legislation imposing civil equality. He kept out of the debate, and his name rarely appeared in the votes. Sumner pushed his measure during the entire session, with all the persistency which was a part of his nature.[1] Some senators became weary of the subject, and one of them (Hamlin) forgot his sense of propriety by rising, when Sumner was insisting on action before final adjournment, and asking, with a serious air, "if it would be in order to sing Old Hundred before voting."[2] Sumner rebuked him for his trifling.

The former controversy as to the force to be given to the Declaration of Independence in interpreting the Constitution was revived, and here Morrill was as far apart from Sumner as Carpenter had been. He refused to treat it as a source of power, although allowing it to be "an inspiration" and "a pervading and all-powerful influence." He was a clear-sighted lawyer, and indeed anticipated in his positions the judgment of the Supreme Court. He complained, and had reason to complain, of Sumner's mode of handling a constitutional question, — his drawing on sublime doctrines of human rights rather than looking sharply at the written text. Sumner was disappointed at finding some Southern Republican senators who had been chosen by colored votes opposed to coupling his civil-rights bill with amnesty, and worried them by his remarks, which called the attention of their colored constituents to their action. Naturally they resented this mode of "cracking a whip over them." Carpenter nominally supported the measure, though in a way to leave a doubt whether he was really in favor of any part; but he objected strenuously to its interference with churches and juries as of doubtful constitutionality.[3] The two senators renewed their contention over the Declaration, and Sumner went so far as to place the authority of that document higher than that of the Constitution itself, as "earlier in time, loftier, more majestic, more sublime in character and principle."[4] Sherman and

1 Works, vol. xiv. pp. 417–473.

2 This remark was at first left out of the Congressional Globe, but afterwards restored (Jan. 26, Feb. 7 and 9, 1872; Globe, pp. 622, 866, 906). Gerrit Smith, in a letter to Sumner, January 29, rebuked Hamlin's levity.

3 Carpenter had in a friendly way asked Sumner to leave out churches and juries, but Sumner determined, on reflection, that they should be retained. Feb. 5, 1872, Congressional Globe, p. 825.

4 The scene between Sumner and Carpenter, February 5, is described by J. R. G. H. in the New York "Tribune," February 7.

Frelinghuysen were on the whole with Sumner, though disagreeing on one or two points; and the Senate, on the latter's motion, exempted the churches. The Chinaman again appeared, as one section struck out the word "white" from all statutes of the United States. Sherman was unwilling to open the gates to "the heathen races;" but Sumner declined to modify the section, justifying its scope, and the Senate voted to retain it. There was a tie vote on Sumner's amendment,[1] which attached his civil-rights measure to the amnesty bill, and it was carried by the Vice-President's casting vote,[2] which was received with cheers from the galleries. This sealed the fate of the amnesty bill, as the Democratic senators withdrew from its support, and left it considerably short of a two-thirds vote. Sumner cordially sustained the bill, now "consecrated and elevated," as he said, by the amendment.

Sumner wrote to Longfellow, February 25: —

"Your handwriting, dear Longfellow, is like sunshine from my large pile of letters, and is next to seeing you. To-day is charming; but I am at home, working always. There is no end to it. I am weary, and often say, How much longer must this last? I have been gratified by the success of the civil-rights bill. I begin to believe it will become a law; then will there be joy. Very few measures of equal importance have ever been presented. It will be the capstone of my work. Then, perhaps, I had better withdraw, and leave to others this laborious life."

Three months after the defeat of the first bill, another amnesty bill from the House came up in the Senate, and Sumner renewed his effort. There was the same point of order, overruled again by the Vice-President and the Senate; the same threshing over of former contentions and the revival of personal questions; a motion by Ferry to exempt schools, and another by Carpenter to exempt juries, — both voted down. Trumbull's motion to strike out the first five sections was defeated by the Vice-President's casting vote, which was greeted with applause from the galleries; but Sumner's bill, moved as a substitute, was lost by a single vote. Nothing daunted by this defeat, he moved

1 Among those voting "yea" were Anthony, Cameron, Chandler, Conkling, Frelinghuysen, Hamlin, Harlan, Morrill (Vermont), Morton, Sherman, Sumner, Wilson, and Windom. Among those voting "no" were Carpenter, Ferry (Conn.), Logan, Morrill (Maine), Schurz, Trumbull, and the Democratic senators.

2 The Vice-President (Colfax) explained that he voted for the amendment as a whole, without concurring in all its features.

it a few minutes later as an addition to the amnesty bill, — and now he succeeded, again by the casting vote of the Vice-President; but the amnesty bill, thus enlarged, again failed to receive a two-thirds vote. Unwearied, Sumner placed at once on the calendar another civil-rights bill, with some changes suggested in the recent debates. Within a week he moved his bill as an amendment to an Act to enforce the right of citizens to vote, but withdrew it on an appeal from Sherman in behalf of the pending bill, which it would imperil.[1] A week later, when the Senate was holding a night session for the purpose of reaching a final vote on the supplementary enforcement bill, Sumner, who was ill, remained at home observing medical directions, and not supposing any other bill would be taken up. The bill passed at 5.45 the next morning. Then Carpenter, resorting to an artifice which most of his associates would have deemed unbecoming in a senator, carried a motion to take up Sumner's bill in his absence, a bare majority of the senators being present. After moving an amendment which dropped out schools, churches, cemeteries, and juries, he insisted on an immediate vote; and notwithstanding a protest from a senator against the unfairness of the proceeding, pushed the bill thus amended to a final vote at 8 A. M. The Senate then took up another House amnesty bill, when Sumner, who had been sent for, appeared. He protested against the emasculated civil-rights bill, which had been passed, and moved his own bill as an amendment to the pending bill. This motion being now defeated by a large majority, he declined to vote for the amnesty bill when not associated with equal civil rights; but it passed with only two votes against it, — his own and Nye's. He again renewed his appeal, and "sounded the cry" for the rights of the colored man, which had been sacrificed.[2] The Senate adjourned at 10.20 A. M., less than two hours before another day's session was to begin. Again, three days before the session closed, Sumner moved his bill as an amendment to the civil appropriation bill, but it was ruled out of order. So the amnesty bill became a law; but the civil-rights bill as curtailed by Carpenter was not acted on in the House.[3] It will be hard to find

[1] May 14, Congressional Globe, p. 3425. Sumner, who was absent when the bill passed, was paired with Schurz, who was opposed to it.

[2] Works, vol. xiv. pp. 468-471.

[3] It could not be taken up in the House without a two-thirds vote.

in our history parallels to such pertinacity as Sumner's repeated efforts to carry his civil-rights bill at this session.[1]

Sumner's distinction as the tribune of the colored people deserves emphasis in this connection. Others saw the evil of slavery, and did their best to extirpate it; others saw in the enfranchised slaves a political force, possibly a decisive one in national elections, and then, as later, they devised means to promote and protect their rights as voters; but Sumner alone and at all times insisted on their equal title to all civil rights and privileges, and all the consideration enjoyed by white men, — and this irrespective of any political necessity or advantage. He carried many measures for their benefit, and failed in others; and the comprehensive one on which he set his heart — though after his death placed on the statute book — was declared null and void by the highest authority. But whether succeeding or failing, he established a sentiment and promulgated doctrines of duty and right which for all time will be the hope and protection of the African race.

A resolution of inquiry into the sale of United States arms to France by the war department during the Franco-Prussian war brought on a sharp and somewhat prolonged contest between Sumner and Schurz on the one hand and the partisans of the Administration on the other. Our government had on hand in 1865 a large amount of materials of war, — some unserviceable by reason of new inventions, and others superfluous in time of peace. The statutes of 1825 and 1868 authorized the sale of arms, ammunition, and stores which were "damaged or otherwise unsuitable," and the war department extended these terms to cover arms which were in excess of the needs of a peace establishment. The Secretary of War (Belknap) proceeded to reduce the stock on hand, and was doing so at the breaking out of the Franco-Prussian war, — a war which our government promptly recognized by a proclamation of neutrality. The well known firm of Remington & Son, of Ilion, New York, manufacturers of arms, who were among the largest purchasers, were discovered, Oct. 13, 1870, to be acting as agents of France; and

[1] Sumner reported from the committee on the District of Columbia a bill to secure equality of rights in schools in the District, and to abolish separate colored schools in it; but notwithstanding his repeated efforts to obtain a vote upon it, he did not succeed. April 17, 18; May 2, 4, 6, 7; Congressional Globe, pp. 2484, 2539, 2540, 2985, 3056, 3057, 3099, 3124.

the same day the secretary, with the view of observing forms of neutrality between the belligerents, directed that no further sales should be made to them. While recognizing by this order that a sale of arms to either belligerent would be a breach of neutrality, his department nevertheless treated the order from the beginning as only formal, and made no effort to make the neutrality actual and genuine. The day the order was issued, the war department had agreed orally on the terms of a contract for the sale of arms to Remington's firm before their agency was disclosed; and although there was no binding contract and no deposit had been made by the purchaser, the arms were, when the agency was well known, delivered six weeks later. When the Remingtons withdrew as open competitors, one Richardson, described in the debate as a "little country lawyer," stepped in. He was not in the arms business, was a neighbor of the Remingtons at Ilion, and known to be in close relations with them; and the arms sold to him went at once into their possession, and were thereupon shipped to France.[1] It appeared from Remington's letter — written two months after the secretary's order to the French officer at Tours, who was charged with the duty of buying such materials — that he was still negotiating with our government for the purchase of arms and the manufacture of cartridges. Further, it appeared that Remington still continued to be in business relations with the officers of the ordnance bureau, at whose agency in New York the negotiations were carried on. Finally, on pressure from Schurz, the secretary (Jan. 24, 1871) stopped the sale of arms altogether.[2]

Meantime, however, the ordnance bureau manufactured for Richardson a large quantity of ammunition suitable for the guns sold, although the Acts of Congress authorized only a sale of unserviceable ammunition, not a manufacture of such material.[3]

1 Schurz challenged denial of his charge that Richardson was Remington's agent, but no senator rose.

2 The Secretary of State, to whom Schurz applied, was opposed to the sale of arms to the belligerents. Naturalized citizens of German nativity were sensitive when the sale of arms to France by our government became known. Gustavus Koerner, of Illinois, directed Sumner's attention to the testimony in a French trial, which stated that such sales were taking place. Mr. Bancroft, our minister at Berlin, in a despatch, Jan. 7, 1871, also called attention to them. Curiously enough, however, the Prussian government did not complain of the sales, and Bismarck was reported to have said that it was cheaper to capture the arms on the Loire than to buy them in Washington. Sumner thought this "courageous gayety" no excuse for indifference to a violation of international law. Feb. 16, 1872, Congressional Globe, p. 1072; Works, vol. xv. p. 22.

3 The Senate committee, which fully vindicated the bureau, slides over this irregularity; but Conkling in debate justified it.

There was also a departure from the law in the matter of inspection and notice, which were conditions of a private sale. The only excuse for this illegality was that it was committed with good intent and beneficial results, and under "rather a soldier's than a lawyer's construction of the statute." Some discrepancies in accounts of sales between the accounts of the war and treasury departments, and between the accounts of our departments and those of the French government, which at first invited suspicion, were satisfactorily explained; so also a reported resolution of inquiry in the French Assembly was found to have been forged.

There were suspicions at the time that officials of the war department or persons of political influence outside who were urging the sales had profited by the transactions. Sumner was thoroughly convinced that there was wrong-doing somewhere. It was difficult on any other theory to explain why the show of neutrality was kept up without its substance; why, after a formal refusal to sell to the Remingtons, business relations were still kept up with them through "a man of straw." A telegraphic despatch in French cipher sent to Remington, then in France, by his son-in-law and agent in New York, a few days before the sales to his firm were stopped, was in these words: "We have the strongest influences working for us, which will use all their efforts to succeed." The promoters of the inquiry remained always of the conviction that there was illegitimate money-making at the bottom of the business; but they were unable to penetrate the veil with which astute men know how to cover such transactions. The character of Belknap himself, as subsequently developed in later evidence, is confirmatory of their view.

The person at Washington who first drew attention to the sale of arms to France was the Marquis de Chambrun,[1] then legal counsel of the French embassy at Washington, who took an interest in the trial of one Place, formerly French consul at New York, and accused after his return to his country of misconduct in connection with the purchase of arms. The French government was at the time inquiring how it was that it had paid more for the arms than our government had received. The marquis in the spring of 1871 brought the subject to the attention of Senator Patterson, asking that his committee on retrenchment investigate the subject, and saying that "undoubtedly

[1] *Ante*, p. 265.

certain Americans, and possibly subordinate officials in the war department, would be found mixed up with these transactions;" and further, that "parties in the ordnance bureau must have been in collusion with other parties named in these transactions." Mr. Patterson called Schurz's attention to the subject at the next session, 1871–1872, just before Christmas, and named the marquis in a later interview as one who was informed upon it. About the same time Patterson mentioned some of the circumstances to Sumner, telling him that "it was a bad case, and that it must be looked into." A month later, Schurz, whom the marquis had seen, reported what he had heard to Sumner, referring him to the marquis; and Sumner then communicated with the marquis (their first conversation in relation to it), who stated to the senator the facts within his knowledge.

Sumner was always keen on the point of keeping our government strictly to its duty of observing the obligations of neutrality, and all the more so at this time when our case was pending against Great Britain. Accordingly he moved, February 12, resolutions of inquiry into the sale of arms to France, introduced by a preamble alleging the grounds of suspicion as they appeared. Two days later, without incriminating any one, he stated the reasons which called for an investigation.[1] The inquiry was a surprise to most of the senators, and it arrested at once the attention of Conkling, Morton, and Edmunds. Sumner's opening was not thought equal to the occasion, lacking definiteness and force.[2] An acrimonious debate, lasting over two weeks, followed. Sumner was not well at the time, and on the second day pressed Schurz to speak; and from that time the latter, who was more master of the details than Sumner, was a constant combatant, making four speeches, and engaged often in the running debate. No other senators spoke on the same side; and the democratic senators remained spectators only, watching with satisfaction a division in the Republican ranks. Carpenter, Conkling, Morton, Harlan, Frelinghuysen, and Edmunds threw themselves into the debate with their utmost vigor, and nearly all of them were unsparing in personal epithets. They charged Sumner and Schurz

1 Congressional Globe, pp. 1008–1017. The Washington "Capital" wrote, Feb. 18, 1872: "There is no disguising the fact that Sumner *wrong* is more a subject of admiration in the Senate galleries than any other senator *right*," and that "even his enemies admire him." The editor (Donn Piatt), from his peculiar standpoint, gives an estimate of the senator altogether favorable, offsetting only want of tact against vast and varied resources, readiness as a debater, and perfect integrity.

2 New York Tribune, February 15, 16, 17, 29.

with being false to the obligations of patriotism, because without complaint from Prussia they had volunteered to confess a breach of neutrality on our part, and had thereby invited a claim for damages. They branded the two senators as "emissaries" or "spies" of foreign governments for doing what senators by habit and of right do, — that is, for conversing with foreigners, official or private, who are resident at Washington, both senators having talked with the Marquis de Chambrun, and Schurz having inquired as to certain facts at the Prussian embassy. Puerile as the charge was, Conkling moved an amendment for an inquiry whether any senator or citizen had been in communication or collusion with any foreign power or any "emissary" or "spy" thereof, but was obliged to substitute the terms "agent or officer," being reminded that those of "spy" and "emissary" were applicable only to a condition of war.[1] On the main question, the international one, the senators who justified the Administration (except one) admitted the rule that a neutral power was not allowed to sell arms and war materials to either belligerent;[2] but they reduced it to a formal and purely technical one, denying any duty of the seller to make inquiry as to their destination, and making even knowledge that the purchaser intended an immediate transfer to the belligerent altogether immaterial. Carpenter went even further, contending in his speech and in the committee's report drawn by him that the rule itself did not exist; that the war department in discontinuing the sales to Remington had acted under unnecessary scruples; and that, at least where the sales had begun before the breaking out of hostilities, our government as a neutral had a right to sell arms and war material to either belligerent, even directly to its head, Louis Napoleon or the king of Prussia. While Sumner disclaimed that his resolution was an attack on the President, his opponents insisted that it was "a political move,"[3] specially intended to excite the German vote against the Administration; and the debate was at times diverted into a political and personal discussion as to affairs in Missouri, and particularly as to Schurz's connection with them.

The debate reached its highest point of interest on February

[1] Harper's Weekly, March 16, 1872, while disagreeing with Sumner and Schurz, treated the suggestion of their unlawful intercourse with foreign powers as "ridiculous."

[2] Citizens could of course sell such materials to a belligerent, subject to seizure as contraband of war.

[3] The newspapers took the same view. Harper's Weekly, March 2, 9, and 16, 1872; New York "Independent, February" 29.

19 and 20, — Conkling having the former day, and Schurz the latter. On the first day the friends of the President crowded the galleries, — among whom were conspicuous the ladies from the White House. Conkling's speech was characteristic in manner, gesture, and style. The next day, when Schurz was to reply, ladies were admitted into the Senate chamber, where they filled the sofas and the standing-room. Inspired by the controversy and by his audience, he never spoke in the Senate with such nervous energy, fire, and immediate effect.[1] The galleries were with him, and their outbursts of applause were with difficulty repressed by the chair. Sumner thanked him warmly, and said to others as well as to him that it was the greatest speech he had heard in the Senate for twenty years. Morton led in the debate that followed, and was called to order by the chair for saying that he had "extreme contempt for the senator's extreme insolence." The next day Schurz and Conkling had another encounter, in which the former described the latter's manner in language recalling a similar description of the New York senator by Mr. Blaine some years before in the House.[2] After this the two senators did not speak to each other. Schurz on a later day repelled Carpenter's charge that it is unpatriotic to expose a breach of neutrality on the part of the Administration, saying, "The senator from Wisconsin cannot frighten me by exclaiming, 'My country, right or wrong!' In one sense I say so too. My country, — and my country is the great American Republic, — my country, right or wrong: if right to be kept right, and if wrong to be set right!"[3] a retort which drew applause from the galleries.

Sumner made his principal speech February 28, in which he was more effective than when he opened the debate.[4] It was a calm and dignified statement, without personality towards his opponents; and it won the favor of his audience, which was large and inspiring.[5] The next day he spoke briefly.[6] He de-

[1] New York "Tribune," February 21. See as to Schurz's other speeches in the debate, New York "Tribune," February 26, 27, 28.

[2] *Ante*, pp. 348–350.

[3] Harper's Weekly, April 20, 1872, took exception to Carpenter's standards of patriotism.

[4] Works, vol. xv. pp. 5–44; New York Tribune, February 29; New York Herald, February 29; Boston Journal, February 29.

[5] Hamlin objected to Logan's motion for the admission of ladies to the Senate chamber, which had been allowed on previous days. He was at the time very bitter against Sumner.

[6] February 29. Congressional Globe, pp. 1292–1295.

fended himself against the charge of having taken an unpatriotic position, contending that it was his supreme duty to keep his country right, and pointing for examples under like circumstances to Cobden and Bright at the time of our Civil War, and to Fox and Burke at the time of our Revolution.[1] His preamble with his consent was laid on the table, and the resolution itself was passed by a large majority, only five votes being given in the negative.

To the partisan bitterness of the Administration senators there were some exceptions. Harlan said of Sumner that he was "as patriotic as any member of the Senate;" and Cameron paid a tribute to his magnanimity, justice, and intelligence. Conkling had found other victims of his worrying propensity, and now, as also in later debates, treated him with civility,—almost with consideration.

The strain of the contest on the arms question was too much for Sumner, and brought on another attack of the *angina pectoris*. The mention of his name, the day after the resolution passed, as chairman or a member of the committee of investigation, drew from him a declination, with a statement of his inability to serve; and he was absent from his seat most of the time for two weeks. The committee was constituted in a manner unfriendly to inquiry, with the studied exclusion of its promoters. Hamlin, who had denounced them, was made chairman, while Schurz was refused any place on the committee, although Trumbull and Sumner asked that he should serve on it. The committee, chosen by ballot, consisted of Hamlin, Carpenter, Sawyer, Logan, Ames, Harlan, and Stevenson,—each receiving from fifty-two to thirty-six votes. Schurz received twenty-three, only eleven of which were given by Republican senators, and Trumbull nineteen. The Senate refused the request of Stevenson, the only Democrat chosen, to have Schurz take his place. Sumner was absent at the time, or, as he afterwards stated in the Senate, he would have entered at once his protest against the composition of the committee.[2] His illness drew tender expressions from friends. Lieber wrote, March 2:

"Let your secretary write us how you are, if you are too much occupied. Take care of your health, and remember that it was in 1828 or 1829 that I

[1] This point was much pressed against Sumner, even by some generally friendly to him. New York "Independent," Feb. 22, 1872.

[2] The committee's report stated that Sumner would have been chairman if he had not declined; but the vote on Schurz's name indicates that he would have been excluded.

became acquainted with you. We are not young, and your country wants you, — living, I mean, for it will always have you or keep you in some sense."

Wendell Phillips wrote, March 3: —

"Sorry to hear you are not so well, but glad they have caged you and forced you to rest. Now submit gracefully; consent to play sick for our sakes, who want to lean on you, and so need a strong man. Best wishes for quick recovery, but earnest prayers that you will wait and rest patiently for it."

The committee began its sessions March 6, and closed them April 23, — holding thirty-one meetings, and making a report which, with the evidence, fills a stout volume of eight hundred and forty-nine pages.[1] Schurz, by its invitation, — an invitation which was a confession that he should have been a member, — attended the sessions, examined and cross-examined witnesses, and the committee summoned any whose names he gave. Both he and Sumner testified, though refusing to reveal communications made to them in confidence.

Sumner was requested by the committee in writing to appear as a witness. He came before it and read a protest;[2] and the committee, on Carpenter's motion, then ordered his appearance by a subpœna.[3] He came the next day, and after reading another protest, waived his right, and submitted[4] himself for examination.[5] His protests, while declaring that he had nothing to conceal either in the present case or in all his public life, whether act, letter, or conversation at any time, asserted the right of a senator to confidential intercourse with all who gave him information; but his main insistence was that the committee, assorted as it was, had no right to sit at all. He contended that by parliamentary law the committee should be made up of senators friendly to the inquiry, excluding those who, according to the ancient phrase, were "against the thing," or who took ground that there were no facts or reasons justifying an inquiry, — quoting Jefferson, that a member who is against the bill "ought to ask to be excused;" as well as R. M. T. Hunter,

[1] Forty-second Congress, second session, Senate Reports No. 183.

[2] March 26. Works, vol. xv. pp. 45–55.

[3] No process for contempt would have issued in case of his further refusal. Boston "Journal," April 3.

[4] March 27. Works, vol. xv. pp. 56–60.

[5] Sumner had on previous occasions maintained that the inquisitorial power of the Senate should be kept within strict limits. In the Senate, March 12 and June 15, 1860, Works, vol. iv. pp. 426–440; May 18 and 27, 1871, Ibid., vol. xiv. pp. 284–305.

a former speaker of the House, that "in committees of investigation it is equally clear that the opposition who hold the affirmative should have the majority and the power."[1] He objected particularly to Hamlin, calling him "the acting chairman," and naming him as one who had shown himself in open speech "against the thing."[2] Carpenter moved that the protests be returned to Sumner as disrespectful to the committee, saying then, and repeating the same point in the report, that "it was the first time in the history of the world that a witness has assumed to impeach the capacity of the judge on the bench to examine him." In the course of his examination Sumner replied to Carpenter, who was questioning him in relation to the rule of parliamentary law as to the appointment of committees, that he too was disqualified to sit upon the committee after vindicating the whole transaction in an elaborate speech to show that there was no necessity for an inquiry. While Carpenter was pursuing the examination, Hamlin interposed that Sumner's position was "absolutely insulting to the committee." Further on, when Sumner answered affirmatively a question whether on a rule of neutrality others might be right and he wrong, Hamlin interjected, "That is an admission I did not expect to hear you make." When questioned by Carpenter as to the duty of a senator on hearing a rumor that his own government had wronged a foreign power, Sumner answered, "That again is a broad and abstract question." Carpenter retorted, "But you are a broad and abstract man, and therefore I put the question to you."

The modern practice may not be, as Sumner contended it once was, to make up a committee of investigation wholly of members who recognize suspicions or reasons which justify an inquiry; but the present committee was open to the exception which he took, — in that while it had among its members the stoutest defenders in debate of the transactions in question, all who had in debate maintained the opposite view were studiously excluded from it. The defence was made in the Senate and in

[1] He had previously at the same session made the same point when the majority of the Senate proposed to exclude from the committee of investigation and retrenchment all but one senator who had complained of abuses; and he then urged the unfairness of the exclusion (December 18, Congressional Globe, pp. 160, 167, 168, 173, 190-193); but the Senate refused to arrange the committee in conformity with his idea.

[2] Sumner renewed his protest, May 11 (Congressional Globe, p. 3325), when the report came in; and again he was charged with insulting the committee by denying its competency.

the report for such an irregular and unusual proceeding, that all the members had voted to institute the committee; but that was purely a technical answer.

The report drawn by Carpenter, and signed by all the members except one, fully exculpated the war department and all its subordinate bureaus and officials. It reviewed the relations of Sumner and Schurz with the Marquis de Chambrun, but carefully avoided any declaration as to whether any senator had been in collusion with an officer or agent of a foreign government. Stevenson stated a dissenting view on the main conclusions of the majority. The motion, May 11, to print the report brought on another heated debate, in which Sumner renewed his protest against the composition of the committee, and condemned "the abnormal ultraism" of its new version of international law.[1] He made another effort to have a day assigned for the consideration of the report; but the session was near its end, and the assignment was not made. On the last day of the month, as he began his speech on the Presidential election, he renewed his familiar protest against the committee itself, and pronounced its report "one of the most extraordinary in parliamentary history; unworthy of the Senate in every respect; wanting in ordinary fairness, unbecoming in tone, unjust to senators who had deemed it their duty to move the inquiry, and ridiculous in its attempt to expound international law." Schurz the same day reviewed at length the report, replying to its personal insinuations, as well as controverting its substantial positions. A reply from Carpenter closed the discussion.

The controversy attracted little attention in the country. It was chiefly of interest at Washington, where it drew a crowd to the Capitol, always on hand to witness a display of forensic antagonism;[2] and even with them the debate was wearisome, except when Schurz, Sumner, Carpenter, or Conkling was on the floor. Sumner was, as his manner showed, profoundly convinced of the truth of his position that there had been a breach of international duty, and that there was dishonesty somewhere; but he was in a contest where he was almost sure to be baffled and outwitted by men shrewder than himself, both in the Senate and outside of it. Personal friends felt that he was in no con-

[1] Congressional Globe, p. 3326.

[2] James S. Pike described in the New York "Tribune," February 27, the contest as "a boy's debate, . . . carried on by able men and practised speakers," and affording "the cheapest entertainment to loafers."

dition of health to undergo the strain of such antagonisms; and politicians well disposed towards him, and at the same time supporters of the President, saw with regret the widening breach between him and the Administration. Some thought that he made too much of irregularities which, even if existing to the extent he suspected, are incident to public affairs, and that it was not for him to lead in an exposure which would weaken his own party. To such indifferentism Sumner was at all times proof.

Early in 1872 it became evident that a considerable body, calling themselves "Liberal Republicans," would refuse to support General Grant for re-election. Their objections were largely to his personal characteristics, which were alleged to be unbecoming in a chief magistrate, and to the abuses which he allowed to prevail in the public service. His close alliance with certain leaders in Congress, — Conkling, Cameron, Chandler, and Carpenter in the Senate, and Butler in the House, — whom he allowed to use the public patronage in their respective States in contests with their rivals, stimulated the opposition not only of those who felt the adverse weight of Executive influence, but of others who believed in an entire separation of politics from patronage.[1] His arbitrary methods in attempting to acquire San Domingo and the removal of Sumner from the foreign relations committee as the sequel of his failure, entered largely into the discussion. One of the points made against him was his interference through the army with the governments and elections of the restored rebel States; but in this respect he had only done what Republicans generally had approved, and even demanded.[2] This point was certainly not open to those who had pressed nationalism in the interest of loyal people at the South, of both races, to the limit of constitutional law. Amnesty to the rebels was put by Greeley in the foreground; but the President could not be charged with having been obstructive to this measure, as

[1] General J. D. Cox resigned as Secretary of the Interior in November, 1870; and his resignation was accepted by the President with a tacit admission, as stated by General Cox in a letter to Sumner, Aug. 3, 1872, that he found it impolitic to sustain the secretary against the antagonism excited by his efforts for civil service reform. George William Curtis resigned from the civil service commission for a similar reason, in March, 1873.

[2] His acts in this line in Louisiana during his second term were less defensible; but just before he finally left office he signified that the country had had enough of this kind of interference.

he had signed without hesitation all bills of the kind which Congress passed.

But whatever of justice there was in the objections to the President's policy or conduct, it was clear that the Republican masses, grateful for his military services, were unshaken in their devotion to him, and that he would be the Republican candidate in 1872. The Democratic party had been since the Civil War gaining strength at the North, and was gradually resuming control of the reconstructed States, so that the result of the election could not be predicted with any certainty, and the success of the Republicans would be seriously imperilled by any considerable secession from their ranks. To prevent that danger, Wilson, with a zeal for party unity quickened by his ambition for the vice-presidency, had made the visits to the President which have been referred to.

Schurz early in the year 1872 announced his sympathy with the Republican opposition to the President's renomination which had taken form in Missouri, and his purpose to oppose his election in case he was again selected as candidate. A month or two later Trumbull took the same position. The New York "Tribune," with Horace Greeley and Whitelaw Reid editors, the Chicago "Tribune," the Cincinnati "Commercial," and the Springfield (Mass.) "Republican," each important centres of influence, were moving in the same direction. A national convention, to meet at Cincinnati May 1, was called in January by the Liberal Republicans of Missouri. Sumner, while in relations of confidence with Schurz and Trumbull, kept himself in reserve, avowing his opposition to the President's renomination, but hoping that the Republican convention which was to meet at Philadelphia in June would for the sake of harmony name another candidate. No one but himself, however, counted at all on such a solution of the difficulty; and indeed his own faith must have been slight.[1]

The Liberal Republican movement was from the start in some danger of falling into the hands of enthusiasts or irresponsible malcontents. Its promoters, particularly the editors of the journals already mentioned, who to a great extent took the initiative, did what they could to avert the catastrophe, and to that end invoked Sumner's open and active co-operation. There

[1] His position is indicated, perhaps with authority, in the Washington correspondence of the Boston "Journal," March 19. Compare New York "Evening Post," March 16.

was a moral power in his name which the other leaders did not have; and he had the confidence of the colored people, whose solid Republican column at the South it was important to break. Accordingly, for six weeks before the meeting of the convention its promoters plied the senator with appeals for a public statement of his position, which were so near in date and so alike in substance as to suggest concert among the writers. Among them were Whitelaw Reid of the New York "Tribune," Horace White of the Chicago "Tribune," Samuel Bowles of the Springfield "Republican," Francis W. Bird, Edward Atkinson, David A. Wells, Hiram Barney, George Wilkes, and J. R. Doolittle; and they were reinforced by others who joined in a similar pressure at Washington. They set forth with great urgency the necessity of his taking a stand openly in order to save the new movement at its birth; and they added the personal appeal that one of its inspirations was the indignation felt at the outrage inflicted on him by the President and his partisans in his removal from his committee. Mr. Reid wrote with much concern, March 28, on behalf of himself and Mr. Greeley, as to conflicting reports concerning the senator's position, and pleaded against further delay, saying: —

> "It is needful that you should know at once the grave anxiety that has been inspired, and the light in which Mr. Greeley would regard any prolonged delay in an authoritative expression from you with reference to the combination against Grant. When urging me to go over and see you, he asked me to say that in case you were not going to support us explicitly and with your whole force, it was due to us to know at once, and that it might then become necessary for the 'Tribune' to take a different tack." [1]

The promoters of the movement were perplexed from the beginning as to the choice of a candidate, — it being essential to their success to nominate one strong in public confidence, likely to attract Republican voters and at the same time invite Democratic co-operation. There was an early mention of Greeley; but to sober-thinking people his candidacy seemed preposterous. Trumbull had many points in his favor as an able statesman; but unfortunately just then a charge — doubtless an unfounded one — that he had as a lawyer taken a fee in a matter connected with his public duties stood in the way

[1] Mr. Reid had written, January 25, that Grant's name was not "a symbol of union and victory." He wrote May 16, requesting the senator to contribute leaders to the "Tribune," subjecting the President's qualifications for his office to critical analysis.

of his selection. Sumner's name was one of those proposed. Wilkes presented it in his newspaper,[1] and James M. Ashley was active in bringing it forward, making a visit to New England in the spring for the purpose. Bowles, Bird, and others thought that an open and distinct declaration of sympathy with the movement at an early stage would have placed him at its head. It is not likely — though an opinion on such a matter can be little better than conjecture — that he would have proved the best candidate. His character and fame would surely have attracted a large body of voters hitherto Republican; he might, and probably would, have carried Massachusetts; but his name would not, as was to be expected, have found favor with Southern Democrats, whose undivided support was essential.[2] Though always friendly at heart to that section, he had seemed otherwise in his policy of reconstruction; and he was at the time pushing the civil equality of negroes in a way not at all agreeable to Southern people. Northern Democrats of the "Bourbon" type could not easily accept as leader one with whom they had been long in controversy. He himself did not seek the nomination, or express a desire for it. The Liberal Republican leaders in Massachusetts, who were in close relations with him, did not (presumably following his counsels) present his name, and even discouraged its use. If, however, it had been decided as the wisest course to place him at the head of the ticket, he would doubtless have accepted the place, — as it would have been his duty to do in view of his relations to the movement.

The natural candidate of the new party, and one with whom it would have made its best canvass and perhaps have succeeded, was Charles Francis Adams, minister to England for nearly eight years, — a period including the Civil War, — and at this time (1872) a member of the Tribunal of Arbitration at Geneva. He would have held the Democratic vote, and divided conservative Republicans. At one time his nomination seemed altogether likely;[3] but a peculiar letter from him, made public at the time, in which he spoke of the Liberal Republicans as "that crowd," repelled delegates from his support. Mr. Bird

1 "The Spirit of the Times," Jan. 20 and March 30, 1872.

2 New York "Herald," Feb. 3, 1872. Andrew Johnson signified his opposition to Sumner as a candidate (Chicago "Tribune," Dec. 7, 1871).

3 He led Greeley on all the ballots, but changes on the last one before it was announced gave the latter the nomination.

of the Massachusetts delegation was opposed to his nomination, and was thought, though erroneously, to represent in this respect the senator.[1] Horace Greeley was, however, nominated by the Liberal Republicans at Cincinnati, and afterwards by the Democrats at Baltimore. His nomination, as soon as made, settled the final result. No one in the country among its distinguished men was so unfitted by natural qualities for a high administrative trust. He stood then, as he is always likely to stand, as first of American journalists, and in that career he had done good work for mankind; but he had no aptitude for eminent responsibility. His character has been often drawn, and the portrait need not be reproduced here. The Civil War was still fresh in memory, during which he had appeared strangely at exigent times, — yielding at the outset to dismemberment when heroic resistance was required, interfering later with military movements by clamor of "On to Richmond," and assuming at untimely moments the part of a volunteer negotiator of peace. His personal ways provoked mirth and caricature; and such a man is never a good candidate with a sensible people. His name repelled at once conservative citizens, particularly capitalists, whose frequent comment upon his candidacy was, "There is no knowing what he would do." Altogether it was one of the most singular freaks of politics that such a man should be called to lead a political body like the Liberal Republicans; and what influences effected the selection have not been clearly explained.[2] The members of the convention who had started the movement did not conceal their chagrin and disappointment. Some withdrew from it at once,[3] while others, hoping for the substitution of another candidate, called a conference which was held in New York in June; but nothing came of it. No political sagacity was required to foresee what the decision of the American people, who lean to safe and tried men, would be between Mr. Greeley and General Grant.

[1] In "The Life and Times of Samuel Bowles," vol. ii. p. 184, the erroneous statement is repeated that Sumner was opposed to Adams's candidacy. Sumner and Adams had divided in 1861 on plans of compromise, and Mr. Bird may have supposed that on account of this difference Sumner would prefer another candidate. The senator, however, would have cordially accepted Adams.

[2] The convention at Cincinnati was more a mass meeting than a conference of delegates. Its currents and incidents are noted in Bowles's "Life," vol. ii. pp. 175-200.

[3] Among those in sympathy with the movement who refused to support Greeley were William C. Bryant, Stanley Matthews, George Hoadley, and the editor of the New York "Nation."

Sumner took no part and gave no counsels as to the selection of a candidate. When Greeley's nomination was announced in Washington, and others were commenting on his eccentricities, the senator admitted them, but interposed on the other hand that his success as a journalist and his devotion to good causes were likely to be an attractive force with the American people.

The platform of the Cincinnati convention, which was afterwards adopted without change by the Democratic convention at Baltimore, was in one respect Sumner's handiwork, the draft being received by Mr. Bird at Washington and taken to Cincinnati. The part which came from Sumner, modified perhaps in phraseology, declared the equality of all men before the law; the right of all to equal and exact justice, irrespective of nativity, race, color, or persuasion, religious or political; and affirmed as a finality emancipation and enfranchisement and the three new amendments to the Constitution. Certainly an advance was made when the Southern people accepted even in form such a result.[1]

Sumner, however, maintained reserve as to his definite course in the election till long after the Cincinnati convention, answering inquiries simply by saying that he desired the defeat of Grant, and hoped the Republicans would nominate another candidate. Late in May he wrote to F. W. Bird: —

"Nor have I ever given a hint to a human being as to my future course. My right hand has never spoken it to my left. Of this I shall not speak until I can see the whole field, and especially the bearing on the colored race. I mean to fail in nothing by which they may be helped; therefore all stories as to what I shall do or shall not are inventions. Nobody will know my purpose sooner than yourself, for I honor you constantly. But I seek two things: (1) The protection of the colored race, and (2) The defeat of Grant."

All the while Sumner's position was watched with interest, and by none more than by his old coadjutors. It was given out in March that he was to attend the convention at Cincinnati, and probably take the chair; but this report was promptly contradicted by his authority. Republicans were loath to lose a name which had long been a charm with the moral sentiment of the country, and their journals, in leaders intended for his eye, deplored the possibility of its being lost to them in the election

[1] The New York "Tribune," March 12, 1854, states that Sumner "commended the tariff plank in the Cincinnati platform as 'the most honest expression on the subject ever made by any convention since he had entered public life.'"

at hand. They reminded him that the only alternative of continued allegiance to his party was an alliance with the Democratic party, weighted with its rebellion record and inviting distrust by its hostility to the civil equality of the colored people, which he had so much at heart. They admitted and deplored "the undeserved and gross injury" he had received, but adjured him, for the sake of patriotism and humanity, not to imitate in the coming contest "Achilles sitting aloof in his tent."[1] Friendly appeals of like purport came to him from many correspondents, — from J. W. Forney, Alexander H. Rice, Wendell Phillips, and Rev. William G. Eliot. In his own State a large body of Republicans, probably a majority of those who had decided to vote for the President's re-election, bated not a jot of devotion to their senator. Notwithstanding their own decision, they felt that he could not himself with honor support the President. Some of them, whose sympathies were altogether with him in his position, thought it wiser for themselves to remain with their party so as to be in a better position to support his re-election to the Senate two years later. Generally among Republicans there was no abatement of confidence in him; and in their public meetings his divergence from the party was not mentioned, or if mentioned, he was spoken of with respect and even tenderness. At the State convention in April, which formally presented Grant for President and Wilson for Vice-President, John H. Clifford (former governor) made some thrusts at the President's critics, which were intended for the senator, but they found no favor with the mass of delegates.[2] Republican speakers, both at this time and in their meetings in the autumn, referred to him in terms of respect, and abstained in their resolutions from any formal censure.[3] Some of them, like Charles Francis Adams, Jr., at Quincy, openly declared their purpose to support his re-election; and his declaration represented the spirit of the Republican masses.

[1] Boston Journal, May 6: "Where is Charles Sumner?" March 18: "Where am I to go?" Albany Evening Journal, March 22.

[2] Another former governor, A. H. Bullock, approved Sumner's course, writing to him, March 14: "I congratulate you on the mastery of the situation; for this you have achieved." Samuel Hooper, M. C., though nominally supporting the President's re-election, was in sympathy with Sumner in his course, and gave him advice as to the line of judicious opposition to the President.

[3] E. L. Pierce prepared and reported, as chairman of the committee, resolutions at the Republican State convention which avoided reference to the senator. He also wrote to the senator letters with the view of guarding his personal position.

Sumner was kindly to old friends who did not follow him at this time; but it was a grief to him that he could not draw George William Curtis to his side. One evening in the spring of 1872, when Curtis was at his house and was about leaving, Sumner said to him, as if pleading for his support: "When Brooks struck me down, Douglas stood by; now when Grant strikes, you stand by." The tears fell as he spoke these friendly but reproachful words.[1] Henderson, former senator from Missouri, was witness of the scene.[2]

Sumner's relations with his colleague Wilson were strained at this time, though with no open breach. He felt the need of the latter's sympathy and support, and knew well enough how much he was weakened in his position by the divided representation of the State. Wilson was at heart no believer in General Grant as a civilian, but he was anxious for party unity, and was at the time aspiring to the second place in the national service. Though not sympathetic with all of Sumner's ideas, he had profound faith in the rectitude of his purposes and a genuine affection for him. He had done more than any man in 1851 to place Sumner in the Senate, and four years later the senior senator welcomed the junior to his side. Though greatly unlike each other in training, manners, and ways of living, they had been in general accord on public measures, and their relations had been singularly free from personal questions. Their different courses at this time, though embarrassing, were not likely to lead to any permanent estrangement. Shortly after the close of the French arms debate they had a free conversation with each other, in which Sumner told his colleague that their political paths would shortly diverge, but he hoped they would still remain friends; and he begged him to intercede with Grant to withdraw as a candidate for the sake of harmony. Two days later Wilson wrote Sumner a pathetic letter, reciprocating the hope for continued relations of friendship, and expressing pain at Sumner's separation from the party, — an event which he had feared for months, and done his best to avert. He referred to his own many hours of sadness as he contemplated the calamity, during which he had almost wished himself out of public life, and added that there had been no time for twenty years when he

[1] Curtis, in his eulogy, June 9, 1874, describes Sumner's emotions in 1872, as revealed in intimate intercourse with him.

[2] General Henderson supported, with reluctance, General Grant at this time, but was afterwards a strenuous opponent of the attempt to give him a third term.

would not have done anything in his power for Sumner, — a profession which was in every way sincere.

The managers of Harper's Weekly, while treating in the editorial department (Mr. Curtis's) Sumner, Schurz, and Trumbull with fairness, went beyond the limits of decency in its pictorial exhibitions. Nast, whose caricatures mingled coarseness with artistic talent, had recently been holding up Tweed and other plunderers of the city of New York to public indignation; but those having been disposed of, he turned upon the three senators with the same weapons. His pictures of them had the venom without the wit of caricature; and treating thieves and senators alike, he confounded moral distinctions. His representations of Schurz were the most open to censure,[1] though those of Sumner were hardly less reprehensible.[2] In his support of the French arms investigation he was made one of "The Senatorial Cabal." In another — and this was perhaps a fair hit — he was "Robinson Crusoe" turning his back on his man "Friday." In another, he was kneeling at and placing flowers on the grave of Preston S. Brooks, his assailant in 1856. This brought out a manly outburst from Sumner, who said when told of it, "What have I to do with that poor creature? It was slavery, not he, who struck the blow!" After his speech against the President, May 31, he was represented as holding a broken bow, "bent once too often," or as serving "the old hash" from a dish.[3] The artist delighted greatly in picturing Whitelaw Reid, or "White-lie Reid," as he called him, in various unseemly attitudes. He placed Greeley, whose personal honesty was never questioned, again and again in close embrace with Tweed, known only as a thief who had fattened on public funds. At length journalists as well as moralists saw the impropriety of associating in like ignominy statesmen and editors, even if misguided, with felons, and rebukes were administered to the proprietors of this celebrated weekly.[4] It is a curious fact that twelve years later the managers, the editor, and the artist were all arrayed against Mr. Blaine, the Republican candidate, taking then Sumner's position of dissent from their own party.[5]

[1] March 9, "Mephistopheles." March 23, 30, as "Iago." Justices Chase and Davis are caricatured April 6. [2] New York Tribune, March 21, 1872.

[3] For other representations of Sumner by the artist, see issues March 9, 16; April 27; August 3; November 16, 23, 1872.

[4] "The Use and Abuse of Caricature," New York "Independent," May 9, 1872. Lydia Maria Child, in Boston "Journal," July 2, 1872.

[5] Harper's Weekly approved, Aug. 24, 1872, Blaine's criticism of Sumner's course.

Sumner had been preparing for some weeks a speech against the re-election of President Grant,[1] and Congress had appointed June 3 as the end of the session. The report on the sale of arms to France had come in so late that no time could be set apart for its consideration. Sumner was obliged to take advantage of some opportunity, and moving (May 31) the indefinite postponement of the appropriation bill, he began, unexpectedly to the public, his speech, and held the floor for three hours.[2] He wore on that day the appearance of deep-seated conviction. He knew well enough what he would have to encounter, but there was no hesitation in his manner or voice. Many seats were vacant when he began, as the senators had not been released from the previous session till 3 A. M., and a general listlessness prevailed.[3] In the galleries were a few delegates on their way to the Republican convention, which was to meet at Philadelphia six days later. After a few words on the sale of arms to France, he reached his real subject, and then the scene changed. The Vice-President called a senator to the chair. The telegraph announced that Sumner was speaking, and the galleries filled rapidly; members of the House (among whom were observed Garfield, Shellabarger, Kelley, Butler, Banks, Hoar, and Dawes) came one after another on the floor, leaving their hall almost deserted. Among privileged spectators were Creswell, Belknap, and Robeson of the Cabinet, and the military secretaries Porter and Babcock. The diplomatic and ladies' galleries were filled with distinguished visitors. On the floor Conkling, Carpenter, and Morton gathered in a group, sometimes seeking the lobby for freer conference. Conkling affected at the beginning the indifference habitual with him at such times, but this soon disappeared. He and Carpenter, early in the speech, stood conversing loudly, almost within reach of Sumner, who paused and looked sharply at them till they retired to their seats.[4] One of the senators sitting in front of him called several times for order, and the gavel of the chair was frequently used to quiet the uneasy senators.

[1] Sumner, in interviews, May 16 and 22, and in a letter to the colored people of Arkansas, May 22, had given intimations of his course. New York Tribune, May 17 and 23.

[2] Works, vol. xv. pp. 83–171.

[3] This account is compiled from the Chicago "Tribune," New York "Tribune," Boston "Advertiser," and Boston "Journal," of June 1, and particularly the New York "Tribune," June 7.

[4] The Chicago "Tribune" reported Sumner as saying: "When that conference has ended, it will please make its report;" and laughter came from the galleries.

Shortly after Sumner finished his speech, Schurz took the floor to review the report on the sale of arms to France. The Senate was exhausted, and there was a motion for a recess, on which Sumner proposed to make a single remark; but Conkling raising a point of order that the motion was not debatable, and Sumner claiming that the indulgence was usually allowed, he was given to understand that he had put himself outside the pale of senatorial civilities. "The senator must know," said Conkling, "after what has occurred, that courtesy is not applicable here; we are dealing with sterner things now." The Administration senators yielded to a recess from 6 to 8 P. M., and Schurz finished his speech in the evening. Flanagan, now remembered only for his antipathy to civil service reform, was the first to reply to Sumner; but the day of adjournment being extended for a week, the principal replies were made three days later by Carpenter and Logan.[1]

Carpenter's reply was not wanting in vigor, but it was wanting in decorum of speech. He always found it difficult to rise above the atmosphere of local courts, and this time he fell below even his habitual plane. He said that the senator from Massachusetts had "identified himself so completely with the universe that he is not at all certain whether he is part of the universe or the universe a part of him;" that his presumption was such that he was likely to issue an enlarged edition of the Sermon on the Mount; and with an irreverence natural to the Wisconsin senator, he described the senator from Massachusetts as one of the things seen by the Apostle in conjunction "with the great red dragon" and "the whore of Babylon." Later in the debate Chandler revelled in his native coarseness. Sumner was in a sense at a disadvantage in dealing, as he often had to deal, with associates of Carpenter's and Chandler's class, who were exempt from the restraints which govern gentlemen. Logan, though less trained than the Wisconsin senator, was of a better type. He was personal in his treatment of Sumner, but not more than from his point of view the occasion justified, or than Sumner might well expect.[2] One passage was quite effective, in which he said that the speech "would find an answer in every crutch that helps and aids the wounded soldier, . . . in every wooden arm, . . . in the bereaved heart of every widowed mother," speaking "in defence of one of the most gallant soldiers that

[1] Conkling reserved his reply for Cooper Institute, July 23.

[2] This is true of his speech of June 1, but less so of his later one of June 3.

ever led a gallant band for the preservation of a nation." The sentiment which was here invoked was the one against which Sumner's argument was to beat in vain.

Sumner's speech was a *philippic* of the classic type, such as had been pronounced against Antony and Verres and Hastings. Modern life furnishes few occasions for such efforts, — perhaps none. His was pitched in too high a key. The President had foibles, and had in notable instances disregarded the limitations and legalities of his office. He had given relatives places in the public service, — among them a brother-in-law made minister to Denmark;[1] and others, a dozen or so, of kin to him, whose appointments were mostly of humble grade, — conventional improprieties which Washington and Jefferson would have avoided. He had taken large gifts which circumspect statesmen are accustomed to refuse, but which after the Civil War other officers (Farragut, Sherman, and Sheridan) accepted from a grateful people; and he had committed the indiscretion of naming two of the givers[2] for his Cabinet who had no special fitness for their places. He was less careful than he should have been in appointments to important offices, — as in the case of Murphy, Collector at New York, whom he was obliged afterwards to displace; but in this respect he had among Presidents examples before, as he has had imitators since. He may have enjoyed, as alleged, the good times which the highest office in the government brings to its incumbent; and this may have led him, contrary to the example and self-denying ordinance of his predecessors, to seek a third term, when after a tour round the world he found private life monotonous. He was unfortunate in bringing to the White House staff-officers — "the military ring"[3] as it was called — who had been his familiars in camp, but whose influence was from the first and continuously injurious. His acts most deserving censure were the use of the navy in the waters of Hayti and San Domingo, his methods adopted or proposed for effecting the annexation, and his interposition for the senator's displacement from the foreign relations committee. These points, or some of them, were freely admitted in private by his

[1] Cramer, whom the foreign relations committee were indisposed to approve on account of unfitness. New York "Herald," Feb. 3 and 6, 1871.

[2] This was the distinction made by the senator between the President, who thus returned favors, and other recipients.

[3] Harper's Weekly, March 23, denied the existence of "the military ring," but said that the President had commended to the Collector at New York his former aid, Leet, who was interested in the "general order" scandal.

candid supporters; but they were thought to be altogether outweighed by his services in war. On the other side of the account, too, were his interest in the protection of the Indians,—the starting-point of a movement which has been of great advantage to that race,—and the decisive declaration of his inaugural message that to protect the national honor the public debt should be paid in gold unless otherwise expressly stipulated in the contract. He came to the Presidency with no undue ambition; and if wanting in comprehension of his duties and responsibilities, it might be said in his behalf that it was the fault of the people who thrust the office upon him rather than his in accepting it. But with due allowance for his limitations and shortcomings, he was not what Sumner described him to be,—a Borgia, a Farnese, or a Barberini, founding a family by offices and endowments; least of all was he a Cæsar plotting against the peace and life of the republic. Schurz's description was thought to come nearer the original, when he said in an address that he did not find in the President one who was pondering for the destruction of the State, but rather one who did not ponder at all, or sufficiently, on his duties. Sumner's speech lost by certain omissions,—that of any tribute to Grant's services in the Civil War, and that of approval of his conservative decision on finance. He made also one serious mistake in bringing Stanton (not now living) to the stand as a witness against Grant, adding also that when he inquired of Stanton why he had not borne this testimony in 1868, the latter replied that while in his speeches in the canvass of that year he defended the party, he omitted personal praise of the candidate. It turned out, however, on recurring to the newspapers of that year, that Stanton had in fact commended General Grant in a speech at Steubenville, Ohio. This discovery put Sumner at a disadvantage. There is no doubt that Stanton had said to Sumner and to others, among them Mr. Hooper and Horace White, just what the senator stated he had said;[1] and there is also no doubt that he said the contrary in the speech cited. It is not the first time,

[1] Sumner had a year before his speech freely mentioned in conversation and correspondence Stanton's communication to him. (Edward Eggleston, in New York "Tribune," March 21, 1874; Frothingham's "Life of Gerrit Smith," pp. 331, 334, 336, where the senator's letter of Aug. 28, 1871, is given.) Stanton's statement to Horace White may be found in Senate debate, June 6, 1872 (Congressional Globe, p. 4283). Stanton was not in a pleasant mood towards Grant after the latter took his place as Secretary of War under Johnson. (Badeau's "Grant in Peace," p. 94.) Grant has in several passages of his "Personal Memoirs" perpetuated his unfriendly sentiments towards Stanton.

as it will not be the last, that politicians give one character to a candidate of their own party in private, and quite another on the stump. Truthful though he was in his statement, Sumner was not justified, as no one is justified, in making a dead man's conversation a support in controversy.

Sumner's speech was met the day after its delivery with a leader in every Republican journal.[1] Rarely was any attempt made to reply to it in detail; and often its specifications, instead of being met with a denial, were summarily dismissed as unimportant in themselves, or relatively so at a time when the President's re-election was deemed essential to the best interests of the country; and above all, when it was the alternative of the accession of the Democratic party to power, which was the dread of great numbers of patriotic people. The speech was described as "highly-wrought, . . . exaggerated, . . . pedantic, . . . a distorted picture," a magnifying of small points, and an overlooking of great services, — with an open or implied admission from the critics that there was a measure of truth in the charges. Some who even agreed with its conclusion admitted it to be "overdone."

The Republican opponents of the President's re-election expressed great satisfaction at Sumner's public avowal of his position;[2] but the wise leaders among them did not conceal their regret that it had not come earlier, so as to have exerted a wholesome influence on the Cincinnati convention, enlarged its constituency, given a sober turn to its deliberations, and placed a different candidate than Greeley — perhaps the senator himself — at the head of the movement.[3] Sumner's personal friends, who supported the President's re-election, — as the greater number of his friends did, — credited him with rectitude of intention, and mitigated as far as they could the political resentment against him. Forney in his newspaper made an earnest but kindly protest against his decision.[4] Curtis wrote to the sena-

[1] The New York "Evening Post," June 3, preferring Grant to Greeley, condemned "Mr. Sumner's tirade," though at the same time regarding "the San Domingo plot as a nefarious business of both national and international importance."

[2] Chicago "Tribune," June 3. The New York "Tribune's" leader (probably written by Mr. Reid) began thus: "We are not sure that our greatest senator did not make yesterday the greatest speech of his life." The same journal, with unchanged editorship, said, March 12, 1874, nearly two years later, that the speech was "a portrait in which the historian of the future will seek for the true character of the man under whose lead our armies went to victory, and our politics to demoralized chaos."

[3] Springfield Republican, June 1, 1872; March 12, 1874.

[4] Philadelphia Press, June 2, 1872; Washington Sunday Chronicle, June 3.

tor that he should be compelled to reply to a speech which he deemed terribly unjust to the President, but should do justice to its author's sincerity, and be ever grateful for his services, entertaining the same sincere affection as before. Lydia Maria Child saw much of justice in his "strictures on the President," but dissented from the arraignment as a whole, objecting that he did not look at "both sides of the shield," and that his picture was too dark. Whittier thought him "unduly severe in the tone and temper" of his speech, — a feature which in his judgment diminished its effect; but he as well as Mrs. Child and James Freeman Clarke vindicated in letters to public journals his sincerity and right to be heard.[1] Wendell Phillips wrote: "I have been saying that your speech was all true, only it was not all the truth. You omit Grant's claims; some he can fairly make." Phillips distrusted as well as personally disliked Greeley; and he added this appeal: "Come home and change the air before you follow Greeley's lead. You know no one is more tender of your good fame than I, — almost tempted sometimes to sacrifice principle as I see it in defence of what you do." He said to the writer at this time: "Sumner is right if you judge Grant by men of the antique type; but the difficulty is that Sumner is the only one of that type among public men who is left to us." Longfellow wrote to his friend: "This is a terrible speech of yours; but the terror of it is in its truth. It is not the exposure which is fearful, but the facts. The feeble attempts at reply must convince every one that no reply is possible." Robert Purvis, of Philadelphia, though supporting the President's re-election, wrote, with friendly expressions: "I am free to express my indignation at the onslaught which it has pleased Mr. Lloyd Garrison to make on you." James Freeman Clarke wrote: "I do not know that I agree with you about Grant, but I admire your courage in expressing your opinions openly, and in spite of the partisan clamor of the President's terriers, 'the little dogs and all, — Tray, Blanche, and Sweetheart, — see, they bark at you!' But you who so long stood the fierce assaults of Southern bloodhounds, clamorous for your life, may easily bear the snarls of lapdogs!" Gerrit Smith, a supporter of the President, admitting his own error of statement as to the cause of Sumner's estrangement from Grant, and accepting the senator's version, testified undiminished regard, and

[1] Boston Transcript, June 5, 6; Boston Journal, July 2.

wrote, July 21: "God forbid, my noble friend, that I should wrong you who have suffered more in the cause of freedom than any other living American!" Later, pressing Sumner to be his guest at Peterborough, he wrote: —

"I never wanted to see you more than I do now. How glad I should be to have you spend a week with me on our healthy hills! Here are many Greeley Republicans. My only son is one of them; and here is a beautiful hall which I have just built for my town, and in it we should all love to listen to your happiest speech in favor of our friend Greeley."[1]

These extracts give the temper of mind of Sumner's friends who did not accept his practical conclusion. There was, however, one exception to this fair treatment of his position. Mr. Garrison had written him in recent years, as these pages show, the most earnest tributes to his fidelity, particularly in the San Domingo controversy. He had gone so far as to justify a proceeding for the President's impeachment, and in his letters had given a harsher estimate of Grant's personal qualities than that which the senator gave in his speech. He now turned upon Sumner, and followed him in successive newspaper articles with the same bitterness which he had formerly shown in his newspaper against renowned patriots and philanthropists, — Channing, Birney, Father Mathew, Louis Kossuth, and Frederick Douglass, — being by habit always more bitter towards those who believed in his aims but not in his methods. Though in recent years he had been lauding Sumner beyond any public man for his devotion to the Antislavery cause, he now presented him in an opposite light, — as tardy in its espousal; and this although the first paper for which Sumner subscribed was the "Liberator," and the first time when he appeared in politics was at the age of thirty-four in an Antislavery meeting in company with Garrison himself.[2] Of a different temper was Sumner in dealing with old coadjutors. He thus wrote to Whittier: —

"I have not read Mr. Garrison's letter. Some one said it was unkind, and I made up my mind at once not to read it, — of course, never to answer it. I

[1] A part of Smith's and Sumner's correspondence at this period is printed in the former's "Life," pp. 323-338. Mr. Smith died Dec. 29, 1874.

[2] *Ante*, vol. iii. pp. 103, 104. One observer attributed Mr. Garrison's intemperate criticisms of the senator to "a feeling of rivalry as to what shall be the verdict of history, and what is the estimation of contemporaries" as to the historic figures in the Antislavery conflict. (Warrington's — W. S. Robinson's — "Pen Portraits," pp. 366, 367.) The Springfield "Republican," March 10, 1873, ascribed Mr. Garrison's comments on Sumner at this time, as well as his later action concerning the senator, to "an unreasonable and unnecessary and very unfortunate jealousy."

never allowed myself to have controversy with him in other days when we differed on methods, because I knew he was earnest against slavery. I shall join in no controversy now."

Again, August 11: —

"Never have I acted more absolutely under the mandate of duty, not to be disobeyed, than in my present course. Profoundly convinced of Grant's unfitness, and feeling that a man like Greeley, President, would mark an epoch for humanity, I could not resist the opportunity, especially when Democrats took him as their candidate, and pledged themselves to all that is contained in the Cincinnati platform. From the beginning, while insisting upon all possible securities and safeguards, I have pleaded for 'reconciliation.' This is the word which recurs constantly in my speeches. The South insisted that I was revengeful. Never! And now the time has come for me to show the mood in which I acted. This is a painful experience; but we are not choosers in this world. Certainly, I did not choose this."

To Longfellow, June 7: —

"You are always my friend, dear Longfellow, and I felt so tenderly when I read your note. This is a crisis; and never was I more impelled by irresistible duty than in the speech I have made. I hoped to arrest a demoralizing example; and whatever the immediate consequence, I am satisfied that my effort will make it more difficult for a President to backslide. The Presidential office will be elevated, at least in its requirements. Meanwhile, I am answered by abuse. So it was when I spoke against slavery. The misrule which I now expose is exacting, pertinacious, tyrannical."

Again, June 10: —

"I observe the storm, but I could not have done otherwise; it was my duty to speak. Some generous voices reach me, — some most touching in their trust."

Again, July 31: —

"The present election is the most remarkable in our political history. The Democrats have accepted absolutely a Republican platform, with a lifetime Abolitionist as candidate. This is a revolution; and my hope is to obtain from it the final settlement of all the issues of the war. There will be difficulties and trials; but the object is worthy of any effort."

As the San Domingo scheme was without favor among the people, Republican speakers were disposed to attribute the estrangement of the President and the senator to other and earlier matters on which they may have differed, but at the time without feeling. Whenever this was attempted by persons at all responsible, with whom Sumner was in personal relations, — as Sherman, Boutwell, William Whiting, and Gerrit Smith, — he was prompt with denial, and usually brought a withdrawal or explanation of the statement.

Sumner's speech in the Senate was made primarily to prevent Grant's nomination, which, however, was a foregone conclusion. He was nominated without dissent, and Wilson's name was put on the ticket with his for the Vice-Presidency. But the senator withheld any declaration as to his purpose in supporting candidates; and he was still plied on both sides, — by Republican leaders to maintain his reserve, and by the supporters of Greeley to declare openly his connection with them. At first he thought of abstaining from taking any part; but with serious reflection he saw his duty in a different light. On July 29, in an open letter to colored citizens, he announced formally his support of Greeley.[1] This brought approving letters from Chief-Justice Chase, N. P. Banks, and R. E. Fenton, and a grateful letter from Greeley himself, who had hitherto refrained from any direct communication with the senator.[2] It brought also reproaches from old comrades. Mr. Blaine, Speaker of the House, addressed at once an open letter to Sumner, animadverting on his advice to colored citizens, and reminding him of the unnatural company he was keeping with former secessionists and confederates of Preston S. Brooks. Sumner promptly replied[3] in a caustic vein, saying to Mr. Blaine at the outset, that, serving in the fellowship of men devoted to the Antislavery cause, he had not missed the Speaker until he "hastened to report absence;" and commenting on the reference to his old assailant, said: —

"What has Preston Brooks to do with the Presidential election? Never while a sufferer did anybody ever hear me speak of him in unkindness; and now after the lapse of more than half a generation I will not unite with you in dragging him from the grave where he sleeps, to aggravate the passions of a political conflict and arrest the longing for concord."[4]

1 Works, vol. xv. pp. 175-195. Mr. Curtis in Harper's Weekly, August 17, reviewed the letter, saying to its author what he had said to him (Mr. Curtis) in connection with his support of Grant: "You have taken a tremendous responsibility. God keep your conscience clear!" The New York "Tribune," July 31, gives an interview with Sumner concerning the letter to the colored citizens, and contains a leader approving the letter.

2 Greeley's letter, dated July 30, 1872, was printed after his death in the Boston "Journal," Dec. 30, 1872.

3 August 5; Works, vol. xv. pp. 196-201. The reply to Mr. Blaine brought an approving letter from Rev. A. Toomer Porter, of Charleston, S. C. Invitations to address the Southern people came to the senator. An interview between him and Southern delegates returning from the Democratic convention at Baltimore is given in the New York "World," July 12.

4 July 12. This letter, as well as the speech in the Senate, was warmly praised by Whitelaw Reid in leaders in the New York "Tribune."

Sumner remained at Washington till well on into the heats of August, busy with correspondence and controversy. One evening he addressed the colored people from his doorstep, when they waited on him to bid him good-by, speaking to them for equal civil rights.[1] To one of the San Domingo commissioners he wrote an open letter concerning the discriminations against Frederick Douglass on account of his race while associated with them, which brought out a reply.[2] Appeals were made to him from political leaders (Samuel J. Randall among them), and by Southern men, to make addresses in different States; but he was obliged by ill health to decline the service. While still at Washington he received a note from Longfellow, dated July 27:

> "I wish you could have been at the Club to-day. None of the young members came. There were a dozen of us, all over sixty. It was like a dinner at some Old Man's Home or Hôtel des Invalides. Emerson sat next to me. He was emphatic in his praise of you. 'Such elegant and easy hospitality; such a worker; such agreeable company;' and so on to the end of the chapter."[3]

On reaching home he at once, as was his custom at this season, sought Longfellow at Nahant, where he found as a guest his old companion George W. Greene. One day he drove from the city to Mr. Winthrop's at Brookline. Another day he entertained R. Schleiden, who was on a visit to this country.

Sumner overworked himself at this session, as indeed he was almost always doing. In addition to the controversies in the Senate, which taxed severely his nervous system, he was engaged in the preparation of notes to his Works, of which four volumes had been issued and three more printed; and he was beginning to prepare the eighth and ninth. Twelve or fifteen hours a day were thus given to sedentary work. He had broken down after the debate on the sale of arms to France, and had serious reminders after other excitements. His system lacked strength to withstand such a strain much longer. He experienced a sensitiveness about the heart, and a difficulty of breathing. The day after the session closed he consulted his physician, Dr. J. Taber Johnson, who found that the heart, though

[1] August 9. Works, vol. xv. pp. 202-204.

[2] August 10; Ibid., pp. 205-208. Douglass was, apparently by no fault of the commissioners, not allowed a place with them at the supper table on a Potomac steamer, and was not invited to dine in company with them at the White House. Holland's "Life of Douglass," pp. 324, 325.

[3] Emerson had been entertained by Sumner in Washington.

not enlarged, was beating weakly and irregularly for one of his fine physical organization. The warning symptoms continued after his return home, and abnormal signs were observed in his eyes and face; and he himself was conscious of diminished vitality. His friends and medical advisers decided that he must separate himself from excitement by a journey to Europe; and he yielded reluctantly to their decision, induced to do so in part by the desire to consult Dr. Brown-Séquard, who was then supposed to be in Paris.

A journalist, Charles T. Congdon, who as an editor in New Bedford and Boston had from a Whig standpoint often criticised Sumner sharply, gave at this time the following description of his appearance and estimate of his character:[1] —

"The last time I saw him was in the 'Tribune office during the canvass of 1872. As he sat waiting for the editor, whom he wished to see, I glanced at him from my desk with a feeling of pain, such as I have seldom experienced respecting a public man. The day was warm, and he had evidently been exhausted by the toil of mounting the stairs. 'Eheu! quantum mutatus ab illo!' I said to myself as I saw how hard fortune had broken that noble form, and bitter experience, public and private, stolen its muscular elasticity. I remembered him standing sturdily upon our old platforms, almost arrogant in the consciousness of intellectual and physical strength, full of early vigor, and dilating with the courage of opinion, — the Ajax about whom the young men of Massachusetts rallied for many a moral contest, and followed in the onset of many a forlorn political hope. This then was what they had brought him to, — the murderous, man-stealing oligarchy! This was the martyr made so by the 'institution' in that last death-throe, when it could argue no longer, but could only wildly and ferociously strike! All criticism of the man and of his methods, however much I might be disposed to indulge in it, was silenced by that spectacle. I might doubt much else; I might question whether Mr. Sumner had always been wise in debate; whether his passion for justice had not led him to say things better left unsaid; whether he had not just a trace of the *dilettante* in his great nature; whether he was not somewhat predisposed to personal complaint; but I should as soon question the sunrise, or the ebb and flow of the tide, or the Copernican system, as his entire and perfect integrity.[2] . . . If I have dwelt too long upon the character and conduct of this great man, it has been because, of all the public persons whom it has been my good or ill fortune to know, he seems to me, after the lapse of all these years, one of the brightest and purest. Scholar, orator, philanthropist, reformer, jurist, lawyer, and law-maker, he was never a mere politician, — for which let us thank God and take courage!"

[1] Reminiscences of a Journalist, pp. 161–164.

[2] Mr. Congdon in the omitted paragraph relates the frankness and decision with which Sumner supported Thomas D. Eliot, a member of Congress, whom certain Republicans were attempting to displace with a candidate of less character and strength.

It was Sumner's earnest wish to meet his fellow-citizens once before the election in Faneuil Hall, the place where he had so often met them, and declare to them face to face his convictions as to their duty. He afterwards said to his physician that he was deterred from the effort, not by fear of death, but by fear of paralysis or mental disability as the consequence. Instead thereof he passed the manuscript of his intended speech to his friend Mr. Bird, who had it published in the newspapers on the morning after his departure.[1] In his proposed address he touched briefly on the objections to the President, growing out of his qualities and acts; but in this respect it was less highly wrought than his speech in the Senate. He reviewed his own record on the reconstruction of the South, maintaining that during his support of a thorough policy he had kept in view the time of reconciliation, which he now believed at hand; and he regarded any present outbreaks in that section against the colored people as "sporadic cases, . . . local incidents, . . . sallies of local disaffection or of personal brutality." He accepted the approval by the Democratic party of the Cincinnati candidate and platform as the promise of a new era, as the tender of an olive branch, which for the sake of the country should be accepted.

The third of September was his day of sailing, less than three weeks after his arrival in Massachusetts. Only a few friends knew of his proposed journey. At 11 A. M. he drove with his colored friend J. B. Smith to T. wharf, where a party of friends had gathered to bid him good-by, as he went on board the tender, — among whom were Hillard, Bird, E. P. Whipple, G. H. Monroe, Martin Milmore, and E. L. Pierce. Most of them parted with him at the wharf, but Hillard, Pierce, and one or two others accompanied him to the steamship "Malta," then lying below the lower lighthouse. While the tender was on its way, Sumner and Hillard sat for an hour or more together in the pilot-house. The senator seemed to be in good spirits, and his talk was of the improved facilities for an Atlantic voyage, the galleries he intended to visit, the rest from work before him, and the expectation of meeting his physician, Dr. Brown-Séquard, in Paris. His first anxiety as he reached the ship was, as always in his voyages, to see if his berth was long enough, and the carpenter was sent for to make a new one. Mr. Smith handed him a large

[1] Works, vol. xv. pp. 208-254. The New York "Tribune," September 4, commended the speech and its author.

bouquet, and his friends left him at 1 P. M., giving him hearty hand-shakes, and waving their handkerchiefs from the tender.[1]

For the time there was much party bitterness towards Sumner, which he sorely felt; but the better sort, even among Republican leaders, recognized the rectitude of his purpose. G. W. Curtis, in Harper's Weekly,[2] assured him that "the prayers of thousands of true hearts go with him, invoking for him the health which is here denied;" and speaking from the platform, the same editor said: "I shall never mention Mr. Sumner's name without the utmost affection, respect, and gratitude. . . . May the soft air of the Mediterranean renew that strength spent in our service! May he return — the election over — to find that we have all been true to Charles Sumner!" Agassiz, just returned from a voyage, wrote from Cambridge: —

"MY DEAR OLD FRIEND, — Here I am again and miss you, for you are among those I cared to see first on my return; and as you are far away, I send a few words of greeting. I write on Longfellow's desk. I am very sorry to hear that you are far from well. As I believe I understand something of your illness, let me beseech you to rest. Rest from the agitations of the day is what you need, to enjoy a happy old age. Stand above the contentions of the day; do not allow indiscreet friends to draw you out of your own course. Your record gives you a right to go where your inclinations lead you, and if your contemporaries don't like it, history will do you justice. Remember that a heart's trouble cannot be cured if every day you allow yourself to be exposed to the palpitations which excitement of necessity brings about. Ever truly your friend."

Sumner, when off the Irish coast, wrote to E. L. Pierce, September 13: —

"The sea is to me always a nuisance. I shall not be content until it is all filled up, so that I can always travel on dry ground. Though in constant peril of nausea and with very little comfort, I have had relief in my heart-pains and the cerebral pressure, and am looking forward to delight in pictures at London and Paris; but the thought of the return voyage in November haunts me. I am haunted more by the thought of the wrong[3] which I have received from individuals. I strike out the word 'ingratitude,' for I have always acted on a sense of duty, and I deserve no gratitude on that account; but I do deserve justice. And never in anything in my life did I act more under an irresistible sense of duty than in that opposition to the San Domingo business, which brought on me the anger of the Presidential rings, with the strange co-operation of Massachusetts men calling themselves my friends.[4]

[1] Boston Journal, September 3; Boston Advertiser, September 4; Boston Commonwealth, September 7.

[2] September 21.

[3] "and ingratitude" erased.

[4] A reference to Dr. S. G. Howe.

"The slippers have been a comfort and a pride during this voyage. I have worn them in the cabin and on deck. Thank your wife again for this kind souvenir. Good-by!"

On Saturday, the eleventh day of the voyage, suffering during most of it as he always suffered from the sea, he arrived at Liverpool. Here he was met by Mr. Felt, the secretary of the American Club, and taken to the club-house; also to St. George's Hall and the Free Library, where he recognized in the portraits the faces of old friends. Immediately on his arrival he was greatly disturbed to learn that he had been nominated by acclamation for governor of Massachusetts by the Democratic and Liberal Republican parties at conventions which were held while he was on the ocean; and he sent the same day a cable despatch and a letter declining absolutely the nomination. In the letter he recognized the good-will and desire for peace and reconciliation implied in the action of the Democratic convention, representing fellow-citizens to whom he had been for a long time opposed on important public questions. He also wrote Mr. Bird a private letter insisting that his wishes must be respected. This use of his name was a great surprise to him, and indeed was not contemplated by any one when he sailed from Boston. The nomination was made, not with the view of withdrawing him from the Senate, but for the purpose of attracting voters to Mr. Greeley's support. It was promoted by the younger leaders of the Democratic party and by N. P. Banks, president of the convention of Liberal Republicans. Mr. Bird, as Sumner's confidential friend, only yielded to it after earnest resistance. Sumner's name was, after the receipt of his letter, withdrawn, and Mr. Bird's substituted in its place.

The day after landing, Sumner went on to London, where cordial letters from three Americans sojourning in England awaited him, — from Henry M. Stanley,[1] recently returned from his first African exploration; Hugh McCulloch, who testified his uniform respect for the senator, notwithstanding their differences under Johnson's Administration; and William W. Story, who was passing the summer with his family near Carlisle. In London he "fatigued himself daily with sights, streets, and galleries, and seeing no American papers." Two days were given to the British Museum, and one to the Bethnal Green Museum. His lodgings were at Maurigy's, 1 Regent Street, soon after converted

[1] They had not met before.

into a club-house. His admission to the Athenæum Club, always his favorite resort in London, was arranged by G. Shaw Lefevre. The Duchess of Argyll welcomed him to England and invited him to Inverary. "You could not go back," she wrote, "without seeing your old friends again." Other invitations came from Robert Ingham at Newcastle, Mrs. Adair (*née* Wadsworth) near Dublin, General Sickles at Madrid, and Baron Gerolt at Bonn. After a week in London, during which his weak condition had been aggravated by the tidings of his nomination for governor, he crossed to Paris, where he took lodgings at Hotel Walther, Rue Castiglione. Here, where he remained a month, enjoying various diversions and afar from home politics, he seemed to gain strength. To his great regret he missed Dr. Brown-Séquard, who had suddenly gone to the United States to take up his residence there. He rigidly abstained from the slightest glance at American newspapers. He found American friends in Paris, who gave him a hearty welcome, — Elliot C. Cowdin,[1] A. H. Bullock, Mr. Seligman, Samuel Johnson, J. Watson Webb, James Phalen, and G. W. Smalley. Mr. Cowdin, then representing his New York house in Paris, who had been his friend from early days in Boston, was most kind, giving Sumner the freedom of his bureau for the packing and transporting of his books and works of art. He had always a seat for the senator at his family table in 152 Avenue des Champs Elysées, and brought together to meet him at a dinner distinguished guests, — among whom were Edouard Laboulaye, A. Laugel, A. H. Bullock, Mr. Waite, afterwards chief-justice, and E. B. Washburne, then American minister to Paris.[2] "He was," says Mrs. Cowdin, "very fond of our children, and particularly of our little Alice, who had 'so sweet a name,' he said. He often congratulated me that we were able to give them the privilege of learning to speak more than one language, — thereby, as he expressed it, multiplying their individuality, — while with him it had been only by brute force that he had learned to speak French." He was often with Governor Bullock, once at a breakfast party given for him by the latter at 99 Avenue des Champs Elysées, and made grateful mention of the governor's tenderness after his return home. The governor urged him to remain abroad, in order to

1 1819-1880.

2 Caleb Cushing was then in Paris, but his and Sumner's attempts to meet did not succeed.

restore health and even to preserve life.[1] Sumner was also the guest of Mr. Johnson, Mr. Seligman, and of his faithful friends Mr. and Mrs. Laugel;[2] and on all these occasions he was "the acknowledged head of a large company."[3] His intimate friends remarked not only his physical weakness, but also his depression of spirits, which seemed, however, to pass away when he became absorbed in his search for curious books and manuscripts. He took a keen relish now as always in association with intelligent foreigners. M. de Corcelle, father-in-law of the Marquis de Chambrun, gave him a dinner at the Café Voisin, where Remusat, minister of foreign affairs, and Gouland, minister of finance, were among the guests. He went one evening, with the escort of M. Remusat, to the salon of Madame Thiers, and there met her husband the President, with whom he afterwards dined at the Palais de l'Élysée.[4] One day he passed at Chantilly, where the Duc d'Aumale, whom he had known in England, drove him in the grounds, and showed him in the château the gallery of the battles of Condé. Here he met again the Count of Paris, his visitor at Washington in the Civil War, and since then his correspondent. He received invitations to dine from M. de Caubert, dean of the civil tribunal of Rouen, and from his old friend Madame Mohl.[5] He had an interesting conversation with Gambetta;[6] but while admiring the patriotism of that French leader, Sumner discerned his limitations. Gambetta said, "What France most needs at the present time is a Jefferson;" and the senator replied, "You want first a Washington, and your Jefferson will come afterwards."[7] Laboulaye, who expressed his satisfaction at meeting again "the illustrious senator," as he called him, gave his recollections written in 1878 from the Collége de France:[8]—

1 Governor Bullock, though abstaining from political activity, approved the senator's separation from the Republican party at this time.

2 M. Laugel, in his article on Sumner ("Revue des Deux Mondes," June, 1874), recalls some incidents of this visit of the senator to Paris.

3 Springfield "Republican," October 22. "The distinguished American," whose private letter, dated October 7, gave an account of Sumner in Paris, was Governor Bullock.

4 New York "Tribune," Oct. 18, 1872. Sumner's account of his interviews with Thiers and Gambetta is given by a correspondent in the New York "Tribune," Feb. 7, 1873.

5 M. Chevalier (1806-1879), then absent from Paris, expressed in a letter to Sumner his regret that they were not to meet.

6 The New York "Herald," Nov. 27, 1872, reports an interview with the senator, in which he conversed concerning Thiers, Gambetta, the French people, John Bright, and civil service reform.

7 A. H. Bullock's address at Brown University, June 15. 1875.

8 See New York "Independent," Sept. 9, 1880.

"On his last trip to Paris, Mr. Sumner had a strong desire to see M. Gambetta, and he did not find it difficult to obtain an introduction to him through common friends. I dined with Mr. Sumner the day after this interview, and asked him what impression M. Gambetta had made on him. He replied as follows: 'I found an amiable, intelligent man, who appeared animated by the best motives; but it seemed to me that his political education was very incomplete, and that he had much to experience before he would be capable of regulating such a country as France. On leaving, I said to him: "I am not French, and I know your country too little to be justified in pronouncing judgment on her political principles; but you wish to found a republic without religion. In America we should consider such an undertaking chimerical, and doomed to certain defeat."' I knew Mr. Sumner on his first visit to this country, after the Brooks assault. We were very quickly bound together by a common weakness, — the love of books. I remember the pleasure he experienced upon finding in my library a book which bore the following title: 'Voyage De Newport à Philadephie, Albany, etc. À Newport De L'Imprimerie Royale De L'Escadre.'[1] This was the first sketch of the visit to America of the Marquis of Chastellux, brigadier-general in the French army, under the orders of Rochambeau. It was published in France later (about 1870), in two volumes. But what gave this particular volume its value was the fact that it was printed on board the French fleet, which had carried the army of Rochambeau to Rhode Island. I speedily presented the book to Mr. Sumner, who carried it with him to America. Such are my reminiscences. I need not say that Mr. Sumner was received everywhere as he merited, and that every one did justice to his noble manners, his eminent intellect, and his lofty character. I do not believe that an American has ever made so great an impression in France, and I know he well appreciated the welcome he received in fashionable circles. Sensibility of the kindness which everywhere surrounded him gave new life to his intellect; and whether he spoke English or French (and the latter he spoke fluently), he expressed himself with an ardor and with a gayety which set off still more his superior intelligence. And he left many friends in France, where his untimely death has caused deepest regret."

Sumner observed during this visit a more serious vein in the French people than he had found before, which in his view promised well for the stability of the Republic. Now as always he had faith in the future of democracy in Europe. He felt that it was to be his last visit to Paris, and he made the most of his time, haunting the shops and the quais, and storing up old books, missals, manuscripts, bronzes, and china, which Mr. Cowdin assisted in forwarding. He wrote from Paris, October 17, to E. L. Pierce: —

"I have had much occasion latterly to meditate on the justice and friendship of this world, especially when crossed by the mandate of political power. I

[1] This book is now in the Library of Harvard College, with a memorandum in Laboulaye's handwriting.

know the integrity of my conduct and the motives of my life. Never were they more clear or absolutely blameless than now. But never in the worst days of slavery have I been more vindictively pursued or more falsely misrepresented."

Leaving Paris October 19, Sumner stopped at Brussels and Antwerp, and passed two days with Motley at the Hague, — missing the queen of Holland, then in England, who had wished much to make his acquaintance.[1] Henry Reeve, meeting him at the station there, was "much struck by the change which time and illness had wrought upon his manly form and lofty stature." On the 26th he was again in London, lodging this time at Fenton's, in St. James's Street. His friends were generally absent, not having returned from the country or the continent; but those who happened to be in town — E. Lyulph Stanley, Sir Henry Holland, C. W. Dilke, and Thomas Baring — were prompt to recognize him.[2] Lord Granville came from Walmer Castle to receive him at dinner in his city house. Abraham Hayward invited him with other friends to dine at the Athenæum Club, "where his conversation," as Mr. Hayward wrote, "happening to turn on orators, he poured forth a rich store of examples and illustrations with aptness and effect. He had obviously — as may indeed be collected from his speeches — carefully studied the masterpieces of Pitt, Sheridan, Curran, Grattan, and most especially Burke." One Englishman, departing from his natural catholicity of temper, who thought — very foolishly in each case — that both he and Motley had become enemies of England, though a friend of thirty-four years, refused to answer the senator's card. That was Lord Houghton.[3]

Sumner made a visit to Mr. Sheridan's, Frampton Court, Dorchester, where, the queen of Holland and other notable persons being among the guests, he assisted in the christening of Mr. Motley's granddaughter. While in London he visited the private libraries of Henry Huth, H. G. Bohn, Lord Exmouth, Robert S. Turner, and Edmund E. Benzon; also Cesnola's antiquities of Cyprus and Lord Exmouth's collection of porcelain, and was admitted to a private view of the porcelain and Dutch pictures of Buckingham Palace. Henry G. Stevens, of Trafalgar Square,

[1] Correspondence of J. L. Motley, vol. ii. pp. 354, 355.

[2] He met also Mrs. Grote, who gave him a manuscript of her husband.

[3] Lord Houghton had perhaps forgotten that nearly thirty years before the first American edition of his poems had been prompted by Sumner. Reid's "Life of Lord Houghton," vol. i. pp. 326, 327.

arranged his visits to the libraries. W. W. Story, whom he plied with many questions of a technical character, was his companion on the visit to the Cesnola collection. Two American friends from Boston, — G. W. Smalley of the New York "Tribune," and Henry T. Parker, a co-tenant of a suite of offices at No. 4 Court Street, twenty-five years before, — were assiduous in their attentions to him. He was very busy in the purchase of autographs and rare books, and frequented the shops of Pickering, Quaritch, and Ellis, buying here as in Paris rather lavishly than wisely, and only regretting when he left each place that he had not bought more, even at prices which repelled connoisseurs.[1] His purchases of this kind in London and Paris involved an outlay of $6,000.[2]

Mr. Story writes of him in these days of their last meeting with each other: —

"Again I was enthralled by the old charm. I had now begun to think I was growing old, but to see Sumner again renewed my youth. He treated me as he did when I was twenty, and to his mind and thought I was still a youth. He so pleasantly patronized me that I was delighted and laughed into thorough good-will, and began to think I had still the world before me. He had the same pleased astonishment at all he saw that he had in his early manhood, the same stern and unflinching adherence to his friends.[3] On one occasion when I was breakfasting with him at a friend's house, some bitter remarks were made against a common friend by an unthinking person at the table; at this Sumner fired up at once with a mixture of astonishment and indignation, denied the possibility of the facts stated, and appealed to me to support him, as I did with all my heart. On leaving the table and returning home with me, he expressed himself with great warmth, and declared that he would not let a day pass without informing himself at headquarters in respect to the whole case, so as to be able authoritatively to contradict such assertions; and this he did. He left town when his time was crowded with engagements, sought out all the facts, and returned to me in triumph with a full refutation. That is what I call being a friend.

"Every day of this visit gave him health and strength. Relieved from the toils of politics and the anxieties of public life, he bathed himself in literature, and grew stronger visibly. I urged him with all the arguments I could command to remain for the winter in England, or to go with me to Rome and wander over the old places. At one time I thought I had made an impression on him, but it was for a moment only. 'I should like nothing better,' he said, 'but I cannot, I ought not; tempt me no further.' I pressed the consid-

1 W. H. H. in New York "Tribune," Oct. 18, 1872, and G. W. S. in the same journal, March 9, 1881.

2 It is perhaps needless to refer to a statement (wholly untrue) that the senator's friends made up a purse to pay the expenses of his journey.

3 E. P. Whipple in a conversation with the writer noted this quality of Sumner.

erations of restored vigor and prolonged life as the reward of a six months' or year's absence. He agreed to my view, but said, 'It is useless; I must go. My duty requires it.'"

On his last morning in London he breakfasted at the Westminster deanery, the guest of Dean and Lady Augusta Stanley. It was Monday, November 11, when the tidings of the great fire in Boston had just come. Lady Augusta inquired about Trinity Church, then on Summer Street, where the funeral rites of her brother, Sir Frederick Bruce, had been performed, and Sumner said, "We know not whether Trinity Church now exists." It was indeed a ruin.

Mr. Story adds his recollections of this breakfast at the deanery: —

"The last time I saw Sumner was at the breakfast-table of Dean Stanley. It was a delightful company, and Sumner was in great force, enjoying it thoroughly. We were all gay together, and tried to forget that our parting was so near; but at last the cab was announced which was to carry Sumner to the station on his way to America, and we were to say farewell. We gathered about him; he tried to smile, but the tears were in his eyes. A grasp of the hand, an earnest 'God bless you!' — and he was gone, never again to be seen by any of us. Sumner was a great loss to me, and a great loss to his country; a braver, more high-minded, purer character never informed this mortal clay.

'Quis desiderio sit pudor aut modus
Tam cari capitis? . . .
. . . . . . .
cui pudor, et justitiae soror
Incorrupta fides, nudaque veritas,
Quando ullum inveniet parem?
Multis ille bonis flebilis occidit:
Nulli flebilior, quam mihi.'"

A few moments after parting with friends at the deanery, he was on the train to visit the Duke of Devonshire at Chatsworth, leaving the great city for the last time. It had been his purpose to visit the Argylls at Inverary, but he had not the time to go so far north. The duchess had written him several letters, expressing the most earnest desire that he should not fail to come. When she found that he was unable to visit Scotland even for a day, she wrote: "I cannot wish you to spoil your time of rest by a fatiguing journey, but I assure you it is a great disappointment to me." At last, as he sailed, she replied to his farewell letter in a note of plaintive tone: "If the time has done you good, perhaps you will come again. I should not like to think I am not to meet you in this life again. God knows, and one is thankful. He alone knows the solemn future." From Chatsworth he went to Rochdale. Mr. Bright described, in 1875, his visit, thus: —

"His last night in England was spent at my house at Rochdale; we sat up till after midnight. The conversation, which I remember, was on many topics. Two of them I remember particularly. He spoke of the President and of the estrangement between them; of the San Domingo scheme, and of the offer to him of the mission to England as a proposition to shut his mouth on that question; and he gave me a printed paper with, I think, an unspoken speech or unpublished writing, defending himself and condemning the conduct of the President. I have not kept this paper.

"A more interesting subject of conversation was his visit to England and the quiet time he had spent in London. He wished to see London, and he spent, I think, about a fortnight in making himself better acquainted with it. He spoke of its magnitude, of the excellence of much of its architecture as seen in buildings scattered about in various and distant parts of it, and of its ancient and historic buildings and places.[1] He spoke too of our government and of the working of our constitution. He referred especially to Mr. Gladstone as prime minister, and to Lord Selborne, recently made lord chancellor, — men so distinguished and so admirable. He thought a country was to be envied which could have in its highest positions men so eminent, of such great capacity, of such lofty purpose, and so conscientious. He spoke of the virtue of a people who could call such men to the highest positions among them. He mentioned Mr. Harcourt, now Sir William V. Harcourt, whom he had met and conversed with at some evening party in London, but without knowing him. He spoke of his writings on international law, under the signature of Historicus in the 'Times,' newspaper, as not surpassed in manner or matter by any of the great writers and authorities on that branch of learning and of law. He spoke of England with much feeling, how many friends he had in this country; how sorry he was to leave it under a sad sense that he should visit it no more. His friends advised him to stay longer here, but his duty in the Senate seemed to force him home. He spoke of his illness, and in the morning said he had not been well during the night; he put his hand upon his heart, indicating where was the seat of his malady. There was a great gentleness in all he said, with a sadness and a melancholy which left upon us the impression that he felt himself seriously ill, and that his life of work was nearly ended. My wife remembers that when our little dog would have made friends with him, he remarked that he 'had never had time to play with dogs.'

"He left us for Liverpool; the day was not a pleasant one, — weather unsettled and rough. I was not well enough to go with him to Liverpool, which I much regretted. I was anxious about his voyage during the winter season. I give you these few particulars of his visit; it was a visit most pleasant to me and to my family."

1 In interviews the next winter he dwelt on the vast extent of London and the greatness of England.

Sumner left Liverpool by the "Baltic," of the White Star line, November 14, and arrived in New York the 26th, refusing the offer from the company of a free passage. From Queenstown he wrote to Mr. Bright: "I leave England with regret, wishing I could see more and mingle more with English people, who are for me most agreeable and interesting. Especially do I regret Inverary, which I should have visited. My last day with you was very pleasant, but too brief. Good-by." The vessel encountered a violent gale for two days, and afterwards boats manned from her rescued the crew of a disabled ship. Sumner was chairman of a meeting of the passengers, at which a contribution was raised for the benefit of the shipwrecked seamen and their rescuers. After a day or two in New York to consult Dr. Brown-Séquard, and a night with Mr. Furness in Philadelphia, he went to Washington on the 29th. It was the day that Mr. Greeley died, of whose illness he heard when he arrived in New York. He was much affected by the event, and it was his purpose to commemorate it in the Senate.[1]

The election in North Carolina in August had indicated the drift towards the President's re-election, and the elections in September and October[2] made the result in his favor quite sure. The President received a popular majority of three quarters of a million of votes, and the result in the electoral colleges was still more decisive. He carried all the Northern and a majority of the Southern States. A large body of Democrats would not support Greeley, and either voted against him or abstained from voting. In Massachusetts the President received two to one in the popular vote, and his majority was seventy-five thousand. The result did not, however, express the popular feeling as to the course of the Administration. There was a wide discontent, but it was quieted by various causes, — such as the patent unfitness of Greeley, the distrust of him by capitalists and sober-thinking people; the probability of the President's election, which kept politicians in line; and, above all, the dread of race conflicts at the South, and financial disturbance likely to come from the

[1] Works, vol. xv. pp. 256, 257. Fenton's attempt (December 3) to introduce a resolution in commemoration of Mr. Greeley was defeated by Cameron's insisting on his motion to adjourn, so that Sumner's proposed tribute to Mr. Greeley was prevented. Both houses, however, by unanimous votes, bore witness to "the eminent services, personal purity, and worth" of Mr. Greeley.

[2] Sumner read the meaning of these autumn elections. Motley's Correspondence, vol. ii. p. 355.

success of a party whose strength lay in the Southern States, and among Northern men who were largely Southern in sentiment. It was but seven years since the Civil War, and the uppermost thought was to maintain what had been won by it. The President's critics found that they could not obtain with the masses a hearing of their charges of maladministration, and their voices were drowned by the mention of Vicksburg and Appomattox. When Sumner in his undelivered address said that "the time for the soldier had passed," meaning as a claimant of civil distinctions solely on the score of services in war, he mistook the temper of a people who have always regarded distinguished military services, not always with discrimination, as the best title to civil honors. Reconciliation was put in the foreground by Greeley's supporters; but the President had not been backward in that movement, and the last Congress, both parties uniting, had passed a liberal measure of amnesty.

The President's second term was marked by one most beneficent act, — his veto of the inflation bill in 1874, against the counsels of Morton and Logan, and after he had once decided to approve it;[1] but in civil administration it was not an improvement on the first, and it brought his party to the brink of defeat in 1876. It was the period of the "Whiskey Ring" conspiracy, in which he manifested more sympathy with Babcock, an indicted party, than with the prosecutors, Secretary Bristow and Solicitor Wilson;[2] and of the impeachment of Belknap,

[1] J. R. Young's "Around the World with General Grant," vol. ii. pp. 153, 154.

[2] *Ante*, p. 429, *note*. The investigations concerning "general orders" in New York and the Sanborn moiety contracts may be referred to in this connection. (Forty-third Congress, first session, House of Representatives Report, No. 559, Evidence, No. 264.) As to the safe burglaries, see New York "Tribune," June 25, 1874 (*ante*, p. 429, *note*). Congress, after a prolonged investigation by a joint select committee, which reported June 16, 1874, abolished the existing government of the District of Columbia, chiefly for the purpose of removing A. R. Shepherd, who had obtained the chief control of its administration. To the public surprise, the President promptly nominated Shepherd as a member of the governing commission which the Act had created, and the Senate as promptly rejected the nomination by the decisive vote of six in favor to thirty-six against it. The New York "Tribune," June 24, 1874, commented without reserve on the nomination, calling it "indecent and characteristic," and charged the President, in making it, with "deliberately insulting the country, Congress, and his own party." George F. Hoar, always a sturdy Republican, said (May 6, 1876), as a manager of Belknap's impeachment, "I have heard that suspicion haunts the footsteps of the trusted companions of the President." Bristow left the Cabinet for want of support in these prosecutions, as Cox had left it in 1870 for want of support in his endeavors to improve the civil service. Marshall Jewell, postmaster-general, had been the President's devoted and intimate friend, but he fell under the ban of the Babcock clique, and he had besides become Bristow's friend. One day the President, at the close of some ordinary matter of business, quietly asked him for his resignation, neither then nor afterwards explaining to him why he took the step. This was stated to the writer by Mr. Jewell himself.

Secretary of War, for corruption in office, from whom the President parted with a too friendly acceptance of his resignation. Later Administrations, — those of Hayes, Garfield, Arthur, Cleveland, and Harrison, — have happily escaped the succession of scandals which distinguished the civil service from 1869 to 1877. The demoralization of that period is chargeable in some degree to war, which always brings vices in its train; but it was also due largely to the President's too good opinion of men of easy virtue and his lax treatment of them when they were found out. This came to be the opinion of the American people, who, ever grateful for his service in the army and ready to confer on him any military rank or emolument, were determined in the purpose not to prolong his civil administration by a third election, either at the end of his second term or after the intervening term of his immediate successor. The Republican State convention of Pennsylvania, nearly a year before his second term expired, took a definite position against a third term for the President in a resolution which called out a reply from him, May 29, 1875.[1] He declined a re-election, but there was in his letter an underlying tone of regret that such an announcement from him had been expected.[2] There being still a popular conviction that, notwithstanding his withdrawal, the general might yet be a candidate, the House of Representatives, Dec. 15, 1875, passed a resolution, by a vote of two hundred and thirty-three to eighteen, declaring that "a departure from the time-honored custom [that of a President retiring after a second term] would be unwise, unpatriotic, and fraught with peril to our free institutions." This ended the question of a third term in 1876; but it was revived again in 1880, when the scheme was supported by Conkling, Cameron, Logan, and Fish. The better sentiment of the country was aroused against it, and it again failed, though this time materially aided by the idea that "a strong man" or "savior of society" was needed to maintain order in the Southern States.[3] No State was so fixed against a

[1] New York "Tribune," May 31, 1875.

[2] The New York "Tribune," June 1, went so far as to say of the letter, "It has shown to all intelligent people his desire for a third term and his utter unfitness for it." Estimates of General Grant's character as a civil magistrate may be found in the New York "Nation," March 1, 1877, Dec. 6, 1878; New York "Evening Post," July 1, 1870; New York "Tribune," Oct. 16, 30, 31, 1872, March 3, 1877.

[3] Among Republicans openly protesting in 1880 against General Grant's candidacy were President Woolsey, Thurlow Weed, Murat Halstead, E. R. Hoar, Henry L. Pierce, Rev. Henry W. Bellows, and Rev. James Freeman Clarke. For articles and opinions adverse to a third term, see New York "Nation," Aug. 22, 1878, Oct. 16, 1879; Boston "Transcript,"

third term for General Grant as Massachusetts, where, in 1880, the Republican State convention by a large majority chose delegates to the national convention who were elected because of their avowed opposition to his nomination, and who resisted it during all the ballots, which finally ended in the nomination of James A. Garfield of Ohio. The people of the State, cherishing the memory of their senator, still remembered the indignity which had been visited upon him nine years before at the instance of Executive power.

The patriotism of the Republican seceders of 1872 as a body, whether leaders or undistinguished citizens, cannot be questioned. They were largely men of superior intelligence, keenly sensitive to the low standards of character in public officials then prevalent, and to the demoralization ensuing on the Civil War, manifest particularly in the service at Washington and in the federal offices in the city of New York. It is curious to note how cordially leaders and masses alike were welcomed back to the old fold, and how many of them became again in high favor with the party which they then left. Among them, in New York, were Frank Hiscock, senator in Congress, Chauncey M. Depew, whose nomination was supported in 1888 by the Republicans of his State as a candidate for the Presidency, and who was afterwards offered the post of Secretary of State,[1] and Whitelaw Reid, minister to France, and Republican candidate for the Vice-Presidency in 1892; in Massachusetts, N. P. Banks, member of Congress, United States marshal and presidential elector, John D. Long, governor, and Albert E. Pillsbury, attorney-general; in Missouri, Carl Schurz, Secretary of the Interior; in Ohio, James M. Ashley, twice Republican candidate for Congress, Murat Halstead, nominated minister to Germany, and Stanley Matthews, Republican senator and justice of the Supreme Court of the United States.[2] The New York "Tribune," the Chicago "Tribune," and the Cincinnati "Commercial," which joined in the

Jan. 21, 1880 (containing opinions of college presidents); and address of General John B. Henderson at St. Louis, April 10, 1880.

[1] Mr. Depew, as the anti-Grant candidate for lieutenant-governor of New York, made about forty addresses, the tenor of which may be found in the New York "Tribune," Sept. 6, 20, 21; Oct. 17, 25; Nov. 3, 1872. What he said on the platform, and what Mr. Reid the editor said in his leaders, in the description of General Grant's personal and official qualities, was quite as severe as anything to be found in Sumner's treatment of the same subject.

[2] Judge Matthews was a member of the Cincinnati convention, but refused to support Greeley.

revolt, became again the leading Republican journals. On the other hand many of those who in 1872 were the sharpest critics of dissent and separatism became themselves twelve years later dissenters and separatists,[1] — as the managers of Harper's Weekly, the New York "Times," the "Nation," and Henry Ward Beecher. Even Conkling, who had treated the Republican opponents of President Grant as if they were no better than rebels in arms, was in 1884 a potent influence in the defeat of Mr. Blaine.

Grant is not reported to have spoken unkindly of Sumner after the latter's death, except, when under promptings from the state department, he stated what was untrue, but what he believed to be true, — that the senator had not done his duty concerning treaties. What Sumner's final estimate of Grant would have been if he had lived to be the survivor, it is not possible to say; but it is easy to suppose that he would at the last have colored the picture differently. He would have seen the Ex-President a modest citizen in retirement, with his nature softened and his will subdued; finding out slowly the quality of the creatures he had trusted, like Belknap, Babcock, and Badeau; cheated in business as he had been often cheated in politics, but ever wishing well to his country, ready to reverse his judgments adverse to his military contemporaries when new evidence was brought to him,[2] reconciled to men whom he came to realize had been honest critics of himself and his acts, rebuking agitators who sought to keep alive the passions of civil war, counselling confidence in the Southern people, bearing misfortune with more than a soldier's fortitude, and dying at peace with all men. Whatever President and senator may have thought of each other, the final judgment will be that both, one in military and the other in civil affairs, deserved well of his country.

1 J. W. Forney, who pleaded most earnestly with Sumner to keep aloof from the secession of 1872, became a seceder in 1880, and supported Hancock against Garfield. Henry Ward Beecher, who was another of Sumner's critics in 1872, left his party in 1884, and remained outside of it for the remainder of his life.

2 As in General Fitz John Porter's case.

## CHAPTER LVIII.

THE BATTLE-FLAG RESOLUTION. — THE CENSURE BY THE MASSACHUSETTS LEGISLATURE. — THE RETURN OF THE ANGINA PECTORIS. — ABSENCE FROM THE SENATE. — PROOFS OF POPULAR FAVOR. — LAST MEETINGS WITH FRIENDS AND CONSTITUENTS. — THE "VIRGINIUS" CASE. — EUROPEAN FRIENDS RECALLED. — 1872-1873.

SUMNER'S health as the season opened was no better than when he left the country in September, and a sad winter was before him. Complying with his physician's directions, he asked to be relieved from service on committees. He attended the Senate only for the first sixteen days, during which he spoke briefly on pending matters,[1] and pressed without avail his civil-rights bill and his bill to enforce equality in the schools of the District of Columbia. His last words for the session were on December 18, when he paid a tribute — one of his best offerings — to Garrett Davis of Kentucky.[2] He did not appear in the Senate after the next day till the beginning of March, and then not to take part in the proceedings.[3] At the special session which followed in that month he went only once to his seat, and then to present the credentials of Mr. Boutwell, who had been chosen to succeed Mr. Wilson, — leaning on his cane when conducting his colleague to the Vice-President's desk to be sworn.[4] Sumner held at the time the position of "a man without a party." The call for a caucus of the Republican senators was drawn in novel terms, inviting those only who had supported the platform and candidates of the party at the late election. A copy was sent to him, probably as notice that he was not expected to attend. The caucus assigned no places

[1] A bill to admit free of duty materials used in rebuilding the burnt district of Boston, Dec. 12, 1872 (Works, vol. xv. pp. 258-260); December 13 (Congressional Globe, pp. 179, 180), a bill to purchase land for the new post-office in that city (Globe, p. 170).

[2] Dec. 18, 1872. Works, vol. xv. pp. 261-265.

[3] He wrote to Wilson asking for pairs, and for deferred action on the flag resolution. Boston "Journal," Jan. 9, 1873.

[4] He called March 12 at the treasury department to congratulate Mr. Boutwell on his election.

to those who had supported Greeley.[1] The Democrats placed Schurz on the committee on foreign relations, of which he had been a member, notwithstanding his disclaimer of a political connection with them.

A proposition made by Sumner in the Senate a few moments after it met on the first day — it was the first time that he asked the attention of the chair — led to an excitement which is a curious illustration of the passions of the period. He asked leave to introduce a bill as follows: —

"Whereas the national unity and good-will among fellow-citizens can be assured only through oblivion of past differences, and it is contrary to the usage of civilized nations to perpetuate the memory of civil war; therefore, be it enacted, etc., that the names of battles with fellow-citizens shall not be continued in the Army Register, or placed on the regimental colors of the United States."[2]

This proposition accorded with the practice of civilized nations, ancient and modern.[3] Sumner, with the approval of high military authority, had twice before made efforts of a similar intent, — one in 1862, against placing on the regimental colors the names of victories obtained over our fellow-citizens; and another in 1865, against placing in the national Capitol any picture of a victory or battle with our own fellow-citizens, — without incurring criticism or indeed attracting any general attention.[4] What had been done without censure and with little

[1] Partisanship in the Senate, the smaller body, is intensified by personal jealousy. It was more temperate at this time in the House, which insisted that Mr. Banks, though a supporter of Greeley, should retain the chairmanship of the committee on foreign affairs.

[2] Works, vol. xv. p. 255.

[3] Smith's Dictionary of Greek and Roman Antiquities, article "Triumphus." Mr. Schurz, in his eulogy on Sumner, in Boston, April 29, 1874, illustrated the practice of modern nations thus: "The Irishman, when fighting for old England at Waterloo, was not to behold on the red cross floating above him the name of the Boyne. The Scotch Highlander, when standing in the trenches of Sevastopol, was not by the colors of his regiment to be reminded of Culloden. No French soldier at Austerlitz or Solferino had to read upon the tricolor any reminiscence of the Vendée. No Hungarian at Sadowa was taunted by any Austrian banner with the surrender of Villagos. No German regiment from Saxony or Hanover, charging under the iron hail of Gravelotte, was made to remember by words written on a Prussian standard that the Black Eagle had conquered them at Königgratz and Langensalza."

[4] *Ante*, p. 77; Works, vol. vi. pp. 499, 500; vol. ix. pp. 333–335. Adam Badeau, in the Century Magazine, May, 1885, p. 160, states that Sumner waited, at the head of a committee, on General Grant, soon after the close of the war, and proposed (Badeau present) a picture of the surrender at Appomattox to be placed in the rotunda of the Capitol, and that the general declined. This statement was replied to by C. W. Eldridge in the same magazine for October, 1885, p. 957. It is incredible on its face, and exhibits well the quality of that untrustworthy narrator.

observation in the midst of the intense heats of the Civil War strangely enough now provoked indignant protests in the name of patriotism, at a time when there had been an opportunity for the passions of war to subside, and the policy of restoration and reconciliation to take their place. Time and circumstance showed that the professed sentiments were unreal, and that the occasion was taken advantage of to punish the senator's divergence from his party at the late election. Sumner was thought to be rather reckless in opening fresh wounds anew; but it is not likely that he foresaw the clamor he was to provoke, and it is certain that he would not have hesitated in his purpose if he had foreseen it. Hale of Maine offered, a few days later, in the House, a counter proposition, which was passed, without debate, by a party vote. This, as well as Sumner's bill, was laid over in the Senate on account of his illness, as he expressed his desire to take part in the debate. Edmunds, though yielding to a postponement, avowed his earnest opposition to Sumner's bill.

At the time Sumner introduced his bill the Legislature of Massachusetts was holding an extra session, called solely to meet exigencies growing out of the great fire in Boston. A member of the House (Hoyt of Athol), who had been a soldier, but not one remarkable for any service, introduced a resolution condemning severely the senator's bill. The committee to which it was referred heard him and two of his friends in its behalf, but advertised no public hearing and gave no opportunity to remonstrants. Three members, not a majority (three being for and three against the resolution), made a report on the day before the final adjournment; but the fact that the report was not submitted by a majority was overlooked in the confusion. The one colored member of the committee, be it remembered to the honor of his race, stood with Sumner, saying cleverly that his only offence was that what he had done was fifty years too soon. The committee's resolution condemned the senator's bill as "an insult to the loyal soldiery of the nation, . . . depreciating their grand achievements in the late rebellion," and "meeting the unqualified condemnation of the people of the Commonwealth." The debate began the same afternoon, and continued the next morning. There was no critical or historical treatment of Sumner's proposition; but instead of this, the partisans of censure indulged in loose rhetoric and passionate harangues. Here and in other quarters Sumner was coarsely accused of seeking the overturn of soldiers' gravestones, the ploughing up of the national cemeteries, the discontinuance of pensions, and the obliteration of Union victories from histories and school-books.[1] Colonel Charles R. Codman, who had served his country in the Civil War, and Willard P. Phillips, led the opposition to the committee's report. The sober sense of the members was adverse to the proposed censure; but too many of them were of a type of men who yield readily to clamor, and they feared, quite erroneously, that the veterans of the war were watching them. The sense of responsibility was weak, as less than one-fourth of the members had been re-elected to the next Legislature, which was to meet in a few days. The roll-call on a motion to postpone indefinitely showed a tie, and the Speaker (Mr. Sanford) gave the casting vote in the affirmative; but a recount showed a majority of one against it. The resolution was then hurried through the House, and the same afternoon, after a brief debate, it was carried in the Senate. Its passage was thus forced in two days, and those the last two days of the session. Members freely expressed in conversation their regret at being compelled to vote on the resolution, but they shrank from making a different record. One or more wrote to Sumner, confessing remorsefully that they had voted against their better judgment.[2] Sumner wrote to W. P. Phillips, December 21:[3] —

"I cannot comprehend this tempest. The resolution which is treated so severely is an old inhabitant. I have already brought it forward in substance twice before this last motion, and received the warm commendation of General Scott, General Anderson, etc. . . . I know that I never deserved better of Massachusetts than now. It was our State which led in requiring all safeguards for liberty and equality; I covet for her that other honor of leading in reconciliation. First in civilization, Massachusetts must insist that our flags shall be brought into conformity with the requirements of civilization."

The action of the Legislature at once called out a popular protest, not confined to those who had acted with the senator in the late election. There was a general feeling among sober-minded people that the Legislature had not behaved in a de-

[1] Nast's caricature in Harper's Weekly, Dec. 28, 1872, gave countenance to such absurd ideas.

[2] The resolution, as required by its terms, was sent to the senators and representatives of the State in Congress, but none of them presented it in the House or Senate.

[3] Boston Herald, Jan. 15, 1893.

cent and honorable way towards a public man who had rendered illustrious service to the State and nation. Whether they had joined with him or not in the contest with the President, they felt that he was not without justification for his course, and it was their purpose to keep him in the Senate. Rev. James Freeman Clarke promptly denounced from his pulpit the legislative resolution, and justified Sumner. As soon as the session of the new Legislature began, in January, 1873, a movement for rescinding and annulling the resolution of censure began under the leadership of John G. Whittier. It was supported by more than five thousand petitioners, the number of whom could have been easily increased many fold. Among them were the names of those in the State most distinguished for learning, public spirit, philanthropy, devotion to the Antislavery cause, and courage as soldiers in the Civil War. The annals of the State contain no paper of such import in its list of names as this one now addressed to the Legislature.[1] Scholars, merchants, politicians, and veteran Antislavery leaders gladly gave their names to it. Among the signers were soldiers of distinguished rank in the Civil War, who bore in several instances on their persons the marks of their heroism, — William F. Bartlett[2] and Joseph Tucker, each of whom lost a leg in battle; A. B. Underwood, severely wounded at Wauhatchie and maimed for life; Charles Francis Adams, Jr., who led the colored troops into Richmond, the first to enter the Confederate capital; and Henry S. Russell, who served in Libby prison as well as in the field. The petitioners were supported by an appeal from other States, in which Chief-Justice Chase, William C. Bryant, Frederick Douglass, Gerrit Smith, and Governor Noyes of Ohio joined. A remonstrance was sent in, but it contained few signatures, and those not of persons well known in the State.

The committee on federal relations, to which the petitions were referred, gave public hearings. At the first one, Ex-Governor William Claflin, who opened the case briefly for the petitioners, was followed by Ex-Governor Emory Washburn the jurist, and by

[1] Among the signers were Whittier, Longfellow, Holmes, Agassiz, R. H. Dana, Jr., J. T. Fields, S. G. Howe, George S. Hillard, Charles W. Eliot, J. Ingersoll Bowditch, W. Endicott, Jr., Franklin Haven, Amos A. Lawrence, Wendell Phillips, A. H. Rice, T. W. Higginson, William Claflin, Henry L. Pierce, and Mr. Wilson, Vice-President elect. Boston "Journal," Feb. 22, 1873.

[2] The correspondence of General Bartlett and Sumner on the subject is published in the former's "Life" by F. W. Palfrey, pp. 246–248.

Rev. James Freeman Clarke.[1] These last two gentlemen spoke with earnestness and power; but their free comments on the action of the last Legislature offended the members who by re-election were members of the former as well as the present body. Hoyt appeared, on the other hand, to object to any interference with the action of the last Legislature of which he had been the promoter. To the surprise of the public, he was supported by William Lloyd Garrison, who had been bitter in his censures of Sumner for opposing the President's re-election.[2] He was joined by Mrs. Julia Ward Howe, who having signed the petition for rescinding now appeared to oppose it. E. L. Pierce, at Mr. Whittier's request, closed the hearing with a reply to the remonstrants, in which he sought to make clear the points of controversy, and took issue with Mr. Garrison.[3] The report was adverse to the petitions for rescinding, and both houses by large majorities concurred in adopting it. The movement for rescinding, which began early in January, thus ended in failure at the last of March. The petitioners had to encounter not only the political hostility of some heated partisans of President Grant and a supposed "soldier feeling," but also certain technical objections, — namely, that the rescinding or expunging of a resolution is not a legitimate parliamentary proceeding, and that the expression of an opinion by one body cannot be recalled by another. The argument, however, which had the most effect was that the rescinding resolution implied a censure of the Legislature of 1872; and the members of that body who were members of the Legislature of 1873, as well as other members of the former Legislature not re-elected but busy as lobbyists, were able to communicate their own sense of offended dignity to the mass of the members of the new body.[4]

[1] An erroneous statement is made in the "Reminiscences of the Rev. George Allen," p. 102, that Sumner requested Mr. Allen to appear before the committee. The senator requested no one to appear before it, by letter or otherwise.

[2] Mr. Garrison's tone in this debate, depreciatory of Sumner, was in contrast with his letters to the senator, already given, and with his tribute in the New York "Independent," March 19, 1874. The Springfield "Republican," March 10, 1873, dealt plainly with Mr. Garrison's participation in the contest.

[3] Springfield "Republican," March 7, 1873. Wendell Phillips, who was unable to attend the hearing, wrote an eloquent defence of Sumner, which was published in the Boston "Advertiser," March 11, 1873. He said of a flag containing emblems of victory in the Civil War: "I should despise a Southerner who would march under such a flag; only I should despise yet more heartily a North that could ask him to do so."

[4] The leader of the opposition in debate in the House to the rescinding became in less than four years a fugitive from justice, and has lived since in South America with an assumed name.

No other consideration or feeling had so much influence as this in setting the current.

The movement for rescinding, however, accomplished incidental results more important than success in the Legislature. It enlightened the public as to the true character of the senator's proposition, which was now seen to be in no sense unpatriotic or unjust to the soldier. It revealed the hold which he still retained on the people of the State. Those who resisted the removal of the censure were driven to stand on apologetic and technical rather than on substantial grounds; and there was a general sentiment to the effect that while what had been done could not well be undone, it would not now be attempted if no action had been taken. The fruit of the agitation was to be postponed for only a few months.[1] Sumner felt keenly the legislative censure, — far more so than he would have felt it when younger and stronger.[2] He at once determined to defend his position, and gathered materials and authorities for the purpose. He wrote on Christmas Day to James Freeman Clarke, who had three days before in a sermon sharply condemned the action of the Legislature: —

"With deep emotion I have read the abstract of your testimony. How a cultivated heathen could differ from me I do not understand. History is full of examples to sustain me; only the sea and tiger are as blind and senseless in ferocity as party hate. I long to state the case. Twice before, once in 1862, I offered this resolution with the applause of General Scott and General Robert Anderson. Where is Massachusetts civilization? Thus far our Commonwealth has led in the great battle of liberty and equality. By the blessing of God she shall lead again in smoothing the wrinkled front of war. Thanks, and God bless you!"

To E. L. Pierce he wrote gratefully for his "effort before the committee, which was so much praised. I feel it in my heart."[3]

Sumner did not anticipate when he arrived from Europe the prostration which was at hand. He wrote, November 28, the day before he reached Washington: "My strength is perceptibly in-

1 The Boston "Commonwealth," July 25, August 1 and 8, 1874, contains "an historical statement," — "Charles Sumner and the Battle Flags," by E. L. Pierce, which gives in detail what the text attempts to give only in substance.

2 Longfellow wrote in his diary, Christmas, 1872: "Carl Schurz came to see me yesterday, and stayed to dinner. He said a good deal about Sumner, and thinks he feels keenly the action of the Massachusetts Legislature. Well he may; for it was vindictive and brutal."

3 His letter to Mrs. Claflin, March 11, 1873, is printed in Chaplin's "Life of Sumner," p. 438.

creasing. I have walked to-day, and with a stronger step and more natural gait than for a long time." The *angina pectoris* now returned, and a week later he wrote to his physician: —

"Two nights ago I heard the lecture of Professor Tyndall, during which I sat one and a half hours, and then walked slowly to the horse-car (two short squares); but before reaching it the pains in the heart visited me so that on reaching the car I was much exhausted with suffering. They gradually ceased, leaving me feeble. Yesterday I walked on Pennsylvania Avenue nearly a mile without any pain or weakness. I mention these things that you may see how fitful is my case."

After December 19 he absented himself altogether from the Senate for the remainder of the session. He was under the general medical direction of Dr. Brown-Séquard, then in New York, to whom he sent daily reports, and under the immediate care of Dr. J. T. Johnson, of Washington, who visited him twice a day. His rest was broken at night by an incidental difficulty, due to irritability in the spinal cord. He was sensitive in his back, shoulders, and neck, so that he was uneasy in sitting. He was weak generally, particularly in his legs, and walked with difficulty, using a cane in the house. There were pains in his chest, running into his left arm, and at intervals of a week, more or less, he suffered severe attacks of *angina pectoris*, sometimes continuing for several hours. His record for Dr. Brown-Séquard, February 13, was: —

"Before bed took bromide of potassium; did not sleep, and at midnight was attacked by the *angina*, which was very severe, and lasted till near morning. The pain invaded the left arm, making the part above the elbow so sensitive as hardly to bear touching. I got up repeatedly and walked the room; took two teaspoonsful of bromide of potassium in addition to the sodium. The pain was hard to bear."

Two nights later, however, he had better sleep than at any time for months. In March he had severe attacks of the *angina* at midnight, as well as in the daytime, calling for the immediate attendance of the doctor, who applied subcutaneous injections of morphine. Relief then came, followed by sleep. He wrote to E. L. Pierce, April 12: "I am sorry to report that I am very feeble, and do not seem to gain strength. The last two days I have taken to my bed. Dr. Howe called yesterday. I think he understands my case precisely; but he is against medicines, especially poisons." The attacks of the *angina* became during this month less frequent, and the last was on the 20th. His restlessness at night continued, and the remedies (strychnine, morphine, and galvanism) were kept up, with occasional cupping, — not applied, however, in the severe way to which he had been subjected in Europe. To his friends who observed the phials on the stand at his bedside he would say, "These are my poisons." On May 9 he reported the preceding day as follows: "Took strychnine not long before dinner. Attempting to eat, found it difficult to put food in the mouth without convulsion; this lasted twenty minutes."

Sumner was at first restive under his enforced absence from his official duties, longing most of all to defend his "battle-flag" resolution in the Senate. His physician feared that such an effort would be fatal; but as the intimation of that result did not deter him, he was held in check by the warning of prolonged disability of brain, — a calamity which he had so much dreaded in 1856 as the effect of the assault. From December to May he rarely left his house, taking only an occasional short walk or drive, and "leading," as he said, "a tranquil existence, seeing friends, and amusing himself with books." He kept his thoughts as far as might be from public business, and suspended annotations and proof-reading on his Works. His mind found most relief in the calls of friends, with whom he was always ready for a talk.[1] They were apt to draw him out on his last visit to Europe, and particularly on his interviews with eminent Frenchmen, — topics which were altogether agreeable to him. Some brought their wives and daughters, to whom, while he took them through his house, he explained the treasures of book and manuscript which he had brought home. His good nature and attractive ways at such times are well remembered by visitors of both sexes. Once, and perhaps only once, and that was in March, he had friends to dine with him; and the same month he was present at a dinner given by Mr. Fenton in honor of Mr. Trumbull, who had just finished his service in the Senate.

He wrote to Longfellow, January 27, of Mr. and Mrs. Agassiz, who had been in Washington just before: —

"I hope their visit has been pleasant. It added much to my happiness, although I could see them only in arm-chair and dressing-gown. I wish I could be as cheerful about my case as he is."

[1] Among his English callers at this time were the Earl of Dunraven (introduced by Francis Lawley of the "Daily Telegraph"), Lewis Clifford (introduced by Sir Stafford Northcote), Sir George Broderick (introduced by James Bryce), and A. Rutson (introduced by Mountague Bernard).

He wrote to Wendell Phillips, February 9: —

"Is it true that you are to lecture here next Friday? Then come direct from the station to my house, where you will be at home and welcome as long as you can stay. I hope you will find me much renovated. If not, then poisons fail in their work. God bless you!"

During these weary months he did not conceal from intimate friends his depression of spirits; and of these were Wendell Phillips and E. L. Pierce, who were his guests, — the latter in January, and the former in February. For this it was easy to detect as the principal cause, in connection with ill health, his shock of disappointment that the country had decided as it had in the last election, and that his appeals and warnings had been ineffectual. He was oppressed by the legislative censure, which in a better condition of health and in a happier mood of mind he would have treated with indifference, or repelled as an impertinence. His friends assured him that partisan clamor never determined the permanent judgment of mankind.[1] His love of life, which was weak with him in youth,[2] was now weaker than ever. To Wilson, his old colleague, now Vice-President, who called to express sympathy and urge cessation from work, he said with great earnestness, as they sat alone in his study: "If my Works were completed, and my civil-rights bill passed, no visitor could enter that door that would be more welcome than Death."[3] By the middle of April, as spring opened in Washington, he attempted short walks and drives more regularly, walking two or three squares at a time; but such light exercise often exhausted him. On the first day of May he assisted at the wedding of his physician, and the same day called on Chief-Justice Chase; it was their last meeting, — six days before the latter's sudden death in New York. Their talk was chiefly of old times, old associates, and old conflicts, in which they had contended side by side; and they were in like agreement on current politics.[4] The senator's ill health obliged him to decline the request of the chief-justice's family that he should serve as pall-bearer at the latter's funeral in New York. The two

[1] E. L. Pierce's letter, Feb. 9, 1873.

[2] *Ante*, vol. ii. p. 287.

[3] Wilson's letter, March 13, 1874, to the meeting in Faneuil Hall.

[4] In the New York "Tribune," May 8, 1873, is an account of the interview. R. C. Parsons, in a letter published in that journal, May 21, questioned some points; but his version does not agree with the evidence.

friends, now as in other days in full accord, were not long to be divided. Sumner wrote to E. L. Pierce, May 10: —

"I shall be sorry not to see you before you go to outre-mer.[1] I envy you the going with health and strength. I improve slowly, walking a little daily, and then taking to my bed. Galvanism is now the order. I am glad to have seen Chase just before he passed away. Our interview was intimate and affectionate. Nothing but my bodily condition — making the journey to New York impossible without stopping, and making walking difficult — would keep me from his funeral. Remember me kindly to Mrs. Claflin, whose visit here was very pleasant to me."

The improvement which was apparent in the latter part of April continued through May, with, however, occasional reminders of weakness at the end of his walks. His daily drives in Washington, never so lovely as in May, were a stimulant to health. Mr. Hooper's horses were at his service. Sometimes he drove to General Cushing's suburban residence, six miles from town. In his drives he was glad to have a sympathetic friend with him. On some of them he invited Mrs. Claflin, wife of Governor Claflin, both always loyal to him. On another he had for his companion on a drive to Arlington the English philanthropist, Miss Mary Carpenter.

Later in May, for the first time since he absented himself from the Senate, more than five months before, he resumed the annotation and revision of his Works; and on that errand began to make visits to the Congressional Library. He wrote, June 2: "I have gained in strength daily for the last month, and begin to have a sense of health, so that for ten days I have done a little work." Two days later he found himself weak again; but this weakness shortly gave way to "an increasing sense of health." The potions of strychnine ended July 11. At the close of the month, Dr. Brown-Séquard returned to Europe, and medical treatment for the present ended.[2]

During his illness he was constantly receiving letters expressing sympathy, and imploring him to rest. They came from friends far and near, — many, indeed most, of whom had not acted with him in the late election. Among the writers were Longfellow, Whittier, O. W. Holmes, Wendell Phillips, Gerrit Smith, Henry Ward Beecher, Lydia Maria Child, Amos A. Lawrence, Sidney Bartlett, Dr. T. W. Parsons, R. H. Dana,

1 His friend was about to make a summer excursion to Europe.

2 The doctor seemed to be keeping up a practice in both hemispheres, and was in Boston the next September, when he met Sumner there.

Jr., the brothers Bowditch, and others in great number. None were tenderer in their expressions than his former secretaries, now members of the bar, who knew him best. From the colored people in distant States came testimonies of gratitude and devotion, often traced in an illiterate hand, and sometimes with a long list of signers. Wendell Phillips wrote at the beginning of the session from Boston: —

December 12, 1872.

DEAR CHARLES, — I wish I could come on and see you. I would were I not tied here by so many engagements. I want to beg you to rest; to strike work for a while. If you must stay in Washington, why, stay! but go to the Senate only semi-occasionally; or if you must cling to your old rule, and go there daily, why then lounge in half an hour, just to report yourself; take no part in debate or business, but go home leisurely. This is what Massachusetts wishes you to do. The time has come again when your simple presence there will be and do work enough for one man. We shall need you too much in times ahead to allow you now to waste your strength on matters other men can handle. Every one will grant your full right to just such relaxation. Every one has a right to claim that you save yourself for the future. Now, don't sacrifice your life for a scruple of too rigid adherence to routine duty. I remember the nights I passed with you when you were ill. They taught me that you are not equal yet to such work as you are undertaking. When we differed, I forbore to urge this on you; now I feel freer to do so. Due care and a fair amount of such relaxation as I advise will save you, in the Senate or foreign office, for many a year. Let me in the names of all your friends beg you to trust us, and be advised, at last, for once to take some care of yourself, — if not on your own account, then for our sakes and for the country and cause to which you belong. Now, be good and listen! With ever thorough and cordial regard,

Affectionately yours,

WENDELL PHILLIPS.

And again, the day after he had parted with his friend in Washington: —

NEW YORK, Tuesday, Feb. 18, 1873.

DEAR SUMNER, — It is useless for me ever to try to say to you what I would of my affection. So my farewell seemed very cold. That was only this foolish Saxon shame of showing emotion, — ashes on the surface, no matter how much fire below. I shall long remember your last nod from the window, and I wondered as the cars rolled along whether your ride seemed lonelier yesterday than the days before. I did enjoy with all my heart, and most tenderly, the opportunity of seeing so much of you. Years — and something more cruel than years — narrow the circle; but the narrower it becomes, we must draw the closer together. I gave up calling on Mrs. Eames, — not caring to leave you. So please forward the apology I inclose, and understand all I would say. Mind, and be lazy; feel sure how thoroughly and affectionately I am your brother,

WENDELL PHILLIPS.

Henry Ward Beecher wrote from Brooklyn, Jan. 13, 1873:

"From day to day thousands look into the newspapers to learn whether your health is better or worse. Your long life devoted to the noblest questions which can occupy the thoughts of Christian patriots; the great courage and fidelity with which in trying times you upheld the cause of justice and liberty; the large contributions which you have made in the interests of humanity to the literature of the world; your unsullied character, and long years without a spot or suspicion of selfishness in public affairs, — have made your name national, and your life a part of the best history of the noblest period of American affairs. That your recent difference of judgment and action in political affairs — and to speak frankly, I differed with you, as you did with your life-long friends — should throw a cloud over you is natural, considering the infirmity of human nature. But it is a cloud that your life-long and noble service will ere long scatter, as the sun scatters darkness. Even should it please God to bring to an end now, or ere long, your career, you have achieved a success which might amply gratify an honorable ambition though it were far greater than yours. I hope that I do not intrude upon your private griefs by these lines, which I send hoping that they may assure you of the warm sympathy and affectionate respect of thousands as well as my own."

Sumner replied, January 14: —

"Thanks, many thanks, dear Mr. Beecher, for your kind words! What I have done has always been at the mandate of conscience, and I could not have done otherwise. My hope has been to help mankind, and advance the reign of justice on earth; nor do I doubt that sooner or later this will be seen by many who now judge me unkindly. As for my health, I am hopeful. Once before I have recovered from these severe injuries. If I must succumb, so be it; I am content. God bless you! Ever sincerely yours." [1]

Whittier wrote, Jan. 27, 1873: —

"I write just to tell thee not to believe for a moment that the people of Massachusetts have any sympathy with the 'resolution' adopted by a dead Legislature galvanized into life by the governor's proclamation for a special purpose. Not a single respectable paper of any party has to my knowledge indorsed it. It is deader than the Legislature itself. I have yet to see the very first man or woman who speaks a word in its favor. Depend upon it, the heart of the old Commonwealth is sound and generous, and turns towards thee with its old love and gratitude. She has learned to value pure-handed public servants. Dear friend of many years, be assured and hopeful! All is safe! Thy future is secure! God bless thee, and have thee ever in his holy keeping!"

And again, February 4: —

"I hope thee will not make an effort to speak this term. The country is coming all right as to thy 'flag' resolution. The pitiful folly of our late

[1] This correspondence between Beecher and Sumner was published in the Boston "Journal," Jan. 23, 1873.

Legislature is already repented of. Believe me, thee never stood higher with the best people of this State of all parties than now. Amidst the miserable muddle of the Credit Mobilier, it is something to be proud of that the smell of fire has not been upon thy garments."

To Mrs. John T. Sargent, who invited him to be a guest, Sumner wrote, June 26: —

"That large airy room in the large house is most tempting; but you know not the size of the elephant you invite. Beyond his own natural proportions and ordinary trunk are other trunks larger still, with supplementary boxes packed with books, papers, and documents, various, vast, extensive; you have no idea of the mass. The porters at the Coolidge House are accustomed to this variety, and know how to deal with it. There I must go unless willing to disturb good friends beyond all right of hospitality. You are good and kind, dear Mrs. Sargent, and I beg you to believe me most grateful. It is pleasant to feel a sense of health, to sleep without narcotics, and to move about as other people, without effort or ache."

Henry Wilson was stricken with paralysis May 19, 1873,— less than three months after his term as Vice-President began. He had before mentioned to his colleague his premonitions of such a fate. A week afterwards, against his physician's orders and in strictest confidence, he used his pen for the first time to communicate to Sumner the attack, which was still being kept from the public. He had been forced to suspend work on his History, though hoping to resume it in a few weeks. "I am conquered," he wrote, "and must submit." He closed his note thus: "I am glad to see you are better after your long sickness. God grant that you may soon be in full health, and that many years of life may be given you!" He recovered a measure of strength, though he was never after equal to any labor involving a strain on body or mind. The two friends were each struggling in a disabled condition with a book on his hands, but neither was to live to complete his enterprise.[1]

Sumner wrote to Mrs. Claflin, June 7: —

"I have your kind letter with better news about Mr. Wilson. I wish I could help him; he must help himself by abnegation. I have often trembled for him, knowing his constitutional tendency, especially since his superadded literary labor. His work on that book was very much that of a horse in a street-car, — one constant pull. I fear he will be restless and uneasy in his enforced idleness. I wish there were some very retired spot, either on the

[1] Curiously enough Wilson, whose life had been passed in politics, and who had recently been advanced to the second office in the government, was convinced that what he had done in public life was soon to be forgotten, and, though no scholar, expected to be remembered only by his book.

sea-shore or in the country, where reporters could not reach him, and he could go and vegetate. One of his penalties as a public man is that he cannot escape observation. I hope that the printing of his book will be stopped at once. If it is allowed to proceed, he will be under constant pressure to work on it, to re-write a paragraph, to correct a sentence, — all of which will be a draft on his brain. But he must have solace and recreation. The best and perhaps the only kind really beneficial will be life in the open air, as in superintending a garden, farming, or fishing. A sea-voyage would do much by cutting the connections with care and duty at home. If his face is soon restored, so as not to excite observation, he might travel and enjoy the heights of Colorado. But it must be under a promise not to speak or to engage in politics. You see how frankly I write. A sufferer myself, I have a fellow-feeling with others in this condition, especially with the friend and colleague of many years. I hope you will kindly let me know how he gets on. It is pleasant to think that he is in your hands."

Sumner's friends were very desirous that he should pass the recess of Congress in Europe, but he would not yield to their persuasions. He was always morbidly sensitive about being in debt, and this time about the debt he had incurred on account of his last journey and his heavy bills for medical attendance. To E. L. Pierce he wrote, April 3: "I am yet in debt for my European trip last autumn, and no temptation can make me repeat this indiscretion, and reduce still more my small capital. Evidently you do not consider my expenses, — my house, clerk hire here, salary to proof-readers at Cambridge, my doctor's bills (two daily visits for months), with Dr. Brown-Séquard's accounts; also poor relations.[1] How to meet these, even with my increased pay, I know not." His friends, who unavailingly urged the journey, were most anxious that he should return well and strong to enter on the next session, — the one next preceding the election in Massachusetts which would choose his successor.

Sumner remained in Washington till July 25, and reached Boston August 2. His last month at the capital was free from pain, and he slept without anodynes. He showed some effort in walking, and other symptoms indicated that he had not the full measure of health; but his face betokened a new vitality. Daily drives, diligent work on his "book," and visits to the Congressional Library filled his time. On his arrival in Boston it was observed that his step was elastic, and that his former vigor had come back. He said himself that he had not been so well for three or four years. To his physician he wrote, September 5:

[1] A maternal aunt, who was dependent upon him, survived him.

"My general health is excellent. I have a sense of health, and a certain elasticity." During August and till late in September he was at his rooms in the Coolidge House, or at Nahant with Longfellow or George Abbot James.[1] While at the sea-shore he received a call from Mr. Wilson, their first meeting since the latter's stroke of paralysis. He made calls in the city on the few friends to be found there during the warm season,—one of them on Henry L. Pierce, the mayor. Early in September, in company with Longfellow, he took a drive of twenty miles in Essex County, calling on Whittier at Amesbury, and dining with B. P. Poore at his house in Newbury. The same month he attended the wedding of the daughter of his friend Mr. Bird at Walpole, and passed a few days with Mr. Hooper at Cotuit. Late in the autumn he was for a day or two at Governor Claflin's in Newtonville. He met there one evening the members of a farmer's club, owners of fine villas and spacious grounds, where, inspired by their presence, he talked for an hour or more on country life, the different breeds of cattle, chiefly the English; and here, as often with those who had not been well affected towards him, prejudices vanished before the charm of his personality. There was surprise at so full a treatment of the topic from one who had never been the proprietor of an estate, or owned a beast, except a span of horses for a few months only.

When he left Mr. Hooper's the third week in September, declining an invitation to visit Mr. and Mrs. John Bigelow at Highland Falls, Orange County, N. Y., where Mrs. Charles Eames was a guest, he gave as the reason for renouncing the pleasure the necessity of preparing at once to meet an engagement with a bureau for delivering a lecture in different parts of the country, appearing four or five nights a week from the middle of October to the beginning of the next session in December. He wrote: "I need rest and play and friendship; instead, I commence wearing toil." He had undertaken the task for the purpose of paying the balance of the debt incurred in his recent journey to Europe. His subject was to be "The Unity of the

[1] In Mrs. James, daughter of John E. Lodge, he took an almost paternal interest. A room in the house was called "the Senator's" when it was built in 1868; and from that time he was usually a guest in the summer. Mr. James wrote in January, 1890: "It made and still makes our summer a different thing,—missing him! We loved him dearly, and he knew it. His relations with my wife were almost paternal. He was the greatest man I have ever known, and one of the most lovable, with all his peculiarities."

Republic." Dr. Brown-Séquard thought him equal to the effort; but there was a general remonstrance among his friends to this hazardous test of his strength.[1] Wendell Phillips was very earnest to arrest his purpose, and intervened to have the debt so placed that it would not be again a matter of thought.[2] Yielding to the pressure, he withdrew very regretfully his name from Mr. Redpath's list of engagements for him. He kept aloof from politics, even avoiding the subject in conversation. If he voted at the State election he doubtless voted the Republican ticket, headed by William B. Washburn, candidate for governor, who had been his associate in Congress, and was always friendly to him. It was the year of General Butler's attempt and failure to obtain the Republican nomination for governor; but Sumner did not take part in the preliminary canvass as he had done in 1871. He wrote to Mr. Bird, August 14: "I do not comprehend the political maze, and am happy to be out of it."

By invitation of Mr. Alexander H. Rice, afterward governor, he spoke at a meeting at the Merchants Exchange in behalf of sufferers by the yellow fever at Memphis and Shreveport.[3] Mr. Rice, with the view to the senator's re-election, was desirous of keeping him in the current of affairs; and this personal reason, not however communicated to him, prompted in part the invitation. Sumner was to have attended a bi-centenary celebration of the town of Wrentham, October 27, but a furious gale with rain kept away guests from other places, and prostrated the tent in which the dinner and speaking were to be. He would have spoken upon Horace Mann, who was a native of Franklin, a parish of the ancient town; and some notes in pencil of his intended remarks aré preserved. He had been in full sympathy with Mann in his early labors for the education of the people, and served with him in his later conflicts for freedom; and it would have been a grateful duty to have paid a tribute to him in a community where the older inhabitants still recalled his youth.

Never in his life was Sumner more genial, more glad to see old friends, — those of his youth as well as of his manhood, —

1 Longfellow's "Life," vol. iii. p. 204.

2 Henry L. Pierce was substituted as creditor, and took Sumner's note, which was duly paid. It is not true, as has been stated, that any gift was made to the senator to relieve him of the necessity of making a lecture tour. F. W. Bird in Boston "Herald," March 18, 1877.

3 October 24. Works, vol. xv. pp. 281–283.

or more ready to make new acquaintances. He enjoyed the monthly dinners of the Saturday Club, where were Longfellow, Agassiz, Emerson, Holmes, J. M. Forbes, Dana, Judge Hoar, and others of like spirit.[1] He was with the Radical Club at Mrs. John T. Sargent's, where, in the midst of a sympathetic circle, which included Wendell Phillips, James Freeman Clarke, and T. W. Higginson, he listened to John Weiss's paper on "Portia." He was twice on the platform at the Music Hall when Mr. Bradlaugh, M. P., was the lecturer (Wendell Phillips in the chair on one occasion), and declined the call of the audience at the close of the lecture. He was one of J. B. Smith's guests in Bulfinch Street at a dinner for Mr. Bradlaugh, where also at the table were H. L. Pierce, Mr. Hooper, Ex-Governor Emory Washburn, William Lloyd Garrison, and Thomas Russell. He took the chair at a lecture by Edward Jenkins, the English writer, and was warmly applauded when he rose to introduce one whom he commended "as an author who by his remarkable pen has drawn attention to the poor and lowly, awakened for them a wide-spread sympathy, and helped the reign of justice on earth." Many of his fellow-citizens then saw him for the last time.

An incident of the autumn was his election as a member of the Massachusetts Historical Society, of which Mr. Winthrop was president, where he took the vacant place of the late James Savage. This is an honor always much coveted in Boston, and would have come to him thirty years earlier if he had kept in harmony with the conservative sentiments of the city. During his last weeks in Boston he dined as principal guest with three clubs, meeting at each from thirty to sixty persons, all prominent in political or commercial life. He met at these reunions many whom he had long known, and others to whom he was then first introduced; and with all he was most cordial. His health was drunk, and he answered without preparation in an easy and unstudied way, appearing, as was remarked, never happier or more in touch with men. He avoided partisan politics, and dwelt rather on topics apart from controversy, recalling agreeable reminiscences of the past, and expressing faith in the future of the country.[2] As old friends and new friends came to take his

[1] He was present, October 28, when the elder Dana was received with honor. Adams's "Life" of Dana, vol. ii. p. 360.

[2] After his death the editor of the Boston "Commonwealth," March 14, 1874, recalling these occasions, wrote: "Not an auditor of these addresses, so full of power, of wisdom

hand he received hearty congratulations on his improved health, and assurances of personal regard and political support. The enthusiasm and devotion which were testified in these individual greetings, and in the responses at the tables, betokened very clearly the sentiment of his State towards him. To Whittier he wrote: "Verily, the heart of Massachusetts is returning!"

The most notable of these festivities was the dinner at the Commercial Club, October 18, at the Revere House, where A. H. Rice, who had pressed his acceptance of the invitation, held the chair as president of the club. Many persons now met him for the first time. He spoke at some length on the importance of a speedy return to specie payments, the proposed centennial exhibition,[1] and the history of clubs. All were charmed with his manner, as well as with what he said; and prejudices were overcome with several who had been repelled from him by what they thought his too absorbing devotion to the African race. It was a common remark among the members that it was the most delightful scene of the kind they had ever shared in. Mr. Slack, an editor who had a critical sense of the effect of an address on an audience, wrote, two days after, of "the freshness, pertinency, and happy current of thought with which it was charged," and described it as "really grand, an old-time renewal of power, suggestiveness, and eloquence." Sumner was urged by editors to write out his remarks for publication, but he declined.

At the Massachusetts Club,[2] November 1, after referring to some features of the Antislavery conflict before the Civil War, and maintaining the necessity of passing the civil-rights bill, he recalled the presence of coadjutors in past contests. "It may seem," he said, "that I am speaking of things which I have spoken of before. Perhaps, however, you have read of the bugle of Munchausen, in which the tunes were all frozen up; but when the warmth had thawed it, the old tunes which once it had been accustomed to play rang out from it again. Warmed by your presence, — the presence of my old friends and associates, — the old bugle of my life-long principles commences to play once more." As he recurred to ancient fellowships and

of the highest and most disinterested suggestion, but was charmed into recognizing him as a master in morals, politics, and social amenities."

1 He gave his views adverse to a world's fair as the proper mode of commemorating the birth of the republic.

2 Composed of Republicans who had supported President Grant's re-election.

common labors there was emotion in his voice and manner. Mr. Bradlaugh's presence suggested some remarks on the liberal cause in Europe, and the senator said: "Republicanism is daily asserting its strength in Europe; and mark my words, that strength will go on until all Europe is republican as America is to-day." He defined "republicanism" not as a mere name, but as government which rests on the consent of the governed, and establishes equal rights for all.[1] At the Bird Club,[2] November 8 (Mr. Bird in the chair, with Vice-President Wilson as one of the guests) Sumner explained his battle-flag resolution, and insisted on a return to specie payments without delay, and paid a tribute to John Bright.[3] The Banks Club,[4] which met at the Parker House November 22, was the last festivity of the kind which he attended in Boston. Here he made kindly mention of Mr. Banks, for whom the club was named, and who had just been elected State senator by the Democrats. He avowed his continued adhesion to his early purpose to promote, now that slavery had been abolished, reconciliation between those who had been on account of that conflict placed in antagonistic positions, and the union of all for the advancement of the common country. He paid a tribute to Massachusetts, — ever dear to him for her leadership in movements for liberty and civilization. His chief topic, however, was the advantages of social intercourse, particularly of conversation as an educating influence.[5] A gentleman well-known in the history of New England journalism, Mr. George H. Monroe, thus sketched this part of his remarks: —

"Passing to the consideration of a subject more specifically appropriate to the occasion, Mr. Sumner said he had once dined in company with Daniel Webster on a social occasion, when there were present William H. Prescott, the historian of Spain and her possessions; George Ticknor, who taught the Spaniards the wealth of their own literature; Joseph G. Cogswell, the most eminent bibliographer the country had produced; Francis C. Gray, and many others of distinction. The subject as to what influence exerted the greatest effect upon men's character and acts came up for discussion. Mr. Prescott declared that a mother's influence was the most potent, and paid an eloquent

[1] Boston Times, November 2; Boston Commonwealth, November 8; New York Tribune, November 4. As to Sumner's early and constant faith in the progress of the liberal cause in Europe, see *ante*, vol. iii. p. 36, and "Personal Recollections of Charles Sumner," by the Marquis de Chambrun (Scribner's Magazine, February, 1893, p. 160).

[2] Composed mostly of members, hitherto Republicans, who had supported Mr. Greeley.

[3] Boston Commonwealth, November 15.

[4] Composed of members of both parties.

[5] Saturday Evening Gazette, November 22.

tribute to the female sex in this relation. Another gentleman expressed the belief that most was owed to schools; another gave the preference in his judgment to books; another to the newspaper. He (Mr. Sumner) sat, the youngest man in the party, and watched Mr. Webster, who was apparently thoughtful for a considerable time, but finally broke the silence to declare that, to his mind, there was more to be derived from the conversation of intelligent men than from any other source. Mr. Sumner then enforced this view by reference to what had been said by men eminent in history. He referred to the declaration of Charles James Fox, that he was more indebted for knowledge to his intercourse with Edmund Burke than to all other sources of information. He spoke of the statement of Dr. Johnson, that Burke could not be met under a tree in a thunder shower without impressing one with the fact that he was in the presence of an extraordinary man. He illustrated his point further by reference to the conversation of Johnson himself, as reported by his biographer, which had so long been among the classics of literature."

One evening Sumner took tea at Jamaica Plain with Rev. James Freeman Clarke's family, where he talked of his last visit to Paris, and his dinner with Thiers. After dining at Longfellow's on the afternoon of November 12, he went to the Church of the Disciples in the south part of Boston to attend a social meeting, to which he had been invited by the pastor, Dr. Clarke. Mrs. Clarke writes as follows: —

"While on his way to the church he asked a gentleman in the street-car about the exact locality. The gentleman told him, and then said, in a tone of inquiry, 'Are you a stranger, sir?' showing that there was a Bostonian who did not know Mr. Sumner by sight. But a boy in the car jumped out when Mr. Sumner reached his destination, and said: 'Mr. Sumner, will you please write your name in my album?' They stopped under a street-lamp, and Mr. Sumner wrote his name. Is not that a scene worth preserving?

"At the social meeting Mr. Sumner with some reluctance consented to speak. Soon 'his heart warmed toward the young people present, and he addressed himself to them, telling them what great opportunities were awaiting them in the approaching years. He said no word of the past; nothing of what he had seen and done; only of the magnificent future which was before the rising generation, and the noble duties which they had to fulfil. . . . Once or twice he said he wished he had been born later, so as to be able to take part in the events which are to come soon. In regard to this, one lady said to him later in the evening that she thought the Lord knew better than he when he ought to have been born.'

"I have taken these extracts from Mr. Clarke's sketch of Charles Sumner in his work entitled 'Memorial and Biographical Sketches.' But I too remember that evening at the church, and the deep pathos in Mr. Sumner's voice as he spoke of the great privilege of having the opportunities of life before us and not behind us. The address was worthy of the man. He seemed to have one single desire, to make the young people before him realize their high calling as citizens of this Commonwealth and Union, and to prove themselves worthy of their privileges. His true nobility of soul showed itself as clearly in that social gathering of the Church of the Disciples as it did on the floor of Congress."

A few days before leaving for Washington, Sumner dined with George S. Hillard, the friend of his youth, already smitten with paralysis.[1] Their themes were by-gone days and the books they had both loved. An eye-witness relates the scene: —

"The two friends talked till nearly twelve o'clock, recalling old and intimate days, — discussing men, books, and affairs, chiefly their European experiences, and the 'Five of Clubs.' I remember an animated difference over a Latin quotation, finally settled in Mr. Hillard's favor, — Mr. Sumner saying some pleasant thing, to the effect that Mr. Hillard was as aggravatingly correct as of old. Indeed, it was an evening to be remembered; roused by the excitement, Mr. Hillard talked like his old self, with hardly a trace of weakness. When they parted, it was almost in silence, with a long clasp of hands, as if each felt it was for the last time. It so happened that we had colored servants. The old cook had been a slave in Georgia, and was greatly excited over the preparations of a dinner for the man who was to her the deliverer of her race. Mr. Hillard told Mr. Sumner what a solemn occasion it was to her. Mr. Sumner said it was the custom in some places to send a glass of wine to the cook when the dinner was unusually good, and begged permission to do so, which he did, rendering the old woman almost beside herself with pride. The servants had told me of their earnest desire to see the great man, and I asked Mr. Sumner if he could gratify them. He assented, simply and readily. I shall never forget how he looked as he stood in the doorway of the dining-room, almost filling it in height and breadth, while those two poor, homely black women, one of them scarred by injuries received in slavery, reverently kissed his hand. It was a scene full of significance. We looked on with wet eyes; but he was rather embarrassed, and glad to escape upstairs. I also remember that the kitchen department was demoralized for some days following."

One day Sumner dined with Dr. George C. Shattuck, a companion of his youth, when, it is remembered, he made kindly mention of all on whom the conversation turned.[2] He dined also with James T. Fields, with whom, as his friend and publisher, he had long enjoyed most agreeable relations.[3] He was obliged by other engagements to decline invitations to dine at Mr. Martin Brimmer's, and also at Mr. Winthrop's. In the late

[1] Hillard survived Sumner nearly five years, dying Jan. 21, 1879, at the age of seventy. To the end he took a constant interest in the preparation of this Memoir, and read the proofs of the first two volumes. It was the writer's privilege to pay a tribute to his memory in the United States Circuit Court, Boston.

[2] Dr. Shattuck in an interview, Dec. 4, 1874, recalled his meetings with Sumner in 1837–1839, and mentioned as his distinguishing traits moral fearlessness and the absence of vindictiveness in his nature.

[3] J. T. Fields's "Biographical Notes and Personal Sketches," p. 197.

autumn he dined occasionally at Mr. Hooper's.[1] The afternoon of Sunday, the day before leaving for Washington, he passed at Cambridge with Agassiz. On the evening of the same day he dined with the son of William H. Prescott, with whom he renewed the memories of friendly and sympathetic intercourse with the historian. Among the guests were the young Lord Rosebery, and Longfellow and his daughter, afterwards Mrs. Dana.

His letters show how he kept English friends and affairs in mind. To Lady Hatherton he wrote, April 3: —

"I was glad that you remembered me, although you could not restrain an allusion which I do not think I deserved. It became my duty to set forth the wrong done to my country by England during our terrible Civil War. The pain that cost me you cannot know. I felt it the more because of my attachment to England, and never did I utter a word which was not more than justified by the speeches of Mr. Cobden and Mr. Bright, — good Englishmen always. But I forbear. For years I have allowed misrepresentation without a word of reply, lest what I said might be tortured into some unfriendly expression. Among my early souvenirs of English politics was the incident so clearly explained in the volume you kindly sent me.[2] I have read it with great interest, and am glad that the family of Lord Hatherton permitted its publication. It is a complete chapter of history. I am sorry that Lord Brougham appears no better. My neighbors here, Mr. and Mrs. Russell Gurney, enjoyed it also. I like them much, and am always happy in long talks with them about England. Last autumn I passed a fortnight in London, which seemed more metropolitan and fascinating than ever. Everybody was agreeable, and I enjoyed my visit much."

To Robert Ingham, July 11: —

"As I am about to leave for Boston I receive the South Shields paper, with the interesting report of the beautiful ceremony in honor of you. I wish I had been there. Such a monument is better than a statue. This recognition among friends and neighbors must be very pleasant. Among those present was Miss Blackett; but where was my ancient friend, Mme. du Quaire? I was unhappy at not seeing her during my fortnight in England. But I did not see you.

"I have been cheered by the vote of the House of Commons on Mr. Richard's motion;[3] that is an historic event marking an epoch. It cannot fail to exert a prodigious influence. I know no reform which promises such universal

[1] One habit of Sumner may be worth noting. Reaching, on his way to Mr. Hooper's, the gate of the Public Garden, at the head of Commonwealth Avenue, he always turned about to look at Story's statue of Everett standing in characteristic attitude with uplifted arm. The design has not escaped criticism, but Sumner liked it. His own statue and Everett's now front each other, though at quite a distance apart.

[2] Memoir and Correspondence relating to political occurrences in June and July, 1834.

[3] For international arbitration, *ante*, vol. ii. p. 382.

good as the release of any considerable portion of present war expenditure, or expenditure on armaments, so that they can be applied to purposes of civilization. It is absurd to call this Utopian. Nothing more practical. Here is an open and incessant waste. Why not stop it? Here is something which keeps human thoughts on bloodshed, and rears men to slay each other. Why not turn their thoughts to things which contribute to human happiness? Mr. Richard has done a great work, and so has the House of Commons. The cause cannot be arrested. But why did not Mr. Gladstone adopt it at once, and place England on heights of civilization which no nation has yet reached? I like him, and am sorry that he allowed himself to be on the wrong side. Such a presentation of the case must have an effect on the continent as well as in England, teaching reason. I shall not live to see the great cause triumph. I often wish I had been born a few years later, and one reason is because I long to witness the harmony of nations, which I am sure is near. When an evil so great is recognized and discussed, the remedy must be at hand. Pray excuse this enthusiasm which I feel in my inmost soul.

"I have not been well this winter and spring. Care and overwork revived old injuries; but I am now better, and this news is better than medicine.

"I am at a loss to understand how that wretch Arthur Orton finds a witness or a shilling. His place is the penitentiary, quick step. Is not the case clear as day? But what a reprobate!"

To Mrs. George Grote, November 2, on the occasion of the publication of her "Personal Life" of her husband: —

"Your most interesting volume, which arrived at the end of the summer, besides its grateful souvenir of your kindness, has made me live again in pleasant scenes of the past. Nothing has so recalled old memories. Valued friends now dead reappear as in a magic mirror. Besides the great author, are others, — Tocqueville and wife at his old castle, Senior in Paris and London, Cornewall Lewis, Molesworth, the Dean of St. Paul's, Hallam, Parkes, John Austin and wife, all of whom I see again! Nor are all dead. I was glad to read of Charles Austin,[1] whose 'talk' I always placed, as you do, foremost. Why does he not appear in Parliament? But these companions, as introduced by you, show the historian, whose serene and glorious life was passed in such an atmosphere of character and talent. Undoubtedly he was one of the most remarkable scholars ever produced by England, and he grew as none other. He was no university plant or graft; he was a rich seedling with an original flavor. In his history he became the philosopher and vindicator of liberal ideas. Posterity will hear and listen. I have a sincere gratitude for the truth he has taught so well. I regret that he saw so indistinctly the terrible trials of our government, struggling for national life with a rebellion whose single animating impulse was slavery.[2]

"Why not complete your work by a volume of his miscellanies, political and literary?[3] His speeches were masterpieces of scholarly politics. I ad-

1 *Ante*, vol. ii. p. 57, *note*.

2 Grote's view of the Civil War is given in his letters to G. C. Lewis, Dec. 29, 1862, and Jan. 12, 1863. "Personal Life," pp. 262-264.

3 Mrs. Grote published her husband's "Minor Works" in 1874.

mired much his first address to his constituents (p. 71), which seems a *chef-d'œuvre* of breadth, both in mass and detail. The essay on Mitford, which marked his original studies in Greek history, ought to be within the reach of those who admire the history. While I write with this execrable pen and ink, I get the first report of J. S. Mills's autobiography. The revelations of his precocious life surprise me. Here he is another Pascal, but without the faith of the Frenchman.

"Among the letters in your book, those of the historian to Lewis (p. 202) and of Hallam (pp. 164-169) are most scholarly. It is pleasant to think that G. G. succeeded H. H. as trustee of the British Museum. The latter once told me that early in life his two special objects of ambition were to be a bencher of the inn where he studied, and a trustee of the British Museum. I was interested in the efforts of the historian to obtain for Lewis a copy of the works of Saint-Pierre. Four years before I had imported from Paris a complete set, — more than twenty-five volumes. While with Tocqueville I enjoyed much a visit to the old ancestral home of Saint-Pierre, some five or six miles from Tocqueville, in a thick wood, gridironed with roads and paths.[1] This reminds me of your residence at St. Germain in the summer of 1858, and of my taking to you Professor Felton, our Grecian just returned from Athens, who seemed to refresh the historian, and came away charmed. He, too, is dead; an admirable scholar.

"I am glad that your husband declined a title. The simplicity of his life was kept perfect to the end, when 'Westminster Abbey' became his peerage.

"The John Fiske[2] whose article is praised so effectively (p. 294) was a young man of twenty-five at the time. His abilities have developed since, and he is now absorbed in 'evolution' and Darwinism. His friends are pleased with this valuable tribute. He is now in Europe, probably in England, especially to publish a work.

"The Baron Degérando whose works amused the historian at Harpton Court (p. 255) was no humorist. I knew him in 1838, dining with him in the Rue de Verneuil, and receiving from him tickets for the Chamber of Peers. The inquiry about Daunou interested me, as I have his works in twenty volumes, which I brought home sixteen years ago. My friend George W. Greene, who is much of an invalid, was cheered by the allusion to him at Rome. I think often of your kindness when we met. By the time you receive this I shall be on my way to Washington, where I expect to find that most interesting manuscript in a binding not unworthy of it."[3]

Among Sumner's published papers during the year were open letters on civil rights to the colored people;[4] a reply to the

1 *Ante*, vol. iii. p. 548.

2 Since distinguished in studies of American history.

3 The original draft of the "Life, Trial, and Death of Socrates," written by Mr. Grote in 1830–1831, and laid by for forty years, another and more complete account being drawn up by the author for his published history. The first was given to Sumner in 1872 by Mrs. Grote.

4 Dec. 19, 1872. Boston "Journal," Dec. 20, 1872; April 16, 1873. Works, vol. xv. pp. 266, 267. June 22, Ibid., pp. 268, 269. July 29, Ibid., pp. 275–278.

President of Hayti, who had testified gratefully to his resistance to the annexation of San Domingo;[1] a note of congratulation to Henry Richard on the success of his motion in Parliament for international arbitration;[2] a letter commending the scheme for the extension of the territory of Boston by the inclusion of suburban municipalities;[3] and a bibliographical memorandum on Archdeacon Walter Mapes, an English writer of the time of Henry II.[4]

The seizure of the "Virginius" by the Spanish authorities in Cuba, with the summary execution of a large number of men on board, on the ground that, though flying the American colors, she was on her way to assist the insurgents in that island, was made the pretence of indignation against Spain, then a republic with Castelar at its head. There is always in the city of New York a filibustering interest which draws to its support a certain class of merchants and a certain class of lawyers. This interest, ever ready to provoke or aid an insurrection in Cuba, held a public meeting at Steinway Hall, November 17, to stimulate a war spirit against Spain. William M. Evarts took the chair and made an inflammatory speech. Sumner was invited to be one of the speakers; but he declined, and instead sent a letter of a spirit directly opposite to that of the meeting, in which he insisted on waiting for evidence and on considerate treatment of the Spanish republic and its noble president, and discountenanced the belligerent preparations then under way in our navy yards, which involved burdensome expenditure and encouraged an unhealthy war fever.[5] These views he expanded in an interview with a correspondent of the New York "Tribune."[6] It was Sumner's characteristic to keep his mind steady in the midst of popular frenzy. He had always the courage to challenge a universal opinion. The sober sense of the best people was with him in this protest. R. H. Dana, Jr., wrote: "Let me thank you for your letter; it is the wisest thing I have seen — I should not be out of the way to say, the only wise thing I have seen — in the 'Virginius' case." Caleb Cushing wrote: "I am delighted to

1 July 4, 1873. Works, vol. xv. pp. 270–272.

2 July 10. Works, vol. xv. pp. 273, 274.

3 October 4. Works, vol. xv. pp. 279, 280.

4 July 23. New York "Evening Post," July 25.

5 Works, vol. xv. pp. 284, 285. New York "Tribune," November 19. Boston "Advertiser," November 19. The letter was not read at the meeting.

6 November 18. The same journal, Jan. 5, 1874, reports a later interview with the senator on the fall of Castelar's ministry.

learn through the newspapers that you continue to have the courage of your convictions, and do not cease to be yourself because of the insanity which infects the citizens of New York on the subject of Cuba." Longfellow wrote on a postal card: "I like your letter to the Cubans extremely. That is the way a statesman should think and speak." J. R. Doolittle, the late senator, with whom Sumner had fought many hard contests, wrote from Chicago: "I deem it wise and most fortunate when all the world would cry out for war, that there is one statesman left in the Senate who can speak boldly and truthfully to our people."

The "Virginius" affair was discreditable to our government. Spain was from the beginning anxious to do justice. The piratical craft, as the attorney-general of the United States found, carried American papers which had been procured by perjury. A show of fight against a power incapable of resistance, and that power a new republic with some hope of perpetuity, was altogether suited to the genius of the two heads of the war bureaus, Robeson and Belknap. The former spent five millions of dollars in his unseemly preparations of a naval armament against a friendly power, and the latter's subsequent career is well remembered. Behind all was the greed for Cuba and the watching of an opportunity to seize that possession of Spain. The whole transaction, reviving the memory of the Ostend manifesto of Buchanan, Mason, and Slidell, ended in a fiasco. The "Virginius" was delivered up by the Spanish government; and while being towed as a trophy by one of our war ships to New York, she went to the bottom off Cape Fear.

I left Boston for Europe, May 20, and was absent till November 13. For the few days after my arrival home Sumner remained in the city. I sought his rooms at the Coolidge House as often as each alternate morning, reaching his door before he had completed his dressing, and remaining till after his breakfast. I brought him a can of honey from Hymettus; told him what I had seen in Europe,—Rome, Sicily, Athens, Constantinople, the Danube, and the exposition at Vienna,—and described the spectacle I had witnessed when John Bright resumed public activity after a season of prostration, in an address to an immense audience in Birmingham. He listened with interest, and thought I had seen much. On Monday morning, the 24th, I happened to be going by the same train with him to Palmer, less than twenty miles short of Springfield, at which latter city he was to remain a few hours to be received by citizens at a club and dine with S. R. Phillips, in company with Governor William B. Washburn and Henry L. Dawes. We passed two hours or more together in the drawing-room car, during which he was looking over parliamentary blue-books, except when I interrupted him. Once I said, "Do you not see how the heart of Massachusetts is with you?" "Yes," he quietly answered, after a moment's thought; "I expected it, but not so soon." Leaving the train at Palmer, I saw him again but for a minute or two in the evening at Springfield when he was taking the train for New York. As he stood on the platform of the car, we shook hands, he saying, "Good-by; God bless you!" and we parted for the last time. In a few moments he had left forever the State he had loved and served.

He was in New York two days. It was always his instinct to seek the relatives of his deceased friends, and this time he searched without success for the widow of Dr. Lieber, who had died October 2. He paused for a day in Philadelphia to see the Furness family, and here Mr. Forney called on him.[1] He reached Washington on Friday of the same week.

It was evident during the summer and autumn that the hearts of the people of Massachusetts were with their senator. The heats of the Presidential contest of 1872 had subsided. Reasonable men, though not voting as he had advised, recognized that after the indignity he suffered when removed from the committee on which he had so long served, he could not, without loss of manhood, do otherwise than he did. The Credit Mobilier scandal had ruined some public men, hitherto of high consideration for integrity, while it had tainted the reputations of others whose apologies, in view of former good service, were accepted. The unseemly greed which had prompted the last Congress in its closing hours to vote itself "back pay,"—an unearned salary which the senator, one of a small proportion of senators and representatives, declined to receive,—added to the distrust of public men.[2] Among all classes in the country, however they differed

[1] Mr. Forney, in his interesting recollections of Sumner ("Anecdotes of Public Men," vol. ii. pp. 253–263), gives an account of his interviews with the senator in Philadelphia at this time, in which he notes "his high spirits and apparently excellent health." pp. 260, 261.

[2] The New York "Evening Post," May 5, 1873, contrasted Sumner's action with that of a member of the House who opposed "the back-pay swindle," but accepted his share of the fund. See New York "Times," May 6.

in politics, religious faith, sectional traits, or personal likings, there was accord in the belief that one life and character stood unassailable, — the life and character of Charles Sumner. He might have this fault or that; he might overdo in some things or fall short in others; but he had, as all men felt, upheld in the Senate for wellnigh a generation a lofty standard of fidelity, dignity, and unblemished virtue.[1] Such a career is a capital which the American people know how to value.

It would have been natural for Sumner to expect when he came home in August to see some averted faces among the people he had left eleven months before with a deliverance which grated on their feelings; but these he did not see. As he walked the streets of his native city, citizens whom he had known and others whom he had not known stopped him to inquire eagerly for his health and to express their warmest interest in him. This cordiality was most noticeable among men of mercantile pursuits, who as a class had never been much attracted by his devotion to the uplifting of the African race. Their friendly greetings in the clubs have already been mentioned. At no time had he felt so sensibly the warm breath of popular favor, always grateful to a public man. It was everywhere the talk that he would be elected for a fifth term by the Legislature to be chosen a year later. This public feeling found expression in the newspapers, and if there was dissent anywhere it was cherished in perfect silence. The repeal of the legislative censure was already assured. As things then looked, he was to receive the unanimous support of the people, again nominated by the Republicans and voted for by the Democrats, — not standing so much now the leader of a party as the first citizen of the Commonwealth. In the contest, if there had been one, the voice of his old colleague, now Vice-President, would have been heard in his behalf, — not with youthful vigor as in 1851, but still potent and inspiring. If in any quarter opposition had developed, — and this would have come only under stimulus from Washington, — the members of the Legislature would have been chosen with sole refer-

[1] George F. Hoar, M. C., contrasting at Worcester, Sept. 4, 1873, General Butler with other political leaders, thus referred to Sumner: "Some of you in spite of recent estrangements have to think of those evenings [in Worcester] when Charles Sumner (applause) moulded the ornaments of literature, the teachings of history, the commandments of law, human and divine, into one of his burning and eloquent pleas for the slave."

ence to his re-election, and without regard to party lines; and a result in his favor would have been certain. When therefore he resumed his duties in the Senate for what proved his last session, he enjoyed the consciousness that his people loved and trusted him never more than now, perhaps never as much.

## CHAPTER LIX.

CORDIALITY OF SENATORS. — LAST APPEAL FOR THE CIVIL-RIGHTS BILL. — DEATH OF AGASSIZ. — GUEST OF THE NEW ENGLAND SOCIETY IN NEW YORK. — THE NOMINATION OF CALEB CUSHING AS CHIEF-JUSTICE. — AN APPOINTMENT FOR THE BOSTON CUSTOM-HOUSE. — THE RESCINDING OF THE LEGISLATIVE CENSURE. — LAST EFFORT IN DEBATE. — LAST DAY IN THE SENATE. — ILLNESS, DEATH, FUNERAL, AND MEMORIAL TRIBUTES. — DEC. 1, 1873–MARCH 11, 1874.

SUMNER received cordial salutations from senators of both parties as he entered the Senate chamber, Dec. 1, 1873. The Republican majority, classifying him as a member of the opposition, placed him low down on two committees, — that of privileges and elections, of which Morton was chairman; and that of education and labor, of which Flanagan was chairman. Wilson, Vice-President, though suffering a permanent disability, made it a point to attend on the first day, with the hope of harmonizing the relations of the majority and the dissenters of 1872;[1] but this well-meant effort found no encouragement with the set then dominant in the Senate and assuming to represent the Administration. Still, outside of a small number, — like Conkling, Chandler, Logan, and Carpenter, — the feeling towards Sumner was in every way kindly and considerate. Even with Edmunds, who had been among the leaders in promoting his removal from the foreign relations committee, he had resumed friendly intercourse. It is Mr. Edmunds's recollection and opinion that during the session "the cordiality between Sumner and the body of the Republicans was almost completely restored, and that had he lived everything would soon have been perfectly friendly, co-operative, and harmonious."[2] This is doubtless a correct view; but while he lived he remained entirely silent as to his political relations. He had too much self-respect while disowned by Republican senators to

1 The New York "Tribune," Nov. 18, 1873, called for Sumner's restoration to the head of the committee on foreign relations.

2 Letter to George W. Curtis.

seem to solicit their favor by announcing himself, uninvited, as of their number.[1]

Immediately after the prayer on the first day, Sumner put on the calendar a list of eight measures, all but one of which he had brought forward before, some of them several times: (1) The civil-rights bill; (2) Equal rights in the schools of the District of Columbia; (3) Compound-interest notes as a substitute for legal-tender notes in the national currency, with the view to restore specie payments, which he explained and defended at some length a few days later;[2] (4) Payment for French spoliations; (5) Election of President by direct vote of the people;[3] (6) Limitation of the office of President to a single term;[4] (7) International arbitration;[5] (8) The protection of children kidnapped in Italy and brought to the United States. This starting of a series of favorite measures showed the zest with which he returned to activity in the Senate, and his confidence in his ability to maintain them during the session.[6]

In the evening of that day he responded from the steps of his house to a serenade by the colored people.[7] On the first day of the session, and again after the holiday recess, Sumner made an earnest effort to have his civil-rights bill, now number one on the calendar, taken up;[8] but Edmunds, who was in favor of some measure of the kind, as well as Morrill of Maine and Ferry of Connecticut, both of whom believed such legislation unconstitutional, insisted, against Sumner's protest, on a reference to the judiciary committee,—a reference which they thought all the more desirable by reason of a recent decision of the Supreme Court in

1 Washington gossip, which often has no basis of truth, reported Sumner as saying that he had changed his views about General Grant, and that he was back again in the Republican party to remain. But he wrote nothing of the kind, and indulged in no such expressions when conversing with his confidential friends.

2 Dec. 11, 1873, Congressional Globe, pp. 142, 143. He voted on the finance bill, Feb. 18 and 19, 1874.

3 Proposed Feb. 11, 1869. Works, vol. xi. p. 98.

4 *Ante*, p. 498.

5 A series of resolutions, the same, with one omitted, as offered May 31, 1872. Works, vol. xv. pp. 80-82.

6 Later in the session he gave attention to private bills for relief. His bill for a bust of the late Chief-Justice Chase is elsewhere noted. He spoke briefly, Feb. 9, 1874 (Congressional Globe, p. 1322), against changes in the Bankruptcy Act calculated to impair its efficiency. He received, February 6, a delegation of the city council of Boston, charged with the errand of promoting an appropriation for the post-office in that city, and his cordiality was referred to in their commemorative meeting, March 12, 1874.

7 Boston "Journal," Dec. 2, 1873.

8 Dec. 2, 1873, Works, vol. xv. pp. 286-290; Jan. 27, 1874, Ibid., pp. 301-313. He presented at this session a large number of petitions for the bill.

the New Orleans Slaughter-house cases.[1] Sumner objected that such action on a bill already fully considered would as before end in an adverse report, and only serve the purpose of delay; but he yielded the point on the assurance that the committee would promptly consider and report upon the bill. In the debate he traced the history of the measure in the Senate for nearly four years, — from its introduction by himself, May 13, 1870, to Jan. 27, 1874, the day when he made what was to be his last appeal. It is evident from the tone of Republican senators in the debate on the reference, as also from their action at a later day, that they were generally well disposed towards him personally, and desirous to go as far in supporting the measure he had so much at heart as their views of expediency and constitutional limitations admitted.

The subsequent history of Sumner's bill may be properly given in this connection. It came back from the judiciary committee, April 14,[2] when he was no longer in the Senate, and was taken up for debate on the 29th. It had not been substantially abridged or weakened, but was left to apply to inns, public conveyances, theatres, and other places of public amusement, common schools, public institutions of learning, cemeteries supported wholly or in part by taxation, and to grand and petit jurors. It did not, however, interfere with churches. Frelinghuysen, who had charge of the bill, said in opening the debate: —

> "Would that the author of the measure were here to present and defend it! To our view it would have been becoming that he, who was in the forum the leader of the grandest victory of the nineteenth century in the western hemisphere, — the victory of freedom over slavery, — should have completed the work he so efficiently aided. But it was otherwise decreed."

There was a full debate, in which party lines were drawn, — Republicans defending and Democrats opposing the bill. It passed by a vote of twenty-nine to sixteen, after a night session, at nearly seven o'clock on the morning of May 23. Carpenter voted against it on account of the provision concerning juries, but Morrill of Maine and Ferry did not vote. Morton, Howe, Frelinghuysen, and Edmunds led in the debate in favor of the bill. The House did not reach a vote upon the Senate bill during

1 Wallace's (U. S.) Reports, vol. xvi. p. 36.

2 Mr. Frelinghuysen stated, March 17, at the first session of the Senate after its adjournment on account of Sumner's death and funeral, that the committee's report was ready and would be submitted as soon as Mr. Edmunds, who was in favor of it, could be present. Harper's Weekly, April 11 and May 9, 1874, commended the bill.

this or the next session; but in February, 1875, a new bill, originating in the House and omitting the provisions as to schools [1] and cemeteries, was carried through both houses and approved by the President. This Act was in 1883 adjudged unconstitutional by the Supreme Court.[2] The opinion of the court was to this effect: (1) That the thirteenth amendment prohibits only slavery, with its incidents, elements, and badges, among which discriminations on account of race and color in inns, places of amusement, and public conveyances are not included; (2) The fourteenth amendment — which forbids the abridgment of the privileges and immunities of citizens, the deprivation of life, liberty, or property without due process of law, and the denial of the equal protection of the laws — is directed only against State laws and proceedings, and not against individual acts which are not done under their authority. It does not extend the power of Congress to the domain of private rights, which still remains with the States; it authorizes legislation corrective of State action, but not primary and direct legislation. Mr. Justice Harlan, of Kentucky, in a dissenting opinion, treated the argument of the court as "proceeding on narrow and artificial grounds, and sacrificing the substance and spirit of the amendments by a subtle and ingenious verbal criticism." It is clear that Sumner would not have been content with this judicial limitation of their scope. The result, however, justified his solicitude at the time they were under consideration in Congress, when he insisted on more specific and comprehensive provisions.

Sumner mourned the death of Agassiz, which took place two weeks after the session began. Their friendship was formed in 1846, when the naturalist arrived in the country, and it had been of late years more intimate than ever. Sumner had been tenderly affected by Agassiz's refusal to have his name count against his friend in the San Domingo controversy. Mrs. Agassiz, in her reply to Sumner's letter of condolence, recalled his letter of congratulation on their engagement twenty years before.

Sumner wrote to the Duchess of Argyll, Dec. 16, 1873: —

"I am sure that you and the duke will grieve at the loss of Agassiz,[3] who died as he was beginning a serious answer to the new doctrine of evolution.

[1] The omission of schools, where Sumner thought equality most important, prompted an expressive cartoon in the New York "Graphic," March 3, 1875, representing the senator in indignant attitude pointing to the mutilated measure.

[2] United States Reports, vol. cix. pp. 3-62.

[3] Sumner had written, Sept. 5, 1873, to Dr. Brown-Séquard, "Agassiz has come home, tired but gay, and with good health, for his sixty-six years."

He had written a first article on primitive types to appear in the January number of the Atlantic Monthly, to be followed by others, and by a course of lectures this winter in Washington. I think you will like his first article, unhappily his last. I have found him latterly singularly gentle and genial, and determined in the controversy before him to avoid all personalities, confining himself to a rigorous scientific treatment. I am sure this is the tone of the article already written, which he sent me in the proof-sheets. I passed my last Sunday afternoon with him before leaving for Washington. I feel his death much, for he had become very affectionate and interesting with me. Rarely have I known so much head and heart together; his nature was large and winning. How much he was in science you know as well as we do. Everywhere and in everything his death creates an immense void. He has been blessed by a wife of rare devotion and intelligence. His last article was written out by her three times, each copy being interlined with his corrections. His English style was excellent and very flowing. Few will feel his death more than Longfellow; they were much attached to each other.

"I always like young Englishmen, — as Lord Roseberry, Mr. Rutson, and Mr. Acland, who have been here some time, and were not displeased with Boston. Together they give freshness to our dull routine, and let in a breath of English air. I was sorry to hear of the death of Mr. Baring, whom I always liked. His pictures were charming."

Sumner had been several times urged to be the guest of the New England Society in New York at its commemorative dinner, December 22, the most attractive festivity which the country annually presents; but a fixed rule had kept him hitherto from any divergence from public duty during the session of Congress. He was, however, now relieved from active responsibility, — a senator still disowned as a political associate, — and he felt more at liberty to waive the rigid rule to which he had uniformly adhered. He accepted the invitation which this time came with strong, friendly pressure from the president of the society, Mr. E. C. Cowdin. The dinner was served at Delmonico's, with two hundred and fifty New England men filling the seats at the tables, and General Sherman, Henry Ward Beecher, L. P. Morton, and Mr. Havemeyer, the mayor, prominent among the invited guests. Sumner was delayed on the train, and entered the hall half an hour after the banquet had begun. He was most warmly welcomed as he passed up to the president's table, at whose right he was placed as the principal guest. When he rose to answer to a toast "to the Senate of the United States," the members stood up in mass, cheering loudly and waving handkerchiefs.[1] At several points he was interrupted with applause, and at the end "the

[1] Works, vol. xv. pp. 291–300.

audience gave cheer upon cheer." These demonstrations were not merely formal and customary, but they were sincere expressions of respect and gratitude.[1] Sumner himself saw how genuine they were, and was deeply moved. In the few weeks of life that remained they were a solace, and a sign to him of the final judgment of mankind on his career. He lodged at Mr. Cowdin's during his four days in the city. In conversation with the family he recurred several times to the warmth and enthusiasm of his reception. Indeed, the exhilaration of spirits which came from his visit had, as his physician observed, a visible effect on his health for weeks to come. The exposure, however, resulted in a hard cough, which kept him awake at night and brought his host to his chamber with the offer of remedies. He wrote from Washington, December 26, to Mr. Cowdin: "Major Poore dined with me last evening, and I dine to-night at the French legation; so that I shall be kept in the line of French souvenirs, so pleasant in your beautiful home. Washington looks more like a village than ever before. My protracted visit has made me feel the grandeur of New York, to say nothing of the elegant hospitality there."

Sumner wrote to F. W. Bird, December 26: —

"I note and value your warning. My case is less menacing than the Vice-President's. I have latterly done my eleven hours work a day. Wilson's work on his book will bring death or worse. I agree with you on the bankrupt law. Mr. Tremain [2] has lost as a legislator by the ill-considered haste with which, without the support of the committee, he rushed through the repeal. Baez has [3] from the beginning been a mercenary, looking out for himself, and a usurper sustained for years by the navy of the United States, illicitly employed at immense cost. Millions! Read my sketch of him, and see how it is veri-

[1] Chauncey M. Depew, in a eulogy on General Sherman at Albany, March 29, 1892, stated that "at a notable gathering in New York" (meaning the New England dinner at Delmonico's) Sumner attacked General Grant as a failure in civil affairs, covertly alluding to him in remarks on Miles Standish, and was replied to by General Sherman. The statement has no basis of fact. Sumner did not then or at any other time after November, 1872, make the slightest reference in public to General Grant. Nothing in the language of either Sumner or General Sherman justified the imputation. No one present, as General James Grant Wilson, one of the guests, certifies, suspected Sumner to have intended any such personal reference. It is surprising that Mr. Depew, who in the election of 1872 was himself bitterly personal against General Grant, should have put such a construction on the senator's speech. The passage of Mr. Depew's eulogy referred to was the subject of criticism in a communication to the New York "Evening Post," May 7, 1892.

[2] Lyman Tremain of New York. The bill of repeal, which passed the House, Dec. 15, 1873, was not acted on in the Senate. A later Congress, however, repealed the Bankruptcy Act.

[3] Again in the United States to promote the annexation of San Domingo.

fied by the result. Howe's first mistake was that he did not follow the example of Agassiz, who refused to be seduced into any co-operation against a friend."

The vacancy in the office of chief-justice was filled at this session. The President first offered the place to Mr. Conkling, among whose qualifications, whatever they were, the judicial temper was not one. Fortunately, he declined it; and then it was offered to George H. Williams of Oregon, whose name was withdrawn when it was found impossible to secure a confirmation. A greater surprise was then in store,—the immediate nomination of Caleb Cushing, who, having been appointed and confirmed as minister to Spain, was about to set sail. This third name struck the Senate and the country with amazement, and a confirmation was at once found to be impossible. Mr. Conkling alone appeared to approve it, and not more than half-a-dozen Republican senators seemed disposed to listen to his persuasions. The senators were at a loss to understand upon what principle the President proceeded in making the several nominations, and he in his turn was quite unable to understand what kind of a man they thought suited to the office. He yielded, however, to the request of a Republican caucus for the withdrawal of Mr. Cushing's name, recalling it five days after it had been sent in. The nominee had run a most eccentric political career,—first a Whig and then a Democrat; a partisan of pro-slavery doctrines; president of the Democratic convention at Charleston in 1860; a supporter of Breckinridge's candidacy the same year, and the author of an inflammatory speech after Mr. Lincoln's election, which was calculated to encourage Southern resistance.[1] He addressed, March 21, 1861, a letter to Jefferson Davis in favor of a clerk about to join the rebellion,[2] similar in purport to the one given by Jesse D. Bright which caused his expulsion from the Senate. His personal as well as political relations with the secessionists ended, however, with the breaking out of the rebellion, and from that time he was not obstructive to the government. He sought at the outset a place in the military service, but found an impediment in Governor Andrew, who thought his record stood in the way of an appointment. Later, his ability as a publicist was brought to the aid of the government at Washington in important matters, and before the arbitrators at Geneva. He acted

[1] *Ante*, pp. 2, 3.

[2] This letter came to light while his nomination was pending, and compelled its withdrawal.

with the Republican party by his votes in the national elections of 1864, 1868, and 1872, and also approved the constitutional amendments and the measures of reconstruction.[1] His loyalty had been recently assumed by his confirmation as minister to Spain.[2] Withal, he was genial, and opened generously his stores of knowledge to all who sought them. Nothing in his life commended him to lawyers, as he had done almost everything but practise law. He was a judge of the Supreme Court of Massachusetts for only a few months, appointed by Governor Boutwell and confirmed by a majority of one, which was obtained only after considerable pressure on the council. The Massachusetts men, on whom Sumner most relied for advice, were all against Mr. Cushing's appointment, — among them F. W. Bird, Dr. S. G. Howe, Wendell Phillips, and George F. Hoar, who signified in letters to the senator their earnest opposition to a confirmation. One Massachusetts lawyer, P. W. Chandler, alone took a different view.

Sumner, as soon as the nomination was made, decided to support it by speech as well as vote; and this decision was almost as much a surprise as the President's action in making it. He knew all the points against Cushing as well as the others, and some of them were more likely to stand with him as vital objections than with most men. No two men could have been further apart than the two had been before the Civil War in their ideas of the Constitution and of political duty; but Sumner was catholic in his views of men, was disposed to credit their sincerity when they changed for the better, and bore no personal grudges, as others in his place might have borne against Cushing, who had been for three months an impediment to his first election.[3] Cushing had, in profession at least, come to adopt Sumner's views of the new order of things, and Sumner believed fully in the genuineness of his conversion. Indeed, his sincerity at this point of his career was as credible as at any other. He was by

1 Cushing supplied Sumner a brief, which stated his political action and his relations to the government during the Civil War. His letter to the President requesting the withdrawal of his name also contained a similar statement. New York "Tribune," Jan. 15, 1874.

2 Shortly after the withdrawal of his nomination as chief-justice, he left on his mission to Spain, which he filled creditably. He was always friendly to that country, and deplored the proceedings in the "Virginius" case.

3 R. H. Dana, Jr., in drawing Sumner's character in Faneuil Hall, March 14, 1874, stated that his action as to individuals was never affected by wounded sensibilities. "He did not deal with men as units. . . . He dealt with them by classes and races."

training and habit of mind a Federalist, and he would not have been troubled with the scruples of a strict constructionist in giving a wide scope to the Constitution. Of the validity of the civil-rights legislation he had, as it appears, assured the senator, even before the suggestion of his name for chief-justice. The two were in accord on foreign questions, particularly those pending with Great Britain. Identity of tastes in literature, a common interest in the history and present systems of Europe, and genial companionship at Washington were doubtless influences which helped to make it easy for the senator to look at Cushing in the best light. While it was a choice which he would not himself have made in the first instance, it was on the whole a better one than any other he thought the President likely to make.[1]

There was a sense of relief when the President made his fourth attempt to appoint a chief-justice in the nomination of M. R. Waite of Toledo, Ohio, who, though without a national reputation as a jurist, except in his part as one of the counsel at Geneva, was credited by those who knew him best as well equipped by study and practice, distinguished for the integrity of his mind and character, and possessing in a marked degree the judicial temper. The appointment was not thought at the time to promise a career equal to that of the great jurists who had before filled the office, but all felt that it avoided the risks involved in the previous selections. The result more than justified this expectation. Chief-Justice Waite held the office for fourteen years, and left a name which bears well a comparison with those of his predecessors.

Mr. Waite was confirmed by a unanimous vote in executive session. Sherman and Edmunds supported the nomination in debate; and besides them, Sumner alone took part in it. Without dwelling on the nominee whom, as he remarked, he had heard well spoken of, he passed to consider the greatness of the office, the qualities it called for, the duty of those who assisted in filling it, and the careers and services of former chief-justices. It was a field in which he was at home. He had been from his youth familiar with the characteristics and work of great judges; he had been drawn as a pupil to the subject by Story's recollections and descriptions; he had seen Marshall preside with his associates, and been admitted to their mess-room;[2] while still

[1] For a statement of a newspaper correspondent as to the senator's views, compare Boston "Journal," Jan. 12, 1874.

[2] *Ante*, vol. i. p. 125; Works, vol. iii. p. 145; Ibid., vol. viii. p. 238.

fresh in professional enthusiasm he had become the intimate friend of the most distinguished English judges, and had been a careful observer of French tribunals. It was easy for him to dwell for a half hour or more on a theme which had interested him for a lifetime; and the Senate always listened well — better than ever — when he was on a topic aside from the beaten track of political controversy. The speech made a great impression on the senators, and they freely spoke of it as the most interesting which he ever made.[1] One of the clerks of the body has written that "it was by far the most learned and interesting of any which I heard delivered by Mr. Sumner during the eight years I was connected with the Senate. I deplore and shall never cease to regret that it was never written out by the senator." Sumner's name is not recorded on the vote. As he was at the time still excluded from Republican counsels, he exercised the privilege of declining responsibility for appointments made by the Administration.[2]

After all, in accepting the President's second nomination, though to the surprise of Antislavery coadjutors, Sumner was right from his standpoint. The civil-rights measure, which he had supremely at heart, would have been safer with Cushing than it proved to be with the jurist finally appointed, who joined with his associates in holding such legislation unconstitutional.

Sumner wrote to F. W. Bird, Jan. 15, 1874: —

"I should never have nominated or recommended Cushing as chief-justice; but I was called to consider, his name being before the Senate, if I could vote for his rejection. Now, I know him well, having seen him for the last ten years constantly; and I know his positions on questions in which I am deeply interested. I trust him absolutely, and believe, if the occasion had occurred, he would have vindicated our ideas judicially far better than any probable nominee of Grant. I do not write in the dark, for I have talked with him on these questions and have seen his sympathy with me. You know that I do not cherish old differences and animosities. How many have I seen advanced to

1 No notes of the speech are preserved, and probably none were made. The outline of the senator's thought is likely to have been in his mind for a speech in support of Cushing's nomination. It is not easy to penetrate the veil of the Senate when sitting in executive session and obtain details of a debate. Three senators, however, and a clerk have given the writer their general impressions. The correspondent of the New York "Tribune," January 22, describes the speech as "one of the best and most impressive which he has delivered in the Senate." The Washington "Chronicle," March 13, referred to it as "something akin to inspiration itself."

2 It was incorrectly stated at the time of Chief-Justice Waite's death that Sumner spoke and voted against his confirmation; but he did neither. The correspondents of the New York "Tribune" and Boston "Journal," who were in personal relations with him, gave in those journals, Jan. 22, 1874, an entirely different impression.

the front who were once bitterly the other way! Knowing Cushing as I did, would it not have been mean and craven for me to turn against him, or to skulk in silence? This is not my way with friends. Such is not my idea of friendship. But no earthly friendship could make me put in jeopardy our cause. I confess that I am glad of the sensibility shown for the safeguards of reconstruction. Thank W. S. Robinson; but what shall we do with other possible nominees? Who will vouch for B. R. C.? And who will vouch for some accepted Republicans with whom technicality is a peril to principle?"[1]

While abstaining at this time from personal questions, Sumner in February spoke and voted against the confirmation of W. A. Simmons as collector of the port of Boston, doing so in conformity with the general opinion of the merchants and the best people. General Butler had presented the name to the President. The nominee belonged to a type of men then much in favor,—like Babcock (the President's secretary), Murphy (collector of the port of New York), and A. R. Shepherd (governor of the District of Columbia). The protests against the nomination from merchants and members of Congress were of no avail,[2] and the President refused to substitute another name. The Senate committee (Boutwell chairman) reported adversely to a confirmation. It was, however, supported in debate by Conkling and Carpenter; but even with their aid it would have failed except for the strenuous efforts of General Butler, whose influence was more effective with the set then controlling the Senate than any public man who was not a member of that body. Two years later, by a similar intervention, he obtained from the same body the rejection of R. H. Dana, Jr., as minister to England. Simmons's career in office was such that President Hayes refused to give him a second term; and his later connection with a department of the municipal administration of Boston appears in court records.

The Massachusetts Legislature, by large majorities in both houses, rescinded and annulled in February, 1874, the resolution of censure which in 1872 had been passed on Sumner for his bill against continuing the names of battles with fellow-citizens in the Army Register, or placing them on the regimental colors of the United States.[3] The rescinding resolution was sup-

1 A similar letter in justification of his intended vote for Cushing's confirmation, written to P. W. Chandler, was published in the Boston "Advertiser," March 12, 1874.

2 W. B. Washburn, governor of the State, Dr. Oliver Wendell Holmes, and John G. Whittier wrote to Sumner in opposition to the appointment. E. R. Hoar, G. F. Hoar, and H. L. Pierce, members of the House, opposed a confirmation.

3 *Ante*, pp. 550–555.

ported in the Senate by Dr. George B. Loring, the president, H. S. Washburn, and Gen. N. P. Banks. As its passage was assured from the outset, it encountered only a feeble resistance and created little excitement.[1] Gov. W. B. Washburn, who was heartily in sympathy with it, deputed J. B. Smith, a member of the committee which reported it, and Sumner's colored friend, to take it in person to Washington. Mr. Smith delivered the copies on March 6. The next day General Butler presented one in the House; but Mr. Boutwell being ill, its presentation in the Senate was delayed till the 10th. Less than two years thus intervened between the swift censure and the sober recantation, making a passage of history which will remain a perpetual lesson for commonwealths and statesmen.

The revocation of the censure contributed largely to the senator's cheerful mood of mind during the last month of his life.[2] He received many letters and calls of congratulation. Whittier wrote, February 17:—

> "The record of the Bay State is now clear. The folly of the extra session of 1872 is wiped out thoroughly. I am especially pleased, as like Senator Benton on a former occasion, 'solitary and alone I set the ball in motion.'"

Mrs. Harriet Beecher Stowe wrote after the senator's death:

> "How glad I am that the injustice was repaired in Mr. Sumner's lifetime! The offence he gave was only a consistent carrying out of his peace principles and of the policy of amnesty and forgiveness now becoming general, but which in the first heat of wrath New England could not accept. In a few years everybody will feel how grand and noble was the spirit of the very thing, especially from one whom the South had so deeply injured. It was the forgiveness of the martyr and Christian."

Henry L. Pierce, recently mayor of Boston, took his seat as a member of the House at the beginning of the session in December, 1873. He was a Free Soiler of 1848, and had been Sumner's earnest supporter during his service in the Senate. The senator welcomed to the capital one in whose friendship and discretion he confided absolutely, and had him frequently to dine *en famille*. Early in February Mr. Pierce gave a dinner at Wormley's to the Massachusetts delegation, at which Sumner was present.

[1] It passed the Senate, February 11, and the House, February 13. For comments of the press approving this action, see Philadelphia "Press," February 27.

[2] When asked on the evening of March 9 if he should speak on the subject in the Senate, he answered, "The dear old Commonwealth has spoken for me, and that is enough." Washington "Chronicle," March 13.

In February the senator prepared a revised edition of his speeches on civil rights, with the view of strengthening public opinion in favor of his bill. He also continued the editing of his Works;[1] and expressing to Longfellow his impatience at the slow progress of proof-readers and printers, the latter answered, January 30: "I do not wonder that you are worn out with tedious delays; but do not despair. Persevere to the end of this good work, if it is to have any end. The work itself is a noble monument to your life and labors in the cause of truth and right." He was from the beginning of the session revising, out of order, his "Prophetic Voices concerning America,"[2] for a separate volume commemorative of the centennial year of Independence; and this work was on his mind during his last day in the Senate. It was fitting that his thoughts should be to the end on the future of the country, and the part that was to be hers in the destiny of mankind.[3]

Among sympathetic friends from Massachusetts who called on Sumner during this session were Governor and Mrs. Claflin. Wendell Phillips, engaged to deliver lectures in Washington, came late in February, and again early in March. On Monday evening, March 2, they parted an hour after midnight. Sumner clung to Phillips, and would not let him leave sooner. The latter reminded him that he was to have a foot-bath, and Sumner said: "Well, I will take it if you won't go." They talked of old times, and of common friends at home. Within a week after, F. W. Bird, ever faithful and true to him, passed some hours with him. J. B. Smith was the senator's guest from the 6th to the 8th,—introduced by him one day on the floor of the Senate, and dining with him at Mr. Hooper's on Sunday.

The senator's views of the President underwent no modification, and he held to those he had expressed in 1872, never qualifying them in any respect; but he refrained after the election of that year, except in one or two confidential letters or a casual remark to an intimate friend, from any recurrence to the subject. E. R. Hoar said in the House, April 27, 1874: "I saw him frequently and familiarly during the last four months of his life, and wish to give my testimony to the gentleness and kindliness

[1] *Ante*, pp. 370, 371.

[2] *Ante*, p. 333. His last correspondence with Longfellow, which was in February, related to the choice of the preposition in the title.

[3] The volume was published a few weeks after his death.

of his temper during all that time, and to the fact that he uttered no word of harshness or censure in my hearing concerning any human being."[1] To E. L. Pierce, who on grounds of expediency had advised reserve as to the President, even in conversation, and also only brief remarks in presenting the rescinding resolution, if it was to be presented by himself, he answered, March 5: —

> "Your brother Henry will assure you that I am not unreasonable or impracticable. For a year and several months I have said nothing of the President, — not a word.[2] While an invalid last winter I was confirmed in this rule, which I have followed since. Therefore, anything attributed to me is an invention. Should the Massachusetts resolutions reach me, I shall present them in words as few as those you select; and to this conclusion I came sometime ago. Certainly, I shall say nothing controversial. I am now opposing the monstrosity of a world's fair linked with the commemoration of the national natal day. I have spoken once, and shall speak again briefly, perhaps in a few minutes."

Sumner's health during the early weeks of the session did not fall below what he had enjoyed at home during the summer and autumn. The severe cold which he contracted in New York in December lasted through January, and then disappeared. Shortly after his return from that city the pains on the heart recurred; but after two nights they left him, and he did not have recourse to the former remedies. Otherwise he had only slight reminders of the *angina*, and this after ascending the staircase to the Senate chamber. At the beginning of March he was waked by it one night, and suffered for an hour or more, until relieved by medicine; but for the week following he was very cheerful and free from pain. From the beginning of the session he kept well up to his former standard of work, — eleven hours a day, retiring at midnight. The debate on the bill for the centennial exhibition at Philadelphia, to be held in 1876 under the direction of a private corporation, with aid from the national and State governments, was the last one in which the senator participated. He was in favor of a national commemoration of the centenary of American independence, — the beginning, as he called it, "not only of the American republic, but of republican institutions on earth;" but he insisted that

[1] The editor of the New York "Evening Post," who had seen him shortly before, made a similar comment, March 12, 1874.

[2] B. P. Poore ("Perley"), who saw him daily, states Sumner's abstinence from reference to the President. Boston "Journal," March 12, 1874.

it should be a national rather than an international affair. He regarded with favor an exhibition of American progress as a part of the commemoration, but he was averse to the idea of converting it into a world's fair, which in his judgment, besides being premature so soon after that recently held in Vienna, could only succeed under the direct patronage and supervision of the United States government. He followed the bill closely, and on two different days (February 27, and Friday, March 6) spoke at length[1] in favor of further consideration and another reference to a committee. The Senate agreed with him, and voted the reference March 6. He was on that day full of spirit and earnestness. His contention with the Pennsylvania senators (Cameron and Scott) was sharp, though friendly. Flanagan of Texas,[2] however, who followed him, and closed the debate on Friday, reminded him of his recent divergence from his party, and his failure "to pull his State from her solid moorings." Sumner's remarks on that day were his last words in the Senate.[3]

On the night of Sunday the 8th his malady, which had been quiet for months, returned with its former severity.[4] The *angina pectoris* attacked him as soon as he retired at midnight, and kept him awake for four hours, — the physician[5] being obliged to resort to the former remedies. The Senate had adjourned from the 6th to Monday the 9th, when there was an adjournment, after a session of a few moments only, in recognition of Ex-President Fillmore's death. That evening he talked freely to a visitor[6] of European affairs and friends, of English politics and the new Germany; read aloud in deep rich tones of tender melody Milton's sonnet on the massacre of the Waldenses; and showed the parchment copy of the rescinding resolution of the Massachusetts Legislature, which had been sent him by the governor. In referring to an intended speech in favor of a

1 Congressional Globe, pp. 1830-1833, 2025-2027.

2 The same Flanagan who in a national Republican convention, when "the spoils system" was under discussion, asked, "What are we here for?"

3 His last words with Thurman referred to the good effect of this discussion. (Congressional Globe, April 27, 1874, p. 3400.) His last vote was on March 6 in favor of a national commission on the liquor question, for which he had spoken briefly two days before.

4 He dined on Sunday evening at Mr. Hooper's in company with Senator Anthony and J. B. Smith, bearer of the rescinding resolution.

5 Dr. J. Taber Johnson, who read a paper, May 4, 1874, at the Georgetown College on the *angina pectoris*, with special reference to the senator's case.

6 Washington Chronicle, March 13.

speedy return to specie payments, he emphasized as at other times his weariness. Later, during the same evening, the pains on the chest returned to some extent, and his physician being sent for he slept after the usual remedies, and felt on awaking less of reaction than usually followed them. Mr. A. B. Johnson, who had been his guest for some days, said: —

"At breakfast [Tuesday] he was more than usually genial. It was his custom to occupy himself with his mail on its arrival, but this morning it failed to come for nearly an hour after its usual time. Of all the breakfasts we had together for the past years, I remember none so pleasant. Waiting for the mail, his conversation was naturally desultory. It touched on many topics; he spoke of many persons, of various events, and always in a kindly, genial, pleasant tone."

He was greatly wrought up on the last two days of his going to the Senate by the report that Baez, who was already in New York, was to receive a complimentary dinner in Boston. He wrote letters to F. W. Bird, Governor Claflin, and E. L. Pierce, expressing indignation that a testimony of honor to the Dominican adventurer was possible. These were his last letters; and when they were received, the hand that traced them was lifeless. The dinner, for which arrangements had been made, did not take place.[1] Though his physician was reluctant to have him leave the house on Tuesday, the 10th, he went to the Senate, fearing that his absence would start a report of his illness in the newspapers, and wishing particularly to be present on that day, as Mr. Boutwell, not yet fully recovered, was to come to the Senate for the express purpose of presenting the rescinding resolution. He was in his seat when, during the morning hour, about 12.30 P. M., his colleague presented it.[2] Though senators and spectators turned their eyes to him, he seemed unconcerned; but he was so only in appearance, for the occasion was to him an event, and deeply moved him. This was the last matter in the proceedings of the Senate to which he gave attention. He received at once congratulations from senators on this testimony of his State. He went to the seat of Mr. Boutwell, who had risen to

1 Mr. J. W. Candler, being in the Senate chamber on Monday, casually mentioned to Sumner the proposed dinner; but finding how he felt about it Mr. Candler assured him that it should be given up, and at once sent a telegram to Boston to have it stopped. Dr. S. G. Howe had taken the leading part in proposing and arranging this compliment to Baez.

2 The account of the last two days of the senator's life is made up from the testimony of eye-witnesses, and of the correspondence of the public journals, particularly of the "Advertiser" and "Journal" of Boston, the "Tribune" and "Herald" of New York, the "Press" of Philadelphia, and the "Times" of Chicago.

return home, and with an affectionate manner, — putting his arm around his colleague's neck, — expressed concern for his health, and walking with him to the door of the chamber bade him "Good-by." Soon after, or perhaps somewhat earlier in the day, he had an interview with Charles Kingsley (they had not met before), whose daughter, with him at the time, wrote that notwithstanding former differences on American matters, "the moment the two came face to face all mistrust vanished, as each instinctively recognized the manly honesty of the other, and they had a long and friendly talk."[1] He conversed at his seat with H. L. Pierce, who had come from the House to advise with him in relation to the scandals growing out of the conduct of informers in New York and Boston, then undergoing investigation; and he invited Mr. Pierce to dine with him at six. He received Mr. John W. Candler of Boston in the Senate chamber, and sitting on the sofa spoke with him of the rumored dinner to Baez in Boston; and Mr. Candler assured him that it was not to take place. He mentioned his own weakness, and his fear of another attack of his malady, and said he should have to put matters already in his charge into Schurz's hands. He took a vacant seat next to that of Mr. Sargent, senator from California, and spoke with him in relation to the centennial exhibition bill, in opposing which they had co-operated, showing some sensitiveness as to anonymous letters he had received upbraiding his action upon it. He expressed his gratification at the recent action of the Massachusetts Legislature, and at the kindness that had cheered him on his last visit to the State. Taking a seat next to that of Mr. Ferry, senator from Connecticut, he mentioned to him symptoms of his malady which he had experienced during Sunday and Monday nights, and compared his own case with that of Mr. Ferry, who had suffered from a spinal affection, — complaining also of severe pain while they were conversing. He expressed to Mr. Schurz the fear that he should not be able to

1 Charles Kingsley's "Life," vol. ii. pp. 426, 427. Mr. Kingsley delivered a lecture in Washington the same evening on "Westminster Abbey." He wrote from Boston, March 23: "Sumner's death has been an awful blow here; I do not wonder, for he was a magnificent man. He and I were introduced to each other an hour before his attack. He was most cordial, and we had much talk about Gladstone and the A's [Argylls]. His last words to me were that he was going to write to the Duchess of Argyll the next day. Alas! I wrote to her for him to tell her particulars of the end." Mr. Kingsley is here in error as to the time of their meeting, as it was several hours before the attack; and in his address at Brooklyn, March 11, he mentions the time as "noonday." He was soon to follow Sumner, dying Jan. 23, 1875.

support him by a speech on finance as he had hoped. He conversed at his seat with Mr. Spofford, the librarian, who came to consult him on the authorship of Hargrave's "Argument in the Case of James Somersett, a Negro," etc., — a book with which he had been long familiar.[1] While in the Senate he felt again, at times severely, the pains in his side, referring to them in conversation as they came, and also in a letter, written the same day, to Dr. Brown-Séquard. To one or more with whom he spoke he said, "I am tired, tired." The employees in the Senate chamber observed signs of illness in his face and manner, and unusual glances as he finally left the chamber, suggesting the possible thought in his mind that he might not see again that familiar scene.[2] He left for his home, as had been arranged, at 4.30 P. M. with Mr. Hooper, whose carriage had come at that time.

Just before six Mr. Pierce and Mr. B. P. Poore found Sumner in his study. He spoke of the rumored dinner to Baez in Boston, and walked the room reprobating the idea. He had been writing letters, and when he had sealed the last one, they went below to the dining-room. The dinner was plain, and host and guests sat about two hours at the table, during which the conversation turned to the investigations already referred to, and the public sentiment in Boston — from which Mr. Pierce had just returned — as to the collector of the port recently appointed. The two friends, to whom the senator seemed in his usual health, noted a peculiar tenderness and gentleness in his manner. He referred, as Mr. Poore rose to leave, to his recent attack of the *angina* on the two previous nights, and the physician's opinion that his malady was not heart disease, but an affection of the spinal cord resulting from old injuries, and communicating with the heart through the net-work of nerves. Mr. Pierce remained behind a few minutes after Mr. Poore left.

Half an hour after Mr. Pierce left, the servants below heard a noise as from a fall; and one of them going to the senator's chamber found him supporting himself partly on the lounge, and apparently suffering severe pain.[3] Dr. J. T. Johnson was at once sent for, and he, followed immediately by his brother, A. B. John-

[1] He talked with Mr. Spofford about the title of his "Prophetic Voices concerning America," saying that Longfellow preferred the preposition "concerning" to "of."

[2] H. F. Hayden, Boston "Journal," June 4, 1883.

[3] The accounts of Dr. Johnson and A. B. Johnson, which were put in writing shortly after, and the oral statements of other persons present, have served in the preparation of this narrative of the senator's last illness.

son, reached the chamber at nine, or shortly after. The doctor found him lying across the bed, groaning, and in great agony. Morphine was administered hypodermically, and a quarter of an hour later the continued pain made another resort to it necessary. The sufferer said, presently: "There, now I have turned the corner; the pain is decreasing. I shall sleep." He then fell asleep, and those present retired to the adjoining room, — the study. The physician, who had been with him in several attacks, had seen none so agonizing as this. Twenty minutes later he awoke with another paroxysm. The morphine and other remedies for deadening pain and keeping up vitality were again applied. The narcotics produced a stupor, after which intervals of full consciousness were infrequent and brief. In the mean time disconnected expressions came from the sufferer, among which, "My book, my unfinished book!" references to the uncompleted edition of his Works, were distinguished. He said: "Doctor, this thing must kill me yet, and it might as well be now; for life at this price is not worth the having." At twenty minutes past ten, after the third attempt to relieve the pain, his pulse was found to be weak, wavering, and slow; and it was apparent that, though it might be prolonged for hours, the final struggle had come. His friends, Wormley and H. L. Pierce, who lived near by, were notified of his condition, and came at once to the house. A messenger was despatched for other professional aid, and Dr. W. P. Johnston arrived shortly. From that time to the end there was little change, save in the still weakening pulse, the diminishing sight, and the increasing coldness of the limbs. The heart beat now and then with a certain force, but for the last six hours of life there was no pulsation at the wrist. At intervals the sufferer came out of the stupor, and spoke briefly, but intelligibly. When the pain had gone, an awful sense of weariness remained, which he implored the physician to relieve. Friends at the bedside heard the words "tired," "weary." In the morning (Wednesday), before sunrise, a telegram was sent to Dr. Brown-Séquard, then in New York, summoning him to Washington; and at nine Dr. Barnes, then surgeon-general, and Dr. Lincoln came for a consultation, but it was of no avail. Judge Hoar and Mr. Schurz heard in the morning of their friend's condition, and came at once. At the bedside, serving as friendly nurses, were Wormley and G. T. Downing, both of the race whose champion he had been; and bending over him was his faithful secretary, Johnson, who was with him to the last. At hand through the day, except in brief absences, and often in his room, were H. L. Pierce, Judge Hoar, Schurz, Hooper, and Poore. Many waited in the study, — among whom were observed Mr. Blaine (the Speaker), Senators Morrill of Vermont and Windom, Montgomery Blair, and Frederick Douglass; and in the same room the chaplain of the Senate read passages from the fourteenth chapter of Saint John's Gospel, and offered a prayer. To Johnson and the two colored friends, who were raising him and changing his position, the senator expressed regret for the trouble he was giving them, saying to his secretary, "You must be very tired; but you can soon rest." To Judge Hoar who, while chafing his hands, said, "I am trying to warm you," he answered, "You never will." To several persons he spoke anxiously, in very few words, of his civil-rights bill. It was the one thought, and the last public thought, bearing heavily on his conscious or half-conscious mind. To Judge Hoar he said three times, varying the words somewhat, in the tone of earnest entreaty, "You must take care of the civil-rights bill, — my bill, the civil-rights bill, — don't let it fail!" and the judge assured him that all that was possible should be done to carry out his desire. Shortly after noon Schurz said to him, "Do you know me?" "Yes," he replied, opening his eyes; "but I do not see you." The weariness continued, and again the words, "Oh, so tired! oh, so weary!" passed his lips. At two he revived, and Dr. Johnson and some friends, who had been constant in their presence in the same or the adjoining room, left on some brief errands, expecting to see him again. Half an hour later he asked for morphine to relieve the weariness and give him rest; but Dr. Lincoln, who had been left in charge, did not think best to apply it. Shortly after, when the end was very near, he said to Judge Hoar, a near neighbor and relative of Ralph Waldo Emerson, "Judge, tell Emerson how much I love and revere him." The judge signified that he would give the message,[1] adding, "He said of you once, that he never knew so white a soul."[2] Almost directly some one said, "Mr. Hooper has come to see you." The dying man beckoned him to a seat, and said, "Sit down." These were his last words. He

[1] Judge Hoar fulfilled the commission at once. His letter to Mr. Emerson, posted the same day, and his clear memory, have assisted in the preparation of this account of the last scene.

[2] At Concord in 1856. *Ante*, vol. iii. p. 499.

then fell asleep, and woke a few minutes later, only to pass through one more convulsion. He died thirteen minutes before three. Johnson and Dr. Lincoln were supporting him in the final moment. Downing was holding his right hand, and Judge Hoar, who having gone out had returned just in time, took his left. There was only a single gasp, a sign from the physician that all was over, and a brief stillness broken by Judge Hoar who still held the dead senator's hand, saying, as he laid it down (Schurz entering at the moment), "Well done, good and faithful servant! enter thou into the joy of thy Lord!"

The tidings of Sumner's illness, announced on Wednesday morning, with the certainty of death at hand, was a shock to his associates in public life who had seen him in his seat the day before. The Senate, meeting at noon, adjourned on Sherman's motion immediately after the prayer, which referred to the senator as yesterday in the chamber with all the presence of his manly form, now prostrate and lying close to the edge of the dark river. The House continued its business, which was interrupted by the reading of telegrams stating his condition; and when the one announcing his death came, it adjourned. In both houses members lingered in conversation on the event. All that was possible was done to pay respect to his memory. The nation, by the action of the two houses the next day, took charge of the body to bear it to Massachusetts, and as soon as that duty was performed they adjourned. Conkling referred to "the vacant chair long held by a senator of distinguished eminence, and one of the most illustrious of Americans," and "joined in sincerity and respect" to pay tribute to "the long and remarkable life now closed."[1] Anthony, always most happy on such occasions, said: —

"It is an event which needs not to be announced, for its dark shadow rests gloomily upon this chamber, and not only upon the Senate and the capital, but upon the whole country; and the intelligence of which, borne on the mysterious wires that underlie the seas, has been already carried to the remotest lands, and has aroused profoundest sympathy wherever humanity weeps for a friend, wherever liberty deplores an advocate. The oldest member of this body in continuous service, he who yesterday was the oldest, beloved for the graces and the virtues of his personal character, admired for his genius and his accomplishments, reverenced for the fidelity with which he adhered to his convictions, illustrious for his services to the republic and to the world, has

1 The New York senator had for some time refrained from the annoying treatment of Sumner which he had heretofore practised.

crossed the dark river that divides us from the undiscovered country. Charles Sumner died yesterday. To-day, in humble submission to the divine will, we meet to express our respect for his character, our veneration for his memory. To-morrow, with solemn steps and with sorrowing hearts, we shall bear him to the Massachusetts which he served so faithfully, and which loved him so well; and to her soil, precious with the dust of patriotism and of valor, of letters and of art, of statesmanship and of eloquence, we shall commit the body of one who is worthy to rest by the side of the noblest and the best of those who, in the centuries of her history, have made her the model of a free commonwealth. But the great deeds which illustrated his life shall not be buried with him; and never shall the earth cover the immortal principles to which he devoted every energy of his soul, the consummation and vindication of which, as his highest reward, a gracious God permitted him to witness."

Judge Hoar, speaking in the House, with deep emotion said: —

"Wherever the news of the event spreads through this broad land, not only in this city among his associates in the public councils, not only in the old Commonwealth of which he was the pride and ornament, but in many quiet homes, in many a cabin of the poor and lowly, there is to-day inexpressible tenderness and profound sorrow. There are many of us who have known and loved the great senator whom this event unfits for public duties, or for any thoughts other than those of that pure life, that faithful public service, that assured immortality."

The country was startled by the intelligence. In the cities on Wednesday frequent bulletins made known the senator's condition. Merchants paused in the rush of traffic to contemplate the impending event. No death, except that of Lincoln, — it was a common remark at the time, — had for a long period so touched the popular heart. For days and weeks the press teemed with narratives of his life and delineations of his character. The Washington "Chronicle" (Forney's journal) recorded the titles, "Honored statesman, true patriot, generous friend;"[1] and recurring to the theme on the day of the funeral, said: "He was no master in the arts of the cunning demagogue. He never for himself asked the vote of a single person or solicited an office." The New York "Tribune" began its leader with the sentence, "The most dignified and illustrious name which the Senate has in recent years borne upon its rolls has disappeared from them forever." In its fuller estimate it said: "His dignity and impressive courtesy sat well upon a princely frame. . . . To the

[1] J. W. Forney, in his "Sunday Chronicle," March 15, paid two tributes to the senator. The New York "Tribune" published leaders upon him March 12 and 16, and April 30.

most elegant accomplishments he added the sternest purity of purpose and the highest conception of moral duty. Indeed, a somewhat familiar phrase, current during his lifetime, is none the less true because he is dead, — 'There is but one Charles Sumner.'" The "Evening Post" of the same city said: "One of the great spirits of the republic, if not already gone, is passing away. . . His name is woven with the same immortal wreath which binds the brow of the redeemed and regenerated republic." The "Independent" said: "History will select for peculiar honor her few grand names; and above the long, low level of shifty statesmen the form of Charles Sumner will long rise grand and solitary, like Teneriffe seen from the sea." Henry Ward Beecher, in the "Christian Union," wrote: "It is not too much to say that in the death of Charles Sumner the nation has lost a statesman of a type in which he had no peer. . . . The negro race will deplore the loss of their mightiest and faithfulest champion; and all the friends of justice and equality will lament the death of a leader whose flaming torch was carried high above all obscuring vapors, leading them ever in the sure path of victory."[1] The Springfield "Republican" began its leader with the words: "The noblest head in America has fallen, and the most accomplished and illustrious of our statesmen is no more." The Baltimore "American" wrote: "The foremost statesman of America has dropped suddenly from the ranks of his associates." These expressions typify the general estimate. His career was likewise the theme of foreign journals.[2]

The Massachusetts Legislature adjourned upon the announcement of the event, and the flags on public buildings were placed at half-mast. The governor the next day, by a message, recognized the death, "from the burden of a disease long and heroically borne," of "the great orator, scholar, statesman, philanthropist, the champion of universal freedom and the equality of man, . . . whose voice was that of an honest man, whose endeavors were those of an upright statesman, whose moral integrity stands out

[1] March 18. Later numbers contained other tributes to the senator.

[2] The English newspapers generally contained full sketches and estimates, the latter colored often, as might be expected, by the senator's maintenance of his positions on the conduct of Great Britain in the Civil War. G. W. Smalley reviewed the comments of the London journals in the New York "Tribune," March 30, 1874. The Duchess of Argyll wrote to Mrs. H. B. Stowe: "America seems to me so much farther off since dear Charles Sumner's death. How many must miss him!" And Mrs. Stowe added: "Sumner was appreciated in England for his real worth." The "Ny Illustrerad Tidning" of Stockholm, May 16, 1874, printed a sketch with portrait.

a sublime figure in these later years." The leading members of both houses paid tender tributes to his memory,[1] and the State assumed the charge of the burial. The Legislature of New York adopted appropriate resolutions; and various public bodies, municipal councils and associations, commercial, historical, and literary, joined in similar testimonies.[2] The citizens of Boston met in Faneuil Hall (the mayor in the chair) while the remains were on the way from Washington, and listened to eulogies. There were gathered on the platform, as speakers or spectators, all that was most distinguished in the noble city for public spirit, philanthropy, scholarship, and eloquence.[3] That historic hall was the fitting place for the commemoration of one who had so often pleaded there for causes of humanity and patriotism. It deserves also a record that the African race in different parts of the country testified by formal action its gratitude to its faithful tribune.

On Friday, a day rare even for March in its bleakness, the funeral services were held in the Senate chamber at midday. The procession, moving from the senator's home in the morning, was led by a body of colored people on foot, at the head of whom was Frederick Douglass. The immediate guard in charge from the police of the Capitol was made up in part of that race. The body lay for some hours in the rotunda, where thousands, only a part of those who pressed for admission, took their last view of it. It was then borne to the Senate chamber, where it was awaited by the President and Cabinet, the justices of the Supreme Court, the diplomatic corps, the high officers of the army and navy, with General Sherman at their head, and the members of both houses.[4] Prayers were offered by the chaplains; and in the absence of Vice-President Wilson, Mr.

[1] Among his eulogists in the Legislature were George B. Loring, Eben F. Stone, N. P. Banks, Charles R. Codman, and Charles Hale.

[2] At a special meeting of the New York Chamber of Commerce addresses were made by William E. Dodge, Jonathan S. Sturges, George Opdyke, Samuel B. Ruggles, E. C. Cowdin, and C. W. Field; resolutions were adopted, and a committee appointed to attend the funeral.

[3] The address of R. H. Dana, Jr., and the letters of C. F. Adams and Henry Wilson, read at the meeting, were interesting in their personal estimates and reminiscences. Other speakers were A. H. Rice, N. P. Banks, William Gaston, and Rev. E. E. Hale. Mr. Winthrop paid a tribute at the meeting of the Massachusetts Historical Society. The resolutions of the city government of Worcester were prepared by Governor Bullock; those passed at the town meeting in Quincy were drawn by Charles Francis Adams.

[4] Nearest to the head of the coffin sat the President and the Secretary of State; and nearest the foot, Senator Schurz.

Carpenter (in the chair) intrusted the remains of the deceased senator to the sergeant-at-arms and the Senate committee, to be conveyed under their charge to Massachusetts. The Senate adjourned, not to meet till the day after the burial. The vacant seat, to which all eyes turned, was draped, and on the desk in front was a vase of flowers. Among the abundant floral tributes was a cross from the President's daughter.

The special train bearing the remains, the committees of Congress, the Massachusetts delegation, and certain intimate friends of the deceased, leaving Washington at 3 P. M., arrived in New York late in the evening. Independence Hall in Philadelphia and the City Hall of New York were tendered by the authorities of those cities as places of temporary deposit, where the people might pay honor to the dead statesman; but the arrangements did not admit of these pauses on the way. The committee and their sacred charge were for the night at the Fifth Avenue Hotel, and the next morning the journey was resumed. A delegation from the New York Chamber of Commerce — Messrs. Low, Chittenden, Cowdin, and Field — now joined the procession. The governor of Connecticut sent a staff officer to accompany it through the State. The arrival at the Springfield station, which was draped with mourning emblems, was signalled by minute guns and the tolling of bells, and the train was met by a committee of the Legislature of Massachusetts. Here and at Worcester and other stations the people gathered as the train passed. It reached Boston early in the evening, where a multitude of people awaited its arrival. The body was taken to the State House and placed on a dais in the rotunda in sight of the memorials of Washington and the flags of Massachusetts regiments. In the dimly lighted hall Senator Anthony addressed the governor: —

"May it please your Excellency, we are commanded by the Senate of the United States to render back to you your illustrious dead. Nearly a quarter of a century ago you dedicated to the public service a man who was even then greatly distinguished. He remained in it, quickening its patriotism, informing its councils, and leading in its deliberations, until having survived in continuous service all his original associates, he has closed his earthly career. With reverent hands we bring to you his mortal part that it may be committed to the soil of the renowned Commonwealth which gave him birth. Take it; it is yours. The part which we do not return to you is not wholly yours to receive, nor altogether ours to give. It belongs to the country, to mankind, to freedom, to civilization, to humanity. We come to you with the emblems of mourning which faintly typify the sorrow that dwells in the breasts which they cover. So much we must concede to the infirmity of human nature. But in the view of reason and philosophy, is it not rather a matter of high exultation that a life so pure in its personal qualities, so high in its public aims, so fortunate in the fruition of noble effort, has closed safely, without a stain, before age had impaired its intellectual vigor, before time had dimmed the lustre of its genius? May it please your Excellency, our mission is accomplished. We commit to you the body of Charles Sumner. His undying fame the Muse of History has already taken in her keeping."

On Sunday, as the body lay guarded by colored soldiers, thousands of citizens passed through the State House. In the churches, not only in New England but elsewhere in the country, the character of Sumner was the theme of the sermon. On Monday, the day of the funeral, business was suspended in Boston. Mourning drapery and inscriptions of honor to the dead were displayed on stores and dwellings and public buildings, bells were tolled, and the flags in the harbor were at half-mast.[1] The trains brought from the country throngs of citizens who passed through the State House or stood in mass in the neighborhood. Never in Boston, noted for good taste, never perhaps in the country, had there been an equal display of floral emblems like those which decorated the capitol where the remains lay in state, and King's Chapel where the last rites were performed. Hayti, whose minister had come from Washington on the errand, sent her offering in gratitude for the senator's early espousal of her right to a place among nations, and for his chivalrous maintenance of her cause at a later period. On the afternoon of Monday the body was removed to the church where the Sumner family had worshipped. A dense mass of people stood about the State House, in the vacant spaces around it, on the Common near by, and at the church. The services were brief, impressive, and faultless in taste. The clergyman, Rev. Henry W. Foote, read selections from Scripture which fitted most aptly the life and character of the dead man. The long procession passed down Beacon and through Charles streets on its way to Mt. Auburn, witnessed by great numbers who rendered freely the tribute of reverence and love which in other days had been withheld. Such honors Boston paid to her son, who had done his duty to country and mankind, as well when she frowned as when she approved. In death he was borne through

[1] There was a similar recognition of the occasion in many cities and towns of New England.

scenes familiar to his life, — through the streets of his native city, over the Cambridge bridge pressed so often by his feet, by the college he loved, by the homes of Story and Longfellow, along the shaded road he had so often trod with classmates and teachers, to that final resting-place of Boston's cherished dead, whose consecration he had witnessed in youth, there to renew companionship with Ashmun, Story, Greenleaf, Fletcher, Channing, Felton, Agassiz, and Everett, and to await the coming of Hillard and Longfellow. Here, beneath a stalwart oak, close by parents, brothers, and sisters, in the presence of classmates, friends, and of a sorrowing multitude, late in the afternoon when darkness was setting in, the "Integer Vitæ" and "A Mighty Fortress is our God" were sung; the words of comfort, "Blessed are the dead who die in the Lord," were spoken, and the benediction given.[1] No one of kin was there; and it fell to him who writes these lines to direct the closing of the grave, and to remain till the undertaker's work was done.

Congress set apart April 27 as a day for eulogies upon the deceased senator.[2] His personal qualities, his character as a public man, and his place in history were reviewed in both houses by those who had known him well in personal relations or had watched closely his career. His limitations were stated to be "a predominance of the ideal over the practical," too great persistency in pressing his favorite measures, his indisposition to yield minor points for the sake of common action, and the habit of exacting the full measure of what he believed to be wise and just, — a catalogue of qualities which may be virtues or blemishes, according to the critic's point of view. From every quarter came testimony to his kindness in personal intercourse; his cordial greeting and genial smile; his freedom from personal hatred and revenge; the amenities of his home where he carefully and skilfully suppressed topics of difference; his scrupulous observance of the rules and courtesies of the Senate; his fidelity and courage; the rectitude and elevation of his purpose; and the absolute purity of his private and public life. A colored member recalled the warm and friendly grasp of his hand and the welcome he always gave. All accorded him the foremost place in the history of his country as "the undoubted leader of the political opposition to slavery."

[1] Longfellow, Whittier, Holmes, and Emerson stood by the open grave: and there also stood Wilson, the Vice-President.

[2] The New York "Tribune," April 28, said of the eulogies: "One cannot fail to be impressed by the commanding presence of the dead senator in the midst of his late associates."

In the Senate, Morrill of Vermont gave him the title of "the model senator." Sargent of California testified to "his courage, his manliness, his singleness of purpose, his high achievement," and to his influence as "the chief inspiring cause and guiding spirit" in the Antislavery revolution. Pratt of Indiana dwelt upon "the purity and simplicity of his character," his courtesy and kindness to all who approached him, his lofty and transparent character, and his position for twenty-two years as a living power in Congress, where he had influenced, in perhaps larger degree than any other, the opinions of men. Thurman, the Democratic leader, avowing his fixed disagreement with him on the questions which had divided parties, recognized his fidelity to his lofty ideal, the charm of his personal intercourse, the absence of offensive egotism in his manner, his habit of discussing in private political questions with opponents without loss of temper or want of respect for their views, and said: —

"And when we add that in the conversation of the deceased there never was anything low or vulgar, but on the contrary, intellect, refinement, and taste marked all that was said, we contemplate a character whose amiability, high breeding, and politeness will ever command our respect and admiration. . . . I speak over his grave my belief that he was great in intellect, profound in learning, sincere in his convictions, true in his friendships, urbane and amiable in his intercourse, and wholly unassailable by corruption."

Sherman, wiser in his judgment of contemporary public men than perhaps any one of our time, speaking with discriminating judgment, and bearing witness "to the purity of Sumner's motives and the lofty purpose of his warfare," at last acknowledged by old antagonists as well as coadjutors, said: —

"The heat of recent contests in this body, unavoidable where debate is free, and where honest opinions boldly expressed necessarily produce some strife and personal feeling, — this was passing away, and Charles Sumner was by the judgment of his associates here, by the confidence of his constituents, by the general voice of the people, the foremost man in the civil service of the United States. This eminence is assigned him for unblemished honor, for high intellectual capacity improved by careful study and long experience, and for public services rendered here with unwavering fidelity and industry, with conscientious consistency, contributing in a large degree to the liberty of millions of slaves, and to the advancement of the power, position, and prosperity of the whole country. We ought not to exalt the dead with false eulogy; but I feel after long association with Mr. Sumner in the public service, continued since December, 1855, sometimes disagreeing with him and conscious of his imperfections, that I would not do justice to his memory did I not place his name and fame above that of all in civil life who survive him. . . . He was profoundly versed in the science of government. It is a common error that he confined his attention to the slavery question; far from it. No one in this Senate was so familiar as he with all the laws and usages that govern our intercourse with foreign nations. He was deeply interested in questions affecting the internal improvement of the country, and of late years has carefully studied all financial questions, and has contributed to their solution."

In the House the eulogies, cordial and affectionate like those of the Senate, were from Dawes and the brothers Hoar of Massachusetts, Conger of Michigan, Kelley of Pennsylvania, Phillips of Kansas, Rainey of South Carolina, Nesmith of Oregon, and notably Lamar of Mississippi, a former Confederate officer.[1] Nesmith, a Democrat, who had served with him in the Senate and was rarely in accord with him in that body, closed his eulogy thus: —

"His chair in the Senate, to which all eyes were turned whenever any great question agitated that grave body, will never be filled by a public servant more pure in his motives, more elevated and courageous in his action, or truer to his convictions. Let us keep his virtues in remembrance. May his monument be of spotless marble, for it cannot be purer or whiter than his life."

Wilson, the Vice-President, visiting the Capitol a few days after his former colleague's death, referred in a company of intimate friends to the sense of a great loss which was felt there, and said: "Taking Sumner altogether, he was the greatest man in the Senate while I was a member of that body. Other men exceeded him in some particular thing, as Fessenden in a debate or an argument on a law question; but taking him 'by and large,' he was the greatest man in the Senate in my time."

The city of Boston and the Commonwealth of Massachusetts, with due ceremonies, commemorated the senator; and on these occasions Carl Schurz and George William Curtis were the orators.[2] Whittier and Longfellow embalmed him in verse. The people placed a monument over his grave at Mt. Auburn, and his statue in the Public Garden of Boston. He coveted, though it never tempted him, the favor of mankind in his own day and thereafter; and well he might be content with the final judgment. Even when burdened by undeserved reproach, assured of what it would be, he wrote to a friend a year before his death: —

"Meanwhile I sometimes meditate on life and its hardships, and the inconstancy of men, — never forgetting the true. There is one satisfaction which

[1] The Boston "Advertiser," April 29, 1874, singled out Mr. Lamar's tribute as "the most significant and hopeful utterance that has been heard from the South since the war."

[2] Curtis's eulogy is printed in Harper's Weekly, June 20, 1874.

cannot be taken from me: I have tried to do my duty and to advance humanity, keeping Massachusetts foremost in what is just and magnanimous. When I am dead, this will not be denied."

Sumner's will, written in autograph and signed the day before he left for Europe in 1872, after certain personal legacies, mostly tokens of friendship, bequeathed his pictures and engravings to the Art Museum of Boston, his books and autographs to Harvard College,[1] and divided his remaining estate between his surviving sister and his Alma Mater, prescribing that the half for the college should be for the benefit of the library, and applied to the purchase of books relating to politics and the fine arts, and adding this explanation: —

"This bequest is made in filial regard for the college. In selecting especially the library, I am governed by the consideration that all my life I have been a user of books; and having few of my own, I have relied on the libraries of friends and on public libraries; so that what I now do is only a return for what I have freely received."

Two of Sumner's literary executors, Messrs. Balch and Pierce, requested their other associate, Mr. Longfellow, to write the senator's life, but failing physical power compelled him to decline. The three then united in inviting successively Motley, Whittier, Dana, and Curtis to be the biographer; but the three former declined on account of inadequate health, and the fourth on account of the pressure of other work already in hand. Finally, at the request of Mr. Longfellow and Mr. Balch, their other associate undertook the duty which he had desired to have fall to better hands. He confesses, in these final words, his debt of gratitude to many who have aided him in his task; but most of all to the late George William Curtis, scholar, gentleman, and patriot, worthy to be placed with Sumner among the supporters of truth, liberty, and good government, who for ten years or more preceding his last illness, which ended Aug. 31, 1892, was always ready with counsels and friendly offices, even to the reading of the entire manuscript.

MILTON, MASSACHUSETTS,
*March* 11, 1893.

[1] His gift to the college for an annual prize essay on peace has been noted. *Ante*, vol. ii. p. 382.

# NOTE.

THE following is a memorandum of the known likenesses of Sumner arranged as nearly as may be in chronological order: —

1. The earliest representation of any kind is Crawford's bust, taken at Rome in 1839, now in the Boston Art Museum (*ante*, vol. ii. pp. 94, 265).

2. Crayon drawing, by Eastman Johnson in 1846, belonging to the Longfellow family, and engraved for this Memoir (vol. ii.). It is held by the artist to have been a good likeness at the time, but others express a doubt.

3. Crayon, by W. W. Story; made from sittings in 1851 at the request of the seventh Earl of Carlisle, with some final touches from Seth W. Cheney, as Story left for Europe before it was quite finished (*ante*, vol. iii. p. 64; iv. p. 261). It has been kept at Castle Howard, Yorkshire; it is a good likeness, and represents Sumner at his best, in the fulness and strength of manhood. Prescott wrote to Sumner in January, 1852: "You cannot expect a better likeness in every sense." It was lithographed by S. W. Chandler before it was sent to England. Epes Sargent wrote of the print, which was published in 1854, that it was a capital likeness, and that nothing could be better. The biographer has a copy of a photograph of the picture, taken at York since the senator's death.

4. Daguerreotype, by Southworth and Hawes, of Boston, in 1853; taken for, and owned by, the biographer, and engraved for this Memoir (vol. i.).

5. Daguerreotype, taken a few months later at Lowell; owned by Mrs. W. S. Robinson.

6. Portrait, by Walter M. Brackett; painted from sittings in 1854, and now in the custody of Edward A. Presbrey, Brookline.

7. Portrait, by W. Wight; painted in the winter of 1856–1857, and given to the Boston Public Library in 1874; has been engraved by S. A. Schoff. The engraving does not follow the portrait closely, and is thought better than the portrait.

8. Portrait, by Wellman Robinson; painted in 1856, now belonging to Harvard College.

9. Photograph, taken in London in 1857 for the late Henry Richard, M. P. (*ante*, vol. iii. p. 547).

10. Portrait, by W. Willard; painted in twenty-one sittings in August and September, 1865, and still in Mr. Willard's possession at Sturbridge, Mass. The artist made a copy in 1877, which is owned by Thomas Mack, of Boston. He also painted the head for Abraham Avery.

11. Bust, by E. A. Brackett; given to Harvard College in 1857.

12. Bust, by M. Milmore; finished late in 1865 (*ante*, vol. iv. p. 199), and greatly commended at the time by Wendell Phillips, W. M. Hunt, John T. Sargent, F. V. Balch, and Lydia Maria Child (see her "Letters," p. 187). The original was placed in the State House, Boston, and the artist's reproduction of it was given by the State of Massachusetts to George William Curtis in recognition of his eulogy on the senator. This copy has been on exhibition at the Metropolitan Art Museum in New York. A picture of the bust is given in Harper's Weekly, June 20, 1874.

13. Medallion, by Margaret Foley; taken from sittings in 1865, and given by the family of James T. Furness to Harvard College.

14. Photographs, by Black of Boston; one reproduced in Harper's Weekly, March 24, 1866; and another in 1869, reproduced in Harper's Weekly, March 28, 1874, and engraved in Sumner's Works.

15. Photograph, by Brady of Washington, in 1869; reproduced in "Every Saturday," March 4, 1871 (a weekly newspaper published in Boston), in "Memorial History of Boston," vol. iii. p. 391, and in this Memoir (vol. iii.).

16. Photographs, by Warren of Cambridge, about 1870–1871, — one standing, one sitting with a cane, one holding a French newspaper, and one reproduced in the Memorial volume published by the city of Boston in 1874.

17. Portrait, by William M. Hunt, not from sittings, but following Allen and Rowell's photograph.

18. Portrait, by Edgar Parker, for which sittings were given in Boston in 1873. Mr. Parker painted three portraits, — one now belonging to the city of Boston, another to the Wallace Public Library of Fitchburg, and the third still belonging to one of the artist's relatives.

19. Two unfinished portraits, by William Page, for which sittings were given in New York in 1872 or 1873.

20. Photograph, by Allen and Rowell of Boston, the last ever taken, made late in 1873; is reproduced in the Memorial volume printed by the State in 1874, and in this Memoir (vol. iv.), and has been engraved by the treasury department at Washington. The photographers have also issued it enlarged.

21. Full-length portrait, by Henry Ulke, for which sittings were given in Washington in 1873–1874; last likeness from life. It was ordered by Hayti in recognition of the senator's opposition to the San Domingo annexation, and now hangs in the Senate chamber in the Haytian capitol. The artist painted two other portraits at the same time, all three alike representing Sumner speaking in the Senate, — one full-length and owned by John B. Alley, of Lynn; and the other three-quarters in length, and given by James Wormley to the State of Massachusetts. This last hangs in the State Library (Senate Doc., 1884, Nos. 272, 323; Boston "Transcript," Sept. 27, 1883).

22. Various busts and statues in plaster, offered for a bronze statue, for which Thomas Ball's design was accepted. The statue was erected in the Public Garden in Boston in 1878.

The oil paintings of Sumner were generally unsatisfactory. Those by Ulke, however, represent well his figure, dress, and attitude in debate, and give a better idea of him in his later years than any other paintings.

Washington
3d Jan '73

My dear Mrs Claflin,

I am touched by yr kind good letter.

The best place for me is my own house where I can take my medicines & pursue the treatment prescribed by Dr Brown-Séquard; but I am none the less grateful for yr hospitable invitation.

Meanwhile I have

times meditate on life, & its hardships & the inconstancy of men, — never forgetting the true.

There is one satisfaction which cannot be taken from me: I have tried to do my duty & to advance humanity, keeping man foremost in what is just magnanimous. When I am dead this will not be denied

Believe me dear
Mrs Claflin,
Sincerely yours,
Charles Sumner

---

Note.—See *ante*, pp. 607–608.

# APPENDIX.

# APPENDIX.

## I.

## THE REJECTED TREATY FOR ST. THOMAS.[1]

SCRIBNER'S Magazine (November, 1887) contained a paper entitled "A Diplomatic Episode," by Miss Olive Risley Seward, which undertakes to narrate the negotiations with Denmark for the purchase of the islands of St. Thomas and St. John in 1866-1869 by Mr. Seward (then Secretary of State), and the connection of the Senate committee on foreign relations (Mr. Sumner being chairman) with its consideration and failure of ratification. With many words, the introduction of superfluous incidents and assertions of facts not verified by reference to sources, she gives an air of mystery to what was a plain transaction and a very simple question. A map is inserted, as if to produce an optical illusion, on which a number of straight lines converge to St. Thomas as a common centre of islands, continents, and commercial marts, just as all roads once led to Rome.

Impartial authorities describe St. Thomas as exposed to hurricanes passing once in twenty years over it, and doing great damage; with very frequent earthquakes coming with serious shocks at intervals; with often-recurring droughts; with no running stream, and only one small spring, the only resource for fresh water being the storing of rain; its only present productions "a few vegetables, a little fruit, and some guinea grass," insufficient for one twentieth of its inhabitants; its population "one tenth white, two-thirds black, and the remainder mixed;" its utility for commercial purposes dwindling from year to year, and its imports falling off one half from 1870 to 1880; abandoned as a rendezvous by the British Mail Company in 1885, with other important lines following its example. From the end of our Civil War, during which its trade had a temporary stimulus, its descent in importance has been constant.[2] This is the prize which Mr. Seward won for us, but which was lost by the mysterious indifference and perversity of all the statesmen of his time! Yet

[1] This reply by the biographer to Miss Seward's paper was published in 1889. In this reprinting a few omissions are made to prevent repetition of what has already been stated (*ante*, vol. iv. pp. 328, 329).

[2] American Cyclopædia. Encyclopædia Britannica. Article, "St. Thomas."

among those statesmen no one, except himself, thought the island worth having at any price, or being taken as a gift for any purpose of peace or war. In a foreign war it would have been useless for offence and difficult of defence; and while during the Civil War, when the Confederates held most of our Southern Atlantic coast, one of the Antilles would have served a purpose as a coaling and supply station, it is no part of national duty to make military preparation for civil war, certainly not a part of ours, with the nation consolidated by the abolition of slavery. Of St. John little need be said here, as scarcely anything was said of it during the discussion. In extent it is somewhat larger than St. Thomas, but so unattractive and repelling that it was "an almost abandoned island."[1] Providence, as if to save us from a wild venture, gave in the midst of the negotiations a triple warning by an earthquake, a tidal wave, and a hurricane, in quick succession.

Ours, too, is a country of the temperate zone, and the aspirations of its people are continental. There has been among us a healthy resistance to going farther southward than we have now reached, or seeking islands either in the Atlantic or the Pacific, — an instinctive reluctance, as shown in the later case of San Domingo, to enter on a career of tropical extension, with dangers and embarrassments to free institutions which could not be measured in advance.

The underlying thought of "A Diplomatic Episode" is that the Senate of the United States, in withholding assent to Mr. Seward's negotiation, put our country in the position of acting in bad faith to Denmark. This contention has no basis in fact or political ethics. The Constitution of the United States, of which all the world in doing business with us must take notice, confers on the President "power by and with the advice and consent of the Senate to make treaties, provided two-thirds of the senators present concur." It confides this great power — an incident of sovereignty — to the President and Senate, each acting with an independent responsibility and discretion, neither having the right to abdicate in favor of the other. This discretion of the Senate has been freely exercised in dealing with strong as well as with weak nations, — for instance, in the rejection of the Johnson-Clarendon treaty on the one hand, and of the San Domingo treaty on the other. All publicists are agreed (among our own the authors of the "Federalist," as well as Story and Wheaton) that treaties bind neither party in law or in honor, until finally ratified by all the bodies in which the authority is placed by the constitution of the State.

Whence comes this gloss on the Constitution that the treaty-consummating power is now wholly lodged in the Executive, and that the Senate has lost its constitutional right of withholding its advice and consent? If this notion were to prevail, some future secretary, chief of a bureau not established by the Constitution, swaying some future Andrew Johnson, might carry our dominion into Mexico, to the Isthmus, to the Amazon, even to Cape Horn, to say nothing of countless islands; and the Senate, representing sixty millions of people, would have to stand aloof in amazement, shorn of all power to arrest the madness! Aside from the merits of the question, the fate of the St. Thomas treaty was of great advantage, in that it established against a monstrous assumption of

[1] C. H. Bithome to Mr. Seward, May 13, 1867.

one-man power the prerogative of the Senate to act on all treaties with absolute freedom of judgment, unhampered by Executive initiation and pledges.

The purchase of Alaska from Russia is not analogous to the attempt to acquire St. Thomas. In the one case the territory was continental, in the other extra-continental and insular; in the one case lying to the north, in the other tropical; the one bringing wealth in fisheries and furs and fair climatic conditions, while the other was without resources, actual or undeveloped, and even subject to derangements of nature unparalleled within the same limited space; the one checkmating the colonial empire of Great Britain in the Northwest, and opening the way to the dominion of the continent which has been the thought of far-seeing statesmen like Sumner and Cobden, while the other was to bring to us two worthless islands of the size of a county, two of the thousand in the Caribbean Sea, with a waste of money in peace and complications in war. Alaska exceeded half a million square miles, and the price was $7,200,000; while the bargain with Denmark called for $7,500,000 for a meagre area of only seventy-five square miles.

It is true that Mr. Sumner added to his main argument for Alaska, made April 9, 1867, the consideration that "the dishonoring of the treaty," as he called it, at that stage would involve a serious responsibility. But he was very careful to confine this *obiter dictum* to the case in hand; and Miss Seward very deftly, as well as abruptly, cuts short her quotation from his speech when she reaches his emphatic exclusion of all other treaties from any implied sanction. He went on to say that "had the Senate been consulted in advance before the treaty was signed or either power publicly committed, *as is often done on important occasions*, it [the Senate] would be under less constraint," — a clear intimation that this should be the practice in such cases. And then, to make his *caveat* emphatic, he said: "Let me add, that, while forbearing objection now, I hope that this treaty may not be drawn into a precedent, at least in the independent manner of its negotiation. I would save to the Senate an important power justly belonging to it;" and he added, "This treaty must not be a precedent for a system of indiscriminate and costly annexion." He also expressed his anxiety that our expansion should come from natural processes, without war and *even without purchase*, the latter to be justified only under peculiar circumstances. Mr. Sumner in this *caveat* gave Mr. Seward and the Danish negotiator timely warning as to the determination of the Senate to hold fast to its constitutional prerogative, which they had no excuse not to keep in mind in the following October when they made their definite arrangement.

No one knew this constitutional limitation better than General Raasloff, the principal negotiator on the Danish side. He had lived among us almost as a citizen when engaged in engineering enterprises, and had already represented his country in the United States as consul-general and minister. He wrote our language without foreign idiom, and spoke it almost without foreign accent. He knew our polity as well as we know it ourselves. Indeed, unlike the case of Russia, where the Czar holds the power absolutely and exclusively without hindrance from any one, the constitution of Denmark contained a limitation analogous to that of our own, making the treaty-consummating power dependent on the decision of the Rigsdag. The treaty was itself explicit, reserving, as conditions, ratification by our Senate and by the Danish

Rigsdag, and also by the islanders themselves. Rejection by any one of the three would have involved no breach of faith.

It was natural that the Danish negotiator, whose personal pride as well as whose party interests were at stake, should make the point of good faith; but he labored hard in insisting upon it when pressed before the committee on foreign relations by Mr. Fessenden's question: "Would, in your opinion, the United States have a right to complain if your Rigsdag had refused their consent to the ratification of the St. Thomas treaty?" His answer was that in that event the Rigsdag would have been dissolved, and a new election ordered; and then, if the new Rigsdag followed the action of its predecessor, the Cabinet itself would have resigned. And this was all the satisfaction he could suggest as possible, — clearly none for a nation disappointed in a bargain and insisting on a point of good faith. He thought, too, that we should still have had the right to complain that his government had trifled with us "in having neglected to secure beforehand the ratification of the treaty," — an intimation that Mr. Seward should have made himself surer of his footing, and have consulted the Senate in advance, as pointed out to be the proper course by Mr. Sumner in his speech on the Alaska purchase.

Whatever color of justice there may have been in Denmark's point of good faith came from Mr. Seward's unauthorized assurances that the enterprise was sure of approval in the Senate; and according to the Washington correspondence at the time, the committee on foreign relations, at their hearing Jan. 28, 1869, thought them to be "an egregious blunder" when General Raasloff made them the basis of his appeal. Mr. Seward said to the Danish negotiator, June 28, 1866, that "the Executive could always count upon the assistance of Congress in matters of this kind, provided the proceedings had been correct," and in other communications gave the Danish government to understand that there need be no fear as to the ratification. Arguments in newspapers and pamphlets at the time put the case for ratification chiefly on the ground that Mr. Seward had committed us to the treaty by his ill-considered and precipitate action. Raasloff's intimate friends laid the blame of his misfortunes on Mr. Seward. Mr. G. V. Fox, writing to Mr. Sumner, Jan. 31, 1869, concerning General Raasloff's appeal for his good offices to assist the treaty, suggested that the foreign relations committee invite his (Fox's) opinion, and said: "This course seems to me the only one which enables me to satisfy my friend, General Raasloff, that I have attempted to aid him in the most unpleasant position in which Mr. Seward's diplomacy has placed him. I can see that there is no possibility of success for him, and that the rejection is fatal to his future in his own country." Raasloff himself, writing to Mr. Sumner, Jan. 12, 1869, and referring to the effect of the rejection on his own career, speaks of himself as "having been more than anybody else (Mr. Seward, of course, excepted) instrumental in bringing such a calamity and humiliation upon my country." The parenthesis, which is his own, is significant.

The writer of the "Episode" insinuates that prejudice against Seward as well as Johnson accounts for the want of welcome which awaited the St. Thomas treaty in the Senate. It is unnecessary to resort to this theory, for the objections against the treaty would have been equally fatal if it had been negotiated by a secretary and a President who were retaining the confidence of the country. The general disfavor into which Mr. Seward had fallen with Republicans may have had something to do with producing the popular distrust of the Johnson-Clarendon negotiation, but it does not appear to have affected the convention with Denmark. One thing is certain, — that the senator at no time prejudged the secretary's diplomatic enterprises, but uniformly came to their consideration with an open mind. They had parted politically, but the spell of an old friendship and common memories was still on Mr. Sumner, probably also on Mr. Seward. Never was Mr. Sumner inhospitable to Mr. Seward's plans or wishes, even after the contest between Congress and President Johnson had begun. As soon as Mr. Seward had negotiated the treaty for Alaska, a few hours before it was signed, he sent for Mr. Sumner, March 29, 1867, to come to his house the same evening to confer with him and the Russian minister concerning it. With what vigor Mr. Sumner sustained that treaty is a part of history. When shortly after its ratification I asked him how he came to take so much interest in it, and to prepare so laborious a speech in its defence, he stated several reasons of a public nature; but first in order of time, he gave Mr. Seward's earnest desire to carry it through.

Mr. Sumner recognized always the duty of co-operating cordially with public officers with whom he might not at the time be in political sympathy. He continued during Johnson's Administration to call often at the state department when Mr. Seward was secretary, and to keep himself informed as to its business and needs, and in debates, even during the heats of the impeachment controversy, contended so vigorously for Mr. Seward's recommendations as to clerical force and the contingent or secret service fund as to invite the suggestion from some associates that he was too much the partisan of that department. Any one curious in such matters may verify this statement by consulting the Congressional Globe's reports for January 30 and 31, February 4 and 7, and June 22 and 23, 1868.[1]

The "Episode" makes and reiterates against the Senate the charge of delay in acting on the St. Thomas treaty, — a charge which lies against the negotiators rather than the Senate. More than three years passed between Jan. 1, 1865, when Mr. Seward opened up the subject of the purchase to General Raasloff at Washington, and the time when the treaty and necessary papers were ripe for the consideration of the Senate. The intervening period was occupied with inaction on both sides, principally the Danish; more or less skirmishing between the parties as to the government from which the first offer of amount should come; prolonged silence and inattention of the Cabinet at Copenhagen after Mr. Seward's first offer, which our minister at that court was unable to break;[2] finally, instead of an acceptance of Mr. Seward's offers, one counter proposition and then another; the Danish minister at Washington going home and leaving no successor; the insistence of Denmark after the price had been fixed on a vote of the islanders, which in view of what they were could be of no significance, and which involved vexatious questions and postponements, so that the treaty was not signed till Oct. 24, 1867, and not submitted to the Senate till December, and the vote of the islanders was not

[1] *Ante*, vol. iv. p. 295.

[2] Mr. Yeaman's letters to Mr. Seward, January 21, March 13, April 27 and 30, and May 2, 1867.

communicated till Jan. 17, 1868. Although in December, 1867, when the treaty was referred, Mr. Sumner promptly requested the papers from the state department, they were not forthcoming for seven weeks; and when they had been printed and were available for use, the time fixed by the treaty for ratification (Feb. 24, 1868) had expired, and an extension of time became necessary. So sluggish were the Danes in the whole business that our minister, Mr. Yeaman, could not control his impatience, and wrote of the national characteristic: "In everything, from cobbler to king, they are the most deliberate and leisurely people in the world." In the purchase of Alaska, on the other hand, between the first broaching by the Russian minister and the final signature there was less than a six months' interval.

No one saw more clearly than Mr. Seward the peril to which the delay at Copenhagen exposed the treaty. Its only chance of approval in this country grew out of the peculiar exigencies of a *civil* war, when a long southern coast was held by the insurgents; and that period was receding. Military considerations were diminishing in force, and ambition for territory was not the passion of the hour. Every day, too, the Administration, of which Mr. Seward was the inspiring leader, was losing the confidence of the country. He telegraphed Jan. 19, 1867, to Mr. Yeaman, "Tell Raasloff, haste important." In a letter to Mr. Yeaman, Aug. 7, 1867, he urged on the Danish government "promptness in the pending negotiation as essential to success;" and in letters September 23 and 28, a month before the convention was signed, he emphasized the hazard to which the procrastination at Copenhagen had exposed the whole business, as in the mean time the people of the country had lost interest in the acquisition of a naval station in the West Indies, and were turning their attention to other and cheaper projects. He wrote: —

"The desire for the acquisition of foreign territory has sensibly abated. The delays which have attended the negotiation, notwithstanding our urgency, have contributed to still further alleviate the national desire for enlargement of territory. In short, we have already come to value dollars more, and dominion less."

It was evident that Mr. Seward, before the treaty was submitted to the Senate, and even before the convention was signed, had lost faith that it would be ratified, — not because of any peculiar adverse influences in that body, but because the American people had become unfriendly to such a purchase. It was a dead treaty when Mr. Seward handed it to the Senate, as he well knew at the time. This appears from his letters to Mr. Yeaman, as well as from his letter to Mr. Sumner, Nov. 9, 1868, when replying to the latter's inquiry as to another matter, he wrote: —

"It is true, on the contrary, that instructed by the debates of Congress and the tone of the public press during the past year, I have declined all recent suggestions in regard to the acquisition of naval stations anywhere in the West Indies, especially the mole of St. Nicholas."

The author of the "Episode" suggests foreign influence at Washington operating against the treaty. This, of which she gives no proof, is the creation of her imagination. When, where, and on whom was it exercised? Was Mr. Seward approached in that way, and does this account for his losing heart in the project? Was Fessenden bought up by some German lobbyist? Did

British gold find its way into Cameron's pockets? How were Morton, Patterson, Harlan, Casserly, and Sumner taken care of? One, without recurring to Horace (*Nec deus intersit*, etc.), ought to be wiser than to resort to such an unnatural explanation.

The Danish negotiator, in his letters to Mr. Sumner and in his speech at Copenhagen, named as his only difficulties "the prevailing ignorance of facts" (which he hoped to remove by proof of the value of the islands as a naval station), and the contest between the President and Congress; but he gave no hint of foreign influence. In fact, the only influence of this kind exerted at Washington was in favor of the treaty, through the attractive qualities of General Raasloff, whom all wished if possible to serve, and the refined hospitality which he freely dispensed. Besides, he argued his case on two different days before the committee on foreign relations, and did what he could to affect public opinion. He called to his service as counsel to enlighten senators a gentleman (the Marquis de Chambrun) who combined social favor with professional accomplishments. He employed an able and well-known writer (Mr. Parton) to prepare a pamphlet argument in favor of ratification, and supplied him with documents concerning the treaty which had been printed by the Senate as confidential; and he sent this pamphlet to senators and to the leading journals of the country, in which it was reviewed. Articles in favor of the ratification appeared in Paris contemporaneously in the "Moniteur" and "Pays," which indicated a prompting from the same source. It is safe to say that a pressure of such various kinds by a foreign power to carry a treaty in the Senate is without precedent.

The paper under consideration seems to attribute to Mr. Sumner altogether the failure of the treaty in the foreign relations committee, for the reason that he was "almost implicitly followed by it." He had indeed with the committee the weight which comes from a combination of perfect integrity, sound judgment, large experience, and technical knowledge; but the other members — Fessenden, Cameron, Harlan, Morton, Patterson, and Casserly — were not men naturally of his type, none of them antislavery leaders like himself, every one of them at times strongly differing from him. Mr. Fessenden was at that time antipathetic to him, and disposed to be critical of what he did. If Mr. Sumner was unfair, if he did aught unbecoming a senator, there were sharp eyes to follow him. Mr. Fessenden, it may be remarked, was the member most demonstrative against the St. Thomas treaty, and he was one of the only two senators who voted against the Alaska purchase. Clearly Mr. Sumner's "over-mastering advocacy" in favor of this last treaty did not influence the senator from Maine; and the latter's resistance to the St. Thomas project came equally from his own independent volition.

There are insinuations in Miss Seward's paper which are unworthy of any kinswoman of the distinguished statesman whose name she bears, and which he, if living, would be the first to rebuke. In three passages, at least, she imputes to Mr. Sumner an unworthy and deceptive silence, and a hypocritical purpose to mislead General Raasloff, and give him false hopes of a ratification of the treaty. In all this, as well as in the other charge of "smothering" the treaty ("secretly and silently done," she says), there is no truth. Happily, the amplest record evidence is at hand to disprove them. As many as twenty-five letters or notes from General Raasloff to Mr. Sumner, — from December,

1868, to May, 1869, the period during most of which he was at Washington urging the ratification, — are preserved, and are in my hands.

The purchase of St. Thomas did not attract Mr. Sumner, but he kept an open mind concerning it, and as far as possible held his judgment in suspense. He had a regard for Denmark as a nation, and a particular friendship for Raasloff, and sought to give every opportunity to him to prove the value of the acquisition. He arranged for Raasloff personal interviews with his colleagues, and (what was quite exceptional, if not unprecedented) formal audiences with the committee Jan. 26 and 28, 1869; obtained documents for him which he sought in order to remove objections to the purchase; distributed pamphlet arguments for the treaty among the members of the committee, which Raasloff supplied; and intervened at his request to obtain the opinion of Mr. G. V. Fox, which was known to be in favor of the purchase. He was the one member of the committee to whom Raasloff applied freely for good offices, which were uniformly granted; nevertheless, he was never converted to the treaty. Raasloff's surviving friend, General Christensen, says that he frequently spoke of Mr. Sumner's connection with it, "always regretting that he could not win the sympathy of that statesman for the transaction."

The committee suspended action, but this was in order that Mr. Seward and Raasloff should have the fullest opportunity to complete all proofs and supply all considerations in favor of the purchase. Mr. Seward never called for a decisive vote, and both he and General Raasloff knew that there was no time when the treaty would have been carried, and they thought with diminishing hope that there might be a favorable turn. It was a ratifying vote which they desired, not a vote with the certainty of a rejection. The non-action of the Senate was at Raasloff's express instance, as proved by a contemporaneous record. Mr. Fish wrote to Mr. Sumner, March 28, 1869, a note containing only these words: —

Dear Sumner, — Raasloff does not wish any action on his treaty. He will probably see you.

H. F.

The imputation of sinister silence on Mr. Sumner's part is effectually disproved by General Raasloff's contemporaneous letters. In December, 1868, probably late in the month, he arrived in Washington with a view to press the treaty. At once he began to send to Mr. Sumner notes and letters about the treaty, as well as congratulations on New Year's Day, and invitations to dine, and they were meeting from day to day. On the evening of Jan. 11, 1869, Mr. Sumner told him frankly that there was little or no chance of his success with the committee and the Senate, and sympathizing with him in the probable effect of his failure on his position at home, said: "I am sorry for you; you are in a tight place," etc., — words which were repeated by Raasloff in a note to Sumner the next morning, and which he said had kept him awake a good portion of the night. In the same note, and in another written a few days later, he said that he was fully prepared for the worst, and had all along been prepared for it. He felt, however, constrained to push his case, and went before the committee on the 26th and 28th of the same month, and otherwise did all he could to save it, but in vain. Toward the last of March he left Washington, never to return. Just before his departure, Mr. Sumner gave him the portrait of Thorwaldsen, which he acknowledged March 28, 1869, saying "it would be very dear to him as a *souvenir d'amitié*." The gift was made after Mr. Sumner had forewarned Raasloff of the doom of the treaty, and had, neither in the mind of giver or receiver, as Miss Seward suggests, any import of favorable action upon it. Raasloff wrote from Copenhagen, May 19: —

"Let me thank you once more for the beautiful portrait of Thorwaldsen. It is much admired, both on account of the historical interest attaching to it and as a work of art. I hope I may be allowed to keep it."

He had gone from our country not to return, but his thought of Mr. Sumner was as affectionate as ever.

An authentic statement of General Raasloff's appreciation of Mr. Sumner's relations with himself and of the senator's conduct concerning the treaty appeared in the general's speech made at Copenhagen after his return, when all active pressure for the ratification had finally ended. The occasion was a celebration of the amalgamation of some telegraph lines. Writing to Mr. Sumner, May 19, 1869, a few days after the speech in which he had mentioned the treaty and Mr. Sumner personally, he said: —

"I felt very much tempted to say more about you than I did, but I know you shrink from ovations and public compliments, all of which, however, you cannot expect to escape. I did not say, as the telegraph (I am told) has it, that you were in favor of ratifying the St. Thomas treaty; but I said that you had done more than anybody else to save the treaty from an untimely death."

Here is a testimony from the person who was most interested and best informed as to Mr. Sumner's course, which assigns to him more effective aid than any given by any one, including Mr. Seward himself, "to save the treaty from an untimely death," — testimony directly in the teeth of Miss Seward's intimation of sinister silence, double dealing, and suppression. No other and contrary statements, it is presumed, were ever made by him; for if made, they would show him to be other than the honest and truthful man he was believed to be. The general, as still further showing his absolute confidence in Mr. Sumner, bespoke his friendly intervention in the embarrassed relations between Prussia and Denmark, and said: —

"I find to my great regret that we are not making any progress in our relations with Prussia; and I wish you would lend a hand in bringing about a really good understanding and sincere neighborly relations between us and the North German Confederacy. We (I mean my colleagues and myself) are anxious for it; but every time we make an overture or an approach, we are repulsed in such a manner as to make it almost impossible with self-respect to make new attempts. . . . I really know no other man in the world who could as well as you, being the friend of both, help us out of this unsatisfactory state of things, and thereby remove one of the existing causes of war."

A European who could solicit in such terms the friendly intervention of an American citizen in the relations between his own and another kingdom must have held in remarkable confidence and esteem the foreigner to whom he applied.

Miss Seward deals disingenuously with this speech. She cites it as made in June, 1869, in the Rigsdag, whereas it was made May 13 at the banquet; but exact time and place are unimportant, except as bearing on her method of dealing with facts. She quotes three sentences from the speech, and at the end of the first one there are stars, indicating an omission. The next sentence was the following, at the beginning of which she was careful to stop: —

"It must, however," continued General Raasloff, "not be forgotten that the treaty has not been rejected; its ratification has only been postponed; and that it is so is owing to the stand taken by some few wise statesmen, foremost among whom is my friend the Hon. Charles Sumner, one of the most prominent and experienced statesmen of the age, for many years the leader of the Senate in regard to foreign relations, and a man who never loses sight of the regard and consideration due from one friendly nation to another."

Miss Seward might well omit this sentence, as it spoils entirely her theory. The omission of Mr. Seward's name from the speech is significant. He had led the Danish negotiator into a pitfall, and his name therefore received no grateful mention. Raasloff's career as a public man ended with his diplomatic failure, and with the fall of his ministry as the consequence; and leaving his country he passed the rest of his life abroad, chiefly in Paris, and died in the suburb of Passy, Feb. 14, 1883, at the age of sixty-seven. He was in New York in May, 1872, but he had become soured by disappointment, and kept aloof from Washington.

Within a month before General Raasloff left Washington in 1869, there was a new President, General Grant, and a new Secretary of State, Mr. Fish, neither of whom showed favor to the treaty, the former dismissing it summarily as "a scheme of Seward's, and he would have nothing to do with it;" and the latter sending to Mr. Sumner notes which indicated an adverse leaning. As appears by one bearing date Oct. 8, 1869, Mr. Fish peremptorily refused, at the urgent request of De Bille, the new Danish minister, to ask for another extension of time for the ratification, leaving De Bille to ask for it, and took pains to guard against any expression in favor of its ratification. A few months later, Jan. 28, 1870, he transmitted to Mr. Sumner, for use at his discretion, a letter from R. C. Kirk, minister resident at Buenos Ayres, dated Dec. 13, 1869, who, in an account of a recent visit, described St. Thomas as "one of the most God-forsaken islands; . . . the great majority of its inhabitants filthy-looking negroes," subject to earthquakes, one of which occurred on the morning of his arrival, and the island itself as "not desirable even as a gift."

Miss Seward undertakes to give matters of record concerning the treaty which at the time she wrote were under the seal of secrecy. But upon the removal of the injunction, Jan. 5, 1888, on Mr. Hoar's motion, it was found that Mr. Sumner did not, as she states, indorse "the one word 'adversely' on the treaty," and that neither he nor any one indorsed that or any other words upon it, it being absolutely free from any notes whatever. Even the wrapper contains only a memorandum of the reference to the committee. The words "suspension of action" which she puts in quotation marks as Mr. Sumner's recommendation, are her words, not Mr. Sumner's or the committee's.

The committee took definite action at the time General Raasloff left Washington finally. It laid the treaty on the table March 30, 1869, and recorded on its minutes the words, "The understanding being that this was equivalent to rejection, and was a gentler method of effecting it." For his sake it held back its report for a year, and then cleared its docket. By the official transcript from the record it appears that on March 24, 1870, Mr. Sumner reported the treaty "with the recommendation that the Senate do not advise and consent to the ratification of the same," with a similar report on the proposed extension of time. Miss Seward's fidelity to facts will be understood on recurring to her article, where she says that "the matter was never brought before the Senate, and may be said to have been smothered in committee!" The record, as now open to the public, it may be added, shows Mr. Sumner's faithful attention to the business in repeated motions for references of documents.

Of the committee on foreign relations to which the St. Thomas treaty was referred, Cameron of Pennsylvania, Patterson of New Hampshire, and Harlan of Iowa, alone survive. Their testimony has been requested by the writer, and after a reading of Miss Seward's "Episode," is cordially given. It should be read in the light of her charges and insinuations of "smothering" and dishonorable reticence, and her assumption that the argument for the acquisition was so self-evident and conclusive that it became "morally impossible to report openly against it," and that neither the committee nor any senator "could assign a reason for an adverse report." This is not the first time that an advocate sorely pressed finds it easier to assume than to argue.

Mr. Cameron writes: —

"The rejection of the treaty was quite a simple matter; there was no mystery about it. No person on the foreign relations committee was in favor of the treaty. The case of Alaska was very different, in which one of the chief motives was to show our regard for Russia for the part she had taken during the war, and to strengthen the Northwestern possessions. The St. Thomas purchase made no impression upon the committee or upon the public either. The smothered attack upon Mr. Sumner in this [Miss Seward's] article is most unjust." [1]

Mr. Patterson writes: —

"I have read the article by Miss Seward with a good deal of interest and more surprise. The Senate generally, I believe, regarded the treaty for the purchase of St. John and St. Thomas about as General Grant did, — as one of Seward's schemes, and determined to have nothing to do with it. Some denied the constitutionality, and more rejected the policy, of entering upon a system of annexing non-contiguous territory and outlying islands to the United States."

He states that the vote of the islanders was regarded by senators as a mere farce, and that not being fit for self-government, how they were to be governed when annexed to a self-governing people was a problem not easily solved; that in time of war the island would have been the first object struck at by an enemy, and would have required for its defence a great increase of our military and naval force; and that the finishing stroke to the treaty, already meeting with no favor anywhere, was given by a contemporaneous earthquake and tidal wave. He adds: —

"The reason why the Senate did not act promptly on the treaty, but allowed it to die on its hands, was a desire, if possible, to save the liberal ministry of Denmark, which had been drawn into that measure, against the natural effect of its rejection."

[1] Mr. Cameron died June 26, 1889, at the age of ninety. Mr. Patterson and Mr. Harlan are still (1893) living.

Mr. Harlan in his letter concurs with his associates in the opinion that "as a mere commercial transaction the proposed purchase at the price named would have been a great folly;" that "as a naval depot and coaling station St. Thomas would be of doubtful value to the United States;" and "as it did not appear to the committee to be specially desirable as a military station, they decided unanimously, I think, not to recommend the ratification of the treaty." As to the charge of unjustifiable delay on the part of the committee, he writes: —

"In this case the committee were not, I think, dilatory. Ample but only necessary time was taken to make the necessary investigations and inquiries, and for the interchange of views; and when they decided not to recommend the ratification, it was thought that it would seem less harsh towards the other power to permit the time for exchanging ratifications to expire than to formally reject the proposed cession."

In relation to the inquiry as to whether the chairman, Mr. Sumner, acted fairly in the transaction, Mr. Harlan adds: —

"None who ever knew Mr. Sumner could have any doubt on that point. He was the soul of candor and frankness. And if he had been disposed to act otherwise in the case referred to, he could not have trifled with the Senate committee on foreign relations as then constituted."

It is perhaps worthy of observation that the Senate appears to have unanimously acquiesced in the views of the committee.

Such is the true version of the "diplomatic episode," or rather of the diplomatic fiasco, and a final question may be asked: If the acquisition of St. Thomas was so manifestly desirable as Miss Seward represents, how does it happen that no one at Washington or among the people during the twenty years since Mr. Seward left office has said a word to revive the scheme? A good thing does not die so easily; there will always be true men and wise men to appreciate what is of enduring value. We have since had six Presidents, — Grant, Hayes, Garfield, Arthur, Cleveland, and Harrison, — and, not counting Washburne, five Secretaries of State, — Fish, Evarts, Blaine, Frelinghuysen, and Bayard; but none of them has coveted this island of the Caribbean Sea, rifted by earthquakes, swept by cyclones, and submerged by tidal waves, the imagined centre of universal commerce and a necessary outpost for our national defence! Journalists and merchants have been alike silent. Foreign nations who were suspected to be greedy spectators have turned away from the prize. St. Thomas remains still a Danish spinster, as she has been for two hundred years, unwedded and unsought. One lone sigh over her continued isolation comes from the namesake of a statesman who saw visions of her fairness and her dowry hidden altogether from the eyes of his own and of this generation.

# II.

## A SENATOR'S FIDELITY VINDICATED.[1]

THE defeated attempt to annex San Domingo to the United States, the recall of Mr. Motley from the mission to England, the removal of Mr. Sumner from the head of the committee on foreign relations, on which he had long served, the rupture of friendly intercourse subsisting between him and Mr. Fish, are likely, both in their public and personal aspects, to prove matters of permanent interest. While many contributions have been made to the discussion, the more elaborate are the letter of Mr. Fish, Oct. 29, 1877, printed in the Boston "Evening Transcript," the reply of one of Mr. Sumner's literary executors through the same journal, November 28, and a paper by Mr. J. C. Bancroft Davis, in support of Mr. Fish, dated Jan. 3, 1878, and appearing in the New York "Herald."

Various persons have at times had relations to the controversy, but lately it has been treated as one which chiefly concerned Mr. Fish and Mr. Sumner. Their respective claims, however, to the public esteem are not the pending question. Mr. Sumner, in 1870, resisted in the Senate with all his power the annexation of San Domingo as fraught with evil to the colored race, and as promoted by measures which violated international law, while Mr. Fish strenuously supported it in the Cabinet. Whether, in this or other measures on which they may have differed or agreed, one or the other is entitled to the higher rank as a statesman, is not now in dispute. The issue is a narrower one, involving chiefly the validity of the reasons alleged at different times for Mr. Sumner's removal, which the public has quite generally attributed largely to the intervention of the President, and of his Secretary of State Mr. Fish. The discussion sweeps a wider field, but it begins and ends at this point of contention.

In an interview with a reporter at Boston, Oct. 19, 1877, Mr. Fish stated that "with regard to the alleged negligence of Mr. Sumner while chairman of the committee on foreign relations, it was a fact, susceptible of proof from the Senate records, that drafts of treaties [meaning treaties], from eight to eleven in number, remained in the hands of the committee for several months, some of them, as near as Mr. Fish could remember, for more than two years." In reply to a written request for a list of the treaties referred to, he answered by letter, October 29, printed in the Boston "Transcript," enumerating nine, — one each with Mexico, Colombia, Guatemala, Nicaragua, Austria, Salvador, and Great Britain, and two with Peru, — as "transmitted to the Senate for its action, and referred by that body to the committee on foreign relations, while Mr. Sumner was its chairman, and which remained unacted upon at the time when he ceased to be such chairman;" and later in the same letter he referred to the nine treaties as having "failed to receive *the consideration of*

[1] This paper was printed in the North American Review, July–August, 1878. Its points are given briefly *ante*, vol. iv. pp. 478–481.

*the committee* at the time when Mr. Sumner's appointment as its chairman expired." By note of November 7, merely correcting a date, Mr. Fish appeared a third time before the public. In an interview held at Garrison's November 10, with a reporter of the New York "Herald," he treated with ridicule the suggestion ascribed to Wendell Phillips that Mr. Sumner had "prepared and digested" the treaties referred to, which thus made final action only a formality, and replied, "with a certain bland smile of contempt," that "on the contrary he had pigeon-holed those treaties; he would pay no attention to them whatever." Again, by letter to the "Herald," November 10, evening, he supplemented with further statements what he had said to the reporter in the afternoon; thus, in the brief period of three weeks, coming before the public five times to make and support charges against Mr. Sumner, and each time with no appearance of being a reluctant witness, — certainly without being governed by any self-imposed rule of silence or reserve.

Before October, 1877, Mr. Fish seems to have been, not publicly but privately, making the same charge against Mr. Sumner. In an interview held early in September, *en route* from London to Edinburgh, General Grant stated that he had said to George William Curtis, at Long Branch, in 1871, that "Mr. Sumner had not done his duty as chairman of the committee, because he had hampered the business of the state department by pigeon-holing treaties for months;" and the Ex-President added: "I told Mr. Curtis that there were nine or eleven treaties before the Senate from the state department that had been there several months, and had been in Mr. Sumner's hands, but had never been laid before the committee. I wrote from the spot — Long Branch — to the state department, and to my own surprise there proved to be more treaties than I had said that had been in Mr. Sumner's own hands for a longer time than I expected. . . . The work of that committee when Mr. Cameron took charge was in a most deplorable state, due entirely to Mr. Sumner's obstructiveness and dilatoriness." General Grant thus indicated the state department as the source of his information, and from it he obtained a formal list of the "pigeon-holed" treaties. Mr. Fish, at its head, being the only officer connected with it who was brought into constant communication with the President, and having six years afterwards been quick to support a renewal of the charge, appears as the author of the original charge which General Grant repeated with so much emphasis in his interview.

The charge of suppressing important public business, thus authorized by Mr. Fish, and many times repeated by himself and others who relied on him as authority, is assuredly a very grave one. It implied official unfaithfulness, and even moral delinquency. Whether a statesman, living or dead, was able, wise, or far-sighted is always a fair question for discussion; but the charge of moral delinquency, such as Mr. Fish originated and spread, and that too against one who could no longer speak for himself, could only be justified by indubitable evidence. Stated so positively and in such a quarter, it was likely to obtain general credence; and but for a fortunate suggestion that the Senate records should be searched and made known, this calumny might have remained forever attached to an eminent senator.[1]

[1] Mr. Fish's letter to the Boston "Transcript" adroitly gave only dates of references to the committee; and the omission of dates of reporting suggested to Mr. Sumner's friends a further inquiry as to the omitted dates.

On November 21 the injunction of secrecy was removed from the Senate proceedings, on the motion of Senator Hoar of Massachusetts, and Mr. Fish's repeated charge found to be untrue. Mr. Sumner's chairmanship ended March 3, 1871. It was found that he reported the Mexican protocol (referred Dec. 8, 1869) on Jan. 11, 1870; the Darien Canal treaty with Colombia (referred April 1, 1870), on July 13, 1870; two treaties with Peru, and one each with Guatemala and Nicaragua (all four referred Dec. 8, 1870), on Jan. 12, 1871; one with Salvador (referred January, 1871), on March 1, 1871; one with Great Britain (referred Feb. 28, 1871), on March 1, 1871; leaving only the Austro-Hungary treaty (referred Dec. 14, 1870) unreported, — eight of the nine treaties being thus reported by Mr. Sumner, which Mr. Fish charged he had "pigeonholed" in his committee. Not only did he report them, but he reported them with more than the despatch customary with committees. Five of the nine were kept with the committee only about a month, and that month a broken one, which included the holiday recess; and a sixth was reported the very next day after it was received. The treaty with Salvador was with the committee seven weeks, the last fortnight of which Mr. Sumner was prostrated with a severe illness which kept him from the Senate. The Darien Canal treaty remained with the committee only three months, although it is still pending in the Senate, which has not been able to come to a conclusion upon its merits for the period of nearly eight years since it was reported.[1] When we consider the deliberation and obstructions to which public business is subjected, particularly in Congress, Mr. Sumner will be regarded by all who study these dates as having dealt with his share of it with extraordinary despatch. Senator Hoar, recently in this Review, recorded his amazement at the proof of diligence which this record gives, all the more impressive because of the various duties pressing on Mr. Sumner, and his belief that no other committee could show such a record.

Eleven days after Mr. Fish had appeared by letter in the "Herald," his charge against Mr. Sumner was shown to be untrue by the solemn record of the Senate. What, then, was his duty? He had made the charge to Ex-President Grant, who was spreading it in Europe and the United States. He had repeated it by letters and interviews. He had made it, not against a living rival, but against a dead senator, one with whom he had often held sweet counsel. The code of honor, the Christian canons, the instincts of human nature, commanded an instant retraction and apology under his own hand. The case did not admit of a vicarious defence. There are some duties which cannot be delegated, and one is that of recalling a false imputation against the character of another, and most of all when cast at the speechless dead. But all at once Mr. Fish was silent. One who had five times in three weeks come before the public, and chiefly as a volunteer, all at once stopped writing letters and meeting interviewers; and from Nov. 21, 1877, when his accusations were shown to be untrue by the publication of the Senate journal, he has maintained an impenetrable reserve. Withdrawing at this interesting stage of the discussion, he seems to have obtained a substitute to take his place. Mr. J. C. B. Davis, his former assistant secretary of state, spares time from new duties on the Court of Claims to write a paper for the "Herald" in his behalf. This

[1] Still pending in 1893, twenty-three years after it was reported.

mode of justifying by proxy has two advantages: it relieves Mr. Fish of the unpleasant necessity of stating at the outset how he came to make such untrue charges against a dead senator, and further enables him to avoid responsibility for new positions taken in his defence, which may be found as unsubstantial as his original charge of "pigeon-holing" treaties. It is even better for the purpose than "interviewing," in which the interviewed, when his statements have been shown to be contrary to the fact, with great facility changes his positions, coolly throwing on the interviewer the responsibility of misapprehending him. Not, however, from Mr. Davis or any other substitute, but from Mr. Fish himself, under his own hand, an explanation is required by every law of moral duty.

Mr. Davis's method of narration is certainly unique. He relates some conversations where plainly he was not present, others in a way that leaves the reader in doubt whether he is reciting another's story or his own; talks of the thoughts, anxieties, remembrances, and states of mind of Mr. Fish, as if the two were one; and recounts frequent and long interviews at Mr. Fish's house (matters concerning which Mr. Fish is the only competent witness), and in some instances he differs radically from Mr. Fish's versions. He undertakes to say, giving no authority, what took place between Mr. Sumner and Mr. Fish, Jan. 13, 1871, at Mr. Sumner's house, when they two were alone together, and what Mr. Fish said to senators when he (Mr. Davis) does not claim to have been present. The paper abounds in vague phrases, as, "it was said;" "it was no secret;" "one Republican senator went so far;" "the President and Mr. Fish stated to more than one senator;" "there appeared on the part of leading Republican members," — in all which the generality of allegation and suppression of names make any attempt to test the truth of the statements impossible. If he is a witness, let him qualify by showing presence and opportunity; and if he is only acting as amanuensis of Mr. Fish, let him say so. A paper of such a character as he has given carries no weight as evidence.

One part — and a large part it is — of Mr. Fish's as well as of Mr. Davis's statements ought to be eliminated from the discussion. They write with facility of the *conversations* of Mr. Sumner which are not now subject to his denial, or the different version he might give; and they undertake to put in testimony of this kind which they did not give in his lifetime. Recent statutes deny to a party the right to testify to the conversations of a deceased adversary, for manifest reasons of public policy. The rule is justly applicable to other than legal controversies, and should be applied more stringently against parties whose previous allegations against the deceased have proved untrue. *Falsus in uno, falsus in omnibus*, is a maxim which, though subject to limitations, holds a legitimate place in the law of evidence. The public will require better proof of Mr. Sumner's conversations, manner, and thoughts than such testimony from such a source.

Mr. Davis in his paper jumps the charge of "pigeon-holing" with an acrobat's dexterity. He says that "at or about the time the change [Mr. Sumner's removal] took place, the President and Mr. Fish stated to more than one senator that the current business of the department of state had been neglected in the Senate during the present session, and particularly that no treaty which had been sent to the Senate during the session which followed Motley's recall *had been acted on.*" This shifting of positions is adroit, but it will not answer its purpose. Mr. Fish's uniform charge, as given to the public and to General Grant, is "pigeon-holing" in committee, not inaction in the Senate; and the list of nine treaties which he gave was one which he alleged had *not been reported*, — not a list of treaties reported, which were *not pressed* in the Senate. If Mr. Fish told senators what Mr. Davis asserts, then he gave them a different account from what he has given in letters and interviews. Mr. Davis very quietly slips in this new charge in place of the old one, without calling the reader's attention to the substitution. Let it be noted, too, that he associates the Ex-President with Mr. Fish in the making of charges to senators, while the former in his interview denied any participation in the removal, though pleased to hear that it had taken place.

Mr. Davis says: "The unrevealed records of the Senate in executive session will show whether Mr. Sumner made any attempt during that winter [1870-1871] to secure the action of the Senate on these treaties." They might, or they might not. Mr. Sumner might have appealed urgently to senators to take up the treaties, and the general expression might have been against his appeal, and there the matter have ended without a record. If Mr. Davis can find anything in the Senate journals to impeach Mr. Sumner's fidelity, let him produce it, and not darkly hint at points against him which do not exist. On the assailant rests the burden of proving his charges. There is a presumption in favor of the right-doing of public business which has passed into a maxim. Reputations are to be assailed only by proved facts, not by cunning insinuations. Mr. Sumner's friends have no occasion to fear records which have already so well exposed the calumnies industriously circulated against him.

The charge which Mr. Davis now substitutes for the original one is, that Mr. Sumner "did not move forward the treaties and secure the Senate's action upon them." No such intimation was made in the caucus or in the Senate when Mr. Sumner's removal was debated, March 10, 1871; nor by President Grant, when giving reasons for it in the summer of 1871; nor by Mr. Conkling, July 23, 1872, when at the Cooper Institute he defended with much elaboration the removal, stating instead, what is now disproved, that Mr. Sumner did not report "six or seven treaties;" nor by Mr. Howe, Mr. Hamlin, Mr. Cameron, and Mr. Anthony, when they explained in the Senate the cause of the removal, April 28, 1874; nor by General Grant, in his interviews in 1877-1878, in Scotland or in Egypt; nor by Mr. Fish, in his five appearances before the public in October, November, and December, 1877. But it is, for the first time, made by Mr. Davis, Jan. 3, 1878, nearly seven years after Mr. Sumner's removal, and almost four years after his death, and only when Mr. Fish's repeated accusation has been completely disproved by the record.

Mr. Davis's assertion that the President and secretary at that time informed senators of Mr. Sumner's neglect of public business is disproved by the facts. Such a statement, if believed, would have inevitably been used in the caucus and in the Senate. The senators who promoted the removal were sorely pressed for reasons which should be distinct from the San Domingo issue, and they would have seized upon an argument calculated to carry public opinion with them. Not one, however, even in that hour of bitterness, saw fit to accept Mr. Sumner's challenge to an inspection of his record as chairman, or to deny his fidelity. Mr. Howe and Mr. Nye expressly admitted it, and the silence of others was an implied assent. If any one of all those who voted for the removal had received the information which Mr. Davis says that some had received from the President and secretary, he could have met Mr. Sumner with a positive denial of his fidelity, and vindicated the propriety of his removal before the country. That no senator received the communication, as stated by Mr. Davis, is shown by the fact that no senator reported Mr. Sumner's alleged neglect to the caucus or the Senate, and that the positive assertions of his fidelity were left unquestioned. The substitute charge, however, is as unfounded as the original one. No affirmative evidence is given of its truth, and Mr. Sumner's friends might rest content with challenging the assailant to supply his proofs. But they can well advance beyond mere negation, and bring his surviving colleagues on the committee and in the Senate as witnesses to his character and fidelity.

No legislator, it may be remarked, can be held responsible for the refusal of the legislative body to act when he has duly reported a measure and brought it properly to its attention. The body may insist on its own order of business, or be averse to the consideration of the measure. The Darien Canal treaty, the French claims, the "Alabama" claims, and the civil-rights measures are all instances of dilatory action, which neither chairmen nor committees could prevent. Some of these Mr. Sumner urged, as is well known, with untiring effort, but without success. If, *primâ facie*, a chairman is to be deemed culpable for the non-action of the legislative body, no chairman could stand the test. It is for Mr. Davis to show, before he can sustain his charge, an occasion when Mr. Sumner should have urged a treaty and did not, and what treaties he so neglected; when, if ever, any senator upon his committee, or not upon it, asked in the Senate for the consideration of a treaty, and found him obstructive or indifferent; or when, if ever, Mr. Fish solicited Mr. Sumner's attention for the purpose, and it was not given. Many notes of Mr. Fish to Mr. Sumner are preserved, mostly of a very familiar character, mingling public and social affairs, and in not one of them is there a suggestion that any treaty has been neglected; not one speaks of delay or calls for action.

The testimony of senators who were serving with Mr. Sumner at the time of his removal in March, 1871, is here given. Messrs. Patterson, Schurz, and Casserly were members of the committee on foreign relations at that time. Messrs. Casserly, Thurman, and Bayard were his political opponents; and with some of the others, for instance Mr. Trumbull, he had at times strong antagonisms on public questions. But whatever their differences, political or personal, they have cheerfully borne their emphatic testimony to the remarkable fidelity of their deceased colleague.

Ex-Senator Patterson of New Hampshire, a member of the committee with Mr. Sumner, writes, Feb. 25, 1878: —

"Mr. Sumner's fidelity in the discharge of his senatorial duties was so generally recognized that I could not have believed that any person would be found to question it, if I had not seen it. I am glad to be able to say, in response to your question, that I think he was exceptionally faithful and prompt in pressing the consideration of all matters referred to his committee, and in urging action upon the same, after they had been reported to the Senate; and my own belief is that Mr. Sumner never exhibited greater activity or ability, and never manifested a stronger desire to expedite the business of his committee, than during his last term of service as its chairman.

I never saw or heard an intimation that he was either slack or obstructive in the discharge of his duties as chairman until I read the paper lately published by Ex-Secretary Fish in response to Mr. Phillips's strictures upon the utterances of President Grant relative to Mr. Sumner. It so happened that I was absent from Washington, attending the annual election in New Hampshire at the time Mr. Sumner was dropped from his committee, and so did not hear the discussions upon that subject, either in the caucus or the Senate. It was, however, a matter of frequent conversation after my return; and I do not remember to have heard any one give, as a reason for his being dropped, a premeditated and wilful holding back of treaties which had been referred to the committee, or even a careless neglect of foreign affairs.

"It was rare, if ever, that the files of our committee were cumbered with unconsidered business. It was Mr. Sumner's habit to drive his work, and not to be driven by it. He kept the table of the committee clear, and ready for new matter as it came to hand. It certainly never occurred to me — and I have no reason to suppose it did to any of my associates upon the committee — that our chairman's zeal in the discharge of his official duties flagged during his last term of service, or that personal feelings toward the Secretary of State influenced his action as a senator in the slightest degree. The charge that Mr. Sumner, simply to gratify personal spite, designedly and maliciously delayed action, either in the committee or the Senate, upon pending treaties, is something worse than an after-thought. The record shows it to be untrue, and a wrong done to the memory of a statesman whose name will be revered and honored in spite of this violation of the rest of the grave.

"Mr. Sumner undoubtedly had great confidence in his own judgment of public affairs, and perhaps was liable through the strength of his feelings to do injustice to the motives and opinions of others; but he was not suspicious or malignant, and his patriotism was too constant and strong ever to have allowed him to gratify his personal dislikes to the sacrifice of a public duty. All the treaties mentioned by Mr. Fish in the article already alluded to, when referred to the committee, were taken up and acted upon with the usual promptness, and were reported back to the Senate by our chairman with no more than the ordinary and necessary delay. Nor did Mr. Sumner's activity stop there. More than once, as I well remember, he reminded the Senate that those treaties were on its table, and waiting its action; but as no one of them was of such a character as to demand immediate action, and as no real interest of the country would be sacrificed by delay, the Senate preferred to go on with the *legislative* business upon its crowded calendar during the short term, and so declined to go into executive session for the consideration of the treaties. Two out of the nine treaties spoken of by Ex-Secretary Fish, it is true, could not be classed among what are called 'stock treaties.' They did not relate to the general questions of international intercourse, but yet were of such a character as would allow them to be held in abeyance without detriment to any public interest. That relating to the Mexican commissioners, it was understood, would meet with serious opposition, and could only be ratified, if at all, after long debate. The Darien Canal treaty had such wide and far-reaching relations, and was to inaugurate expensive and protracted operations in a locality so distant and little understood, that it demanded time for investigation, both in the committee and the Senate. It was therefore thought best that these should go over with the others to the extra session, when there would be ample time to consider them. It is not an unusual thing — indeed I think I may say it is the common practice of the Senate — to allow executive business pending near the close of a session, if it does not press for immediate action, to go over to the extra or special session, if it is understood there is to be one. This gives time for the consideration of legislative business, which always crowds, and necessitates hasty action in the closing days of Congress."

Ex-Senator Schurz, of Missouri, another member of the committee with Mr. Sumner, now Secretary of the Interior, writes, May 15, 1878 : —

"I was a member of the Senate committee on foreign relations during the last two years of Mr. Sumner's chairmanship, and I have never heard his diligence in preparing and pressing forward the business of that committee questioned by any one until now, after his death. I was personally on intimate terms with Mr. Sumner, and know from my own observation that his official duties, especially those connected with foreign affairs, were constantly occupying his mind and engaging his energies. If the charge of negligence had been brought against him while he was at the head of the committee on foreign relations, it would have been unanimously put down as utterly absurd by all those who had any knowledge of the business of that committee.

"Mr. Sumner never hesitated, neglected, or ceased to press the business of the committee upon the attention of the Senate on every available occasion. As to the list of treaties recently mentioned by Mr. Fish in his letter to the Boston 'Transcript,' I do not pretend to have any specific recollection ; but I feel warranted in saying that if those treaties, or any of them, went over from the regular session of Congress to the extra session of the Senate immediately following it and called especially for the transaction of executive business, it was by no means an unusual but a very common and a very proper thing. It is notorious that toward the close of a session of Congress there is a vast accumulation of legislative matter to be disposed of in a hurry ; that there is scarcely time for the calm consideration of anything ; that the Senate at that period devotes most of its time in executive sessions to the confirmation or rejection of the nominations still on the calendar ; and that extra sessions of the Senate, immediately following the adjournment of Congress, are called for the special purpose of transacting business which requires consideration and could not be sufficiently considered amid the turmoil of a closing Congress. To cast blame upon Mr. Sumner, or any one else, for permitting important business to go over to the extra session of the Senate under such circumstances, if in the instance mentioned by Mr. Fish it did go over, seems entirely gratuitous.

"The reasons for which Mr. Sumner was dropped from the chairmanship of the committee on foreign relations were discussed in open Senate, and even the debate which had taken place in the caucus of Republican senators on the subject was drawn into that discussion. No senator who favored the removal of Mr. Sumner ventured to hint at remissness in the conduct of public business on the part of Mr. Sumner, or at a difference of opinion between him and the Secretary of State concerning the acquisition of Canada, as forming part of those reasons. The record in the Congressional Globe speaks for itself. Neither have I ever, until now, heard these two things privately mentioned by any one as making the retirement of Mr. Sumner from the chairmanship desirable. To put his retirement from a post which he had held so long and so honorably upon such grounds appears very much like an after-thought ; and to accuse a man like Mr. Sumner, whose highest pride was in his fidelity to public duty, of negligence or obstructiveness in the discharge of those duties, now that he is in his grave, is, to say the least of it, very ungracious business."

Ex-Senator Casserly, of California, another member of the committee with Mr. Sumner, writes, Feb. 19, 1878 : —

"During the two years, from 1869 to 1871, while I was on the committee with Mr. Sumner, I can say that in the committee, as its chairman, he was faithful and diligent in reporting and pressing treaties. He was equally so in the Senate, where he was apt to be rather persistent with treaties of importance. It is my recollection that treaties sent in to the Senate during the session ending March 4 were, unless the emergency was great, usually laid over for the special session of the Senate immediately following. The Mexican Claims treaty encountered from the first much opposition. I do not recall the circumstances connected with the Austro-Hungarian treaty, or the Darien Canal treaty. Generally speaking, I should say that the delays, whatever they were, in disposing of important treaties were imputable to the Senate rather than to Mr. Sumner. I refer more especially now to the session ending March 4, 1871, when he was excluded from the committee. Whatever specious pretexts for this proceeding may have been given then, or may be given now, I cannot doubt that the controlling motive for it is to be found in Mr. Sumner's unflinching opposition to the San Domingo job. This was the understanding at the time among all of us Democrats in the Senate, and not a few Republicans."

Senator Morrill of Vermont writes, Jan. 24, 1878: —

"I cannot pretend any other than a general impression touching the manner of Mr. Sumner in the discharge of his duties as chairman of the committee on foreign relations; and that impression was and is that he was remarkably attentive to all subjects referred to the committee, and I never noticed that he was dilatory in pressing them upon the attention of the Senate. To the very last he seemed to me especially ambitious not to shirk his senatorial labors. I was also frequently at his room, and there always found him a hard worker."

Ex-Senator Trumbull of Illinois writes, Jan. 25, 1878: —

"I am amazed that there should be any controversy as to the fidelity with which the late Mr. Sumner performed his duties as chairman of the committee on foreign relations. During the eighteen years I served with him in the Senate, no member of the body was more prompt in his attendance or more attentive to business than he, saving only the period while he was physically disabled by the brutal assault of 1856. In 1871, when Mr. Sumner, after a service of ten years, was displaced as chairman of the committee on foreign relations, no one intimated that it was because of any delay or neglect in the discharge of duty either in the committee-room or as a member of the Senate. So far from it, his fidelity was admitted by all; and though my personal relations with him were not at that time of the most agreeable character, I was so well satisfied that the good of the public service required his retention as chairman of the committee on foreign relations, that I did not hesitate to protest against his removal. I regard the accusation that Mr. Sumner, either during the last year of his service as chairman of the committee on foreign relations, or at any other time, failed or neglected properly to bring forward and press upon the consideration of the Senate treaties or any other matter referred to his committee, as cruelly unjust and wholly unwarranted by the facts."

Ex-Senator Fenton of New York writes, Jan. 29, 1878: —

"I know of no senator more faithful and efficient in pressing committee-business committed to him than was Mr. Sumner. During the years I served with him in the Senate I never heard it charged or intimated, nor did I ever for a moment think, that he was careless or remiss in the discharge of duty, whether relating to treaties or other matters before his committee or the Senate. His views relative to the acquisition of Canada, whatever they may have been at the time of his disconnection with the committee on foreign relations, were not urged or referred to privately or publicly, to my knowledge, as a reason for his displacement."

Senator Thurman of Ohio writes, May 24, 1878: —

"I never heard, until after his death, any suggestion that Senator Sumner was remiss in the discharge of his duties as chairman of that committee. The suggestion greatly surprised me, for he was very remarkable for his punctual attendance in the Senate, and I had always supposed that he was equally diligent in the discharge of his committee duties. I cannot but think that those who have intimated the contrary are very greatly mistaken."

Senator Bayard of Delaware writes, Feb. 18, 1878: —

"In reply to your inquiry as to the fidelity of the late Senator Sumner in conducting the business of the committee on foreign relations while he was the chairman, I will say that not having been a member of that committee I can speak only of its business as presented to the Senate; and there I can well attest Mr. Sumner's remarkable assiduity in attending to all the duties of his position. In this he was conspicuous, and I never knew his steady fidelity to fail or flag even when ill-health and suffering would have given him ample excuse. I cannot imagine a more frivolous pretext for his removal from the chairmanship he had held so many years than an alleged lack of attention to its duties. In his lifetime I never heard such a suggestion, for it would have been considered absurd. When he was deprived of the chairmanship, there was no man in the Senate so well equipped as he for the place, and not one more assiduous in his devotion to what he believed to be his duty; and in this there was no abatement until death relieved him."

Similar testimonies have been received from other associates of Mr. Sumner in the Senate, as ex-Senators Morrill of Maine and Logan of Illinois, and Senators Anthony, Windom, and Spencer; but there is not space to insert them here.

Senator Sherman of Ohio, now Secretary of the Treasury, in the debate on Mr. Sumner's removal, March 10, 1871, while considering himself bound by the action of the caucus, declared the change "unjustifiable, impolitic, and unnecessary," and after Mr. Sumner's death, in a tribute to his memory, bore testimony to his remarkable fidelity. The leading promoters of the removal admitted in the debate his perfect fidelity, and no senator alleged or hinted the slightest default either in the committee or in the Senate, whether arising from inattention, obstructiveness, or any other cause. That was left for the fertile imaginations of Mr. Fish and Mr. Davis.

The breach of personal (not official) relations between the secretary and the senator was assigned as the cause of the removal by its advocates in the Senate debate of March 10, 1871. But it was shown at the time that Mr. Sumner was always ready to confer freely with Mr. Fish on public business, and indeed had done so but a few weeks previous, and that the breach of personal relations was caused by "a gross insult," so called in debate, which Mr. Fish had given Mr. Sumner in the despatch to Mr. Moran of Dec. 30, 1870, previous to which they had been engaged in friendly intercourse and correspondence. This "flimsy pretext" of non-intercourse, as it was termed by Senator Schurz, did not avail at the time to mislead the public. The debates in the caucus and in the Senate, and the public journals in their leaders, paragraphs, and correspondence, pointed to Mr. Sumner's determined opposition to the San Domingo scheme and his exposure of the proceedings of its leading promoters as the motive or justification of his displacement.

The reasons for Mr. Sumner's removal heretofore given having failed, Mr.

Davis has attempted a new one, which no assailant of Mr. Sumner hitherto has ventured to suggest; namely, that the senator, by a memorandum of Jan. 17, 1871, sent by him to Mr. Fish, in answer to a call for his advice as to the negotiations with Great Britain for the settlement of the "Alabama" claims and other questions, proposed that "the withdrawal of the British flag from Canada cannot be abandoned as a condition or preliminary of such a settlement." This, according to Mr. Davis, was communicated by Mr. Fish to "leading Republican senators," who were governed in their votes by the communication, making them, as he says, "their practical answer" to the memorandum; and he then states that for diplomatic purposes this reason was not given to the public, but only the reason "that Mr. Sumner was not on speaking terms with the President and with Mr. Fish." The presumption is against senators having been influenced by such an argument, if it had been used. It is not customary, on account of a difference on a single measure involving no party passions, to dismiss a chairman from a post he has held with universal approval for a long period, but it is found easier and more consistent with the proprieties to vote him down on that question than to remove him altogether from his place.

A few considerations show this newly-devised explanation of Mr. Sumner's removal to be absurd. No such reason was given at the time of the removal, either in the caucus on March 9, 1871, or in the Senate on March 10, 1871, or in the public journals of the time. The "non-speaking" reason, and that alone, was insisted on by senators who advocated the removal. If the embarrassment of negotiations had been a reason, it would have been given at once. Mr. Davis intimates that it would have been "the height of indiscretion" to give the reason while negotiations were pending; but why so? The removal of a chairman who was making exorbitant demands against Great Britain would have shown our friendly disposition, and made negotiations easier. But no attempt to conceal a reason operating on the minds of senators could have succeeded. In some way the reporters would have discovered it. Nothing is more easy to detect than the considerations governing the action of public men who are co-operating in the support of a measure.

Mr. Davis's explanation why this reason remained a profound secret will not stand a moment's scrutiny. If reasons of state required senators to keep this cause for the removal a secret, the secret would have come out when those reasons of state ceased to operate; and they ceased entirely to operate when the Treaty of Washington had been concluded and ratified in June, 1871. The fact that this alleged cause for removal was not made public then, or whenever after the causes of the removal were canvassed by senators, proves that it never existed, that it never had any place in their minds, that it was never communicated to them. It was not mentioned by Mr. Conkling when he defended the removal in his speech at Cooper Institute, July 23, 1872; nor in the debate in the Senate, April 28, 1874, when it was explained or defended by Howe, Hamlin, Anthony, and Cameron; nor by Mr. Fish himself in his interviews and letters of October 19, October 29, and November 10, 1877; nor by any one except Mr. Davis, and by him only after the pretext of unreported treaties had been disproved. Mr. Howe, writing so recently as in the last number of the North American Review, gives only the non-intercourse reason, thus lending no sanction to Mr. Davis's latest invention. The memorandum, as a justification of the removal, was thus an after-thought, taking the place of another after-thought, which had failed. The statement, then, that any position of Mr. Sumner in relation to the acquisition of Canada was in the mind of any senator when voting for his removal, or was ever communicated to any senator as a reason for removal, may fairly take its place with the charge that he never reported the nine treaties.

But who are "the leading senators" with whom Mr. Fish is said to have conferred? Were not the two Messrs. Morrill, Messrs. Schurz, Sherman, Trumbull, and Wilson as "leading" senators as any who favored Mr. Sumner's removal? These all, however, sustained him in caucus. Either, then, Mr. Fish did not communicate this argument to them or to any of the twenty-one who voted in Mr. Sumner's favor in the caucus, or if he did they placed no reliance upon it. If he withheld it from the twenty-one, but communicated it to some of the twenty-six who voted for the removal in the caucus, upon what principle of selection did he proceed? Were the senators who voted for removal any more pacific in disposition toward England than those who voted against it? Among the former was Mr. Chandler, who was most zealous against Mr. Sumner; but it was he who made in April, 1869, the most aggressive speech against England ever made in Congress, and who then proposed to obtain by negotiation a surrender of all the British possessions in North America as the basis for a settlement of our claims, and who in the same speech recited the offensive propositions he had from time to time made, such as the withdrawal of our minister from the court of St. James, the repeal of the neutrality laws, the declaration of our neutrality between England and Abyssinia, and who said that "the sixty thousand veteran soldiers of Michigan will take the contract to take possession of the Canadas in thirty days." Indeed, Mr. Chandler, who proposed to seize Canada by force, voting to remove Mr. Sumner for desiring only a peaceful acquisition, with full consent of England and of Canada also, would be an interesting spectacle! Surely, he was not one of "the leading senators"! Nor could there have been among them, for reasons already given, Messrs. Conkling, Howe, Hamlin, Cameron, or Anthony. Who, then, were the nameless, undesignated "leading senators" to whom Mr. Fish made known the memorandum which, as now alleged, he then thought a fatal obstruction to an important negotiation, — a secret, kept so well for seven years, and now first revealed by Mr. Davis?

If it were true that Mr. Fish ever made the communication to senators which Mr. Davis now alleges, such communication would also have been made first of all to the President, before even it was mentioned to a senator. But General Grant, in all his justifications of Mr. Sumner's removal, puts forth two only, — "the pigeon-holing" and "the non-speaking" ones, as in his conversation with Mr. Curtis in the summer of 1871 at Long Branch, and in his interviews in Scotland in September, 1877, and at Cairo in January, 1878, without ever making the remotest allusion to the reason which Mr. Davis now resorts to when the others have failed.

Again, and finally, as showing that no views of Mr. Sumner about Canada ever prompted a vote for his removal, it should be remembered that the removal was attempted at the beginning of the session in December, 1870, and threatened in debate on December 21, some weeks before the memorandum of Jan. 17, 1871, about Canada was written.

Mr. Davis assumes to give the terms of Mr. Sumner's memorandum of Jan. 17, 1871. Taking it as given, Mr. Sumner appears to have thought the proximity to us of the British possessions a cause of irritation and disturbance, by furnishing a basis of operations for Fenianism; and in order to make the settlement complete, and prevent all controversy in the future, he proposed the peaceful and voluntary withdrawal of the British flag from this continent. This proposition was neither dishonorable nor unstatesmanlike, and it is in harmony with the best opinions of our time. The single sentence of the memorandum already given alone invites criticism; but by those words, written not in a formal paper, and signed only with initials, he meant merely to say, as the event showed, that the cession of British America should be our first request in order to reach, as a final consummation, perpetual peace between the two nations. That this was his thought is shown by other expressions in the memorandum, as where, cordially accepting Sir John Rose's idea that all causes of irritation should be removed, he added: "Nothing could be better than this initial idea; it should be the starting-point." That he laid no greater stress on this part of his memorandum appears clearly enough from a letter he wrote the day after to George Bemis, in which, mentioning the fact of his memorandum, he refers to the clause in it concerning the depredations of the different cruisers, but without any reference to the clause concerning Canada. But as demonstrating that he held no impracticable, no obstructive position about Canada this fact alone is sufficient, that he supported in the Senate the Treaty of Washington; and while he criticised some omissions, and moved certain amendments, and spoke at length upon its various provisions, he made no complaint that it did not provide for the cession of Canada, and indeed made no reference to the matter whatever.

This was not the first occasion on which Mr. Sumner had shown his desire for the acquisition of British America, as he had already supported that of Russian America. Always, however, he insisted that it should be made by peaceful annexation, by the voluntary act of England, and with the cordial assent of the colonists. This view appears in his speech at the Republican State convention at Worcester, Sept. 22, 1869, where he recalled the aspirations of our fathers for the union of all Englishmen in America, and their invitation to Canada to join our new nation at its birth; suggested that reciprocity of trade was prophetic of political unity, and pictured our country as hereafter destined to cover the continent "from the frozen sea to the tepid waters of the Mexican Gulf;" but referring to the whispers of territorial compensation for our claims against England with territory as the consideration, he rejected such a solution altogether, except with the full concurrence of Canada herself, declaring with emphasis, "Territory may be conveyed, but not a people." Is there anything in this aspiration unworthy, visionary, or impracticable? Rather is there not something in it lofty and inspiring? Everywhere races of common origin and speech are gravitating to oneness and solidarity. Such is the lesson of history, and such also is the spectacle of our era. This generation has seen Italy rise from a geographical expression to a national entity, — her various kingdoms, duchies, pontifical states, provinces of a foreign dynasty, all becoming one country, which stretches the length of the historic peninsula. It has seen likewise Germany, no longer a mere dream of patriots and idealists, at last consolidated as one people, and realizing the fatherland of patriotism and of song. At this hour it sees in the far East the Greek race, in whose language mankind has found its culture, its philosophy, and its religion, yearning for a nationality commensurate with the common speech, and centred in a renowned capital on the Ægean or the Bosphorus. Such a generation will respond with sympathy to Sumner's thought of Canada joining speedily the sisterhood of American States, even if with a seer's instinct he anticipated, as he often did, the fulness of time. In the final week of his life, even on the very day he left the Senate for the last time, at whose close he was smitten with mortal agony, he was finishing his "Prophetic Voices concerning America," in which he had gathered what from age to age had been foretold of her greatness and destiny; and among these he placed his friend Cobden's contemplation of the coming union of Canada with us. What nobler epitaph can be written of an American statesman than this, — that after an illustrious career of devotion to universal liberty, carrying into age the fresh hopes of youth, he died, cherishing fondly the vision that the country he had loved and served was to grow in peace to an empire wide as the domains of the English-speaking race on this continent!

# INDEX.

# INDEX TO VOLS. III. AND IV.

## DATE DUE

| | | | |
|---|---|---|---|
| | | | |
| | | | |
| | | | |
| | | | |
| | | | |
| | | | |
| | | | |
| | | | |
| | | | |
| | | | |
| | | | |
| | | | |
| | | | |
| | | | |
| | | | |
| | | | |
| | | | |
| | | | |